Faith, Life and Witness

The Papers of the Study and Research Division
of
The Baptist World Alliance 1986-1990

Edited by

William H. Brackney
with
Ruby J. Burke

Publication of this volume is a thank-offering to God and to the international Baptist Community from Samford University in gratitude for the Lord's Providential watchcare over Samford University these one hundred fifty years.

SAMFORD UNIVERSITY PRESS
BIRMINGHAM, ALABAMA
1990

Supervisor of Production, Laverne A. Farmer

Production Assistance, Charlotte Fleagle, Edith Hutson
and Judith Williams

Library of Congress Card Number: 90-060092

Copyright Registration Number TXu 410-752
by Baptist World Alliance

ISBN 0-9625634-0-4

McLean, Virginia USA

All Rights Reserved

Manufactured in the United States of America

Printed by

Interface, Incorporated

STUDY AND RESEARCH COMMITTEE
1986-1990

Cora Sparrowk, Chair

Douglas Waruta, Vice Chair

James M. Dunn, Vice Chair

J. Ralph McIntyre, Director

Members:

Samuel T. Ola Akande
Alexei Bichkov
William Brackney
Keith Clements
Russell Dilday
Peder Eidberg
Ralph Elliot
Paul Fiddes
Edna Gutierrez
Welton Gaddy
Mark Heim
William Hull
Glenn Igleheart
B. C. Jenkins

Birgit Karlsson
Lorenzo Klink
James Lai
Thorwald Lorenzen
Thomas Mackey
Glenna McNeill
Joao Makondekwa
Morgan Patterson
Armando Pereira
George Peck
Wiard Popkes
David Priestley
David Shannon
Nalla Thomas
Tairas Wagey

Editorial Committee

William H. Brackney

James M. Dunn

C. Welton Gaddy

William H. Brackney is Principal and Professor of Historical Theology at McMaster Divinity College, Hamilton, Ontario.

Ruby J. Burke is a staff member at Eastern Baptist Seminary in Philadelphia, Pennsylvania.

Table of Contents

Samford:
The Missions-Minded University With a World View

From its beginning as a Baptist college named for a British social reformer, to its emergence as an internationally-minded university approaching its 150th anniversary, Samford University has held high the Christian ideal of world missions. Alabama Baptists began Howard College in 1841, taking its name from John Howard, who devoted his life during the 1700s to the betterment of prison conditions throughout Europe and Russia. John Howard's statue stands today in St. Paul's Cathedral in London, and the college named for him now prospers as Samford University. Established to train ministers and laymen, the University offers a variety of fully accredited university-level programs within a Christian context.

Throughout its existence, Samford educated ministers have taken the message of Christ to all the world. In 1987 through the generosity of a dedicated layman, Ralph W. Beeson, the University began Beeson School of Divinity, to educate prospective ministers at the graduate level, through the Master of Divinity degree. For many years Samford has led the nation's colleges and universities in the number of students involved in summer missions work. A few students participate in a summer missionary internship program at mission sites around the world. Realizing that today's students will live and work in the multi-national, multi-cultural world of the 21st century, Samford began an extensive international program during the early 1980s. Converting a small family hotel in London, England to a Study Centre, the university instituted a Semester Abroad program to ensure that students develop global vision. Other credit programs take students to Spain, Germany, Mexico, and the a cappella choir has travelled to Germany, Korea and England in recent years.

Today, with its continuing emphasis on world missions and preparing students for the global village of the 21st century, Samford University is truly America's missions-minded university with the world at heart.

Alabama's only comprehensive, *private*, non-government university, Samford opened the decade of the "90s with more than 4,100 students from 43 states and 39 nations. Enrollment has increased almost 200 percent during the past three decades. A striking campus of approximately 40 structures of Georgian-Colonial architecture has been built. The size and stature of the faculty has kept pace with growth in other areas. Today, Samford faculty members hold degrees from more than 100 universities in the United States, Canada, Europe, Latin

America and the Far East. During 1988-89 *USA Today* newspaper rated Samford one of the nation's 182 most selective universities. The Templeton Foundation selected Samford its 1989 "best of the best" listing of character-building colleges and universities. And Samford was recognized in the 1990 edition of *U. S. News & World Report* magazine as one of the "rising stars of American higher education," an up-and-coming university noted for its innovative educational achievements.

Samford sprang from humble beginnings. Inspired by a missionary movement in America during the early 1840s, three Baptist leaders—planter E. D. King, pastor James H. DeVotie and educator Milo P. Jewett—collaborated to establish Howard College. The first class included nine young men studying to become preachers. Under its first president, Vermont native Samuel Sterling Sherman, the college grew rapidly. By 1846 the curriculum reached the level of a standard four-year college. After surviving two destructive fires during the 1850s, Howard struggled during and after the Civil War, never closing its doors but at times graduating only one man per year. Thus, in the 1880s, when offers of financial support came from sources in the rapidly growing new city of Birmingham 80 miles to the northeast, the college relocated.

Enrollment increased at the new site in Birmingham's East Lake area, and by 1920, Howard had opened its doors to women (1913), begun a summer school (1915) and received accreditation by the Southern Association of Colleges and Schools (1920). The college took first steps toward university status as early as 1927, when a pharmacy division was established. Although Howard struggled again during the Depression of the 1930s, enrollment held and no major activity was suspended. Harwell G. Davis was named president in 1939, signalling the beginning of a period of significant growth. By the mid-1940s, Howard had outgrown its East Lake campus.

Moving six miles South of downtown Birmingham to a new campus in the Homewood area in 1957, Samford began its most prosperous era under the presidency of Leslie S. Wright. The college took another step toward university status in 1961, acquiring the renowned Cumberland School of Law. Four years later, Master's degree programs were instituted. This development, coupled with growth in professional programs such as pharmacy, business, and teacher education, resulted in Howard's official elevation to university status and renaming as Samford University in November of 1965. The school was renamed for longtime chairman of the board Frank Park Samford, a Baptist layman whose influence and generosity had helped guide the institution from the dark days of the Depression.

Today, Samford offers 19 degree programs through eight units—the Howard College of Arts and Sciences, Cumberland School of Law, Beeson School of Divinity, Orlean Bullard Beeson School of Education, Ida V. Moffett School of Nursing, the School of Business, School of Music and School of Pharmacy. The University unites rigorous academic training and Christian principles, seeking to equip well-qualified, dedicated and responsible leaders for all walks of life. Samford has more than 36,000 alumni around the world.

Under the leadership of Dr. Thomas E. Corts, who became president in

1983, Samford has worked to strengthen programs of service to students, educational innovation, faculty renewal and Christian commitment. Samford celebrates its Sesquicentennial during 1991. It does so mindful of the role it has played and will play in fulfillment of our Lord's great commission. The finest tribute to the past, says Dr. Thomas Corts, is to make the future even better. And at Samford, "the best is yet to be."

Preface

The Division of Study and Research is vital to the life of the Baptist World Alliance. Through this channel scholars call upon member bodies to examine critical issues in our contemporary world and challenge the church to assume its responsibility. Study papers growing out of commission deliberations are collated and sent to Baptist schools of higher learning worldwide. They become ongoing library resources. In addition, international theological conversations with world church bodies enable us to know and understand the wider Christian community.

This volume is a collection of selected study papers of the six commissions: Baptist Heritage, Baptist Doctrine and Interchurch Cooperation, Christian Ethics, Human Rights, Ministry of the Laity, and Pastoral Leadership. These present a sample of their work covering the 1986-1990 period. The papers are the views of the writers and not necessarily the Baptist World Alliance. A summary preceding each commission gives an overview of the group's activities.

The Division is mandated in the By-Laws "to assist member bodies in their mission" and "bring about the exchange of ideas on topics relating to Christian experience and mission; to encourage creative new solutions to problems of Christian mission in today's world." It is the hope that these pages will not only be informative and challenging, but also, deepen the spiritual foundation of our Baptist family around the world and create a renewed commitment to the work we do together for Jesus Christ.

We express appreciation to Dr. Thomas E. Corts and Samford University for underwriting this project as part of the 150th anniversary celebration of the University. We are indebted to Dr. William Brackney and Ruby Burke for editing and compiling the material for publication, and to President Noel Vose who kept the vision alive.

Cora Sparrowk, Chair
Study and Research

A Message From The President

Amongst other structural features of the Baptist World Alliance are five Divisions designed, as the Constitution asserts, "to carry out the ministries and programs of the Alliance".

One of these is the *Division of Study and Research,* whose unprepossessing title hides an exciting aspect of the World body's work. The Division is made up of six Commissions each averaging about thirty members who deal with such areas as doctrine, inter-church co-operation, Baptist heritage, ethics, human rights, laity and pastoral leadership.

For many years the Study Commissions have been an integral part of the life and work of the Alliance. Their origin and development make fascinating reading. Over the past forty years they have changed shape many times but the vision lying behind their genesis remains: that leaders of the Baptist world should meet periodically to wrestle with matters of concern to the whole Baptist family, and to motivate us all to creative thinking about every aspect of our Christian commitment. And so it has proved. But dreams and visions take time to mature. The difficulty of gathering the right people, and severe limitations of time and resources, produced more frustration than results among many involved. By some, the Study Commissions came to be viewed as the Cinderella of the B.W.A. But their enthusiasm persisted. Since 1985, more time has been allotted to their meetings at each General Council, with results that are plain to see.

With the greatest pleasure therefore we offer this volume - the first of its kind - which gathers together a small sample of the extensive and valuable work of a much larger body of Commission members. It is designed to be more than an expression of academia; rather, an attempt to point up some of the big issues facing us as we move towards the Twenty-first Century.

Our resources are still too limited for this large enterprise, it is true; but with the help and example of such people as President Corts of Samford University, we believe that this volume will be the "first fruits" of an increasing stream of valuable materials to be shared in published form by Baptists around the world.

My warmest thanks and congratulations go to the Editor, contributors, and to many Commission members whose sterling work warrants much wider circulation.

G. Noel Vose
President, Baptist World Alliance
1985-1990

The Commission On Baptist Doctrine and Interchurch Cooperation

The Baptist World Alliance Commission on Doctrine and Interchurch Cooperation has attempted to address both of its assigned emphases this quinquennium.

(1) In the doctrinal area, the Commission has read papers and held discussions on such concerns as the separation of church and state, (cf. Deiros paper in this section), religious liberty, Christian unity, ecumenism, (cf. Geldbach's paper in this section), baptism, and ministry. We have responded to the Faith and Order Paper No. 111 on *Baptism, Eucharist, and Ministry,* and No. 140 on *Toward the Common Expression of the Apostolic Faith Today.* Case studies pertaining to religious liberty and churchstate relations are being prepared for Central America, Latin America (southern part), South Korea, Asia, India, China, Indonesia, Eastern Europe, Africa, and South Africa.

(2) In the interchurch cooperation area, the Commission has sponsored and reported on a number of dialogues between Baptists and other groups: five sessions with Roman Catholics, 1984-1988 (cf. report in this section), four sessions with Lutherans, 1986-1989, one session with Mennonites, 1989. Proposals for Baptist-Jewish dialogues and conversations with Anglicans are being considered.

An Ecumenical Strategy Paper for receiving, summarizing, and distributing information from the dialogues was finalized in the 1989 meeting.

The papers included in this publication are representative of the work of the Commission during the quinquennium:

"A Response to *Baptism, Eucharist, and Ministry: Faith and Order Paper No. 111,*" by William R. Estep, U.S.A.

"Freedom and Its Limits: The Problem of Church State Relations," by Pablo A. Deiros, Argentina.

"Baptists and the Ecumenical Movement — a Strategy Paper," by Erich Geldbach, West Germany.

"A Draft Response to the Faith and Order Commission Paper No. 140, *Confession One Faith,*" Keith Clements, Great Britain.

"The Theology of the State," Janos Viczian, Hungary.

Russell H. Dilday, Chair

Russell H. Dilday is president of Southwestern Baptist Theological Seminary, Fort Worth, Texas, USA.

A Response to *Baptism, Eucharist, and Ministry: Faith and Order Paper No. 111.*

William R. Estep

Introduction

In response to the invitation of the Faith and Order Commission of the World Council of Churches, the Baptist World Alliance wishes to submit the following document. While the Alliance recognizes that it does not represent the highest authority in Baptist life, but in keeping with Article 3 and its constitution to "promote understanding and cooperation among Baptist bodies and with other Christian groups, in keeping with our unity in Christ," it wishes to frame a reply in keeping with the spirit of *Baptist, Eucharist and Ministry*.

Before the specific answers can be given to the request made on page X in the "Preface" of BEM, it is important for the Faith and Order Commission to understand something of the nature of the *Baptist concept of the church* since baptism, eucharist, and ministry are such an integral part of ecclesiology. Without this context, the response would hardly be adequate and surely not very well understood. Therefore, first we will delineate something of the Baptist understanding of the nature and purpose of the church and the relationship of the Commission on Baptist Doctrine and Interchurch Cooperation to the Baptist World Alliance and in turn the make up of the Baptist World Alliance to the Baptist constituency which make up its fellowship. After these preliminary statements, however inadequate they may appear, the response to the specific issues raised by the "Lima Report" will be attempted.

The Church and the Churches

Historically, the concept of the church has been at the very heart of the Baptist movement. The Baptist doctrine of the church has distinguished it as W. O. Carver wrote years ago, "From their Protestant brethren as from the Roman and Orthodox Churches, the difference on which they justify their separate existence within the Christian following and on which rests their conviction of duty to maintain their witness to their brethren and to mankind." Therefore the vocabulary of the World Council of Churches and many ecumenical organizations is quite foreign to that of the Baptists. For an example, very few national Baptist unions or conventions refer to themselves as the Baptist Church. The term church is generally used only of local churches and of the Church universal.

The universal Church to which Baptists refer when they use the term "The Body of Christ" is made up of all regenerate believers as indicated in Ephesians. Baptists find these two uses of the term church in the New Testament to which they look for the criteria in determining the nature of the church, its purpose, and mission in the world. W. O. Carver stated it very well:

.

"In general, we all (Baptists) recognize three proper uses of the word "Church" and think all other uses more or less misleading and dangerous for the true understanding of "our most holy faith." These uses are: (1) The whole number of spiritual, regenerate believers, constituting "the body of Christ" in this world, expounded particularly in Ephesians. This Church, for Baptists, is not, and cannot be ecclesiastically organized; and it has no local seat nor any administrative human head or headship. (2) The organized church, the functioning body of Christian believers, which should always be limited to a community in which convenient assembling and functioning are possible. It is a democratic body under the recognized authority and headship of its Lord and Savior. (3) The abstract, generic use of the term, as the church, the school, the state, the court, etc.

"It will thus be seen that the organized church as an institution is not for Baptists primary but secondary, functional and instrumental. It was intended to be, and exist as, the functioning agency of the Kingdom of God on earth and of its gospel. Ideally, it should concretely and socially embody the universal spiritual Church as the Body of Christ in each community. It is the declarative agency of that power that has no direct saving authority or power. It proclaims salvation and offers it to man in the name of the Redeemer; it does not definitely administer or withhold salvation. It has no vicarious mediatorial function, but is committed to the proclamation of the complete, exclusive priesthood and sacrifice of Jesus Christ as the Lamb of God that taketh away the sin of the world. Baptists thus find no place in, and no place for, any hierarchy and no saving value in any sacrament.[1]

Baptists from their very beginning have recognized that Jesus Christ is the only Lord of the church. This is spelled out quite succinctly in the very first Baptist Confession of Faith set forth in Amsterdam in 1611, Article 9 of which reads:

"That JESUS CHRIST is Mediator off the New Testament betweene GOD and Man, I Tim. 2.5, haveing all power in Heaven and in Earth given into him. Mat. 28.18. Being the onely KING, Luke 1.33, PREIST, Heb. 7.24, and PROPHET, Act. 3.22. Off his church, he also being the onely Law-giver hath in his Testament set downe an absolute, and perfect rule off direction, for all persons, at all times, to bee observed; Which no Prince, nor anie whosoever, may add to, or diminish from as they will avoid the fearefull judgments denounced against them that shal so do." Revel. 22.18,19.[2]

In Baptist understanding, the state has no right to intrude into the life of the church, therefore, the state is limited. It can never assume the authority to dictate the nature of the church's witness or worship. Article 84 of the 1612 Confession of Faith of the Smyth congregation remaining in Amsterdam set forth this principle of religious freedom which has been basic to Baptists' understanding of the relationship of church and state ever since.

84. That the magistrate is not by virtue of his office to meddle with religion, or matters of conscience, to force or compel men to this or that form of religion, or doctrine: but to leave Christian religion free, to every man's conscience, and

to handle only civil transgressions (Rom. xiii), injuries and wrongs of man against
man, in murder, adultery, theft, etc., for Christ only is the king, and lawgiver
of the church and conscience (James iv. 12).[3]

The first particular Baptist Confession of Faith of 1644 is in essential agreement on the nature of the church with the previous confessions quoted.
The essence of Article 23 reads:

The Church, as it is visible to us, is a company of visible Saints, called and
separated from the world by the word and spirit of God, to the visible profession of the faith of the Gospel, being baptized into that faith and joined to
the Lord, and each other, by mutual agreement, in the practical enjoyment
of the Ordinances, commanded by Christ their head and king.[4]

The Second London Confession adopted in 1677 speaks of the Universal
Church which "consists of the whole number of the Elect, that have been, are,
or shall be gathered into one, under Christ the head thereof; and is the spouse,
the body, the fulness of him that filleth all in all."[5] The confession goes on
to characterize local functioning churches:

"The Members of these Churches are Saints by calling, visibly manifesting and
evidencing (in and by their profession and walking) their obedience unto that
call of Christ; and do willingly consent to walk together according to the appointment of Christ, giving up themselves, to the Lord and one to another
by the will of God, in professed subjection to the Ordinances of the Gospel."[6]

In 1963, the Southern Baptist Convention adopted a revision of the 1925
Confession of Faith which was itself a revision of the New Hampshire Confession of Faith. The article on the church (VI), in addition to recognizing the
functioning local church, made up of "baptized believers," said, "the New
Testament speaks also of the church as the body of Christ which includes all
of the redeemed of all ages."[7]

The above excerpts from the various confessions Baptists have formulated
through the centuries are representative of the two concepts of the church held
by most Baptists. To be a member of the universal Church which is invisible
and known only unto God, a faith commitment to Jesus Christ is the prerequisite. Whereas, to be a member of a local Baptist church, a confession of faith,
which is accompanied by believers baptism that signifies a commitment to Christ
and an experience of regeneration, is required. Each local church recognizes only
the lordship of Jesus Christ and while churches cooperate with one another in
associations, unions, and conventions, these organizations do not exert authority
over the churches but are the means by which the churches work together in
accomplishing that which they could not possibly accomplish alone.
The theological diversity of Baptists, ethnic, and cultural differences have
dictated many different but cooperating bodies. This diversity is reflected in the
Baptist World Alliance, the primary function of which is to provide a forum

for fellowship for the widely scattered Baptist constituency and the various national Baptist bodies of the world.

The Baptist World Alliance

Some three hundred years after the formation of the first English Baptist church of record, Baptists from around the world met in London on July 17, 1905 to form the Baptist World Alliance. The Baptist World Alliance is open to "any organization of Baptist churches...which desires to cooperate in the work of the Alliance...." Presently, the Alliance is composed of more than 128,289 churches with 33,190,977 "reported" members in 134 member bodies of 143 countries. (Some member bodies failed to send in their statistics and others are notoriously inaccurate. Still other Baptist denominations do not belong. The total Baptist constituency is estimated at 45,000,000.) Among the first three objectives of the BWA are: first, "promote Christian fellowship and cooperation among Baptists throughout the world; second, bear witness to the gospel of Jesus Christ and assist unions and conventions in their divine task of bringing all people to God through Jesus Christ as Savior and Lord; third, promote understanding and cooperation among Baptist bodies and with other Christian groups, in keeping with our unity in Christ." It is this third objective that calls forth this response to BEM. However, it should be noted, as Walter Shurden states in *The Life of Baptists in the Life of the World,* that the BWA

"is *not* a Baptist super church. It is not a worldwide Baptist judicial or legislative body seeking to violate cherished Baptist principles of congregational autonomy or the rights of individual believers by imposing its will upon an individual, a local church, or a convention of churches. The BWA is designed to protect, not usurp, cardinal Baptist convictions."[8]

This statement by Shurden is amply confirmed from the earliest years of the Alliance to the present. Dr. John Clifford speaking on "The Baptist World Alliance: It's Origin and Character, Meaning and Work" in 1911 said,

"First, this must not be doubted, that we rejoice in the efforts now being made on behalf of unity of the followers of Jesus Christ, and gladly cooperate with these endeavors. We crave it. We pray for it. We should hold ourselves guilty if we created or upheld any ecclesiastical division on mere technicalities of the faith or on insignificant details of the practice of churches. We endeavor to keep the unity of the Spirit in the bonds of peace.
But with equal frankness we say that a visible, formal, and mechanical unity has no charm for us whatever. It is not the unity Jesus prayed for; nor is it the unity that increases spiritual efficiency, augments righteousness, or advances the Kingdom of God."[9]

Dr. Josef Nordenhaug, general secretary of the Baptist World Alliance in addressing a plenary session of the BWA Congress in Miami Beach, Florida echoed the sentiments of John Clifford when he said,

> "In regard to Christian unity, as in all other matters, our ultimate authority
> is Jesus Christ. He is the one and only Lord. Any impetus toward unity must
> flow from him. We recognize no intermediary between Christ and the individual
> believer. But this does not mean that Christian faith is merely pietistic in-
> dividualism: For the purpose of God through Jesus Christ is in the fulness of
> time "to unite all things in him" (Eph. 1:10). It was I believe, in this context
> that Christ prayer for the unity of His followers (cf. John 17:20-24).[10]

The Baptist World Alliance is made up of numerous, diverse bodies of
Baptists. Some of these are members of the World Council of Churches, but
the majority of Baptist denominational groups, even while affirming their interest in ecumenical movements and acknowledging the essential oneness which
they have with all those who know Jesus Christ as Savior and Lord, choose
to remain outside the structure of the World Council of Churches. In spite of
this diversity and sometimes confusing and ambivalent attitude toward
ecumenical movements, there is a commonality of Baptist faith and practice that
makes possible a deep and abiding fellowship around the world in the BWA.
Dr. Nordenhaug underlines this common confessional bond that holds Baptists together in a world fellowship when he said in addressing the Eleventh Congress of the Baptist World Alliance in 1965,

> In most of the nations of the world there are Baptists who have stood up to
> profess the faith they have in the Lord Jesus Christ. They have professed this
> through baptism upon their profession of faith. They believe in the sovereign-
> ty of God, in the lordship of Jesus Christ, in the guidance of the Holy Spirit,
> in the personal nature of faith, in believer's baptism, in the regenerate church
> membership, in the memorial nature of the Lord's Supper, in the priesthood
> of all believers, and in obligation upon all to bear witness to the Lord Jesus
> Christ.[11]

Baptism

I

In evaluating the baptismal section of the Lima Report we would express
immediate appreciation of the endeavor made to do justice to the biblical and
historical understanding of baptism.

To an extent far greater than the sections on "Eucharist" and "Ministry"
the exposition of baptism is more closely related to the biblical evidence, particularly in the exposition of the meaning of baptism (II, 2-7) and in the treatment of baptism and faith (III, 8-10). The opening paragraph is general enough
to invite unanimous consent, but two questions may be asked:

How are we to understand the words, "baptism is...incorporation into
Christ...is entry into the New Covenant"? Is the verb here merely copulative,
or does it express *essence*? To put it differently: is the text saying "Baptism signifies

incorporation into Christ" or "Baptism is in essence incorporation into Christ"?

And what weight is to be put upon the phrase, "Baptism is a gift of God"? Is it to be interpreted: "Baptism as a gift is an expression of the pure objectivity of the grace of God"?

II

The relation between baptism and conversion is affirmed in remarkably strong terms, such as we have not met in an ecumenical report of this kind. (e.g. "The necessity of faith for the reception of the salvation embodied and set forth in baptism is acknowledged by all the churches: (III, 8). This, of course, is wholly in line with Baptist witness through the centuries. But our difficulty lies in the fact that the language used identifies the sign with the thing signified. For example, "Baptism *is* incorporation into Christ..." it *is* entry into the New Covenant between God and God's people" (I.1) Baptism *unites* the one baptized with Christ and with his people"; it "*is* participation in Christ's death and resurrection." The implication of these verbs is that being baptized, in and of itself, necessarily and mechanically brings about these results (II.2). "Those baptized are pardoned, cleansed and sanctified by Christ," etc. (II.B.4), implies that they could not receive God's grace from the Christ-event unless they *were* baptized. We have similar difficulty with such statements as, "Through baptism, *Christians* are brought into union with Christ..." (II.D.6) This seems to imply that they are Christians *before* they are baptized, but, if not, does it mean that unbaptized believers in Christ are denied such union? "Baptism, in its full meaning, signifies *and effects* both" (participation in Christ's death and resurrection and the receiving of the Spirit (IV.B.14). To speak of the sign *effecting* what it signifies is to lead us straight into the *ex opere operato* views of the sacraments which Baptists have never accepted. Surely, personal faith in Jesus Christ is the only means of grace — the ordinances or sacraments are a graphic means by which the gospel is proclaimed. We must not confuse the sign with that which it signifies. Of course, baptism and that which it signifies are closely related.

We acknowledge that the New Testament itself sometimes uses such language in relation to baptism. "All of us who were baptized into his death" (Rom. 6:3); "Having been buried with him in baptism and raised with him..." (Col. 1:12). However, we must remember that in the New Testament believers alone are baptismal candidates. If baptism is conceived as a response to the saving grace in Christ on the part of the baptized, the problem disappears. Baptism is an act of confession and public identification with Christ and his people on the part of one who has voluntarily committed himself to Him in faith.

Dr. Nelson Thomson, Principal of the French Baptist Seminary in Montreal, writes:

On this matter we cannot, in conscience, negotiate. There is some pressure on Baptists to recognize infant baptism as being Christian baptism, albeit less well-attested in the New Testament. We would reply that infant baptism is not attested at all in the New Testament — and as long as we hold to the latter's authority, we shall have to reply firmly that we cannot go in that direction.[12]

III

The work of the Spirit in relation to baptism is well stated in the brief affirmation, "The Holy Spirit is at work in the lives of people before, in and after their baptism (II.5). Linked with this is the reminder, important also to Baptists, "Baptism is related not only to momentary experience, but to life-long growth into Christ," with which the ethical implications of the new life in Christ are also emphasized (III, 9-10). However, we would question another sentence, "God bestows upon all baptized persons that anointing and promise of the Holy Spirit...," if it implies that such anointing and promise are withheld from believers who are not baptized. Baptists recognize a spirit of unity with all who acknowledge Jesus Christ as Lord and Savior, whether or not they have been baptized. That is why we question the statement in II.D.6 that Christians find their unity in one common baptism. Ephesians 4:5 hardly applies to the present situation. When these words were written, there *was* only one baptism — that of believers.

We appreciate the emphasis that baptism is "a sign of the Kingdom of God and of the life of the world to come," and the way in which this insight is developed (II.D.7).

While Baptists will genuinely welcome these, and other elements in the exposition of baptism in the "Report", there are difficulties for them, some of which appear to arise out of contradictions within the text. It is possible that the latter owe their place in the "Report" through the adoption of concepts from varied traditions which are inharmonious and what lie side by side in unresolved opposition. We give some examples:

i. Over against the affirmation of the necessity of faith for the reception of the salvation represented in baptism, the "Report" largely assumes that baptism effects what it signifies, and that at the time of its administration. The recommended order of baptism, for example, should contain "a declaration that the persons baptized have acquired a new identity as sons and daughters of God, and as members of the Church..." (V.D.20). However, we would have to interpret "the necessity of faith" as meaning the faith of the one being baptized, as well as that of the believing community. We hold that "personal commitment is necessary" for baptism as well as "for responsible membership in the body of Christ," because, as V.D.19 points out, "Within any comprehensive order of baptism" the persons baptized *are* "members of the Church, called to be witnesses of the Gospel." With III.9 and III.10 we are in complete agreement, as we certainly hold to the need for spiritual growth throughout life. As pointed out earlier, the Great Commission of our Lord admonished us to make disciples, baptize them, and to teach them to observe what he has commanded, and in that order. Again, it is stated, "God bestows on all baptized persons the anointing and the promise of the Holy Spirit, marks them with a seal and implants in their hearts the first installment of their inheritance as sons and daughters of God" (II.C.5). The term "all" in that sentence is disturbing; it comports neither with what is said as to the necessity of faith for the reception of salvation nor with the harsh facts of life (witness e.g. what Brunner called the millions of baptized pagans in Europe).

ii. It is stated (in IV, 11) that baptism on personal confession of faith is the most clearly attested pattern in the New Testament documents. This admission should lead to the recognition, common among biblical scholars, that the theology of baptism in the New Testament assumes conversion and faith (so in Acts, and the important baptismal declarations in Galatians 3:26-27, Colossians 2:12, I Peter 3:21). To apply, as does the "Report," the entire theology of baptism in the New Testament to the baptism of infants is to sunder unwarrentedly baptism from that which is signified. Inevitably this leads to a sacramentalism which is foreign to Baptists.

iii. The Report assumes that the baptism of infants normally takes place in the community of faith and for families of faith. That the latter feature (faith in the families) is not always present is implied in the gentle admonition that churches practicing infant baptism must "guard themselves against the practice of apparently indiscriminate baptism" (IV.C.16). The compilers of this "Report," however, must surely be aware that the actual situation is other than assumed: witness the fact that in many countries of western Europe almost whole populations are still receiving baptism in infancy. For this situation to be brought into line with the presuppositions of the "Report," a gentle admonition is insufficient; it requires a revolution in the practice of baptism in such areas. More than 200 years ago Baptist churches began to conduct services of parental dedication, in which God is thanked for the gift of a new life upon which occasion the parents and congregation commit themselves to rear the new born child in the Christian faith. Preparation for baptism, in this sense begins at birth. However, we believe that baptism should be received only after careful instruction, when the candidates are prepared to accept the responsibilities of Christian discipleship in both church and the world. We deplore the practice in some Baptist churches of what we can only call "deferred infant baptism" in which little children who have hardly reached the age of moral responsibility or understanding of the basic significance of the baptismal act are baptized.

iv. In light of these observations Baptists view with mixed feelings the statement, "Baptism is an unrepeatable act. Any practice which might be interpreted as "re-baptism" must be avoided" (IV, A.13). Ideally, the former sentence is correct. The name "Re-baptizers" (Wiedertaufer) given by opponents to the forerunners of the modern Baptist movements has always been repudiated by them. The question at issue for them has been the justification of equating the rite of infant baptism with the baptism which the New Testament appears to attest, wherein the faith of the person baptized is integral to the rite. The earliest Baptists believed that the equation was unjustified and so they sought *biblical* baptism *for themselves*, and then for others. This same crisis of conscience perpetually confronts the successors in persons who regard themselves as casualties of the general bestowal of baptism on infants and who, on coming to faith in later years, believe that they should receive the baptism which they find in the

New Testament, and they come to Baptist churches with the plea that they should be given it. The existence of such casualties of the prevalent system is a prior question that requires more serious consideration than is commonly given.

v. While readily recognizing that there are many churches which strive to administer infant baptism in the kind of setting envisaged in the "Report," it must be acknowledged that Baptists continue to find it difficult to acknowledge infant baptism as authentic biblical baptism, by reason of their conviction that baptism is rightly applied to those who personally confess their faith in Christ. The "Report" asks them to contemplate that "both forms of baptism embody God's own initiative in Christ and express a response of faith made within the believing community (Commentary, 12), the confession of faith being made in believer's baptism *at* baptism and that of baptized infants being made later." Certainly this proposition envisages a different situation from that which brought forth the original Baptist protest in the context of state-church Europe during the Reformation. Baptists will continue to evaluate their own practice of baptism and that of other Christian communions in the light of their understanding of the New Testament. It is also fervently hoped that the difficulties which they find in infant baptism, such as those voiced in the preceding paragraphs, will be further contemplated by their sister churches. Persistent dialogue between Baptist and paedobaptist confessions will surely see a furthering of the progress that has undoubtedly been made during the present century in the interpretation and administration of baptism. In this search for understanding it is also to be hoped that the insights of notable theologians within the paedobaptist communions who are urging reform in the practice of baptism with a view to an administration more closely approximating the primitive apostolic practice, will be heeded, which is hardly apparent in the "Lima Report"; such "reformers" may be able to aid us all in our endeavors to walk together in obedience to the revelation of God in Christ Jesus.

The Eucharist

I

Baptist theologians have written much about baptism, and indeed, about ministry, but rather less on the "Eucharist" (We use the term, as in the "Lima Report"). This is not to say that the Eucharist has not been a regular part of Baptist worship, but that there has been relatively little Baptist reflection upon its meaning and practice. This section of the BEM, therefore, may well have much to say to Baptists.

There are many things in this section which should immediately commend themselves to Baptists.

1. We should welcome the way in which the Eucharist is set against so rich and diverse a biblical background both of Old and New Testaments (Paragraph 1). To recognize that the Eucharist is prefigured in the Passover reminds us of the vital Old Testament background. To understand that the meal on the Emmaus Road links the celebration of the Last Supper with the glory

of the Resurrection adds an essential dimension of our communion services.

2. In the section on the "Meaning of the Eucharist" there is a richness of description which Baptists have at times failed to recognize. However, we are puzzled by the statement, "every Christian receives this gift of salvation through communion in the body and blood of Christ." This appears to imply that salvation comes through the Eucharist which Baptists have never held. The following sections also present problems for Baptists because they seem to indicate that grace and forgiveness are mediated by the Eucharist.

A.3. For baptists the Eucharist is also an act of thanksgiving to our heavenly Father for the gift of his Son for our redemption. This has always been a part of a complete observance of the Lord's Supper on the part of Baptist churches.

A.4. Indeed, we welcome the concept of praise. For Baptists the observance of the Lord's Supper is among the most sobering and sacred moments of worship in the life of a given church.

B.5. The Eucharist is for Baptists and *anamnesis*. It is much more than the English term *memorial*. It is a remembering again, that is, to call to mind the Christ-event, the passion, crucifixion, death, and resurrection of our Lord. Just as the Passover calls to mind for the Jewish people and celebrated the Exodus, so the Lord's Supper calls to mind the agony of Him who died for us. In so doing it elicits anew a fresh commitment to the living Christ, to live for him in faith, hope, and love.

B.6. For Baptists the Eucharist is also *kerugmatic*. It is a gospel-proclaiming act in which the Christ-event is celebrated but also the promise of the *parousia* is always present.

B.8. Baptists have always held with the Reformers of the sixteenth century that the Eucharist in itself is not a fresh sacrifice but a thanksgiving celebration of the one unique sacrifice of Christ which can never be repeated for in Him God historically mediated his supreme revelation of love and grace for which we can but give Him thanks in communion with the risen Lord and the assembled brethren.

B.12. There is much in articles 9-11 that enriches our thinking in regard to the proper observance of the Eucharist but article 12 is of particular importance.

B.13. This paragraph presents a number of problems for most Baptists. The word sacrament as used here is quite unacceptable. It is not found in the New Testament nor used by Christ. The implication of the opening sentence and the use of the term "real presence," which is used twice carries with it historically theological connotations the Lord's Supper was never intended to convey. "But Christ's mode of presence in the Eucharist is unique. Jesus said over the bread and wine of the Eucharist: "This is my body...this is my blood...." What Jesus declared is true, and this truth is fulfilled every time the Eucharist is celebrated." This interpretation sounds very much like traditional positions on the Eucharist which Baptists cannot accept. The statement is qualified somewhat by the assertion, "all agree that to discern the body and blood of Christ, faith is required." However, to accept the view of the Eucharist as set forth in this paragraph is to do violence to the true nature of the ordinance and rob it of its spiritual significance for both the individual believer and the church.

C.14. There is much in this paragraph that strikes a resounding chord in Baptists' hearts. We believe in the living presence of Christ whenever two or three are gathered together in His name. We recognize it is the Holy Spirit that makes His presence possible. However, once again the overtones of a sacramentalism and the concept that the sacrifice in the Eucharist found in the last sentence must be rejected.

C.15. This paragraph is of concern to Baptists since it focuses upon the sacramental aspects in the elements rather than upon Christ.

C.17. This is a good statement with which we heartily concur.

C.18. The "blessed hope" of the Lord's return is a welcome emphasis.

C.20. This paragraph is a particularly important one. One of the aspects of communion for Baptists is that it is a means of expressing gratitude to God and love for one another. Preparation for partaking of the Lord's Supper demands self-examination, repentance, renewal of faith in the crucified savior and renewed dedication to do His will in word and deed — to truly pray "Thy kingdom come, thy will be done in heaven and earth."

D.21. There is much that is challenging in this paragraph but Baptists must take exception to some of the ideas found therein. Most Baptists believe that the Eucharist is communion, that is, it cannot be taken alone nor administered to the sick. It is for the gathered congregation of baptized believers. Some Baptist churches hold that only members in good standing of a particular church may partake. Others invite all "of the same faith and order." Still others hold that all who know Christ as Savior and Lord may participate in celebrating the Lord's Supper. Many Baptists have no hesitancy in joining in interdenominational celebration of the Eucharist in that of other communions when invited. The ambivalence here is due to a number of factors too numerous and varied for explanation at this point.

E.26. Baptists would question the last statement in this paragraph. The strength of the missionary witness for them is dependent not upon a common table but upon fidelity to the unique revelation of God in Christ.

III

F.27. This is suggestive. Surely a variety of services where the Word is preached and the "sacraments" are properly observed is the essence of such worship. This may take place for Baptists once each month, every three months, once a year, or in a few churches, weekly. This to Baptists is wholly a matter for local churches to decide.

Ministry

Baptists warmly welcome *Section I*, where the priority is given to the People of God, but will be disappointed with *Section II*, with its description of an order of ministry "which may appropriately be called" priestly (17), and which (apparently) has the exclusive right to celebrate the Eucharist (14). In particular they will be baffled by the restriction of the celebration of the oft-repeated communion to an ordained officiant, while lay celebration of the once-for-all baptism is permitted. The Baptist view is that "any member of the Church may be authorized by it, on occasion, to exercise the functions of ministry..., to preach the Word, to administer baptism, to preside at the Lord's Table."[13]

The emphasis of *Section III* on the Three-Fold Order of Bishops, Priests and Deacons is a further difficulty for us. The structure of leadership in Baptist congregations all over the world is that of minister (ordained) and deacons (lay). Baptists very early in their history struggled to determine the nature of the ministry as set forth in the New Testament. Consequently they rejected the four-fold ministry of Geneva and the three-fold ministry suggested here. Hence from their beginning Baptists have held to a two-fold ministry for local churches of pastor (bishop, presbyter, elder are synonyms in the New Testament) and deacons. The development of monarchial, metropolitan bishops, and archbishops or patriarchs, and other hierarchical forms of the episcopate they cannot justify in the light of scripture. The New Testament does not distinguish between bishop and presbyter for the double-named office of the leader of the local Christian community, nor is it clear that deacons were other than lay leaders. In some parts of the Baptist world, a distinction is made between the function of elders and ministers.

Although emphasizing the autonomy of the local church, Baptists, since their earliest history, have been in fellowship with sister churches, and very soon formed themselves into district associations, and ultimately into national Baptist unions or conventions, which may make decisions on agreed areas of common tasks (e.g. ministerial training, evangelism, and social action). While there is nothing to prevent an association or union from appointing officers to aid church planting and nurture, or missionary appointment — an example of the former would be the "messenger-apostles" of the 17th century, and of the latter the English area superintendents or American executive secretaries or directors of missions today — these are purely leadership rather than authoritarian roles.

A.19. Baptists concur with the opening sentence, "the New Testament does not describe a single pattern of ministry which might serve as a blueprint or continuing norm for all future ministry in the church." However, the report inserts its "nevertheless" and goes on to affirm that the traditional three-fold ministry may serve today as an expression of the unity we seek and also as a means of achieving it. (22) This is an implication which Baptists find both inconsistent and unhelpful.

A.23. This paragraph is acceptable provided that the ministry of the *episkope* (oversight of the Christian community) is not necessarily identified with any one of the particular forms of the episcopacy as historically developed in certain churches. Baptists, from their inception, have recognized the importance of the *episkope* as a gift of Christ to his church for the care and discipline of the people of God. it is a commission which is ultimately inherent to the gathered community itself, which, meeting together, seeks to discern and minister the will of Christ under the guidance of the Holy Spirit. This community has both the responsibility and freedom under God to commission certain persons to fulfill particular aspects of *episkope* especially the ministry of the word, pastoral care, and teaching.

B.26,27. For Baptists, ordination is the recognition on the part of the church of the gifts of the Spirit already bestowed. Ordination then makes no qualitative difference between the ordained and the unordained but rather indicates certain functions. The earliest Baptist confession of 1611 recognized women as well as men for the deaconate. Today in many Baptist churches both men and women are ordained to various ministries. However, it must be admitted that historically some of our most effective ministers were never formally ordained by the laying on of hands, e.g., Charles Haddon Spurgeon. Some Baptist churches still do not use the laying on of hands but simply recognize the call of God in the life of the minister or deacon by congregational affirmation and prayer. Some Baptist unions and associations accept the responsibility to ordain and commend the ordained to the churches.

The "Commentary (21) is helpful with many suggestive ideas for helping churches to come to grips with the need of relating the call of God to minister to the needs of a suffering humanity.

C.28-31. Some Baptists claim a succession back to John the Baptist in an unbroken line of churches or baptized believers. Even though this theory, known as the "John, Jerusalem, Jordan" theory of Baptist succession, is not subject to documentation, it has been persistent in helping to form the Baptist identity. Even though no denomination can document an historical succession through bishops, presbyters, churches or baptism, succession has been an attractive argument for maintaining the purity of the faith from Irenaeus to the present. Notwithstanding, perpetuity is no guarantee of orthodoxy.

While contemporary Baptists reject the so-called "apostolic succession," they recognize that no Christian communion stands outside the stream of Christian history. For them, however, apostolicity is seen in the degree of faithfulness to the historically mediated revelation of God in Christ to which the apostles bear witness in the pages of the New Testament. This is the witness which the Holy Spirit honors with his presence and power and which brings fallen humanity into a saving relationship with Jesus Christ.

VI

C.51-55. This section is based on a series of assumptions foreign to Baptist faith and order. *The New Delhi Report* echoes for most Baptists a viable concept of unity:

"It is in Jesus Christ, God's Son and our only Mediator, that we have union with God. It is he who has given this gift to us through his coming into our world. Unity is not of our making, but as we receive the grace of Jesus Christ we are one in him.[14]

Conclusion

We wish to express our gratitude to the Faith and Order Commission for the formulation of this document and to the World Council of Churches for making it available. We further commend its careful study to the churches of the Baptist World Alliance. However, the distinct impression persists in spite of many fine and noble sentiments expressed in this *Faith and Order Paper No. III,* for which we are truly grateful, that entirely too much emphasis is eventually given to apostolic succession of the episcopacy which is said to be essential to Christian unity. We are convinced this is to seek unity where it cannot be found.

For Baptists, unity can best be achieved not in a uniform liturgy or ecclesiology but in sharing a common faithful witness to Jesus Christ in word and deed.

William R. Estep is Professor of Church History at Southwestern Baptist Theological Seminary in Ft. Worth, Texas, U.S.A.

Endnotes

1. W. O. Carver, "The Baptist Conception of the Church," originally appeared in *Christendom* but was printed in a section entitled "Denominational Statements" as "6. Baptist Churches" in *The Nature of the Church,* edited by R. Newton Flew. (New York: Harper and Brothers Publishers, 1951), p. 289.

2. William L. Lumpkin, ed., *Baptist Confessions of Faith.* (Philadelphia: The Judson Press, 1959), p. 119.

3. Ibid., p. 140.

4. Ibid., p. 165.

6. Ibid., p. 286.

7. *Annual of the Southern Baptist Convention.* (Nashville: The Southern Baptist Convention, 1963), p. 275.

8. Walter B. Shurden, ed., *The Life of Baptists in the Life of the World: 80 Years of the Baptist World Alliance.* (Nashville: Broadman Press, 1958), p. 13.

9. Ibid., p. 141.

10. Josef Nordenhaug, ed., *The Truth That Makes Men Free.* (Nashville: Broadman Press, 1965), p. 7.

11. Tape of Josef Nordenhaug, "Summary and Highlights," Eleventh Congress of the Baptist World Alliance, June 25, 1965. Recorded by the Radio and Television Commission of the Southern Baptist Convention, Fort Worth, TX.

12. R. F. Watts, "Baptists and Baptism in the BEM Consultation" (unpublished paper), p. 4.

13. W. A. Visser 'T Hooft, ed., *The New Delhi Report* (New York: Association Press, 1962), pp. 117-18.

Freedom And Its Limits: The Problem Of Church-State Relations

Pablo A. Deiros

Introduction

The proclamation of the Gospel of Jesus Christ requires an atmosphere of freedom for its accomplishments. Freedom is a must if the Christian community of believers is going to obey its duty to comply with Jesus' commandment of carrying the Good News to the ends of the earth. Christians around the world without any distinction of denominations and traditions have recognized freedom as an important precondition that guarantees the success of their missionary commitment.

In the fulfillment of its responsibilities the church is only limited by its disposition to be subject to Christ's lordship (Acts 4:19-20; 5:29). A responsible witness to the Gospel, then, first of all takes seriously its duty to the Lord Christ and his kingdom. Any compromise of this freedom to be obedient to Him would endanger the effectiveness and consistency of the Christian testimony of both church and individual believers. The Christian church should be free to be the church, that is, a confessing community of disciples of Jesus Christ.

Freedom to witness, however, has to be a responsible exercise that takes into account the fact that the church is a historical entity. As such, it is in the world although it is not identified with the values and perspectives that rule over the world in opposition to God's eternal purposes. The church itself is one spiritual body but a heterogeneous reality, united but not uniform. Diversity is part of its richness, and not a negative aspect of its character. How, then, to understand freedom to witness from the inside of the confessing body? In other words, how do the diverse members of the same spiritual body of believers put into practice their obedience to the missionary duty with regard to their brethren of different traditions?

Moreover, it is because the church serves the world in the name of Jesus and is committed to bear its witness to the Gospel in the world that its freedom to do so must be also taken into account. The church is not only responsible for freedom within itself but also freedom outside itself. As stated above, the church is bound to its exclusive loyalty to Christ. But the mere fact that it is in the world creates limits that should be taken into account.

It is because of its obedience to the mission given by its Lord that the church has the obligation to promote law and order in society and do its best to foster the welfare of each individual and society as a whole. Since the field of action in which the church gives its service and testimony coincides with the arena of the state's action, it is inevitable questions should arise concerning the relationship that should be developed between them. Should the church be subservient to the state? Should the state be at the service of the church? Should church and state recognize their own spheres of sovereignty? Should they come to an association which unites their actions for the welfare of society?

Baptists have always considered Christian witness as the major responsibility of the church. They have claimed freedom as the necessary condition to better accomplish the Christian mission. In order to express most effectively religious freedom, they have considered separation of church and state to be an indispensable requirement. Without separation freedom is a fallacy; without freedom a responsible witness to the Gospel is not possible.

The present paper does not pretend to be a complete discussion of the proposed topic. It is, rather, a preliminary and concise approach to the issue of separation of church and state from a Baptist perspective. The discussion is focused on those aspects of the principle which are most closely related to the responsibility of witnessing to the Gospel in an ecumenical age. Questions for further discussion are raised in the conclusion.

I. DEFINITION OF THE PRINCIPLE BY BAPTISTS

Baptists believe that the spiritual principle of religious liberty can only be guaranteed by its corollary, the political principle of the separation of church and state.[1] This principle has its roots in the Scriptures, rather than in any historical or cultural factor. It is necessary to make clear that the principle of separation of church and state is not just a political expression of the American idiosyncracy. Although it is a historical fact that the principle was incorporated for the first time since the days of Constantine in the political system of the United States, it has been sustained by many dissenters during the late Middle Ages and the Reformation period.[2] Certainly, these influences were incorporated into the Constitution of the United States during the eighteenth century. But the principle grew out of a Biblical interpretation applied to politics and not on the contrary.

Baptists have been insistent upon the proclamation and application of this doctrine throughout the history of their denomination.[3] Robert G. Torbet explains the consistency with which this principle has been sustained saying that, "It has been to safeguard their beliefs in the priesthood of believers and in religious freedom that Baptists have insisted upon the complete separation of church and state."[4]

The Concept of Church-State Separation Among Baptists

According to Baptists, the principle of separation of church and state expresses their conviction that the Bible does not teach nor in any way does it justify that the church be dominant in political matters, nor that the state regulate the religious teachings or practices of the church. Furthermore, Baptists do not accept that a church or denomination should receive pecuniary help from public funds.[5] By this, "they have meant that the state has no right to interfere with the religious beliefs and practices of individuals or congregations; and that the church on its part, has no claim upon the state for financial support."[6]

In the light of the Bible, it is evident that neither church nor state should control the spirit of man and his convictions with regard to God. The relationship that binds God and man is eminently spiritual (John 4:24). This is the reason why no external factor should interfere. An association of church and state may create a situation of pressure which can make impossible such a spiritual relationship. On the other hand, the state is an institution ordered by God (Romans 13:1-2), as is also the church (Matthew 16:18; Ephesians 5:25). Besides, each sphere has responsibilities which are their own.[7] So then, from a Biblical perspective, the union of church and state is inadmissible for the Christian conscience. As Henry C. Vedder has pointed out, the "union of Church and State is contrary to the Word of God, contrary to natural justice, and destructive of both parties in the union."[8]

Biblical Basis of the Concept of Church-State Separation

Most of the Biblical statements that support the principle of religious liberty support also the principle of separation. The Bible teaches that law and order are part of God's design for the welfare of man. Accordingly, the state should be, in its own sphere, an instrument to serve this divine purpose (Romans 13:17; 1 Peter 2:13-14). The Bible recognizes the existence of the state and encourages believers to respect, obey, support and pray for the state (1 Timothy 2:1,2). These passages, however, do not imply the approval of evil rulers or an unjust authority. They simply recognize the fact of a principle of government, "ordained by God". Jesus himself recognized the state (Matthew 22:21), although he carefully made a distinction between the duties of citizenship in this world and in his kingdom. He made it clear that the state, within its own sphere, has its authority, which is only limited by the authority of God himself. "Render unto God the things that are God's" means that the supreme loyalty of man belongs only to God.[9]

However, there is not an explicit declaration of the principle of separation in the Bible. The doctrine is implicit if the spiritual character of God's relation to man is taken into account, as well as the nature of Christ's kingdom and the differences that exist between the functions of the church and the state.

Baptists consider that this is more than a mere political postulate or a principle that finds its roots in the development of political sciences. They insist that the principle springs out of the Bible itself. According to Justice C. Anderson, the Bible and not any political system constitutes the foundation for the doctrine of separation. The principle is the result of Biblical interpretation applied to politics. He states that "the interaction between these Biblical truths and their application to modern politics, in the light of historical mistakes, has produced the Baptist doctrine of separation of church and State, or rather, the ideal of a free church in a free State."[10]

One of the most systematic and condensed attempts to summarize the Biblical basis for the principle of separation of church and state is found in an article by Jimmy Allen.[11] The author presents, in the form of an outline, the basic ideas that have been vital for Bible-believing Baptists through the years, and the Biblical passages that support them. The Scriptures quoted are not used as proof-texts but as expressions of principles which are central throughout the Bible. These ideas are those which Baptists have traditionally used to substantiate their understanding of the principle of separation of church and state.

According to Allen there are three reasons why state and church should be and remain separated. First, both church and state are bound by the Biblical teachings concerning the nature of man. Second, both church and state are institutions ordained by God. Third, both church and state have distinctive contributions to make to the development of individuals in society.[12]

Among all of Allen's considerations, the most important one seems to be the first, which emphasizes the fact that man is made in the image of God, who is spirit (Genesis 1:26-27; John 4:24). In consequence, man, like God Himself, is spiritual in his nature (1 Corinthians 15:45). This spiritual nature requires that the relationship between them be a spiritual one rather than an outward form arbitrarily enforced by legal means (Romans 14:12). Besides, man has not only infinite worth, but also individual freedom. This means that the state has no right to legislate and the church has no right to dictate so as to attempt to control man's inner religious convictions (Acts 5:29). On the other hand, the state has no moral right to force one person to support the religious institutions of another (2 Corinthians 9:7). The state has the unique responsibilities of restraining evil and preserving law and order (Romans 13:3-4; 1 Timothy 2:1-3; 1 Peter 2:13-15). The responsibilities of the church are those of witnessing to individuals and society about Christ (Acts 1:8), of instructing believing individuals in their Christian responsibilities (Matthew 28:20), and of providing an atmosphere of Christian fellowship in which Christians will grow into the likeness of Christ (Ephesians 4:11-13).[13]

There are some other Biblical teachings that support the doctrine of separation, namely, the Lordship of Christ (Matthew 28:18), the nature of Christ's kingdom (John 18:36), man's sinful condition (Romans 3:23), the universal priesthood of all believers (Ephesians 2:5-10), the spiritual nature of the church (Matthew 16:18), and the double citizenship of the Christian believer (Matthew 22:21).

Baptists consider as very important their assertion of a Biblical basis for the principle of separation, since there are many others that advocate separation but for different reasons and ends. Atheists, humanists, skeptics, human rights champions and numerous ideological, social, cultural and political groups fight for separation of church and state. Baptists are not looking for the separation of social life from religion, but the triumph of a free religion. Their struggles have been not to free man from religion, but to free man for religion.

Historical Background for the Concept of Church-State Separation

Historically speaking, the principle of separation of church and state has been one of the major contributions of Baptists to the development of Christianity. E. Y. Mullins has summarized the way Baptists came to the appropriation of this doctrine when he says:

> There is no evidence that Baptists came to their view of soul freedom and separation of church and state gradually. There is nowhere a wavering note on this great theme. It seems to have been a divinely given prophetic insight into the meaning of the gospel and the implicit teaching of Scripture. Mark the phrase, implicit teaching. For Scripture nowhere enjoins in so many words separation of Church and State. It required a spiritual discernment to discover the doctrine, prophetic insight of a high order, and yet when once discovered by the unbiased mind it was accepted as a self-evident truth.[14]

The Reformers, with many different views, sustained in general the idea that the state should not be separated from the church—at least, spiritually. The more radical religious groups of the sixteenth century, however, insisted in the need of such separation. This is why they came to be know as "free churches", that is, not official or national churches. At the same time, the advance of the new political ideas which were springing to life during the seventeenth and eighteenth centuries led to a rupture, in some cases violent, of the relations between church and state. The idea of a religious state and also that of the religious foundation of the state suffered so much because of the criticisms levelled against them from various groups that it can be said that they almost disappeared in the Western world.[15]

The relations of church and state have followed different alternatives throughout history and have assumed various forms. The view of the Roman Empire was that the church and the state were antagonistic. The state persecuted the church with the purpose of razing it. Physical persecution and social prejudice were the means employed. Today it is not so common to see open persecution against the church. But there are many subtle forms in which the state can hinder the testimony of believers.

The view of the medieval Roman Catholic Church was that the church should dominate the state. This doctrine was the result of a long development from the times of Constantine (313) to Innocent III (1215). Even today there are many indications that the ideology coined throughout the centuries still exerts its influence in the Roman Church in spite of the laudable achievements of Vatican II.

The erastian view, taught by the Zwinglian Thomas Erastus (1524-1583), was that the state should dominate the affairs of the church. This was also the idea of Constantine, and represents the position of several Protestant and Orthodox churches. In some cases, the church is nothing else but a department of the state, under the supervision and protection of civil authorities. History teaches that in many occasions this meant a legislated uniformity of religion and as a consequence the persecution of dissenters. This view fosters the idea that the state has the obligation to protect and promote the national church.

Baptists and their spiritual ancestors, the Anabaptists, are historically responsible for the view of separation, that is, that church and state have different spheres of action, and that each one must operate within its own sphere without interference of coercion from the other. This view is what Leo Pfeffer calls the "concept of mutual independence".[16]

The Anabaptists and English Baptists stated this principle in the sixteenth century, but it was Roger Williams (1603-1683) that put it into practice in New England in the seventeenth century. He was the first one to challenge politically the Constantinian view. His foundation was a political ideal based on the Bible. he called it "the doctrine of the two tables". According to it, civil authorities had the responsibility to prosecute everything that had to do with the Second Table, man vis-a-vis man, but the magistrate had no right to punish breaches of the First Table of the law, that is, man vis-a-vis God. Here lies the germ of the doctrine that the church and the state should be entirely separate and independent of each other.

After his banishment from Salem Williams made his way to Rhode Island, where he bought land from the Indians and founded a settlement. Providence became a "lively experiment", since it was a refuge not only for Baptists, but

also for Quakers, Catholics and Jews. Williams spent his life propagating his doctrine. He advocated separation in the socio-political sphere, but also sustained
that Christianity should be separated from the idea of Christendom.[17]

In his book, *The Bloody Tenent of Persecution,* which marked a landmark
in the literature on freedom, Williams states that separation of church and state
is the necessary corollary to the principle of freedom. He considers them as just
one principle. Williams ideas were not only fundamental for the development
of democracy in his country but also were influential all around the world.[18]

Some other prominent Baptists helped to introduce the principle of church-
state separation to the laws of the United States in North America. Isaac Backus
(1724-1806) and John Leland (1754-1841) lived in times of political and ecclesiastical effervescence in North America. Both were pastors and writers, but their
major contribution was their struggle for the principle of church-state separation.

Backus excelled in his performance at the Continental Congress of 1774,
where he layed before its members the claims for religious liberty and separation of church and state. He was also active in the ratification of the American
Constitution; he fought for his Baptist views in Massachusetts until his death,
but separation had to wait until 1833. Isaac Backus is considered to be one of
the founders of the American republic. Being himself a victim of religious oppression, Backus committed his life to the elimination of this evil.[19]

John Leland used his contacts with James Madison and Thomas Jefferson
to advocate for the doctrine of separation. Leland considered that the establishment of a Christian Church by Constantine had created the terrible monster
of Christendom.[20] His life was a saga of litigations in favor of the principle of
separation. He and the Baptists were those responsible for the abolition of a
state church in Virginia, Massachusetts and Connecticut.[21]

These champions of separation were followed by many other Baptists that
built one of the most outstanding democracies of the modern world.[22] But the
defense and promotion of the principle of separation of church and state is not
an exclusive feature of Baptists in the Anglo-Saxon world. It is characteristic
of Baptists everywhere.

Practical Meaning of the Concept of Church-State Separation

For Baptists, separation of church and state means a double separation.
On the one hand, it has to do with a separation in organization. This discards
any attempt to impose an established church, as well as any effort on the part
of any institution to use another as an instrument to promote its own ends.[23]
On the other hand, it means separation in their functions. Church and state
should recognize that their functions are different, and that they should not
interfere in the affairs of each other. Nevertheless, an absolute separation of
church and state is not possible since both of them are performing their service
in the same society.[24]

The last statement means that church and state fulfill functions which
overlap in that they necessarily deal with matters which touch the sphere of
the other. So then, the state with regard to the church has the responsibility

of protecting it as long as it functions as such and fulfills its specific mission. Furthermore, it has to promote a healthy environment so that the church, together with school and family, may accomplish its vocation of service for the betterment of society. But the state should also put limits to the freedom of any church or religious group, when the free exercise of such a privilege and right restrains or threatens the freedom of others.[25]

On its part, the church also has duties toward the state. The Christian community of faith should provide citizens that will respect the authority of the state and its officials. It should proclaim to the state and its magistrates the message of God, espousing the Christian ideal for the state and the basis for God's judgement over the present state. It should also encourage its own members, whether they are officials of the state or simple citizens, to be active participants in the life of the nation, in order to be the bearers of the Christian principles and spirit to the total life of the community.[26]

In summary, the basic proposition of Baptists has been to keep a free church in a free state.[27] This proposition recognizes the distinction between both terms of the relation. However, it does not propose a mechanical separation, but the sovereignty of each entity in its own sphere. Church and state, in this sense, are related by their two sovereign spheres of life. The church should not put limits or coerce the state, nor should the state act in this way with regard to the church, as both develop and express their own sovereignties.

II. APPLICATION OF THE PRINCIPLE BY BAPTISTS

Walter Rauschenbush has said: "The separation of church and state has the double advantage of removing the clerical influence from political life, and the political influence from church life. It leaves the church unmuzzled to speak out, if it has anything to say."[28] An absolute separation, however, is almost impossible in a changing world in which prevails the idea of the growing role of the state for the well-being of society. Baptists recognize that an absolute separation is not feasible nor convenient. Although in the United States the expression "a wall of separation" has traditionally been used by most Baptists to describe their understanding of separation,[29] this expression is not the most adequate way to describe Baptists' claim in the light of a world wide perspective. Perhaps it is necessary to find other language to express the dialectic tension that exists between church and state. Both church and state have their own sphere of action and fulfill specific responsibilities. However, both of them are part of historical reality and deal with the same human circumstances.

Separation and Relation

The relation between church and state is more like an old Medieval castle. There was a moat surrounding the fortified place, but there was also a bridge that gave access to and from the castle. The Baptist understanding of the principle of separation provides for the necessary protection and separation as with the moat of a castle, but at the same time recognizes the church's need of communication with the world around it, just as the bridge of the castle opens the way to the outside world.

The church is like the embassy of a nation in a foreign country. The doctrine of separation points to the diplomatic immunity enjoyed by an embassy. The church should be independent. Otherwise it will run the risk of loosing its own Christian identity and its prophetic calling. Without the principle of separation, Christianity is in danger of turning into Christendom. The church should never forget that it is in the world, but is not of this world (John 17). The Christian community of faith should ideally be a free church in a free state.

Separation is the only coherent possibility, since the nature and character of church and state are so different. The church was ordained by God to proclaim the Gospel; the state was ordained by God to administer justice. They have a different constituency: the church is composed by believers, while the state is made up of all the inhabitants of a given jurisdiction. They also have different methods to achieve their ends, since the church uses voluntary persuasion while the state enforces law by coercion. Their administrations are not the same: the church is under the lordship of the living Christ; the state is under the authority of the magistrate or the elected ruler. Their economic resources are different in their origin, because the church receives its support from the voluntary offerings of believers, while the state supports its activities by the collection of taxes from its citizens. In the sphere of education, they are also different in that the church pursues a sectarian educational program oriented toward personal conversion and Christian discipleship, while at the same time the educational program of the state is oriented to the pluralistic formation of the citizens.

Baptists do affirm that Jesus Christ is Lord over both the church and the state. But, his lordship is explicit for the first, and implicit for the second. He is the recognized Lord of the church, but he is the Lord *de facto* of the state. The church proclaims his lordship to the world. The state lives under his lordship, whether it recognizes it or not. For the church the lordship of Christ is a matter of faith and commitment, but for the state his lordship is a matter of historical understanding. Christian believers live and serve in obedience to their Lord on the basis of a voluntary covenant in the church; citizens are bound by law to keep order and be subject to the state in its pursuit of the wellbeing of all. In summary, church and state have functions, loyalties, methods and activities that are different, even when both are under the lordship of Christ.

The major responsibility of the church to the state is just that of being the church. Today more than ever a decaying world is demanding the church to be exactly that for which it was created by its Lord. In recovering its own identity as a witnessing community of faith under the direction and power of the Spirit, the church will be the first to be benefited. As Winthrop Hudson has stated:

> The constitutional provision for the separation of church and state has the great merit of making this responsibility of the churches explicit and of fostering those qualities of initiative, responsibility, relevance, resourcefulness, liberality, missionary zeal, and lay participation, which...(are) the characteristic consequences of the acceptance of the voluntary principle in religion. The separa-

tion of church and state has the additional virtue of guaranteeing the freedom of a church to be a church, to determine its own life, and to appeal to a "higher law" than the statutory enactments of the state. For this reason alone, if for no other reason, the separation of church and state ought resolutely to be guarded—the more so when the prevailing culture is so largely secular.[30]

A committed and separated church will also be a blessing to the state. The state needs to hear the judgement of God as it is expressed through the prophetic ministry of the church. A church mingled with the state has not the necessary critical distance to be the leaven that is required for the betterment of society.

Separation and the World Today

The principle of church-state separation raises several issues in the light of the present world scene. Baptists around the world agree in stating the following practical suggestions which result from their understanding of this principle.

1. Church and state should be separated in the public and legal sphere. No church or denomination should be declared or considered by law an official, established, national, or supported church by any state, nor have the recognition of a "favored" church or the church of the majority in the nation. This does not mean an absolute separation in terms of moral and spiritual matters, but a clear distinction between the functions, loyalties, methods and activities of both church and state.

2. All churches should be constituted on the basis of a voluntary decision of faith by each individual, in the light of the teaching and practice of the New Testament. This principle of voluntarism demands an equal standing with regard to law and government. No discrimination should be made by the state because of religious convictions or church affiliation. Governments should not discriminate in order to favor any given church to the detriment of others.

3. Ecclesiastical or religious taxation represent violation of the principle of separation and constitute a trampling of the rights of the individual. The state should not use public funds to support any church. In a pluralistic society this practice is an open act of injustice. The church should not be an accomplice to the crime of coercing individuals to support financially any church when they do not share its doctrines. The church and its program should be voluntarily supported by those who freely have agreed with its teachings and practice. This does not preclude the possibility that church and state collaborate in a given project oriented to the well-being of society.

4. Religious education is the proper responsibility of the church, and therefore it should not be imparted in public schools. It is not the responsibility of the state to teach religion, nor the task of the church to use the public system to fulfil its mission. This does not mean that religion should be excluded from schools or that the state will teach against religion or promote a secular understanding of reality. Religion is as much a part of the world as mathematics, history or literature. But the state should teach religion as an historical fact and not as a doctrine or dogma. The responsibility of the church is not to inform

the world about God, but to proclaim his gospel.

5. The principle of separation has as its end the benefit of church and state. Each one is sovereign in its own sphere. Both have responsibilities toward individuals and society. In keeping their independence and freedom they will be beneficial each to the other, and their separation and communication will result in the well-being of everybody.

The doctrine of separation of church and state, put into practice, will undermine the foundations of collectivism and totalitarianism, will suffocate the growth of secularism, will resist the excesses of nationalism, will dismantle the intrigues of clericalism, and will dilute the rigidness of ecclesiasticism. Religious freedom can only be more than an expression of good will in a society where the separation of church and state is a reality. Separation is not an impossible ideal, but a possible reality. Today's world is waiting for Christians to demonstrate in facts their vocation for freedom as it is taught in the New Testament. Such a living testimony of religious freedom has to result in its corollary, the separation of church and state. The church bears first responsibility to witness to the new life in Christ, separating itself from any compromise with the state.

Phillip Schaff has said with regard to one of the most accomplished democracies in the world: "The glory of America is a free Christianity, independent of secular government, and supported by the voluntary contributions of a free people.... This is one of the greatest facts in modern history."[31] The dream of Baptists is that this ideal of a free church in a free state be a reality all over the world. They are ready, as ever, to give their lives for the sovereign exercise of this principle in the world today.

Conclusion

Several centuries of consistent struggle for religious freedom and separation of church and state have granted Baptists a valuable experience. Any serious student of modern history will recognize the contribution made by Baptists to the advance of freedom in the world. They have not only been responsible members of society and good citizens in almost every nation of the world, but their distinctive convictions and practices have been their major contribution. This positive attitude toward the state and society has been possible not in spite of their principles, but because of their principles and their faithful adherence to them.

The right of every individual to direct access to God, the understanding of religion as a voluntary matter, the church conceived as composed by believers freely associated in obedience to Christ and for purposes set forth by him, the universal priesthood of all believers—all these doctrines constitute the basis to the conviction on religious freedom and church-state separation. Baptist believe these principles are of a great value, even from a civil and political perspective, to the present world.

In the light of the Baptists' concepts of church-state separation there are several questions that deserve to be discussed in a Baptist-Roman Catholic dialogue.

1. Religious freedom and church-state separation is one of the issues that has mostly filled the agenda of reflexion in the modern world. How can Baptists contribute to enrich the development of the Roman Catholic reflexion on religious freedom, which has been fostered in the last two decades due to the initiatives of the Second Vatican Council? Are Roman Catholics ready to be critical and open minded so as to accept Baptist contributions that could question some traditional and dogmatic postures?

2. In many areas of the world religious freedom is a fantasy if not totally absent. Baptists and Roman Catholics suffer equally arbitrary restrictions to their rights to live and worship according to their religious convictions. What can we do, as fellow Christians, to stimulate the legal recognition of religious freedom and the inalienable right of individual believers and churches to share the Good News of Jesus Christ? In which ways can we join forces so as to dream together in a world without religious restrictions nor discrimination?

3. Throughout history and in many areas of the world the Roman Catholic Church has suffered the oppression of states that have sought to dominate the church and use it as an engine for its purposes. Baptists have been successful in overcoming any temptation or pressure from the state everywhere. What can Baptists do to help the Roman Catholic Church to be separated from domination by the state and obtain the necessary freedom to be the confessing church the lost world needs it to be?

4. It is the understanding of many Baptists that during temporary periods of history and in certain nations the Roman Catholic Church has dominated the state. In Latin America, for example, Baptists and other Christian believers have suffered from discrimination and serious restrictions to their religious responsibility of witnessing to the Gospel. Is there any way in which the Roman Church could make the necessary corrections in regional or national situations that should take into account the new ecumenical understanding that prevails in the world? What contribution can Baptists offer to help Catholic believers and hierarchy in Roman Catholic dominated areas?

5. The principle of separation is closely associated with that of religious freedom. Baptists are convinced that separation guarantees freedom, and freedom requires separation. Do Roman Catholics share the same conviction? If so, what concrete measures and attitudes is the Roman Catholic Church assuming to secure the separation of church and state in those countries where they are united?

6. The church is always faced with the temptation of compromising its character and mission to obtain advantages, privileges and power. The union of church and state appears to be too seductive. The ideal of an absolute separation is almost unattainable within the limitations of human communal society. Baptists have been very careful in avoiding any compromise with the state. How can this experience be shared with Roman Catholics? Will Roman Catholics be willing to seriously consider the experience of Baptists throughout history and seriously take into account their basic convictions?

7. The fact that the Roman Catholic Church is closely associated to a recognized state in the world, the Vatican state, is quite confusing to Baptists. How is it possible to be at the same time the church of Jesus Christ and a state

of this world? If complete separation of church and state is best for church and
best for state, and secures freedom for both, how is it possible for a Christian
church to be a state? Baptists consider the Vatican state to be an open contradiction to the nature of the church according to the teachings of the New
Testament. To them it is also a historical anachronism in the modern world.
A state-church or a church-state is not only a political absurdity but a religious
impossibility according to the Baptist understanding of the Christian faith.

8. In the fulfillment of their responsibility of witnessing to the Gospel,
Baptists have reached many people of Roman Catholic affiliation that were integrated to Baptist churches. In areas with a Roman Catholic majority this proselytism has been understood by Roman Catholics as a sectarian attitude, giving
place to discrimination and state coaction particularly in those countries where
the Roman Church is closely associated to the state. This has resulted in the
scandalous fact of Christians fighting against Christians, instead of giving a common witness of faith, hope, and love to an unbelieving world. Baptists ought
to recognize that in many occasions they have been more prompt to preach
against the Roman Catholic Church than for the kingdom of Christ. Is it possible to find ways in which Baptists and Roman Catholics can create a wider
common ground of confidence, dialogue and consciousness of their duty of being salt and light in the world? Will Baptists and Roman Catholics be willing
to recognize their historical mistakes and give concrete steps toward a better
understanding of each other? What can Baptists and Roman Catholics do to
give a responsible witness to the gospel in an ecumenical age?

Pablo A. Deiros is president of the Baptist Seminary in Buenos Aires, Argentina.

Notes

1. Robert G. Torbet, *A History of the Baptists,* 3d ed. (Valley Forge: Judson Press,
1963), p. 490; James D. Mostellar, "Basic Baptist Principles and the Contemporary
Scene," *Southwestern Journal of Theology* 6 (April 1964): 75; Adolfo Robleto, *El mensaje
de los bautistas para el mundo* (San Jose, Costa Rica: Mision Bautista en Costa Rica, n.d.),
p. 136.

2. Donald F. Durnbaugh, *The Believer's Church: The History and Character of Radical
Protestantism* (New York: Macmillan, 1968), p. 245-249.

3. Edgar Y. Mullins, *Axiomas de religión* (El Paso: Casa Bautista de Publicaciones,
1948), pp. 41-42.

4. Torbet, *History,* p. 490.

5. J. E. Dillard, "Por que son distintos los bautistas y que es su mensaje?" *El Expositor Bautista 16 (February 15, 1923):* 6. *See also James E. Giles, Esto creemos los bautistas,*
3d ed. (El Paso: Casa Bautista de Publicaciones, 1984), pp. 93-94.

6. Torbet, *History,* p. 490.

7. *Encyclopedia of Southern Baptists,* s. v. "Separation of Church and State, Baptist
Concept," by C. Emanuel Carlson.

8. Henry C. Vedder, *A Short History of the Baptists* (Philadelphia: American Baptist
Publication Society, 1907), p. 415.

9. Oscar Cullmann, *The State in the New Testament* (New York: Charles Scribner's

Sons, 1956), pp. 35-36.

10. Justice C. Anderson, *Historia de los bautistas*, vol. 1: *Sus bases y principios* (El Paso: Casa Bautista de Publicaciones, 1978), p. 87. See also Robleto, *Mensaje*, pp. 139-40.

11. Jimmie Allen, "...and the State," in *These Folks Called Baptists*, ed. by Jimmie H. Heflin (Grand Rapids, Mich.: Baker Book House, 1962), pp. 71-76. Allen's article has also been included in a pamphlet published by the Christian Life Commission of the Baptist General Convention of Texas, under the title "Basis for Separation of Church and State".

12. Ibid., pp. 72-73.

13. Ibid.

14. Mullins, *Axiomas de religion*, pp. 41-42.

15. Robleto, *Mensaje*, pp. 137-39.

16. Leo Pfeffer, *Church, State and Freedom*, rev. ed. (Boston: Beacon Press, 1967), p. 84.

17. Edwin S. Gaustad, "Roger Williams and the Principle of Separation," *Foundations* (January 1958): 61.

18. In Latin America, Domingo F. Sarmiento, great Argentine educator and statesman, was a zealous admirer of Williams' views. Pfeffer says: "Seventeenth century America was not ready for Roger Williams. In view of the still current attack on the principle of separation of church and state,..., we are perhaps even now not ready for those ideas. Nevertheless, they do represent the great contribution of American democracy to civilization" (Pfeffer, *Church, State and Freedom*, p. 88).

19. T. B. Maston, *Isaac Backus* (Rochester, N.Y.: American Baptist Historical Society, 1962), pp. 11-20.

20. Edwin S. Gaustad, "The Backus-Leland Tradition," in *Baptist Concepts of the Church*, ed. Winthrop S. Hudson (Philadelphia: Judson Press, 1959), pp. 128-33.

21. Anson Phelps Stokes and Leo Pfeffer, *Church and State in the United States*, rev. one-vol. ed. (New York: Harper & Row, 1964), pp. 62-63.

22. See Joseph Martin Dawson, *Baptists and the American Republic* (Nashville: Broadman Press, 1956).

23. See C. Emanuel Carlson, *The Meaning of Religious Liberty* (Washington: Baptist Join Committee on Public Affairs, n.d.); and Philip Jones, *A Restatement on Baptist Principles* (Philadelphia: American Baptist Publication Society, 1909), pp. 69-70.

24. Anderson, *Historia de los Bautistas*, p. 97. See also Herschel H. Hobbs, *The Baptist Faith and Message* (Nashville: Convention Press, 1971), pp. 142-43; idem, What Baptists Believe (Nashville: Broadman Press, 1964), pp. 122-23.

25. Karl Barth, *Community, State and Church: Three Essays* (Garden City, N.Y.: Doubleday, 1960), pp. 122-35.

26. Ibid., pp. 135-48. See also Giles, *Esto creemos*, pp. 94, 96-98; Cullmann, *State in the New Testament*, pp. 90-91.

27. This phrase comes from Camilo Benso de Cavour, the renowned Italian statesman of the last century. See S. William Halperin, *The Separation of Church and State in Italian Thought from Cavour to Mussolini* (Chicago: University of Chicago Press, 1937), pp. 11-14. According to Thomas Armitage, Cavour was inspired in the ideals of Roger Williams. See Thomas Armitage, *History of the Baptists* (New York: Bryan, Taylor and Co., 1889), p. 645. The Cavour's formula—*Chiesa libera in Stato libero*—was introduced among North American Baptists by E. Y. Mullins, who synthesized with what he calls

the "religious-civil axiom". Mullins, *Axiomas de religión*, p. 166. See also Anderson, *Historia de los bautistas,* p. 87; Robleto, *Mensaje,* pp. 136-37; and Edgar Y. Mullins, *Baptist Beliefs* (Philadelphia: Judson Press, 1912), pp. 72-73.

28. Walter Rauschenbush, *Christianity and the Social Crises* (New York: Macmillan, 1911), p. 188.

29. The phrase was coined by Thomas Jefferson in a letter to the Danbury Baptist Association in the state of Connecticut, January 1, 1802. Since then Baptists in the United States have used it extensively. See Dawson, *Baptists and the American Republic,* p. 38.

30. Winthrop S. Hudson, *The Great Tradition of the American Churches* (New York: Harper & Row, 1953), p. 262.

31. Philip Schaff, *Germany: Its Universities, Theology and Religion,* quoted in Durnbaugh, *Believers' Church,* p. 249.

Baptists and The Ecumenical Movement. A Strategy Paper

Erich Geldbach

What is the Ecumenical Movement?

"The symbol of the boat to represent the World Council of Churches in particular and the ecumenical movement in general is a correct one. We are passing through troubled waters, negotiating all sorts of storms, and endeavoring to keep on course. But our problem seems to be that we have settled down in the boat, and are enjoying the voyage⁣ We know how to get around obstacles and can cope with critical situations. What we lack is the longing to arrive, the passionate desire to glimpse the harbor ahead, the goal of unity". These words were spoken by Emilio Castro, the Secretary General of the World Council of Churches of Methodist background, in his report to the Central Committee of the WCC in Buenos Aires in 1985. However one may define the "goal of unity", it is certainly true that the boat of the ecumenical movement is steaming or sailing through rough waters.

But this is not only part of the current situation. Ecumenism has always been on a difficult course. Once a division had occurred, it became difficult, if not impossible, to turn back the clock or to repair the damage. Even during the time of the Reformation those efforts were unsuccessful. Not only did the irenic spirit of Melanchthon turn out unsuccessful in his attempt to prevent a further breaking apart of Lutheranism and Romanism; even within Protestantism a division into a number of parties could not be avoided. The effort of Philip of Hesse failed to establish a pan-Protestant alliance through a dialogue between the key theologians of the new faith: Luther, Jonas, Melanchthon, Zwingli, Bucer, Hedio, Brenz, Oecolampad, Osiander, Bugenhagen (Marburg Colloquy 1529).

And yet, within the history of Protestantism, there has always been a tendency to overcome division and party spirit. These attempts were accompanied by further splits, sometimes caused by theological, sometimes by non-theological factors, most often by a combination of both.

Within Puritanism it was e.g. John Durie (Dury, Duraeus 1596-1680), who made a tremendous effort to reunite the churches (except the Roman Church). The Lord Protector Cromwell himself sent Durie to Scandinavia and to the European continent to seek support for an ecumenical cooperation of Protestant churches. Underlying these efforts were strong convictions of the essential unity of the church and the eschatological restoring of that unity. The "return" of the Jews to England as initiated by Cromwell upon a letter by the chief rabbi of Amsterdam, Manaseh ben Israel, must be seen in this context.

In Pietism and later revival and awakening movements the tendency toward unity is clearly noticeable. Thus, when Count Zinzendorf held his famous councils of all Protestant parties in Pennsylvania in 1742, it was resolved: "The real aim of the Assembly of all Evangelical Religions is this, that if a poor soul would like to know the way (of salvation) it would not be directed toward twelve different ways, but to the only One, it may ask whomever of us it wish. If someone thereafter loves the man who has shown him the way so much so that he wants to travel in like manner and he has not yet been part of another (religious) society, he may do so." (Budingische Sammlung einiger in die Kirchen-Historie einschlagender sonderlich neuerer Schrifften, Budingen 1742, p. 740; my own translation)

The different denominations are called upon to speak with one voice when the central question is asked. There may not be any discord among churches when it comes to the centrality of Jesus Christ as the only way to salvation. Not only harmony but unity is required in this most important area. The denominational ways may part and each may travel in slightly different route once the Way to salvation has been found.

Inter-church work became a feature of life in England among Bible Societies, Tract Societies, agencies for Foreign Missions and Mission to the Jews. It was therefore only a matter of time for such Christians to call for an organizational platform. This was done in 1846 when the Evangelical Alliance was organized in London. It was a trans-denominational and an inter-national agency for prayer and cooperation in evangelism and mission and has since its inception exerted considerable influence among like-minded brethren. The chief disadvantage of the Evangelical Alliance is its disregard for denominations and church structures. It operates on the assumption that the "awakened" spirit of brethren is enough Christian unity and that, consequently, the factors that divide churches need not be discussed. There can be little doubt, however, that the Evangelical Alliance has contributed to a no small degree to a better understanding among Christians of various denominational background. This contribution continues to be made through other evangelical agencies, like the World Evangelical Fellowship.

Another factor in the rise of the ecumenical movement were the organizations that attracted young people. Two years before the Evangelical Alliance was formed, George Williams (1821-1905) organized the Young Men's Christian Association (YMCA) in London. Within two generations the "Y" developed into a worldwide lay movement that provided the leadership of the ecumenical movement.

The evangelist and president of the Chicago area YMCA, Dwight L. Moody (1837-1890), organized in 1886 the Mt. Hermon Conference in Northfield, Massachusetts where the Student Volunteer Movement was initiated and where the Methodist layman John R. Mott (1865-1955) dedicated his life to mission work. He was to become the apostle of church unity and the ecumenical architect of the twentieth century.

After some preliminary conferences the International Missionary Conference which was held in Edinburgh in 1910 was the great stepping stone of the modern ecumenical movement. It is not surprising that the urgent call for Christian unity was first raised by missionary people and societies. Nowhere was the scandal of church divisiveness more apparent than on the mission field. It not only was a practical question whether denominational mission agencies ought to "export" their particularities to the mission field, it was also a very subtle theological issue. Was not the witness of the church rendered ineffective and even lacked credibility if churches began to "battle for souls" on the mission field? The conference chairman was none other than John R. Mott who also served later as President of the International Missionary Council (founded 1921, Lake Mohonk) and was active in the "Life and Work" movement (f. 1925, Stockholm). Together with the "Faith and Order" movement (f. 1927 Lausanne) these three movements eventually were brought together in the World Council of Churches founded in Amsterdam in 1948. The Council with its various Commissions and branches now serves as an umbrella organization for more than 300 churches of the Eastern Orthodox, Anglican and Protestant traditions.

In recent years there has emerged an ever-growing number of renewal movements of various kinds. Most of them are charismatic in orientation, but a considerable number are active in the field of promoting peace, racial equality or other social action concerns. These groups are bringing people of different denominations together and are therefore part of the ecumenical movement. The unity that Christians find in these groups while sharing common concerns is of such quality that the traditional dividing issues between churches become very small, indeed virtually extinct.

Another factor which has contributed to the ecumenical movement needs to be pointed out. The different churches and denominations became aware of the fact that most of them are globally, at least internationally at work. For this reason the different world bodies were organized such as the Lambeth Conference of the Anglican communion, the World Alliance of Reformed Churches, the Baptist World Alliance, the World Council of Methodist Churches, the Lutheran World Federation et al. These organizations have done much to enhance the ecumenical cause by rendering important intraconfessional services. BWA, therefore, can be called an ecumenical agency.

These historical facts were somewhat extensively recalled to suggest that the modern ecumenical movement grew out of and was at least in the beginning firmly rooted in the evangelical-awakening branch of Christianity. It is important to keep this in mind as the Baptist movement, at first developing within the stream of Puritanism, owed much of its strength to revival preaching and sound gospel teaching.

In recent years yet another church emerged as a champion of ecumenism: the Roman Catholic Church. Although its record of ecumenical achievements covers only the last 25 years since Vatican II (1962-65), it is nonetheless astounding. This is even more so when one considers the earlier anti-ecumenical pronouncements of Vatican authorities. Anglican orders were considered "null and void" (1896); freedom of the press, religious liberty, labor unions and other achievements in modern democratic societies were condemned (*syllabus errorum* 1864), and in *mortalium animos* (1928) ecumenism was rejected as theological indifference. When the World Council of Churches was created in 1948, Roman Catholic theologians were forbidden to attend the meetings as observers, and at the second General Assembly of that body in 1954 in Evanston no Roman Catholic theologian was expected to enter that town.

This high wall of separation between the Roman Church and the rest of Christianity was shattered with the accession of good Pope John XXIII and the creation of the Vatican Secretariat for Promoting Christian Unity immediately preceding the second Vatican Council. The Council firmly committed itself to ecumenism and passed an important declaration on religious liberty. Since then the Roman Catholic Church has given up its self-imposed ecumenical isolation. The process of *aggiornamento* which Pope John XXIII envisioned for his church is both expressed and supported by the involvement of the Roman church in the ecumenical movement.

To sum up the discussion thus far, it may be stated that there are major centers of ecumenism:

(1) the World Council of Churches
(2) the Evangelical Alliance and related organizations
(3) the YM/WCA and other organizations for young people
(4) renewal movements, such as the charismatic movement
(5) the World confessional families, including the Roman Catholic Church

Whereas the WCC seeks to solve interconfessional/interdenominational problems, and whereas the world confessional families concentrate mainly on interconfessional issues, the Evangelical Alliance is dedicated to a certain interpersonal piety and life-style. The young people's and renewal movements are devoted to certain age groups and/or are preoccupied with particular issues.

The present inter-church situation can best be described as an ongoing process of intensive dialogue. Two centers can be depicted. One is the Commission on Faith and Order of the WCC where the multilateral dialogue is carried out. The recent fruit of this endeavor is the Lima document on "Baptism, Eucharist and Ministry" (1982). Currently the Commission is working on a project entitled "Towards a Common Expression of the Apostolic Faith Today".

The second center of dialogue is constantly changing as it involves any two churches which are engaged in a so-called bilateral dialogue. The Roman

Catholic Church, when it gave up its fortress mentality and decided to enter into the ecumenical arena, stimulated both centers of dialogue noticeably. Although the Roman Church is not a member body of the WCC, its theologians are nevertheless fully integrated into the Commission on Faith and Order. This church has also sought and carried out an amazing number of bilateral dialogues with major world Christian communities. These latter include the Lutherans, Reformed, Methodists, Orthodox, Pentecostals and of late the Baptist World Alliance. The world confessional families have, therefore, also displayed *inter*-confessional leadership roles by creating and supporting bilateral dialogues on a world level.

In answer to the question "what is the ecumenical movement:, it may be stated that all forms of inter-church dialogue and cooperation, and all inter-denominational agencies, platforms and organizations are an expression of the multiform but *one* ecumenical movement. Although there are several centers of gravity, the over-all goal of the *one* ecumenical movement is "that the world may believe" (John 17:21).

Are Baptists Anti-Ecumenical?

Church history lasted for roughly 1600 years before it pleased God to raise up Baptist churches. They came into existence because they vehemently op-posed the Theodosian concept of the church within a given political realm. This model, going back to emperor Theodosius (380), elevates the Christian church and later on: one particular denomination - to the only religion in the Empire, later on: a given territory. Thus in European Christendom there developed a monolithic state-church system, and it mattered little whether the church was Orthodox, Roman Catholic, Lutheran or Reformed: they all tried by means of coercive and oppressive power to subdue each other and to prevent other groups from gaining a sizeable foothold.

When Baptist churches emerged, they were labeled dissenters, separatists, nonconformists, sectarians, enthusiasts, *Schwarmer*. All of these pejorative terms were to suggest that Baptists had little regard for church unity; they would, instead, break away from the church of a given territory and organize a new church. Over the years Baptists acquired a reputation for being very divisive: "When in doubt, let's split."

It must be stressed, however, that originally the Baptists were committed to the one church. They thought the state-church system and its coerciveness to be out of step with the teachings of the Bible. The Baptist call for liberty of conscience (cf. Leonard Busher, *Religious Peace: Or a Plea for Liberty of Conscience*, 1614) was not an anti-church, but a pro-church demand. It was thus directed toward the entire church. It was a call for the church universal to abandon its unbiblical alliance with worldly, ungodly powers. In Busher's words:

> "Kings and magistrates are to rule temporal affairs by the swords of their temporal kingdoms, and bishops and ministers are to rule spiritual affairs by the Word and Spirit of God, the sword for Christ's spiritual kingdom, and

not to intermeddle one with another's authority, office, and function."[6]

Thomas Helwys, in similar fashion, looked at the king as a mortal being who has no authority over the immortal souls of his subjects. The true church must, therefore, be a church which severs all ungodly ties. When a Baptist body in 1689 met in London, they adopted with a few alterations the Westminster Confession which had been drafted in 1643 by other Christians. Baptists wanted as much as possible to be in harmony with other Christian people. Great Baptist leaders in the past addressed themselves not just to the Baptist constituency, but to the whole church. Thus William Carey (1761-1834) referred to all Christians when in 1792 he published his "An Enquiry into the Obligations of Christians to Use Means for the Conversion of the Heathens." He was also actively involved in the creation of the first interdenominational mission society, the London Missionary Society (1795) and proposed a missionary conference for the year 1810, much along the lines of the Edinburgh conference 100 years later .

Walter Rauschenbusch (1861-1918) called upon all Christians, not only his fellow-Baptists, to consider the social implications of the gospel so that all of God's erring children would at last find their way from the City of Destruction to the City of Love. Another example would be Billy Graham whose evangelistic crusades have always been interdenominational in scope. There is no ground to suppose that by definition or theological outlook Baptists are anti-ecumenical.

Why Should Baptists Be Involved In the Ecumenical Movement?

In our present "global village" no church can stay aloof or retreat into its little clamshell. Nothing within the Baptist denomination will go unnoticed. Even a fierce anti-ecumenical stand is an indication that ecumenism is here to stay. It is healthier to pass in the ecumenical ship through trouble waters than to try to swim all by oneself through the rough sea.

Those Baptists who are critical of the ecumenical movement must be asked on what ground they justify their reservations. As was pointed out earlier the ecumenical movement was firmly rooted in that tradition of Christianity which also gave guidance to the Baptist movement. If ecumenism today differs from what it was 80 years ago and if Baptists today feel less at home in the oikoumene, is not one critical factor the great lack of Baptist involvement in the ecumenical movement?

To be ecumenically active requires of Baptists to know who they are, where they came from and what they stand for. Ecumenism forces Baptists to re-assess their tradition and to enter into a process of self-appraisal. This is not to be confused with an experience of l'art pour l'art, but it is in the interest of both the Baptist movement and the Church universal that such a self-appraisal ought to take place. A dialogue with another church or different churches cannot take place without a firm commitment to Baptist principles.

An illustration of what active participation in the ecumenical movement by Baptists can accomplish is the Lima document, particularly the section on baptism. Whereas this section may not claim to include a full-fledged Baptist theology on baptism, it cannot be denied that it reflects Baptist concerns. In fact, some responses from paedebaptist churches criticize that the Lima document puts too much emphasis on believer's baptism as the "real" model for Christian initiation from which other modes may be derived. This input of Baptist theology into the ecumenical stream of thought would not have occurred, had it not been for active Baptist delegates in the Faith and Order Commission and had not the Baptist seminary in Louisville hosted a consultation of the Commission on baptism in 1979, i. e. a few years before the final draft of the BEM-document was voted upon at Lima in January 1982.

Within the ecumenical movement the Baptist tradition would certainly be located at one extreme end of the spectrum of churches. Baptists are part of the left wing of Christianity. At the other extreme are the traditional churches of the Eastern Orthodox rite. The latter are so exclusivistic in their claim to be the only true and authentic Christian church that they will not even recognize as valid the rite of baptism which is administered in another "sacramental" church, i. e. the Roman Catholic Church (cf. the International Orthodox-Roman Catholic Commission's report "Faith, Sacraments and the Unity of the Church"). The only truly baptized are those who receive the sacrament of baptism in the Orthodox church where the authentic expression of the Christian faith, as elucidated by the seven ecumenical councils, is kept. The claim, therefore, is that for sacraments to be rightly administered, an authentic church is the prerequisite. As the Orthodox church is the only authentic church, which preserved fully the Apostolic faith, it is only within its bound that the building-up of the church, as performed through the initiating act of baptism, can be achieved. Baptism in a Roman Catholic Church is not an empty rite however; it does bestow grace upon the baptized, but in an abnormal way.

Several points need to be stressed here:

(1) It is the Orthodox claim to be the only, true, authentic, apostolic church (as exemplified above in the case of baptism and its recognition);

(2) There is a growing influence of Orthodox theology in the ecumenical movement, especially in the Faith and Order Commission. The Lima document is a reflection of this tendency. More so, the new project "Towards a Common Expression of the Apostolic Faith Today" points in that direction.

(3) Among Western churches (other than the Roman Catholic Church which feels very close to the Orthodox tradition anyway), there is a tendency to look to Orthodoxy for guidance and help in the cultural crisis of the day. Orthodox theology and the expression of piety - often within hostile societies - are sometimes considered vital for the survival of Christianity (cf. dialogues of the Protestant &establishedé Church of West and East Germany and the Russian as well as Rumanian Orthodox Church; Lutheran Church of Finland and the Russian Orthodox Church of Finland et al.).

In light of this situation the question may be asked if it is not the ecumenical task of Baptist churches to call to the attention of the ecumenical movement that adherence to the principles as expressed in the seven ecumenical councils does not necessarily constitute the community of the faithful and will not help the Church much as it moves into the third millennium? Must not Baptists - at the other end of the ecclesiastical spectrum - raise their voices to expound that merely looking back to a time of an allegedly "undivided" Christendom is a form of romanticism and that the "strangeness" and the "exotic" that Westerners experience in their encounter with Orthodoxy is not necessarily a test of the validity of the Orthodox claim? Who else would be better equipped than the Baptists to perform this task on behalf of ecumenism?

The point is not to diminish the accomplishments of the Orthodox churches; they are, in fact, enormous. The point is that Orthodoxy lacks certain experiences, e. g. the experience with democratic institutions and with matters concerning human rights, that the ecumenical movement would be ill-advised to be overwhelmed or have its policy shaped too much by Orthodoxy.

To put it yet another way and very bluntly: could a devout Orthodox Christian be the head of a state in an Orthodox environment without doing harm to or endangering religious liberty? (cf. Greece and the trouble Papendreou has with the Orthodox establishment). The answer would have to be the same as in the case of a Baptist fundamentalist (cf. below, especially the dangerous consequences their interpretation of prophecy could have for the world): No.

These points are but a few examples why Baptist involvement in the ecumenical movement is necessary for the well-being of both the Baptist and the ecumenical movements.

Obstacles to Baptist Participation in the Ecumenical Movement.

The origin of the Baptist movement and a certain portion of its history reveals that Baptists "broke away" from other churches to organize their own denominations. It further became apparent as the movement grew that even within one country Baptists would often be ready to split up and form unions and conventions independent of one another. There seems to be little concern for unity and much more concern for the freedom of expression. Often the Baptists are accused of a subjective, individualistic approach to the Christian faith which contributes to, rather than prevents, divisions. This charge must be honestly faced.

The impact of the fundamentalist movement upon Baptist churches further added to the readiness of Baptists to separate. In fundamentalism the call for separation is a key element. It is based on the assumption, first expounded by John Nelson Darby (1800-1882), that salvation history must be divided into a number of successive dispensations. Each dispensation is characterized by God's gracious dealings and man's failure to act according to God's economy. However God's patience carries on a dispensation, man's failure in the outset of a dispensation is "departure from God...and all is gone in principle."[2] There can not be any human attempt to re-establish a dispensation.

The church dispensation soon after its inception also ended in apostasy; the church cannot be restored according to a New Testament model. All denominations are part of the failure now, and the believer must abandon all human institutions in order for the "two or three to gather together" at the Lord's table (Matt. 18:20). The believers are called upon to separate in order to form the true spiritual body of Christ. Separation from evil is the path of the saint and God's principle of unity for Christ's bride. This true church is to keep its heavenly conversation and citizenship (Phil. 3:30). "It is this conviction, that the church is properly heavenly, in its calling and relationship with Christ, forming no part of the course of events of the earth, which makes its rapture so simple and clear; and on the other hand, it shows how the denial of its rapture brings down the church to an earthly position, and destroys its whole spiritual character and position:. This secret rapture has nothing to do with Christ's appearance to judge the world.[3]

This premillennial dispensationalism is further complicated by a distinction that is made in regard to prophecy. "The great point I judge needed, is a clear apprehension of the difference of the church called for heavenly places, and the government of the world in respect of which the Jews form the centre of the ways of God."[4] From this statement follows the hermeneutical principle that all Scripture must be reviewed as to whether it applies to the church or to the Jews.

Dispensationalism as the root of fundamentalism introduced a divisive spirit into many Baptist churches. Separation became a necessary article of faith in order to keep the bride "pure". When in the ecumenical movement the church hierarchies became apparent, and as the goal of unity was perceived by many fundamentalists to mean *one* unified church, it looked as though the forces of Antichrist had taken control of the ecumenical movement and that this movement would contribute to the ecclesiastical as well as to the civil apostasy as prophesied for the end-times.[5]

The dispensationalist-premillennial system, however, is based upon a very biased reading of Holy Scripture. This system with all its hermeneutical presuppositions is not, as Darby claimed, "the only true scriptural one." As a matter of fact, it is very arbitrary and had no precedent in the history of Christian thought. It was, at first, one man's sectarian opinion and later had a tremendous impact upon various denominations and church leaders through the Niagara Bible Conferences, Bible Schools and the *Scofield Reference Bible,* all of which popularized Darby's eccentric points of view.

However, the wide-spread acceptance of Darby's system does not make it any better. It must be stated very clearly and poignantly that premillennial dispensationalism and fundamentalism are totally out of step with the original intent of Baptist principles. Baptists thought that it was clearly possible and, indeed, necessary to restore the church along the lines of the New Testament. They rejected false claims by established churches which had aligned themselves with worldly powers; yet their aim was not the creation of a separated, spiritual remnant, but the visibly congregated people of God who are ready to evangelize and missionize the world and thus make known the saving power of Jesus Christ. There is no reason to assume that this aim was or is incompatible with the ecumenical movement.

Moreover, the onslaught of present-day fundamentalists on denominational structures and seminaries, as is particularly visible in the Southern Baptist Convention, not only reveals the divisive character of fundamentalism, but also runs counter to the original intent of dispensationalism. "Separation from evil: cannot be realized by a power struggle for control of boards, theological seminaries or entire conventions.

The high regard of Baptists for the Bible and its role in church life and church polity has sometimes been contrasted to the role that tradition plays in the ecumenical movement. Whereas Baptists rely on the Bible, so it is said, the ecumenical movement appeals to tradition as its authority. Again it is in fundamentalist circles that this argument is widely accepted. It should be understood, however, that bibliolatry may be a fundamentalist point of view, but it certainly is not a Baptist position. There can be no doubt that the Bible is at the center of every church that participates in the ecumenical movement and that it is in accordance with Baptist principles that there are pluriform ways - and not a uniform way - to approach the Bible and to listen to its heart-shaking and soul-searching message.

Among Baptists there is a wide-spread fear of Roman Catholic involvement in the ecumenical movement. Baptists were especially struck by the refusal of Popes to accept freedom of the press, liberty of conscience and religious liberty. Although the claim is still made and will continue to be made that the Pope is the guarantor of Christian unity, it must also be stressed that Roman Catholic theologians and Vatican authorities have greatly profited from the ecumenical movement since Vatican II. To talk about ecumenism and leave out the Roman church has become totally impossible.

Some churches which are very conspicuous in the ecumenical movement are characterized by a high degree of authoritarianism and sacramentalism as expressed in the hierarchical structures. Indeed, some churches, especially those with formerly strong ties to the civil authorities - like Eastern Orthodoxy, Roman Catholicism, Anglicanism and Lutheranism - display a high, if not an alarming amount of trust in their hierarchies and seem to have little regard for the laity. The very fact that a distinction between the ordained hierarchy and the laity is considered "essential", as a Roman Catholic pronouncements[6] is provocative for Baptists. The question, however, remains whether this one-sidedness is sufficient for Baptists to abstain from the ecumenical movement.

Separatists have always held that the Baptist movement should not be tainted by theological liberalism and modernism which they see at work in the ecumenical movement. Anyone with eyes to see will acknowledge that there are "liberal" tendencies in the ecumenical movement, however one may define liberalism. But this is only one expression of the pluriformity. Baptists have in the past never adhered to *one* approach when it came to Christian faith commitment and they should not in the case of the one ecumenical movement depart from this heritage. The Lima document on "Baptism Eucharist and Ministry", moreover, runs counter to the charge of liberalism.

The charge is often made that the ecumenical movement has little regard for evangelism and mission. As was pointed out the missionary movement was one powerful contributing factor early in the century to the formation of the ecumenical movement. Baptists, for the preceding 100 years, had been the champions among advocates of a strong foreign mission program of the Church. If there really has been a shift in the ecumenical movement away from evangelism and mission, is it perhaps largely so because Baptists and other who are committed to this task withdrew from active participation in or support for the ecumenical movement? Again, it must be pointed out that the document "Mission and Evangelism" (passed by the Central Committee of the WCC in July 1982) runs counter to this charge.

Critics point to an active support of political radicalism, liberation theologies, socialism or even communism on part of the ecumenical movement, notably the World Council of Churches. One may resort to Baptist theologian Walter Rauschenbusch and his Christian socialism or to the black Baptist leader Martin Luther King and his civil rights movement to stress that Baptists have voiced opinions in a "radical" fashion. It may also be crucial to note that any political viewpoint and any economic system is not beyond criticism from churches, groups or individuals. The church is not to fall into the trap of culture-religion as European Christendom and its coercive state-church system, or the German Christians of the Third Reich, or some dreamers of liberation theology or some fundamentalist Baptists with their call for a "Christian America" did or are presently doing. if the church must play its role as a counter-culture instead, which derives its criteria from a higher source than political science and economics or a political or economic system, then the church must be free to place all systems under rigorous scrutiny and to criticize injustice, discrimination, inequality and lack of human rights wherever and under whatever circumstances these occur.

The charge is raised that the ecumenical movement in its search for unity rests on doctrinal minimalism or on the lowest common denominator and settles for compromises at the expense of truth. Certainly, there needs to be a wrestling with the issues, and in some isolated cases a compromise may have to be reached. But as the Lima document indicates and as the entire work of the Faith and Order Commission reveals, it is with strenuous effort that truth is sought.

Many of the above-mentioned attacks on the ecumenical movement, which serve as serious obstacles for Baptist involvement, are raised by Baptists as well as other Christians. There is one distinctly Baptist obstacle that remains to be mentioned. Baptists have a time-honored tradition of the autonomy of the local church. In Baptist polity a convention or the World Alliance has no authority over the local churches and hence the resolutions and other pronouncements are non-binding on the local level. This tradition of decentralizing the activities of a Union or Convention may be very confusing for other Christians and raises the serious question who, in dealings with other churches, can speak representatively and authentically for Baptists.

Which Contributions Can Baptists Make to the Ecumenical Movement?

Many of the obstacles, if positively interpreted, may serve as illustrations of particular Baptist contributions. The last point may serve as an illustration.

What looks as a typically Baptist obstacle, may turn out to be an advantage. Grass-root ecumenism may develop if a local Baptist church gets involved in the oikoumene. Even if a Convention is against entering into closer ties with other churches, a local congregation may still go ahead and become an active ingredient in local ecumenism. What is confusing for other Christians is the fact that in a town only two miles away a Baptist congregation of the same Convention may be militantly anti-ecumenical.

The protest against a coercive style of religion led Baptists to call upon civil authorities not to grant, but to respect and protect religious liberty and other human rights. No other denomination has such a long and dynamic tradition when it comes to human rights concerns (and it is truly saddening that some Baptist fundamentalists are feverishly working to destroy that tradition).

Another distinctly Baptist principle is the high respect for the laity and its involvement in church policy-making decisions. Whereas in a hierarchically-structured church like the Roman Church, *bishops talk* about the role of the laity, in Baptist churches lay-people act and would reject the notion of being talked about by superiors. The priesthood of all believers, which was rediscovered during the Reformation of the sixteenth century, but only half-heartedly and reluctantly introduced in Reformation churches, has become a dominant feature in Baptist church life and is one of the treasures that Baptists have to offer to ecumenism.

Closely related to this principle of lay-involvement is the decision-making process. Baptists are a democratically-minded people. In fact, they have immensely contributed to the rise of democratic societies, and they ought to share their insights with the Church universal. The ecumenical movement as a whole must contribute to the spread of democracy and not be entangled by hierarchs who derive their power not from the people of God and are not accountable for their actions to the people of God.

The high regard for the Bible has Baptists administer believer's baptism. This is a thorn in the flesh of all paedo-baptist churches and ought to be so. The particular ecclesiology that goes hand in hand with the principles of believer's baptism, the priesthood of all believers, church polity, evangelism and mission as well as respect for human rights must be brought to bear on the ecumenical movement.

How Should Baptists Be Involved?

All through the history of the modern ecumenical movement Baptists have been involved. The experiences of individuals, groups and entire Unions or Conventions must be shared with other Baptists who are reluctant to give up their isolationism or their anti-ecumenical fortress mentality. How can all Baptists profit from those who have had previous experiences?

The first question that requires an honest answer is this: Is the Baptist movement committed to the whole Church of Jesus Christ? Are Baptists interested in the renewal of the Church and would they see the ecumenical movement as an agency for renewal? Is the Baptist movement "catholic" or "sectarian"?

Next Baptists must be asked whether or not they would be ready to accept that certain misconceptions and misunderstandings about the one ecumenical movement were deliberately spread among them and if they are willing to be corrected? What are Baptists afraid of vis-a-vis ecumenism and are the objections sound or based on distortions and prejudices? Would the ecumenical movement care to listen to sound objections and allow corrections in its course? Are there reasons to suppose that prejudices can be effectively attacked and myth-making rejected?

As was pointed out earlier, the ecumenical movement is to a large degree characterized by interchurch dialogues. In different countries Baptists are involved in such conversations on a local or a national level, e.g. the Southern Baptist Convention and the Roman Catholic Church in the USA, the Baptist Unions in East and West Germany with the Protestant Church, Baptists and Lutherans in Norway etc. It has also been pointed out that Baptist theologians take part in the Faith and Order Commission of the WCC. Reference needs to be made also to the fact that on the international level, there have been talks between the World Alliance of Reformed Churches, the Roman Catholic Church as well as the Lutheran World Federation on one hand and the Baptist World Alliance on the other hand. It follows that Baptists are firmly established in the vast network of dialogues that are currently taking place. Some serious problems arise as far as form and content of the talks is concerned. This is of prime strategic importance.

Dialogues on local, national and international levels should be encouraged by Baptist leaders. At this stage of the ecumenical game, it is still a high priority to inform one another of the other's beliefs, principles, religious life, mission work, social action programs etc. The aim must be to develop a mutual understanding and a sense that the dialogue partner is also a fellow believer who seeks to be obedient to the Lordship of Jesus Christ. It is only a matter of time before certain differences are detected. They must be squarely faced.

As there is a wide ecclesiastical spectrum, it follows that there are some churches closer to the Baptist tradition than others. It is deemed advisable to enter into a dialogue with those denominations with whom Baptists are thought to share many areas of common understanding. It may also turn out that the closer one feels to another church, the more prominent the remaining (few) differences may become. Churches which in faith and order are close to Baptists are the Mennonites, the Brethren, the Disciples of Christ, some Pentecostal churches and the churches in the Reformed tradition.

For the Baptist World Alliance it is recommended that it take up an international dialogue with Mennonites. It may be advisable to include the Church of the Brethren and the Disciples in the same process. Confessionally speaking all four traditions have much in common and conversations between churches who profess and practice believer's baptism may be a clear signal in the ecumenical movement.

The conversations between the Baptist World Alliance and the World Alliance of Reformed Churches which were conducted between 1974 and 1976 have yielded substantial agreements in the areas then touched upon. A second round of talks should be taken up to further the bonds between the two world communions.

It is also imperative that the Baptist World Alliance take up conversations or continue to hold them with those churches which constitute an overwhelming majority in certain areas of the world, where Baptists are a sizeable or small minority. This must be done to help Baptist churches resist the charge that they are not a church, but a "sect" or "cult". From this point of view the conversation with the Roman Church is helpful for Baptists in a Catholic environment, notably Southern Europe and Latin America, and the talks with the Lutheran World Federation may have positive effects in Germany and the Scandinavian countries. Following this line of thought the BWA may consider opening conversations with the Russian and Romanian Orthodox Churches. In both countries the Baptists are a very active and recognizable community. The encounter between two church families of the extreme ends of the ecclesiological spectrum could be very helpful for both communities and would require a close communication with the national Baptist leadership in both countries. In fact, they should be the determining factor as to whether or not a dialogue should be started.

One of the many beneficial factors of a dialogue is a mutual recognition of the partners. It may not involve a full recognition as churches in the dogmatic sense of the word, but it may ease the pressure that is often exerted by majority churches on minorities.

How Could Baptists Define the Goal of the Ecumenical Movement?

The key question in conjunction with all dialogues is that of the ultimate aim. From the beginning of the ecumenical movement there has been a longing for "visible unity". Although this goal has never been clearly defined, there are several models as to how this visible unity should look like or be achieved.[7]

According to the 1975 General Assembly of the World Council of Churches, the churches should seek a "conciliar fellowship of local churches who are themselves truly united". The Lutheran World Federation is advocating the concept of "unity in reconciled diversity". Here the question must be raised which factors need reconciliation. The answer can only be that the church-dividing issues are to be reconciled. If they are reconciled, however, why should a diversity continue to exist and be of church-dividing quality? The Lima document and the work of the Faith and Order Commission seems to go on the assumption that visible unity must be achieved by a process of convergency which will eventually lead to a consensus of all churches on key issues, e. g. the mutual recognition of baptism and the ministry. As the process of reception of Lima clearly indicates, there is at least the danger that some churches may confuse consensus with conformity to their own tradition or theological insight. Visible unity would then mean uniformity.

Even if there is no clear definition of visible unity, there is general agreement that it must *not* be confused with uniformity. The goal of visible unity has nothing to do with creating one uniform church. Although this charge has been repeatedly made against the ecumenical movement, it is the express intention of all theologians, churches, commissions, ecumenical agencies et al. *not* to establish a super-church.

For Baptists, in addition, uniformity is dangerous because of their past experience. Would not a uniform church again be tempted to use illegitimate power against others who decline to conform?

The goal of visible unity is expressed in particular by those churches with formerly close ties to worldly powers. Is one uniform Empire (East or West) and one uniform church still a guideline for them? It is also very conspicuous that leaders of hierarchically structured churches speak of the "scandal of a divided Christendom". But is it really the sin of the churches to be divided? Count Zinzendorf's answer was: "The Savior had a hand in that fact that there are so many denominations, and even if one had it in his power to diminish them by a single Sect, one ought first to ask if one should (do so)".

Baptists will have to raise the question whether or not the goal of "visible unity" should not be abandoned altogether. Is a process toward visible unity really necessary and is the proof text of the ecumenical movement (John 17:11 ut omnes unum sit) based on sound interpretation? Is there really an underlying unity beyond the denominational diversities? Is it the aim of dialogues to overcome diversities and to go beyond to those "everlasting" *notae ecclesiae*? Could Baptists not advocate a communion of churches that can withstand the divergences and differences? Is this not the model of the New Testament and the early church which allowed four gospels to be incorporated into the canon and rejected Tatian's attempt to harmonize them into one gospel (*Diatessaron* c. 172). Is not the quest for visible unity more like Tatian's harmony of the gospels and should not the gospels with all their divergences, differences and even contradictions remain as they are?

However, just as the four gospels are part of one canon so should the churches be part of one communion as a realistic goal of the ecumenical movement. No one church would have to give up its particular gifts that it feels were given to it by the head of the church for the good of the entire koinonia of churches.

The envisioned communion of churches as a goal of ecumenism is not to be confused with a mere coexistence of different denominations. In order to realize a communion amidst all the diversities and contradictions of present churches, the Baptist ecumenists would have to appeal to *all* churches to give up their claims to be the exclusive Church of Jesus Christ. This appeal would first have to be directed toward the Roman Catholic Church.

The Second Vatical Council conceded that the true Church "subsists in" (not: is) the Roman Catholic Church. This opened the door for many ecumenical activities of that church (cf. 1.11). However, postconciliar documents and even Roman Catholic theologians who are committed to the ecumenical task (like Otto Hermann Pesch) seem to indicate that the traditional equation of the Church of Jesus Christ with the Roman Church still holds true. Christian unity, so it is argued, has never been lost. It has always been realized in the Roman Catholic Church. This church, as Vatican II proclaimed, must undergo a constant process of repentance. The church will not be the same in the future because of this process of repentance. As a result, however, there will in the days to come be room for the "separated brethren" within the Roman Church. The Pope is the guarantor of Christian truth and Christian unity. Unity can only be conceived of as unity *with and under* the Pope, and all churches must eventually yield to that claim if unity is to be achieved.

Next, Baptist ecumenists would also have to appeal to the Orthodox churches. Their responses to the Lima document clearly put forth their contention to have throughout history remained the true heirs to the apostolic church of undivided Christendom. Christian unity must necessarily involve a "return" of all churches to the fullness of the holy tradition which only the Orthodox churches have preserved.

In both cases unity is defined by an exclusive claim: either "full" Roman Catholic teaching of "fullness" in the Orthodox tradition becomes the sole criterion which determines whether or not other churches are in "full" communion with the one, holy, catholic, and apostolic church.

Next, Baptist ecumenists must also appeal to their fellow-Baptists and other Protestants to give up the assertion that only they are "biblical" and that all churches must adhere to these biblical insights.

Only if those exclusive claims are given up can a koinonia of churches emerge that is not only strong enough to withstand differences, but that can celebrate divergences and contradictions as enriching and beneficial for all and as expressing the fullness of life in the togetherness of divided churches. The witness to the world would thus be that, in spite of divisive issues, the churches would recognize each other as under the same Lordship.

As the koinonia of divided churches is not a mere coexistence, this communion must also have a structure. This would include:

(a) an initial act of affirming fundamental articles of faith which all Christian churches share. There are certainly fundamental differences, just as there are fundamental areas of agreement. Are the latter more important than those aspects in theology, faith and order that make churches separate entities? Are the divisive factors to be seen in the light of fundamental agreements or do the points of disagreement cast their dark shadows over that which Christian communities hold in common? (b) an affirmation of the principle that churches should act together as much as possible. There needs to be a search for areas of common action. What can churches do together that they could do less effectively each by itself?

(c) the ongoing process of bilateral and multilateral dialogues should not be viewed as preliminary steps to a future koinonia, but as an *expression* of a communion that already exists. The dialogues would thus be upgraded to a structural element of the koinonia.

(d) Eucharistic hospitality: hospitalite eucharistique. If all churches who participate in the koinonia realize that it is truly the Lord's Supper they are celebrating, they then have no "jurisdiction" to exclude other Christians only because these hold membership in a different church. Christians who are in good standing in their own community must be received as guests by all participating churches at the Lord's table.

(e) a council or synod of all churches. This would be the communion's highest organ. It would function on the basis of *ius humanum* and may not interfere in the individual churches' own synods, conventions or councils. Its purpose would be

    1) to receive reports of the dialogues;

    2) to oversee the process of dialogue and reception;

    3) to release common statements on theological as well as non-theological or ethical issues;

    4) to plan concerted actions.

Baptists and Reception

Reception, in recent years, has become the new "holy word" of the ecumenical movement.[8] Why is this so? The answer has to do with two astounding observations. On the one hand theologians have reached in bilateral and also in multilateral talks an amazing amount of agreements on formerly controversial issues. Years of hard work in doing theology together are beginning to bear fruits and yet there is a wide gap between convergence or even consensus statements produced in the dialogues by delegates who were officially appointed by the churches and, on the other hand, the situation in the life of the churches. It seems that nothing or very little has changed in the churches as a result of the official conversations. The work of commissions in conferences and consultations is apparently not "received". The institutions and church structures seem to resist for whatever reasons what commissions are recommending. Both the leadership and the general membership of churches are not very interested in ecumenical results. This observation applies to all churches. Reception of the fruits of inter-church conversation, therefore, becomes a key to future ecumenical developments.

It is amazing that even hierarchically-structured churches have difficulties with the reception process. It would seem that, once the hierarchy gets behind a certain convergence document, its content would be received by the general membership in no time. But the experience is different. However, for Baptists the reception process is infinitely more complex because of the decentralized organization of Baptist bodies. Who is the authority to "receive" other than each individual congregation? Ultimately in each church the people of God are those who must be the subjects of the reception process. This is not any different in the Orthodox or in the Baptist tradition. But how are results of ecumenical dialogues handed down to the people of God?

Some Practical Sugggestions

Research conducted by the Lutheran World Federation has shown that ecumenical activities on a local level depend largely on the ministers and a few people in leadership positions. Once flourishing ecumenical enterprises collapsed overnight as soon as a minister, who emphasized oikoumene in his work, left a given church. Apart from the fact that this shows how little ecumenicism is rooted in the general membership, it also goes to show that ministers must be sensitized to the ecumenical task. Therefore, all Baptists seminaries should be asked to offer courses in ecumenism and include ecumenical issues in seminary training.

Because of the importance of inter-church dialogues and in view of the particular problems that Baptists face with the reception process, there ought to be an appointment by the Baptist World Alliance of a dialogue coordinator. His/her job would be

1) to seek contact with other denominations as prospective partners in dialogue;

2) to be present at all international dialogues with Baptist participants;

3) to serve as advisor and resource person for Baptist delegations;

4) to make sure that Baptist delegations which are involved in talks with different churches use the same language so that one partner in a dialogue may not be irritated or disturbed by what Baptists are saying in a parallel dialogue with another partner;

5) to find ways to promote the cause of ecumenism in unions, conventions and congregations;

6) to organize meetings for Baptist theologians to discuss ecumenical issues.

The selection of Baptist delegation for a dialogue should be made with utmost care. Women should be adequately represented as well as the laity. If the impact of a dialogue may be felt in particular areas of the world, as e.g. Southern Europe or Latin America in the case of the Roman Catholic-Baptist talks, people from those countries/regions should be well represented.

One practical step would be to investigate how other churches are treated in books, in Sunday School material or audiovisual material put out by Baptist publishers or on behalf of Baptist churches or agencies.

Finally all of these ecumenical goals within the Baptist family cannot be accomplished without proper financing. Baptist delegations or a dialogue coordinator must be paid for their expenses and research to prepare for meetings. As the budget of the Baptist World Alliance allows only small sums of money for ecumenical ventures, the proposal is made that a Baptist Ecumenical Foundation be set up. Initial funding should be solicited from Baptist Conventions and Unions, Baptist agencies and Baptist individuals who are interested in advancing ecumenism in order to overcome Baptist self-righteousness and the narrowness of denominationalism, as well as to promote the ecumenical movement through making the Baptist voice be heard.

Erich Geldbach is a Professor at the Confessional Institute of the Protestant Union, Bensheim, Federal Republic of Germany.

Notes

1. Quoted in A. P. Stokes, *Church and State in the United States*, vol. I (New York: 1950), p. 113.
2. J. N. Darby, *Collected Writings*, vol. I, p. 115.
3. Ibid., vol. II, p. 155 f.
4. Ibid., *Letters*, vol. I, p. 118.
5. Ibid., *Letters*, vol. II, p. 321 ff.
6. Presbyterorum ordinis No. 2; Lumen Gentium No. 10.
7. International Roman Catholic-Lutheran Commissions's document "Unity before Us"; No. 13-34.
8. Thomas Ryan: "Reception: Unpacking the New Holy Word", Ecumenism 82, 1983, p. 27-34.

A Response to the Faith and Order Commission Document No. 140

Keith W. Clements

The Faith and Order project "Towards the Common Expression of the Apostolic Faith Today" has been examined and discussed at the meetings of the BWA Commission on Doctrine and Inter-Church Co-operation at Amman (1987) and Nassau (1988). At the Amman meeting Keith Clements presented an extended report on the project, subsequently published in the April 1989 *Baptist Quarterly*. At Nassau, Clements presented a further paper on the Study Document No. 140 "Confessing One Faith", to which Erich Geldbach and Glenn Hinson made responses. This draft draws upon these presentations and the discussions which they evoked.

The document at the centre of the discussion, *Confessing One Faith* was issued by the Standing Commission on Faith and Order in 1987. It is in the form of an "explication" of the Nicene-Constantinopolitan Creed (381) as a means whereby all the churches might express their common faith, and as a basis on which concrete confession of the faith in particular circumstances might be made. It must be stressed that this document is a provisional one (hence being called a "study document"). It does not have the finality of the "Lima" text *Baptism, Eucharist and Ministry* (1982), and responses to it should be made with a view to its further development, not as a definitive "reception" of it. This draft therefore attempts to identify, positively and in a spirit of constructive criticism, those elements which Baptists see as significant in the continuing development of this, the most wide-ranging and inclusive attempt hitherto made in Christian history, to express the essentials of belief in the biblical, apostolic faith.

I. The Project as a Whole

A Welcome and Appreciation

Baptists have always believed that the unity of God's people on earth must be based upon a common understanding and proclamation of the gospel of Jesus Christ as testified in the Scriptures. We therefore welcome the project "Towards the Common Expression of the Apostolic Faith Today" as an important attempt by all the Christian traditions to state the essentials of Christian belief. We particularly appreciate the emphasis that is given in *Confessing One Faith* to the purpose of this explication: to aid the fulfillment of the churches' calling "to confess their faith in Jesus Christ in their common mission and service to the world" (p.2).

We welcome the significant place given to Scripture in this explication, and the attempt made throughout to see the Nicene Creeds as founded in the biblical faith.

We acknowledge that while Baptists have always claimed to recognize Scripture as the supreme authority for faith and obedience to God, their understanding and proclamation of the gospel have not always reflected the whole range and balance of the scriptural faith. For example, "salvation" has sometimes been emphasized to the detriment of the doctrines of creation and the last things; and the understanding of salvation itself has often taken a highly individualistic turn, ignoring God's loving purpose for a new community and indeed a renewed creation. We therefore recognize in the project a challenge to us to recover the wholeness of the faith.

The Nicene-Constantinopolitan Creed: A Qualification.

We recognize that for a great number of Christians and churches throughout the world the Nicene-Constantinopolitan Creed (NC) is a revered expression of their belief, regularly used in their worship, and containing for them the essentials of the faith which unites them with the universal church, past and present. We can thus understand why many see it as the most long-lasting and widely-recognized ecumenical symbol, and therefore a highly appropriate basis for an explication of the apostolic faith today.

Baptists, however, have some hesitations over this procedure. Let it be said at once that as such the *content* of the NC would not be disputed by Baptists (indeed many would claim that in their evangelical emphasis some of the items find at least as wholehearted an acceptance as in other traditions).

The hesitation is over the status of creeds as creeds. Baptists stress that faith, being our obedient response to God's grace, is an essentially free and personal relationship to God. While faith cannot be without its intellectual element of understanding, an emphasis on a credal formulary can lead to the intellectualization and formalization of belief to the loss of the personal, relational element which is the living heart of faith. Equally, while faith is never simply faith of the isolated individual, but a faith by which the believer is united with the community of the church, such faith cannot be coerced and compelled by external authority.

Baptists are among those whose historical experience gives them good cause to beware of the role of creeds in the formalization of faith, and the use of creeds by political power to compel uniformity of belief without regard to conscience. We would not suggest that any such danger lies within the present exercise but we would ask that in the Introduction, paras. 11 and 12, some acknowledgment be made of this side of the story of creeds in Christian history. We are grateful that the document states: "The main content of these Creeds is also present in the thinking and life of churches which do not officially recognize these Creeds or use them in their teaching and worship" (Introduction, para. 12), but we wonder why this very significant fact—which might seem to relativize the status of the Creed itself—receives no further reflection.

Further, some surprise has been occasioned among us by the sentence: "The decision [to use NC as basis for the study] was also taken in the recognition that the Nicene Creed served as an expression of unity of the Early Church and is, therefore, also of great importance for our contemporary quest for the unity of Christ's Church." The first part of this sentence makes an historical judgment which needs close historical scrutiny. How much "unity" was there, and of what kind was it, in the churches of the 4-5th centuries? How much of it was owed to the Creed itself—or to what extent was NC the *product* of a certain kind of unifying process which was highly ambiguous in its motivation? What, for example, of the coercive role of the Emperor—especially at Nicea in 325? Secondly, even if this judgment is historically sound, the second part of the sentence in question, °and is, therefore, of great important ..." cannot really be considered to follow logically from the first, unless considerable assumptions are made. Why should a fourth-century statement be assumed to be crucial for our contemporary quest for unity? For one thing, the subsequent history of Christianity could be held to demonstrate all too clearly that *despite* the existence of NC unity was not achieved or maintained. Further, how inclusive is the account of essential Christian belief given by NC, when no explicit reference is made in it to such vital doctrines as atonement, for example? What is more, does not the extent to which the creed now requires explication indicate its inadequacy as a statement of unifying faith for today?

These critical questions do not militate against the project as such. But we do feel that the problematic aspects of the creed for many Christians today should be more fully acknowledged. Baptists would not wish to dissociate themselves in any way from the Nicene-Constantinopolitan Creed, considered as a summary statement of biblical doctrine necessitated by the requirements of a particular and crucial moment in Christian history, and as indicating a direction always to be followed. Indeed, at certain moments in their history (as in seventeenth century England for example) Baptists have explicitly commended the Apostles', Nicene and Athanasian Creeds, both on account of their utility in teaching in the biblical faith, and of the felt need of Baptists to be identified with the mainstream of Christian orthodoxy. But NC will be significant for us in so far as it refers beyond itself to the Scriptures, within which is found the

Word of God.

It is therefore of some concern to us to know what rules are governing the use of Scripture in *Confessing One Faith*. The "biblical foundation" given to each sub-section is often impressive in the range and detail of biblical exposition. Is the possibility adequately recognized, however, that as well as being a foundation for the Creed, the Bible might itself at times offer a critique of it, or at least indicate that the Bible might have more to say than the Creed itself? The example of the atonement was cited above. This receives lively and lengthy treatment in the exegesis and explication of the credal term "for our sake" (114-132). But after the biblical foundation there appears to be little reference back to the Creed. Is the Creed as such actually being given an "explication", or is it merely providing a series of "titles" or "headings" of significant items of Christian belief which are then being explore biblically?

II. Key Elements in *Confessing One Faith*

Faith: Apostolic and Personal

We are glad to see in *Confessing One Faith* a real acknowledgment of Christian faith as personal decision, trust and commitment in response to the gracious initiative of God in Christ (for example paras. 2, 130, 131, 162, 163). We wholly identify with the repeated emphasis upon the Christian experience as one of a life transformed through encounter with Christ, one in which we must expect both joy and suffering in obedient decipleship and witness. We see here a true concern to reject any notion of an impersonal, formalized faith which belongs to an abstract notion of "the church" divorced from its living members.

At the same time we recognize the strong element in *Confessing One Faith* of the corporateness of Christian belief, and the concept that "The individual's faith is made in communion with the faith of the whole church" (para. 2). Baptists customarily speak of "the fellowship of believers' rather than "the communion of faith". There is need to examine the ecclesiology of *Confessing One Faith* to discover what are the implications of such differences in language. Certainly, there is a stimulus here for Baptists to recover more of their classic emphasis that the local church is in truth a community of people who covenant with the Lord and with each other, not just an association of believing individuals; and equally, a belief in the church universal, comprising all those in Christ.

The three biblical images, People of God, Body of Christ, Communion of Saints, would certainly find Baptist endorsement in their understanding of the Church. It is also good to see in the section on the Church, "The Church and the Trinitarian Communion", an emphasis upon the church as local as well as universal, and indeed as being fully manifested "wherever people are gathered together by word and sacrament and obedience to the apostolic faith" (para. 205). This sentence however is followed by: "This *local* church is fully the church of God when all it preaches, celebrates and does is in communion with all that the churches in communion with the apostles preached, celebrated and did, and with all that the churches here and now are preaching, celebrating and doing in communion with the apostles. In this way the *universal* church consists in the communion of local churches." (para. 205)

Most Baptists would see the "catholicity" of the church residing in the local church itself, since they see the essence of the church being the fellowship of committed believers to whom is given the promise of Christ's presence (Matthew 18.20). The church is thus the living Christ with his people who acknowledge him by faith. They would find some difficulties in speaking about such a "local" church being "fully the church of God" by fulfilling the conditions of "communion" thus described—not because Baptists do not believe in the universal church but because in this statement they do not find any direct reference to Jesus Christ himself as sole Lord of the Church, known through Scripture, who makes his will known to his gathered people. Precisely what does "in communion with…" mean? What criteria would indicate such "communion"? Agreement in every detail? Uniformity of practice? Or what? *We would therefore wish for some further exploration of the ecclesiological assumptions behind this section of the document.*

A particular example of the language of *Confessing One Faith* which seems indicative of a "catholic" tendency is the frequency with which the adjective "Eucharistic" appears, for example in para. 213 ("The church is the *Eucharistic community*…") and para. 214 ("This *Eucharistic vision* unites the universality of God's design with the uniqueness of Christ's death and resurrection…"). Again, most Baptists would affirm the importance of the Lord's Supper in their life and worship. But many would want to ask why "Eucharistic" seems to become such a normative description of the church and Christian living in an explication of a creed in which there is in fact no mention of the Eucharist. *We would therefore wish for explanation as to why "Eucharist" has become such a favoured term instead of, for example, "kingdom of God".*

Baptism

We deeply appreciate the connection made in paras. 225-234 between baptism and the new life of faith, transformed by encounter with Jesus Christ. "A decisive and fundamental change…" (para. 230) is indeed how we would express the significance of baptism, together with lifelong growth into Christ (para. 233).

However, as in Baptist responses to the Lima text *Baptism, Eucharist and Ministry,* we must point out that many Baptists will wish to distinguish between baptism itself, and that which it indicates, namely the union with Christ by faith. Thus for example the statement: "The baptism which makes Christians partakers of the mystery of Christ's death and resurrection implies confession of sin and confession of heart" (para. 232), will be accepted by many Baptists if "implies" means "accompanied by". And to speak of baptism as such, making Christians partakers in Christ, will be acceptable to most Baptists only if "baptism" is in fact read to mean "the faith which confesses Christ in baptism".

We are glad to see in the "Commentary" to para. 230 a clear recognition that there are in fact two rather different modes of conceiving the relationship between the prior activity of God's grace and the acceptance of that grace by faith—and the relationship of both to the "new birth". We would wish the difference between the "sacramental" and "symbolic" views to be explored further. We would especially emphasize that Baptists who take the "symbolic" view, no less than "sacramentalists" regard the prevenience of God's grace in Christ as absolutely foundational to the meaning of baptism. (Incidentally, the first sentence of the second paragraph of this commentary is surely intended to be the conclusion of the first paragraph.)

Commendation

We hope that such points as these will be considered by the Faith and Order Commission in the continuation of this important project, which is accompanied by our interest and prayers, and anticipation of a final document which has the potential of great significance for the proclamation of the gospel by all God's people in all the world.

Keith W. Clements is Senior Tutor at Bristol Baptist College, Bristol, England, U.K.

Commission on Baptist Heritage

The Study Commission on Baptist Heritage is a new component of the Division of Study and Research. Formed at the World Congress in Los Angeles in 1985, it is composed of 25 members who include historians, archivists, theologians and church and institutional leaders. At its meeting in Singapore, the Commission voted as its purpose, "To investigate and promote the meaning of Baptist heritage and identity."

The tasks of the Commission are subdivided into working groups for archives, historical preservation, publication and bibliography.

The theme of the Singapore meetings in 1986 was the "origin of the people called Baptist" from a global perspective. Papers were presented by Kenneth R. Manly (Whitley College, Australia), William R. Estep (Southwestern Baptist Theological Seminary, USA), with a response from Heather M. Vose, University of Western Australia.

At Amman Jordan in 1987 the focus was upon the international regional development of Baptists. Gunter Balders, FRG, focussed upon Northern Europe, David Priestly, North American Baptist Divinity College, presented the history of Canadian Baptists.

Due to a lively interest in the subject, the sessions in Nassau, the Bahamas were devoted to Baptist achievements in education. The major presenters were John Briggs (University of Keele, U.K.) William Brackney (Eastern Baptist Theological Seminary, USA) and Glenn Hinson (Southern Baptist Seminary, USA). W. Morgan Patterson (Georgetown College, USA) Arthur Walker (Southern Baptist Convention, USA) and Thomas Corts (Samford University, USA) comprised a panel discussion on Baptist collegiate education in the southern U. S. context. Lynn May (Southern Baptist Historical Commission, USA) presented a most encouraging progress report on the additional data survey authorized in Singapore.

The final full meeting of the Study Commission was held in Zagreb, Yugoslavia and explored the role and perception of women in Baptist life. Paper presenters for this session were John Briggs (University of Keele, U.K.), Edna Gutierrez (Women's Division, Mexico), Heather Vose (University of Western Australia, Australia), Eljee Bentley (SBC Woman's Missionary Union, USA). Ruth Lehotsky of Novisad, Yugoslavia served as a resource person for those sessions.

The larger interests of Baptist Heritage have been articulated in the Study and Research Committee meetings and within the General Council. Two resolutions, developed by the Commission, were approved by the General Council. "In an era of concern over Baptist identity, this Council endorses the request of the BWA Baptist Heritage Commission to urge Baptists worldwide to recover their rich heritage and to conduct their mission as a part of Christ's church with a deeper understanding of their history, and indicates the availability of the Commission as a resource body." The second resolution states: "Recalling the historic Baptist understanding of religious liberty for which our forbears were persecuted and put to death, this Council calls upon its constituent members to uphold continually that vision of freedom granted in the gospel of the living Christ, and therefore to allow for varieties of practice and interpretation."

William H. Brackney, Chair

William H. Brackney is Vice President and Dean, Eastern Baptist Theological Seminary, Philadelphia, Pennsylvania, USA.

Origins of the Baptists: The Case For Development from Puritanism - Separatism

Kenneth R. Manley

"Whether the first appearance of a Baptist ecclesiology within English dissent arose primarily as the result of dynamics inherent to left-wing Puritanism and Separatism or as the cross fertilization of Separatist and Anabaptist ideals, is a problem likely never to be solved to every historian's satisfaction."[1]

This frank admission from Stephen Brachlow, who, however, does not hesitate to argue persuasively for the Puritan-Separatist thesis, is a salutary reminder as once again this complex issue is considered. An appropriate humility, however, is not the same as despair and the dialogue engendered by these B.W.A. Commission meetings will hopefully further our awareness of both the complexities and significances of our Baptist origins.

I

What exactly are the questions posed about the origins of English Baptists? They may be reduced to four.[2] To each of them different answers have been offered with the inevitable result that different answers have been given to the larger question of Anabaptist influence. The questions range across the possibility of a general Anabaptist influence on an ecclesiastical movement to questions of specific points of contact.

The general question is: Did the Anabaptist influence the development of Puritan Separatism? Specific questions include: Did the Waterlander Mennonite church influence John Smyth in his decision to be baptised? Did the Anabaptists influence Smyth and Helwys in other ways not least in modifying their Calvinist beliefs towards an "Arminian" theology? Did the Rhynsburg Collegiant Church influence the later emergence of the Particular Baptists?

II

These simple questions might at first seem to be capable of simple answers. But there are many problems which complicate the answers and in turn make us suspect the simplicity of our questions.

Certainly some have confidently offered simple answers. Words like "obvious", "inevitable", "undisputed" adorn much of the literature on this topic. At first sight the parallels in the theology of the English Separatists and the continental Anabaptists seem "obvious". That "Anabaptists" were active in England prior to the clear emergency of Separatism is demonstrable. When it is noted that the old Lollard-Anabaptist dissent seems to disappear at the precise time that Separatism emerges, then it seems "undisputed" that the Separatists are simply a new stage in the history of Anabaptism in England.[3]

But many respected historians have refused to accept the "obvious" and the "undisputed". B. R. White, who has been the leading exponent of the Puritan-Separatist theory for our generation, claims that the question of the possibility of Anabaptist influence on the Separatists is made "virtually insoluble" by three complicating factors.[4]

First, it was possible for both groups to reach independently the same conclusions because both groups appearled to the Bible as providing the one unchanging pattern for the church's life and order.

Secondly, even if the Separatists did learn anything from the Anabaptists they would be unlikely ever to admit it. For one thing, their claim was that they derived their truth directly from the Bible, and, moreover, to acknowledge the Anabaptists as a source was a quick way to ensure that 16th or 17th Century hearers would give the idea no sympathetic thought. Accordingly English Baptists strenuously opposed the term "Anabaptist" when applied to them, anxious to avoid any "libel" by "label".[5] It is therefore, "next to impossible to measure the impact of Anabaptist ideas in a situation where their impact is bound to be denied or ignored *even if it were considerable*—a possibility for which there is not the least explicit testimony?.[6]

Thirdly, and this is White's own strongly-held viewpoint, there does exist in the development of the English Separatists a plausible explanation for the development of their ideas which does not require the introduction of any Anabaptist influence. Accordingly Dr. White concludes:

"It may, therefore, be fairly claimed that, when a plausible source of Separatist views is available in Elizabethan Puritanism and its natural developments, the onus of proof lies upon those who would affirm that the European Anabaptists had any measurable influence upon the shaping of English Separatism."[7]

III

But before reviewing White's "plausible" account for the development of Separatism, it will be helpful to give a brief review of how previous Baptist historians have interpreted this question. Ian Sellars of Manchester in an instructive discussion, shows that during the Edwardian period Baptist historians generally rejected the older claims of Anabaptist connections to advance the Puritan-Separatist thesis.[8]

Certainly the earliest Baptist historians (T. Crosby, J. Ivimey, D. Benedict, T. Armitage, B. Evans, A. H. Newman, H. C. Vedder) all held to the Anabaptist connections. But there came a remarkable revolution earlier this century and Sellers has identified four factors which gave rise to this different interpretation.

First was the development of methods of historical criticism and especially an emphasis on a strict documentary approach. All generalised propaganda myths were rightly rejected. Some Non-conformist historians, notably the influential Champlin Burrage, believed that their approach was more strictly historical.[9] Burrage was the first closely documented account which advocated the Puritan-Separatist thesis.

Secondly, certain events in the United States had an impact on the development of Baptist historiography in Britain. The successionist school of Baptist history which claimed a line of succession from John the Baptist to modern Baptists and which often, though not invariably, claimed Anabaptist links was often associated with the Landmark movement.[10] This successionist theory was attacked by both H. S. Burrage and, in what developed into a famous controversy, by W. H. Whitsitt, of Southern Baptist Seminary.[11] Moreover Walter Rauschenbusch, regarded with suspicion by more conservative Baptists, became an enthusiast for Anabaptists. Sellers suggests that "for a generation only Baptists of the theological and political left would care to appropriate the Anabaptists as their spiritual forebears".[12] So, from two differing movements there was an impetus towards the Puritan-Separatist thesis being advocated.

A third explanation offered by Sellers is that during the Edwardian period "three scholars representing three other and very different groupings wrote powerfully to claim the Anabaptists for themselves". These were the Marxist Socialist Belfort Bax, the Unitarian W. H. Burgess and the Quaker Rufus M. Jones.[13]

The fourth factor is somewhat more tentatively proposed. This is the sociological thesis that "denominations at a certain stage of their evolution seem to compensate for a loosening of theological bonds by a tightening up everywhere else...there is a search for academic and social respectability, not least in respect of origins and history".[14]

Certainly Champlin Burrage in his *Early English Dissenters* (1912) had little sympathy for the Anabaptists and revealed an iconoclast's delight as he rejected earlier undocumented histories. Burrage was a major influence on the leading Baptist historian, W. T. Whitley who in 1908 had accepted that the General Baptists were an outgrowth of continental Anabaptists acting upon the Lollards but who a few years later insisted that Baptists should be "sharply distinguished" from the Anabaptists.[15] G. P. Gould, J. H. Shakespeare and (eventually) H. Wheeler Robinson denied Anabaptist links.[16] During this process and accompanying debates Baptist historical studies were developed in a more professional manner.

But the Puritan-Separatist thesis has not, of course, been universally accepted as standard orthodoxy. The exciting developments in Anabaptist research since World War II have led to a much calmer, more positive and balanced assessment of the Anabaptists. Baptist scholars conducted a vigorous debate on this question in the 1950s and 60s. On the one side J. D. Mostellar from the U.S.A. and the dean of British Baptist historians, E. A. Payne argued for the Anabaptist links whilst on the other side W. S. Hudson, H. Wamble and L. D. Kliever argued for the Puritan-Separatist thesis.[17]

It cannot be claimed that the debate was always conducted with appropriate professional detachment. W. S. Hudson felt that to insist on the Anabaptist connections (though E. A. Payne was to reject his distorted definition of an Anabaptist) led to serious consequences: "The origins of the Baptists are distorted, the quest for theological foundations is destroyed, and the ecumenical thrust imperilled".[18] Others, of course, seemd to feel that any Anabaptist connection was a cause of true pride. But significant scholarly debate was stimulated by the exchange. W. Estep published *The Anabaptist Story* in 1963 (revised edition, 1975) which argued powerfully for the Anabaptist connection relying in part on the researches of I. B. Horst on Anabaptism in England.[19] R. G. Torbet in *History of the Baptists* (1963 ed.) argued that Baptists are spiritual descendants of *some* of the Anabaptists but cautiously commented, "No historical continuity between the two groups can be proved".[20]

Meanwhile B. R. White's 1961 Oxford thesis was the basis of his definitive work, *The English Separatist Tradition* (1971) in which he argued for the development of the Baptists from the Separatists.

A recent exchange of articles in *The Baptist Quarterly* has renewed the debate. James Coggins reviewed the theological positions of John Smyth and observed that "there is no evidence to suggest Smyth received any Anabaptist influence prior to his baptism".[21] Douglas Shantz argued, however, that Smyth's emphasis on the place of the resurrected and ruling Christ in the life of the community was more central to his theology than the notion of covenant and suggested that this was a sign of Anabaptist influence.[22] White was unrepentant in a thoughtful rejoinder to these articles whilst Stephen Brachlow drew on his research into Puritan theology in two articles to strengthen the claim that there is an even more convincing case for regarding Smyth's Baptist convictions as developing from radical Puritanism and Separatism.[23]

These have been the major contributions to the debate.[24]

IV

An excellent summary of the Separatist theory, using all relevant material as then published, was made by L. D. Kliever in 1962. His arguments and those subsequently developed, especially by White and Brachlow, form the substance of this present review.

No one seriously claims a *direct* and *demonstrable* continuity of Anabaptists and Baptists. The question is rather whether there is significant *indirect* influence and whether at some specific points of contact there is a *direct* influence. Confining himself to the General Baptists Kliever argued that there are no specific points of contact with the Anabaptists which *caused* the General Baptists to emerge from their Separatist background, that theological continuity cannot be claimed because the Anabaptists and Baptists belong to different traditions and, positively, that the rise of the General Baptists was "a leftward movement of Puritanism and an extension of Separatism".[25]

The four questions raised earlier may now be considered separately.

(1) *Did Anabaptism play any significant part in the rise of Separatism?* Despite the researches of I. B. Horst the whole question of the role of Anabaptists in England in the 16th Century remains a confused one. Problems of terminology are familiar to the student of the period. Many "Anabaptists" were executed.

But what exactly was an "Anabaptist" and how widely known were the views of a largely underground movement? When Horst concludes that "English anabaptism was not separatist and did not institute rebaptism of believers" the reader may wonder whether "anabaptist" is the correct term for the radicals he describes.[26] However, Michael Watts follows Horst in his judgment that whilst "concrete literary evidence" is lacking there is a good deal of "circumstantial evidence" to suggest a link between Lollardy, Anabaptism and the General Baptists".[27] He notes, for example, that the early General Baptists appear in precisely the same geographical regions as the old Lollard strongholds.[28]

But there *is* a lack of concrete literary evidence. It is not that proponents of the Separatist theory lack historical imagination. Of course, as Payne observed, ideas "had legs in the sixteenth and seventeenth centuries".[29] The possibility of Anabaptist influence cannot be denied in such an excited and volatile age. Nor can it be demonstrated.

There is, moreover, a clear, logical and *demonstrable* development from Puritanism to Separatism which does not need to posit any Anabaptist influence. White has clearly stated the thesis.[30] He begins with the claim that John Foxe's *Acts and Monuments* played a significant part in the foundation and nourishment of the English Separatist tradition. His account of the Marian persecutions "familiarized several generations of Englishmen with the arguments which had been used and the precedents which had been created, for withdrawal from a "false" Church".[31]

B. R. White then discusses the underground congregations which met in London during the early years of Elizabeth I and suggests their theology was supplemented by the Genevan ecclesiology promoted by Presbyterian Puritans. For this reason the role of Robert Browne in developing a Separatist ecclesiology, though significant, may not have been as central as sometimes has been assumed. Certainly the "mutualist" concept of the covenant as taught by Robert Browne was essential to his ecclesiology and "provided the theological dynamic" for his act of separation.[32]

Did Anabaptists influence Robert Browne? Norwich was a centre of radical Protestantism. Estep suggests that the radical nature of the Puritan movement in the area "may have been due to the influence of the Mennonites in the area".[33] He quotes Schaffer's view that similarities between Browne and the Mennonites were so similar that "dependence is obvious".[34] Horst is more cautious, noting that "conclusive evidence has never been presented" but that "on theological and spiritual grounds" the evidence is more convincing.[35]

Browne's view of the church and his views on the magistracy are thought to be very similar to the Anabaptists and Estep ventures the observation that the migration to Holland may indicate sympathy with the Mennonite view. Similarities between Browne and the Mennonites "seem to have been more than coincidental".[36] Again, Estep points out that Anabaptists virtually vanish from the English scene as the Separatists emerge and that Anabaptist ideas are prevalent among the Brownists and the Barrowists. He concludes that "it seems more than a chance" that the Separatist movement bore such a close resemblance to the Anabaptists.[37]

There are several comments to be made on this type of argument and on the specific details. It is important to distinguish between using a term *descriptively* and using it *derivatively*. An idea may perhaps be called "Anabaptist" but it is quite another thing to conclude that the idea derives from specific Anabaptists. There is a tendency to convert parallels into influences and influences into sources which should be carefully avoided.

We must return to Robert Browne's ecclesiology. The most likely influence on Browne's "mutualist" or "conditional" nature of convenant was William Tyndale.[38] Brachlow has argued that the mutualist concept may possibly be linked with certain theological modifications that had begun to occur within Calvinism. Radical Puritans did employ the mutualist interpretation of the covenant as early as the 1570s, a decade before Browne, in their confrontations with those who supported episcopacy. There is no need to look beyond the immediate Puritan Context for this central concept of Browne's ecclesiology.[39]

Again, both Anabaptists and Puritans were reading the same Bible and believed it gave them clear directions concerning church life and order. Asking the same kinds of questions it would not be surprising if they came up with the same kinds of answers1

White shows that Browne's covenant teaching was not so influential on Henry Barrow and John Greenwood but his distinctive emphasis was revived, c. 1606, by Francis Johnson, Henry Ainsworth and John Smyth. In particular the role of Francis Johnson on both John Smyth and John Robinson is to be stressed. Their viewpoint received classic statement in the 1596 Separatist *Confession*. Accordingly White has traced the development of the Separatist tradition and concludes that there is no evidence of "anything approaching direct influence upon the English Separatists before John Smyth arrived in Amsterdam".[40]

Specific aspects of Separatist ecclesiology may be considered. Both groups shared a desire for restitution of the Apostolic pattern of church life but the Separatist concern may more readily be linked to the first *Admonition to the Parliament* (1572). This pamphlet revealed a "shrewd application of the New Testament golden-age standard to the current establishment".[41]

Again, the Anabaptists characteristically made use of "the ban" in their understanding of Matthew 18:15-17. Douglas Shantz has sought to argue that this notion of the ruling Christ was more important than the covenant to Smyth's ecclesiology[42] but B. R. White has reasonably replied that it was the covenant which needed to be fulfilled in order for Christ to reign.[43] Church discipline was a major concern of Martin Bucer and John Calvin and Matthew 18:15-17 was an important text therefore to the Puritan-Calvinists of England.[44]

Congregational autonomy is an aspect of ecclesiology clearly demonstrable in the Puritan context. Presbyterian Puritans had argued for congregations to choose their own ministers. Separatists stressed the same principle in pleading for congregational autonomy.

White has also commented that if G. H. Williams is accurate in his judgment that "England's Anabaptism was exclusively Melchiorite"[45] then the absence of any discernable weakness in that direction in English Separatist Christology provides a further indication that Anabaptist influence is not clearly to be discerned in the English Separatist tradition.[46] Michael Watts has noted that these views did appear among the General Baptists but this is much later by which time Melchiorite views had become more widely known, not least by negative condemnation.[47]

Again, Brachlow has shown that the Separatist emphasis on an "experimental" approach to man's knowledge of election was employed by Puritan contemporaries. The two distinctive marks of saving faith, so the Separatists held, were knowledge of orthodox doctrine and visible obedience. Here John Smyth, for example, echoes the sentiments of William Perkins. The emphasis on visible active faith as evidence of saving faith was a feature of radical Puritanism and the Separatists.[48]

In these ways the general thesis that there is a logical development towards Separatism from radical puritanism has been developed. There is no need to posit what cannot be proved; the Anabaptists did not play a significant part in the development of Separatism.

(2) *Did the Waterlander Mennonite Church influence John Smyth in his decision to be baptized?*

John Smith, Thomas Helwys and their companions moved from Gainsborough to Amsterdam in 1608. Smyth was soon in conflict with the "ancient" Separatist church of Francis Johnson. The first dispute concerned the use of the Scriptures in public worship and Smyth insisted that to read the Scriptures in translation was wrong. The second dispute related to church government in which Smyth insisted that the congregation had ultimate authority in the church.

But the most radical and certainly most controversial development was that Smyth rejected infant baptism. He not only opposed baptism in the Church of England, he rejected all infant baptism. Smyth insisted that baptism was not only "washing with water" but involved "baptism of the Spirit, the confession of the mouth, and the washing with water".[49] How then can an infant receive baptism? Smyth's church agreed. In 1609 his church was reconstituted on the basis of baptism. Smyth first baptized himself, then Thomas Helwys and then the whole company by the pouring of water over the face.

Smyth subsequently defended his re-baptism but on one point was disturbed. His critics asked why he had not sought baptism from the Waterlander Mennonites of Amsterdam who already practised believers" baptism. Smyth met this criticism by making contact with them and so, says Knappen, established the first discoverable tie between the English Separatists and the Anabaptists.[50]

This development led to the famous breach between Smyth and Helwys. Smyth's followers eventually joined the Waterlanders whereas Helwys and a smaller group returned to England. Helwys had been especially distressed by the thought that Smyth's action demonstrated an improper concern for apostolic succession.

The principle reason for suggesting Smyth was not significantly influenced by the Anabaptists is that he did not seek baptism from them. Of course he knew that they practised "re-baptism". He stayed in a Mennonite house for part of his time there. Their existence may have encouraged him in a general way to think about the issue but there is no hint of any dialogue with them. He may well have been suspicious because of a Christology which was thought heretical. This all suggests his contact was not a very close one.[51]

Once again, there is (at least in retrospect) an inevitable logic in Smyth's religious pilgrimage from Puritan to Separatist to Baptist. Smyth simply refused, as other Separatists, to modify the requirements of church membership for the children of church members. L. D. Kleiver summarises Smyth's action:

"The logic of his own beliefs was too strong to resist. The Reformation understanding of justification by faith, the Puritan view of the sacraments, the Separatist concept of the church comprised of believers only in covenant with God and one another, The separatist conviction that the Established Church was totally corrupt - all of these coupled with a thorough study of the Scriptures brought Smyth to the decisive act in which "he took a stance so logical, so radical, so scriptural that he inaugurated a new era"."[52]

The question is often quite reasonably asked: if the logic of Separatism leads so naturally to the Baptist position, why didn't all the Separatists make the same pilgrimage? William Estep, for example, suggests that this move was because of Smyth's contact with the Waterlanders and was independent of his Separatist beliefs.[53] But there are other ways of understanding this lack of more general Separatist support. As K. Sprunger has commented, Separatism did not lead to Anabaptism for most English Separatists because they themselves practised something very close to the believers' church ideal. This made the revolutionary, and for many of them repugnant, step into Anabaptism unnecessary.[54]

J. R. Coggins has also observed that the Church Fathers cited by Smyth in defence of his position on baptism are unlikely to have been suggested by Anabaptists. "Moreover, influences are not passed on by osmosis through proximity. There is evidence that the language barrier severely restricted meaningful contact between English Separatists and Dutch Mennonites."[55]

(3) *Did the Anabaptists influence Smyth and Helwys in other ways, not least in modifying their Calvinist beliefs towards an Arminian theology?*

Before Smyth and Helwys had separated there was another important shift in their theological position. Smyth and Helwys both adopted a modified Calvinism as is clearly revealed in their confessions of belief.[56] There are several possible sources for this Arminian modification of their beliefs.

L. D. Kliever has claimed that "no Anabaptist influence need be considered significant" in this regard.[57] He points to the criticisms which were levelled against Calvinism by Peter Baro at Cambridge in the 1590s whilst Smyth was at Cambridge. He presumably would have known of this debate. Again, Arminius was professor at Leyden where he died in 1609. The Arminian issue must have been known by the English Separatists. Or again, Kliever suggests, the Bible might have been the direct source of Smyth's theology in this regard. On the other hand, Michael Watts and J. R. Coggins incline to the judgment that the timing of Smyth's conversion to "Arminianism" suggests it was the Mennonite influence which was the decisive factor.[58]

Stephen Brachlow, however, has been able to show that here again there are "intriguing indicators" that in this matter also there is an "ideological continuity" which may be traced in Smyth. He traces this in the new emphasis among second-generation English Calvinists upon visible faith and conditional convenant theology. Indeed, he suggests that the change in doctrine and the change in polity clearly belong together.[59]

There were clear differences between the English Baptists under Helwys and the Mennonites (and John Smyth's group). L. D. Kliever has traced these differences by careful reference to the main confessions of faith and concluded that they are "two different and dissimilar traditions".[60] The key areas of disagreement, as they emerged, were the taking of oaths, whether a Christian should serve as a magistrate, pacifism, and Christology.

One other key issue requires special comment. Timothy George has recently traced the English Baptist doctrine of religious toleration and suggested that their position is between radical Anabaptist pacifism and the Calvinist tradition of magisterial reformation. He insists that Smyth's views on church and state were influenced by the Waterlander Church. Certainly Smyth's final position was pacifist. Helwys on the other hand had a different view. George shows that the English Baptists remained faithful to the Puritan tradition on war, and the role of Christian magistrates, but differed from them with regard to religious toleration.[61]

There seems, that here also, a reasonable case for tracing this emphasis can be found within Separatism. The inviolability of conscience was a Puritan concern. But that is not to diminish the radical and significant contribution which English Baptists made to the struggle for toleration in England.

(4) *Did the Rhynsburg Collegiant Church influence the later emergence of the Particular Baptists?*

This takes the discussion to a later stage in the story of Baptists in England. The story of Particular Baptists arising from the Jacob-Lathrop-Jessey Church is well-known, although there are still some points of uncertainty.[62] On one point there is no doubt. Richard Blunt was sent to the Netherlands because he understood Dutch and could consult with those there who practised believers" baptism. Blunt went to consult with the Rhynsburgers. Clearly that they had knowledge about them is significant but the clear evidence of the Kiffin manuscript is that the group had already become convinced about the truth of believers" baptism by "diping" (sic.). Glen H. Stassen discussed the questions of Anabaptist influence on the origin of the Particular Baptists and made the interesting suggestion that they were indebted to Menno Simon's *Foundation Book* "or to another treatise or Mennonite whose position was extremely similar to its contents".[63] This indebtedness, however, is scarcely convincing, since the divergences are so clearly apparent.

The case for decisive Anabaptist influence on the origins of the Particular Baptists seems distinctly uncertain.

For each of these questions, a case can be made for Baptist development from the Puritan-Separatist background.

V

Some concluding comments may be ventured.

(i) It is interesting to note that those who develop a specialised knowledge in one area of study, whether it be Puritanism or Anabaptism, tend to posit a case for Baptist origins from their own special perspective. Here Baptist historians may profitably note the observation of Patrick Collinson concerning the early dissenting tradition that "denominational history is engaged history, never more passionately engaged than in this ecumenical age".[64] A concern to trace a linear progress, whether the line be from Anabaptist or Puritan, may not finally be the most important or most helpful way of proceeding. Geographic, social, economic factors may yet give us more of an understanding of our tradition than we presently have. Perhaps we have to think more of polygenesis and less of monogenesis.[65]

(ii) How does our quest for an accurate understanding of our origins influence contemporary Baptist life?

Donald Durnbaugh has suggested that all three theories of Baptist origins (successionist, Anabaptist kinship and English separatist descent) have important ecumenical implications.

> "In all cases, they present a Baptist position vis-a-vis other churches. All seek to place Baptists correctly within the long sweep of Christian history. In some ways they reflect apologetic or polemical considerations. In other ways they reflect the need to establish a tenable Baptist position in the face of denominational rivalries. Implicitly or frankly, they intend to establish a Baptist ecumenical posture."[66]

This was certainly the concern of Winthrop Hudson, as has been noted.[67] But the strictures of Christopher Hill on such an apologetic or polemical approach to our origins or our "pre-history" need to be carefully heeded.[68] Indeed B. R. White is right in his insistence that "no amount of theological or historical sleight of hand can make *either* of the main groups of 17th Century English Baptists comfortable participants in 20th Century ecumenical debate".[69]

Accordingly, whether the Anabaptist or Separatist origin is championed, what finally matters is what Baptists *across their entire history* have contributed. On either theory of origins the respected judgment of Daniel Day Williams is unaltered:

"Here is a form of the Christian community which rests upon an experience of the Gospel which is personal, rather easily intelligible, vividly symbolized, calling for personal dedication, and open to the promptings of the Spirit. The Baptists seem to prove that the Christian Church can live and grow as a personal fellowship based on a directly shared experience, provided it is interpreted through a commonly accepted language of Scripture symbols."[70]

That is our contribution to the ecumenical scene.

Of course there are pastoral and denominational values which we need to discern from our heritage. Not infrequently recourse is made to the "historic Baptist position" on some contemporary issue. This justifies and necessitates an accurate concern to recover our heritage. But it must be an accurate and complete recovery, not ignoring the complexities and diversities of our heritage. Scholars and apologists debate what is the essence of the Baptist faith. Most would include religious liberty and this dimension is urgently needed in our pastoral and denominational activities. But here again, whether we affirm the Anabaptist or Separatist descent theory, the fact remains that Baptists have championed religious toleration from their birth.

The larger question is the authority that our Baptist, and indeed, whole Christian heritage has for our contemporary faith and life.[71] Clearly our heritage is meant to be a golden coin, something to be treasured and used. It is not a golden chain, beautiful but binding us to old ways. For Baptists, as for all Christians, Jesus is Lord. God's truth and purposes are mediated through the Scriptures, and through the traditions of the church as they reflect the Scriptural revelation. This Christian heritage includes, but is wider than, our Baptist traditions. However as we seek to be obedient to our Lord we will have a special family concern to test the Baptist part of our Christian heritage against the self-authenticating Word of God. We are most surely Baptist when we take our stand on the Word of God. For whatever their limitations that was what John Smyth, Thomas Helwys and many others whom we honour (including Anabaptists, Puritans and Separatists) sought to do.

Kenneth R. Manley is principal of Whitley Theological College, Melbourne, Australia.

Notes

1. Stephen Brachlow, "Puritan Theology and General Baptist Origins", *Baptist Quarterly*, XXI (1985), 189.

2. As suggested by L. D. Kliever, "General Baptist Origins: The Question of Anabaptist Influence", *Mennonite Quarterly Review*, XXXVI (1962), 292.

3. See I. B. Horst, "England", *Mennonite Encyclopaedia* (1972). II, 215-221.

4. B. R. White, *The English Baptists of the Seventeenth Century*, (London: 1983), p. 22.

5. L. D. Kliever, loc. cit., 291.

6. B. R. White, *The English Separatist Tradition*, (Oxford: 1971), p. 164.

7. Ibid.

8. Ian Sellers, "Edwardians, Anabaptists and the Problem of Baptist Origins", *Baptist Quarterly*, XXIX (1981), 97-112.

9. Champlin Burrage, *The Early English Dissenters*, (Cambridge, 1912), I, p. 14.

10. See W. M. Patterson, *Baptist Successionism. A Critical View*, (Valley Forge, 1969).

11. Sellers, loc. cit., 100. For a popular account of the Whitsitt controversy see W. B. Shurden, *Not a Silent People: Controversies That Have Shaped Southern Baptists*, (Nashville, 1971), pp. 21-33.

12. Sellers, loc. cit., 101.

13. Sellers, ibid.

14. Sellers, loc. cit., 105.

15. Sellers, loc. cit., 106 and sources cited there.

16. Ibid.

17. J. D. Mostellar, "Baptists and Anabaptists", *The Chronicle*, XX (1957), 3-27; 100-115. E. A. Payne, "Who were the Baptists?" *Baptist Quarterly* XVI (1956), 303-12; "Contacts between the Baptists and Anabaptists", *Foundations* IV (1961), 39-55. "Contacts Between Mennonites and Baptists", in *Free Churchmen Unrepentant and Repentant*, (London: 1965), pp. 75-92; W. S. Hudson, "Who were the Baptists?", *Baptist Quarterly* XVI (1956), 303-312; "Baptists were not Anabaptists", *The Chronicle* XVI (1953), 71-79; Hugh Wamble, "Inter-relations of Seventeenth Century English Baptists", *Review and Expositor* LIV (1957), 407-425; L. D. Kliever, loc. cit., 291-321.

18. W. S. Hudson, "Baptists were not Anabaptists", *The Chronicle*, XVI (1953), 176.

19. See note 3, and I. B. Horst, *The Radical Brethren*, (Nieuwkoop: 1972).

20. R. G. Torbet, *A History of the Baptists*, (Valley Forge: 1963), p. 29.

21. J. Coggins, "The Theological Positions of John Smyth", *Baptist Quarterly*, XXX (1984), 247-264.

22. D. Shantz, "The Place of the Resurrected Christ in the Writings of John Smyth", *Baptist Quarterly*, XXX (1984), 199-203.

23. B. R. White, "The English Separatists and John Smyth Revisited", *Baptist Quarterly*, XXX (1984), 344-347; Stephen Brachlow, "John Smyth and the Ghost of Anabaptism", ibid., 296-300; and "Puritan Theology and General Baptist Origins", *Baptist Quarterly*, XXX (1985), 179-194.

24. There is a 1974 Southern Baptist Seminary Th.D. thesis by G. Saito, "An Investigation into the Relationship between the Early English General Baptists and the Dutch Anabaptists", but I have not seen this. Timothy George, "Between Pacifism and Coercion". The English Baptist Doctrine of Religious Toleration", *Mennonite Quarterly Review*, LVIII (1984), 34, note 20 comments on this thesis. "He concludes that there was a minimum of Anabaptist influence on Smyth's initial act of self-baptism, but allows for significant influence on the later General Baptists." I also have not seen Joseph Ban, "Were the Earliest English Baptists Anabaptists?", *In The Great Tradition*, (Valley Forge: 1982). B. R. White, "English Separatists and John Smyth Revisited", *Baptist Quarterly*, XXX (1984), 347, note 2 comments about Ban: "This is a sound and judicious discussion of most of the issues involved."

25. L. D. Kliever, loc. cit., 294.

26. I. B. Horst, *The Radical Brethren*, p. 178.

27. M. Watts, *The Dissenters*, (Oxford: 1978), p. 8.

28. Ibid., pp. 13-14.

29. E. A. Payne, "Who were the Baptists?". *Baptist Quarterly*, XVI (1956), 340.

30. *The English Separatist Tradition, passim*.

31. Ibid., p. 160.

32. Ibid., p. 54.

33. W. R. Estep, *The Anabaptist Story*, (Grand Rapids, 1975), p. 214.

34. Ibid.

35. I. B. Horst, "England", *Mennonite Encyclopaedia*, II, 219.

36. W. R. Estep, op. cit., p. 214.

37. Ibid., p. 215.

38. B. R. White, *The English Separatist Tradition*, p. 55 cf. his more recent comments on "covenent" in "English Separatists Revisited", *Baptist Quarterly*, XXX (1984), 345.

39. Stephen Brachlow, "Puritan Theology and General Baptist Origins", *Baptist Quarterly*, XXXI (1985), 181.

40. B. R. White, op. cit., p. 162.

41. M. M. Knappen, *Tudor Puritanism*, (Chicago: 1939), p. 234.

42. D. Shantz, loc. cit.

43. B. R. White, "English Separatists and John Smyth Revisited", *Baptist Quarterly*, XXX (1984), 346.

44. B. R. White, *The English Separatist Tradition*, p. 162.

45. G. H. Williams, *The Radical Reformation*, (London: 1962), p. 790.

46. B. R. White, op. cit., p. 163.   .

47. M. Watts, op. cit., p. 14.

48. Stephen Brachlow, "Puritan Theology and General Baptist Origins", *Baptist Quarterly*, XXXI (1985), 183-186.

49. J. Smyth, *The Character of the Beast*, 1609, in *The Works of John Smyth* (ed. W. T. Whitley), II, (1915), 567.

50. M. M. Knappen, op. cit., p. 330.

51. B. R. White, op. cit., p. 133.

52. L. D. Kliever, loc. cit., 318. The quotation is from W. T. Whitley, *Works of John Smyth*, I, xc.

53. W. R. Estep, op. cit., pp. 220f.

54. K. Sprunger, "English Puritans and Anabaptists", *Mennonite Quarterly Review*, XLVI (1972), 128; S. Brachlow, loc. cit., 180.   55. J. R. Coggins, loc. cit., 251.

56. For details see (for example), L. D. Kliever, loc. cit.

57. Ibid., 317.

58. M. Watts, op. cit., p. 46; J. R. Coggins, loc. cit., 258.

59. Stephen Brachlow, loc. cit., 179-180. For the developments in Calvinism see R. T. Kendall, *Calvin and English Calvinism to 1649*, (London: 1981).

60. L. D. Kliever, loc. cit., 315.

61. Timothy George, "Between Pacifism and Coercion: The English Baptist Doctrine of Religious Toleration", *Mennonite Quarterly Review*, LVIII (1984), 30-49.

62. See M. Tolmie, *The Triumph of the Saints*, (Cambridge: 1977), pp. 22-27 and Appendix A (pp. 192-195) where he disagrees with the views of B. White. A relevant extract from the "Kiffin Manuscript" may conveniently be seen in W. H. Brackney (ed.) *Baptist Life and Thought: 1600-1980: A Source Book.*, (Valley Forge: 1983), pp. 29-31.

63. G. H. Stassen, "Anabaptist Influence in the Origin of the Particular Baptists", *Mennonite Quarterly Review*, XXXVI (1962), 322-348.

64. Quoted by Ian Sellers, loc. cit., 109.

65. Cp. the approach to Anabaptist origins in J. M. Stayer, W. O. Packull, K.

Deppermann, "From Monogenesis to Polygenesis: the Historical Discussion of Anabaptist Origins", *Mennonite Quarterly Review*, XLIX (1975), 83-121.

66. Donald F. Durnbaugh, "Free Churches, Baptists, and Ecumenism: Origins and Implications", in *Baptists and Ecumenism* edited W. J. Boney and G. A. Igleheart (Valley Forge: 1980), p. 11.

67. See note 18.

68. See the quotations from Hill listed in M. Tolmie, op. cit., p. ix and Christopher Hill "History and Denominational History", *Baptist Quarterly*, XXII (1967), 65-71.

69. B. R. White, *The English Baptists of the Seventeenth Century*, p. 22.

70. D. D. Williams, "The Mystery of the Baptists", *Foundations*, (1958), 9. See W. S. Hudson, *Baptists in Transition: Individualism and Christian Responsibility*, (Valley Forge: 1979), p. 16.

71. On this issue see B. R. White, *Authority: A Baptist View*, London, 1976; George Peck, "The Baptist Heritage: Practice, Polity and Promise", *Andover Newton Quarterly*, 19 (1979), 215-222; Glen Hinson, "The Authority of the Christian Heritage for Baptist Faith and Practice", Paper presented to B.W.A. Commission on Baptist, Doctrine, typescript, 1973.

The State of Baptist Studies in Germany

Gunter Balders

I. GENERAL STUDIES

For more than 150 years there have been Baptist churches on the European Continent, starting in Germany. The scientific research of their history has seldom been part of the vision of the German Baptists. There are two main reasons:

First in a country with big Protestant national Churches and the Roman Catholic Church, the Baptists as a very small free church were of almost no interest for the academic world. The Baptists have not contributed to the history of theology in the land of Luther and Bonhoeffer. For a long time they were described as an "Anglo-American sect" or separatist group which did not need to be taken seriously.

Also, the Baptists themselves were (and are) practically oriented. Winning men and women for the Lord and the building of churches, according to the New Testament, has always been the primary interest. That's why a reflection on their own history or even a reflection on the present was hardly possible. Before World War II those few people capable of scientific research were urgently needed as qualified workers in each and every area of the church; in the training of new pastors they were especially needed as interpreters of the Bible and as teachers of the doctrine and of practical theology. If they dwelt at all with their own history they did it more or less to underline one's own identity and to strengthen the motivation for mission.

When in 1924 the centennial of continental European Baptists was

celebrated, a book came out which for the first time did not solely take into
account Baptist sources. Hans Luckey presented *Johann Gerhard Oncken und Die
Anfange des Deutschen Baptismus* (1934) after thorough research at church and
public archives and careful analysis of the historical and theological situation.
A short time later (1939) he published a second scientific biography: *Gottfried
Wilhelm Lehmann und die Entstehung Einer Deutschen Freikirche*. (Lehmann was
the founder of the first Baptist church in Prussia and Berlin, which celebrated
it's 150 years jubilee some weeks ago). But Luckey didn't have any time for
further research. The situation during the Third Reich, World War II and the
years of rebuilding took up all his attention and energy. He became principal
of the Theological Seminary at Hamburg and taught Exegesis and Systematic
Theology until 1970.

Only after the founding of the Theological Seminary in Ruschlikon by
our American partners, were hands and minds free to present the history, practice and doctrine of the Baptists. This was done by John D. Hughey (1959)
in a book with the same (but German) title as well as in the important contributed volume *DIE BAPTISTEN* in the series *DIE KIRCHEN IN DER WELT*
(1964). It can generally be noticed that a lot of qualified works concerning the
Anabaptists came from Ruschlikon, but hardly any concerning the Baptist history
of Europe.

During 1958-60 the Oncken Verlag published two books on the history
of the German Baptists by Rudolf Donat, a retired pastor *(WIE DAS WERK
BEGANN/DAS WACHSENDE WERK)*. It was a painstaking work and consists of such a quantity of details that it is impossible to obtain a general view.
After more than a thousand pages he has only reached the year 1909. A third
edition of Luckey's Oncken biography was published in 1958, but only 1000
copies were sold. German Baptists and 16 years earlier lost their Baptist name
and began to forget their history.

Twenty years later I presented an illustrated biography of Oncken, *Theurer
Bruder Oncken* when the Oncken Publishing House had its 150 years sesquicentennial. This book was received gratefully. Then, in 1984 when the German Baptist Churches had their jubilee, I edited an extensive *Festschrift ein Herr
ein Glaube eine Tauffe*. In this volume are found, among other topics a thorough
treatise on the confessions of faith and one about the church life done by my
successor as church historian at the Theological Seminary in Hamburg, Edwin
Brandt. After having edited our hymnbook *GEMEIMDELIEDER*, My task was
to revise books written by other people. But along with that I wrote for the
above mentioned *festschrift* an extensive "Short History of the German Baptists" (Gunter Balders, *KLEINE GESCHICHTE DER DEUTSCHEN BAP-
TISTEN*) which is according to some non-Baptist reviewers, scientifically well-
founded and at the same time popular. It is said to be "largely a critical clearing
up of the German Baptist history." As there were hardly any publications during the periods from 1909, I had to do extensive original research work and
at the same time compress the material on a limited number of pages. The era
includes two world wars, the Third Reich, the uniting of our Baptist "Bund"
with another group into the "Bund Evangelisch-Freikirchlicher Gemeinden"

as well as the rebuilding ear of our country and churches and structural crises before and since 1945 (a stiff job; sabbaticals are unknown in our country).

II. REGIONAL STUDIES

During the last years a lot of regional or local studies have been published on the occasion of lots of jubilees. They were mostly written by laymen and cannot be presented here. Often they offer important background material for research; there is a growing knowledge that it is not sufficient to screen the record books or registers of the local churches in order to develop the history of one's church. Kaspar Schneiter wrote in a similar way a *Geschichte Des Baptismus in der Schweitz* 1847-1978 and published it himself.

III. BIOGRAPHIES

Several biographies and biographical articles have ben published. I'd like to mention a revised biography by Eduard Scheve (1834-1909), a leading man of the second generation in our country who funded the deaconesses-house "Bethel" Berlin, a hundred years ago. All his time he was a supporter of female contributions in the church. He is also the founder of the German Baptist (Foreign) Mission in Cameroun, etc., today European Baptist Mission: E. S. DEM HERRN VERTRAUEN: BLUTEN UND FRUCHTE EINES LEBENS FUR GEMEINDE, MISSION UND DIAKONTE. The 1978 EVANGELISCHES GEMEINDELEXIKON focused on the neopietist evangelical wing in the Protestant churches and on the freechurches. In this book you find information on persons and matters and also a lot about the German Baptists which are not to be found in such large encyclopedias as RGG, EKL, LThK, TRE and others. C. H. Spurgeon's (abridged) *Autobiography* was also for the first time published in Germany. &Up to now Spurgeon is the most-read Baptist in our country, he is especially favored by neopietist groups and the strict Darbyites (his opponents in his own time₁).é

IV. ENCYCLOPEDIAS AND HANDBOOKS

The new theological encyclopedias contain on the whole strong articles about the Baptists, almost written by Baptist scholars (because they have better information?). In the new 2nd edition of the EVANGELISCHES KORCHENLEXIKON or "International Theological Encyclopedia" Eduard Schutz, until 1986 Principal of the Theological Seminary, Hamburg, has written about Baptists. This encyclopedia contains in careful and accurate articles a lot of references to Baptists all over the world. An American edition is being prepared for Eerdmans. Author of the corresponding article in the OKLUMENELEXIKON was Claus Meister of Ruschlikon; of that in the EVANGELISCHES GEMEINDENLEXIKON: Erick Geldbach (member of the BWA Commission on Doctrine and Interchurch cooperation; Geldbach is a specialist on Ecumenics and—as far as a German can be—an expert on American Church history). For

the TASCHENLEXIKON RELIGION UND THEOLOGIE, Otmar Schulz
has done this, for several Handbooks of denominations I have written the corresponding articles; in F. Heyer, KONFESSIONSKUNDE (especially for
students) H. Stahl is the author. Some of the best presentations are to be found
in the big Catholic Handbook KONFESSIONSKUNDE of ALGERMISSEN
as well as in another Catholic book on FREIKIRCHEN IN DEUTSCHLAND)
by Wilhelm Bartz (1973). In 1977 there was an urgent demand for an article
on Baptists for the new THEOLOGISCHE REALENZYKLOFADIE (a work
of more than 30 volumes). Within that short time J. D. Hughey, in cooperation with Rudolf Thaut, wrote a short contribution—too short for this important encyclopedia and in my opinion hardly sufficient in this context.

Theological Themes

The Baptist inheritance is - in a certain way - reflected in several exegetical
and systematic theological works. It is generally known that the German speaking Baptists (Austria, Switzerland, German Democratic Republic and Federal
Republic of Germany) have presented a new Confession of Faith
(RECHENSCHAFT VOM GLAUBEN) in 1977. Detailed information can be
obtained from the important book by Keith Parker, *Baptists in Europe: History
and Confessions of Faith, 1982*. (The history is only summarized in short introduc-
tions to the Creeds.) In this book you also find an English translation of the
1977 Confession. Those who know the oldest continental-European Confessions of Faith, all of which depend more or less on the German one of 1847,
can examine the change in contents and form, a change important for the history
of theology. (A simple example: while in the old document evidences from Acts
of the Apostles, were clearly dominant they are now taken from Romans and
1 Corinthiansı). Wiard Popkes, (Professor of New Testament at the Hamburg
Seminary), has presented two studies with exegetical and historico-systematical
and practical aspects: ABENDMAHL UND GEMEINDE ("Lord's Supper and
the Church") and GEMEINDE - RAUM DEES VERTRAUSENS (Church
Place of Trust).

Since the translation of the standard work by G. R. Beasley-Murray,
nothing has been published concerning the question of baptism, although there
is an urgent need for new contributions. It was not by chance that the section
about "Faith and Baptism" in the "Rechenschaft vom Glauben" in the GDR
version got a different form by Adolf Pohl; Pohl is professor of New Testament
and Systematics at the Theological Seminary in Buckow, GDR. Since the Lima
Document, a new study of the theology of baptism is necessary. Because of the
still unchanged practice of "closed membership" in the FRG and GDR (with
the exception of two churches in Hamburg) and the resulting strict practice of
baptism there have lately been new debates on proselytism for instance in Thur-
ingia and in the Eifel (cf. the interchurch dialogues in the GDR (1982-83) and
in the FRG (starting 1988?)

It is probably known to you that in the question of hermeneutics (Schrift-
verstandnis) there has been a controversy. So far the struggle has kept us busy

for five years, not only in the theological field, but more concerning essentials of our brotherhood. Historians of generations to come will find many files of letters and documents. We are convinced of the necessity of intensive theological work not only by theologians but also of the churches.

VI. SPECIAL CONTRIBUTIONS

In *New Move Forward in Europe* (1978) William Wagner is concerned with "Growth Patterns of German Seeking Baptists in Europe." His studies show that the methods of Pasadena can only be applied in a very modified form with regard to an analysis of a Freechurch in a context of a territorial established or State Church.

Historically precise and new materials were presented by Wayne Detzler in his study about *British and American Contributions to the "Ermeckling" in Germany, 1815-1848* (Manchester, 1974). He shows once again how strong especially the first generation of Baptists on the Continent were linked with the various mission efforts of the Anglo-saxon societies. Detzler gave evidence that for instance Oncken is not only the founder of the continental British movement but also an outstanding activist with regard to the Bible distribution.

At this point I should also mention another work of J. D. Hughey: *Baptist Partnership in Europe* (1982). It is non-scientific but yet important for our present state of Baptist studies. A Baptist professor and sociologist, Dienel has presented a sociological study on five Evangelisch Freikirchliche Gemeinden (*"De Freiwilligkeittskirche"*, 1962). Several smaller new essays in this field also convey important insight into how the churches are interwoven and their special socio-cultural environment. Unfortunately there still are no studies by theologically trained sociologists (or vice versa) on the Baptist "minority".

VII. SOVIET UNION

As already mentioned the German Baptists have—by reason of the small number of members—not much energy or time for profound research. All the more pleasant is that others give a helping hand. Two outstanding examples, written by Lutherans, have to be mentioned, both with the topic "Freechurches in the Soviet Union": Wilhelm Kahle, *Evangelische Christen in Rußland und der Soviet Union*; Ivan Stepanovic Prochanov (1869-1935) *Und Der Weg Der Evangeliums - Christen und Baptisten* - a study of 600 pages published by Oncken Verlaag in 1978; Hans-Christian Diederich, *Ursprunge Und Anfänge des Russischen Freikirchentums*, (Erlangen 1985), a very thorough study of the Russian sects (of the "Molokanen" and "Duchoborzen"), and also the Mennonite-Brethren, the Russian-German Baptists and of the Russian Stundism as well as Stundo-Baptism. In the GDR (where the author lives) an abridged version was published: *Siedler, Ektierer Und Stundisten, Die Enstehung Des Russischen Freikirchentums*. (Berlin 1985).

The author succeeds in presenting the many sources of the Russian Freechurch movement. One appreciates once again the prophetic view of Oncken who travelled through South Russia when he was almost 70 years old - a journey "of historical relevance" (p. 96). Oncken did a lot for an orderly and disciplined church life. In a letter written in 1869 he said: "I bid the churches to pray especially for the movement among the masses. It can light a fire which cannot be extinguished by an power on earth. After my visit to Petersburg (1864) I was filled with hope that the Lord will gather for himself a great many people in this vast nation." (B. G. *Theurer Bruder Oncken*, p. 137; Diedrich, "Siedler...", p. 106: "prophetic words").

After the German Bund has shared his part in the financing the large edition of this extensive work by Diedrich, a publisher should be found who is willing to publish at least an English edition of the abridged version.

VIII. (PLYMOUTH) BRETHREN-MOVEMENT IN GERMANY

Not only the Union of the Evangelical Christians-Baptists in the Soviet Union is a federation of several movements, but also—since the Third Reich—the German "Bund Evangelisch-Freikirchlicher Gemeinden"; since 1942 we no longer officially show the name "Baptists". The "Brudergemeinden" (Christliche Versammlung, that is Plymouth Brethren) who at present unfortunately are only partially united with us suffer up to now from the genesis of the union during the Third Reich. For them the union has become a heavy burden and has cast them into an identity crisis without comparison. That's why there are so many publications on the part of the "Brudergemeinden" which are concerned with their history - especially with their more recent one.

In this context, Erich Geldbach was the first to present a scientific study of John Nelson Darby, *Christliche Versammlung und Heilsceschichte Bei John Nelson Darby*. (Theologischer Verlag Rolf Brockhaus, Wuppertal 1971). One of Geldbach's students has presented a dissertation containing a lot of references: *Ulrich bister, Die Bruderbewegung in Duetschland von Ihren Angangen Bis Zum Verbot Des Jahres 1973* (Marburg 1983). Three volumes were written by Gerhard Jordy: *Die Bruderbewegung in Deutschland* (Wuppertal (1979). In addition, four books were published which deal with the topic "prohibition of the Plymouth Brethren by the Gestapo in 1937: and the founding of the BFC, a new federation which was meant to enable the movement to survive and which then united with the "Bund der Baptistengemeinden". Not all joined in, and after the War many left our federation (Bund EFG), some returning to the traditions of their fathers, others seeking a new way.

Historians specialized in denominational studies might find this quite puzzling: the Darbyite Brethren who had always been concerned about not adapting to or being integrated into any kind of church "system", united with the Baptists who were (and are) always in favor of organization and structure - this can only be understood with the context of the special situation during the Third Reich.

IX. THIRD REICH

The history of the German Baptists during the Third Reich has still not been written. Those Baptists of the previous generation who would have been able to do that work in a scientific way were without exception jointly responsible for the extremely problematic way of the Baptists "under the swastika." Younger ones have made minor efforts in this field. But one has to place oneself in the context of the German Baptists who had been influenced by Calvinism and Lutheranism and Neopietism. This is the only way to understand what the sources say. And what's more, it helps us to find out where those sources can be found which should be studied apart from the "official" sources by the Bund.

In addition to that, the studies of this era are also encumbered with the mortgage of the still unmastered past. The justification of the then chosen path in the middle of the road between absolute bondage and resistance, of diplomatic proceeding and making pacts was more obvious than to try courageously to strike the balance soberly and also to confess the common guilt. It was only on the occasion of the 150 years jubilee - in connection with the European Baptist Congress 1984 - that the younger ones, together with some of the older generation still living, could strike the balance "in the last hour". It was a moving experience for me and many others that the sober, and in many cases sobering, historical working off the past which was done in 1984 resulted in an historic document. This was presented by our Bundesleitung, then passed by the Bundesrat almost with one voice (1) and afterwards read aloud to the European Congress by the President of our Union. It was even more moving to experience the spontaneous reactions of our foreign guests. We thank God that at last 40 years after the War we could breathe freely as if a heavy burden had been taken off our shoulders.

In the meantime an abridged version of an extensive scientific study has been presented by a Methodist historian, living in the GDR: Karl Zehrer, *Evangelische Freikirchen und das "Dritte Reich"* (Berlin und Gottingen, 1986). This work offers a lot of material and good observations concerning the events as well as the analysis. The author has for instance been able to use sources which are not available to us in the West—for example the files of the "Reichskirchenministerium" which are kept in the GDR. Unfortunately, Zehrer has examined all freechurches at once with the emphasis on the Methodists, the Baptists, the Salvation Army, the Freien Evangelischen Gemeinden (i.e. Covenant church), the Darbyites and others like the Mennonites and different separate groups of strict Lutherans (Altlutheraner). As a result, none of the reviewers from these free churches is fully satisfied because the author couldn't resist sweeping judgments, standardizations and simplifications. Additionally the book unfortunately contains theologically anachronistic judgments. Nevertheless this book has expedited the research work.

I myself have tried to picture the way of our Baptist churches and our "Bund" in the background of the presentation of the history of the German Baptists as mentioned. But a vast amount of material is waiting to be documented and analyzed. I hope that a thorough research work can be seen from the brief study I published with regard to a special point, that is the temporary fulfill-ment of the "Fuhrerprinzip" in the Baptist Union: "Gunter Balders, *Eine Theologie des Fuhrerprinzips*"? and "*Heilige Gefolgschaft*" (Theologisches Gesprach, 1979). There is also a doctoral thesis on the years 1933/34 by Gunter Koesling, Marburg 1980. (I have to skip the smaller works of several students.)

By the way - a study of this era is certainly important for a history of the BWA, because the World Congress was held in Berlin 1934.

It will be our task to take more seriously into account the sources from the public archives and libraries and those of the other denominations, especially the Established Churches (Landeskirchen). Moreover, we should consider sources and opinions in other countries.

In his essay *A Question of Freedom? British Baptists and the German Church Struggle* in *Baptists in the 20th Century* (London, 1983), Keith Clements offers valuable material and good theological judgement, in my opinion. On the other side, he quotes only English records. Similar studies, for example, from the Dutch or Scandinavian background would be very welcome.

Gunter Balders is professor of Church History at the Baptist Theological Seminary in Ham-burg, Federal Republic of Germany.

Canadian Baptist Historiography

David T. Priestley

It does not take long to compile even a twenty-page typewritten bibliography of materials written and/or edited by Canadian Baptist historians. The assignment of this paper, however, is not so much to provide such a bibliography as it is to provide an introduction to what is found in such a bibliography. If a comprehensive listing of primary and secondary sources is of interest, there is forthcoming a Canadian bibliographic guide in the next several months; the project is the labor of Jarold K. Zeman of Acadia Divinity College (Wolfsville, NS), George A. Rawlyk of Queens University (Kingston, ON), and Philip Griffin-Allwood (Halifax, NS).

The historiography of Baptists in Canada struggles in search of cohesion for its story. At least four factors contribute to this incoherence. In the first place, Canada itself has no integrating "myth" by which to interpret and relate the events by which it has stumbled from French and English colony to nineteenth-century dominion to present nation among the nations. The nation-building process has been motivated more by a counter-revolutionary attitude toward the United States and by a British colonial possessiveness (combined with a Canadian nostalgia for the Old Country) than by a national vision. Its borders are only partly due to topography; most of the country has been carved rather arbitrarily by war and negotiation out of what some of her politicians like to boast is "the tough part of North America."

In addition, Canada exists in an uneasy tension among its five regions: Atlantic provinces (Nova Scotia, New Brunswick, Prince Edward Island, Newfoundland), central Canada (Ontario, Quebec), and the North (Yukon, Northwest Territories). The regionalism is natural enough—the process of settlement and development, influenced by geography, has produced significant differences among the parts—but it is expressed locally as a kind of umbrage that each is ignored by the others surprise that the others feel ignored. The Baptist story is also usually a regional tale in which the inter-regional connections are more rhetorical than objectively verifiable or actually felt by the constituency.

Furthermore, the Christian ecclesial picture is dominated by the Roman Catholic Church, the Anglican Church, and the United Church of Canada; these stand as a multiple quasi-establishment in a land formally without an established church. The church-sect distinction, therefore, has some validity as a conceptual tool in Canadian church historiography—greater than in the United States, probably less than in the United Kingdom. The Baptist story, as a consequence, though very important to us, is rather peripheral to the larger Christian story here (with the single exception of the establishment controversies in central Canada in the 1820s-50s). A survey of the historiography in other confessional groups offers some consolation to the Baptist researchers; for example, a detailed narrative of the Roman Catholic Church in Canada is yet to be written.

Finally, the Baptists themselves are divided into more than ten groups which variously share a common history and preserve a distinct past. Four groups are united in the Canadian Baptist Federation (CBF): United Baptist Convention of the Atlantic Provinces (UBCAP), Baptist Convention of Ontario and Quebec (BCOQ), Union of French Baptist Churches (UFBC), and Baptist Union of Western Canada (BUWC). They have roots farthest back in Canadian history, roots which are American, English, and Scottish. Three other bodies are offshoots of CBF unions from which congregations and individuals separated in the wake of the modernist-fundamentalist controversies of the 1920s and since then have pursued vigorous church-planting policies: Association of Regular Baptist Churches (ARBC), Canadian Convention of Southern Baptists (CCSB), and Fellowship of Evangelical Baptist Churches in Canada (FEBC). Two others have theological distinctions of longer duration through the former extend into the eighteenth century, the latter appear in 1978: Free Will Baptist (FWB) and Seventh-Day Baptists (SDB). Three fellowships persist out of ethnic origins among Scandinavian, German, and Ukrainian immigrants. The Baptist General Conference in Canada (BGCC) and the North American Baptist Conference (NABC) have denominational structures; and in the urban and suburban communities where their churches minister the ethnic roots have no relevance. The Ukrainian national organizations (Ukrainian Evangelical Baptist Convention of Canada, and Union of Slavic Churches of Evangelical Christians and Slavic Baptists of Canada) are more of an ethnic fellowship and most of their churches are dually aligned with one of the other Baptist bodies.

Census of Canadian Baptists[1]

	Churches	Members
Association of Regular Baptist Churches	10	1,500
Baptist General Conference of Canada	71	6,028
Canadian Baptist Federation	1,120	137,590
UBCAP 555/67,078		
BCOQ 389/47,378		
UFBC 19/ 2,572		
BUWC 157/20,562		
Canadian Convention of Southern Baptists	80	5,440
Fellowship of Evangelical Baptist Churches	450	53,468
National Association of Free Will Baptists (in Canada)	17	1,875
North American Baptist Conference (in Canada)	113	17,331
Seventh Day Baptist Conference (in Canada)	1	40
Ukrainian Baptists (UEBC/USCEC & SB)	[c.18]	[c.700]
TOTAL BAPTISTS IN ASSOCIATIONS	1,862	223,272

A count of the unaffiliated Baptist churches and the independent baptistic "community" churches is impossible, though the total might be significant. While this fragmentation complicates the story, Baptists are considerably more unified in Canada than in the United States.

If narrative cohesion is difficult due to lack of national myth, to regionalism, to the quasi-establishment of Roman Catholic, Anglican and United Churches, and to Baptist fragmentation, Baptist historiography generally suffers from the congenital malady which plagues any denominational history—a narrow, partisan, pious, and uncritical, rather than scholarly, approach. B. R. White observed about twenty years ago that Baptist historiography should not only tell a plain tale plainly but should defend and explain the Baptist case as well as mould the thinking, even the policy, of their denomination.[2] Case-making has been patent in most of the historical writings of Canadian Baptists. There is a naive egocentricity and triumphalism in much of the "official" and even the free-lance histories. They make the case, in most instances, for the current status of the respective body or agency. D. G. Bell, in an exemplary essay on the historiography of Maritime Baptists, succinctly said of it: "Single-mindedly devoted to a "rise and progress" theme, it has been a fair example of what gives the genre of religious history a bad name."[6] Though he believes things have taken a turn for the better in the Atlantic provinces, the few signs of it elsewhere are not quite so strong.

In general, the Baptist story follows the drift of immigration from the Maritimes, though central Canada, to the prairies and Pacific coast. Two publications exemplify the regionalism which is the customary pattern for the Baptist narratives, all the more noteworthy as they intend to tell the national story.

Fitch, E. R., ed. *The Baptists of Canada: A history of their Progress and Achievements*. Toronto: Standard Publishing Co., 1911.

Kirkconnell, Watson *et al.* "The Baptist Federation of Canada" in *Baptist Advance,* ed. Davis C. Woolley. Nashville, TN: Broadman Press, 1964, pp. 131-85.

Though written more than fifty years apart, the format is the same: first, the events and individuals of the Maritimes; then, of Ontario and Quebec, finally, of the west. A newly written dissertation on Canadian Baptists uses the same design, though it also intends to give a more national view.

Griffin-Allwood, Philip G. A. "The Canadianization of Baptists: From Denominations to Denomination, 1760-1912," unpublished Ph.D. Dissertation, Southern Baptist Theological Seminary, Louisville, KY, 1986.

In an as yet unpublished paper I attempt to illustrate that periodization—colonial (1755-1867), early dominion (1867-1920), and contemporary (1920-)—can overcome the customary tunnel vision of both regionalism and sub-denominational bodies.

Priestly, David T. "The Canadian Baptist Story in National Perspective".

The state of the literature, however, forces a regional kind of presentation; in a concluding section of the present paper some methodological and topical issues will be introduced.

Atlantic Provinces

The oldest narratives are based on the recollections, opinions, and sources accumulated by Edward Manning (d. 1851), a Nova Scotia Baptist minister influential in the founding of Acadia University; his was "a carefully selective view."[4] These regional histories aim to improve their predecessor(s), rather than to correct or revise what had been done; journal articles do the same, sometimes shamelessly rehashing the books.

Bill, I. E. *Fifty Years With the Baptist Ministers and Churches of the Maritime Provinces*. Saint John, NB: Barnes ¿ Co., 1880.

Saunders, E. M. *History of the Baptists of the Maritime Provinces*. Halifax, NS: Press of John Burgoyne, 1092.

Levy, George Edward. *The Baptists of the Maritime Provinces*. Saint John, NB: Barnes-Hopkins, 1946.

Allwood, Philip G. A. *Atlantic Baptist Roots*. Wolfville, NS: Baptist Historical Committee, UBCAP, 1980. Mimeographed.

Levy, George Edward. "Milestones in the History of Maritime Baptists," *Chronicle*, 8 (1945).

Sinnott, Frank. *History of the Baptists of Prince Edward Island*. (N.P.: by the Author, 1973). Mimeographed.

Levy, George E. "A Yankee New Light in Nova Scotia," *Chronicle,* 10 (1947), 65-74, 103-12.

Gibson, M. Allen. "Isaac Chipman of Nova Scotia," *Chronicle,* 14 (1951), 167-75.

Rawlyk, G.A. *Ravished by the Spirit: Religious Revivals, Baptists, and Henry Alline.* Montreal: McGill-Queen's University Press, 1984.

Rawlyk, George A. "Henry Alline and the Canadian Baptist Tradition," *Theological Bulletin.* McMaster Divinity College. 4:4 (1977).

Similarly, the story of Negro Baptists has been repetitious and idealized though the revisionist mode in North American black history is reflected in more recent titles.

McKerrow, Peter E. *A Brief History of the Coloured Baptists of Nova Scotia (1832-1895.* Halifax, NS: Nova Scotia Printing Co., 1895. Rev. Ed. by Frank Stanley Boyd, Jr., Halifax, 1976.

Oliver, Pearleen &Althea?é. *A Brief History of the Coloured Baptists of Nova Scotia 1782-1953.* Halifax, NS: by the Author, 1953.

The Baptists in the Maritime provinces were divided between Calvinist "Regular" Baptists and Arminian "Primitive" or "Free Will" Baptists until 1905 when the United Baptist Convention of the Maritime Provinces organized as a fusion of the two movements. Actually, not all joined the UBC. But because the merger was a milestone of "progress", the histories have tended to ignore the Free Will story despite the fact that some of the congregations persist into the present. A correction is beginning here as elsewhere in Maritime Baptist historiography.

Stewart, I. D. *History of the Freewill Baptists.* Dover, NH, 1862.

Baxter, Norman, *History of the Freewill Baptists.* Rochester, NY: American Baptist Historical Society, 1957.

The recovery of a scholarly, rather than a polemical, history as part of the larger story of the Maritimes is sketched lucidly by Bell. Beginning with biographies of Henry Alline, a Nova Scotia "New Light" Congregationalist whose evangelistic success gave impetus to the earliest permanent Baptist churches, in the last twenty years there has been an investigation of Baptists and their relationship to the Nova Scotia Great Awakening (associated with Alline), the American Revolution, and the larger Maritime story. This renaissance promises much for the study of Baptists in the Maritimes and offers Baptists elsewhere a challenging standard to emulate.

Benzanson, W. B. *Romance of Religion: A Sketch of the Life of Henry Alline.* Kentville, NS: 1927.

Armstrong, Maurice. *Great Awakening in Nova Scotia, 1776-1809.* Hartford, CN: 1948.

Bumsted, J. M. *Henry Alline, 1748-84.* Toronto: University of Toronto Press, 1971; repr. Hantsport, NS: Lancelot Press, 1983.

Stewart, Gordon and George Rawlyk. *People Highly Favoured of God: Nova Scotia Yankees and the American Revolution.* Toronto: 1972.

An ongoing publication project of the historical commission of the Atlantic Baptists is making available sources for further research as well as some assessments of the past. Already released in the *Baptist Heritage in Atlantic Canada* series are:

Levy, George E., ed. *Diary and Related Writings of the Rev. Joseph Dimock.* Hantsport, NS: Lancelot Press, 1979.

Cuthbertson, Brian C., ed. *Journal of the Rev. John Payzant.* Hantsport, NS: Lancelot Press, 1981. Beverly, James and B. M. Moody, eds. *Journal of the Rev. Henry Alline.* Hantsport, NS: Lancelot Press, 1982.

Rawlyk, George, ed. *New Light Letters and Songs.* Hantsport, NS: Lancelot Press, 1983.

Bell, D. G., ed. *New Light Baptist Journals of James Manning and James Innis.* Hantsport, NS: Lancelot Press, 1984.

Rawlyk, George A., ed. *Sermons of Henry Alline.* Hantsport, NS: Lancelot Press, 1986.

Several conferences in the past decade signal a widespread interest in scholarly Baptist historiography and give hope of the improvement of the craft elsewhere. The second volume in the *Baptist Heritage in Atlantic Canada* series contains papers read at a 1979 Baptist Heritage Conference held at Acadia Divinity College.

Moody, Barry M., ed. *Repent and Believe: The Baptist Experience in Maritime Canada.* Hantsport, NS: Lancelot Press, 1980.

Rawlyk, George A. "From New Light to Baptist: Harris Harding and the Second Great Awakening in Nova Scotia".

Deweese, Charles W. "Church Covenants and Church Discipline Among Baptists in the Maritime Provinces, 1778-1878".

Williams, Savannah E. "The Role of the African United Baptist Association in the Development of Indigenous Afro-Canadians in Nova Scotia, 1782-1978".

Allwood, Philip G. A. "Joseph Howe is Their Devil": Controversies Among Regular Baptists in Halifax, 1827-1868".

Moody, Barry M. "The Maritime Baptists and Higher Education in the Early Nineteenth Century".

Trites, Allison A. "The New Brunswick Baptist Seminary, 1836-1895".

Davison, James D. "Alice Shaw and Her Grand Pre-Seminary: A Story of Female Education".

Sinnott, Frank H. "The Union of the Regular and the Free Will Baptists of the Maritimes, 1905 and 1906".

From the same conference, papers pertaining to other regions were published in a separate volume and in issues of *Foundations* and of *Baptist History and Heritage*. An essay Deweese composed in preparation for the paper read at Acadia (see above) was also published.

Deweese, Charles W. "Prominent Church Covenants of Maritime Baptists, 1778-1878," *Baptist History and Heritage* 15 (April 1980), 24-32.

Two other conferences have subsequently been held at McMaster Divinity College: and the school also published those papers for a wider audience. Of them, two pertain to the Maritimes.

Mitton, Harold. "Theological Education Among Maritime Baptists: A Preliminary Summary", in *Canadian Baptist History and Polity*. Murray J. S. Ford, ed. Hamilton, ON: McMaster University Divinity College, &1982é, 56-65.

Rawlyk, G. A. "Maritime Baptist Contributions", in *Celebrating the Canadian Baptist Heritage*. Paul R. Dekar and Murray J. S. Ford, eds. Hamilton, ON: McMaster University Divinity College, /1984/, pp. 27-37.

Yet another Baptist Heritage Conference is scheduled at Acadia this fall (October 19-23) on the occasion of the University's sesquicentennial at which papers focussing on aspects of the Baptist story in other regions will be presented also.

Central Canada

Among the earliest reports of Baptist work in this region is that of F. A. Cox and J. Hoby. These ministers were sent to North America in 1836 as fraternal delegates of the Baptist Union in England. Their travelogue devotes sixty of its nearly 500 pages to describe their itineraries in what later became the provinces of Ontario and Quebec; but they seem not to have visited in the maritimes, where some of the churches were already more than fifty years old.

Cox, F. A. and J. Hoby. *The Baptists in America: A Narrative of the Deputation From the Baptist Union in England to the United States and Canada*. New York: Leavett, Lord & Co., 1836.

They marvel at the frontier and reflect the optimism of missionary beginnings.

Though the editor was on the faculty of the Canadian Baptists' McMaster University and the three authors of the sections on Canadian Baptist work were professors at McMaster and Acadia, *A Century of Baptist Achievement* seems to stake an American claim to progress in Canada.

Farmer, J. H. "The Baptists of the Dominion of Canade: Part I. Ontario, Quebec, Manitoba, and the Northwest" in *A Century of Baptist Achievement*. A. H. Newman, ed. Philadelphia: ABPS, 1901, pp. 137-45.

Keirstead, E. M. "The Baptists of the Dominion of Canada: Part II. The Maritime Provinces", pp. 145-52.

Wallace, O. C. S. "American Baptist Education Work: Part IV. In the Dominion of Canada", pp. 347-54.

The narratives are suffused with the optimism of nineteenth-century American evangelicalism; they enthusiastically expect the Baptists will influence, if not overwhelm, all Christian efforts in the new century. J. Gordon Jones is just as enthusiastic on the eve of World War II.

Jones, J. Gordon, ed. *Our Baptist Fellowship: Our History, Our Faith and Polity, Our Life and Work.* N.p.: Baptist Convention of Ontario and Quebec Jubliee Editorial Committee, 1939.

The French mission supported by Canadian, American, and European evangelicals produced mostly promotional materials, but they are of historical value even in themselves.

Cyr, Narcisse. *Memoir of the Rev. C. H. O. Cote.* Philadelphia: ABPS, 1852.

Therrien, Leonard A. *Baptist Work in French Canada.* Toronto:; ABPS, n.d.

Therrien, Leonard A. *Grand Ligne Mission: Is it Really Worthwhile?* N.p.: Grand Ligne Mission, 1906.

Wyeth, Walter N. *Helen Feller and the Grand Ligne Mission: A Memorial.* Philadelphia: ABPS, 1898.

Black Baptists appeared in Ontario in the early nineteenth century also.

Lewis, James K. *Religious Life of Fugitive Slaves and Rise of Coloured Baptist Churches, 1820-1865, in What is Now Known as Ontario.* New York: Arno Press, 1980.

Two post-war studies illustrate the scholarly investigation of Baptist work in this region like that which has arisen more recently in the Maritimes, although at present there is not so visible a development of Baptist study there as these two publications portend.

Ivison, Stuart and Fred Rosser. *The Baptists in Upper and Lower Canada Before 1820.* Toronto: University of Toronto Press, 1956.

Pitman, Walter G. *The Baptists and Public Affairs in the Province of Canada 1840-1867.* New York: Arno Press, 1980.

The Baptist Heritage Conference at Acadia in 1979 which resulted in Moody's *Repent and Believe* (see above) also included other papers on central and western Canada that were published in a separate volume.

Zeman, Jarold K., ed. *Baptists in Canada: Search for Identity Amidst Diversity.* Burlington, ON: G. R. Welch Co., 1980.

Milolaski, Samuel J. "Identity and Mission".

Wilson, Robert S. "British Influence in the Nineteenth Century".

Thomson, W. Nelson. "Witness in French Canada".

Zeman, Jarold K. "They Speak in Other Tongues: Witness Among Immigrants".

Link, Edward B. "North American (German) Baptists".

Dekar, Paul R. "Baptists and Human Rights, 1837-1867".

Carder, W. Gordon. "A View of Some Canadian Headlines, 1860-1914".

Moir, John S. "THE CANADIAN BAPTIST and the Social Gospel-Movement, 1879-1950".

Ellis, Walter E. "Baptists and Radical Politics in Western Canada, 1920-1950".

Bullen, R. Fred. "World Relief, Development and Inter-Church Aid".

Pinnock, Clark H. "The Modernist Impulse at McMaster University, 1887-1927".

Tarr, Leslie K. "Another Perspective on T. T. Shields and Fundamentalism".

Richards, John B. "Baptist Leadership: Autocratic or Democratic?"

Davis, Kenneth R. "The Struggle for a United Evangelical Baptist Fellowship, 1953-1965".

Beverly, James A. "National Survey of Baptist Ministers".

The bibliographic references in the Zeman and Moody volumes are extremely helpful in identifying specific sources for further investigation. Likewise, the McMaster conferences of 1982 and 1984 demonstrate the possibilities for research and the resources available. A number of these papers introduce specific issues of polity, theology, and personalities which can keep historians busy for many years to come.

Ford, Murray J. S., ed. *Canadian Baptist History and Polity: The McMaster Conference.* Hamilton, ON: McMaster University Divinity College, [1982].

Mikolaski, Samuel J. "Canadian Baptist Ordination Standards & Procedures".

Hillmer, Melvyn. "Baptist Theological Education in Ontario & Quebec, 1838-1982".

Mitton, Harold. "Theological Education Among Maritime Baptists: A Preliminary Summary".

Churchill, G. Keith. "Educational Policy of the Baptist Union of Western Canada, 1873-1975".

Thompson, Eugene M., *et al.* "The Status of Transcongregational Polity".

Aldwinckle, Russell F., *et al.* "Believers" Baptism as an Ecumenical Issue".

Wood, William R. "A Study of Church Membership in Relation to Baptism".

Ban, Joseph D. "Canadian Baptists and Renewal: Some Movements

Deserving Historical Consideration".

Allis, Walter E. "Baptist Missions Adaptation to the Western Frontier".

Woods, Bruce A. "Theological Direction and Cooperation Among Baptists in Canada".

Dekar, Paul R. and Murray J. S. Ford, eds. *Celebrating the Canadian Baptist Heritage: The McMaster Conference.* Hamilton: McMaster University Divinity College, *[1984].*

Zeman, J. K. "The Changing Baptist Identity in Canada Since World War II".

Rawlyk, G. A. "Maritime Baptist Contributions".

Dekar, Paul R. "The Gilmours: Four Generations of Baptist Service".

Ellis, W. E. "Baptists Visions of the New Jerusalem in Western Canada".

Thomason, W. N. "Two French Canadian Baptist Pastors 1821-1920".

Allen, J. Stanley. "Roger Williams".

These recent essays are varied, interpretive, and strive for objectivity. The 1982 McMaster Conference had the strength of assigning study committees to make advance preparations, so the papers in some cases were not the work of just a single scholar. Yet they have a parochial, even patronizing, tone for they deal with matters largely from the perspective of the BCOQ and the CBF. While that is appropriate for those bodies, it belies the announced intention of dealing broadly with Canadian Baptists (unless that was meant as a CBF-specific term, not a generic one). Nonetheless, these papers continue a less polemical and triumphalist historiography which bodes well for future work.

The BCOQ in the 1920s experienced a split which has produced not only distinct bodies of churches but also a historiography of its own. The "fundamentalist" Regular Baptists which sprang up in the train of controversies over modernism at McMaster University and Divinity College are writing their story as a vindication of truth against error. A national fellowship was formed in the 1960s as the Ontario and Quebec group merged with Alberta, British Columbia, and Saskatchewan Regular Baptists who originated in their areas on the same issue of modernism, though at the BUWC's Brandon College in Manitoba.

Tarr, Leslie K. *This Dominion His Dominion: The Story of Evangelical Baptist Endeavour in Canada.* Willowdale, ON: Fellowship of Evangelical Baptist Churches in Canada, 1968.

Tipp, Charles A., ed. *10 Years of Fellowship: A Historical Review and Year Book.* Toronto: Trans-Canada Fellowship of Evangelical Baptist Churches, 1962.

Watt, J. H. *The Fellowship Story.* Willowdale, ON: FEBC, 1978.

The West

Baptist work in the Maritimes had been underway for a century before the first missionary was sent from Ontario to evangelize and plant churches. Western Canada experienced development only after confederation in 1867 brought the former fur trading territories of the Hudson Bay Company and its earlier rivals under Canadian administration and exposed them to massive immigration. The West, therefore, is less Canadian, more of an adolescent, than are the regions already discussed. Likewise, the issues of the nineteenth century are less significant among their churches than are those of the twentieth. Nonetheless, the Baptist story in the West remains more in the pious style than in the scholarly one which has begun to make headway in eastern and central Canada.

The earliest publications are jubilee celebrations or- reminiscences of missionaries and denominational executives; not all the reminiscences can be verified from other sources, as is characteristic of the genre.

Baptist Union of Western Canada. *Western Baptist Jubilee: 1873-1923*. N.P.: n.d.

McLaurin, C. C. *Pioneering in Western Canada: A Story of the Baptists*. Calgary: By the Author, 1939.

Smalley, William C. *Come Wind, Come Weather: Reminiscences From a Life of Christian Service*. Saint John, NB: Lingley Printing Co., 1969.

A flurry of histories appeared in the 1970s, written by people with longtime involvement in the Baptist Union of Western Canada.

Bentall, Shirley. *Buckboard to Brotherhood: The Baptist Church in Calgary*. The Century Calgary Historical Series. Vol. IV: The Search for Souls—Histories of Calgary Churches. Calgary, AB: Century Calgary Publications, 1975.

Harris, J. E. *The Baptist Union of Western Canada: A Centennial History 1873-1973*. Saint John, NB: Lingley Printing Co., 1976.

Thompson, Margaret E. *The Baptist Story in Western Canada*. Calgary: BUWC, *[1974]*.

A significant amount of historical interest has been shown among those who diverge from the existing stream during the modernist-fundamentalist controversies in the 1920s; despite their apologetic casemaking, there is a coolness in the styles which gives the impression of objectivity even in what is clearly one side of the story.

Bonham, J. S. H. *FEBCAST [*Fellowship of Evangelical Baptist Churches in Alberta, Saskatchewan and the Territories*]: Our Lord, Our Roots, Our Vision*. Three Hills, AB: E.M.F. Press, *[1980]*.

Pousett, Gordon H. "Formative Influences on Baptists in British Columbia, 1876-1918," *Baptist History [Heritage*, 15 (April 1980).

Richards, John B. *Baptists in British Columbia: A Struggle to Maintain "Sectarianism"*. Vancouver, BC: Northwest Baptist Theological College and Seminary, 1977.

Ruhlman, John J., Jr. *History of Northwest Regular Baptists*. Schaumburg, IL: Regular Baptist Press, 1975.

Baker, J. C. *A Baptist History of the North Pacific Coast*. Philadelphia: ABPS, 1911.

The last book mentioned recounts the nineteenth-century origins of Baptist work under the auspices of the American Baptist Home Mission Society. The efforts in the United States at that time naturally extended themselves into British Columbia. Some would see the restored links in the 1950s as a kind of recovery of a temporarily broken relationship.

Issues in History and Historical Writing

These references just given introduce again what has been for Baptists in North America the theological watershed of the present century. This period of the 1920s needs careful investigation from a Canadian perspective, all the more since the related "Social Gospel Movement" in Canada bears little resemblance to what is called by the same term in the United States. The polemics of attack and defense have left truth a victim not yet much tended, let alone recovered. Bruce Woods in *Canadian Baptist History and Polity* appeals for and Clark Pinnock in *Baptists in Canada* attempts the rectification of the pride and dishonesty which surround the modernist-fundamentalist controversies at McMaster Divinity College in Ontario; no similar move has been made regarding Brandon College in Manitoba over which the western union split. The dominance of this theological polarity throughout conservative Christianity in North America raises questions about the casual treatment of earlier disputes over open and close communion, between Free and Regular Baptists; may parts of those "dead issues" still lurk as disturbers of our peace?

The Canadian Baptist story contained in the sources cited above can be sorted out as it is in terms of geography and time, of topic and personality. The majority of them is regional. Those essays may deal with 200 years of development or a temporary figure or issue, but for the most part they are geographically localized. The recent spate of research and publication shows the same specificity of place. The characteristic regionalism of Canada may continue to make localized histories inevitable; but something of broader sweep is needed, even if only provisionally formulated in order to integrate the events into a picture with national proportions. H. A. Renfree, retired Executive Minister of the BUWC, is at work on a Canada-wide history; but whether it will be CBF-focused and regionally patterned, remains to be seen.

What is surmountable in writing Baptist history in Canada is the parochialism of the various bodies represented in each region. Familiarity, in this case, breeds infatuation; contempt, or at least condescension, is reserved for others. This may be innocent as any "in-group feelings" or due to the reality that "we know what the people we know know"; but the polemics of the twentieth century require conscious effort to cultivate light-hearted generosity toward others. We need historians who are as affectionately interested in one or more "them" as they are in "us".

Various denominational periodicals and annuals tell of developments within those bodies and their agencies. The only supra-denominational instrument in which Canadian Baptists can find parts of their story are scattered issues of *Foundations* and its predecessor *Chronicle*; the current journal of the American Baptist

Historical Society, the *American Baptist Quarterly*, has yet to include an article pertaining to Canadian Baptists.

Bristol, Lyle O. "Baptists in Central Canada," *Chronicle*, 18 (1955), 111-18.

Ellis, Pierce W., Jr. "Baptists and the War of 1812," *Chronicle*, 11 (1948), 124-34. (from the U. S. perspective)

Gibson, M. Allen. "The Baptist Press in Canada," *Chronicle*, 16 (1953), 158-63.

Gibson, M. Allen. "Isaac Chipman of Nova Scotia," *Chronicle*, 14 (1951), 167-75.

Levy, George Edward. "Milestones in the History of Maritime Baptists," *Chronicle*, 8 (1945), 77-93.

Levy, George E. "A Yankee New Light in Nova Scotia," *Chronicle*, 10 (1947), 65-74, 103-12.

Longley, R. S. "The Background and Early History of Acadia University, Educational Centre of the Maritime Baptists of Canada," *Chroniclt9.*, 5 *(1941), 125-32.*

McLaurin, C. C. "The Story of Western Canada and the Baptists," Chron-icle, 2 (1939), 23-32.

Moore, John F. "Baptists of British Columbia," *Chronicle*, 18 (1955), 129-40.

Nobles, "Canadian Baptists and the United Church of Canada," *Chronicle*, 1 (1938), 23-29.

Albaugh, Gaylord P. "Themes for Research in Canadian Baptist History," *Foundations*, 6 (1963) 42-56.

Aldwinckle, Russell F. "The Fellowship of Believers and the Nature of Belief," *Foundations*, 23 (1980), 6-21.

Carter, W. Gordon, "Controversy in the Baptist Convention of Ontario and Quebec," *Foundations*, 16 (1973), 355-76.

Ellis, Walter F. "Gilboa to Ichabod: Social and Religious Factors in the Fundamentalist-Modernism Schisms Among Canadian Baptists, 1895-1934," *Foundations*, 20 (1977), 109-26.

Handy, Robert T. "The Influence of Canadians on Baptist Theological Education in the United States," *Foundations*, 23 (1980), 42-56.

Harrop, G. Gerald, "Canadian Baptists in Their North American Context," *Foundations*, 4 (1961), 216-24.

Harrop, G. Gerald. "The Era of the "Great Preacher" Among Canadian Baptists," *Foundations*, 23 (1980), 57-70.

Hudson, Winthrop S. "The Interrelationships of Baptists in Canada and the United States," *Foundations*, 23 (1980), 22-41.

Levy, I. Judson. "Canadian Baptists Ecumenical Relationships," *Foundations*, 23 (1980), 84-96.

Pitman, W. G. "Baptist Triumph in Nineteenth Century Canada," *Foundations*, 3 (1960, 157-165.

Perkin, James R. C. "Many Confessions, One Creed," *Foundations*, 24

(1980), 71-83.

Russell, C. Allyn. "Thomas Todhunter Shields, Canadian Fundamentalist," *Foundations*, 24 (1981), 15-31; rpr. from *Ontario History*, 70 (1978) 263-80.

Zeman, Jarold. "Baptists in Canada and Cooperative Christianity," *Foundations*, 15 (1972), 211-240.

The British seem to have ignored their trans-Atlantic cousins; in a rapid scan of the past twenty-five years of the *Baptist Quarterly,* one can find articles on American Baptists Isaac Backus, Walter Rauschenbusch, and (?) Roger Williams, but nothing on Canadian Baptists. This is all the more remarkable in view of the regular solicitation in the United Kingdom by Baptists from central and western Canada throughout the nineteen century for financial support of their educational and home mission efforts. The Southern Baptists have published only three articles in a special Canadian issue of *Baptist History & Heritage* (Vol. 15, No. 2, 1980) which included two of the 1979 Baptist heritage Conference papers that dealt with Southern Baptists in Canada; six years earlier another sketch had appeared in a seminary journal.

Harrop, G. Gerald. "The Canadian Baptists—An Historical Sketch." *Southwest Journal of Theology*, 6 (1974), 26-37.

Denominational histories for the minor Baptist bodies need to be written, for themselves and for the larger Baptist and Canadian audience. The BGCC, only five years old, has not pulled together any narrative which focuses on the Swedish work in Canada, although their parent-body has some historical materials in print.

Olson, Adolf. *A Centenary History as Related to the Baptist General Conference of America.* Chicago: Baptist Conference Press, 1952.

Anderson, Donald, ed. *The 1960s in the Ministry of the Baptist General Conference, 1945-1960.* Chicago: Harvest Publications, 1961.

Guston, David and Martin Erikson, eds. *Fifteen Eventful Years: A Survey of the Baptist General Conference, 1945-1960.* Chicago: Harvest Publications, 1961.

The details of editor/author and title for a decadal history of the 1970s have not been obtained, although such a volume is reported.

The NABC, whose first church appeared in Ontario in 1851 and in the West in 1889, includes the Canadian developments as part of its larger story. The specifically Canadian facet has been outlined in one of the 1979 conference (mentioned above) papers. Post-World War II immigration is narrated by the official responsible for arranging most of it.

Link, E. B. "North American (German) Baptists," in *Baptists in Canada*. Ed. Jarold K. Zeman. Burlington, ON: G. R. Welch, 1980.

Sturhahn, William J. H. *They Came From East and West. . .: A History of Immigration to Canada.* Winnipeg, MB: North American Baptist Immigration and Colonization Society, 1976.

Woyke, Frank H. *Heritage and Ministry of the North American Baptist Conference*. Oakbrook Terrace, IL: North American Baptist General Conference (1979).

CCSB, currently has an emeritus pastor at work on the story of their churches in Alberta; otherwise, the only version of their beginnings designed for public distribution is a little booklet of forty pages, a photo-reduced typescript.

Hood, Roland P. *Southern Baptist Work in Canada*. Ed. Allen Schmidt. Portland, OR: Northwest Baptist Convention, rev. 1977.

Biographies and autobiographies have appeared occasionally about Baptist leaders from various parts of the country. Oddly, the Shields biography shows great historical integrity even though it is written by a partisan of a very controversial figure.

Gibson, Theo. T. *Beyond the Granite Curtain: The Story of Alexander McDonald, Pioneer Baptist Missionary to the Canadian North-West*. N.p.: n.p., [1975].

Jones, J. Gordon. *Greatness Passing By: Biographical Sketches of Some Canadian Baptists*. N.p.: Baptist Federation of Canada, 1967.

McLaurin, C. C. *My Old Home Church*. Calgary: By the Author, 1937.

Tarr, Leslie K. *Shields of Canada: T. T. Shields (1873-1955)*. Grand Rapids, MI: Baker Book House, 1967.

Several of the papers above raise the question of Baptist identity. In part this is a search for a conceptual framework to "tell the tale plainly"; in part it reveals Baptist ambivalence amidst currents of ecumenism, Canadian state-churchism, and generic evangelicalism. In fact, what is perhaps the best attempt to face the question was produced for an ecumenical forum.

Ivison, Stuart. "Is There a Canadian Baptist Tradition?" in *The Churches and the Canadian Experience: A Faith and Order Study of the Christian Tradition*. Ed. John Webster Grant. Toronto, ON: Ryerson, 1963, pp. 53-68. See also John S. Moir, "Sectarian Tradition in Canada," pp. 119-132; and H. H. Walsh, "A Canadian Christian Tradition," pp. 145-61.

For some Baptists the concept of the "believers' church" offers a helpful conceptual label. Papers presented at a 1978 conference on the subject attempt to reflect on their history, rather than to present new facts from or facets of it.

Zeman, Jarold K., Walter Klaassen, and John D. Rempel, eds. *The Believers' Church in Canada: Addresses and Papers From the Study Conference in Winnipeg, May 1978*. N.p.: Baptist Federation of Canada and Mennonite Central Committee, 1979. See especially:

Dyck, C. J. "The Believers' Church in Canada: Past," pp. 29-33.

Renfree, Harry A. "Church and State in Canada: Co-operation and Confrontation," pp. 207-19.

Ellis, Walter E. "Divisive and Unitive Forces in the Baptist Church Tradition in Canada," pp. 221-32.

As one looks around the tangles of Canadian Baptist history, questions arise and puzzles are uncovered. Work needs to be done. Investigations and interpretations are needed about the Free-Will Baptists of the Maritimes, the Gaelic mission there, French missions in various places, ethnic evangelism and church planting among European, African, Asian and South American immigrants. The relation of Canadian Baptists with those in the United States, even with the larger evangelical movement there, needs to be examined, without the nationalist impulse to prove dependence or autonomy. Here even a sociologist may help.

Hiller, Harry H. "Continentalism and the third force in religion," *Canadian Journal of Sociology*, 3 (1978), 183-207.

The modernist-fundamentalist controversies are far from dead, though currently nuanced by half a century's development among all the parties to those arguments. Historical integrity must pave the way for Baptists in Canada to relax with one another again. The various views of a set of developments need to be articulated in an intentionally partisan manner in order to be coordinated in a later stage of writing the Canadian Baptist story.

Immigration, so dominant a reality especially in the West due to its recency, poses the question whether the riddle of "identity" is soluable in the face of such imported diversities. Ethnicity and ecumenicity are opposite impulses but equally real in their impact. Historians need to discuss Canadianization, continentalism, evangelicalism, interpretive motifs: e.g., church-sect, believers' church. Regionalism, partisanship, and denominationalism contribute to blind spots in even the most well-meaning researcher (in my own case, I grew up in the United States, live in Western Canada, and belong to the North American Baptist Conference—a 7% minority among Canadian Baptists).

The sources must be found: how can we get things into archives; and how can we find things in archives? The best-managed Baptist archives are those of the UBCAP at Acadia (Wolfsville, NS) and of the Canadian Baptist Archives at McMaster (Hamilton, ON). The various denominational offices of each body and their schools offer archival assistance of varying quality. Public libraries (university, municipal, and provincial) offer surprises to the diligent Baptist mole. Acadia and McMaster have encouraged the writing of historical theses by divinity students; they provide teasers to investigate amidst a great mass of reworked familiar sources. But MA, ThM, and PhD theses of interest to Canadian Baptist historians have been written in a number of public and private universities. For example,

Hill, Mary Bulmer Reid. "From Sect to Denomination in the Baptist Church in Canada." Unpublished PhD dissertation, State University of New York at Buffalo, 1971.

Outlets must be discovered and created where people can publish what they are finding and thinking. The historical interests of individuals guarantees the continued submission of narratives. Many of the various conventions, conferences, and unions among which Baptists are distributed have established historical commissions. Their work in most cases is rather preliminary, perhaps even the product of a single interested pastor, layman, or professor. Maritime Baptists, e. g., have made a small industry of colonial Nova Scotia as the citations above and further references in those writings reveal. But the materials are accumulating. The research and writing of our history is hobby and discipline for numerous people among us. The most promising sign is the frequency with which conferences of Baptist historians have been held in the past decade. The agenda for and the participation in these continuing symposia, however, need to be broadened just as correspondence and the awareness of students, publications, and archives among those interested throughout the country needs to be cultivated.

Baptist historians in Canada are not excavating a dead past but are exploring a past with which a vital present has still active nerves to signal delight and pain.

David Priestley is Professor of Theology at North American Baptist Divinity School, Edmonton, Alberta, Canada.

Endnotes

1. Drawn from Constant H. Jaquet, Jr., ed., *Yearbook of American and Canadian Churches* (Nashville: Abingdon Press, 1986) and personal inquiries.
2. B. R. White, "The Task of the Baptist Historian", *Baptist Quarterly* 22 (1967-68), p. 399.
3. D. G. Bell, "All things New: The Transformation of Maritime Baptist Historiography", *Nova Scotia Historical Review* 4:2 (1984), pp. 69-80; quotation from p. 70.
4. Ibid., p. 69n.

Baptists and Higher Education in England

J. H. Y. Briggs

Introduction

Quotations from a nineteenth-century Anglican Bishop and a contemporary Baptist theologian may be allowed to set the parameters for this discussion.

Of John Smyth, Mandell Creighton, sometime Dixie Professor of Ecclesiastical History at Cambridge and later Bishop of London, said "None of the English Separatists had a finer mind or a more beautiful soul than John Smith (sic). None of them succeeded in expressing with so much reasonableness and consistency their aspirations after a spiritual system of belief and practice. None of them formed their opinions on so large and liberal a basis". George Beasley-Murray confesses of the present day "...leading members of other denominations do not expect to hear anything profound from a Baptist and are surprised when they do. Our stock is pretty low... There is cause for this judgment upon us and it must be plainly faced. It is the theological shallowness of much of our preaching and the ignorance of many of our members."[1]

Higher Education and Baptist Origins

Part at least of our heritage was born in the universities of seventeenth century England and the reflexions of thoughtful Puritan scholars, like John Smyth, academically trained at Oxford or Cambridge in a period of theological ferment, upon the nature of the church and its ministry. The calculation as to how many of the early leaders of both General and Particular Baptists were trained at Oxford and Cambridge and what that contributed to their leadership of early Baptist life is a task that would be well worth undertaking.[2]

But some caution would be necessary. The excellent practical education provided by the Inns of Court to men like Thomas Helwys and William Kiffin would also need to be recognised, nor would it be right to write off "cobblers, button-makers, soap-boilers and furriers" as illiterates. Indeed therein lies the root of a question that has run through Baptist concern for higher education as a preparation for ministry throughout the succeeding centuries: can preparation for ministry be fairly left to be determined by the academic measures of the university, what is the relationship between personal experience and formal education in equipping the future minister for his task, of what use is the rigour of academic discipline without spiritual insight and how far can the latter exist independent of the former?

In the context of such questions, it can be seen how the widening of the categories from which ministers were drawn in general, and the advocacy of lay preaching in particular, at once challenged not only ecclesiastical tradition but a wide range of assumptions about educational qualifications and above all the social exclusiveness of the clergy. Consider the title of the Puritan Lazarus Seaman's tract in support of "Gangraena" Edwards' Presbyterian favoring of a closed shop of university-trained clerics. The tract, which lists twenty preachers by name, including the Particular Baptists, William Kiffin, Paul Hobson and Thomas Patient and the General Baptists, Thomas Lamb and Jeremiah Ives, is entitled *'Tub Preachers Overturn'd or Independency to be Abandon'd and Abhor'd...in a Satisfactory Answer to a Lybellous Pamphlet, Intituled a letter to Mr. Thomas Edwards...Shewing the Vanity, Folly, Madness of the Deboyst Buff-Coate, Mechanick Prize-Coate, Lay Illiterate Men and Women, to Usurpe the Ministery"*.[3]

Against such superiority, Thomas Collier, the evangelist of the West Country, from a Baptist position, was confident that there were many in England who lacked a higher education but who knew more natural philosophy, logic and rhetoric than the clergy. Not only so, he argued that God, following the argument of 1 Corinthians 1, uses the weak and the foolish to confound the wise and to overcome individual intellectual pride, for some of the university men were "none but asses in the things of God, who study Arts and Sciences, to help them to preach and prophesie". Similarly, Jeremiah Ives, a General Baptist autodidact, in *Confidence Encountered; or, a Vindication of the Lawfulness of Preaching Without Ordination* (1658) contended that any man possessing a spiritual gift had the legal right to preach. "Higher education, was not mentioned as a necessary prerequisite", notes Professor Greaves, who goes on to note that the question, which began with the issue of preparation for ordination and licensing to preach, soon came to embrace other questions such as the validity of classical studies, the development of the natural sciences and the whole question of the social role of education.[4]

But the association of ministry with sound learning would not easily be put on one side. The first history of the Baptists, by Thomas Crosby, was largely provoked by the fact that he had made available to Daniel Neale, the historian of the Puritans, Benjamin Stinton's notes towards a history of Baptist life, only to find Neale's treatment of seventeenth century Baptists wholly inadequate, repeating contemporary slanders against their character and their education: "The advocates of this doctrine were, for the most part, of the meanest of the people; their preachers were generally illiterate and went about the countries (sic) making proselytes of all that would submit to their immersion, without a due regard to their acquaintance with the principles of religion, or their moral characters". This provoked Crosby into a discussion of learning as a prerequisite for ministry. Thus he calls on Keach and Delaune's affirmation that "Tis certain that no sort of men have more need of *learning,* than the *ministers* of the gospel, because their employment is of the highest concern;" though they also confess "most certain it is, that human literature without grace, is a dangerous enemy to the true christian religion" for such knowledge in itself provides no right to ministry "any more than the meanest of mechanick arts". Conversely, the epithet "unlearned" must be discerningly applied: "For if a man should attain to some perfection in this seven liberal arts and sciences, and besides these gain the knowledge of several languages, and be a proficient in moral and natural philosophy, these would be rare accomplishments, make him a lovely man, useful, and set him in a station above his fellows; but yet he might be ignorant of the things of God, and consequently an *unlearned* man in the account of St. Peter".

Crosby, with approval, cites an episcopal condemnation of "*school* divinity" as the source of all heresy from Alexandria to the present day. Knowledge of languages is useful but it is doubtful if it can be called essential to the ministerial task. Such an argument leads Crosby to parade a series of biographies of Baptist ministers to show "that men of the greatest *learning* and *piety* have neither been ashamed nor afraid in the worst of times to stand up in vindication of a principle truly *apostolical*".[5]

A comparison of the earlier with the later leaders is illuminating in so far as a high proportion of the former were university-trained whereas in the latter list, though there appear some graduates, the general pattern is quite different. Thomas Harrison, "obtained full liberty for study...under the tutorship of the learned Mr. Thomas Rowe", an independent minister, tutor-in-charge at Newington Green Academy from 1678. Joseph Stennett, "having finished his gram-mer learning at the public school in Wallingford, .. soon mastered the French and Italian languages, became a critic in the Hebrew and other oriental tongues; successfully studied the liberal sciences, and made a considerable proficiency in philosophy". Ebenezer Wilson was trained at Mr. Jolley's Academy at Attercliffe in Yorkshire before entering the ministry in Bristol.[6]

By contrast, Dr. Benjamin Grosvenor entered the same academy as a Baptist but left it a Presbyterian. Of Richard Allen it is said, "by his own industry, after he was called to the work of the ministry, he attained to such an acquaintance with the *oriental languages*, or other parts of useful learning, as to exceed many who enjoyed the benefits of a learned education in the schools". Benjamin Stin-ton also had no formal "academical education" but with the aid of "the famous Mr. Ainsworth' equipped himself in both language and literature to exercise a learned ministry. John Gale's parents were well enough off to send him to Holland for his education where he graduated from the University of Leyden with an M. A. and Ph.D. before the age of nineteen. He later turned down Leyden's D.D. offered on condition that he assent to the articles of the Synod of Dort. Edward Wallin was self-taught, the persecution of his parents disabl-ing them from providing him with a formal education.[7]

Of Academies, Societies and Funds

It was in the context of this change noted in Crosby that nonconformity began to formalise its concern for higher education with the establishment of various funds, societies and academies.[8]

As early as 1675 a group of ministers in London had sought subscriptions for the education of young men called to the ministry. This was formalised by the Particular Baptist Assembly of 1689, when the first subscriptions were secured, "to assist those with a disposition to study and have the gift for it" to become equipped in Latin, Greek and Hebrew, that is to say not only the languages of the scriptures but also those of classical literature, still the inherited culture of the world of learning. The General Baptists resolved to establish a "school of universal learning" in 1702, though no practical programme seems to have followed. By contrast the Particular Baptist Fund was early found sup-porting a man like Richard Sampson who was tutored by William Thomas, not himself a Baptist, in Bristol.

John Piggott, minister of Little Wild Street, warned his contemporaries not to "expect that preachers will drop down from heaven, or spring out of (the) earth; but due care must be taken for the encouragement of humble men that have real gifts, and let such be trained up into *useful learning,* that they may be able to defend the truths they preach". In 1702, Hercules Collins, though not himself a possessor of "a learned education; and well aware that mere human learning could be a snare, expressed concern that although the churches were themselves "the schools of Christ", they make so little provi-sion for the future of their ministry;" and went so far as to suggest that senior London ministers should set aside time every week to instruct potential ordinands. Joseph Stennett was one who did just that.[9]

Such aspirations were formalised in 1717 with the establishment of the Particular Baptist Fund, one of the first beneficiaries of which was the formidable John Gill of Kettering who received £17 for the purchase of Hebrew Texts. A candidate so assisted was not required immediately to abandon his secular calling but he was required not to "decline or neglect the frequent exercise of his ministerial gifts" in the period during which he undertook academic preparation: an early pattern of theological education by extension in which the analysis of the study was kept in harmony with and informed by pastoral and expository experience. In 1752 a further development took place with the establishment of the London Baptist Education Society which was later to be subsumed into the history of Stepney College.

The Particular Baptist Fund was very particular. It refused subscriptions from both the Barbican Church, served by a succession of Calvinist ministers from its foundation in the Commonwealth period but anxious in the early eighteenth century to be known as neither Particular or General, and the open membership church at Pinner's Hall, though the building itself became the headquarters of the Fund, which also accepted donations from its proprietors, the Hollis brothers, who were baptized members of that same open membership church, one of three churches which used the hall for worship. Shortly afterwards, in 1725, the Barbican Church established its own fund for ministerial training which later came to be known as the General Baptist Fund. The Hollis brothers seem not to have been offended when their wishes were not agreed by the other managers of the Fund, of which they were themselves treasurers: "You have greatly grieved us, and some other brethren, hearty well-wishers to the cause we wish to engage in, by the narrow principles you tied yourselves into at the last meeting and particularly refusing our worthy friend and his church, that might be likely to be useful in the pious design" they wrote in February, 1719 but still offered £200 from their father's will to the fund managers, to which John added a further £1,100 on his death in 1735. His brother, also a protester at the "narrow principles" of the Particular Baptist Fund, whilst continuing to support the fund, found a greater outlet for his philanthropy in establishing the twin Hollisian chairs of philosophy and mathematics (as also divinity) at Harvard, as well as ten scholarships for ministerial students, and other miscellaneous donations including rare books, equipment and Hebrew and Greek type-face, gifts which far exceeded that of any other benefactors of that institution at that time. He did all this notwithstanding the fact that Harvard was not a Baptist foundation: indeed the President noted that in the previous century his predecessors in the faith had been formidable persecutors of anyone holding Baptist beliefs.

The Massachusetts' eulogy of Hollis on his death commemorates particularly the fact that though "he was not strictly of our way, nor in judgment with us in the point of infant baptism" he overcame that "narrow party spirit which is so much the disgrace and detriment of the protestant interest" in offering such munificent support. For his part, Hollis rejoiced that Harvard was an institution "where protestants of every denomination may have their children

educated and graduated". Significantly, the Hollisian Professor of Divinity at
the time of his death noted his concern for all human knowledge not just
theology.[10]

Institutionally more significant than the various funds and societies were
the academies. Some saw academies as temporary devices pending the reopen-
ing of the ancient universities to dissenters. A legacy of 1677/8 establishing ex-
hibitions at the academies required that the holders of these should be
simultaneously entered for an Oxford or Cambridge college "to obviate any delay
in their proceeding thither as soon as permitted". A beneficiary of a similar be-
quest made by John Owen confessed that it was Owen's wish "to have us entered
at the *Publick Universities*, though educated at these *private ones*". The longer
penal legislation was deployed against dissent, the more realism demanded that
it was necessary to see the separation between nonconformity and the established church as something other than temporary.[11]

Dissent increasingly came to represent not only ecclesiastical nonconformity but a comprehensive alternative culture which was to play an increasingly
important part in the development of English life. In helping nonconformity
to fulfill this task, the academies clearly faced a task of fundamental importance.
The most prestigious of them as "private universities" accepted lay as well as
ministerial students and in so far as they came to provide a more modern form
of higher education than the universities, received the compliment of attracting
episcopalian students as well. However, their most important task was to train
succeeding generations of ministers, once the casualties of the Great Ejection,
and those who had benefited from access to the universities prior to 1662, became
older and fewer. This was well understood by their Anglican opponents who
accordingly contrived the Schism Act to attack the academies as crucial agents
in perpetuating dissent.

Whilst there was a fair measure of co-operation between the different
dissenting denominations in the running of these institutions, at some questions were raised about the wisdom of accepting Baptist candidates in rather
disdainful terms, as at Taunton in 1696, where the issue was raised: "Whether
we are not concerned to promote the education of Tailors etc. and the sending
out of Tools in two or three years' time after they are taken from the Plough
or Shop to do jobs for Anabaptist." For all that, a number of Baptists were
trained at non-Baptist academies, including Hugh Evans (Carmarthen), Professor John Ward of Gresham College (Bethnal Green), Andrew Gifford (who,
with Bishop Butler and Archbishop Secker was trained at Tewkesbury), and Caleb
Evans (Hoxton), amongst others. Indeed it has been said of the King's Head
Society and Academy, founded as a bastion of orthodoxy in 1730 when other
academies appeared to harbour doctrinal laxity, that of its alumni who became
tutors in other institutions, "the best known seem to be Baptists".[12]

Baptists were slow to establish their own separate institutions: the only
early academy with Baptist associations was that established in Trowbridge by
John Davisson, a Particular Baptist who was minister there from 1669-1721.
In his teaching he showed himself committed to the importance of reason,
deprecated the use of commentaries, and stressed the functional importance of

instruction in elocution for future ministers. In 1737 the Trowbridge Academy then under Thomas Lucas (d.1743), whom Ivimey suggests was not orthodox, received from the Library of the Barbican Church in London such books as it could use in its work.[13] Lucas died in 1743: his successor in the pastorate was William Waldron, who seems to have supported himself as a clothier rather than through the academy. Some authorities associate the distinguished Baptist classicist, Dr. Thomas Llewellyn, who was wholly orthodox, with Trowbridge Academy but when and for how long is unclear.[14]

Of similar importance was the academy at Trosnant, Carmarthenshire, in the 1730s, where some forty ministers as well as laymen were trained under the guidance of John Matthews, and the academy associated with the name of W. N. Clarke in Southwark, 1762-85.[15]

The most significant of Baptist ministerial institutions was undoubtedly Bristol now the oldest surviving Free Church College, the fruit of Edward Terrill's munificent bequests of 1679 (which became available for ministerial training on his wife's death in 1697) and of Bernard Foskett's pioneering work with students from the beginning of his ministry in 1720. A number of histories of Bristol College exist: suffice it to note here that its effective starting date was relatively late and its purposes limited to ministerial training, albeit with a fairly broad syllabus, so that its work was more confined than some of the more celebrated institutions with their distinguished alumni on the bishops' bench and within the world of law and science. But as Gordon Rupp has recently noted, Foskett and the Evans brothers addressed themselves to the essential task of the academies, namely, "to keep alive the tradition of Biblical learning and piety and be able to stand against the storms of cultural repression from without and a recurrent anti-intellectual peril from within."[16] Until 1770 the scale of the work at Bristol was domestic: in about forty years Foskett, with the assistance of Andrew Gifford for a short period and of Hugh Evans for almost twenty years, trained some sixty-four men for the ministry.

The Evangelical Revival and the New Academies

Nineteenth century Baptists could never wholly forget the story of Arian and Socinian decline in the eighteenth century, and that memory served to foster a suspicion of the intellectual world. In fact, the history of Baptist Colleges during the century was relatively peaceful: in so far as the denomination was troubled by religious controversy, the controversy was in the churches, not the colleges, where such matters were handled with the utmost discretion.

It is tempting to say that the colleges were essentially the fruit of the Evangelical Revival and that would be broadly true, save that those who have studied the Bristol situation increasingly emphasise the evangelical continuity of the west country Particular Baptists by comparison with the prevalence of the heavy scholarship of hyperism in the capital. But even in Bristol, 1770 marked something of a new beginning with the launching of the Bristol Education Society, effectively the first of the Baptist educational societies of the post-revival years, followed a generation later by the Baptist Education Society that fathered

Stepney, and the Northern Education Society, the parent of Horton-Rawdon, both founded in 1804.

These institutions were the fruit of a new theology. In a bibliography with commentary that Caleb Evans supplied to one of his students in 1773, he acknowledged John Gill as a writer who "excels in rabbinical learning", apparently in Bristol. By contrast, Doddridge "is to be valued for sublimity, perspicuity, penetration and unbounded love" whilst Jonathan Edwards was thought of as "the most rational, scriptural divine and the liveliest Christian the world was ever blessed with". By like token, the moderate Calvinism of Andrew Fuller was an important intellectual restatement of the tradition, symbolic of the new thinking which both reflected a changed attitude amongst Baptists, which, in its time, made them look again at their doctrine of ministry, of the church and of Christian mission.[17]

The French historian, Elie Halevy, draws attention to the decay of the older academies in the latter decades of the eighteenth century and the emergence "of new schools of another type, orthodox and pietist", "a new generation of evangelical academies" is Deryck Lovegrove's language: "theologically grounded in moderate evangelical Calvinism and in consequence displaying a strongly practical bias, the new seminaries (the term itself indicates their divergence from the earlier pattern) afforded regular opportunities for practice in evangelical preaching and encouraged the growth of personal devotion." The model for these new schools was the Countess of Huntingdon's foundation at Trevecca, which had its effect on what was happening at Bristol, Horton and Stepney, though these institutions did not generally reflect the anti-intellectualism that at times seemed to threaten Trevecca. But even at Bristol, as sympathetic a commentator as Joseph Hughes of the Bible Society, reckoned that as a theological college, the institution was deficient "both in system and in stimulants". Part of the problem was constituency demand, still suspicious of the intellectualism of the old academies and its associated heterodoxy, still opposed to the concept of "man-made" ministers.[18]

In the meantime students at the new academies were put to work as evangelists and church planters, making the college not just a place of training but an immediate ministerial resource effective in the life of the churches. As early as 1773 the Bristol Education Society organized a Gospel Mission into Cornwall with Benjamin Francis as its itinerant, following the injunction of Caleb Evans "that the society's work was not only to offer basic theological education but to encourage missionaries to preach the gospel wherever providence opens a door for it." In the north, the work had been pioneered by John Fawcett at Hebden Bridge, who educated a series of ministerial candidates in his own home, ran a distinguished private academy, and in 1773 sought, with the encouragement of Hugh Evans, to establish a northern college but to no avail. It was to be more than twenty years before the education society got off the ground with William Steadman as principal, whose ideal a punster has said was always for "evangelism *steadied* by education".[19]

Holding that balance was to prove very difficult. The new evangelical academies moved fairly swiftly from indifference to intellectual attainment to a more traditional academic outlook, shedding on the way something of their concern for aggressive evangelism. Partly, it was argued, to meet the needs of a better educated society, partly because prosperous urban and suburban churches demanded well-educated and respectable ministers - just one aspect of what to-day would be called the gospel and culture, the need to communicate the eternal message in language and concept meaningful to the new industrial world, but more, it would seem, the world of employers, managers and skilled artisans than the serried ranks of the poor, the unskilled and those only partially employed.

Exclusions, Alternatives and Assaults

Another aspect of that culture was a history of political and educational disability. In the nineteenth century the processes of exclusion which had been introduced after the Restoration were put into reverse with the repeal of the Test and Corporation Acts in 1828 which terminated the old Anglican constitution governing the Administration of the State and its corporate boroughs. The principle therein enshrined was not immediately extended to the ancient universities on the argument that they were private, ecclesiastical, rather than national, institutions. For their part nonconformists argued to the contrary, "these institutions being national in their character and so regarded by the legislature". They argued against the medieval identification of education at all levels as a church function and, therefore, entered into alliance with the educational reformers of the period to break the Anglican monopoly.[20]

The first stage in this process was the movement to secure a non-denominational institution of higher education in London. Baptists, and particularly Dr. F. A. Cox, minister of Mare Street, Hackney, alongside philosophical radicals like Lord Brougham, played a large part in this campaign. As early as May 1820, a sketch had appeared in the *Baptist Magazine* entitled "Protestant Dissenting Academy".[21] This was almost certainly the work of a university of dissenters' and gives him equal status with the poet, Thomas Campbell in fathering the university. Indeed, Professor Lardner, writing in 1830, said "the first notion of a university is said to have been suggested by a dissenting clergyman named Rev. Mr. Cox".[22]

Cox was not slow to form a committee, initially of Baptists only, but later expanded to include other dissenters and Scottish churchmen resident in England. The enlarged group met together in April 1825 at the King's Head Tavern in the Poultry, the hostelry where so many Dissenting, and Baptist agencies in particular, had their birth. The upshot was the appointment of a delegation of dissenting laymen and clergy to meet with Brougham and Campbell.[23]

Amongst these were included Benjamin Shaw and Cox himself, both Baptists, as well as the charismatic luminary, Edward Irving, of Regent Square Scots Church. There immediately ensued a debate as to whether or not to include theology chairs in the new institution. Brougham and his friends apparently wrote to Campbell, "We think with you that the introduction of Divinity will be mischievous; but we must yield to the Dissenters with Irving at their head. We must have a *theological* college". The immediate reaction of Anglican subscribers was predictable: the theology was to be Church of England or there should be no theology at all. The dissenting interest was apparently flexible. Presented with the Anglican response, the reply was, "Enough, enough. We are convinced and concede the point that the University shall be without religious rivalship". Irving, however, had his doubts and confided to Carlyle: "It will be un-religious, secretly anti-religious, all the same", the origin of the popular designation of the new university as "godless Gower Street" in reference to its location. The issue of the inclusion or the exclusion of theology was to rumble on for several years.[24]

Meanwhile, Cox's counsel was particularly important as one of the few amongst the planners who had experience in teaching in higher education by virtue of his tutorship at Stepney; accordingly he became honorary secretary of the provisional committee of the new university and it was he who presented the plan at the first public meeting chaired by the Lord Mayor, calling for "a palace for genius". The support of the London dissenters was very important to the new venture: they offered the new project a well-developed connexion, not only in London but reaching out into the provinces, whose wealth was needed for the new institution to get off the ground, not to mention their experience of the academies, and their close ties with the Scottish universities, who, for their part, together with some North American institutions, gave dignity to dissent by the recognition of nonconformist scholars and leaders by the award of honorary doctorates.[25]

Ironically cautions as to the secular nature of the new institution led to the exclusion of all clergy from the Council of the College and therefore of Cox, (though he continued to serve as clerk and secretary until September, 1828). Instead, Baptist interests were represented on the Council by Olinthus Gregory, Professor of Mathematics at the Royal Military Academy at Woolwich, eminent theologian and biographer of Robert Hall, who sat on the education committee and whose name is to be found on the foundation stone of University College. He was supported by Benjamin Shaw, Treasurer of the Baptist Missionary Society 1821-6 and sometime MP for Westbury.[26] With John Smith and I. L. Goldsmid, Shaw underwrote the purchase of the site for the university college at his own risk until the new institution had accumulated sufficient funds to secure it. The combination is an interesting one: liberal Whig MP, Jewish emancipationist and Baptist man-of-the-city. Indeed the whole enterprise involved a remarkable interplay of interest, with Cox increasingly intimate with Lord Brougham during whose rectorship of Glasgow University in 1824 he was awarded an honorary LL.D. At Gower Street, perhaps as a substitute for not being a member of Council, he was appointed Librarian in 1827, Brougham having suggested it was a possibility two years earlier, at a salary of £200 p.a., out of which it was supposed he would fund an assistant. However, financial exigencies led to this appointment being terminated in 1831.

The funds for the new institution were to be secured by the sale of 1,500 shares of a nominal value of £100 each with Cox as a foremost advocate. One of the principal purchasers was the Duke of Bedford for many years President of the non-credal British and Foreign Schools Society "of which he regarded Brougham as the founder". The religious issue still obstructed the project. As Irving's comments earlier indicated, whilst conscientious dissenters could convince themselves without difficulty of the necessity of proceeding on a purely secular, non-credal, basis, Evangelical opinion, represented on the Council by Zachary Macaulay, was less certain. Regretfully declining an invitation to Brougham Hall, Cox wrote with regard to the sale of shares, "Some of our *Evangelicals* however are at work in another way, and I or you or some of us may expect an attack (besides the caricatures shop) of which I am by no means sorry!" He encouraged Brougham to support the idea of launching the sale of a further thousand shares when most of the first issue were secured and also supported Joseph Hume's recommendation that large share holders be encouraged to split their holdings to increase the number of sympathisers for the new venture.[27]

But religion remained a problem. Professor New notes that whereas Evangelicals were troubled by a university not teaching religion, High churchmen were shocked at the thought of a University not teaching the religion of the Church of England. Wilberforce suggested "a separate endowment for lectures on the Evidences of Christianity", begging Brougham to "reflect seriously on the consequences of imparting to so influential a body of men ... all branches of philosophical knowledge knowledge, leaving them wholly ignorant of the grounds and basis of Christian truth". Fundamental questions were being raised about the nature of the new world being ushered in by the industrial revolution and associated changes. On the one hand, the Established Church stood for a Christendom view of society with only one legally promoted exposition of Christian truth. Dissent could not agree to that, and was even at this early date moving to a pluralist position, occasioned by its co-operation with establishment men, a powerful Jewish financial interest, those of no religious commitment at all, as well as both orthodox and heterodox dissenters. A long history of disabilities coupled with the insistence of the established church on total control of educational institutions made secularists of pious dissenters, that is to say, made them supporters of an educational institution which itself would be deliberately detached from the advocacy of religious values.[28]

The coalitioning involved in this was not unknown to Evangelicals. Of their project against slavery Halevy says, "By a strange paradox men who were Protestant to the backbone, zealots of the dogma of justification by faith, were so devoted to philanthropy that on the common ground of good works they were reconciled with the most lukewarm Christians, even with declared enemies of Christianity". Indeed both Brougham and Goldsmid had both been involved in the Slavery campaign and in the struggle won the confidence of the Evangelicals. But education was, apparently, another matter, though a younger Macaulay, that is the historian, came to the defence of the new college in the pages of the *Edinburgh Review,* arguing, "We entertain a firm conviction that the principles of liberty, as in government and trade, so also in education, are all important to the happiness of mankind. We do in our souls believe that they are strong with the strength and quick with the vitality of truth".[29]

For his part Brougham went on record. "It was not because they disregarded religious education that the Council had omitted theological lectureships, but because they deemed the subject too important to be approached lightly or inconsiderately. Their object was to leave the religious instruction of the students to their parents and clergymen".[30]

That statement may have been the spur which led three Anglican clergymen who held chairs at the college to announce in *The Times* that, with the approbation of the Council, at a place near the University "a course of divinity lectures will be delivered during the academic session". The Dissenters could hardly stand by and so Cox, and the Congregationalist Joseph Fletcher, announced that they would run a similar course outside the university on the Evidence of Christianity, Biblical Literature and Church History. The Council disclaimed approval of either, whereupon church and dissent joined forces to try and secure the Council's blessing with Cox nominated privately to secure Brougham's support, which he did by arguing that such a way of proceeding would disarm the opponents of the college of the frequently uttered changes of godless secularism. They were apparently right, for Lord Althorpe was soon writing indicating that the additional lectures had quite satisfied his qualms about the venture, asking if he could now become a shareholder. For the committed Anglican, however, an alternative was soon provided with the establishment of the credally based King's College in 1828. Brougham was quite sanguine about the competition which he likened to that betwixt British and Foreign, and National Schools. Thereafter what had originally been called London University adopted the title of University College and the two institutions became parts of the federal University of London on its incorporation in November 1836: its degrees were to be open "to persons of all religious persuasions, without distinction and without the imposition of any test or disqualification whatsoever."[31]

Here, it should be noted that the same pattern was also developed in the schools, where Baptists for the most part supported, first the non-credal British and Foreign Schools, and after 1870, the Board Schools with their simple Bible instruction. Baptists were not quick to enter private secondary education though they did share in a number of general nonconformist ventures such as those at Mill Hill and Taunton, and those functionally-necessary establishments that made special provision for missionaries' children such as Eltham for boys and Walthamstow Hall for girls. By contrast the Congregationalists, the Quakers and especially the Methodists, set up a fair number of denominational secondary boarding schools. Not so the Baptists, who put their weight behind the state system. This is reflected in Spurgeon's desertion of an earlier voluntaryism in favour of the Board system which alone seemed to meet the scale of the need of urban England. This was symbolised by his campaigning for W. R. Selway, a tutor at Pastor's College for election to the London School Board, which perhaps explains why Colonel Griffin's proposal, when President of the Baptist Union in 1890, that a Baptist University be established at a cost of £250,000 was met with thunderous silence.

Although the establishment of London University opened up admission to higher education for dissenters, exclusion from the ancient universities still smarted. The first stage was to secure the admission of dissenters to first degrees following the wish of the Royal Commission of 1850, and this was achieved for Oxford and Cambridge in 1854 and 1856 respectively. But a declaration as to bona fide membership of the Church of England remained necessary for all University and College offices, thus denying to dissenters the possibility of a scholarly livelihood. Whilst religious tests were abolished in the University of Durham in 1865, at Oxford and Cambridge exclusion still obtained. A series of cases of dissenting scholars whose future careers were denied to the universities began to accumulate, totalling some fourteen in the 1860s, amongst them several Baptists who paraded their disabilities on the platform of the Liberation Society. Henry Bompas of St. John's College Cambridge, subsequently a Q.C., was Fifth Wrangler in 1858. William S. Aldis, Senior Wrangler in 1861 (following the Presbyterian W. Sterling in 1860, the First Trinity man so to distinguish himself for thirteen years), James Aldis, Sixth Wrangler in 1863, and Thomas S. Aldis, Second Wrangler in 1866.[32]

In 1869, the Senior Wrangler was a Jew named Hartog who was unwilling even to take his degree under the trinitarian formula with which it was offered. But therein lay a problem, for another statute said that until the Senior Wrangler had taken his degree none other could proceed to theirs. The Senate was, therefore, confronted with the problem of issuing a Jew with a degree by special grace, or excluding 114 good Christians from theirs. The grace was allowed. The situation was further heightened by a Classics Fellow at Trinity resigning his Fellowship because he believed he could no longer conscientiously hold to the declaration he had once formally signed. A special lectureship was created for him, but again the case of the nonconformists was powerfully underlined.

In 1871 religious tests at Oxford and Cambridge, with only a few exceptions, were abolished by Parliament. But vigilance was thought to be necessary to capitalise on this and so the existence of the Cambridge University Society for the Promotion of Religious Equality. At Oxford lawyers got rich quickly when J. H. Tillyard, probably of Baptist origins, presented himself as a candidate for election to a Hertford Fellowship announced as restricted to those in orders in the Church of England, contrary, it was argued, to both the 1871 Act and the legislation that converted Magdalen Hall into Hertford College. A second case, also involving Tillyard, witnessed the Liberation Society taking action against the College in Queen's Bench, which did indeed find that Tillyard had not been properly examined in contravention of the 1871 Act, giving judgment that a new election should be held, but the Court of Appeal overruled Queen's Bench, thereby provoking additional legislation in 1882, which opened all headships to competition (save three), whilst clerical fellowships were confined to those exercising a chaplaincy function, conducting services, and giving religious instruction. Even so, R. F. Horton was still opposed as a theology examiner in 1883 though he had the support of the Vice Chancellor and the House of Congregation.[33]

But that was not the end of the story. Leading nonconformist families, having secured access to the ancient universities for their offspring, soon found that those institutions, and Oxford in particular, represented a severe corrosive of dissenting commitments, and consequently many were lost to dissent, and indeed in some cases to Christian faith altogether. As sympathetic a commentator as T. H. Green, who accepted office as Vice President of the Oxford University Nonconformists' Union, spoke of access to Oxbridge as "an injury rather than a help to nonconformity", pleading with dissenting leaders to make better provision for the defence and maintenance of the religious life and faith of those who came there from their churches. This was the situation that promoted the founding of the Oxford University Nonconformists' Union in 1881, whose life seemed to centre around the person of R. F. Horton. Mainly Congregationalist in character, Baptist involvement seems to have included W. J. Ashley, who eventually became an Anglican, and Frank Tillyard, with external support from people like H. M. Bompas, now a Q. C.[34]

More significant was the decision to relocate Spring Hall College, the Birmingham Congregational Theological Seminary, in Oxford as Mansfield College in 1886, amidst much talk of nonconformity returning to the universities. Apart from the desirability of educating congregational ministers, and a fair number of Baptists as well, with the benefits of Oxford theology, the strategy was to provide a cultural focus in Oxford for nonconformist students. Trevelyan, appositively argued that hitherto exclusion had provided nonconformity with its leadership, distinctively trained in its own principles, their aggressive loyalty to dissent sharpened by that very experience. The opening up of Oxford and Cambridge, by contrast, meant that such men, "have been absorbed in the general stream of national life", concluding: "This change has contributed with other causes to the diminution of the dissenting bodies both in self-consciousness and power."[35]

The Work of the Denominational Colleges

Whereas the history of Congregational Colleges in the nineteenth century is full of crises and controversies, the record in the Baptist colleges is far less patent. At Bristol, in 1837, three students were dismissed and others censured, in the conviction that "no greater injury can be inflicted on the churches of Christ than to send among them ministers of unsettled principles and doubtful piety". In 1872 there was concern at the views of a particular tutor (the layman, E. W. Claypole), the college committee resolving that "the tutors be in general agreement with the vital doctrines entertained by the Baptist denomination". In the Report of Regent's Park College for 1871 the old spectre of Socinianism reasserted itself in the committee's "dissatisfaction with the views of four of the students on some vital truths". Two of the four resigned whilst the courses of the other two were discontinued. The Downgrade Controversy, with all its potential peril, was not directed specifically at the colleges even if those whose names were most often mentioned in association with it - J. G. Greenhough and James Thew - had both been trained at Rawdon under the Principalship of S. G. Green.[36]

Some had hoped that the strict communionist, Henry Dowson, minister of Westgate, Bradford and the college secretary, would have become Rawdon's principal, but Green was chosen instead. It was not long, however, before such conservative spirits were objecting to what they called Green's "latitudinarianism" and began to offer their support elsewhere.[37] So it was that the founding of what was to become the Manchester College related to that older controversy on closed and open communion that had been debated by Robert Hall and Joseph Kinghorn at the beginning of the century. William Newman, the first president of Stepney, like many of the leaders of the denomination in the first half of the century, had been a closed communionist, pressing that view on the Stepney students to the point at which some of them rebelled against his leadership in something like a fully-blown academic strike1 In the North West a generation later, a separate strict-communionist association which was loyal to the Baptist Union, and which eschewed that high Calvinism "which lifts the believer above normal obligations and sinks the sinner below normal responsibility, and which dishonours the doctrines of grace while professing to exalt them," separated from the Lancashire and Chester Association in 1860.[38]

The college, founded at Bury in 1866, was established as the agency of this association for training candidates of a strict-communionist persuasion with Dowson as its first Principal. The new institution sought to embrace distinctive principles: it was not to be resident (for that "had some of the disadvantages of the Monkish system"), it eschewed "classical, mathematical and secular studies" which all too often interfered with the study of theology, and the study of the ancient languages was not to be insisted upon being seen as unrealistic for the talents of many candidates; "to take them from the loom, the plough, the shop or the counting house, unaccustomed to habits of study and only imperfectly acquainted with their own language" and expect them to master Latin, Greek and Hebrew was in a majority of cases "simply an absurdity". Such skills were not now necessary in view of the tools available for Biblical exposition, though of course, "The principal book for the ministerial student is the English Bible". Beyond the academic course, practical work in city missions was presented as an essential part of training. Notwithstanding the eschewing of general education the syllabus still included English Literature and the written and spoken use of the English Language, General History, Geography, Natural Philosophy, Logic and Mental Science as well as Theology, Church History and Pastoral Studies. There was also a Voluntary Latin Class but no teaching in Greek or Hebrew. In the event those languages, and classical literature, could not be kept out, and for all the early protestations came to occupy a central place in the curriculum within a decade.[39]

Moreover, when the college moved to Manchester in 1873, it was to a residential suite of buildings. Spurgeon, who necessarily distanced himself from the total viewpoint of the college, (for the principal of his own college was a paedo-baptist) preached at the stone laying and addressed himself to the accusation that the colleges were producing more men than pastoral vacancies required, but he was not at all daunted by this for he believed they were training men to take charge of churches yet to be founded. The college in Manchester developed strongly not least because of its location and the development of healthy relationships first with Owen's College and then with the Victoria University.[40]

The pattern of development in England was generally for the Baptist Colleges, whilst retaining their independence, to develope university relationships. Beyond Oxford, Cambridge and Durham, the pattern of development was for the University of London with its federal structure to be the sponsor of new institutions of higher education. In like fashion when in 1884 the new Victoria University was established in the North, it too was a federal institution with a presence in Liverpool, Manchester and Leeds. The University of Wales, established in 1893 was once more a federal institution embracing several separate University colleges. Such a structure made it easy for Baptist colleges both to retain their independent status but to affiliate to a university discipline. Accordingly, aided by the Unitarian, James Martineau, both Stepney and Bristol affiliated to London University in 1841, followed by Horton by 1852.[41]

Such association it was hoped might bring some relief to the small overstretched staffs of the Baptist Colleges in so far as ministerial candidates would be able to attend the local university or university colleges for that contextual education in arts and sciences which was still considered very important, allowing the college staffs to concentrate exclusively on biblical work, theology, and pastoral studies. This never seems fully to have occurred, perhaps because too few candidates were able to matriculate (as required from 1858) to take advantage of the university courses, though a large number of Baptist leaders possessed London BAs and MAs. Economies and improvements in teaching were, however, secured by cooperation with other free-church colleges in the same location; even so the tutorial resource remained pitifully slender so that the denomination's best academic talents were exhausted in teaching, and not able to contribute as much as they might otherwise have done with their pens to wider debates.

The pastorate as much as the college, therefore, became the likely location for Baptist contributions to scholarship: thus, for example, neither John Foster nor Andrew Fuller, John Howard Hinton nor Samuel Cox, J. H. Shakespeare nor John Clifford held college office, rather were they publishing pastors who wrote from the manse.

The problem with the relationship with London was that institution's exclusion of theology from its curriculum at the time of its foundation, the only exception being what was called the "First Scriptural Examination" available to BAs from 1839 and a Further Scripture Exam made available from 1840. The syllabus covered the Hebrew and Greek Scriptures, Butler's *Analogy* and Paley's *Evidences* and Biblical History. No questions were allowed on topics disputed by Christians and no answer provided by a student was to be objected to for "peculiarity of doctrinal views". From 1847 King's College offered an associateship in theological studies (A.K.C.) to those of its graduates who were successful in a special series of theological papers - but for theological degrees as such students still had to go to Oxford, Cambridge, Durham or Scotland. Thus it was that S. W. Green argues that the University of London gave great benefits to the various theological colleges in general but not direct stimulation to theological studies in particular. This difficulty led to the Congregational colleges establishing a Senatus Academicus in 1879 which was swiftly subscribed to by many other theological institutions. Its function was to set an annual examination, both internally and externally examined, of approximately degree standard. After two years of study an ATS (Association of the Senatus Academicus) could be obtained, with a Fellowship (FTS), at the equivalent of Honours standard, available after four years. To all intents and purposes London University students were thereby taking the equivalent of theological examinations, thus preparing the way for the establishment of London Theological Faculty and of the B.D. degree in 1901, once more to be available "without the imposition of any test or disqualification whatsoever". The B.D. was available not only to internal students but also through the Council for External Students, who also made available a Certificate in Religious Knowledge for those not able to matriculate, a provision which was to prove most helpful to many Baptist students without formal secondary education.[42]

Candidates offering themselves for training for the Baptist ministry represented a very wide range of backgrounds and abilities. The absence of a decent standard of secondary education, not publicly available in England until 1903, was a major reason for the inability of the colleges to confine themselves to theology and pastoral training. Even Regent's Park, the academically most prestigious of the colleges by the end of the century, which had set itself the task of "showing that between nonconformity and mental incapacity there is no inseparable relation as is sometimes taken for granted," was unable or unwilling to confine its entrants to those able to matriculate. There still remained a double-think about the inter-relatedness of academic ability and achievement and potential for ministry in a society of many diverse educational, not to say spiritual, needs. This double-take is most perfectly represented in a report on the work of the colleges presented to the Baptist Union Council in 1896: whilst not wanting to "discourage any man who has received from the Lord the gifts and call which qualify for the work of a pastor and teacher", it did want to exclude "unworthy men", with significantly the rider that non-graduates were to be encouraged to go to college, with the Union assisting financially where this was necessary. Perhaps at a slower speed than other free churches, Baptists were becoming increasingly denominational, and one of the agencies of that change were the colleges. Whereas as late as 1870, less than half of the ministers in charge of English Baptist churches had been trained in denominational colleges, by 1901 the proportion had risen to some 64%, although it has been shown that the colleges were seriously under-providing for the denomination's needs at this time, for whereas 1165 men left the ministry between 1890 and 1901, the college input was only 605, falling far short of the Spurgeonic ideal of providing for causes yet to be planted.[43]

Diversity of work, it was argued from the mid-century onwards, called for some rationalisation of resources. But such proposals as were forthcoming, sensible as they might seem, foundered on the independency of the separate colleges, backed by differences of theological outlook, regional sentiment, and functional focus: proposals to amalgamate the old New Connexion Midland College, Rawdon and Manchester foundered as much on Trans-Pennine mutual suspicion as on the number of guaranteed close-communionist tutorships in the new institution, whatever the vital significance of that to Baptist life on the eve of the twentieth century.

The most distinctive of all the colleges was Spurgeon's (originally Pastors') College. Founded in 1856, the same year that Dr. Angus's institution moved from a Stepney that was becoming socially problematical to the salubrious environment of Regent's Park, it was well-placed to become an arm of Baptist advance in the Second Evangelical Awakening in Britain, when it has been calculated, there was something like a 40% growth in Baptist Church membership. Behind the new college lay Spurgeon's judgment on the existing theological scene. After referring to costs and social class, he concludes, "I may have been uncharitable in my judgment but I thought the Calvinism of the theology usually taught to be very doubtful and the fervour of the generality of the students to be far behind their literary attainments." Spurgeon believed that the academies had a monitory history, citing the decline of Doddridge's in particular; it "sought to make ministers rather than to aid them" and therein imperilled its success. Of course there was also the bogey of incipient Socinianism which many saw re-emerging in the extremer forms of liberalism, particularly that associated with the popular Congregational preacher, John Baldwin Brown of Brixton. One who followed his line was a young Baptist minister named Carey Walters recently described as a "key figure" in the preparation for the Leicester Conference on the terms of religious communion. A graduate once more of Rawdon, his first pastorate was at Whitchurch, Salop., but soon after his arrival, he left the pastorate to form a Free Christian Church, which subsequently followed the example of that other very unorthodox Baptist, George Dawson of Birmingham, in assuming the title of the Church of the Saviour, "where neither minister nor congregation had to offer assent or subscription to any theological creed." Baldwin Brown preached at the dedication of the new church with the President of the British and Foreign Unitarian Association in attendance. Brown's action as Chairman Elect of the Congregational Union, thought *The English Independent*, "will afford additional ground for the charges of our opponents and fears of our friends that an incipient Socinianism is slowly progressing among our ministers and churches." For his part, Walters was soon writing proudly of his own Unitarianism; the Leicester Conference already had Spurgeon pondering the Evangelical soundness of historic dissent a decade before the Downgrade.[44]

In his own college Spurgeon set himself the task of producing Preachers of the Gospel: not scholars or cultural adornments but those who could "get to the hearts of the masses, to evangelise the poor - this is the College ambition, this and nothing else," and if for this purpose it was necessary to allow a "lowering of the average of scholarship", so be it. The curriculum of the college embraced classic Puritan theology set within a broad context of scientific, philosophical and historical knowledge with appropriate instruction in Biblical language and contemporary church work. The principal problem in the running of the college was not the syllabus but the length of a student's course. Initially set at two years, with only short vacations, it was increased to three in 1880, it being argued that the third year was "more useful than the other two". But all too often students contracted their courses as deacons of vacant churches seduced them into early service; Spurgeon was thought a "harsh jailor" when he detained men in college when there was urgent work to be done in the churches. Like all institutions, Spurgeon's grew into conformity with its sister colleges, increasing its interest in academic education per se; the key date, which is yet to be determined is probably the first year in which a Spurgeon's man secured his London B.D.[45]

Twentieth Century Tailpiece

The twentieth century has witnessed the mushrooming of institutions of higher education in England in several successive waves. For Baptist Colleges this has meant increased relationships with the local university and a decline of the partnership with London. In many provincial centres, college staff have provided the backbone of teaching in theological faculties, and today, when all university budgets are under attack, are regarded as a very valuable asset. Provincial faculties of theology have also provided opportunities for Baptist scholars to hold chairs, and in particular the distinction in Old Testament scholarship should be noted in the work of Professors T. H. Robinson, Aubrey Johnson, (Cardiff), H. H. Rowley, (Bangor and Manchester), Henton Davies, (Durham), and R. E. Clements, (King's College, London). At the same, a sizeable number of laymen have achieved distinction in other disciplines; their presence has also played an important part in the development in Christian discipleship of Baptist undergraduates.

Their needs were also catered by the two interdenominational societies, the Student Christian Movement and the Inter-Varsity Fellowship. The former was very important in the pre-war years and immediately following the Second World War in providing a positive and creative ecumenical forum. In the "sixties it adopted an increasingly radical stance which led to declining support both amongst the student body and from the churches. At the same time some evangelical student groups became less pietistic, more prepared to wrestle with both intellectual and social responsibility issues. Today, by far the larger number of candidates for the ministry, have a background in one of the evangelical Christian unions, and it is in their fellowships that most Baptist students will be found.

An earlier generation formed specifically Baptist societies, the oldest of which was the Robert Hall Society in Cambridge, in the establishment of which T. R. Glover played an important part. Such local initiatives came together in the establishment of the Baptist Students' Federation in 1947 which established societies in all English societies. Personally fostered by Dr. E. A. Payne during his general secretaryship of the Baptist Union, it trained several generations of Baptist leaders. By the 1970s not only was the tide turning against denominationalism with the growth of the charismatic and restorationist movements, but with the expansion of higher education beyond the universities into the

polytechnics and colleges, the identification of students, as over against youth
more generally, became much less clear, and the Baptist Student Federation was
terminated though individual societies continued to offer programmes to a much
reduced clientele, probably now dependant on the energies and enthusiasms
of the local chaplain who woos their support.

Within the English churches an increasing number of candidates, both
men and women, are offering themselves for training for the ministry. Following initiatives taken by the Northern College in Manchester, other colleges have
also experimented with patterns of training which are congregation-based. These,
reflecting newer insights into ministerial training in other parts of the world,
put more emphasis once more on the practical aspects of training, and upon
learning through theological reflexion on particular pastoral situations. This, in
its turn has had its effects upon processes of selection as well as bringing about
the enrichment of the pastoral studies of all ministerial students. The rigours
of academic analysis are still, however, necessary for all who hold leadership positions, whether locally, nationally or internationally, if the besetting sin of Baptists, namely pragmatism and an easy seduction by the anticipation of easy short-
term success, is not to prevent a world-wide fellowship, which is currently enjoying a new spiritual buoyancy, being of maximum usefulness to the work of the
kingdom. Part of the reason for that harsh judgment on Baptists
by members of other denominations, noticed by George Beasley-Murray, is our
over-concern with the question "Will it work?" as a defining criterion for policy-
making. Though often frustrating in the perplexities and complexities which
it throws up, the academic tradition reminds us of the need to ask that other
question, namely, "Is it true?"

*John H. Y. Briggs is chair of the Victorian Studies Program at the University of Keele
in Staffordshire, England, U.K.*

Footnotes

1. Mandell Creighton: *Historical Lectures and Addresses*, ed. L. Creighton, 1903,
p56; G. Beasley-Murray: "Confessing Baptist Identity" in A Perspective on Baptist Identity, ed. D. Slater, 1987, pp79-80.

2. R. L. Greaves and R. Taller: *Biographical Dictionary of English Radicals*, 3 vols.,
[1983], provides the basic information for such an analysis. Baptists who achieve academic
distinction in this early period would include Sir Jerome Saxbery, sometime Sub-Warden
of All Souls, Oxford, and Dr. Peter Chamberlen, Seventh-Day Baptist, a graduate of
the universities of Cambridge, Heidleberg, and Padua, an early pioneer in improved
midwifery.

3. Noted by R. L. Greaves: *The Puritan Revolution and Educational Thought*, New
Jersey, U.S.A., 1969, p18

4. Ibid p18-19, 143 (citing T. Collier, *The Pulpit Guard Routed*, 1651), 24-5, 151

5. T. Crosby: *The History of the English Baptists*, Vol I, 1738, piv and 260ff. Lists
of ministers and others with attention to their education is given in Vol I chapter IV,
in Vol III, 1740, chapter I, [an account of ministers silenced or ejected] and Vol. IV,

1740, chapter III and the latter part of chapter II, p266ff.

6. Crosby, Op. Cit., Vol. IV, p266, H. McLachlan: *English- Education under the Test Acts*, 1931, pp50-59.

7. Crosby, Op. Cit., Vol IV, p326 and McLachlan, Op. Cit., p106-9; Crosby, Op. Cit., Vol IV, p346; Ibid., p348; p366; p390

8. The standard accounts are I. Parker: *Dissenting Academies in England*, 1914, H. McLachlan: *English Education under the Test Acts*, 1931, J. W. Ashley Smith: *The Birth of Modern Education*, 1954, with the chapter on the academies in E. G. Rupp: *Religion in England, 1688-1791*, 1986, providing something of a revisionist approach to some of the more grandiose claims of earlier writers. Seymour Price's article "Dissent Academies, 1662-1820" in *The Baptist Quarterly*, Vol VI, 1932, p125-137, is partially right in suggesting Baptist additions to McLachlan, but does not sufficiently distinguish between what were essentially schools and what were academies for older students.

9. R. Brown: *The English Baptists of the Eighteenth Century*, 1986, p48ff, Crosby, Op. Cit., Vol III, p129

10. J. Ivimey: *History of the English Baptists*, Vol 3, 1823, p153-5, 208-10, 386-99.

11. Ashley Smith, Op. Cit., p10.

12. McLachlan: Op. Cit., p71; Ashley Smith, Op. Cit., p198.

13. Davisson wrote *De Ordinatone Dissertatio Historica* in 1704, published a series of *Sermons*, and also *A Vindication of the Protestant Minister's Mission* in 1720; J. Ivimey, Op. Cit. Vol II, 1814, p586-8; W. T. Whitley: "Bampfield's Plan for an Educated Ministry" in *Transactions of the Baptist Historical Society*, Vol III, 1912, p17.

14. Ashley Smith, Op. Cit., p206 suggests it was at a later date; H. Foreman: "Baptist Provision for Ministerial Education in the Eighteenth Century" in *The Baptist Quarterly*, Vol. XXVII, 1978, indicates that Llewellyn was operating from Trowbridge 1752-1760, but Seymour Price, Op. Cit. p135, and *Dictionary of Welsh Biography*, p568 together with Ivimey, Op. Cit., Vol IV, p393 suggest that from 1747 he was in London, and that he founded an academy to train men for the ministry in Hammersmith which he ran until the 1760s or '70s, more probably the former.

15. Seymour Price: Op. Cit. p134-5, S. Gummer: "Trosnant Academy" in *The Baptist Quarterly*, Vol. IX, 1939, p412-24; Ivimey, Op. Cit., Vol IV, p397-8. One of the most famous of Trosnant's alumni was Morgan Edwards, (1722-95) who after further training at Bristol and emigration to the United States became the historian of the American Baptists and prime mover in the foundation of Rhode Island College (today Brown University) which in the eighteenth century played a significant part in according academic status to many English ministers by conferring degrees upon them in a period when they were excluded from English universities. One such was W. N. Clarke of Unicorn Yard, Southwark.

16. E. G. Rupp: Op. Cit., p179.

17. L. G. Champion: "Evangelical Calvinism and the Structure of Baptist Church Life" in *The Baptist Quarterly*, Vol. XXVIII, 1979, p204.

18. E. Halevy: *England in 1815* (rev'd edn.), 1949, p418-9; D. Lovegrove: *Established Church; Itinerancy and the Transformation of English Dissent, 1780-183*. 1988, p67-8; J. Liefchild: *Memoir of the late Revd Joseph Hughes*, 1835, p39 as cited by Lovegrove, p76.

19. R. Brown: *The English Baptists of the Eighteenth Century*, 1987, p115; N Moon: *Education for Ministry: Bristol Baptist College*, 1679-1979, 1979, p20, Lovegrove: Op. Cit.,

pp3, 70, 79; A. C. Underwood; *A History of the English Baptists*, 1947, p176.

20. Minute of 6th March 1854 of The Liberation Society, cited in W. H. Mackintosh: *Disestablishment and Liberation*, 1972, p84.

21. C. W. New: *The Life of Henry Brougham to 1830*, 1961, p362. Eight years earlier Daniel Bogue (and J. Bennett) in his *History of the Dissenters*, 1812, had penned this sentence: "Were an institution established in a central part of England, upon a liberal plan, open to all denominations, Christians or Jews, and were the incomes of the professors to arise, like those of Scotland, in great measure from the students, whom their celebrity would attract, it would find sufficient support." Later this turned into a plan for a Dissenting University, and created a specific group of leading dissenters who were able to turn their energies to promoting the new London University when its establishment first began to be canvassed. H. H. Bellott: *University College, London, 1826-1926*, 1919, p21.

22. New: Op. Cit. p362.

23. Bellott: Op. Cit. p22, offers the innocent but spurious judgment that the committee remained sectional because confined to "Baptists and Pedo-Baptists"; Seymour Price: "The Centenary of the Baptist Building Fund" in *The Baptist Quarterly*, Vol. III, 1926, p81ff.

24. Bellott: Op. Cit., p22-3.

25. New is too extreme in his judgment that "Birkbeck alone (and Cox, the Secretary) had been associated with any educational institution except as a student." Cox's prior experience was, of course, as a tutor at Stepney, but Gregory also, from the dissenting side, was by then well-experienced in his appointment at the Military Academy at Woolwich. Both were graduates of Scottish Universities.

26. Westbury was a famous pocket borough purchased in 1810 by Sir Manasseh Masseh Lopez, a convert from Judaism to the Established Church, who established something of a reputation for bribery and corruption in parliamentary elections for which he was both fined and imprisoned. For his part, Shaw was active in debates in the House of Commons, 1813-18, speaking mainly on commercial topics. He was apparently a Lloyd's underwriter and it was thus presumably his professional interests in the city that introduced him to Lopez whose wealth was largely in East Indian stock. In 1823 after being unseated by the House for corruption, Lopez took his own seat of Westbury which he held until 1829 when he resigned to provide a seat for Sir Robert Peel on the latter's rejection, over Catholic Emancipation, by the University of Oxford. Benjamin Shaw became an important patron of dissenting societies, becoming involved in the work of the Dissenting Deputies, the Particular Baptist Fund, the Baptist Building Fund and Stepney College. In a skit on the new university, printed in *John Bull* and entitled, "Cockney College: An Invitation to Stinkamalee", Gregory is portrayed as "Dr. Olympus Gregory" who "will instruct the junior fishmongers in the science of throwing shells", whilst of Benjamin Shaw, it is said "will explain the Rights and Privileges of the Underwriters at Lloyd's Coffee-House." Cited in Bellott: Op. Cit., p70-71. Shaw does not appear in Dr. Bebbington's *List of Baptist MPs in the Nineteenth Century* but will appear in the *Corrigenda* to the same. He is, of course, particularly interesting as adding to the number of dissenters who sat at Westminster prior to the Repeal of the Test and Corporation Acts in 1828.

27. New: Op. Cit., p364; Brougham Mss 2 August 1825, cited New Op. Cit.,

p365. Not that Cox, himself, was other than an Evangelical Dissenter. In his memorial sermon, *Maturity in Death Exemplified*, Daniel Katterns, his successor at Hackney, said "He was always a preacher of the gospel, yet more richly evangelical as he proceeded", though, at the same time, he noted that he was a well-finished Biblical critic. Page 8, 23.

28. New: Op. Cit., p366.

29. E. Halevy: Op. Cit., p383; *Edinburgh Review*, February 1820, cited New: Op. Cit.,- p370-1.

30. *The Times*, 28 February, 1928, sited by New: Op. Cit., p379.

31. University College Correspondence No. 647 of 27 September 1828, cited New: Op. Cit., p382 S. W. Green "Sketch of the History of the Faculty" in *London Theological Studies*, 1911.

32. M. D. Johnson: *The Dissolution of Dissent, 1815-1918*, 1987, p172 Henry Bompas was the *brother*, not the *son*, pace Mackintosh: Op. Cit., p178, of the first bishop of the Yukon. The Bompas parents, described as "strict though not narrow Baptists" were members of Baptist Noel's John Street congregation which may explain why Henry, at St. John's College, Cambridge, took communion in his College Chapel, though at the same time becoming more convinced in his Baptist views. He, therefore, refused to sign the declaration approving all the rubrics of the Book of Common Prayer and was thus excluded from a Fellowship in favour of an inferior scholar. Turning to the law, he had a distinguished legal career; serving for more than twelve years as a county court judge, he was an energetic patron of dissenting and Baptist enterprises, including the work of the Liberation Society. He married the eldest daughter of the Revd Edward White, of conditional immortality fame, who whilst rejecting not only traditional doctrine in this area but also the validity of infant baptism, proceeded to the chair of the Congregational Union in 1886. The three Aldis boys were the sons of the Revd John Aldis of Maze Pond, London and King's Road, Reading, their mother being a daughter of Dr. Steadman, first President of Horton Academy. *Dictionary of National Biography, (Compact Edition)*, 1975 Vol. 2, p2522 J. H. Aldis: "Reminiscences of the Abolition of Religious Tests in the Universities of Oxford and Cambridge" in *The Baptist Quarterly*, Vol. IV, 1929, p249.

33. Ibid., Johnson: Op. Cit., chapter IV.

34. Johnson: Op. Cit., p186.

35. G. M. Trevelyan: *British History in the Nineteenth Century and After*, 1937, p284.

36. N. Moon: Op. Cit., p46-7; L. G. Champion: "The Contribution of Bristol College from 1770 to 1970" in *The Bristol Education Society, 1770-1970*, (1970) p15. In 1845, Bristol also suffered the loss of one of its tutors, Edgar Huxtable, who served at the college from 1834-45. Sometime scholar of St. John's College, which presumably suggests non-Baptist origins, he moved away from Baptist views on Church and Baptism, and accordingly resigned to join the Established Church (subsequently becoming A Canon of Salisbury Cathedral); significantly four students resigned with him. Moon: Op. cit., p. 43. R. E. Cooper: *From Stepney to St. Giles: The Story of Regent's Park College, 1810-1960, 1960*, p63-4.

37. E. A. Payne: *A Short History of the Baptist Union*, 1958, p130; A. C. Underwood: *A History of the English Baptists*, 1947, p209.

38. Charles Rignal: *Manchester Baptist College, 1866-1916*, 1916, p36-7. By comparison with the Bristol incident in note 36 above, a list of Past Students on p247-66

shows that of more than 200 graduates in the first 50 years, eleven joined the Established Church, two the Wesleyans and one each the Presbyterians and the Congregationalists. Such changes of denomination concentrate on the period after the turn of the century.

39. Ibid., p34, p48-51.

40. Ibid., p63-5, 150ff.

41. When Bristol became a separate university in 1909, the Baptist College affiliated to it, eventually helping to establish its faculty of theology. Similarly Rawdon affiliated to Leeds in 1915. Manchester became active in the Theology Faculty of Manchester University, having first negotiated the inclusion of Hebrew, Greek Testament and Philosophy as subjects within its arts degrees; it was also involved in the teaching of a separate B.D. established in 1904.

42. E. A. Payne: "The Development of Nonconformist Theological Education in the Nineteenth Century, with special reference to Regent's Park College" in ed. E. A. Payne: *Studies in History and Religion*; ed. S. W. Green: London Theological Studies, 1911; W. T. Whitley: "Our Theological Colleges" in *The Baptist Quarterly*, Vol I, 1922, p16.

43. K. D. Brown: *A Social History of the Nonconformist Ministry in England and Wales, 1800-1930*, 1988, esp chapters 2 and 3. J. E. B. Munson: "The Education of Baptist Ministers, 1870-1900" in *The Baptist Quarterly*, Vol. XXVI, 1976, p320ff.

44. Johnson: Op. Cit., Walters, passim.

45. M. Nicholl: "Charles Haddon Spurgeon, Educationalist" in *The Baptist Quarterly*, Vol. XXI, 1986, p384ff and Vol. XXXII, 1987, p73ff.

Nurseries of Piety or the School of Christ?
Means and Models of Baptist Ministerial Education In Early America

William H. Brackney

"Drunkards, uncleane persons, dumb Idoles or at the best cruel malignants"[1] was the assessment of contemporary learned ministers, according to Edmund Chillenden, a seventeenth century English Baptist writer. Chillenden, and others like him, associated education, titles, elaborate church buildings and vestments with Anglican or Roman Catholic characteristics which had no warrant in Holy Scripture. The average convert or second generation Baptist apparently agreed, for only meagre attempts were made to improve the training and lot of the clergy until the 1680s when a West Country church leader died and left a trust for that purpose. Baptists were to be called, possessed of a blameless lifestyle, gifted to preach and students of the Word. Education was incidental…to…unnecessary.

American Baptist ministers in the seventeenth century were a bit more fortunate, but not due to an intentional turn toward formal education. Several of the earliest clergy were graduates of English universities, trained as Anglican or Puritan divines. Among these were Roger Williams, John Clarke, John Myles,

Henry Dunster and Hanserd Knollys. This "gift" from the Reformed tradition created a major type of ministry and enabled the Baptists in general to achieve a higher recognition than many others in the dissenting tradition by 1700.[2]

More typical, however, was the second group of clergy who answered the call in a local church thence proceeding to preach, gathering aptitude and knowledge through experience. Such was the case with Elias Keach, William Screven, Thomas Goold and Valentine Rathbun. This route to the Baptist ministry picked up momentum during the Great Awakening when several young men were moved by the preaching of George Whitefield, or one of the other revivalists, and entered the ministry. Isaac Backus, Hezekiah Smith, Elias Smith, Benjamin Randall and Shubal Stearns took this route. With little or no formal education, several of these folk would assume life-long pastorates and make large contributions to the life and thought of early American Baptists.[3]

A final cluster of influential ministers provided a model and an urgency to improve the quality of pastors, elevating the social and political standing of the denomination at the same time. Essentially eighteenth century urbam folk who were educated in non-Baptist institutions, they brought a style and skill which others vividly lacked. Most prominent were Elisha Callendar (Harvard, 1718) Morgan Edwards (Bristol, 1756), James Manning (Princeton, 1762) and William Staughton (Bristol, 1793).[4] One can point to specific links between these ministers and the roots of intentional ministerial education for Baptists in the United States.

For the most part, then, Baptist ministers in America from 1650 to about 1770 were self-taught or mentored by older, seasoned pastors. Typically, a young man would live with the pastor's family, read theological treatises, learn Greek and Hebrew, study the Scriptures, and then gain experience in preaching, pastoral visitation, and in some cases evangelism.[5] In the New England area, pastors like Samuel Stillman, Asa Messer and Thomas Baldwin took the mentoring responsibility very seriously and sent several young persons into the ministry. Sometimes associations provided the unique option of service for the summer months on preaching tours on the western or northern frontiers.[6] In fact, it was the rapidly expanding frontiers, stretching from Nova Scotia to Alabama, which increased awareness of the inadequacy of early entry patterns to the Baptist ministry.

Funds and Societies

Specified benevolence and the emergence of voluntary societies for religious purposes provided the vehicles for a major change in the landscape of ministerial education. Money for, and interest in, education made it possible for long term plans to be realized and for a solid Baptist institutional life to emerge.

The first means of providing for the training of ministers were "funds" established and administered by associations of churches. Perhaps the first was the London Particular Baptist Fund with roots in 1689 among the London area congregations. A similar model was encouraged among the English General Baptists in England in 1704 who were concerned about the "great decay, sinking and languishing condition" of the churches.[7] Similar to these collective "funds" was the Edward Terrill Trust at Bristol, England which granted support for tutors and student aid for study under a local church pastor.[8] During the seventeenth century, prior to the chartering of societies which could invest the principal monies, ministerial candidates drew upon the "funds", and general collections among the churches replenished the treasuries. This, of course, proved to be precarious or insufficient in times of increased need.

A major watershed was created with the establishment of the early societies for the promotion of education. These organizations, growing out of the dissenter/voluntaristic tradition, combined with progressive business models of the early eighteenth century industrial revolution and brought new capital and investment interest to Christian endeavor. Persons who responded to appeals such as the "funds" had earlier made, could focus together their interest in a common ongoing project with a sense of participatory management as members of a society. Examples of these in the Baptist tradition were the Bristol Education Society (1770), the natural outgrowth of the Edward Terrill Trust, and the Baptist Missionary Society at Kettering, founded in 1792.[9]

William Staughton was aware of both of these organizations when he arrived in America in 1793. First in Hopewell, New Jersey and later in Philadelphia, Staughton expanded his pastoral labors through the formation of voluntary, single purpose societies, most of which were devoted to education. Another series of societies was founded in New England among Congregationalists and Baptists, for missionary endeavor and to promote ministerial education. By 1820, Baptists had adopted wholesale the principle of societies.[10]

The first of the American Baptist education societies was that of the Middle States, formed in Philadelphia in 1812. Its constitution, penned by William Staughton, was directed to "the assisting of pious men in obtaining such literary and theological aid...to fulfill the duties of the Christian ministry." Plans were laid for the trustees to evaluate suitable candidates for the ministry, to employ tutors, and eventually to erect a building where instruction would take place.[11] Each member subscribed five dollars per year and had full voting privileges; the society's geographical constituency included Pennsylvania, New York and New Jersey, a region in which most of the prominent congregations were located. With the full support of Philadelphia area clergy William Rogers, Henry Holcombe, William White and Burgess Allison, the Baptist Education Society of the Middle States had an auspicious beginning.

The Baptist ministers in New England were next in line, forming the Baptist Education Society of Massachusetts in 1814. Their goal was to provide for a tutor and living expenses for ministerial candidates in Massachusetts, New Hampshire and Maine. Three years later, partly in overt competition with their missionary-minded Massachusetts brethren, frontier New Yorkers founded in 1817 the Baptist Education Society of the State of New York at the small village of Hamilton, on the Indian frontier. These local pastors wished "to provide instruction to persons of the Baptist denomination who showed evidence of personal piety and call to the gospel ministry."[12]

From the outset, the New Yorkers envisioned an institution which would provide pastors for destitute churches plus others who would pioneer new mission congregations. While their field was upstate New York, the Hamiltonians looked to wealthy entrepreneurs in the city of New York for their support.[13]

The pattern of regional education societies continued to evolve with the formation of state conventions. In 1821 when the first convention was created in South Carolina, an auxiliary society was formed for education which had the unstinting support of the eminent Richard Furman. In 1831 Ohio Baptists form-ed a group which would create a frontier manual labor school for the training of ministers.[14] Similar to the Massachusetts model which focussed upon sup-port for ministerial candidates, Connecticut, Rhode Island and New Jersey churches all ratified education societies by 1835. This was to be the means by which Baptists recruited and supervised young ministers prior to the coalescence of institutions.

Collegiate Education—The First Step

It was inevitable that societies created to support candidates should themselves move to establish institutions. There were essentially three reasons for this metamorphosis: (1) the society trustees tended to favor certain outstand-ing tutors; (2) institutions became tangible entities worthy of support; (3) in-stitutions fulfilled a larger regional and socio-cultural agenda for the denomination.

Among the first specifically collegiate institutions which Baptists founded were the College of Rhode Island (1764), Georgetown College, KY (1829), Mercer University, GA (1833), Acadia College, N.S. (1839) and Richmond Col-lege, VA (1840). In each case, the trustees or founders looked to a single Bap-tist clergyman to give shape to the dream. At the beginning of what became Brown University, the Philadelphia Association chose a twenty-four year old recent graduate of Princeton, James Manning, to be principal, tutor, dean and president of their school in Warren, Rhode Island. Manning's first "class" was a group of five men who lived with him in a spacious home in Warren where they worked and studied. Similarly, Jeremiah Chaplin, the most popular tutor in the Massachusetts Baptist community, was called from his church at Danvers to be president and sole faculty member at Waterville, Maine in 1818. William Staughton, who had started a theological school in his parsonage in Philadelphia for five to seven young men, was asked to assume the presidency at Columbian in 1821 and later at Georgetown in 1829. This pattern evolved in the South as well, where Wake Forest grew up around Samuel Wait's teaching (formerly of Columbian), Mercer's roots were in Silas Mercer's private school from 1793 to 1796, and Richmond's beginnings were to be found with Robert Ryland of Lynchburg. Not all of these early mentor/pastors were educated in the classical style: Nathaniel Kendrick of the Upper Hudson Valley lacked any formal educa-tion but was the unanimous choice for the position at Hamilton, largely because he knew the domestic mission field and was an unreconstructed Calvinist. Thus a handful of leaders actually created the entire foundation of denominational colleges primarily for the education of ministers.[15]

There can be little doubt that a tangible program with a faculty, campus, library, etc., attracted more attention that a scholarship fund. Trustees, for instance, took proprietary ownership of land and buildings. A promoter of Waterville College observed that "the fertility of the soil in this section of the country cannot fail to afford...a plentiful supply of the necessities and comforts of life."[16] The Board of Hamilton Institution purchased a large farm for their campus and at once developed a site plan with a scheme to interest wealthy Baptist merchants in selecting a name for the buildings.[17] The greater the reputation of the founding president, the more likely the chances of financial success. William Staughton, for instance, was said to be the leading pulpiteer of his era with the most elaborate meeting house in the denomination built for his worship services. Luther Rice believed Staughton to be the key to success for Columbian College when he induced Staughton to come to Washington, D.C.

Frequently, much more was at stake than education in raising a college. Rice thought that Baptists would have a *national* opportunity if they could build their school and mission base in the Nation's Capital.[18] Morgan Edwards saw great value in placing a Baptist college in Rhode Island where it would become the principal institution of the colony. The founders of Waterville College believed that a respectable institution on a par with the other colleges in Maine, would advance the Baptist reputation greatly in that Commonwealth. An outstanding accomplishment among all the institutions was the founding of Acadia College. It represented a valiant struggle against the Anglican Establishment where Baptists across the province of Nova Scotia sounded a note for complete religious freedom in education. To make their point certain, a Baptist Board elected a third principal for the school, Edward Blanchard, who was a Presbyterian.[19]

Baptist collegiate education was based on the eighteenth century tradition of a heavily classical program designed for clergy and lawyers. Insofar as clergy were concerned, the assumption was that generalist community leaders needed a broad exposure to the history of classical civilization, the discipline of language arts and well-developed skills of elocution and debate. A modest amount of biblical study and ethics was added to the baccalaureate degree to meet the demands of the clergy trustees.

At the College of Rhode Island, entering students were expected to have a complete command of the Latin language, having mastered Virgil and Tully, two authors of intermediate difficulty. In Greek, each freshman was to be able to read and grammatically analyze the New Testament. When many students fell short of these qualifications, Manning felt obliged to institute a grammar school preparatory to collegiate studies.[20]

The classical tradition continued to dominate the college curriculum. Manning and his first tutor, David Howell, covered the advanced Latin writings of Horace, Cicero and Lucian; in Greek, Homer and Xenophon were the rule. By the third year the class was introduced to French and Hebrew grammar. So great was the emphasis upon languages that students were challenged to converse in Latin and their commencement exercises exhibited their skills in debate, oration and pronunciation before large congregations of hearers.[21]

Studies under Manning were rounded out with the most advanced textbooks of the day in English. Students mastered Bolingbroke's *Remarks on the History of England* (1743), Hammond's *Algebra*, Isaac Watts' *Logick, Or the Right Use of Reason in the Enquiry After Truth* (1747), Benjamin Martin's *Philosophia Britannica* (1747), and Guthrie's geography,[22] accompanied by readings in surveying and navigation. (Geography was the cutting edge of scientific inquiry along with chemistry and electricity in the Revolutionary Era). Completing the requirements were readings in Philip Doddridge's *Lectures on The Rise and Progress of Religion in the Soul* (2745) and Francis Hutcheson, *A Short Introduction to Moral Philosophy* (1747).

Although Manning was available for tutorial work in biblical studies and theology, as time went on, he devoted his energies more to the liberal arts and sciences and institutional promotion. While no one could fault the quality of the classical approach or its contemporary social, scientific and political values, Baptist churches found that the collegiate program was inadequate in practical experience and biblical studies necessary to their ministry. Relatively speaking, fewer than 25% of the graduates between 1764 and 1825 actually entered the Baptist ministry.

It was in the Baptist community of the Southern states that the collegiate model blossomed more quickly and directly than in the North. When Columbian College encountered financial exigency in the 1820s, most of the states formed education societies with plans to develop academies or colleges. A few, like Richmond and Furman, embarked upon a course combining theological and classical studies in separate programs; most determined rather quickly that pre-theological or collegiate education was more appropriate. Georgetown, Mercer, Richmond and Wake Forest all developed baccalaureate degrees on a modified classical plan to meet the needs of their regions. The most significant modification from the eighteenth century model was less dependance upon Latin and Greek. Texts were chosen from English authors and modern languages like French were offered on a Latin grammar foundation. Scientific and technical courses also frequently replaced the former heavy stress upon history and rhetoric. Baptist colleges in the West and South also offered manual labor and agricultural experiences as a means of financial assistance for students from modest socio-economic backgrounds.

Literary and Theological Institutions

A combination of high admission standards, inadequate practical divinity and the rapid growth of the Baptist movement from 1800 to 1815 necessitated a new approach to ministerial training. A hybrid called the literary and theological institution (L&T) was the result. These schools fulfilled the expectations of some that colleges would be more palatable to state legislatures which issued charters, while also meeting the needs of the churches for new leadership. The plan for the Maine Literary and Theological Institution (later Colby College) was the vanguard, and it reflected all of these realities.

Maine's frontier, with a growing number of revivalist-centered Baptist churches, was the context for a bold experiment. Leading pastors in the territory saw the need for localized theological studies, yet realized that the pressing need of the region was a system of academies and a college. In fact, there was strong opposition in the legislature to a Baptist school, many fearing a sectarian outpost which would threaten the Congregationalist system. Against high odds, a charter was granted for a school at Waterville which would benefit primarily those who were "desirous of engaging in the learned professions" and secondarily the gospel ministry, "open to every religious sect." The proponents justified the wedding of divinity with literary studies by observing that

> in a (seminary) where many are truly pious, the rest can hardly fail of being overawed and may be expected to refrain from the many vices into which their unhallowed passions would otherwise hurry them. Associating daily with those who pay a sacred regard to the precepts of the gospel, they can hardly fail to impose a restraint on their words and actions. Parents who intend to give their sons a classical education should be excited to patronize an Institution, the plan of which is so eminently adapted to promote morality and piety as well as to facilitate the acquisition of useful knowledge.

Although a charter was drafted in 1813, the grand design for Waterville would wait until 1818 and the close of hostilities in the War of 1812.

For a founding professor, the trustees were led to a highly qualified candidate, already engaged in tutoring ministerial students: Jeremiah Chaplin (Brown, 1799) of First Baptist Danvers, Massachusetts. In 1818 Chaplin had seven students living with him, similar to his own theological training pattern earlier with Thomas Baldwin in Boston. Chaplin and the trustees in Waterville were able to persuade the Massachusetts Baptist Education Society to agree to a merger of Chaplin's theological students with the new school at Waterville on the basis that Maine and Baptist missions there were logically and politically related to Massachusetts.[23]

During the first seven years of the Main L&T's history, Chaplin built a strongly classical program with a ministerial course which stressed theological readings and biblical exposition. Pressure from the trustees eventually forced the modification of the program to create baccalaureate and master of arts degrees and to remove all denominational restrictions from the trusteeship. Prior to the advent of the new entity called Waterville College, a total of fifteen students completed the theological course. After a successful term as president-fundraiser and pastor of the Waterville Baptist Church, Chaplin returned to the full-time pastorate in Massachusetts, his energy depleted from his far-ranging responsibilities.

A second fertile ground for the L&T model was in Hamilton, New York. There, the intention of the founders was to provide prospective ministers with "the whole amount of instruction in the classics and the higher branches of English and mathematics, as well as theological studies, which their profession might require."[24] Almost from the beginning, President Kendrick and his colleagues recognized both the deficiencies of entering students and the high interest in the school by persons who had no inclinations toward ministry. Their response was to invent several tracks or courses, totalling eight-years duration, including a preparatory department, a collegiate course, a theological course and an English course. The Hamilton Literary and Theological Institution was perhaps the most open and flexible program available to the denomination between 1819 and 1833.[25]

What emerged in 1833 out of the experimentation at Hamilton was a four year course of literary and scientific studies which in 1846 was given university status. Although the trustees of the Baptist Education Society of New York continued to support theological instruction, by 1833-34 there were no students enrolled in that track.[26] Rather than remain at Hamilton for post-graduate studies, several of the graduates of the classical course actually went on for ministerial studies at either Newton or Andover Seminaries. In the face of such evolving realities, two schools were created in 1846 on the campus that was to become Colgate University: Madison University and the Theological Seminary at Hamilton.

Columbian College was the least successful of the literary and theological models. From the beginning, an unhappy union of a theological school from Philadelphia and a college from the Nation's Capital, plus an unworkable integration of a church-related college and a government-supported national university, Columbian was also doomed by regional and economic strains. Baptists in the South wanted a strong college and the James Monroe Administration was willing to grant a charter. Luther Rice and William Staughton favored a theological emphasis; Rice even urged a law school and medical college. When a national recession occurred in 1821 and a series of real estate ventures failed to produce needed income for the college, theological studies were discontinued, the law and medical schools were closed, the General Baptist Missionary Convention lost confidence in the venture and Columbian closed for a time. Perhaps most damaging was the loss of President Staughton who resigned to take the presidency of Georgetown College in Kentucky, an institution of the classical/collegiate tradition. When it reopened in 1829, Columbian became a partly public liberal arts college serving the District of Columbia.[27]

Other attempts were made to establish combination literary and theological institutions, notably Furman Academy and Theological Institution in South Carolina, Wake Forest Institute in North Carolina, Granville Literary and Theological Institution in Ohio, Michigan and Huron Literary and Theological Institute in Michigan, and Acadia University in Nova Scotia. In the latter instance, Baptists had started a dissenter academy which offered scattered theology courses for advanced students from 1829 to 1838. Much of the early curriculum was designed by Edward A. Crawley who studied carefully the plan at Waterville College in Maine. Crawley persuaded Irah Chase of Newton and Alexis Caswell (Brown, 1822) to visit Halifax to assist in the formation of the Nova Scotia Baptist Education Society and to advise on the academy program. Caswell urged that the school should broaden its subjects to include general education in order to receive government aid. What became Acadia University probably had the longest tenure as a literary and theological institution, in part due to the Baptist support for serious theological courses and partly because of limited resources and the isolation of the Maritime region with its closely-knit church community.[28]

The importance of the literary and theological institution model for Baptists cannot be overestimated. More than a classical college—in fact too much for practical purposes of limited resources and students—these schools sought to meet evolving needs in a rapidly changing frontier society and religious denomination. Although led by some of the ablest theologians, the theological studies were always secondary to the literary and scientific which most students preferred. Moreover, most Baptists still sought a shorter route to the ordained ministry. Gradually these institutions naturally evolved into church-related colleges and universities.

Birth of Theological Seminaries

As noted earlier, most Baptist candidates for ministry lacked even a long-term secondary school education well into the nineteenth century. Thus the first step in developing an adequate educational plan was to provide for collegiate studies. The vast majority of ordinands prior to 1920 possessed a baccalaureate degree or less, even with over 100 colleges in the denominational family. Post-graduate seminary studies would be reserved for a few qualified students who typically moved into significant pastorates, missionary service or educational ministries.

In the late eighteenth century American context, the word "seminary" could be applied to a variety of institutions, including preparatory schools, public academies, female institutes and theological schools. In the latter instance, "seminaries" focussed upon professional religious education and did not offer degrees of any kind until the 1880s. In some cases, theological programs were little more than clusters of clergy who served on a college faculty and also taught some of the general education or language courses.

The first formal attempt at a discrete theological education program in the Baptist family was William Staughton's School in Philadelphia. Staughton and Irah Chase (Andover, 1807) with the generous sponsorship of the Baptist Education Society of the Middle States and the General Baptist Missionary Convention, commenced classes in 1818 in a venture which Chase described as "a general school, sacred to the gospel ministry."[29] Richard Furman and Luther Rice expected this beginning to supply both pastors for U. S. churches and candidates for the foreign missionary enterprise. From 1818 to 1821 a total of twenty-one students finished the course in Philadelphia before Luther Rice persuaded Staughton to move the program to Washington, DC where it would be merged with Columbian College's baccalaureate degree in the literary and theological school model. Unfortunately, Staughton's pioneering efforts did not materialize into a permanent theological institution largely due to the overarching concerns discussed earlier.

Theological education in America itself became much more highly focussed in 1807 with the founding of Andover Theological Seminary by the Congregationalists. Partly as a reaction to Harvard's Unitarianism, partly a new concept in post-collegiate studies, Andover became a model for virtually every other theological school by mid-century. Given the fact that a number of prominent Baptists attended Andover, including Luther Rice and Adoniram Judson, it is not surprising that Baptists adopted the model for their own purposes.

Briefly described, the Andover plan was developed by the first professor, Eliphalet Pearson (Harvard, 1790). He envisioned a three year residential program where students would specialize in one area each year and live and work together with a resident, ordained faculty. The chief difference at Andover was the requirement of a baccalaureate degree which laid the foundation for advanced studies. Distinguished professors, like Leonard Woods, Moses Stuart, and Edward Griffin, could then intensify a student's effort and provide the maximum intellectual experience before taking a church.[30]

In the years from 1807 to 1825, while only twenty of Andover's graduates were Baptist, the pattern was set in New England. When prominent Boston area pastors Thomas Baldwin and Joseph Grafton determined in 1825 to strengthen preparation for the ministry, it was the Andover model which they imitated rather than the literary and theological institute or classical/collegiate traditions. Newton Theological Institution thus became in 1826 the first Baptist theological seminary; its program was designed by Irah Chase (Andover, 1817) and predicated upon a bachelor of arts degree. Chase understood well the new direction, from his work at Columbian and his familiarity with Hamilton, as he opted for the graduate model. The combination within New England of Brown as an undergraduate college, plus Newton as a professional school, gave Baptists as complete and vigorous a program for ministerial education as any Christian group in the United States.

Other New Englanders soon followed Newton's example. At New Hampton, New Hampshire, a theological department grew out of an English language academy and flourished for about a decade, providing pastors for several thousand Baptists in the state. E. B. Smith, a Newton graduate, and J. Newton Brown (Hamilton, 1823) built a four year program which combined classical subjects with biblical theology, exegesis and pastoral care. Because the demand for immediate placement in churches was so great, the New Hampton Institution eased its classical requirements in favor of intensified theological studies by 1838.[31]

The story of the evolving Baptist institution at Hamilton, New York also deserves careful attention in this context. After Newton's founding in 1825, President Nathaniel Kendrick and the faculty at Hamilton recognized the need for a separation of programs in the literary and theological tradition and began to refer to the ministerial course as the "theological department" in 1833. Eventually, when the Hamilton Institution was transformed into Madison University in 1846, the theological department became a post-graduate program on the Newton plan and the second graduate Baptist theological school in America was born as the Hamilton Theological Seminary. The school continued to accept many students without a bachelor's degree, however, owing to the needs of its missionary context.[32]

The content of Baptist theological education was dominated by biblical studies. Each institution had to determine on the basis of prior qualifications in linguistic facility, upon what basis instruction would be given. For students who had a strong classical collegiate education, the original languages were the norm. For those who entered professional studies directly or those who had a weak background in Latin and Greek, an English course was developed. In William Straughton's school, students worked primarily with textual interpretation and sermon preparation, modelling Staughton's own renowned style which he doubtless learned at Bristol. Public exams were given on various subjects of biblical theology such as "the character and offices of the Holy Ghost."[33]

In contrast at Newton, students spent their first year in the study of Hebrew and Greek, supplemented by lectures in biblical geography, harmony of the gospels, and New Testament interpretation. In the second year, further work in Chaldee (Aramaic) was expected, together with Jewish history, introductory issues for both testaments, Hebrew prophecy and the Messianic literature. Hamilton's program, after 1835, was blessed with the services of Thomas Jefferson Conant who stressed linguistic evidence for theology and the necessity of general "Oriental" studies which amounted to comparative Semitic work.

Theology, historical studies and practical courses completed the first curricula. In Newton's plan, seniors focussed on Christian apologetics and systematic analysis of biblical doctrines with particular attention to historical theology. Church or Ecclesiastical History was usually treated by theologians until after mid-century when librarians frequently doubled in the field. Of all the practical work, the preparation and delivery of sermons was foremost from the original Andover plan where a chair had been endowed in Sacred Rhetoric. Not only were sermons written and critiqued by the class each week, students also made presentations demonstrating their elocution at the commencement exercises. Pastoral theology was a generic term covering guest lectures from local pastors and visiting specialists who spoke to visitation, church administration, the ordinances and polity.[34]

Of the three areas of study across the three year model—biblical, systematic and pastoral theology—it appears that the professors of systematic theology were the dominant figures. It was the task of the sytematician (usually the president) to organize the study of theological subjects into a usable whole—in short to add structure to the educational plan. At Newton, Irah Chase emphasized biblical evidences of classic doctrines such as the trinity, the authority of the bible, ethics, and evangelism. His goal was to "awaken the efforts of a genuine disciple of Christ and lead him to search the Scriptures."[35] In contrast, Professor Kendrick at Hamilton used the classical theologians of the Reformation in an interrogative lecture style which stressed the bible as divine revelation. Kendrick also stressed a quiet, studied, simple preaching style which avoided the excesses of New School revivalism.[36]

It is evident from the priority placed upon original language study, historical theology and a critical approach to pastoral work, that the design of the postgraduate seminary program was to produce a sophisticated ministry. For the most part, those who endured six to seven years of studies were rewarded with significant roles in the churches and denominational institutions. A few, however, felt that seminary work delayed their entry into the church and fatigued their constitutions; they frequently elected to leave seminary before finishing the course. And, of course, the vast majority of Baptist ministers in the nineteenth century were still overwhelmed by serious study and remained self-taught, usually through the published writings of the seminary professors and older classic divines reaching back to John Gill.

Conclusion

In little over a half century, Baptists in America progressed in their concepts and plans for ministerial education from a tutorial or self-taught system to a network of colleges and theological seminaries. Like other Christian groups, Baptists experienced rapid growth and inadequate models. The late eighteenth and early nineteenth centuries thus were a period of experimentation and continual modification.

Not only were Baptist leaders concerned with educational content, but also with form and structure. Funding and church relationships had to be organized and established before institutional advancement. Here the Baptist proclivity to voluntary societies was of paramount importance.

Various models of education in other countries and religious denominations were important to Baptists. The most attractive models were Princeton, Bristol, Waterville and Andover, all of which blended into the major streams of Baptist institutional life. The literary and theological school tradition was especially useful, for it served as a laboratory in which to test the integration of professional and classical education. In many ways the L&Ts enabled Baptists to develop a philosophy of church-related higher education.

A relatively small group of dedicated and intellectually keen individuals masterminded the development of Baptist ministerial education in this era. Men like Manning, Chaplin, Kendrick, Staughton, Chase, Mercer and Wait drew upon their own experiences and their theological commitments to the integration of faith and learning to erect lasting contributions in Christian education. They were indeed "giants in the land" who cast long shadows into the future.

The Baptist achievement in ministerial education is all the more significant when one considers the opposition to formal education which was a part of the "life in the Spirit" which energized the denomination. As one leading Baptist preacher put it,

"Nothing gives me greater pain than to hear education spoken of as the first consequence in regard to our rising ministry, while the work of the Spirit is...is put down as of secondary or inferior importance...Oh, I don't object to the Latin, the Greek and the Hebrew, but let them be placed at the feet of Jesus, and not inscribed, as by Pilate, over his head."[37]

William H. Brackney is Professor of the History of Christianity at Eastern Baptist Theological Seminary, Philadelphia, Pennsylvania, USA.

Endnotes

1. Edmund Chillenden, *Preaching Without Ordination* (London: George Wittington, 1647), p.2. Chillenden was likely a General Baptist.

2. Most early Baptists in the Puritan Tradition were Cambridge graduates as this list testifies.

3. Backus was the major political theologian and historian of Baptists in New England; Hezekiah Smith was the leading New Light evangelist from Massachusetts to Northern New England, who distinguished himself in the Revolution; Elias Smith was a New Light Separate who started the first magazine devoted to free thought; Benjamin Randall founded the Freewill Baptist movement and Shubal Stearns took the Great Awakening among Baptists to the South.

4. Edwards and Staughton were the links with English Baptist education and held high standards for theological studies. Edwards was less influential in curricular and institutional design than was Staughton. Callendar's ordination was an event of singular importance because it symbolized the maturing of the sect in New England, and its recognition by the Standing Order.

5. Unfortunately only diaries and hints suggest precisely how this process worked. This was a method long used by Congregationalists for college graduates and others, as in the case of Jonathan Edwards who interned with his grandfather, Solomon Stoddard of Northampton, Mass.

6. In Vermont (Shaftesbury Association), Massachusetts (the Missionary Society) and New York (associations and missionary groups) itinerant evangelistic teams worked during the summer months beginning about 1798 in upstate New York, Lower Canada and northern New England. See my article, "Yankee Benevolence in Yorker Lands: Origins of American Baptist Home Missions", *Foundations* (Dec., 1981).

7. For the London project, consult *Origin and Design of the Particular Baptist Fund* (London: Perkins, Bacon and Company, 1887), p. 2; a note on the General Baptists is found in *Minutes of the General Assembly of the General Baptist Churches in England, 1654-1728*, edited by W. T. Whitley, Vol. I (London: Kingsgate Press, 1908), p. 95.

8. Norman S. Moon, *Education for Ministry: Bristol Baptist College 1679-1979* (Bristol: The College, 1979), pp. 1-3.

9. Ibid. pp. 11-13; a society was established in London in 1752 but it lacked the structure of its successors; F. A. Cox, *History of the Baptist Missionary Society of England 1792-1842* (Boston: Damrell, 1843).

10. In fact, the entire denominational fabric called the General Missionary Convention of the Baptist Denomination in the United States for Foreign Missions was essentially a voluntary society: see William H. Brackney, *The Baptists* (Greenwood Press, 1988), pp. 79-84.

11. "Constitution of the Baptist Education Society of the Middle States, America" *Baptist Missionary Magazine*, Vol. II, pp. 211-13.

12. "The Baptist Education Society of the State of New York: in Ibid. Vol. III, pp. 9-10.

13. The trustees of the BESSNY were aware of a group in new York City called the New York Baptist Theological Seminary which had no school, but generous support from families like William Colgate. Eventually, the upstate group absorbed the New York City folk.

14. *Annual Report of the Meeting of the Ohio Baptist Education Society and of the Trustees of the Granville Literary and Theological Institution, 1832.*

15. On Manning, see Reuben A. Guild, *Life, Times, and Correspondence of James Manning* (Boston: Gould and Kendall, 1864) and Walter Bronson, *The History of Brown University 1764-1914* (Providence: University Press, 1914); on Chaplin, Ernest C. Marriner, *The History of Colby College* (Waterville: College Press, 1963); and for Staughton, Irah Chase, "The Theological Institution at Philadelphia, 1818-21", *Baptist Memorial and Monthly Chronicle*, Vol. I, No. 4, pp. 101-06.

16. "An Address to the Public on Behalf of the Maine Literary and Theological Institution May 21, 1819" in Marriner, *Colby College*, appendix I.

17. Howard D. Williams, *A History of Colgate University 1819-1969* (New York: Van Nostrand, 1969), pp. 25-29.

18. William H. Brackney, "Dissenter Religion, Voluntary Associations and the National Vision: Private Education in the Early Republic" *Baptist History and Heritage*, Vol. XVIII, No. 4., pp. 37-40.

19. R. S. Longley, "The Background and Early History of Acadia University, Educational Centre of the Maritime Baptists of Canada", *The Chronicle*, Vol. V, No. 3, pp. 130-31.

20. Again, Manning drew upon his own experience: he had been the first student at Rev. Isaac Eaton's Latin Grammar School in Hopewell, New Jersey, founded in 1756 under the patronage of the Philadelphia Baptist Association. The rigor of Eaton's tutelage had qualified Manning for studies at Princeton College.

21. Guild, *Manning and Brown University*, pp. 304-07; for the dependence upon the Princeton model see Thomas Jefferson Wertenbaker, *Princeton 1746-1896* (Princeton: University Press, 1946), pp. 97-102.

22. William Guthrie's "geography" was actually a thirteen volume contemporary travelogue, *A General History of the World, from the Creation to the Present Times, including all the Empires, Kingdoms and States, their revolution, forms of government, laws, religions, customs and manners...together with their antiquities, public buildings and curiosities of nature and art* (London: J. Newberry, 1764-67).

23. Marriner, *Colby College*, p. 18.

24. This arrangement paralleled the missionary work as the Massachusetts Baptist Missionary Society encompassed the district of Maine in its scope. Maine, of course, was not an independent state until 1820.

25. In defense of the peculiarity of "New York's Zion" and the need to combine liberal arts and theological studies, the historian of Colgate University stated that, "the New England seminaries expected their students on entering to have had a college education or its equivalent..they would set up and maintain these standards because the tradition of a well-educated clergy was, of course, older and stronger in new England than in New York." c.f. Williams, *History of Colgate University*, p. 43.

26. *Catalogue of the Faculty and Students of Hamilton Literary and Theological Seminary 1833-34* (Utica: Bennett and Bright, 1834), pp. 3-6, indicates there were 40 in the collegiate course, 72 in the preparatory course, and 12 in the English course for a total of 124.

27. Brackney, "Dissenter Religion", p. 39. Staughton's health failed and he succumbed en route to Kentucky.

28. Longley, "Acadia College", pp. 128-29; *Memorials of Acadia College and Hor-*

ton *Academy, for the Half Century 1828-1878* (Montreal: Dawson, 1881), p. 88, indicates that in the original minutes for the University there was to be an institution for literary and scientific instruction and a Theological Institute. George E. Levy, *The Baptists of the Maritime Provinces 1753-1946* (St. John: Barnes-Hopkins, 1946), pp. 116-118 states that by 1841 ten men were studying theology among others in law, medicine and general subjects. Theological studies were transferred to a collaborative effort with Toronto Baptist College in 1880, until Acadia again revived its divinity college in the present century.

29. Chase, "Theological Institution at Philadelphia", p. 102.

30. For a complete analysis and history of the Andover Plan, consult Henry K. Rowe, *History of Andover Theological Seminary* (Newton: The Seminary, 1933), pp. 26-27, 40-61.

31. William E. Wording, "Academical and Theological Institution at New Hampton, N.H.", *Baptist Memorial and Monthly Chronicle*, Nov. 1843, pp. 325-331. New Hampton was later merged with the New London (N.H.) Academy.

32. *Seventeenth Annual Meeting of the Baptist Education Society of the State of New York, June 3, 1834* (Utica: Bennett and Bright, 1834), p. 9.

33. Chase, "The Theological School at Philadelphia", pp. 105-106.

34. *Catalogue of the Officers and Students of the Newton Theological Institution 1833,34* (Boston: Lincoln and Edwards, 1834), pp. 18-19.

35. Ibid., p. 8 (1834).

36. Williams, *History of Colgate University*, pp. 42, 51.

37. John Davis, *The Life and Times of Harris Harding* (Charlottetown: 1866), pp. 124, 135.

The Ministry of Women
In the Baptist Churches of the USSR

Heather Vose

In this paper, it is important to understand two things at the outset. First, documentary evidence, for some of the material given here is non-existent; therefore a word is necessary about sources.

I have been dependent to an unusual extent upon oral accounts of experiences, personal memories and general background data from individuals in widely scattered areas of the USSR. These contributors range in age from the very old to the early twenties. Their recollections have been translated by brethren in Moscow, and included a statement from manuscripts held in Tbilisi, Georgia.

Correspondence with a few Soviet sisters, stemming from the time I took on this writing assignment, has provided us with many valuable perceptions and assessments of the ministry undertaken by evangelical Christian-Baptist women in their various republics. In addition, some of the information contained here has been drawn from press releases of the European Baptist Press Service (EBPS); and Sister Vera Kadaeva of the publications department of the All Union Council of Evangelical Christians-Baptists (AUCECB) has sent us a copy of her significantly helpful article "Women's Work in Churches of Evangelical Christians-Baptists and Their Participation in the Life of the Society" (1988).

Secondly, the on-going process of democratization of the Soviet Union is constantly bringing about new developments in church-state relations that are likely to have already expanded the visions and the present ministry of Soviet sisters, even since the preparation of this paper. From an historical viewpoint, the era of *Perestroika* is responsible for enormous change regarding avenues of Christian service—for the sisters as much as for the brotherhood. With the realization, then, that we may be trailing behind events rather than looking backward, let us try to glimpse a panoramic view of Baptist women in the vast land of the USSR.

Perhaps the best method is to recall initially a few general facts, without entering here into a detailed pre-history.

In broad, over-simplified outline, three distinct periods of social change have determined the context of Baptist life. These are as follows:

1. The pre-revolutionary time of hardship in Czarist Russia, when the Orthodox Church was the instrument of persecution, and when Free-Church believers were called "sectants" and unrecognized by the State.

2. The era of the revolution (beginning in October, 1917), when all churches were placed on an equal footing. Baptists gained in freedom in the 1920s; but the next decade brought worse repression than before. Under Stalin (beginning 1919) most leaders were at least imprisoned or exiled, many died, and only two or three Baptist churches functioned in the entire country. The years of World War II saw a temporary alleviation of restrictions and suffering: then by the 1960s the situation deteriorated further, under the harshness of Krushchev's 1959-1964 campaign for the complete eradication of the Church. Brezhnev's ascendancy brought about some normalization of State relationships with the Church; and so began a fluctuation in State policies and religious responses to them that continued into the 1980s. Then came a dramatic change.

3. "Before *Perestroika*," stated one reliable source, "we lived in a psychological ghetto."[1] Bare toleration and lack of many citizen's rights gave way to a new climate of thinking, conceptualized in the word *Perestroika* itself. "When Gorbachev gave the intellectual elite freedom, they spoke in favor of the Church." Thus the last three years have witnessed the appearance and growth of hitherto undreamed-of ministries that encompass all aspects of Church life and involve men, women, young people and children.

One further comment by way of clarification: Evangelical Christians-Baptists mainly embrace Christians of four confessions: Evangelical Christians (Brethren roots), Baptists, Christians of Evangelical Faith (Pentecostalists) and the Mennonite Brethren. The Evangelical Baptist movement goes back about 125 years, rising first in the Caucasus, in the south of the Ukraine, and in St. Petersburg (Leningrad). Uniform structures of women's services have never been the context for their Christian activity. Consequently we must look elsewhere for evidence of their work. It is not hard to find, especially within the milieu of *Perestroika* where Evangelical Christians-Baptists function today. But it is against the historical backdrop of social upheaval, of profound suffering at times and of the loss of almost a whole generation of men in war-time that the women of Soviet churches can be observed. These, "our faithful and courageous ones", as an elderly correspondent from Leningrad described then, have had "clear sight, great patience and hope, in incredibly dark circumstances."[2]

"Believing sisters," declares Kadaeva, "have cooperated with brothers since the very conception of the Evangelical movement. They have been especially successful in proclaiming the Gospel..."[3] We will touch more on this aspect shortly. But there is no doubt that the activities of Soviet Baptist women, without any formal organizational structure, have nonetheless provided them with rich and varied experiences, both within their churches and in their society. Forget now about all the avenues of service that are considered "normal" for women in Baptist churches and examine a few different examples of ministry illustrated in the lives of particular people.

Come back to the last century, to St. Petersburg, where Shuvalova Elena Ivanova (1830-1900) was one of the first believers converted through the preaching of Lord Radstock. Taking advantage of her husband's position as head of police, this sister intervened repeatedly to help persecuted brethren. At times of great need, she pleaded with him to invite influential persons to their home; and over dinner presented the case for a softening of conditions under which arrested brothers were forced to live. She was directly responsible for freedom being granted to some while they were actually on their way to prison. "Sister Shuvalova considered her activities as service for the Lord," concluded the one who gave evidence of this.[4]

Consider Chertkova Elizabeta Ivanovna (1834-1923), known also as Princess E. I. Chertkova. The death of her husband and two young sons brought her to Christ; and she not only arranged for Radstock to begin his ministry in St. Petersburg (1874), but she undertook regular prison visitation in the city, visited the dying, supported the formation and activities of the society for "Encouragement of spiritual and moral readings" (which published evangelical literature), managed sewing workshops for women from poverty-stricken circumstances and built a shelter near her home on Vasilievskii Island for Christian meetings.[5]

The noted Russian writer N. S. Leskov referred to Yulia Zasetskaya, daughter of D. Davydov (prominent guerilla fighter during the Patriotic War of 1812, converted under Radstock) in these words: "She had such a compassion to tribulations of hard-working laborers that she was ready to help anyone. She was the first to build a rest-house in St. Petersburg . . . In short, she was a very kind, well-educated woman and a devout Christian, but she was by no means Orthodox."[6]

Extremes of persecution, exile and suffering created a situation where mothers frequently died from malnutrition, other illness or exhaustion. This left fathers, themselves in precarious circumstances, to care for the children who survived. One unusual avenue of service comes to light in the writings left behind. Baptist sisters, from sometimes faraway places, volunteered to share the exile, to marry the unknown fathers, and to care for the household.[7] One such example is that of Vasilii Gurievich Pavlov, whose wife and children joined him in exile in 1892. Orenburg was a city of hunger, cholera and death; so that "Moslems, Jews, Orthodox believers, sectants appealed to the Lord for mercy..." Pavlov's wife and four out of five children died. Finally "a sister from Petersburg came to us in answer to my letter . . . And on the 2nd of January we had a wedding. One of our local pastors from the village of Gumbet blessed us in the village church that consisted of 40 members."

Another such illustration concerns Pelageia Sazontovna Kapustinskaia (1888-1960), daughter of "sufferer for faith" Sozont Evtiheevich Kapustinskii. Together with her parents she spent time in Girusi—"valley of tears and sorrow, where the Tzarist government sent the evangelical believers." With the death of her mother in 1892 from typhus, the family was in dire straits. When she was four years old, news of her father's illness reached central Russia. A sister accepted this as a call from God and travelled to Girusi to be "wife to unknown ill man and mother to orphan children...she was a real loving mother to them." This four-year-old child herself became a Christian, married Jacob Zhidkov Ivanovich with whom she had 13 children (our brother Michail is one of them) and 52 years of ministry in times of joy and deep sorrow. Her particular service was in prayer, each day setting aside her own hour for being alone with God. She also cared sensitively for those in situations such as she herself had experienced.

In a slightly different vein the story of Slegina Domnikia Grigorievna (1872-1958) emphasizes the fact that not only marriage was involved in the raising of bereft children. This sister, born to a peasant's family of Old Believers in the Samarskii region, lost her sight at age three. Nevertheless she passed all her gymnasium exams and became a teacher. Converted in 1909, she set about translating Christian music and literature for the blind. "During World War II the church of Kuibishev had no leading brothers or sisters. Slegina cared for the believers as a mother. Her house was a shelter for the evacuated people many times . . . She had a daily hour of prayer in her house. Believers prayed much for Christ's Church . . . After the war, the Kuibishev Church, preserved by many prayers, was restored in a short period of time. Slegina worked as a teacher for 38 years . . . After the death of her brother and his wife, she brought up and educated three orphans . . ."[8]

This matter of raising children in the absence of parents has been a recurring problem for Christian women in the USSR. After the Stalinist prohibitions of 1929, many children were sent to State institutions, sometimes as nameless orphans even though parents might still be alive. It was dangerous to take these children into the home - "people were arrested and sentenced to 10 years in prison for sending warm clothes for children" recalls one elderly sister. "But all the same - our Baptist women did the impossible . . ."[9] A number of such instances have been included in letters sent to me. Often, the pastors' children were especially vulnerable; not only them, but clothing for them and for "widows" exchanged hands by night. "And this situation," continues one correspondent, "was really as written; right hand doesn't know what the left is doing . . . They (her parents)kept silence to keep *me* alive, to protect each other from dangerous knowledge.[10]

The same contributor, speaking of the strong prayer life of many Baptist women known to her, spoke also of her mother's death: "Dying, after 12 years of tuberculosis. Church is ruined, friends perished, home is destroyed (by Fascist bomb), all her work gone—she was a teacher in the Bible courses, historian of the church, leader of Christian youth, writer (her beautiful songs of Russia's spiritual awakening were never published) and both her daughters unbelievers . . ." Yet she died strong in faith, concentrating heart and mind only on the Lord at the end. And now? Church life newly revived, both daughters are Christians and active in the fellowship of prayer and community service, and a whole range of options lie before them.[11]

During the Second World War, vegetable growing, soup kitchens and giving shelter to the homeless was the fabric of daily life for Baptist women, as for most others. Some went further: "Another sister didn't have anything, but she had hot water. She gave it in the winter to frozen, dying people and saved some of them." Yet another, only a girl, was at the front, dragging wounded people from the battlefield "and told to everyone—Pray, my dearest; God will help you." These were ministries of survival.[12]

Turning to less traumatic fields, it is clear that women have played a considerable role in both establishing and maintaining new churches, or acting in a pastoral capacity when, for one reason or another, no pastor had oversight of a group. Vera Kadaeva relates the account of M. G. Antonenko, a student at the Bible courses in Leningrad, who in 1924 went to the north of the country to preach to Yakuts and Nentsy. Working with Sister Sukhoteuva in the city of Yakut for two years, they established a fellowship of ten believers.[13] Other women obtained some theological education through Bible courses. Six were among the 50 students who were studying in those conducted by the Baptist Union in Moscow in 1927.[14] While it is true that the Orthodox tradition of a male clergy has affected Baptist thinking, it is also true that there have always been preaching and pastoral opportunities for Baptist women. Today, there are more than 100 churches without pastors in the Russian Republic alone. Women lead and preach, and carry out all duties except for conducting baptisms and communion services, and performing marriages.[15]

In the Moscow Bible school, there are many women in music courses. All who take part, whether men or women, must be approved by the Superintendents and the churches. Since in pre-*Perestroika* times it was forbidden to educate young people in Christian doctrine, the role of mothers, but especially grandmothers, assumed large proportions. A great part of responsibility for spiritual understanding and Christian life rested, and still rests, on the women. This fact is gladly acknowledged by the leadership of the AUCECB.

Furthermore, the literary tradition is strong amongst Baptist women. Going back to the 1920-1926 period of intense activity, when Bible study groups and literary circles were formed (in Irkutsk), the talents and creativity of a long line of writers have been manifested in the Church. Kadaeva points to such sisters as V. A. Ozhevskaya (1896-1983) who wrote over 200 poems - many of them dedicated to the resurrection of Christ and are set to music. Evgeniya Siora, a very elderly writer, has made her mark. And the contemporary poet Lidiya

L. Zhidkova of Moscow is concerned, amongst other themes, about peacemaking.[16]

Even in churches which have pastors, Soviet women participate in many ways. Thus they can be found offering prayers, singing in choirs, playing in orchestras, reading poems. Sisters direct choral music in the Baptist churches of Moscow, Kiev, Novosibirsk, Orel, Nikolaev etc. Though they have no share in church councils, they serve as accountants and treasurers for executive bodies. And some make exceptional contributions to the life of the wider fellowship. One such was Maria Samoilovna Bezhenaru, who was notable in Moldavia and Bukovina, and who died in July 1988 at age 80. Baptized in 1926 in Kishinev, and having graduated from the convervatoire, she worked widely in the field of music, singing and choir organization in Kishinev, Moldavia and Bukovina. She translated Psalms for choral performance from Russian, German and French, and also translated several religious books. The Moldavian fellowship honored her greatly.[17]

Generally, respected older women fulfill the role of deaconesses in Baptist church life by undertaking what may be called an auxiliary ministry. They assume responsibility for the charitable activities within the congregation, they give assistance during baptisms, weddings and funerals (these have always been used as opportunities for evangelism), and make the preparations for Communion. Older deaconesses enjoy considerable respect and have a good deal of authority in Baptist churches.

Before moving on to more recent developments, and seeing the dramatic change that marks new options for the ministry of women, we should note that the first congress of sisters was held in Kiev (1926). The 48 participants considered issues relating to what forms their service could take, for example sick-visiting, care for orphans and aged church members, and help to the needy, both in the fellowship and in the community.[18] Another consultation took place in Minsk, on March 21, 1987. Some thirty ministers' wives participated in the extended council of the Republic of Byelorussia. Also present were Rev. Alexei Bichkov, General Secretary of the AUCECB, and the Deputy Superintendents of Latvia and Byelorussia, Brothers Janis Elisans and A. I. Firisyuk. The theme under discussion was "The role of women in the church." The group approached this topic from three directions: the ministry of women in the church; the ministry of women in the family, and the role and ministry of Christian women in society.[19] The last of these aspects is exercising Baptist women in a new way, in view of the marked social change that is overtaking the church.

Subsequent to this meeting, Baptist churches in the USSR have launched a program of education aimed at helping pastors' wives understand better their role in the continuing ministry of the local congregation. The initiative came from the churches of the Kazakh, SSR, region. The General Secretary of the AUCECB reports that very positive results have emerged from several seminars in that region. These confirm, he says, that "the effectiveness of the pastor's ministry depends on his wife's dedication . . ."[20]

To proceed, now, to some of the recent avenues of service that have opened up as a direct consequence of the social restructuring that became State policy in April, 1985. This means that though the old law prohibiting charitable work still exists, the State has anticipated the new law on freedom of conscience (due at the end of 1989), and encouraged Christians to undertake various forms of social service, which of necessity involves women.

Thus since May 3, 1988, Moscow Baptist Church members have been carrying out a regular visitation program in two geriatric sections of the Kashchenko First Psychiatric Hospital. Sisters care for patients, giving comfort, support and friendship for several hours each day. They render assistance to junior medical staff, and in fact, fulfill any functions they are able to perform. Since October of the same year, two other geriatric wards have been included. About 100 sisters (many of them are younger women) work, four in each of four wards per day, twice a month). This ministry has received widespread recognition in the Soviet Union, with the Medical Director of the hospital, psychiatrist Dr. Vladimir Nicolaivic Kosirev, who commended it in an unqualified manner during a special service to honor this work on September 24, 1988.[21]

Furthermore, in January 1989 a similar work was begun at the Children's City Hospital No. 41 where approximately 25 sisters visit on a regular basis. In both Moscow and Leningrad, special attention is given to crippled adults and children in State care, with many young people from the fellowship helping the women. (TEAR Fund assists with the purchase of specialized equipment for these institutions, and so strengthens the witness of the Christians).[22]

Baptist women are given time each month after the communion service to relate to the Moscow congregation what they are doing. And on February 25, 1988, young girls and boys visited the traumatological ward of the Republican Children's Hospital where children injured during the Armenian earthquake are being treated. The visitors were accompanied by their parents. The youngsters gave a concert, a service was held, the Moscow Church folk orchestra played special music, gifts and children's Bibles were distributed.[23] So it is apparent that this new form of ministry is being interpreted as a way of introducing even young girls to the whole idea of Christian service to the community at large—that is, quite outside the confines of the fellowship of believers. Though it has not yet spread to all parts of the country, there is great interest in its development in many quarters.

The same could be said for the new choral concerts being held in many centers throughout the USSR. These all involve younger women, as choir members, soloists, instrumentalists, etc. Benefit concerts for Armenian earthquake victims have been given by a number of Baptist churches, including those in Syktivkar in the autonomous Republic of Komi (where city authorities and Communist Party leaders were present, and which resulted in invitations from Ministers of Culture to repeat the concerts in ten other cities) and Leningrad. The 75-voice youth choir and 25-member orchestra of the Moscow Baptist Church has undertaken train tours to cities such as Kiev, Kaliningrad, Mitichi, Kalenga, etc. with other engagements ahead.[24] We could go on. A concern has been voiced that greater participation of women should be envisaged when large conferences such as the February 1987 "Christian Responsibility in the Modern

World" gathering are held. To this end, firm proposals were made and cover increased representation of Baptist women at future peace conferences also.[25]

At the same time, it would be misleading to suggest that these avenues of ministry would constitute a major field of Christian service for the Baptist sisters of the USSR. There is still the extremely practical and necessary role for older women especially in the sewing and mending, the care of fatherless families—"and, of course, we take care of our own sick, old people." And many have chosen the way of prayer, according to Kadaeva; regular, intercessory prayer always on an individual, private basis, and sometimes "women of prayer are united in prayer groups in some churches. Their commitment to this work can be compared to the devotion of the prophetess Anna, who never left the temple, but worshipped day and night, fasting and praying (Luke 2:37)."[26]

To summarize, then, while recognizing that there are still many new experiences ahead for Baptist women in the USSR, the fact remains that their contribution to the life of the church has been massive, and their witness astonishing, in the face of sometimes fearful adversity. Sharing prison, exile and death with their brethren, upholding the struggling congregations and giving succor to the wretched, nurturing homeless children, attending to the spiritual needs of Christian and non-Christian alike—and now, rising to fresh challenges of much more public service than ever before, these sisters, young and old, have found ways to minister to both Church and society. This has been repeatedly acknowledged by the leadership in earlier times and in our own day. And the women have themselves travelled a long way from the prohibitions against their meetings and auxiliary activities that were inaugurated by the April 1929 law on religious cults.

The expectations of younger sisters will be quite different from those of their antecedents. It remains to see how history will write *their* story in days to come.

Special Notes

1. You may wonder why there is virtually no mention of women's ministry in the few early publications that deal comprehensively with Baptist churches in Eastern Europe. Even the worth *Baptist Work in Europe* by Charles A. Brooks and J. H. Rushbrooke (1920) omits any references to women or their service, when dealing with the Baltic countries of Lativia, Estonia and Lithuania, or its notes on Russia. Though one reason could be that theirs was a "whistle-stop" tour throughout these countries, the real answer is, simply, that no one was looking at the women's presence with any sort of enquiry in mind. They were *there* and nothing more needed to be said.

2. Re. *Pelageia (Polia) Sozontovna Kapustinskaia*:

This sister's background is of particular interest and importance in the history of Soviet Baptists, and makes clear her own commitment to the ministries of prayer and aid to bereft families. Her father, S. E. Kapustinskii, a Ukranian Bible colporteur, had, in the purge of evangelicals in 1899, been exiled (in iron shackles) to the Trans-Caucasus region. Sent first to the town of Orel, he then was transported under guard to Tiphlis. My documents state: "Most Baptists were exiled in the remotest depths of the Zakavkozie region—the hot valleys where there was fever, to the distant towns and villages located at the very frontier with Persia and Turkey. These families suffered privations...hardships undermined their health. Many sickened and died in Girusi, Dzembrail, Terter, etc...Kapustinskii and his family lived in an old deserted hut about a kilometer from the village. There were six in the family. Sozont, his wife, three boys and a girl" (Pelageia was that girl). Soon Ivan was born...After the mother's death, "Sister Lasotskaia took the baby and nursed him till he was two. Then little Ivan (John) lived with other believers who later adopted him...: (From Tbilisi ms.)

Heather M. Vose is a Lecturer in Medieval History at the University of Western Australia, Austr.

Endnotes

1. Personal comment, Michael Zhidkov, June 16, 1989.
2. Private letter from Sr. Maria Karetoikova, 12/6/89.
3. Kadaeva, Vera, *Women's Work in Churches of Evangelical Christians-Baptists and their Participation in the Life of Society* (Moscow, 1988), 2. 4. MS from Michael Zhidkov brought to Ruschlikon, June 1989.
5. Also in MS form brought to Ruschlikon, June, 1989.
6. Contained in Kadaeva, as above, but extracted from *"Division in High Society"*.
7. Personal comments, Michael Zhidkov, Sergei Nikolaev, Alexi Bichkov, and others; also the examples of individuals that follow are drawn from MS sources brought to Ruschlikon, June, 1989.
8. This story is recounted in the manuscript statements brought to Ruschlikon by Michael Zhidkov, June 1989.
9. Extract from Karetnikova's letter, as above.
10. Ibid.
11. Ibid.
12. Ibid., drawing on another's experience.
13. Kadaeva, op. cit., pp. 2-3.
14. Ibid., p. 3.
15. Personal comment from Michael Zhidkov, but confirmed from many sources, e.g. Kerstin Ruden's notes and observations, Kadaeva paper, area superintendent reports.
16. Kadaeva, op. cit., p. 4; also personal comment by Lidiya Zhidkova, April, 1988, Moscow.
17. *Information Bulletin*, No. 10 AUCECB, Moscow, (1988), p. 2.
18. Kadaeva, op. cit., p. 3.
19. Ibid., p. 6; also *European Baptist Press Service*, May 3, 1988, bulletin from Minsk, USSR.
20. *European Baptist Press Service*, Oct. 14, 1988, Moscow.
21. All information bearing on this activity is drawn from personal comments of

many people, including Michael Zhidkov, Vasile Logvenienko and Alexei Bichkov of Moscow; Kadaeva's paper and comments and reports in the *European Baptist Press Service*, Oct. 14, 1988; and *Information Bulletin* of the AUCECB, No. 3, 1989.

22. This information comes from Ibid. p. 2; from personal comments of Michael Zhidkov and Vasile Logvenienko; and from letters of Sr. Karetrikova, Leningrad.

23. Extracted from the *Information Bulletin* of the AUCECB, No. 3, 1989, and noted also in Michael Zhidkov's personal comments.

24. See reports of *European*, Feb. 8, 1989, p. 4; AUCECB, *Information Bulletin*, No. 10 (1988), p. 4. There are also many personal accounts.

25. AUCECB *Information Bulletin*, No. 3 (1987), pp. 5-6.

26. Letters; but that particular set of quotations from Sr. Karetnikova.

Women of the Southern Baptist Convention

Eljee Bentley

Women are the majority in churches with membership in the Southern Baptist Convention (SBC). Women fill the pews on Sunday morning. They sit at the organ and in the choir. Before the service they will have arranged the flowers and made certain that the offering plates are dusted and polished. If the Lord's Supper is to be celebrated, women will have washed the cups. They will wash them again when the service is over.

Women work in the nursery and in "extended service" or "children's worship," caring for those who might disturb adults in the regular worship service. They teach preschoolers, children, youth, and adult women in Sunday School, Church Training, and in missions education programs. They lead Vacation Bible School and take young people to camps and conferences. They lead the congregation to understand and support the work of the Home and Foreign Mission Boards.

Women cook and serve church suppers and entertain at church socials. They cook for and entertain visiting evangelists, missionaries, and denominational representatives. They make phone calls, visit door-to-door, write post cards and letters. They keep records. If appointed to a committee or a board, they usually serve as secretary and are expected to do whatever work is done between meetings.

Women manage the church's ministries to the larger community. They visit shut-ins and look after the sick. They operate kindergartens and daycare centers for working mothers. They arrange outings for senior citizens and take meals to those who live alone. They run soup kitchens for the homeless, find clothing for the destitute, teach English to those who wish to learn it, and take in refugees.

Women are church secretaries and bookkeepers. They get out the church newsletter and the printed program for Sunday services. They protect the pastor and other professional staff from unwelcome disturbances. They handle the mundane, the details that keep the church operating from week to week.

Women seldom serve in professional positions. Women pastor only 23 of Southern Baptists' 37,286 churches.[1] Some women are employed to direct church education and music programs, but the number is small. In the past, when churches were less affluent, directors of education and music were quite often female. Now, churches that can afford to pay a man (It is assumed that women will work for less money, and they usually do.) hire one. They prefer that he be ordained, and they call him minister of education or music. If they can afford additional staff, they may hire women to direct the activities of children or preschoolers.

It is the rare church that has women deacons. Women serve on other boards and committees, but in few churches do they chair or are they in the majority on any committees or boards with administrative or financial responsibilities. Women can vote in church business meetings, but only the foolhardy have the temerity to express an opinion contrary to those held by the male establishment.

Beyond the local church Southern Baptist women have even less authority. They can be chosen as messengers to associational, state convention, and SBC meetings; but the women so chosen are often the wives, daughters, and mothers of the men the church wants to send. The clear expectation is that each man can control his own women.

Messengers elect men to lead their associations, state conventions, and the SBC. This year messengers to three state conventions—Virginia, District of Columbia, and Hawaii—chose women to lead them, but no one believes that this unusual happenstance betokens a trend. In 144 years those registered at a Southern Baptist Convention have only three times elected a woman to office. Messengers in 1963 chose as vice president Marie Wiley Mathis, in 1976 Myra Gray Bates, and in 1981 Christine Burton Gregory. Of course, the vice presidency is more of an honor than an office. No woman has been elected president. Only once has a woman been nominated: Marie Mathis in 1972.

Messengers elect men to associational, state convention, and SBC committees and boards. In an article printed in the January 1977 *Baptist History and Heritage* Norman Letsinger compared the number of women chosen for SBC committees and boards in 1961 and the number chosen in 1975. He saw a significant increase. "In 1961 women filled 2.5% of all positions, and in 1975 over 7%."[2]

Sarah Frances Anders, Professor of Sociology at Louisiana College, has recently studied the membership lists of both state convention and SBC committees and boards. She found that women's names were most frequent in the middle 1970s: "peak representation was approximately 13%. Women members fell to a bare 8% in the mid-eighties; representation is now back to just under 11%."[3]

In 1974 the Christian Life Commission recommended that at least 20% of the total membership of SBC committees and boards be female, a recommendation the messengers rejected.[4] In 1921 the women themselves had suggested a more ambitious plan, one that would have guaranteed them a substantial number of seats on the Executive Committee and on each board. The Convention referred the matter to a committee for study and, in 1922, refused to accept the committee's watered-down version of the women's plan. The convention used words familiar to women and other groups denied equal opportunities by the establishment: nominations would be made "according to personal qualifications, regardless of sex."[5]

The women of 1921 had been bold. In that year the only women on any SBC committee or board were the president and executive director (the office was then called corresponding secretary) of Woman's Missionary Union (WMU), who served by virtue of their office on a special money-raising committee known as the Conservation Commission. They served because WMU had proved to be successful in raising money for convention causes.[6]

Only in 1918 had the SBC altered its constitution to permit women to be messengers to its annual meetings. Women were admitted as messengers by most of the state conventions and associations before 1900. Prior to 1885 women had not been specifically excluded from SBC meetings. The constitution spoke of "messengers" until that year when two women from Arkansas presented their credentials. Then "messengers" became "brethren."[7]

The women's boldness achieved something. In 1921 one woman was elected. She was named as a local member of the Education Board, a board headed by the husband of the president of WMU. The next year 23 women were nominated, 21 as local members of boards. But the women wanted the more prestigious positions as state convention representatives, and thirteen years later an Arizona woman was elected to represent her state on the Foreign Mission Board.[8]

Not until 1927, however, were women elected to the powerful SBC Executive Committee. They would not have been elected that year had not their sponsors waited until late at night, when most of the convention crowd had left for their beds, to present the women's names. Once elected, they were more easily reelected. Even so, prior to 1946, only four women sat on this committee, one being the executive director of WMU who has been a member by virtue of her office since 1933.[9]

The other two women elected in 1922 were chosen for the committee that would present the WMU report at the 1923 convention. A man continued to chair that standing committee of the SBC until 1938. Since 1940 WMU's officers have presented their own report.[10]

Woman's Missionary Union has sent a report to the Southern Baptist Convention each year since 1888, the year of the Union's founding. The long delay in allowing the women to speak for themselves stems in part from a reluctance to hearing them speak. At Southern Baptist gatherings women sing but rarely talk, at least not from the platform.

Strangely enough, the forebearers of Southern Baptists, the Separate Baptists, were notorious for their women preachers. Their "women prayed and spoke freely in public," scandalizing members of established (Episcopalian) and Regular Baptist congregations. Separate Baptists ordained deaconesses and eldresses as well as women pastors. To quote Leon McBeth, "Baptist women had their most active leadership roles in the South."[11]

But he points out, in an article in the *Baptist History and Heritage*, "After 1800 this freedom diminished."[12] The Separate Baptists had combined with the Regular Baptists. Separate Baptists had arisen out of the Great Awakening, and their evangelistic fervor proved most successful in frontier, backwoods areas. Times changed, and women learned to be silent.

Today's Southern Baptist woman may speak in public, but few are encouraged to do so. On rare occasions a woman is invited to speak from the pulpit on Sunday morning, but in most churches the woman is said to be giving a talk. She is not preaching. After all, even if she is seminary-educated, she is not ordained.

Ordination has become the Southern Baptist weapon of choice. Southern Baptists prevent their seminary-educated women (over 30% of those graduating from Southern Baptist seminaries are female) [13] from holding positions of leadership by depriving them of ordination. Ordination is formal, public recognition of God's call to ministry; it serves as affirmation that one's call is from God; it authorizes the use of one's gifts in response to that call. Southern Baptists refuse to recognize that God calls women to function in any office that requires ordination.

Ordination, in Southern Baptist polity, is a function of the local church. Some local churches have ordained women. In 1964 a North Carolina church ordained Addie Davis, a recent graduate of the nearby Southern Baptist seminary who had accepted a call to pastor an American Baptist church in New England.[14] To date over 500 Southern Baptist women have been ordained.[15]

But those local churches who ordain women or who employ ordained women have not been treated kindly. When the Prescott Memorial Baptist Church of Memphis, Tennessee, called Nancy Hastings Sehested as its pastor, the Shelby County Baptist Association voted the church out of the association.[16] Prescott's experience received more press coverage, but it was not unusual.

The Southern Baptist Convention has never refused to accept a church's credentials on doctrinal grounds, but it has spoken against women's ordination. In 1984 at Kansas City messengers voted that women could serve in all but those pastoral and leadership roles that require ordination. Women were excluded "in order to "preserve a submission God requires because the man was first in creation and the woman was first in the Edenic fall"."[17]

Convention resolutions are not binding on local congregations, but the convention and its boards can and have acted to prevent the employment of ordained women. The Home Mission Board currently refuses pastoral aid to churches that choose to call women. The Foreign Mission Board has refused to appoint as missionaries an Oklahoma couple, both of whom were ordained by the church they served.

Women want to be ordained in order that they may be chosen "according to personal qualifications, regardless of sex", and because Southern Baptists have come to require ordination for the more desirable jobs.

As a matter of fact, women in the SBC are losing professional positions to men. Note these statistics from North Carolina. In 1950, 68% of the ministers of youth and music employed by the Southern Baptist churches in that state were female. In 1980 the percentage had dropped to 16%. The job of director of missions (the employee who directs the work of a Southern Baptist association) used to be open to women. In 1950 15% of North Carolina's associations had women directors, in 1980 5%.[18]

In 1979 Southern Baptists' only female directors of missions were in North Carolina. The official list named six, but only three were still serving when contacted. One had just retired after 25 years. She had been replaced by a man and believed that the current denominational feeling was that director of missions is "a man's position." Associations want an ordained person, a man.[19]

Campus ministry was pioneered by women. By 1966 only 25% of student workers were women; by 1971 the figure was 14%. No state convention employed a woman to head its program; only three had women as associates to the directors. Salaries of female campus ministers averaged $2,000 a year less than their male counterparts.[20]

The most famous Southern Baptist missionary was a woman, Lottie Moon. And missionary service has been and remains an attractive career choice for Southern Baptist women. On the mission field, particularly if the field is in another country, women can perform in many roles they are denied access to at home. When home on furlough, they are the women invited to speak before mixed-sex audiences. They (and their husbands) are Southern Baptist saints.

Of course, Southern Baptist women pay for the right to see their own sex on the mission fields. The boards did not wish to appoint women. The female missionary societies offered their salaries, and since these societies contributed a substantial portion of each boards' budget, the boards saw fit to send women to the fields. The two annual offerings sponsored by Woman's Missionary Union continue to be the major source of income for both the Home and Foreign Mission Boards.

Women, however, constitute a much smaller percentage of Southern Baptists' missionary contingent today than they did 60 years ago. As late as 1953, the executive director of the Foreign Mission Board said the board had 300 husband missionaries, 300 wife missionaries, and 300 single women missionaries. In 1983 the percentage of single women was 7.8%. Among the Home Mission Board's 3,500 appointees in 1984, only 174 women were designated as primary worker.[21] Spouses are appointed as missionaries but may be only peripherally engaged in missionary activities.

The boards claim that they would appoint more women, but they must fill requests from the fields. The people in the areas served by missionaries want evangelists and pastors, ordained persons. They request men. Nonetheless, any interested observer can note how few women are among the professional staff of either board.

A large number of women do work for SBC boards, its associations and state conventions, but they work for low pay and predominantly in non-managerial positions. Baptist Book Stores, a division of the Sunday School Board, once had women managers. From 1969 to 1971 the percentage of female store managers dropped from 71% to 47%. By 1987 it had declined to 24%; only 14 of 58 book stores were managed by women. "In 1985 Southern Baptists had no female college presidents, hospital administrators, (or) directors of children's homes." Only two of their 25 retirement facilities had women directors.[22]

No woman has ever been chief executive of a Southern Baptist state convention or of an SBC board or institution. Few women have made it to division-level management. Reba Sloan Cobb, publisher of a newsletter for Southern Baptist women in ministry, says: "It appears that women reach a level above which they are unable to rise, regardless of education, ability, or calling." She calls this phenomenon the "glass ceiling."[23]

Sarah Frances Anders compared the status of Southern Baptist women with women in other U. S. Protestant denominations for an article in the Winter 1975 issue of *Review and Expositor*. She found that American Baptist women also faced a glass ceiling.[24] And American Baptist women do not have the separate route to fame, if not fortune, open to their Southern Baptist counterparts: The Woman's Missionary Union.

Woman's Missionary Union is an independent auxiliary to the Southern Baptist Convention. It has its own elected board, composed entirely of women, that employs women to manage its affairs. WMU, SBC, and state convention WMUs employ some 200 Southern Baptist women in professional managerial roles. Through the years these jobs have provided women with fulfilling ministries and, on occasion, have served as effective stepping stones to careers in other Southern Baptist arenas. They have given their holders visibility in the otherwise all-male Southern Baptist world.

Southern Baptist women organized Woman's Missionary Union just a few years after their northern sisters organized their missions boards. The other women's boards appointed and sent their own missionaries; they were fully independent. WMU was formed as an auxiliary, a helper to the Southern Baptist Convention and its boards. WMU encouraged the volunteering and sending of missionaries, it raised their support; but the SBC boards employed the missionaries and managed their work. Southern Baptist women adopted a more limited role in the beginning, but they have not lost their separate organization.

In the US 19th and early 20th century women were expected to stay in their place, the home, and play the roles of homemaker, wife, and mother. They managed to redefine their place to include church and local community and their roles to include making the community a fit home and nurturing other people's children. They were allowed to do their own thing so long as they did not interfere with the more serious activities conducted by men.

So American women, Baptist women among them, formed their own missionary organizations. They were phenomenally successful. In nearly every denomination their activity brought missions to the attention of the average churchgoer, inspired missions volunteers, and filled the treasuries of sending boards. The male-dominated denominational structures took notice. Originally, they had rejected female participation. Now, they offered merger. Women would be treated as equals they said.

The Southern Baptist Convention never made this offer to the Woman's Missionary Union. Thus, the union continues as that separate place where women play their separate roles. In the local church, in the association, in the state convention, and at the denominational level WMU offers women the opportunity to follow the Lord's call, to develop and practice their gifts, and to minister among equals.

Through the years WMU has contributed greatly to Southern Baptist life. Its major contributions are in the areas of missions education and stewardship, but it began or helped to begin many other activities that are now carried on by others within the convention. Catherine Allen assembled these lists for the centennial history of WMU.

Activities in Which WMU Was an Innovator

Student ministries on college campuses
Vacation Bible School
Theological education for women
Professional training for religious education
Women serving in church-related vocations
Promotion of tithing
Emphasis on systematic, regular giving
Blacks serving in professional positions
Camping as a means of religious education
Missions as a content area in religious education
Age-graded missions education
Direct missions in one's own community
Social work ministries in the denomination
Study of and action to meet community social problems
Publications in Spanish, Romanian, Korean, Japanese, Chinese
Weekday church activities for children and youth
Financial system that provides major avenues of revenue for the Home and Foreign Mission Boards
Use of nonsalaried volunteers in missions work
Systematic prayer plan for daily devotions
Education of missionaries' children
Women speaking at SBC meetings and holding SBC office

Activities in Which WMU Assisted or Was One of the Innovators

Cooperative Program (program through which members of local churches support their state conventions and SBC boards and committees)
Local church budgeting and collecting processes
Age-graded religious education: from bed babies through senior adults
Correlation and coordination of church programs
Recruitment of missionaries
Use of radio and film for promotion and education[25]

Only a minority of Southern Baptist women belong to WMU. The majority of churches have organizations, but in each church only some women choose to participate. Women who are in WMU and those who are not may be equally active in other church programs. In both groups are women who are Sunday School teachers, choir members, visitation coordinators, even deacons.

Some Southern Baptist women do not like WMU. Some believe it too feminist, and they prefer a male-dominated world. Others do not like it because of its separate status. They want to be accepted as equals in the regular structures.

Anne Davis, who is a friend of Woman's Missionary Union, made a plea in the issue of *Review and Expositor* devoted to women and the church. In a piece entitled "Liberation, Not Separation" she pointed out that churches fall into cultural patterns of male-female identifications and assign tasks according to sex. She urged Southern Baptists to adopt the biblical concept of relationship: a "unity in freedom" that allows men and women "the possibility of being free to choose to share (their) gifts to actualize a community of faith under God."[26]

Anne Davis' plea is echoed by many women, but in the real world cultural patterns are the norm. Even when the rules say "according to personal qualifications, regardless of sex," women know they do not have equal opportunities. And in the Southern Baptist Convention they are once again hearing the words they have heard through the centuries: "It's in the Bible."

Eljee Bentley is Archivist for the Woman's Missionary Union of the Southern Baptist Convention, Birmingham, Alabama, USA.

Endnotes

1. Sarah Frances Anders, "Has a Generation Really Passed," *Folio*, Summer 1989, p. 5.

2. Norman Letsinger, "The Status of Women in the Southern Baptist Convention in Historical Perspective," *Baptist History and Heritage*, January 1977, p. 44.

3. Anders, op. cit.

4. Letsinger, op. cit.

5. *Annual*, Woman's Missionary Union (WMU), 1921, pp. 10-11; *Annual*, Southern Baptist Convention (SBC), 1921, pp. 66-67, 70, 109; *Annual*, SBC, 1922, pp. 32-33; see also *Annual*, WMU, 1922, p. 27.

6. *Annual*, SBC, 1921, pp. (3)-(12); see Also Catherine Allen, *A Century to Celebrate* (Birmingham: 1987), pp. 125-129.

7. See Leon McBeth, *Women in Baptist Life* (Nashville: Broadman, 1979), pp. 107-112.

8. See Catherine Allen, op. cit., pp. 308-313.

9. Albert McClellan, *The Executive Committee of the Southern Baptist Convention* (Nashville: Broadman, 1985), pp. 131-132; *Annual*, SBC, 1933, pp. 42-43.

10. *Annual*, SBC, 1922, p. (11b); *Annual*, SBC, 1937, pp. 68, 8; *Annual*, SBC, 1939, pp. 62, 8; *Annual*, SBC, 1940, p. 102.

11. Leon McBeth, op. cit., pp. 42-46.

12. Leon McBeth, "The Role of Women in Southern Baptist History," *Baptist History and Heritage*, January 1977, p. 4.

13. Reba Sloan Cobb, "The Glass Ceiling," *Folio*, Summer 1989, p. 2.

14. Addie Davis Oral History, WMU Archives.

15. Reba Sloan Cobb, op. cit., p. 2.

16. Sehested/Prescott materials, Southern Baptist Women in Ministry Collection, WMU Archives.

17. Bill Stancil, "Divergent Views and Practices of Ordination Among Southern Baptists Since 1945," *Baptist History and Heritage*, July 1988, p. 46.

18. Carolyn Blevins, "Patterns of Ministry Among Southern Baptist Women," *Baptist History and Heritage*, July 1987, p. 43.

19. Eljee Bentley, "Meet Some Women Directors of Missions," *Associational Administration Bulletin*, June-July 1979, pp. 6-7.

20. Sarah Frances Anders, "Woman's Role in the Southern Baptist Convention," *Review and Expositor*, Winter 1975, p. 36.

21. Catherine Allen, op. cit., pp. 176, 179, 183.

22. Carolyn Blevins, op. cit., pp. 43, 47.

23. Reba Sloan Cobb, op. cit., p. 2.

24. Sarah Frances Anders, "Woman's Role," p. 39.

25. Catherine Allen, op. cit., pp. 359-360.

26. Anne Davis, "Liberation, Not Separation," *Review and Expositor*, Winter 1975, pp. 63-68.

Towards a Baptist Identity: A Statement Ratified by The Baptist Heritage Commission in Zagreb, Yugoslavia July, 1989

Preamble

This statement on Baptist identify was produced by the Commission on Baptist Heritage as a working document for the 1986-90 Quinquennium and arises out of a brain-storming exercise at their Singapore meeting. It is deliberately intended to be a *descriptive* rather than a *credal* statement, and it is recognized that there may well need to be flexibility in translation for use in particular local situations.

The Scriptures

Baptists start with the Scriptures, which afford us God's self-revelation, first in the unfolding of a concern for His People, but supremely in the life, death and resurrection of Jesus Christ. The Scriptures, as related by the Holy Spirit to our contemporary situation, are our authority in all matters of faith and practice.

What is the Gospel?

Men and women everywhere are alienated from God and from the world as God designed it. The Biblical word for this is Sin, which the Bible says is so serious that we cannot remedy this condition ourselves: there must be a radical new start which, in John 3, Jesus calls the "new birth". The first word of the Christian gospel must always be Grace: not what we aspire to do but what God has done for us without any claim or work on our part. The grace of God, expressed in the crucifixion of Jesus Christ, makes possible the restoration of the relationship with God that sin has spoiled. But this grace which is God's free gift to all of us, like every other gift, has to be received or accepted for its purpose to be secured. This is the response that the Scriptures call Faith: a free, total and unconditional entrusting of our lives to Almighty God. We are invited to put our trust in Jesus Christ because, in Him, God has reached out to touch our sinful humanity.

Clearly this is an action that no one can take for anyone else;- each individual must make a free and unfettered response for him/herself. Equally clearly, that act of trust must involved an intention to obey God's declared will, for unless this be so, the word trust is evacuated of all possible meaning and effectiveness.

What is the Church?

Unlike many others, Baptists do not define the church in terms of structures of ministry or by the regular celebration of the ordinances. Rather, they believe that as individuals come to put their trust in God and confess Christ as Saviour and Lord, (which they believe to be the scriptural conditions for baptism) so the church is created. This is why they have been advocates of what has been called the Believers' Church or the Gathered Community (of believers gathered out of the world). From this conviction as to the nature of the church as constituted by believers covenanting together in common confession of the name of Jesus, it is seen that their practice of confining baptism (by immersion) to believers only, is entirely logical.

A local church so constituted represents in any place the church in that locality; it is fully the church, not a branch of some national or wider institution. Under the Lordship of Christ and before the open Scriptures, it is competent, when properly summoned, in church meeting to govern itself, to determine a strategy for mission in its locality, and to appoint its ministers (deacons and pastors) and other officers. These officers will serve its interests and execute its will in matters pastoral, educational and practical, but the first authority for all decision-making in a Baptist church must remain the whole church meeting.

Baptist churches reject all state interference in their activities. Each local church is free, and indeed duty-bound by the concerns of the gospel, to enter into covenant relationship with other Christians, both nationally and locally. In Baptist life, relationships have traditionally been in associations, conventions and unions, in support of missionary work at home and abroad, and internationally through the Baptist World Alliance.

Baptists ordain men, and in some, but not all parts of the family, women to the Ministry of the Word, and expect their ministers to be respected for their sacred calling. The witness and service of the church is not seen by Baptists, however, as exclusively the work of the ordained ministry but as inclusively the responsibility of the whole membership.

Most Baptists find no difficulty in a lay person celebrating at the Lord's Table or in the Baptismal Pool, ordinances which are seen by Baptists as symbolic of the death and resurrection of Jesus, and of each believer's identification, by faith, with Him, in both dying to sin and rising to new life in Him. This same Christocentric gospel is preached from Baptist pulpits Sunday by Sunday, for proclamation retains a central place in Baptist worship.

What is Discipleship?

Personal commitment is the starting point for every Christian, yet all need to discover the corporate dimension of the church: in common worship, in generous giving to fellowship needs, and in loyal participation in the mission of the local church.

Baptists are an evangelistic people who have always been committed to sharing their faith, to the extension of the church, and for the last two hundred years to overseas missions as well. In the name of their Lord they have given themselves to the care of the needy and oppressed. Increasingly in the twentieth century (although also in earlier times), they have seen the need to speak and act prophetically, denouncing structural evil wherever it puts God's "Shalom" at risk. Opposed to everything that denies the rule of Christ, some even suffer imprisonment and martyrdom for their steadfast witness, imposing an obligation on all the family to support them in both prayer and action.

Recognizing the vast demands of Christian witness and discipleship, Baptists have always been a praying people, in both corporate prayer and in encouraging a pattern of individual spirituality that requires each church member to engage in regular prayer and Bible study, for the whole of Scripture rather than any abstracted creed is for Baptists the determinant alike of corporate belief and individual action.

Because Baptists delay baptism until an individual has made a personal confession of faith, they are especially concerned for the Christian nurture of children and young people until they come to acknowledge Christ as Saviour for themselves, thus fulfilling promises made at services of thanksgiving and blessing that have become a common celebration of the gift of children among Baptists.

Baptists were among the first to campaign for liberation of opinion and religious practice, not only for themselves but for all people, including the unbeliever, for they believed that each individual needed to be free to make choices about faith and commitment unfettered by any outside agency. Such freedom has led the Baptists to be a diverse people with no over-arching rule demanding common thought or practice among them. But amidst that diversity there is a unity because freedom from the state or from ecclesiastical hierarchies has also meant freedom to develop in each situation a style of churchmanship which, under the guidance of the Holy Spirit, they believe best serves the interests of the kingdom.

Many of the characteristics described here, if not all, are held by other Christian groups. Baptist distinctiveness is best seen in holding all these attitudes together in a way that is at once loyal to the traditions of Reformed Christianity without being sectarian. They are aware that they are but one part of the whole family of Christ's church here on earth, and seek in different ways (some within and others outside formal ecumenical structures) to lend support to the whole of the Church's work as the witness to the kingdom that Jesus proclaimed.

Baptists are:

—members of the whole Christian family who stress the experience of personal salvation through faith in Jesus, symbolized both in baptism and the Lord's Supper;

—those who under the Lordship of Jesus Christ have bonded together in free local congregations, together seeking to obey Christ in faith and in life;

—those who follow the authority of Scriptures in all matters of faith and practice;

—those who have claimed religious liberty for themselves and all people;

—those who believe that the Great Commission to take the Gospel to the whole world is the responsibility of the whole membership.

Commission
On Christian Ethics

The Commission on Christian Ethics of the Baptist World Alliance has the special responsibility of helping Baptists apply Christian principles in every area and relationship of life. The Commission's goal is "to bring about the exchange of ideas on topics relating to Christian ethics and to "encourage creative new solutions to problems of Christian mission in today's world" as these relate specifically to Christian ethics.

To that end, the Commission on Christian Ethics, in its first meeting in the current quinquennium at Singapore on July 1-4, 1986, adopted the general theme for this five-year period, "Baptists Living the Gospel."

The 1986 program consisted of the following topics and speakers, with formal responses and general discussion designed for each:

Domingo Diel, Jr., "Christian Ethics: A Biblical-Theological Perspective"
Christian Wolf, "What is Christian Ethics? A Personal Perspective"
Charles Adams, "Christian Social Ethics in Formation of Community"
Foy Valentine, "Implementing Christian Ethics"

The 1987 program in Amman, Jordan focused on "ethical issues confronting today's families"; and the speakers and their topics were:

O.M. Rao, "Planned Parenthood and Family Planning"
Daniel B. McGee, "Making and Having Babies: A Christian Understanding of Responsible Parenthood"
David Charley, "The Christian Challenge of an Aging Population"
Pablo Alberto Dieros, "Family in Crisis in Latin America"
Manual Alexandre, "Responsible Human Sexuality"
James G. Johnson, "The Church for the Strengthening of Families"

The 1988 sessions of the Commission dealt with the following speakers and topics:

Heather M. Vose, "Our Baptist Heritage: Christian Citizenship and Church-State Relations"
Piero Bensi, "Church-State Relations in a Catholic-Dominated Country"
Gustavo A. Parajon, "Christian Responsibility is a Conflicting Political Situation"
Christian Wolf, "How One Manages Christian Citizenship in a socialist Society"
James M. Dunn, "Christian Citizens in the State and in the World"

The Commission decided in 1986 that the 1989 "sessions should deal with contemporary moral concerns not previously dealt with in the current quinquennium." Among the general topics agreed on as worthy of consideration were Drugs and Alcohol, Human Sexuality, Women's Issues, World Hunger, Human Migration, Justice in the Economic Order, and Ecological Issues. Actual speakers and topics for the 1989 meeting were:

Ruth Lehotsky, "Abortion and Sexual Education"
Beth MacClaren, "Women's Issues"
Domingo Diel, Jr., "Economic Justice-World Hunger"
Donald Black, "Drug Abuse"
John N. Johnson, "The Modern Diaspora"

Choosing study papers for publication in this volume has been difficult for several reasons. (1) The subjects for all of the papers have been of such importance that none deserves to be omitted. (2) The authors of all the papers have come from such varied and fascinating backgrounds that every one of them without exception could be appropriately and profitably read by Baptists around the world. (3) Omission of any papers leaves obvious and painful gaps in the record of the total effort of the Commission on Christian Ethics, which gaps can only very reluctantly be accepted as mandatory constraints necessitated by inevitable limitations of space in a single volume such as this.

From the 1986 meeting of the Commission in Singapore, the several research papers presented in this book have been included in order to provide a general overview of the Commission's task. These papers are somewhat more general than those chosen from the meetings of subsequent years. They seek to prepare the groundwork and lay the foundation for the work of the Commission in the years to follow. They are presented here in the hope that they may undergird Baptist around the world in the task of doing the gospel of our Lord Jesus Christ in the world.

Two papers from the 1987 meeting in Amman, Jordan are included as illustrative of the Commission's concern to help the larger Baptist family of the world to relate Christian principles in some of the specific challenges confronted by Baptist families in today's world. Accordingly, the two study papers dealing with responsible parenthood and with aging are included are included and commended to our entire Baptist constituency.

From the 1988 Commission meetings held in Nassau in the Bahamas, three study papers dealing with different dimensions of Christian citizenship are included for publication in this volume. The paper on "Our Baptist Heritage: Christian Citizenship and Church-State Relations" by Heather M. Vose illustrates the combination of Baptist insights, sensitivity to our heritage, responsible scholarship, and authentic spirituality which make the Commission's annual meetings unique, informative, and worthwhile. The Presentation by Christian Wolf on "How One Manages Christian Citizenship in a Socialist Society" is illustrative of the variety, vigor and vision characterizing the talent from which the Commission in particular and the Baptist World Alliance in general are privileged to draw in building an ongoing program of study and research. The paper by James M. Dunn uses a strong biblical base to make a compelling case for theology in public policy.

Two papers from the 1989 conference held in Zagreb, Yugoslavia have been included in this volume. The one by Beth MacClaren deals with "Women's

Issues" and was chosen because an extensive global survey was done which reflects the need for greater partnership in the mission of the Church. The paper by John N. Jonsson, deals with "The Modern Diaspora" and is included here in order to sensitize our Baptist family to the human migration and plight of refugees worldwide.

The Commission on Christian Ethics commends these studies to our people throughout the member bodies of the Baptist World Alliance and vigorously supports the application of Christian principles in every area and relationship of daily life by all Baptists everywhere.

Cora Sparrowk, Chair

Cora Sparrowk, of Ione, California, USA, a former president of the American Baptist Churches, USA, currently serves as chair of the Baptist World Alliance Division of Study and Research and chairperson of the Commission of Christian Ethics.

A Biblio-Theological Perspective on Peace and Justice
Domingo Diel

To deal with the subject of Christian Ethics from the biblical-theological perspective is to raise the question of its source of authority. For Baptists and a number of other Christian denominations or groups, there may not be any question as to the primary source of this authority—it is the Bible. And perhaps to avoid a strictly biblicist approach to the source of authority for Christian Ethics, theological reflection must still be exercised not only in terms of the biblical witness to the faith and its practice, but also in terms of the present human realities with which a Christian must live and practice his or her own faith in a meaningful way.

Paul Lehman defined Christian Ethics as "the reflection upon the question, and its answer: What am I as a believer in Jesus Christ and as a member of his church, to do?" By this definition, we understand that the areas where this reflection on the question and its answer could take place, are the scriptures, on the one hand; and the situation on the other hand. Consequently then, the doing or the practice of the faith, or the norms of Christian behavior will not be fixed for all Christians at all times. When there is reflection/action on the *being* and *doing* of a Christian in the contexts of the Scriptures and the situation, there will be growth into mature manhood and unto Christ (cf. Eph. 4:13). This subject can be treated under four sub-headings: 1) Affirmations of Tradition, 2) The Reality of Diversity, 3) Some Biblical Examples and 4) The Unity of Purpose.

1. Affirmations from Tradition

One of the earliest documents that contained an affirmation about the

Scriptures was the English Declaration of Faith at Amsterdam in 1611, formulated by those whom we might call spiritual ancestors of the Baptists. Section 23 of that document states:

> That the scriptures of the Old and New Testament are written for our instruction, 2 Tim. 3:16 and that wee ought to search them for they testifie of Christ, John 5:39. And therefore to bee used with all reverence, as containing the Holie Word of God, which onlie is our direction in all things whatsoever.

The "Orthodox Creed" 1678, formulated by General Baptists, says of the Scriptures. . . "that all people ought to have them in their mother tongue, and all diligently, and constantly to read them in their particular places and families, for their edification and comfort; and endeavor to *frame their lives according to the direction of God's Word, both in faith and practice* . . ."

Today, the many different Baptist groups speak consensualy of the Holy Scriptures as the Word of God, written by men divinely inspired and the sole authority of faith and practice. Or as the New Hampshire Confession of Faith of 1833 has it . . . "written by men divinely inspired, and is a perfect treasure of heavenly instruction . . . *the supreme standard* by which *all human conduct, creeds, and opinions should be tried."*

Undoubtedly, according to these documents, the source of authority for Christian faith and practice is the Bible. It is well-known that there is not one formatted statement or articles of faith acceptable to all Baptists; neither is there one pattern of Christian behavior and church practice for all Baptists throughout the world.

Illustrations of this can be found in Baptist tradition. IN the 16th and 17th centuries, election of church officers was preceded by fasting and prayer by the whole church. Marriage was an ordinance of God, indissoluble except in cases of adultery (cf. Matt. 19:3-12; Mark 10;2-123; Deut. 24:1-4). A document entitled "Discipline of the Church, how a Christian ought to live, 1527," attributed to the Anabaptists, has this to say in Article 8:

> In the eighth place: when the brethren assemble they shall not fill up with eating and drinking, but avoid expenses *[reduce expenditures]* to the least *[eat]* a soup and vegetable or whatever God gives (I Cor. 11; I Peter 4: Gal, 5; Rom. 13; Eccles. 37; Luke 21), and when they have eaten, all the food and drink shall again be removed (*Geschicht-Buch*: "from the table") (John 6; Matt 4; Luke 9; Mark 6), for one should use with thanksgiving and moderation the creatures which God has created, our and good, for our substinence.

How much change/transformation had occurred in Christian behavior, conduct and church practices among Baptists since then, one could easily imagine; in spite of the one supreme source of authority for faith and practice, in reality there is diversity.

2. The Reality of Diversity

Since it came into being, the Ecumenical Movement has been working for church unity in many forms. Nevertheless, it has never ignored the diversity of the church's tradition in beliefs, forms of worship, and ethical norms of behavior. In fact, it looks at diverse traditions as enrichment not only to the movement, but also to the total Christian heritage.

However, a question must be raised whether diversity in belief and practice among the churches came about because of the churches'' adaptation to and accommodation of the world, or whether it is because of the nature of the biblical record of God's relevation itself that allows for a diversity of interpretations and/or understanding? To find an answer to this question would be a difficult task; I do not intend to do so. But as we look at our own Baptist tradition or tradition we might discover the basic nature of our diverse perceptions of the Christian faith and how we practice/project this faith in service and proclamation, living and witnessing, and/or in behavior and verbal expression.

In his book *Baptist Confessions of Faith,* 1959, W. L. Lumpkin concluded: ". . . it is obvious that Baptists have continuously sought to formulate and articulate their faith by means of doctrinal summaries. No single confession has yet appeared which would be acceptable to all Baptists. These confessions represent the sincere desire of *many Baptist communities* to set forth *their interpretations of the Scriptures regarding Christian belief and practice* . . . In every instance, they bespeak the *theological* and *biblical* awareness, the *freedom,* and the sense of responsibility of the movement through succeeding generations."

These diverse Baptist Confessions are indicative of a variety of Church practices and norms of behavior. The designations of the different Baptist groups as General, Particular or Regular, Southern, Northern, Seventh Day and.or Pentecost to cite a few, have not only religio-theological roots, they (at least some) have also socio-political connotations. As such, they should be critically evaluated or assessed regularly, and corrected accordingly when necessary, so that they do not become simply a reminder of the past in places, where they originated. In countries, where they have been exported, and in the meanwhile have become, if not an irrelevant, a scandalous historical load.

In matters of Christian behavior and ethical conduct, the diversity is much more pronounced, partly because of the different socio-cultural backgrounds that helped shape this diverse understanding of norms of Christian behavior, values and outlook. While they differ from country to country and region to region, they are at best approximation, at worst, distortion of the biblical teaching and instruction. For example, this is true in the way we deal with foreigners/strangers who live work among us; Chinese in Southeast Asia, Blacks in America, foreign workers and or Muslims in Southeast Asia (cf. Acts 17:26F; 10:34; 1 Peter 1:17); how we value family life and marriage; the aged living in old age homes, instead of living with the children; one divorce for every three or four marriages, or simply dissolution of marriage without due process, or marriage for better and for worse till death parts the couple (cf. Matt. 19:3-12, Mark 10:2-12; I Cor. 7:10-16; Deut. 24:1-4); in how we manage population growth for no-growth; in zero-growth population, there is subsidy for every new-born baby; in over-populated countries, more taxes or less privilege for every new born child, while another under-populated regions of the world, the question is not even raised; in how we handle harness nature and environment; it is being exploited harnessed to the full to serve the needs and wants of man, or it is being used and or developed as the inexhaustible source of life and livelihood of man; or it is being restored and preserved as a natural habitat of man and animals, without which human and animal life becomes impossible (Gen. 24:9, 15; Gen. 9:9ff; Ps. 24:1-2; Ps. 8, 19:1; 148:7-14); and finally, in how we look and behave in the face of impending nuclear holocaust. Here the question on how we live for and make peace and pursue justice needs a longer comment, to which we now turn.

3. Some Biblical Examples

Two biblical passages illustrate peace and justice:

Jer. 6:13-15. "From the least to the greatest all are greedy for gain; Prophets and priests alike, all practice deceit. They dress the wound of my people as though it were not serious. "Peace, peace", they say, when there is not peace. Are they ashamed of their loathsome conduct? No, they have no shame at all; they do not even know how to blush. So they will fall among the fallen; they will be brought down when I punish them," says the Lord.

Matt. 10:34-39 "Do not suppose that I have come to bring peace to the earth. I did not come to bring peace, but a sword. For I have come to turn "a man against his father, a daughter-in-law against her mother-in-law; a man's enemies will be the members of his own household. Anyone who loves his father or mother more than me is not worthy of me; anyone who loves his son or daughter more than me is not worthy of me; and anyone who does not take his cross and follow me is not worthy of me. Whoever finds his life will lose it, and whoever loses his life will lose it, and whoever loses his life for my sake will find it."

World in War

There is conflict everywhere and violence and war in many countries. People all over the world long for peace; leaders of nations work for it, and they say "peace, peace, when there is no peace."

Two small Muslim oil-rich sheikdoms in the Persian Gulf threatened to wage war against each other; Iran and Iraq, both Muslim countries, have been warring against each other for years; Protestants and Catholics in Ireland have been at war for decades; in India there are communal riots between Hindus and Sikhs; in the Philippines, there seems to be no end to the violent strife between Christians and Muslims and between government forces and the New People's Army.

From these examples, one can see that war and/or violent conflict has a variety of causes—religion, ideology, rivalry in the exercise of power, or simply madness. It cannot be stated that war or conflict has been waged only by those who are not Christians. In fact, the two World Wars started in the so-called Christian countries of the West. The chosen example texts in Jeremiah 6:13-15 and Matt: 10:34-39, reveal to us in a more basic way the cause/causes of war and conflict, and thus knowing them, work out possibilities for peace for the individual, family and/or society.

Two Biblical Witnesses

1. When a reformist king named Josiah came to power and instituted wide-ranging reforms in Judah, Jeremiah supported the king's move. At first, the reforms had appeared as an option to avert the judgement of God on Judah; but soon Jeremiah discovered that reforms of the outward expressions of religion, such as offerings and sacrifices, were not enough. Unless there was a genuine national repentance for Judah, her sinfulness would inevitably bring her to judgment and the Exile. She was so sinful that she had become incapable of any moral transformation for herself.

Jeremiah had expressed this state of affairs of the nation vividly in the text, thus:

"from the least to the greatest of them, every one is greedy for unjust gain, and from prophet to priest, every one deals falsely." Greediness and avarice were widespread. It was not only a matter of the rich (the greatest) being greedy and exploitive, it was also the problem of the poor (the least). The supposed guardians of morality and "spiritual values", i.e., the prophet and priest, were in fact perpetrators of falsehood and deceit. This could mean that falsehood had become the general practice, since even those who were to propagate and protect truth and righteousness had betrayed their reason for being.

As a result of this widespread and de-seated sinfulness of the nation, the people became insensitive to callousness and wickedness, to justice and unrighteous deeds. They had become shameless and Jeremiah used a more picturesque statement: "they did not know how to blush" (vs. 15B) at their wickedness. Thus, there could not be peace for these people even if they declare and/or aspire for it. In fact, they were saying: "Peace, peace when there is no peace" (vs. 14B) In other words, in the midst of greed and falsehood, there could only be war and conflict, not peace and Shalom. The prophet Jeremiah knew that it would take a national and genuine repentance before God's judgment could be averted and Shalom could be established in the land and among the people.

2. The main message of the second example in St. Matthew is the coming of the Christ, the Messiah, who in turn inaugurated the Kingdom of Heaven among men/women. This had happened in the person and work of Christ. His mission, embodied in this teachings and deeds, wherever it happened has place individual persons or groups of persons in a position to make a decision and a choice. It has been and will continue to be a choice between the claims of

the Kingdom of Heaven through Christ and the claims of the world, that is opposed to Christ. This initial decision to choose between the two, already results in a "division", a "separation" and/or conflict. And one is reminded of the word of God which is a two-edge sword that divides. It is along this line, that the statement of Jesus Christ can be understood: "Do not think that I have come to bring peace on earth; I have not come to bring peace, . but a sword" (Matt. 10:34).

This could be a division of conflict between principles and/or values. But above all, it is the question of following, obeying and loving Jesus Christ and the will of the Father as against following/obeying the rulers and claims of this world. In other words, a *yes* to Jesus Christ and the Kingdom of Heaven, He represented and embodied is a *no* to the forces/values of the world that oppose him. Such a moment of conflict or "war" between the flesh and the Spirit can and does happen in the individual, family, community or country. In his time, these forces included even the guardians and faithful practitioners of religion. The conflict or "war" then took many forms: from the observance of the Law on food, cleanliness and the Sabbath to the questions of who can forgive sin and who this Jesus really was, whose authority had placed in question the demands of the Mosaic Law, and had claimed for Himself, loyalty and obedience far greater than to the King, parents, sisters and brothers. Today, whenever and wherever an encounter with Jesus Christ and the claims of His kingdom has taken place, and decision made by individual persons or people for or against it, a moment of conflict has set in, but also the reality of peace for such individuals and people becomes a possibility. In this regard, mention should be made that the Christian Church and the Christians themselves are involved in the continuing encounter with the Lord. Thus they are placed also in moments of conflict/war on the one hand; and in the reality of peace on the other hand. Nonetheless, it is they who are to show in word and deed the way to lasting peace and the hope of making it a reality in the life of an individual person or in the community, country and the world.

4. The Unity of Purpose

It may be concluded that war and violent conflict and their consequences, which oftentimes are blamed on God, can be traced back to the very nature of man himself. His greed for profit and power, his ways of falsehood, deceit and unjust dealing with fellowmen individually and corporately, have resulted in institutions and social conditions that have been characterized by oppression, exploitation, injustice, fear and violence. Examples of this, both ancient and contemporary, can be seen in societies and countries throughout the world.

And yet, the longing for peace is as widespread as are occurrences of war and conflict. For example, the condemnation of many nations of international terrorism and the declaration of 1986 as International Year of Peace are indications that nations, and mankind as a whole, are still looking and aspiring for lasting peace as a matter of survival. We cannot overemphasize that enough.

From our limited perspective and situation, it may be beyond us to talk about peace and justice in world-encompassing terms. Thus, let us note that wherever and whenever healing of broke relationships between persons and people takes place, peace has won a place. When alienated husband and wife, parents and children, people and nations are reconciled, peace has become effective. This can happen in a home, in the church, or anywhere we are. Christians need to work for peace, even in small ways such as righteous living with God and just relationships with their fellowmen, by standing up and being counted for the sake of the Prince of Peace.

This would mean a Christian Education program that will gradually change our generally negative attitude toward the Chinese, toward Blacks and Muslims, Buddhists, etc., who are living among us; it would mean a re-examination of our use of power and authority over people, even in the institutional church which is the Body of Christ. What is the motivation of its use: Nothing but a changed heart and a transformed spirit can use power in the service of peace.

Finally, it would mean just and honest dealings with our fellowmen. Christians should be in the forefront of this kind of lifestyle. It is an ethical mandate from Jesus Christ himself, which if lived out faithfully could spell out the difference in the ordinary affairs of men and women. And such could inspire trust and confidence in the people of any community. On the foundation then of justice and truth, we can help build and make peace among our peoples who need it in order to survive and live in peace and dignity.

Domingo Diel is on the staff of the Convention of Philippine Baptist Churches, Inc., Iloilo City, Philippines.

Christian Social Ethics
In the Formation of Community

Charles G. Adams

The question of Christian ethics is, "What am I to do as a believer in Christ and a member of his church?" The presupposition of Christian ethics is faith—not faith as intellectual assent to or cognitive acceptance of propositions and statements, doctrines and principles, but faith as a dynamic, transformative, determinative relationship with God in Jesus Christ. Faith is a radical encounter between the human person and the holy God. It involves total surrender to God who alone is ultimate and absolute. "When I say him, I fell at his feet as though dead." (Revelation 1:17) In Paul Tillich's terms, faith is the exercise of one's ultimate concern. Schleiermacher defined faith as the person's absolute dependence on God. No serious modern theological of international note understands faith according to the commonly misperceived notion that is cognitive belief in the articles or propositions that comprise the doctrine of the church: i.e., the virgin birth, the literal interpretation of Genesis 1-11, the miracles or the bodily resurrection of Jesus. Faith is the I-Though relationship through which human personality is transformed, the human will is redirected, human action is both mandated and generated and human society is changed for the better. It is through the relationship of faith that God continues to bless, heal and deliver humankind. Faith therefore, is not belief in something, it is surrender to someone, the one who "alone can order the unruly wills and affections of sinful people."

Faith inevitably mandates and potentiates human action in response to the divine action that made is possible. The old conflict between faith and work is as unnecessary as it is silly. Radical encounter makes decisive action inevitable. The wonderful indicative of faith inevitably flowers into the tremendous imperative of ethics. My sense of who I am drives me to consider what I shall do. Being and doing are interrelated and interdependent orders - Descartes', "cogito ergo sum" should be transposed to declare, "I am therefore I act." It is this critical and crucial relationship between faith and action that keeps the verticle reality of faith necessarily connected to the horizontal plane of action. The relationship of faith is not shaped like a spurious pole which reaches up to heaven without reaching out to anybody. Faith is better described as assuming the shape of the cross. With the verticle plank it reaches up to God for salvation and power, and with the horizontal beam it reaches out to humanity with love.

Anselm said that faith seeks understanding. Who can dispute the fact that the history of intellectual pursuits and academic institutions is rooted in faith and its inevitable thirst for knowledge? The idea of the university was conceived in the womb of the church as faith became the father of intelligence. It is intelligence divorced from faith that makes knowledge so dangerous, lethal and the imminent threat to human existence that is has become. How necessary it is to keep intelligence growing self-consciously as the child of faith It is faith that creates, stimulates, perpetuates and appreciates the university. "If any of you lacks wisdom, let him ask God, who gives to all people generously and without reproaching, and it will be given him. But let him ask in faith. . ." (James 1:5, 6a) Everything that is true depends on Absolute Truth. Everything that is real is a derivative of Reality Itself. Everything that can be known points beyond itself to the "Beyond come into the midst of our life." (Dietrich Bonhoeffer's definition of God). Athens and Jerusalem converged and became the university. Let not the tension of that relationship be relaxed or resolved into a faith that is alienated from its child, intelligence, or an intelligence that has discarded the dynamic and fruitful reality of its parent, faith. Faith that is denuded of intelligence is superstitious, unrealistic and irresponsible. Intelligence that is independent of faith is delusive, arrogant and dangerous. But faith conjoined with intelligence is the poser of God expressing itself in marvelous ways. Faith makes and keeps the university a transforming frontier of curiosity, creativity, community and hope. If our science is to be our servant and not our master, our helper and not our destroyer, faith must be active at the core of our intellectual pursuits.

The world by its wisdom does not know God, cannot find truth, cannot establish justice, cannot create beauty, cannot contrive national security nor compel world peace. The work in all its wisdom is wiser than ever and closer to annihilation than ever, more estranged than ever, more frustrated than ever, more fearful and fretful than ever. Our wisdom without faith has driven us to the boundary where it will either find faith or it will self destruct in the total atomic extinction of human life. After W. W. 1 Karl Barth noted that just at the moment when the state thought it had succeeded in making men out of wild animals, it found it necessary for national security to make wild animals out of men. Such is the futility of intelligence lost from faith.

Socrates said in his last hours that all the best of human- wisdom amounts to no more than a "raft, to which one must needs, trust and make in peril the voyage of life unless", he added, as a great hope flashed across his mind, "unless it were possible to make the voyage more securely on some firmer vessel, even some divine word." Socrates' vain hope is faith's piercing proclamation: The Messiah has come! Something has happened to create and fulfill our desire to know. The truth of God has been revealed. God's self-disclosure has transversed our intellectual searching. God's healing has embraced the human brokenness of the world. God's liberation has issued eviction notices to all our resident captors. The kingdom of the world is becoming the kingdom of our God and of his Christ, and He shall reign forever and ever: Wisdom can be found. Science can be redeemed. The university can be sustained. Knowledge can be responsible. THe world can be united. Peace with justice can become realized. Humanity can be humanized into a community. The church can make a difference in the world. Society can be reconstructed. Nicaragua can come to rest. Germany can be reunited. The American dream can be actualized. South Africa can find peace with justice because "All this is from God, who through Christ reconciled us to himself and gave us the ministry of reconciliation; that is, in Christ God was reconciling the world to himself, not counting their trespasses against them, and entrusting to us the message of reconciliation." (II Corinthians 5:18, 19).

But does this not take us from the vestibule of the intellectural quest to the very threshold of social action? Indeed! As gorgeously impressive and pompous as may be the pageantry and potency of university life, intelligence is not the most profound or effective offspring of faith. The indicative of faith yields much more than the imperative to inquire. Faith's best child is social action. Who has beguiled the church to think that it is better to know than to do, better to contemplate than to act, better to enjoy than to share? Too much of the Church's energy is spent on enjoyment without utility, worship with work, thought without action, devotion without duty, contemplation without total transformation and social reconstruction. Too often the church has been tempted away from the prophetic criticism of society and the radical reconstruction of national and international relations into the easier preoccupations with personal contemplation and spiritual self indulgence. We have not kept up the tension between enjoyment and use. For example, in the theology of Thomas Aquinas, Aristotelion rationalism influenced him to regard rational any mystical contemplation of the divine as religious superior to ethical action. What a change from the social ethics of Jesus Christ who gave eschatological value and congratulations not to thought but to action! We will not be commended to the

Kingdom of God on the basis of how good we felt or how validly we contemplated a how regularly we mediated but how obediently, faithfully, creatively and lovingly we acted. "Truly, I say unto you, as you did it to one of the least of these my brethren, you did it to me." (Matt. 25:40) The social action that Jesus mandates is specifically directed to the down trodden, the disinherited, the dispossessed, the disfranchised: "For I was hungry and you gave me food, I was thirsty and you game me drink, I was a stranger and you welcomed me, I was naked and you clothed me, I was sick and you visited me, I was in prison and you came to me." Christian ethics is not contemplation but action on behalf of the oppressed. It is redemptive movement toward those who are weak, worn, weary and discouraged. In explanation of his spiritual mission in the world Jesus read from Isaiah 61: "The Spirit of the Lord is upon me, because he has anointed me to preach good news to the poor. He has sent me to proclaim release to the captives and recovering the sight to the blind, to set a liberty those who are oppressed, to proclaim the acceptable year of the Lord." (Luke 4:18, 19 see Isaiah 61:1-4) Also notice Jesus' answer to the disciples of John, the Baptizer (Luke 7:18-23).

That Jesus does not require beatific contemplation nor superior knowledge but liberating action is farther substantiated by the Old Testament's witness to who God is and what God is doing in the world. The God who is revealed to the matriarchs, patriarchs and prophets of the Old Testament is a God of action who redeems human life, redistributes wealth and redesigns social structures: "I will sing to the Lord for he has triumphed gloriously; the horse and his rider he has thrown into the sea. . . Who is like thee, O Lord, among the Gods? Who is like thee, majestic in holiness, terrible in glorious deeds, doing wonders?" (Exodus 15:1, 11) Unlike the nature deities of the Ancient Near East who do not challenge the perennial relationships of the social order, the God celebrated in the Old Testament is Yahweh, who acts in history to deliver slaves from bondage. What God performs in history is the key that unlocks the door that leads to the character of God and the content of ultimate reality. God is as God does. God is not a Grand Deceiver whose actions bare no relationship to his character. God is true to his word and credible in his actions and reliable in his self-disclosure as Liberator and Enabler in the human struggle for justice, freedom, social equality and peace.

> Then Moses said to God, "If I come to the people of Israel and say to them, "The God of your fathers has sent me to you", and they ask me, "What is his name?" what shall I say to them?" And he said, "Say this to the people of Israel, "I am has sent me to you. . . This is my name forever and thus I am to be remembered throughout all generations." (Exodus 3:13 ff)

In Ancient Near Eastern culture, the name of a person is his/her nominal reality. Thus the question concerning the name of the Revealer in the above passage is a crucial issue concerning the identity reality (self-relatedness) of God. The very name Yahweh means that He is by self-understanding the Sovereign Deity who binds Himself to the oppressed as their Liberator. Yahweh means the God Whose nature and purpose is to set at liberty those who are held in captivity. Dr. Raymond Abba shows that in the Hebrew sentence which names Yahweh, "ehyeh 'aser ehyeh", "I am who I am", Yahweh is identifying Himself as essentially a "Bundesgott" and Israel, as a "Bundesvolk".[1] God binds himself and commits himself and his people to his self-disclosure as Liberator of the captives. This is the essential character of God. Abba says, "This is the significance of the repeated statement, "I am Yahweh", which is expressed more fully in Malachi 3:6 "I am Yahweh, I change not". Yahweh is the faithful, trustworthy God, the one who is ever (on the side of the oppressed) the same and upon whom his people can rely, their dwelling place in all generations."

Another critical passage in the Old Testament that might be brought to the support of liberation ethics is the "Sheman Israel" of Deuteronomy 6:4,5 "Here, O Israel: Yahweh is our God, Yahweh alone, therefore you shall love Yahweh you God with all your heart and with all your soul, and with all your might."

Yahweh will accept no presumed or alien sovereignty over his people. No power shall dominate humankind but God. No authority shall determine and capitate the human spirit or dictate the shape of society but the Spirit of Yahweh which is the spirit of freedom.

The ancient Israelites gave to humanity, through their apprehension and comprehension of the revelation of God, the blessing of social action based on historical consciousness. They were the first to recognize God as Lord of history thereby exalting and appreciating history as the locus and the focus of divine revelation, activity and salvation. While the other religions of the Ancient Near East focused upon nature with its unchanging cycles of relentlessly recurring seasons, the Israelites focused upon history and its unique, unrepeatable events that gave ground for the creation of hope, progress, expectation and eschatological fulfillment. It was the ancient Jewish religion that delivered the human consciousness from the circular futility of nature into the linear mode of history and hope. The Old Testament is a profound polemic against conservation f the status quo and a conscientious champion of social, political and economic change. All other religions of the Ancient world practiced a conservative ethic of maintenance. The Jewish religion proclaimed a liberal ethic of change. History not nature, transformation not conservation, change not maintenance, justice not repetition, hope not futility, expectation not despair were the unique emphases of the history, the law and the prophets of the Old Testament and the Christ and Church of the New Testament. It is not the creation of the universe in Genesis I but the call of Abraham in Geneses 12 that is the beginning of Heilsgeschichte, salvation history.

The God of the Bible acts in history, breaks into human events, forms nations, calls Abraham, gives Isaac, blesses Jacob, preserves Joseph, commissions Moses, defeats Pharaoh Ramases II, delivers the Hebrews from the Egyptian bondage, beings them safe through the wilderness, sustained them in the desert, took them across in the Jordan, granted them the Promised Land, drove out their enemies, established the monarchy, sent the holy prophets to challenge monarchic and nationalistic pretentions, sounded forth his universal love, defined

Israel's unique, ethical role in the salvation, liberation and unification of all humankind, centered himself in the middle of human history by the birth of his son, invaded the temporal world: The abstract became concrete, the eternal became external, divine majesty put on human misery, the superior got involved in the inferior, the apriori got married to the aposteriori, the holy entered the profane, the spiritual embraced the carnal, Perfect changed into action, principle became person, God became man in order to redeem, transform and enhance humanity. Something has happened to make Christian social action both possible and necessary.

Social action is the human response to a holy God who has acted decisively in the social order. Social action flows powerfully from divine revelation. "He has shown you, O man, what is good; and what does the Lord require of us but to do justice, and to love kindness, and to talk humbly with your God?" (Micah 6:8) The God who reveals Himself through history, challenges his people through history, gives himself a name and a purpose in history. That history is our judgement and our grace. Therefore we must never forget it, ignore it, take it for granted, revise it, demean it, undermine it nor subvert it; but we are enjoined to know it, receive it and apply it. History is not to be re-written, it is to be rehearsed, received and passed down from generation to generation. We are not in charge of Heilsgeschichte, Heilsgeschichte is in charge of us! The worst think that Christian ethicists can do is forget and therefore to withdraw from the social struggle for peace with justice. To lose our God-given consciousness of history is to lose our identity and integrity. It is to throw away our sense of ethical accountability. "In darkness (moral blindness) walks a people which knows its annals not." It is when we remember the loving-kindness of God manifested in our history that were are confronted and challenged by the revelation of the divine to be ourselves compassionately committed to the work of universal human betterment. Human social action is based upon the mighty acts of God. Law is based on gospel. Prophecy is poised on memory. Ethics if founded on history, Heilsgeschichte. This point is poignantly made by George E. Mendenhall. He has well demonstrated that the mandates of God are inevitably attached to the acts of God. The historical recitation of God's might acts in history precedes the stipulations of the Ten Commandments and the Covenant Code. And God spoke all these words saying, "I am the Lord your God, who brought you out of the land of Egypt, out of the house of bondage. (Now therefore based upon my prior action, prevenient grace, initiative loving kindness and pre-existent mercy) You shall have no other gods before me. You shall not make for yourself a graven image. You shall not take the name of the Lord, your God in vain." (Exodus 20:1-7).

Without historical consciousness, there can be no God consciousness, and without God consciousness there can be no ethical consciousness, no openness to others, no advocacy of other people's rights, no improvement of public life. Without a sense of the holy, there can be no appreciation of the human and no formation of human community.

An important New Testament support for Christian social action is John 1:14 "And the word became flesh and dwelt among us." The word "flesh" is the English translation of the Greek word "Sarx". It means the whole of man in the totality of his historical relationships. That is the content of the self-disclosure of God in Jesus Christ. God did not stay neutral or uninvolved in the struggle for human freedom, but entered the area of historical struggle as a living, breathing, loving, liberating "sarx", a human being, fighting on the side of the least of his oppressed brethren.

The critical support from Christian tradition that favors the social ethics of liberation is the Chalcedonian confession of 451 A.D. which proclaims that Jesus Christ is fully God and fully man unconfusedly, unchangeably, indivisibly and inseparably. This repudiates a docetic Christ who is God, but is not related intricably to the struggle for human liberation or the liberal Christ of the 19th Century theologians tho is so swallowed up in history and humanity that he ceases to be divine and therefore can't be normative and authoritative. Chalcedon, if heeded, protects the liberation ethicist from so identifying the divine with the human as to truncate and destroy His transcendent nature. It also checks the transcendentalist who so declares the infinite qualitative distinction between God and man as to keep God separated from or indifferent to the strivings of His people to be free.

Another support for rigorous, vigorous ethics is found in Paul Tillich's theology of culture which avers that man's apprehension of the Being of God must arise from the historical situation and the cultural context. God is not to be understood apart from the historical dilemma to which He is the answer. Thus the empirical experience of oppression calls for the revelation of God as Liberator.

In the social ethics of Karl Barth, Jesus Christ alone is the normative center and determinative reality. Barth serves as a check on the Christian ethicist who uses some other norm than that God revealed in Christ to arrange ones ethical mandates and priorities. This is the mistake that is perennially made by conservative politicians and theologians who make "order" and "stability" their normative center and the ultimate concern of ethical reflection and action. This tendency to make social chaos the ultimate evil and social stability the ultimate good has caused Christians to submit uncriticlly to the tyrannical governmental regimes of Naziism and fascism. Such submission is echoed and encouraged in these words of Emil Brunner.

> The projection of ideal (political) programs is not only useless, but harmful, because it creates illusions, dissipates moral energy and tempts its proponents to become self-righteous critics of their fellows. The most important consideration for a better social order is that of practical possibility, since the question is one of order and not of ethical ideals. The prophetic demand, which does not concern itself with the possible and the impossible, has, of course, its own relevance as proclamation of the unconditioned law. But it has this significance only if it is presented not as a specific program, but as a general demand - i.e., if it does not involve immediate political realization. When the questions one of the immediate and practical problems, the rule must be: The given order is the best as long as a better one cannot be realized immediately and without interruption. . .The Christian must submit himself to a social order - which

is in itself loveless. He must do this if he is not to evade the most urgent of all demands of the love commandment, the demand to protect the dyke which saves human life from chaos." (quoted in Niebuhr op. cit. p. 141)

Niebuhr rejects this conservative tendency in Christian orthodoxy because for him, the love of God revealed in the Old Testament and declared incarnate by the New Testament is the norm and mandate of Christian social ethics. How relevant today is Niebuhr's stern rejection of the an ethic which in the name of "order" and "stability" refuses to confront, challenge and change the social order:

> This logic manages not only to express an excessive fear of chaos and to ob-
> viate any possibility of a Christian justification of social change by allowing only
> such change as will create a new order "immediately and without interrup-
> tion"; but it nearly dismisses the Christian ideal from any immediate relevance
> to political issues. The same type of logic and the same theory of government
> as a dyke against chaos carries Gogarten completely into the political philosophy
> of fascism. If fascism may be regarded as being informed by a frantic fear of
> the chaos which might result if an old social order broke down, and as leading
> to the very anarchy which it fears through its futile attempt to preserve a
> disintegrated order artificially, after history has dissipated its essential vitality,
> we might come to the conclusion that fascism is government justified mainly
> by the negative task of checking chaos is held in common by both fascism and
> Christian orthodoxy. It may be that the political principles of the former are,
> at least partially, derived from the latter."[2]

It is the wisdom of the New Testament that it can speak of the ethical norm in such way as to disclose and declare its eminence, relevance and power simultaneously, thus bridging the gap between truth and action. This amazing feat is accomplished by referent to the Absolute Reality, the Ethical Ideal, the Incarnate Truth and the Redeeming Power as love. It is God revealed in Christ who is defined as love (John 4:9). This same love is not only the mandate but the will and the power to act accordingly, courageously and creatively. It is the new Testament emphasis on love that guards Christian Ethics from social stagnation and political inertia—

> you shall love the Lord your God with all your heart, and with all your soul,
> and with all your mind. This is the great and first commandment. And the
> second is like it, you shall love your neighbor as yourself. On these two com-
> mandments depend all the law and the prophets' (Matthew 22:34)

In this passage we encounter the basis for Christian social action which guards Christian ethics from cruel indifference to human suffering in the world. The God whom we are commanded to love is both immanent and transcendent, in history yet beyond history, active in the world yet reigning over the world. Our God is the ground of existence and the essence which transcends existence. It is this reality of transcendent and existential love which is both absolute and historical, divine and human which enables humans to give themselves to values actually embodied in persons and society, but also transcending every actuality and achievement. The same love that energizes and empowers us also judges and condemns us lest any persons should boast. How skillfully the New Testament concept of love makes us avoid "both the glorification of human, temporal, and partial values, characteristic of naturalism and also the morally enervating tendency of mysticism to regard "love of creatures" (social action) as disloyalty to God and to confine the love of God to a rational or mystic contemplation of the divine essence which transcends all finite existence. . . The Christian love commandment does not demand love of fellowman because he is with us equally divine (Stoicism), or because we ought to have "respect for personality" (Christian liberalism), but because God loves him." (Niebuhr, opCit p. 191)

That social action is superior to reason and mystical contemplation is nowhere more powerfully proclaimed than in 1 Corinthians 13.

> If I speak in the tongue of men and of angels, but have not love, I am a noise gong or a clanging cymbal. And if I have prophetic powers, and understand all mysteries and all knowledge, and if I have all faith, so as to remove mountains, but have not love, I am nothing. If I give away all I have, and if I deliver my body to be burned, but have not love, I gain nothing.
> Love is patient and kind: love is not jealous or boastful; it is not arrogant or rude. Love does not insist on its own way; it is not irritable or resentful; it does not rejoice at wrong, but rejoices in the right. Love bears all things, believes all things, hopes all things, endures all things.
> Love never ends; as for prophecies, they will pass away; as for tongues, they will cease; as for knowledge, it will pass away. For our knowledge is imperfect and our prophecy is imperfect; but when the perfect comes, the imperfect will pass away. When I was a child, I spoke like a child, I thought like a child, I reasoned like a child; when I became a man, I gave up childish ways. For now we see in a mirror dimly, but then fact to face. Now I know in part; then I shall understand fully, even as I have been fully understood. So faith, hope, love abide, these three; but the greatest of these is love.

Was it Edmund Burke who said that the only thing that is necessary to cause evil to triumph in the world is for good people to do nothing? Certainly it was Martin Luther King, Jr. who said, "the world is being destroyed not so much by the vitriolic words of bad people as by the appalling silence (inertia) of good people." Christian social ethics is not merely an intellectual discipline or a mystical encounter, it is deliberate and resolute action to advance goodness, promote justice, secure peace and glorify God in human life by making human life more human. We have recently seen what a courageous and active church was able to do in the Philippines to humanize human life, liberalize political structures and liberate human people. That their work is neither perfect nor finished is the continuing judgment and challenge of amazing grace which is Absolute Love. That their work exists and is fruitful is witness and testimony to a relevant love ethic and passion that cannot be complacent or indifferent toward social inequality, political tyranny or human suffering.

As an American Baptist I am proud of the fact that a Baptist patriarch,

Roger Williams founded a colony in the New World of the seventeenth century which guaranteed religious liberty and human rights. It was a "state" where Baptists could be Baptist, Jews could be Jews, Catholics could be Catholics and Atheists could be Atheists until persuaded to believe otherwise. The principles of Roger Williams survived deeply into the late eighteenth century and were etched into the U.S. Constitution and Bill of Rights.

Baptist leaders and scholars of the long ago played an indispensable role in the formation of American democracy which is unique, in that it guarantees religious liberty in the form of civil liberty and predicates civil liberty upon religious liberty, seeing the two liberties as inherently inseparable, correlative and interacting. The separation between church and state is necessary if these two interacting and inseparable mutual liberties are to be maintained. If the church is merged with the state, giving the state absolutism which is not rightly due it, or the state identified with the church, giving the church enforcing powers that would enslave rather than liberate the human personality, both liberties will be lost and American democracy destroyed.

Baptists have been creative statespersons because they practiced the New Testament love ethic passionately. Roger Williams founded Rhode Island as a secular commonwealth where the church was free to define and pursue its mission, and the state was restrained from religious pretentions and absolutist delusions. That is a distinctive Baptist contribution. Rhode Island was religious because it did not pretend to be a religious state. It became the prefiguration of an America in which religion has thrived precisely because it has stood on its own.

We wish the Baptists of the world enlightened and empowered by divine love, could have been as effective in the area of race relations. Only the American African Baptist Church represented by the ministry and work of Martin Luther King, Jr. and his students and his ilk have been as responsible and effective in creating better race relations in the world as Roger Williams was successful in the creation of American democracy.

The worsening situation in South Africa that threatens the peace of the world and the life of humanity calls and challenges the Baptists in South Africa and the world to decisive action energized by Christian love. We cannot stand idly by while 87% of the people of South Africa are pushed and crowded onto 13% of the land the deprived of South African citizenship and the right to participate in the political order. The recent publication of the Commonwealth Report submitted by the Commonwealth Group of Eminent persons is as frightening as it is shameful. The report is not anti-South African propaganda or rhetoric designed to inside indignation against a foreign nation, whose practices differ from ones own. It is a sober, objective, empirical analysis of a social situation that has reached crisis proportions in its destruction of human life and its potential via atomic conflagration, to extinguish the human race. The group was modest, practical, pragmatic and limited in its expectations. It epitomized the necessary conjunction of reason and action in Christian ethics. Though action is superior to reason, it is not independent of reason and it must be informed and regulated by reason if it is to be effective in the world and responsible to God. In its consultations with the African people, the Group rejected as impractical the suggestion that the whole complex web of apartheid legislation be repealed as a prelude to negotiation, yet on the other hand the Group was concerned to insure, however, that there should be a firm and unambiguous commitment by the South African Government to ending apartheid in order to provide integrity to the negotiating process. After many discussions with South African Government officials, South African church leaders, political party leaders, White citizens, coloured citizens, Black non-citizens and others, the Group was struck by the overwhelming, multiracial desire on the country for a non-violent negotiated settlement and the quickest possible establishment of a truly democratic state. The Group submitted to the Government the following proposal:

> The South African Government has declared its commitment to dismantling the system of apartheid, to ending racial discrimination and to broad-based negotiations leading to new constitutional arrangements for power-sharing by all the people of South Africa. In the light of preliminary and as yet incomplete discussions with representatives of various organizations and groups, within and outside South Africa, we believe that in the context of specific and meaningful steps being taken towards ending apartheid, the following additional action might ensure negotiations and a break in the cycle of violence.
>
> On the part of the Government:
> (a) Removal of the military from the townships, providing for freedom of assembly and discussion and suspension of detention without trial.
> (b) The release of Nelson Mandela and other political prisoners and detainees.
> (c) The unbanning of the ANC and PAC and the permitting of normal political activity.
> On the part of the ANC and others:
> Entering negotiations and suspending violence.
> It is our view that simultaneous announcements incorporating these ideas might be negotiated if the Government were to be interested in pursuing this broad approach.
> In the light of the Government's indication to us that it:
> (i) is not in principle against the release of Nelson Mandela and similar prisoners;
> (ii) is not opposed in principle to the unbanning of any organizations;
> (iii) is prepared to enter into negotiations with the acknowledge leaders of the people of South Africa;
> (iv) is committed to the removal of discrimination, not only from the statue books but also from South African society as a whole;
> (v) is committed to the ending of white domination;
> (vi) will not prescribe who may represent black communities in negotiations on a new constitution for South Africa;
> (vii) is prepared to negotiate an open agenda.
> The South African Government may wish to give serious consideration to the approach outlined in this note."

The Group's effort failed miserably because of the Government's intransigent insistence that as a prerequisite to the negotiating process the African National Congress renounce and disclaim any use of violence forever while during the talks with the Group on May 19, 1986, the South African Government raided ANC offices in Harare, Gaborone and Lusaka. These violent bombing raids by the Government helped to wreck the arduous task of bringing all pertinent parties to the negotiating table.

The question of violence is a difficult one. While love in the absolute envisions a beloved community where violence is neither possible nor necessary, love operating in the context of a sinful world where life is opposed to life is sometimes compelled to "take up the sword". Love cannot be non-violently passive when the beloved is violently subjected to mortal danger. Neibuhr points out that absolute pacifism may be possible for the extrapolated individual; but it is not possible for the person who lives in loving commitment to family, race or nation. Not to fight to preserve other life is deemed cowardly at best and cruel at worst. Those who are absolute pacifists or who enjoin others to be absolutely pacifistic and non-violent are not honest because they are parasites existing under the protection of a standing national militia and the Government's arsenal of atomic weapons. The sudden introduction of the mandate of non-violence into a situation that is already full of violence - the violent denial of human rights and civil liberties and the violent suppression of political dissent - is as irresponsible as it is unrealistic. It is the epitome of the duplicity and deception that continues to frustrate peace in South Africa and the world. One cannot demand of others what one is not willing to do. The most realistic demand that Government of South Africa could make of Nelson Mandela and the ANC is that they "suspend" all violence for the political purposes during the negotiating process. In turn the Government would suspend all its violence presently unleashed against unarmed political dissenters.

But since the negotiations have not gotten started and are not imminent, and the situation becomes more critical by the hours, the next best thing to do is the international application of tough economic sanctions against South Africa in order to encourage the Government to negotiate in good faith. "The question in front of Heads of Government is in our view clear. It is not whether such measures will compel change; it is already the case that their absence and Pretoria's belief that they need not be feared, defers change," (Report p. 140).

Will the Baptists in South Africa and the Baptists of the world stand idly by and allow the cycle of violence to spiral toward a cataclysmic holocaust? Or will we who love the Lord take concerted action to promote justice in South Africa as a prominent step toward building peace in the world. It is such action which may offer the last best opportunity to avert the destruction of South Africa, and the annihilation of the human race. Christian social action is not *an* answer, it is *the only* answer to the human dilemma in a world of conflict.

Charles G. Adams is pastor of Hartford Memorial Baptist Church, Detroit, Michigan, USA.

Endnotes

1. *Journal of Biblical Literature*, V. 80, 1961, pp. 320-328.

2. Ibid. pp. 141, 142.

Implementing Christian Ethics

Foy Valentine

In his preface to *A Baptist Treasury*, Dr. Sydnor L. Stealey says, "The chief criterion for selecting has been to try to help the average reader discourse intelligently on "Why I Am a Baptist." Therefore, the essay by Walter Rauschenbusch entitled "Why I am a Baptist" was the very first choice." Later Dr. Stealey calls in "one of the best statements ever written on our distinctive principles." I heartily commend that statement to the attention of today's Baptists. While I am not following its outline in these introductory, personal observations I am about to make, I would like to see every Baptist familiar with its important insights. I am convinced that a careful rethinking of this subject will deliver us from some of the serious perils that beset us in the Baptist movement today: creeping creedalism and resurgent Fundamentalism on the right, non-experimental religion on the left, and cheap grace in the radical middle.

I am a Baptist for historical reasons. My parents were Baptists. My father was a deacon and the song leader while my mother was a Sunday School teacher in a little one-room, open country meeting house in East Texas where from time to time there gathered the Pleasant Union Missionary Baptist Church of Christ. (It was reasoned that the Baptist Missionary Association had no corner on the cause of missions and that the Churches of Christ had no corner on the name of our Lord; so, in spite of our affiliation with the Van Zandt County Baptist Association, the Baptist General Convention of Texas, and the Southern Baptist Convention, we, in not untypical Baptist fashion, chose that name.)

Revivals played a big part in being a Baptist. I was converted when I was about ten during a summer revival meeting. I answered the call to preach during a revival meeting about six years later. Early in my ministry I preached in literally hundreds of revival meetings; and this experience deeply affected the course of my life and work. My formal training was at Baylor, the largest Baptist University in the world, and at Southwestern Baptist Theological Seminary, the largest Baptist theological seminary in the world. I began by being a Baptist because my parents were; but today I am a Baptist because with my convictions I could not well and happily be anything else.

I am a Baptist for intellectual reasons. I believe passionately in freedom, in the rightness of our Baptist emphasis on a regenerate church membership; and I cling to the importance of freedom for every human being. I believe that religious liberty's corollary is separation of church and state, and I refuse to equivocate about this. I believe in democracy for the churches as well as for the nations; and I rejoice that I grew up in a church that was genuinely, though sometimes appallingly, democratic. With my whole mind and heart, I believe in radical Christianity. Absolutely repugnant to me are baptism for unbelievers, hocus-pocus religion, and hierarchy, creedalism, scholasticism, phariasaism, and all the mass of paganism which has leaked into religion through the centuries. Radical Christianity insists on holiness "without which no man shall see the Lord" (Hebrews 12:14). Radical Christianity is biblical Christianity as opposed to creedal Christianity; it is experimental in Christianity as opposed to confessional Christianity.

I am a Baptist for intuitive reasons. Baptist, more uncompromisingly than any people I know, have emphasized the priesthood of the believer; and God's Spirit bears witness with my spirit that this is right. It is a part of Baptist strength that we have encouraged individual encounter with God Almighty. We believe that mystic, spiritual apprehension of God is not only possible, but that it is the norm, with no ifs, ands, and buts, for Christians. We believe with Paul that we can "know" whom we have believed. We feel that experience is the one great thing in our religion, the one essential thing in our religion. The more we look around us and the more we understand history, the more we see how great and fruitful is this emphasis on experience.

I am a Baptist for practical reasons. There are many things wrong in the Baptist movement. I know these better now than I did when I started preaching in 1940; and I know them far better than I did some thirty-three years ago when I left the pastorate to work fulltime among Baptists in the area of Christian ethics. For me, the Baptist movement is home; and for me there is simply nowhere else to go. Within the Baptist framework, I believe that I can better preach and work to proclaim liberty, maintain freedom, develop the biblical understanding of the worth of the individual, engage in genuine evangelism, be involved in true Christian missions, and implement Christian ethics than anywhere else.

So, it is as a Baptist that I come to deal with "Implementing Christian Ethics."

Christian involvement in the world has been a plank in the Baptist platform from our earliest days. I think we have our personal commitment to Jesus Christ as Lord to thank for that, our personal experience with the Almighty who leads us into right relationships with others. We also have the Bible to thank, along with our free church, grassroots, plain folks heritage and the working of God's Holy Spirit who never lets His people be at ease in Zion, who never lets them permanently pull away from the real world of blood, sweat, and tears, of broken relationships, lost identities, and raging animosities.

History

When Baptists in a reasonably organized sense were aborning, we were a frontier people. We assembled in simple, one-room, frame meeting houses erected close to our cabins in the clearings. Baptist preachers were common folks who had heard God's call to preach and who, like nearly everybody else in the churches and out of them, had very little formal education. We had no great stake in society. Affluence was no problem for us then. We had no debilitating debts, for we had no institutions, no church programs, no huge church buildings for which we were gloriously in debt. Now, we can say with Paul, "Would God you were even as I am, save for these bonds." Identifying with the poor and needy, existential involvement in social concert, pursuing an agenda of engagement, was natural for Baptists because of who Baptists were sociologically but more especially because of who Baptists were biblically and spiritually and experientially.

Christian social concern, as a distinct movement, came into being toward the latter part of the nineteenth century. Its chief theoretician and most powerful proponent was a Baptist, Walter Rauschenbush. Born in Rochester, New York of German Baptist parents, Walter Rauschenbusch graduated from the Rochester Theological Seminary in 1886, served for eleven years as pastor of the Second German Baptist Church in New York City, where he was called at a salary of $900 a year. In 1897 he became a teacher in the Rochester Theological Seminary and in 1902 he became professor of Church History in the English division of that Seminary where he served for the rest of his life. In 1907 he published *Christianity and the Social Crisis*, which thrust him into national prominence. In 1912 he published *Christianizing the Social Order:* and in 1918 he published *A Theology of the Social Gospel*. The influence of this Baptist on the life and work of the churches not only in America but throughout the world is incalculable. These three books were, I think, the most influential religious publications in America and possibly in the world in the first two decades of the twentieth century. While Walter Rauschenbusch was the personal symbol of the social gospel and the author of the classic books of Christian social concern, he was always closely connected with the church's evangelistic tradition. He never veered from the strictist kind of pietism, personal integrity, and sense of Christian calling. His life was filled with deep compassionate concern. He was unalterably convinced that personal regeneration and social reform ought to go hand in hand. He maintained a unique combination of evangelistic commitment, doctrinal orthodoxy, and social consciousness. He wrote in 1890 in an article entitled, "Society and the Individual", "Most Christians say: wait till all men are converted, then a perfect social order will be possible. Most social reformers say: wait till we have a perfect social order, then all good men will be good. We say: go at both simultaneously; neither is possible without the other.

They all say; wait! We say: repent for the kingdom of God is at hand."[1]

In spite of Walter Rauschenbusch's personal piety and personal evangelistic commitment, social Christianity in America tended to be identified with theological liberalism while theological orthodoxy tended to be identified with the establishment in opposition to social change. Linking financial success to virtue and poverty to laziness, the Baptist lecturer, Russell Conwell, declared, "Ninety-eight out of one-hundred of the rich men of America are hones. That is why they are rich." Making short shrift of the poor he said, "The number to be emphasized with is very small. To sympathize with a man whom God has punished for his sins, thus to help him when God will still continue a just punishment, is to do wrong, no doubt about it . . ."[2] More Baptists were influenced by Russell Conwell, or at least more were in basic agreement with him, than were influenced by or were in basic agreement with Walter Rauschenbusch. In spite of Rauschenbusch's personal credentials as a Baptist, the social gospel movement lost its theological footing.

The incredibly naive belief in the inevitability of human progress and the inconsequentiality of sin received a death blow with the first World War. The social gospel movement was essentially dead by about 1925. The forces of God which brought it into being and the biblical truth which underlay its basic concerns, however, have assured the cause of Christian ethics a continuing place on the Christian agenda in general and on the Baptist agenda in particular.

Christians have social responsibility. Social structures in their particular forms are not necessarily ordained of God. A commitment to relieve the oppressed, help the weak, feed the hungry, and let justice roll down as waters and righteousness as a mighty stream, as Amos put it, are inescapable responsibilities for the people of God. We have a divine imperative to implement Christian ethics.

There is an increasingly strong consensus that God calls His people to an agenda of engagement, that the Christian faith has meaning and relevance in society. There is among Baptists a generally growing sense of social responsibility; and the place of this Christian Ethics Commission in the life and work of the Baptist World Alliance attests to that fact.

Problems

Baptists who would express their faith and their witness by implementing Christian ethics are faced with some serious problems. Controversy attends such implementation as bees attend honey, as it is the nature of the institution to fend off challenges, to reject rebukes, and to press to maintain the status quo, so it is the nature of the prophetic word to challenge, to rebuke, and to press for change. Let it be remembered, however, that controversy attends the clarification of doctrines, mission programs, education, any emphasis on pease, and even stewardship. It is the teaching of James that "the friendship of the world is the enmity of God." Paul clearly says that "all who will life godly in Christ Jesus shall suffer persecution." Indeed, in the light of Jesus' world that if anyone will come after Him, he must deny himself, take up his cross daily, and follow Him, I am prepared to insist that a life without controversy is a life without Christ. It is He, the Great Divider, who said, "Think not that I am come to send peace on earth: I am cone not to send peace, but a sword. For I am come to set a man at variance against his father, and the daughter against her mother, and the daughter-in-law against her mother-in-law. And a man's foes shall be they of his own household. He that loveth father or mother more than me is not worthy of me; and he that loveth son or daughter more than me is not worthy of me. He that findeth his life shall lose it; and he that looseth his life for my sake shall find it." When the choice must be made between conformity to the world and controversy for Christ, the Christian has no choice but to contend. It is not only unchristian but it is extremely unbaptistic of us to fear controversy and shun confrontation as much as many do today.

Baptists interested in implementing Christian ethics must wrestle with a very grave problem caused by the rugged individualism which has been characteristic of Baptists from the beginning. Many Baptists today are intensely angry at those within our fellowships who agitate for engagement and press for social change. These believe there is no place in the Baptist movement for such concerns. They want the Bible preached in the truncated form to which they have become accustomed in the culture religion of their established churches. They would obliterate from Baptist life any emphasis on public affairs or social concerns. They insist that it would be a great service to God and to Baptists to rid the movement of such concern for behavior or with society. In the most social era of man's history, they are obsessed with the radical individualism that in some measure is harbored in the heart of every Baptist. That rugged individualism which has made Baptists strong could, in today's world, now prevent us from claiming our share of the future. What has pushed us forward could now hold us back. These radical individualists view religion as purely personal and the church's task as that of providing preaching, Bible study, and a soul-saving service. They hold that on their own initiative saved souls may then find whatever avenues they can to do whatever God may want done in the world. As one of those saved souls, however, I understand my special christian calling to be that of helping changed people to change the world as we implement our Christian ethics.

Another problem encountered by Baptists who seek to implement our agenda of engagement is the tendency of any church to identify with its culture. You simply get in less trouble if you assume a pastoral or priestly stance rather than a prophetic one. The shepherd's pastoral staff does not traumatize like the prophet's painful goad or his thundering, "Repent." In addition, a lot of Baptist pulpits during political elections sound ominously like the Republican Party or the Tory Party or the established conservative party by whatever name, gathered for prayer. All of this willingness to be used and this identification with the culture suggests that at least many Baptists are lacking in that singleminded commitment to God and concern with the doing of His will in the world without which we shall surely be tossed about by every wind of doctrine. Baptists cannot do the work of God in the world with regard to our agenda of engagement if we are the other-directed rather than inner-directed people, if we have lost our first love, if our trumpet gives an uncertain sound.

Another problem with which Baptists must deal in the area of social concern has to do with the general Baptist acceptance of social evils without moral outrage. It is a fearful thing to consider that much of the current moral outrage regarding the great social sins of our time has been primarily registered by journalists, jurists, editors, and lawyers rather than by the people of God in general or Baptist in particular.

Opportunities

Those of us who are seeking to get Baptists to move forward with this agenda of engagement are not interested in becoming Unitarians and in singing hymns to the Nuclear Freeze, hunger relief, race relations, sewage disposal, and sex education. We are just interested in being God's people and in doing His thing and in helping Baptists to do the things that make for peace, to follow righteousness, and to do what is right in the world. Within our own fellowships there are treasons which must be challenged. We believe in the Christian faith has profound social consequences and that the blessings of God will not abide on a people who refuse to preach the whole word of God in Christ, including the moral word.

Baptists today have a numerical strength and a base of influence for good in society which our Baptist forebears could hardly have dreamed of. Prospects for a significant impact for Jesus Christ were never better. If Baptists today will both accept and communicate the fullness of the Christian gospel, our total witness can be expected to come to life as it most certainly would never do if it were distinguished by visionless irrelevance, selfish commitment to the *status quo*, and a passionless refusal to implement our Christian ethics. It is our opportunity as Baptists and our Christian imperative to communicate God's good news as it relates to family life, race relations, citizenship, daily work, and such special social concerns as peace with justice, hunger, pornography, child abuse, gambling, immoral television programming, and the consumption of alcohol and other dangerous drugs. Both to our own constituents and to the world around us we have a responsibility to communicate these concerns. The gospel is, indeed, good news in all of these difficult arenas of daily life.

The task is to convert the modernists around us and among us who have turned away from Moses and the prophets and Paul and John and Peter and James, and from Jesus, to embrace that wretchedly false and abominably misleading dualism which never ceases to plague the Christian church. Our task is to convince our alienated brethren who seek to turn the church away from the great moral issues of our time that if, indeed, we did turn away, the world would be impoverished and the church's whole life and work would be invalidated, for if God's people cannot confront the issues that affect humanity with the reconciling gospel of Jesus Christ in such a way as to convince unbelievers, then evangelism is empty and missions is mockery.

Our task is to help Baptist people at every level of Baptist life to understand that God's basic concern is not religion but life and to see that there can be no turning back from responsible involvement in the world and responsible commitment to an agenda of engagement to effect social change for God's glory and humanity's good. A continued rejection of social fads, unbaptized humanism, unbiblical pietism, and moral posturing—yes. But disengagement—no. Uninvolvement in this age is simply not a live option for the people of God. Our task is to help Baptists understand that sin is both personal and social, and that we cannot be true to God and wink at the great social sins of nuclear roulette, ecological rape, white racism, unbridled militarism, poverty in the midst of plenty, crime, business exploitation of consumers, male chauvinism, inflation, unemployment, and political corruption. In the escalating battle for the soul of the church between those who in the name of Christ and purely personal religion would retreat from the great social issues and those who in the name of Christ and His full gospel with its social imperative seek to confront and solve these issues, our task is to help Baptists work out their salvation with fear and trembling in this world and in this age and do the work of God regarding social change as we implement our Christian ethics.

Contrary to what today's humanistic activists are saying, Christ cannot be Lord without being Savior. And contrary to what today's pietistic fundamentalists are saying, Christ cannot be Savior without also being Lord. Our task is to help Baptists see that God has joined together Christ's saviorhood and His Lordship. God has joined together evangelism and ethics, withdrawal and involvement, conservation and innovation, worship and work, reflection and action, practicing and preaching, the indicative and the imperative, the personal and the social—these must be everlasting linked in the life and work of the church or else the church goes off into grievous and inexcusable heresy.

Baptists have peculiar resources in our heritage and in our understanding of the Bible to steer us away from the heresy which retreats into private religiosity to escape the tension of the prophetic word. We likewise find in these insights a way to avoid the equally serious error of equating Christian responsibility with every special program of social engineering.

Prospect

On the authority of the Bible and God's revelation of Himself in Jesus Christ, it must be insisted that the implementation of Christian ethic is not an option but an imperative for the people of God.

The waves of Pentecostalism and Dispensationalism, of Pharisaism and Fundamentalism, of escapism and narcissism, which have washed over the gospel and battered the church in the past are now washing over us and battering us again. These waves shall pass. They are tidal waves and not a change in the water level. However temporary they may be, though, they are now doing substantial damage to the witness of Baptists and to the cause of social concern among Baptists.

It is of special concern to all those interested in extending the kingdom of God that an epidemic of immortality has overwhelmed the nation and is threatening to engulf the churches. The Bible's emphasis on Christian morality and responsible engagement in the world was never as desperately needed as it is today.

Because God has made humanity free, His promises are conditional. He blesses in accordance with His own righteous character and so as not to violate our nature as free moral agents. His blessings are not promise and will not be given to a people who embrace culture while rejecting Christ. His blessings are promised and will be given to a people who ascertain the mind of Christ and conform to His mind in doing justice, loving mercy, and walking humbly with God (Micah 6:7-8) as we implement our Christian ethics. If as God's people we will now move to love God with our whole heart and to love our neighbors as we love ourselves (Matthew 22:36-40), then God's blessings all will abundantly come, beyond anything we know to ask or think. The prospects for new life for Baptists and a significant witness to the world are as bright as our real commitment to Jesus Christ as Lord, here and now, in this world.

And now, as a practical conclusion, I set forth ten suggestions as to practical things Baptists can do to implement Christian ethics.

(1) Let us preach Christian ethics faithfully in our pulpits for righteousness, justice, peace, moral values, integrity, mercy, and right relationships are great biblical themes which may not be neglected with impunity by the people of God.

(2) Let us teach Christian ethics as an integral part of the educational programs of all our Baptists churches.

(3) Let us sing about Christian ethics, making sure that the doing of the gospel of God in Christ is not excluded while only expressions about heaven and the sweet by and by are included in this vital part of Christian worship and life and work.

(4) Let us incorporate the various dimensions of Christian ethics in our family life so that Christian concern about family life, human relations, economics, citizenship, and morel decision making in daily life are a vital part of home life in Baptist families everywhere.

(5) Let us conscientiously spread the word of truth related to Christian ethics when, as Baptist Christians, we have opportunity to use the mass media for direct preaching, teaching, or for indirect testimony related to the relevance of the gospel to all the great issues of life.

(6) Let us write about Christian ethical concerns when we have opportunity to write lessons, bulletins, reports, program materials, or personal letters so that practical moral concerns are more and more woven into the reading of those with whom we have anything to do.

(7) Let us include Christian ethics in our planning of the programs for our Baptist conventions, assemblies, conferences, and stated meetings, not neglecting to include and to emphasize matters which are of great consequence in the Bible, in human relationships, and to progress for the kingdom of God.

(8) Let us press for the inclusion of ethical concerns, moral values, and enduring ideals in public life, knowing that Christian ethics is not at cross purposes with authentic values which may be embraced, supported, and promoted by responsible persons throughout society.

(9) Let us organize whenever, wherever, and however we can to further the cause of Christian ethics realizing that structures such as Christian ethics committees, interest groups, commissions, and departments can serve the cause better than mere talk or unstructured dreaming.

(10) Let us practice Christian ethics in our own daily life and work remembering that the basic call of God to us all is to live under the lordship of Jesus Christ every area and relationship of life.

Foy Valentine is the former director of the Christian Life Commission of the Southern Baptist Convention, Nashville, Tennessee, USA.

Endnotes

1. Doris R. Sharpe, *Biography of Walter Rauschenbusch* (1942), p. 92
2. Marquis W. Childs and Douglass Cater, *Ethics in Business Society.* (New York: Menton Books, 1954), 137.

Making or Having Babies: A Christian Understanding of Responsible Parenthood

Daniel B. McGee

Parenting is one of the most awesome, intimate, and value-laden human activities. It is simultaneously exhilarating and intimidating, fulfilling and depleting. The most central human values are involved in parenting. For the reason recent developments in reproductive technology have raised serious and sometimes heated discussions about the ethical legitimacy of our newfound procedures of human reproduction. Two major governmental studies reflect the widespread interest and concern within the general population. In the U.S. a 1982 study is entitled *Splicing Life: The social and Ethical Issues of Genetic Engineering with Human Beings,* and it reflects the views of a broad-based presidential commission that was assigned the task of making recommendations to the U.S. Government.[1] The Warnack Report of 1984 reflects the efforts in Britain to formulate some societal guidelines for these methods of reproduction.[2] The Christian church also has been active in these discussions. The proceedings from a 1973 conference by the World Council of Churches,[3] and a 1987 statement from the Congregation of the Doctrine of Faith of the Roman Catholic Church have enriched the discussion.[4] In addition, there have been a number of important works by individual Christians.[5] The Christian Ethics Commission of the Baptist World Alliance is to be congratulated for entering into this discussion by including this topic in your overall consideration of family life. Indeed, I am especially pleased that you have placed this discussion of the ethics of human reproduction within the context of a larger discussion of family life. This is where our attention belongs because this is not primarily a question about technology or science. For us, it should be a discussion of the shape and purpose of family life and relationships. For this reason I want to focus our discussion on the nature of responsible parenthood and how these new reproductive technologies impact our efforts to be responsible parents.

A brief examination of the new technological realities will help set the state for our ethical analysis. Here, I will use the term genetic modification in its broadest sense—descriptive of a number of different technologies by which we can design our descendants. This involves such procedures as artificial insemination (AID or AIH), in-vitro fertilization (IVF), cloning, surrogate motherhood, or gene therapy. The full range of possibilities is reflected in the distinctions that can be made among euphenic engineering, eugenic engineering, and genetic engineering.

Euphenic Engineering

Euphenics is the use of standard therapeutic techniques to improve the health of those persons who have a genetic disorder. The euphenic therapy provides whatever hormone, enzyme, antigen, or other protein which the body fails to provide normally because of the genetic flaw. The best known of such treatment is the provision of insulin injections for diabetics. There are many other such compensatory treatments which seek to control the expression of genetic information so as to minimize deleterious affects. Note there is no attempt here to alter or control genetic material itself, but rather to deal with the consequences of the genetic information.[6]

Euphenic efforts have been promoted by Joshua Lederberg and others as an effective way to deal immediately with genetic diseases without having to wait for the long term benefits of eugenic or genetic engineering.[7] The one serious objection that has been raised about euphenic engineering is that it can contribute to the pollution of the gene pool.

Eugenic Engineering

Eugenic engineering involves the selection and matching of genes existing in the gene pool of a population. This practice has been in existence for centuries, but the term and the proposal to use this procedure systematically to improve the human race is associated with Sir Francis Galton in 1883. Since then, many eugenic proposals have been made, some of then elitist and racist. Today most eugenic efforts are designed to assist couples to avoid undesirable matching of genes for the welfare of the child. Some of the techniques that can be used in a eugenic effort are artificial insemination by donor (AID), clogging, in-vitro fertilization, embryo transfer, and surrogate motherhood. There has been a significant growth in the effectiveness of and public support of these techniques in recent years.[8]

Genetic Engineering

Genetic engineering can be defined as ". . . the direct manipulation of the genetic message by changing, subtracting, or adding to the instructions received by the cell."[9] This process has come to be called gene therapy and can be achieved by several different techniques of altering the genetic material. When these alterations are made in somatic cells of an individual, they affect only that person's biochemical functioning. When the alteration is achieved in the germ cells (reproductive cells), then the change could be passed on to the genetic descendants of the individual.[10]

Gene therapy represents the most scientifically advanced and, therefore, the most promising or the most threatening of the new reproductive technologies, depending upon your assessment of these new possibilities.

An Ethical Analysis

There are a number of ethical issues raised by these new reproductive technologies that are worthy of our attention. We do not have the time here to deal with all of them. Some that are important, but which will not be the focus of our attention, are: (1) the moral validity of the research necessary to advance these new reproductive technologies; (2) the danger of psychological and social stress placed upon the first children born through the new technologies; (3) many moral-legal questions about the definition of parenthood and status of children born through the new technologies; (4) the question of priorities when we seem to be compulsive in our attention to these new esoteric technologies, but negligent of many proven but mundane technologies (like adequate nutrition) that have dramatic impact on the quality of our children.

In our discussion today, I want to focus on the question of responsible parenthood and how we understand this in the context of our new reproductive technologies.

Our language reflects a change in our understanding of reproduction and parenthood. Traditionally, prospective parents would say, "We are going to have a baby." Today the literature is filled with language about "making" a baby. "To have" and "to make" suggest different understandings of the reproduction process and the nature of parenthood.

"To have" a baby suggests the parental stance of receiving or accepting the baby. It is a rather passive pose in which parenthood is something that happens to them. To speak of "making" a baby suggests a quite different stance in which the parents are understood as much more active. "To make" suggests that the parental role involves creating or even designing the baby. The new technologies of human reproduction cast us more often in the role of "making." In this role our power as parents has increased in two areas. In the first place, our power to become parents has increased as we are able to overcome various forms of infertility. Second, our power to control the characteristics of our children has increased. In both of these areas we are more inclined to think of ourselves as "making" rather than just "having" babies.

I do not want to overstate the difference. There has always been a sense that the reproduction role of parents involved both "having" and "making." The difference is one of degrees. Today, and increasingly in the future, parents will think of themselves more in terms of controlling the reproductive process and thereby making or designing their children. It is my purpose to analyze these changes in the perception of parenthood and to suggest both positive and negative consequences of these changes.

1. "To make" a baby can heighten the parental sense of responsibility as co-creators with God.

To make involves a conscious and deliberate act in which the child is desired from the very beginning. In such a reproductive act, no parents could ever refer to the child as an "accident." To have a child reflects a more passing stance in which parenthood is viewed as a happening that is imposed upon the parents. In this more passive stance, parenthood is often viewed as an unexpected or even undesired side effect or by-produce of sexual activity.

The difference between the active and the more passive stance is significant both for the parents' understanding of their relationship with God and their relationship with the child. The more activist stance understands us as co-creators with God. It finds support in the New Testament accounts of stewardship and talents. In these stories the person of faith is given great responsibility with the expectation that one is to be active in exercising whatever ability or resource with which he or she has been entrusted. In these metaphors of faith, sin is burying your talent or ability. The same activist stance is reflected in the creation stories of Genesis. There God calls Adam to name the animals. In semitic cultures to name was to participate in the creation. The dominion passage of Genesis highlights the responsibility of humanity in the historical process. Such a sense of responsibility in the reproductive act can serve to strengthen the relationship between God and parent. Parenthood in this context can never be an accident. It is a commitment entered into with deliberate intention and purpose. In this model parenthood is unlikely to be received as a burden that is imposed. Rather, it is a vocation to be fulfilled.

The danger of the activist stance is obvious and will be dealt with more completely later in this paper. The danger is that the activist role will evolve into our arrogant rebellion against God. The Tower of Babel story of Genesis 11 portrays this sin where humanity seeks to climb up into God's domain. This arrogance can be expressed through human efforts to use genetic modification to redesign humanity. Some see this arrogance as the only or the necessary consequence of "making." I content that this need not be the case, and indeed, the new methods of human reproduction can be used to strengthen the relationship between God and humanity.

"Making" babies can also affect the parent-child relationship positively by increasing the parents' sense of commitment to the child. If the child is wanted from the beginning, the chances of parental commitment to the child is increased. The child does not begin its life as an unexpected or even unwelcomed intrusion.

2. To "make" a baby can encourage a manipulative paternalism.

One of the ironies of human experience is that we have a way of bending that which is good into an evil shape. We have long recognized a dark side of parental love, i.e., the love that turns compulsive and oppressive. Traditionally, we have spoken of these as a love that smothers the child, denying it the opportunity to become itself beyond the boundaries defined by the parent.

My concern is that the process of "making" or designing a child exposes it to this parental wish-fulfillment that can be very destructive of the child's autonomy and freedom. Having a baby places some restraints on this parental excess. The parents have to wait and be surprised by who is presented to them. This waiting contributes to a parental restraint that is more willing to support the child in fulfilling its own potential. The more designing that is involved in the reproductive process, the more established the parents become in the process of "calling the shots" for the child's destiny. If from the moment the child is a twinkle in the parents' eyes and dreams those parents are involved in concrete efforts to dictate the child's characteristics, then those parents are more likely to be habituated to controlling the destiny of the child. It is a habit that will be difficult to break. Our inclination is to see a project through to its intended conclusion. "Making" or designing our children will incline us to see parenting as a project with an end-result defined at the beginning.

There is another feature of making that contributes to manipulative paternalism. We generally understand that making implies ownership. That which I make is my property and is thus subject to my control. Thus my control of the child's destiny is legitimated by two factors: my ownership and my role as original designer.

The Christian understands parenthood on the stewardship model. We do not own our children. We do have great responsibility toward them, but it is a limited responsibility. As the good steward, we do not possess that which God has entrusted to us. We function as caretaker of those who ultimately belong to God. We can fail at this task by either neglect or by obsessive control of God's children. The new reproductive technologies tempt us toward the sin of compulsive paternalism.

3. To "make" a child encourages the valuing of the child in terms of his or her approximation to the parental design.

The danger is that the parental evaluation of and, therefore, commitment to the child is based on the child's fulfillment of the parents' design. This introduces a conditional commitment into the parent-child relationship.

The tendency is to evaluate people in terms of how well they fulfill their potential or their reason for being. The more we as parents contribute to the design of a child, the more it appears that we define its reason for being. The stage is then set for parents to evaluate the child by the degree to which it fulfills the parent-defined purpose of the child. On the other hand, the "received" child is more likely to come on its own terms, bringing a purpose that the parent is called upon to recognize and accept. To the degree that the child's reason for being is not defined by the parents, they are not tempted to treat the child as a means to a parental-defined end. Every child should be loved as God loves—unconditionally. We live in an age when many factors are weakening the ties that bind families. We do not need another element of tenuousness in the parent-child relationship.

This danger of tenuous commitment can express itself at the societal level as well. There have been suggestions that the new reproductive technologies might be used to create persons to perform specialized tasks. This suggestion matches the spirit of a utilization value system that permeates most of our societal-desired end. We should be alert to rejecting reproductive procedures that promote or encourage such values. Indeed, there should be concern that parents in a society that works hard to avoid a specific genetic disease in a child may be less willing to accept the child from whom the disease is absent but who has some other imperfection. The danger is that, as we become more skilled in eliminating genetic health problems for our children, we will become less tolerant of those who slip through our well-intended net and do not measure up to our dreams for them.

Parental love and commitment should be unconditional—stable—secure.

It can be if we remember that God defines the value and purpose of our children. We must not base our commitment to our children on a purpose that we have created for them.

4. To "make" a child is to run the risk of faulty designs.

Traditionally, parental designs for children have reflected a high level of provincialism and myopia. This parental tendency toward fads and fashion is reflected in the names given children. Even this modest effort to define the child reflects the short-sighted vision of the parents when names are chosen that soon lose their luster. Such mistakes in naming can, at worst, be a source of embarrassment later for the children. However, the mistake would be much more serious if the design of the child is flawed. This provincialism of designing others is reflected in the expressed designs of the past. Hermann Meuller, noted human geneticist, promoted the dream of designing future generations through sperm donation from superior humans. In the first edition of *Out of the Night* (1925), he made an enthusiastic plea for such intelligent planning for the future human race and suggested as an example a promising sperm donor, Lenin. In later editions of this work, Lenin's name was dropped and replaced by Lincoln, Descartes, Pasteur, and Einstein. The crucial point is not the ideal types he chose, but that he changed. We have always been fickle with our heroes. Should we subject future generations, or even just one of our children, to such fickleness? Even if we select a good design, who is to say that the specific genius of one generation is the genius that is needed for the next generation.

A more realistic example and, therefore, a more real danger of provincial parenting is the possibility of selecting the gender of one's child. Surveys show that, if this choice were available at each birth, approximately 70 percent of the children would be male. This would be a tragic mistake and demonstrates the wisdom of Mother Nature.

A specific and prominent limitation in our view of desirable characteristics is our tendency to strive for homogeneity. We tend to become fixed upon a particular ideal type and to narrow the boundaries of what is desirable. The truth is that diversity is probably the greatest strength of the human race. A very real danger in genetic engineering is that, in our enthusiasm to achieve excellence, we will eliminate valuable characteristics from the gene pool.

When we reflect on these differences between "having" and "making" babies, three general ethical concerns emerge.

1. Some are concerned about the involvement of persons other than the husband or wife in the process of reproduction. Some are concerned that this violates the one-flesh relationship of marriage. There is also concern that there is confusion in the parent-child relationship as the traditional understanding of parenthood is threatened. In this regard, there is an interesting case in the Onan story of Genesis 38:8-10. Here, God is displeased when Onan will not sire a child for his deceased brother because Onan realizes that the child will not be his own. It seems to me that, just as the responsibility of nurturing children can be shared with a community larger than the parents, a larger community could participate in the creation of the child.

2. Some are concerned about the separation of human procreation from

the act of sexual intercourse. I sense that here much of the objection is based on an attachment to the past. These methods of reproduction are new and are rejected for that reason. There is a tendency to be traditional in matters sexual or reproductive.

There is a more substantial objection based on a concern to assure that human life is created within the context of love. I agree with the basic premise of this analysis. Every child should be created out of an act of love. What I do not agree with is the assumption that lovemaking is limited to the act of sexual intercourse. There could be no more loving act, i.e., an act filled with commitment to both one's mate and the desired child, than all that is involved in the process of artificial insemination, in-vitro fertilization, etc. I do not see how the absence of coition from the particular event in which conception occurs necessarily excludes love from the reproductive process.

These first two concerns raise questions about the procedures involved in "making" babies. The third concern focuses on the purposes and consequences.

3. There is concern about the use of the new reproductive technologies to design human life. The concern is that such efforts extend beyond the morally legitimate rights or wisdom of humanity. I share this concern.

As indicated above, there is reason to be concerned about the limits of our parental wisdom in determining the characteristics of our children. There are also grounds for concern about how the exercise of this parental power tempts us to become irresponsible parents, yet there are circumstances where the goal of reproductive designing is a parental responsibility. When we have the capacity to prevent a clearly dysfunctional condition in our children, I believe we have the responsibility to do so. Thus, I would support any clearly therapeutic purpose, but nothing beyond that. As parents, we should be open to the rich diversity of humanity in our children, and we should have the humility to recognize that our wisdom in regulating the life of another, even our children, is limited.

Conclusion

The new methods of human reproduction are challenging and, in some ways, frightening. To be sure, they can be used for unethical purposes, and they may even tempt us to be less than responsible. In the final analysis, however, I do not believe that Christians should view them as inherently immoral. Our task is to accept the challenge of new responsibilities and avoid the temptations that are present in these new powers.

Dan Magee is Professor of Ethics at Baylor University in Waco, Texas, U.S.A.

Notes

1. President's Commission for the Study of Ethical Problems in Medicine and Biomedical and Behavioral Research, *Splicing Life: The Social and Ethical Issues of Genetic*

Engineering with Human Beings, U.S. Government Printing Office, Washington, D.C., November 1982.

2. Dame Mary Warnack (Chm.), *Report of the Committee of Inquiry into Human Fertilization and Embryology*, Her Majesty's Stationery Office, London, July 1984.

3. Charles Birch and Paul Abrecht (eds.), *Genetics and the Quality of Life*, Pergamon Press, Oxford, 1975.

4. "Instruction on Respect for Human Life in Its Origin and on the Dignity of Procreation: Replies to Certain Questions of the Day," Vatican City, 1987.

5. These works include: J. Kerby Anderson, *Genetic Engineering*, Zondervan Corporation, Grand Rapids, 1982; D. Gareth Jones, *Brave New People: Ethical Issues at the Commencement of Life*, William B. Eerdmanns, Grand Rapids, 1985; Karen Lebacqz (ed.), *Genetics, Ethics and Parenthood*, The Pilgrim Press, New York, 1983; Oliver O'Donovan, *Begotten or Made?*, Clarendon, Oxford, 1984; Paul Ramsey, *Fabricated Man*, Yale University Press, New Haven, 1970; Thomas A. Shannon, *What Are They Saying About Genetic Engineering*, Paulist Press, New York, 1985.

6. I. Michael Lerner and William J. Libby, *Heredity Evolution and Society*, W. H. Freeman and Company, San Francisco, 1976, pp. 383-5. 7. Joshua Lederberg, "Biological Future of Man" in Gordon Wolstenholme (ed.), *Man and His Future*, Little, Brown and Company, Boston, 1963, pp. 264-70.

8. Lerner and Libby, p. 277-83.

9. Ibid., p. 384.

10. Warren T. Reich (ed.), "Gene Therapy," *Encyclopedia of Bioethics*, Vol. II, "The Free Press, New York, 1978, pp. 513-27.

The Christian Challenge of An Aging Population

David Charley

"They shall not grow old, as we that are left grow old, age shall not weary them nor the years condemn. At the going down of the sun and in the morning we will remember them."

These imperishable words of Lawrence Binyon appear on the memorial to those from Blenheim Chapel, Leeds, England, who gave their lives in the First World War. I see them every Sunday and remember with gratitude.

But we that are left to grow old—to what are we condemned? Certainly the years weary and that cannot be controlled but the situation of the elderly is something over which we can have some control and which demands our thought and action as compassionate Christians.

The expected longevity of those being born today throughout the world is greater than it has been at any time in recorded history. I believe that discussion as to whether true longevity, far beyond anything we can appreciate, ever existed in the time of Methuselah only results in sterile and unrewarding argument. This tendency to live longer has gradually taken place within the nations of the developed world of today but it is now, with increasing speed, also involving the new emergent nations all over the world. In the west an aging population is already a demographic fact, in other countries it soon will be, though that may not seem apparent when one considers countries such as Thailand with over half its population under 25.

This paper endeavours to investigate in what ways this demographic change should alter our Christian thinking and planning, if indeed any alteration is necessary as we seek to serve Christ. Christ who came to call "all to repentance" and who came to bring life and to bring it abundantly—to young and old, as well as to rich and poor, black and white.

In the past, mistakes have been made and mistakes are still being made in our attitudes towards the elderly. Attitudes of society, often condoned by Christians, which have not been conducive to the development of optional ability, personality and spirituality in the elderly. The elderly have not been able to integrate into the society in which they live in a way which can bring the greatest benefit and co-operative well being to all. The "generation gap" has been allowed to grow to a greater extent than it need have been and unnecessary antagonisms have developed.

Many nations are now beginning to grapple with this problem. What have we, as members of the Baptist World Alliance Commission on Christian Ethics to say to them? Can we help them avoid making the same mistakes that have been made? Have some of us words of warning and of hope to take back to our emergent nations?

I write as a physician, trained in the scientific evaluation of facts and try to equate these evaluations with the insights gained from a Christian upbringing, faith and experience. Reference to figures and statistics cannot be avoided when approaching a subject such as this. Attention to statistics is a valid Christian exercise and necessary to evaluate our Christian service. When medical missionaries were first allowed into the Kingdom of Nepal they approached the Nepalese Government to ask in what way they could be of most help in promoting the health and well-being of the country's population. The answer to that question was "by the collection of accurate statistics". For until those were available, the identification of major problems and the best use of available resources could not be defined.

The expectation of life in developed countries has increased rapidly in the last half century. This is largely due to the antibiotics and other measures which have resulted in the effective treatment of the great infective scourges of mankind, which previously caused such horrendous mortality. I find it hard to believe today, that, when I was a medical student just prior to the advent of the antibiotic era, a man over 45 years of age who contracted pneumonia was not expected to live. If he did the credit was rightly given to his nurse for there was little his doctor could do. The time when an epidemic of diphtheria could decimate the children of a village in one short epidemic is just within my lifetime.

One effect of overcoming these diseases has been the liberation of medical time and personnel to deal with the great degenerative diseases of aging which now play such a large part in many doctor's practices.

Out of the multiplicity of figures available, a small and, I hope, representative selection must suffice. In France, since 1900 life expectancy at birth has increased by 24 years for makes and 29 years for females. I spent eighteen months in Sri Lanka in 1944 to 1946 and life expectancy at that time was 43 years. In 1970-1972 it was 66 years an increase of 23 years in quarter of a century. In all countries newborn females have a better life-expectancy than males, averaging 3 years but increasing to 8 years in Finland. Amongst the Kibbutzim in Israel life-expectancy in both sexes is equal and the only community showing a reversal of this trend is that of the Amish of Pennsylvania in the U.S.A. where the men outlive the women.

Let me give you some recent figures and predictions from my own home town, Leeds, in the United Kingdom. Leeds is an industrial city in Yorkshire in the North of England with a population of 3/4 of a million. In 1981 the population contained 15% of persons over 65 years of age, 6% over 75 years of age and 1% over 85 (i.d., nearly 7,500 over 85 years old!) It is estimated that in 1991 the number of persons over 85 will be 12,000 and in 2001 it will be 15,000 and I may be amongst them! It is expected that numbers in the age groups 65-75 and 75-85 will actually drop during the decade 1991-2001 whereas the 85+ group will continue to increase. Our Queen will be spending more and more money on telegrams as she sends a message to everyone of her subjects who reaches their 100th birthday!

Any definition of "old" has cultural and regional connotations. In a shanty town in Peru it would be 45-50 years, in the United Kingdom it is commonly equated with retirement age, i.e., 60 for a woman and 65 for a man (an unnecessary and unjust distinction!) It must be remembered that "retirement" is a recent and a western concept. There can be no retirement where every day brings a renewal of the struggle to obtain enough food just to stay alive. With the increasing tendency towards earlier retirement in those countries where this is possible, there are now four ages of mankind rather than three. There are Youth, Middle Age, Young Old Age (up to 75) and Old Old Age (75 and beyond). In 1980 the more developed regions of the world contained one quarter of the world's total population but three quarters of those in Old Old Age.

There are special insights of relevance as we consider attitudes to the elderly as they approach the extreme end of physical life in this world. The Hospice Movement has, within the last twenty years, revolutionized attitudes toward the dying. The essential change of attitude taught by the Hospice Movement is that such persons are not "dying", although death may not be far distant, but they are persons who are not going to get better and yet still have some living to do. Living which, with the right support and caring love can be happy, creative, rewarding and achieved to the Glory of God.

The Hospice Movement has resulted in a vast improvement in the control of symptoms and thus an improvement in their physical well-being. The Movement has also created an atmosphere in which the psychological needs of patients are better understood and in which the spiritual content of life is fully recognized. It is essential that all these three aspects of care be kept in balance. There are some who feel that good "counseling" is the be-all and end-all of the care of the terminally ill; they forget how to use God-given drugs. Carers should never forget that kindness is no substitute for efficiency and what a patient expects and desires most of all from his careers in their integrity.

Respect for the dignity of the dying patient and the realization that, in the majority of cases, death can occur in comfort and with dignity, has removed one of the main arguments for euthanasia and has influenced the practice of medicine away from the dehumanizing effect of reliance upon high technology. There is no longer an attempt to refuse to accept the inevitability of ageing and death. Instead of treating diseases, men and women with their personalities and their idiosyncracies are being cared for. Cure is still being sought but, where cure proves impossible or inappropriate, care is seen to be a continuing necessity.

In the care of patients who are not going to get better there is one factor which weight heavily against any legislative attempt to allow euthanasia. Towards the end of life there is often a time when sheer physical weakness or other infirmity makes it impossible for the dying patient to respond to their environment, even though they can still take in and understand stimuli and information. The last sense to disappear at death is hearing, a fact which should always be remembered in the presence of the dying. If the patient near to death is unable to communicate with me that may be my fault and not theirs. I may not be listening attentively enough or I may not be sensitive to the nuances of a flicker of movement of the face or an almost imperceptible grasp of the hand. Close and attentive listening as well as recognition of the value of touch are paramount in such a situation.

However, if I, as an attendant upon such a persons, cannot converse with them because of their proximity to death, have I any right to assume that they cannot converse with God and God with them? I think noti So, until death does indeed take place that potential must be cherished and maintained. This is to my mind, is one of the most powerful arguments against any action which might precipitate death and thus cut off the possibility of such dialogue between the dying person and his or her Creator.

In countries of the Third World greater respect is shown to the aged. There are several reasons for this. Firstly, this has traditionally been the situation and there are fewer old people in less sophisticated societies. In technologically developed societies emphasis is put on the young, the virile, the new and the constantly changing. They are following Shakespeare who said, "Age I do abhor thee, Youth I do adore thee". Would that they would pay more attention to Robert Louis Stevenson who wrote, "To love playthings well as a child, to lead an adventurous and honourable youth and to settle when the time comes into a green and smiling age, is to be a good artist of life".

With advancing technology experience matters less. It is the elderly who can bring to any community the value of their experience and when experience is devalued then their status is reduced.

This tendency to devalue the elderly is beginning in the third world but in the western world it has already developed to an extent which is not in keeping with compassionate Christianity. Simone de Beauvoir wrote "The meaning or lack of meaning that old age takes on in any given society puts that whole society to the test, since it is this that reveals the meaning or lack of meaning of the entirety of life leading to that old age".

The elderly are a deprived group in most developed societies. In the United Kingdom two-thirds of pensioners live on the poverty line or within 10% of it. Scandinavia does rather better. The usual experience of old age is deprivation. Financial deprivation leading to deprivation of the physical necessities of life, particularly warmth and deprivation of family ties, especially now that so many families are fragmented. One often reads of the effect of a divorce upon the children of a marriage but the effect upon the elderly of this human catastrophe can be equally devastating. Deprivation of human contact and concern; the value of touch in the care of old people must never be underestimated. Deprivation of respect and dignity resulting in the agony of not being wanted, of being a burden to others.

One of the aspects of modern society which affects all ages, but to which the elderly are particularly vulnerable, is the increasing speed of change. Change in laws and regulations, change in prices, change in timetables and in the many aspects of the daily routine of life. Any individual can only adapt, *without stress*, to a certain quantity of change in unit time. Much of today's stress is due to the fact that many people are having to adapt to change at a rate beyond their capacity. The ability to adapt to change reduces with age and consequently many of these people living under this stress are elderly. It is not practical for Christians to "slow the world down" but rather we should pray "may all change be blessed", remembering that the poet Tenneyson wrote, "The old order changeth, yielding place to new and God fulfills himself in many ways, lest one good custom should corrupt the world".

The elderly should not necessarily be regarded as reactionary because they wish to stick to well tried, well loved and well understood methods and ideas. Often they are proved right as the wheel of change turns full circle to where it started - but not without much stress. Nevertheless the elderly must also recognize their responsibilities in making use of new ideas and not utilizing an unnecessarily large share of available resources.

We as Christian citizens should be aware of the potential dangers if this were carried to extremes. Already those over 65 are filling the majority of all hospital beds in the United Kingdom and occupying them for a longer time. The stark potential of inappropriate use of resources was predicted some years ago, by Sir George Pickering, then Regius Professor of Medicine in Oxford. In an address he gave in New York, he said "Beware the triumph of the senile. The senile, and they would be the rich senile, might demand to be kept alive with somebody else's heart, somebody else's liver and somebody else's kidneys. - *BUT* with their own senile brains". That possibility is greater today than when Sir George issued his warning.

Retirement, as presently experienced in the West, is an- arbitrary event bringing problems of adjustment - mental, physical and emotional. Such traumatic readjustment could be avoided in countries beginning to face the problem of an ageing population. Status and influence and, above all power of choice, should be maintained as long as possible. The elderly should not, by virtue of age alone, be regarded as dependent or as being sick. Old people get sick just as the young do, but just because one is old, one is not necessarily sick. An old person who does not feel sick does not like to be treated as though he or she were sick. Their normal desire is to reach their greatest potential in activity, in service, in spirituality; and we must help them so to do. The old, at the present time, were brought up in a social and economic climate which forced them to develop a spirit of independence; a desire, often of necessity, to stand on their own feet. They are carrying this independent spirit into their old age and ask that it be respected and so it should

The Care of the elderly two generations from now may be completely different. Then, those involved will have, throughout life, been used to the conditions of a welfare State, of protection and support from the cradle to the grave. Will our children in their old age present an easier or a greater problem to their children's children?

The provision of facilities making the elderly dependent upon others, as in so many old persons' homes, may be bureaucratically tidy; but such provision increases dependency. It takes away autonomy, problem-solving ability and above all, challenge. It removes the daily challenge to live to the Glory of God which is to be truly human. Such provision also inevitably takes away private space and creates enforced intimacy. No wonder the elderly submitted to such a regime become apathetic. Yet this has been the pattern of care for the elderly in the United Kingdom and elsewhere and it needs changing. I have visited homes for the elderly and seen them sitting round the room in sullen silence or in agitated self-seeking. They have no choices to make, sometimes not even that choice, so dear to the heart of a lady - "what shall I wear?"

This type of management provides creature comforts and satisfies the authorities that they are fulfilling their obligations. But is it truly kind? It is a policy which we as Christians should condone? Certainly many confined to such an existence are unhappy. However the alternative, that of helping the elderly to maintain their independence, is costly in term of service from others.

Every winter in England there is an outcry in the press when an old person, living alone, is found dead in their home. Death may be due to hypothermia, malnutrition, pneumonia or just "old age" (a doctor cannot put "old age" on a death certificate - it is not a recognized cause of death). Someone is always to be blamed for such a tragedy, if tragedy it is, and it is usually the often maligned social services who take the blame. Might this not be the triumphant end of a fiercely fought battle to maintain independence? The old person may have died in squalor but has been successful in doing things their way.

Hospice patients sometimes express a wish to die at home, even though they have required total care for some time and even if such a move seems quite inappropriate from a medical and nursing point of view. With the willing and often sacrificial support of the nursing staff responsible for domiciliary care, I have sometimes arrange for such a patient to be discharged home solely in order that such a wish shall be met and the patient be able to spend their last hours surrounded by their familiar things.

For many of the elderly the end of life is overshadowed by Dementia -

Altzheimer's Disease. A recent report entitled "Logins a Million Minds" predicts a five fold increase in cases of senile dementia in the U.S.A. by the year 2000! This is directly related to the expected increase in longevity and the figure in the United Kingdom is likely to be similar.

The care of these persons (I do not say patients as it is so important to remember the persons that they once have been) will be a challenge to Christians in any society.

As I see it the two great challenges to Christian caring in the next two decades are going to be the care of demented old people and young people dying of AIDS.

Officially organized schemes for the care of the elderly often provide lots of "services" but little "help". Such schemes need to be flexible and delivered in a caring way. Sometimes in bureaucratically organized services Christian staff, imbued with the desire to serve and help people, become worried by their own loss of sensitivity and leave. They feel unable to give expression to their caring concern within the organizational structure laid down. Their challenge is to remain within the system and slowly and persistently work to change it and give it a more loving aspect.

Another aspect of concern regarding Christian attitudes to the elderly is the way in which we regard the deaf. It is said that the blind get all the sympathy and the deaf get all the ridicule. Yet deafness is equally isolating and tragic, the more so as it is not easily seen and appreciated. The Christian virtue of patients needs full expression in dealing with the deaf.

In Paul's letter to Titus (Chapter 2, verse 2) we read "Bid the older men to be temperate, serious, sensible, sound in faith, in love and in steadfastness". One's spiritual needs are greater as the end of life approaches. In my hospice work I was surprised how many patients referred back in memory to Sunday School days, maybe 60 years ago. In between there is a spiritual blank, but faced with imminent death their spiritual life is re-awakened and needs nourishment. Likewise those, who have led an active Christian life throughout, feel concerned; they see the deterioration of their physical and mental state and naturally may imaging that their spirituality is suffering similarly, just as they are preparing to meet their God and they are worried. The Psalmist cries out (Psalm 71, verse 9) "Do not cast me off in the time of old age; forsake me now when my strength is spent".

So much current evangelistic zeal and drive is directed towards the young. There is great need to evangelize the elderly. One of their deprivations can be the knowledge of the love of Christ. Job, in his distressful old age ways (Chapter 12, verse 13 and 20) - "With God are wisdom and might; He takes away the discernment of the elders".

In summary our aims for improving the care of the elderly should be:

(1) Recognizing their needs and challenging any legislation, attitudes or schemes which may prove unkind.

(2) Recognize their desire for independence, their concern for their spirituality and the natural desire to live positively to the end. (There is a verse

of a hymn which begins "The whole wide world for Jesus' - there could be another verse - "The whole of life for Jesus, this shall our watchword be").

(3) Fostering human relationships throughout life that resentful old age does not develop. This includes helping the young to live with concern for the sort of lives they will be able to live in old age. Young people today are said to fear old age more than they fear death. (Isaac Watts, the hymn writer, put is succinctly when he wrote - "My days of praise shall Na'er be past while life and thought and being last.")

Help is better than care. Love is better than service. The fruit of the spirit is not good works but in showing the love of God. It is only as we walk in the spirit showing the love of Christ and not depending upon our own love or caring or strength that we shall be able to measure up to the Christian challenge of an aging population.

May we all adapt words of the prophet Joel - "So let our young men see visions of service that our old men may dream dreams".

David Carley is a physician and Baptist layman in Great Britain.

Our Baptist Heritage: Christian Citizenship And Church/State Relations

Heather M. Vose

This paper constitutes the first of a five-part series focusing on the general topic of "Christian citizenship and related ethical issues". During the course of these presentations, both local and national concerns are to be raised as fully as possible within prevailing limits. In order to facilitate useful and enlightened discussion it is therefore important to outline plainly the historical background from which, broadly speaking, contemporary Baptist thinking emerged and upon which it builds.

History, then, will be both the context and resource of succeeding papers. This introductory study takes up the specific question of "Our Baptist heritage - Christian citizenship and Church-State relations". Even as we set about examining such a large subject, one critical fact must be borne in mind - indeed, before, during and after our discussion. It is this: we must draw on our heritage, but not be bound by it. Baptist heritage rejects binding as a completely alien notion.

Necessary restrictions upon the paper itself dictate the exclusion of certain material. At points we must rely on sketches of those who became prototypes and exemplars of religious currents. Such a methodology is perfectly legitimate since the spiritual history of Baptists is linked to the experiences of men and women and to records bearing evidence of their human destiny. Here the notion that history is itself selective has considerable consequence; evidence chosen from the available bulk automatically conceals or reveals, while firmly-held beliefs or affinities may never be chronicled. Perhaps this is one reason for the historiographical dispute that clouds Baptist beginnings and categories what may be too embryonic for clearcut disposition.

One place to begin is with the Christian experience of individuals who voluntarily united with others of like mind in community, with membership based on personal faith and not on infant baptism. We must ask - what common factor marked the "gathered Church" patterns emerging from the Puritan-Separatists of 17th century England and the Swiss Anabaptists who turned away from Zwingli's reform in the 1520s? Primarily, a high and radical concept of the Church based on Scripture, rather than a particular view of baptism. This lies at the heart of Baptist doctrinal heritage. It was expressed not in organizational terms, but in the formation of comparatively small groups maintained apart from the State, with no attempt to either solicit the influence of the ruling classes or become part of the social order. It involved rejection of a sacerdotal system administered by an ecclesiastical hierarchy and was accompanied by insistence on individual, unmediated responsibility before God and renunciation of many secular values. The Church was perceived to have not holiness apart from its members.

Such a view stood in direct contrast to the comprehensive, institutional, State-related, socially-conservative model of the Church which pervaded Christendom until the 16th century. Here there were dominating elements of State and ruling class control, patronage, influence and integration with the social order.

In this context, infant baptist inextricably linked Church and community. Consequently, a new concept of the Church as a company of believers meant also a fresh vision of baptism as the right and duty of confessed Christians, and pointed to disintegration of Christian society. This was because the medieval pattern of Christendom dictated that an acceptance of religious pluralism was inconceivable, on political as well as religious grounds. Baptists as citizens thus from the beginning posed a threat to the most vital traditions of Church and State. (As for the Anabaptists, of course, such a threat was multi-faceted, involving in its complete disavowal of magisterial authority a refusal to take the citizen's oath of obedience, to shoulder arms or to accept civil office. It is obvious that in Imperial free cities such as Strasburg, when continuity of its favored standing was dependent upon a strong civil defense, Anabaptists were at least a social burden, if not a cause of civic disruption.[1] The political dimension involved the fact that the legal basis for proceedings against them was the ancient Imperial law concerning re-baptist, originally instituted against the Donatist heretics. Anabaptists were not only religious heretics, but political outlaws.)

Though a smaller number of Anabaptists had existed and been persecuted in England from the reign of Henry VIII (d. 1547), by the accession of Queen Elizabeth I (1559) any signs of the movement seem to have disappeared.[2] Contacts between Separatists and Anabaptists in England still await documentation. "Nobody doubts", says historian B. R. White, "that English General Baptists first evolved from the English Separatists, but there is dispute as to whether the 16th century Anabaptist movement, either in England or on the Continent, had any measurable influence upon the development of

Separatists".[3] In view of this, and without closing the debate about Baptist origins, we proceed now from the 1612 formation of the first Baptist church in England by Thomas Helwys and members of the Gainsborough congregation, recently returned from Amsterdam.

Examination of the Scriptures had led them to see that the dynamic presence of the risen Lord in the midst of the believing congregation spelt freedom; not relaxation of discipline, but joyful participation of all members in decision-making. Significantly, their Amsterdam leader John Smyth took the question of freedom further. He stated in his Confession of Faith, Article 84,

> (We believe) that the magistrate is not by virtue of his office to meddle with religion, or matters of conscience, to force and compel men to this or that form of religion, or doctrine but to leave Christian religion free, to every man's conscience, and to handle only civil transgression - Rom. 13 - injuries and wrongs of men against, man, in murder, Adulterie, theft etc. for Christ onlie is the king, and lawgiver of the church and conscience Jas 4:12.[4]

If Smyth made the first case for full liberty of conscience, shortly after, Thomas Helwys published his famous tract dedicated to King James I in which he stated what has been described as the "finest and fullest defence" of religious toleration.[5]

Such challenges to a monolithic view of Church and State constituted a major re-thinking of the social order.

Civil war and revolution became the milieu within which Baptists of varying kinds began to develop. Throughout the remainder of the 17th century, violent fluctuations in the political arena resulted in changed attitudes to civil power. Baptists, like others, shared in this; their petitions and propaganda reflected their concerns. For instance the 1765 position of several London groups towards civil government was set out in *The humble representation and vindication*. Signatories confirmed their loyalty and obedience to Cromwell's protectorate, except in matters of religion when obedience to God must come first.[6] In addition, they averred, the saints would not rule the world until the return of Christ, - effectively negating any thought of a Christian state.[7]

Similar "confessions" appeared in 1654 and 1660. The latter, presented to King Charles II, opposed magisterial support for Christian ministers.

Meantime, from the American colonies came another voice: Roger Williams, a fugitive from repressive English State policy towards religious affairs, a fugitive from Massachusetts, refuter of magisterial authority over liberty of belief, and Baptist since 1639. His *Bloody Tenent of Persecution for Cause Conscience* appeared in 1644. Forerunner of many later voices opposing the "sad evil of the civil magistrate dealing in matters of conscience and religion . . .", Williams addresses the whole problem of Church and State whose functions, he declares, are disastrously confused. Citizens should be dealt with by the State as citizens; people must be free to associate themselves with the Church if they so desire. The corollary of all this is clear - perhaps more so in retrospect: if the State is to deal with individuals as citizens (that is, members of the State), then it applies equally that citizens are to relate in that *standing* to the State. Thus they cannot expect or demand that the State should be or act in any mode other than secular. Once again, we come back to the non-validity of a "Christian State".

In Europe, Johann Gerhard Oncken (1800 - 1884), a young Lutheran, became convinced that the State Church pattern did not fit the Biblical ideal. His conversion, baptism, preaching and lengthy persecution at the hands of the State make stirring reading; the Baptist historian J. H. Rushbrooke holds that Oncken was indeed "Father of the Continental Baptists".[8]

Each of these examples - a 17th century Puritan, Smyth; a Welsh-American colonizer, Roger Williams; and a German Lutheran, Oncken - came to embrace views that thrust them into the society of a Christian minority which challenged State control of religious matters.

The universally-accepted dictum against which Baptists originally stood was that truth alone has rights, error has none. Proponents of this view were, at various times, Catholic, Orthodox, Reformed and Lutheran. By all of them, small groups of Baptist believers were persecuted. Baptists views were seen as heretical; but they were based upon strong theological premises. Some of these were:

1. Coercion negates faith. The ministry of Christ focuses upon love (John 3:16; I John 4:10). But love, by its nature, cannot be coerced. God Himself does not negate the individual's right to say "no" to the gospel. Christians cannot deny to others what God grants to all, i.e., the liberty to believe or not to believe.[9]

2. Authority as the right and power to command obedience can only operate in the context of responsible freedom.

3. Since in the perception of truth the light is always refracted through human fallenness, definitive judgments on others" doctrines have dire elements of risk.

4. A regenerate church gathered in the name of Christ allows no room for the secular ordering of its conscience. It is true that leading English Baptists (Like other sectaries) from Cromwell's time were politically active. Their concern was two-fold: first, that they should continue to enjoy such freedom as had already been won - by no means sure if either the Episcopalians or Presbyterians regained power; and secondly, they sought more radical reform - not just extended toleration, but complete liberty including freedom from financial burdens imposed by the State such as taxes to pay for the clergy of an established church.

As Baptists spread (especially in Europe) in the 18th century, they confronted to a greater or lesser degree varying forms of State-church patterns. Undoubtedly some of these were absorbed into Baptist life, affecting their forms of worship and social expression. Perhaps this is connected with historian Winthrop Hudson's comment that "Baptists are not the heirs of any single, consistent, ecclesiastical tradition" but have absorbed many influences.[10]

Whatever the circumstances, Baptists have consistently maintained that while the magistracy—that is, civil officialdom—has a proper role in society, the office has no place in the community of believers.[11] State and Church belong to different spheres and should be kept separate.

As we have seen, this principle when first proclaimed was contrary to the thinking not only of medieval Christendom, but also to mainstream European Protestantism. It brought Baptists into profound disrepute;[12] but until this present generation it has remained the denomination's signal and unquestioned heritage.

To be a Christian citizen of Baptist persuasion today demands far more rigorous examination of the Biblical doctrine of the State than it has hitherto received. Such a source would involve consideration of at least the following points:[14]

1. **God over-arches all human government.** Biblical emphasis is clear; Ps. 22:28 "Dominion belongs to the Lord, and he rules over nations". Also II Chron. 20:6. Prov. 8:15-16. God, Who is Creator, Redeemer and Righteous Judge over all the world is also Supreme Governor. Human justice in government reflects God's righteousness.

2. **Government is not intrinsically evil, but is meant to restrain evil.** Our natures demand that human sinfulness must be held back in check for the preservation of civic and communal life. Thus ideally the authority of the State and the rule of law are designed as aids to every citizen's welfare, not as "powers hostile to our freedom".[15] The State with its laws ought to manifest the common or universal grace of God, as distinct from special or redeeming grace.

3. **Government exists to bring dignity, decency and equity to every normal association of persons within the nation.** Hence the frequent apostolic injunctions that citizens honor the emperor and obey magistrates, that masters be considerate to servants and servants diligent in pleasing masters, that parents should carefully raise their children and that children respect and obey their parents.[16]

4. **Those in positions of civic authority are also citizens of the State and members of the nation.** Therefore the obligations of citizenship extend to them, and notwithstanding their office they are also accountable. Indeed, they should exemplify the standards they both represent and demand.

5. **Responsible citizenship should characterize the behavior of the Christian,** who has already received God's love and justice in redeeming grace who should in turn show these to others. Love must motivate all actions; hence Paul's exposition of Rom. 12:9-21 on the State and its authority.

6. **Heavenly citizenship (Phil. 3:20) and freedom in Christ for His service** emphasizes the necessity for Christians to submit to secular authority. Dual citizenship is involved: temporal, with its obligations to a fallen, worldly authority (though still the instrument of grace operating for the general benefit of society); and eternal citizenship, giving God absolute allegiance as the source of *all* human authority. Thus, if civil or ecclesiastic authorities demand of the Christian citizen what is plainly contrary to the Word of God, it must be a case (as for the apostles) of Acts 5:29.

Yet even where temporal authorities are hostile, their claims cannot be summarily dismissed. Moreover, the Christian citizen shares in the responsibilities that belong to the human community. This may mean suffering; but it is behind Paul's admonition to members of the Church at Rome that they be subject to governing authorities (Rom. 13:1). His reasons are explicit:

a) There is no authority except from God, and that which exists is instituted by God (Rom. 13:1). The human faculty to exercise authority is itself God-given.

b) It follows that "he who resists the authorities resists what God has appointed, and those who resist will incur judgment" (Rom 13:2). The Christian citizen must uphold the *ideal* of order in society. For Baptists - indeed for all committed Christians - the point of greatest tension arises when decision must be made as to whether the office of the magistrate (i.e., the State) has so far departed from God's design as to become demonic.

Always there is the dominical word: "Render to Caesar the things that are Caesar's and to God the things that are God's" (Matt.22:21). But what does the Christian do when Caesar demands that he be deified?

To amplify: we should note that since for the Christian Jesus Christ is Lord - involving His absolute authority as transcendent Law-Giver Who revealed the ethical standards of righteousness and love - His ethical authority is absolute. Jesus' own attitude to the State in His Galilean days was concerned with the rule of God in the lives of men and women rather that with the rulers of State. When forced to deal with the governments of His day (that is, those of Herod, the Jews or Rome) He plainly differentiated between them and His Kingdom. His followers, as citizens of earthly States, should show loyalty to them unless it clashed with loyalty to Him. Here the words of Henry Townsend help us:

> Of earthly States His disciples were to be as the light, and as salt, never hiding their light of divine truth and wisdom, and ever acting as an antiseptic against immoral corruption. His most direct reference to Caesar is that he was entitled to the taxes due him. If an unjust tax was exacted Jesus does not indicate what attitude the taxpayer should adopt. At the same time Jesus never referred to Caesar as a ruler by divine right. . . The universalism of His ethical demands transcended those of the Jewish Church and the Roman Empire.[17]

Ever since the State related to the Church in the fourth century in a way it had never done before, all differentiation between the Kingdom of God, the Church and the State has been blurred. The spiritual independence of the Church was largely lost. Examples of despotic States allied to persecuting Churches abound in history. Is there ever a case for Christian citizens attempting to overthrow them?

Undiscerning exegesis of Romans 13 has been repeatedly used by Churches and States to secure submission. And on the other hand, history records the witness of Free Churches, including Baptists, in resisting tyrannical rulers of Church and State (examples, the English Civil War and the "Glorious" Revolution of 1688).

The State's function is law-making, administering justice and restricting evil-doers. The Church's functions is preaching the Gospel in the State, leavening society and educating people in Christian principles, in order that they elect rulers and law-makers approximating to the Christian ethical ideal. Hear Townsend again:

> Training the people for citizenship, promoting tolerance and self-government, affecting the social and political structures of the nation for good - such is the Free Church conception of its function in the State.[18]

Spiritual independence of the Church is the "indispensable condition"[19] of its highest service to the State.

For Baptists, then, the historical tension between Caesar and God has been endless and often a cause of internal division; and just as our Baptist forefathers fashioned the historical process, so Baptists today will, for better or worse, do the same.

Bearing in mind that Caesar is *not* God but is due the respect appropriate to his sphere, the Christian is to exemplify good citizenship in terms of Titus 3:1. Godless and tyrannical governments do not nullify God's supreme sovereignty. It is helpful to remember that New Testament teaching on the State was formulated in a distinctly hostile environment presided over by the pagan and, at points, corrupt rule of Imperial Rome. Paul's attitude towards his citizenship provides an interesting model. When his rights were violated, he complained to the State. When the Lordship of Christ was in question, his heavenly citizenship took precedence over everything and he embarked on a course of civil disobedience - fully aware that in disturbing Imperial peace he was inviting the judgment of the secular State and liable to its punishment.

Christian martyrs confronted civil government and bore the full weight of the law. Part of the Baptist heritage in the area of citizenship is the great load of suffering that has accompanied similar stands by later brethren, dissenters wherever there was an established Church-State relationship. Yet we must return to the point that secular government *as such* is *not* the enemy of God; Baptist forebears saw it as *different in nature* to the Biblical concept of the Church.

Another part of the Baptist heritage is its commitment to the defence of religious liberty for all. This concerns the rights and responsibilities of others. Thus, as Charles Adams points out, Baptists who "pervert their own heritage by clamoring for a theocracy or a Christian nation, turning their backs on the rights of non-believers and non-Christians to exist as full and free citizens" are no longer truly Baptists.[20] They have abandoned their heritage.

It may be helpful now to try to formulate some principles drawn from history for practical application to contemporary situations - and here we are addressing our *obligations* as Baptist citizens. These may include such matters as allegiance to the State or Sovereign, military duties, civil duties (magistracy) such as jury duty and civic service, religious duties such as marriage/burial/provision of statistics. Then there is the field of education: taxes for buildings/education. It is no secret that considerable diversity exists among Baptists from country to country and within any one country on almost all these matters. How can it be otherwise? With their historic emphasis on the priesthood of all believers, Baptists find scriptural warrant for a surprising number of alternatives for such issues. Whenever the Bible becomes the authority, hermeneutics becomes the ground of debate.[21]

Nevertheless it is all too easy to use the reality of diversity for avoidance of either hard facts or the proposition of firm guidelines. Our forebears could afford few such qualms, and neither can we.

While recognizing the need to differentiate between the relative and absolute in drawing out principles, we must take into account three factors:

1. imitations of knowledge: obviously some Baptists are more fully informed of their historical roots, more theologically aware and/or more conscious of the implications of specific social issues.

2. the pervasiveness and diversity of culture that causes Baptists in one place, reflecting the influence of their particular culture and acting on the basis of their experiential relationship with it, to take a different position on some matters from their brethren in another place and of another culture.

3. the ever-present factor of human fallenness through which is refracted all light in the perception of truth, as earlier stated. This means that the self and its interests becomes, even unconsciously, a determinant.

To reiterate: tension always exists between Church and State when the Church is true to its mission, even when the two co-operate for various purposes. This tension may be creative or the reverse.[22] So then to some principles:

1. The Church must oppose any idolatrous claim of the State. Baptist citizens today stand in an historical line that stretches back to the denomination's forerunners and Christian martyrs in maintaining this resistance.

2. The Church must uphold the principles of religious and political liberty and social justice. Here the witness of the Church and the individual is doubly involved. The Baptist citizen, recognizing that all citizens are members of the State and possess the right and responsibility of participation in State affairs, and holding also the tenet of individual liberty in the context of grace (and also within the context of the greater good) sees the members' participation for the ultimate good of the State's life. This necessarily calls for condemnation of injustice and oppression when it occurs, and the witness of Christ's love towards persecuted minorities or those who are otherwise marginalized and deprived of a voice. There is a neglected corollary to this: Baptists have no right to coerce the State in respect to fellow citizens with different values. This means their liberties must be protected even while their ideology is deplored. This is an area of difficulty. It reminds us that the argument over the distinction between executing an Anabaptist for his religious views and executing him because his religious views led him into political sedition is a fine one, and certainly of limited significance to the victim. But the distinction is nevertheless meaningful.

3. Since political and economic injustice is not confined to local and national spheres, the Christian citizen should act as a responsible sentinel in the international affairs of his/her nation.

4. As the local congregation should be for Baptists a center of witness, of evangelical mission and nurture in Christian growth, so the principle of liberty

in the Spirit must rule in the hearts and daily lives of members. Baptist history demands that, according to God's Word, each gives to the other respect, freedom to interpret scripture differently, and support in the transmission of Christian values to the surrounding society. The principle of love for the brethren as the identifying mark of Christians, is paramount.

Though not a principle, there is the necessity to guard against inclusion of Old Testament theocratic ideas since they do not belong to the Church. Baptists have no mandate to impose quasi-theocratic ideas on the State. Nor can they, in all conscience, look to Calvin's rule of the saints for guidance. Compulsory morality, it must be remembered, is a contradiction in terms. Baptist citizens can guide and illumine moral life - by persuasion and example, but not by force.

Christianity cannot be interpreted in terms of dominance or rule, as it was in medieval Catholic social and political thought. This perspective was not limited to the kingdom of Europe, says historian John Tonkin, but found daily expression in the hundreds of virtually independent towns of late medieval Europe whose city councils understood their role to be securing the advance of God's rule throughout society.[23]

Even for Luther, the Gospel was not an instrument of social and political control, but an inward perception of faith to be preached and confessed, not imposed.

We are at an end. In retrospect, it is clear that the commitment of Baptists to principles which evolved from a position of symbiotic solidarity of Church with State, to complete separation of Church and State, grew out of insight and experience. This discernment of the inherent evils of religion established by law should not, however, blind us to the fact that other non-Baptist agencies also contributed to this new historical context for citizenship. We are pointedly reminded that it is "unbecoming braggadocio" to claim Church-State separation as Baptists' private property.[24] Nevertheless of necessity this paper deals only with the *Baptist* heritage.

Professor Charles Villa-Vicencio states that "the Christian doctrine of Church and State is today being assessed and rewritten in virtually every situation of conflict around the world".[25] He is right, but it is not without irony that if in some places traditional Church-State relationships are being newly questioned, in others, theocratic movements appear to be gaining around among Baptists though these are entirely alien to their heritage.

We might well conclude, then, with a reminder from our more recent history that the B. W. A. has traditionally concerned itself with these issues.

Amongst the resolutions adopted unanimously by the Congress in Atlanta, Georgia on July 27, 1939, is the declaration stating that "State Churches and Church States are alike in direct conflict with the principle of freedom. A free Church in a free State, each contributing freely and helpfully to the legitimate sphere and functions of the other, is the idea. . ." In this context, the Baptist believer is able to exercise the rights and responsibilities of citizenship, holding each component in tension.

But the ideal is, in fact, far from the context in which many Baptist citizens find themselves. For them, their heritage is none the less valid; more than ever, it is their resource and strength.

Heather M. Vose is a lecturer in history at the University of Western Australia.

Endnotes

Hence the horrors of the Inquisition and later, more civilized but quite as determined persecution.

There is evidence also that prominent Baptist "laymen" used their social standing to intercede for their brethren in times of persecution and to influence State authorities where possible. For example William Kiffin, wealthy London merchant and Master of the Company of Leathersellers did both in the 1680s, making a ten thousand pound gift to King James II at the same time he was leading an illegal congregation. Nevertheless, Kiffin twice suffered imprisonment.[13]

1. For a clear enunciation of this, see Miriam Usher Chrisman, *Strasbourg and the Reform* (New Haven ¿ London, 1967)

2. A group of Dutch Anabaptists was executed in London in 1575. 3. B. R. White, *The English Baptists of the Seventeenth Century* (London, 1983), p.21.

4. *The Works of John Smyth*, ed. W. T. Whitley (Cambridge, 1915, vol. 2, p. 748.

5. W.K. Jordan, *Development of Religious Toleration in England* (London, 4 vols., 1932-40) vol. 2, p. 274.

6. White, op.cit., p. 56.

7. It might be recalled that this declaration was made at a time when Parliamentary Debate was heavily weighted with Puritan sermonizing.

8. J. H. Rushbrooke, *The Baptist Movement in the Continent of Europe* (London, 1915), p.1.

9. "Statement on Religious Liberty" in the *New Delhi Report: The Third Assembly of the World Council of Churches* (N.Y., 1962) p. 160.

10. Winthrop Hudson, ed., *Baptist Concepts of the Church* (Philadelphia, 1959) p. 11.

11. G.N. Vose, *Focus on Faith* (Sydney, 1985) p. 13. I am indebted to this work and have drawn upon it at points in the foregoing discussion.

12. See G. Hugh Wamble, "Baptist Contributions to the Separation of Church and State", *Baptist History and Heritage*, vol. 20, no. 3, 1985, p. 5.

13. See B. R. White, "William Kiffin, Baptist Pioneer and Citizen of London", *Baptist History and Heritage*, vol. II, 1967.

14. I am indebted to the work of Philip E. Hughes, *Christian Ethics in Secular Society* (Grand Rapids, Mich., 1983) for thoughts on this section, even though I have modified his thinking at points.

15. Ibid., p. 184.

16. Ibid., p. 185.

17. Henry Townsend, *The Claims of the Free Churches* (London, 1949) p. 197.

18. Ibid., p. 199.

19. Ibid.

20. Charles G. Adams, "The Scrutiny of History", *Baptist History and Heritage*, vol. 20, no. 3, 1985, p. 67.

21. Leland D. Hine, "A Second Look at the Baptist Vision", *American Baptist Quarterly*, June 1985, p. 121.

22. *Church and State: Opening a New Discussion*, Faith and Order Paper N. 85 (Geneva, 1978), p. 156.

23. "Doctrinal Conviction and Religious Toleration: The Reformation as a Case-Study", *Proceedings of the Fourth New Norcia Humanities Symposium*, May 1988, p. 12.

24. Wamble, op.cit., p. 3.

25. Charles Villa-Vicenio, ed., *Between Christ and Caesar* (Cape Town and Grand Rapids, 1986), p. xi.

How One Manages Christian Citizenship In a Socialist Society

Christian Wolf

The verb in our theme aims at practice. How to conduct Christian life in accordance with God's promises and commandments within a society that is ruled by a government the roots of which are not in Christian tradition and principles?

Yet, the problem is not restricted to socialist societies, since it has to be seen in the wider horizon of the modern secular state at all. We do not live in this century in a so-called Christian society. The Constantinian era·has passed by. Separation of church and state is a matter of fact irrespective of the set-back in a few Islamic states. The Christian is, according to biblical view, a stranger in whatever society. The question to be considered is not, how we should or could transfer a secular society into a Christian one but, with Biblical thought on our side, in which way and to what measure a Christian or church shall relate to a secular, say socialist, society.

Biblical ethics is not a philosophical theory discussion on the idea of state. Jesus or Paul didn't fathom the origin and nature of the Roman Empire or the Herodean regime. What they were doing was to guide their audience to act and react in a given socio-political situation which they believed to be under God's control. That guidance put civil law in the light of the rules of God's kingdom. In so far Baptist citizens from socialist and other contexts do well to share their citizenship-managing problems with a greater Christian community, in expectation that they find ethical guidelines in order to relate in a Christian manner to an overall secular world.

The other side of the problem emerges exactly from the fact that biblical ethics doesn't occur as an abstract philosophical tract. I always aims at practice. This is the reason why guidelines for doing never appear in Biblical texts in a timeless statement, but mixed up with concrete historical situations. Therefore, we have to explore what a socialist society today is, and who the one is who tries to manage his Christian citizenship in it.

The subject requires a sociological and theological approach. In order to reach social-ethical action, both of them have to be combined. The church is the church of belief, the "invisible" church, its nature and identity is defined by theological categories. Nonetheless church appears as a social institution in various denominational shapes. Marxist analysts sometimes complain of the multiple identifications the church is being given especially within Protestantism, while they are claiming a relatively uniform ideological system. Thus dialogue may be easier for Christians than for their Socialist partners.

Dealing with Christian churches in Socialist societies further relies on two methodical aspects, the synchronous and the diachronou. You have to take into account an historical process and several social levels if you want to understand what is happening in the present situation.

The socialist society is not homogeneous. Historically speaking the USSR looks back on a 70 year history, starting with a lengthy violent revolution that threw the vast land of numerous nations from the Middle Ages to Modern times. To Central European states socialism came as a result of World War II introduced by the socialist partner of the victory powers 40 years ago. The differences of cultural background and economical preconditions amongst Socialist nations were enormous and still have effects on their homogeneity to today. Also, the attitude toward religion has been different in the various states, ranging from the first self-declared Catholic church with a native pope.

The principle of separation between state and church gave equal rights to the minority churches like Baptists, which they had never had before. Since that time, the challenge constantly increased who they would use their new position to meet responsibility on all levels of society. On the other hand the principle of separation was used by the state to uninhibitedly promote atheism of which important educational manuals bear witness.[1]

In recent times the socialist world is being confronted with the new ideas, the reformation and openness inaugurated by M. Gorbachev which is a revolution comparable to that of 1917, but soft and peaceful, although conflicting. The Central Committee of the Soviet Communist Party declares a new quality level to be the aim of the reconstruction: development of democracy and openness, creativity, moral purification, and "the buildup of a real pluralism of opinions and open confrontation of ideas and interests."[2]

Regarding religion the doctrine has been changed that religious belief is a remnant of class society. Nowadays it has been stated that religion even in socialism will meet human needs for an unpredictable time. Concepts of humanism, truth, liberty, tolerance, belief and others are being discussed by Marxist-Leninist philosophers in a new sense that doesn't stamp religious citizens as obstacles of progress but acknowledges their faith and service as helpful for the survival of the human race.

Given these radical theoretical changes, the fact remains that in every kind of Socialist society the Communist party claims the leading role regardless of its specific attitude towards religion.

The people of God take that fact as historically given as with the Babylonian or Roman Empires. The church must not necessarily see socialism with its own eyes, but from the aspect of the kingdom of God. In that view it is by no means eternal, its doctrines are not unalterable, and its practice on religious affairs is not always in accordance with its theory. In other words, the believer's church and the church of belief survives and exists in whatever sort of society, including socialist, because God rules history, as it shows in China after the Cultural Revolution and just now in the Perestroika era.

Regardless of God's lordship, the Church everywhere has to consider how it survives, exists, acts and reacts in society.

The church in socialist society is of similar multiformity as its social environment. Christian citizenship is approached by a Russian, Bulgarian or Romanian orthodox tradition in a rather different way than by Polish Roman-Catholic or Central European Protestant churches. Sometimes the following observation was made by Christians from the USSR: "You in the West are Martha. You are always busy doing things. We in the East are Mary, praying and worshipping at the feet of Jesus."[3] Certainly most of the Protestant and Evangelical Christians in Hungary, CSSR, DDR wouldn't agree to be included in the pure Mary type of faith. Otherwise, the statement says implicitly something about the different approaches to the social-ethical involvement from a more Orthodox or Protestant tradition.

Despite their pluriformity, churches in Eastern Europe have some characteristics and circumstances in common, both sociologically and theologically speaking.

The Church in a socialist society is weak. It is of no influential power. In terms of DDR, about 3% of the population are practicing Christians, a minority, one partial section of society, but with a special status, since it is the only non-socialist institution. The latter explains the relatively great interest Christian testimony and service is of in public, despite the institutional decline of the former state churches. There is no more ideological function left to the churches to legitimate and interpret society and state. While the single Christian in accordance with the institutional right of religious liberty is asked to "plan, work and rule along with" society, the church as an institution has no legal claim of decision-making. In that respect it can only be reactive to law and order.

On condition that the institutional differences between state and church are that enormous, the handling of Christian citizenship in terms of church-state relations depends to a high degree on dialogue between persons. Christians must seek contacts with authorities on all levels, exchange ideas and criticism, coordinate actions of public interest, in order to "seek the welfare of the city." Especially to Baptists in Eastern Europe this is a strange new task, since they were traditionally pushed, and used to the backyard of society.

But isn't the shape of the weak church in the socialist society similar to that of God's people in the Babylonian exile and of the New Testament diaspora churches? Aren't our Anabaptist forbears justified in the light of history, when they struggled for an autonomous church of of true believers being a "welfare of the city"? They suffered from a Church, then coupled with the state and supplying the ideological justification of its power and crime, that forced them into the ghetto, at least nearly eradicated. The Anabaptists were not allowed to realize their "salt and light of the world" principle as a productive power of society, but their seed came up. We learn from those, future times anticipating churches that the Christian church is always likewise the church of the Crucified, the tortured body of Christ, "from whom men hide their faces" (Isaiah 53:3). Church will become non-church at the moment when it believes to be its own creator, savior and completer. The characteristic ministry of the church reads: "When I am weak, then I am strong" (2 Cor. 12:10).

The Church in a socialist society is strong. Its strength derives from its cross-character. The crucified Jesus hung on the cross in order to save the world. Also, the church will be without meaning to whatever society, if it "lives for itself" but not "for him who for their sake died" (2 Cor. 5:15) and that means to live for "the least of these his brethren" (Matt. 25:40) with whom he identifies. Church has to be "church for others."

A miracle happened. Despite loss of formal power the spiritual strength of the church grew. The more it discovered its position in the socialist society (and that took a way of decades) to be a community of testimony and service in, not against or besides society, the more attractive Christian presence became to the people. It is not only the traditionally institutionalized service of healing and caring for the sick, aged, handicapped and drop-outs that is very much appreciated by the citizens and by the state. There are many people frustrated by the opacity, cold bureaucracy and anonymity of social processes, who are looking for a warm human fellowship, where they can communicate their problems spontaneously, uncensored and tolerated. Thus churches provide a free zone of safety, social criticism and sometimes protest for mostly young people, while the majority of middle-aged "happy pragmatists" live satisfied with their senseless materialism.

At this point the strength of the church is challenged twice. At first it needs, for a person-to-person testimony and service, people filled with the spirit of Christ being at home in the Biblical message and aware of the needs of the world. Secondly, the worship service has to be reconciled with group activities. In DDR house-churches and theme-centered groups gained much of attractivity, while the monologue-structured worship service is losing interest. Many of the groups offer true Christian fellowship and interaction. Since they attract a lot of frustrated non-Christians, the danger of any asymmetrical approach to society emerges in the sense that citizenship would be considered totally negative, the church changed into a (this time not state-occupied but anti-state) political movement.

Compared with this, Christian citizenship must be shown as an eschatalogical existence with a prophetic vision, neither in total adjustment nor in total denial to society. Group concerns have to appear on the agenda of central church meetings, in sermon and prayer. Dealing with social-ethical problems helps the church to maintain an autonomy which is productive. Autonomy without establishing social relations means ghetto.

On the other hand, the Christian church can never be a socialist church. It is not possible to translate "a Christian socialism" from other continents to the Eastern European context, where atheism is still a fundamental component of Marxism-Leninism. In the eyes of both Marxists and Christians a "Christian-

Marxist" is a contradiction in terms.

We observed the strength of a weak church in socialist society being reactive to needs and defects of the people. Let me, finally, just mention here, that churches also develop an active attitude. Many Christians feel responsible for peace, justice and integrity of creation. Some of their desires and proposals, once criticized and denied by the authorities, are now on the political agenda. It is likewise true for other than a socialist society that the prophetic voice of the church preaching "goodness to the poor. . . release to the captives. . .liberty for those who are oppressed" may lead to the "brow of the hill" (Luke 4:18, 29) like Jesus in Nazareth. How can we "walk in the light of the Lord (Isa. 2:5) like him "passing through the midst of them" (Luke 4:39) unless in close connection to him? The spiritual strength to manage Christian citizenship between total adjustment and total denial comes from the very heart of Christian faith. Communion with Christ makes the church a temple of God and his Spirit, gives to it value and power, and a mission that means devotion to God's so loved world (John 3:16), devotion in manifold ways from cooperation over objection to resistance.

The spiritual reality active behind managing problems of Christian citizenship transcends the sociological statistics and prognoses. A. James Reichley wrote in +itPolitical Science Quarterly: "Modernity does not establish some inescapable progression of religious decline; surely the experience of the United States establishes this".[4] This is true also regarding the socialist countries, if "religious" isn't merely taken in terms of sociology, statistics and numerical church growth. On the other hand, religious awakening must not necessarily be the enemy of modernity in the sense of a more just, peaceful and human society.

Personal-ethical Conclusions[2]

The question was, how a Christian, being a stranger in every kind of society, shall relate to a socialist society. Because of the variety of both socialism and Christianity attention has been paid to fundamental church-state relations. Within this framework the decisions to be made by the individual Christian are numerous and varied. They necessarily correspond to the specific historical situation. That is why cooperation of ethicists and pastoral counsellors is urgently needed.

Which conclusions should a Christian draw when he has arrived at the present corner on the street of history where socialism is forced to go? Let me reply, not in doctrinal phrases, but by describing some sequences of a recent, first-prize awarded DDR movie. It has been produced by the national film company and directed by a former student of theology. The title is a Scripture quote: "Bear one another's burdens". (Gal. 6:12)

A Communist policeman and a Protestant vicar, hit by the same disease, are forced to live together in one hospital room for a long time. As both of them are confessors the one pins a portrait of Stalin on the wall, the other that of the Crucified. While shaving they sing, competing with one another, the

"International" and Luther's "A Mighty Fortress is our God". They eagerly press for separation. But there is the director of the hospital, former member of the Nazi party and now willing to enter the Communist movement: "To save my job and to have the possibility of carrying out my healing profession I will join either party". He orders the squabblers to make arrangements for survival on both sides.

This is exactly the present situation. Amongst a vast agnostic and pragmatic majority in a hospitalized society two minorities of confessors, the Communists and the Christians, are thrown together. Sitting on the same boat, what are they obliged to do? To condemn and persecute each other? Or to strive for survival of their own and the society?

The Communist on the move organizes a party meeting in the sanitarium. The Communist turns to his typewriter to type the Christian's sermon of which he is critical, because of its criticism of Marxist ideology. He leaves the warm room trudging the snow outside despite a heavy cough, in order to make possible a rendezvous of the vicar and his girlfriend. When the young lady with whom the Communist had fallen in love became severely sick and died, his desperate run through the woods ended in the church, where the vicar mourned with him, kept silence in the presence of eminent death, and finally prayed for him.

One day the Communist learned how seriously ill he was and at the same time could get help from a new medicine produced in the West. But only a few packages were available for privileged persons having suffered in concentration camps. Death seemed to be inescapable for the young man who wanted to change society and work for a better world.

Surprisingly, however, he got the medicine. After his recovery by chance he learned the medicine was the gift of the vicar who received it from an ecumenical relief organization for his own healing.

The Christian citizen may draw a number of conclusions from that movie. Above all, we are reminded that we were called to be yeast in society (Matt. 13:3). That means transforming it from the inside out.5 We are not be the salt and not the bread, the bread is Jesus Christ himself announcing his reign. To be salt of the Kingdom and yeast of the world makes the ethical basis of our Christian citizenship.

So often Christianity was transformed by the culture it headed. We must be transformed by God and then follow him who is transforming societies of all kinds throughout history. We must not expect ideological consensus with Communists. On the other hand, we shouldn't play up philosophical dissent, but rather see the person first. The "agape", our Christian tool, works in a personal way, even when we help change social structures. Look on the Communist with the eyes of the saving God. Even he reaches his limits when it comes to suffer or to die. Learn from him that there is something to be transformed from outside in, to keep a society in balance and ensure the world's survival. Tell him that we must be transformed from outside out, in order to complete this task.

Towards the end of the movie, the Communist citizen types the sermon of the Christian citizen who has turned from his former biblical text to "if possible, so far as it depends upon you, live peaceably with all" (Rom 12:18).

Is it an unattainable idea? Or, on the contrary, a resignation from Christian principles? It is neither, but a practical way of responsibility, worthy to be included in an ethic of discipleship. "So far as it depends on you"—that marks out limits. Christians don't have "all authority in heaven and on earth" (Matt. 28:18). But Jesus Christ rules, even in a socialist society. Under his rule, we discover what depends on us, and do it without fear and anger.

Christian Wolf is Professor of Old Testament and Hebrew Studies at the Baptist Seminary in Buckow, German Democratic Republic.

Notes

1. K. Feireis, *Philosophie in der DDR*, in *Theological Bulletin* 20 (1988), p. 1, 35.
2. Thesen des ZK der KPdSU sur XIX. Unionsparteikonferenz: ND v. 28/29. May, 1988. P. 9.
3. *Review and Expositor*, Louisville, KY, Vol. LXXXII, 2 (1985), 237.
4. quoted in Dialogue, Washington, 3 (1988) 47.
5. G. E. Mann, *Of Yeast and Myths: A Fresh Look at Christians and Government.*

Gospel Worthy Citizens, Anywhere
Christians Citizens in the State and in the World

James M. Dunn

Philippians 1:27 reads, "Show yourselves citizens worthy of the good news of the Christ," in the Goodspeed translation. This prompted T. B. Maston to say, "One cannot be a good Christian unless he is a good citizen." Welton Gaddy puts it this way, "Responsible citizenship in one's nation is an essential characteristic of faithful discipleship in God's Kingdom."

The point is clear but the task is difficult. Our specific challenges to good citizenship are different. Some dedicated Christians are so glad simply to have the opportunity for public worship that they would never do anything to endanger that blessing. Others are convinced, as they believe by God's Holy Spirit, that political revolution is necessary as a matter of basic discipleship. Still others engage in the political process as individuals but believe deeply that the churches as local bodies of believers or "the church" as organized, institutional religion has no business at all in the political realm. Yet others see the use of their churches as logical, essential extensions of personal witness as required by the Lord to be faithful followers of His will, members of His Body.

How do we make sense of it all?

To whom do we turn for understanding?

New Testament passages are pivotal, first, because of their apparent differences, but later because of their striking convergence. As Dr. Welton Gaddy points out:

> Romans 13:1-7 is crucial both because of its use in understanding the nature
> of government and the Christian's role in it and because of its abuse by those
> who would assign to government more power than any human institution can
> legitimately claim. Paul wrote to Christians who lived in the shadow of the
> capitol in Rome. He sought to disassociate Christianity from those insurrec-
> tionist Jewish sects which were violently anti-government. However, he did
> not give a blanket endorsement to every government of any kind.
>
> Here is a helpful, positive word about the value of government, the pur-
> poses of government, the servant nature of a government office, and the import-
> ance of believers' supportive behavior within the government. Yet this is not
> the only word or the final word on this subject in the New Testament.
>
> Revelation 13 describes government gone bad. The same government
> commended by Paul in Romans 13 became so utterly corrupt that the author
> of Revelation labeled it a beast. What happened in Rome can happen anywhere.
> Servant can seek to become master. An institution intended for good can become
> the incarnation of evil. Government—a plan for community ordained by God—
> can become a system so devoid of good that it is opposed to God.

Jesus' own words in Matthew 22:15-22 help to put in perspective the
Christian's duty to the state. Discipleship and citizenship are intersecting values.
The state does have legitimate claims on the life of Christians. These claims include practical demands upon one's material possessions. Those claims are
justified by the Divine order of things. But the duties owed to the state and
God are not the same. The difference is a matter of God's intent, at least in
this sinful world. The different responsibilities to God and government must
be determined anew, over and over by Christians in every time and circumstance.

Because the church is a divine-human institution, because the Christian
life is a divine-human experience, because the Bible is a divine-human book and
our only rule for faith and practice, we must continue to decide what is Caesar's
and what is God's. It will never be settled once and for all.

We do so depending upon the Bible as it is interpreted by the Holy Spirit.
We test what seems to us to be God's leading within biblical warrants. We are
helped by learning the way God has lead faithful followers in the past. Billy
Graham points out that we need not fear tradition, "the living faith of the dead,"
by traditionalism, "the dead faith of the living."

We have the sanctified intellects given to us by God, the fellowship of
believers within which we seek to know God's will, the positive and helpful
structures of society, home and church and school. We have the practical tests
of service for the greatest good, protection for the weak and disadvantaged,
restraint of evil and reward of virtue. We have history from which we may learn
of courses and of consequences.

Yet, when all is said and done in the competition between church and
state we must depend upon God's Word to engage us in creative tension, to
enable us to learn and grow, to sustain us in the inevitable misunderstandings,
ostracisms and sufferings when anyone is a faithful follower of Jesus Christ confronting the principalities and powers of this world.

Baptists, of all people with our emphasis upon soul freedom, experiential religion and the priesthood of all Christians, must develop a theology for public policy. It will not be equally relevant in all nations. It will not lend itself to universal application. It will demand expansion at times, evaluation by biblical norms, and interpretation by informed disciples in every culture, economy and political dispensation. Yet, we dare not run from the challenge.

We may not know all the right answers but under God we're bound to try to ask the right questions. As Christians saved by grace not works, we are free to fail but we're not free to fail to act.

If we do not alarm anyone morally, we'll remain morally asleep ourselves. Not to decide on the vital issues of the day is itself a decision. To do nothing in the political realm is to contribute to the drift towards a coming human hell. To refuse to take part in the public debate on some religious grounds is to say either that Jesus doesn't care or that the Living Lord is helpless to bring change.

The least a theology for public policy can do is *affirm persons*, call for justice, *insist upon freedom, teach stewardship, act on faith* and *pursue the heavenly vision*.

Augustine said, "Christ died for me as much as if I were the only one for whom he had to die." Simple extension of that biblical idea acknowledges that each of those children on the other side of the world is worth it all. The late F. J. Sheed wrote, "The concept that man is made in the image of God is an idea of such transcendant importance that *any* difference between this person and that fades into nothingness by comparison." This notion of dignity and worth of the individual is the bedrock foundation of Christian social ethics. This respect of personhood puts people ahead of pigs and politics and profits. This doctrine of democracy deals a death blow to elitism and racism and economic theories that posture as help for the common man by strengthening the wealthy and powerful: trickle down righteousness.

A theology of public policy calls for justice, sees social systems from the vantage point of the victim, cares about the loneliest, most isolated minority of one.

Perhaps every teacher should write on the chalk board or enter into the word processor the words of Thomas Jefferson, "I have sworn upon the altar of God eternal hostility against every form of tyranny over the mind of man."

A sound religious public policy teaches stewardship. Aristotle said, "Politics is the chief of sciences, since it alone has the power to allocate the always scarce resources of any society to the various elements of that society."

The Judeo-Christian ethic has fostered a public policy that is positive, forward looking. It acts with an explicit faith in the future. How different has our history been from the defensive, self-serving escapist mentality of those who see public institutions doomed. Woodrow Wilson, the President of the United States during World War I, insisted, "the next generation is my true constituency."

A responsible public policy informed by religious values pursues the heavenly vision, Augustine's City of God, whose "alabaster cities gleam undimmed by human tears;" Martin Luther King's dream: "I have a dream that my four little children will one day live in a nation where they will be judged not by the color of their skin but by the content of their character."

The minimum requirement for Christian citizens in any form of government is to hold faithfully to one's own convictions of New Testament goals for the human family. Every policy of government should be measured by those goals. One should never lose sight of the biblical standards. To the degree that it is possible even in the most repressive regime, the implications of clear teachings from God's World should be shared within the family of faith, taught to one's children, handed from generation to generation. As opportunity presents itself, the deepest held insights of our Faith about the common life should be made a matter of public witness.

Even when believers must live in a state so foreign to their understanding of Gospel values that their lives would be at risk to challenge the powers that be, we must never pull down the clear teachings of scriptures. We must never attempt to justify our own sub-Christian behavior by watering down the biblical ideal. We must cling stubbornly to the high calling in Christ Jesus, admitting our accommodation, confessing our sin, recognizing our acceptance of lesser evil, pursuing doggedly the highest good.

Somehow we need to reaffirm the inexorable connection between freedom from want and freedom to worship. Precisely the spark of the Divine in us all that ignites the flame of human worth and divine adoration demands guarding and defending in every person. The poignant recognition that "nothing human is alien to me" makes me care about the victims of mass starvation anywhere in the world, and in the same way it also moves me to intense indignation at the thought of religious liberty for anyone being limited or denied. We care for the hungry. Harry Hopkins once reminded President Franklin D. Roosevelt that ". . . people don't eat in the long run; they have to eat every day."

Thus, we struggle to keep belief and behavior consistent. We wrestle with the disparity between idealism and realism. We test our political philosophy against practical consequences.

Jesus' inaugural address begins with these words: "The Spirit of the Lord is upon me, because he has anointed me to preach good news to the poor." (Luke 4:18)

Many of us see the person of God as source of all human freedom. Because God is person and not principle, because our personhood is in some way rooted in the personality of the One Jesus called "Father," and because in ways beyond understanding we replicate even the Creator of the universe, all liberty flows from religious liberty. Being made like God is the only substantial clue we have for interpreting the human hunger for freedom, *and* our dedication to freedom from hunger.

Freedom from war as well as freedom of worship relates to the *imago Dei*. Julius K. Nyerere, President of Tanzania, pled this point, "We say man was created in the image of God. I refuse to imagine a God who is miserable, poor, ignorant, superstitious, fearful, oppressed and wretched—which is the look of the majority of those He created in His own image."

Fortunately we do not have to choose between the war on hunger and the struggle for human rights. We cannot set aside our dedication to helping the starving until we have brought to oppressed peoples tangible guarantees of political freedom. Economic freedom is an aspect of the good news in its purest form. Therefore, when we claim to be gospel people without any evidence of passion for the poor, we are guilty of doing a life.

Biblically we have no business waiting until we have converted suffering peoples to our way of thinking before we respond from our plenty to their need. The book of Matthew, Chapter 25, categorically rules out the use of food as a weapon. What good is all our freedom talk if one is not actually free to eat and live? High hypocrisy speaks of remote liberties to those whom it lets starve. The world's hungry are, indeed, those whom we *let* starve.

So, contemporary Christians must engage in both the pursuit of political freedom, providing individual rights on one hand, and economic justice, meeting basic human needs on the other. The biblical revelation calls us to be "both/and" not "either/or" persons.

Likewise, in the pursuit of peace we cannot "trust in chariots" like the unredeemed in all our lands. A Baptist Senator in the United States Congress, Mark Hatfield, has held up for ridicule the folly of the arms race. He cartoons our warring madness saying the military build-ups of the superpowers remind him of two men standing in a cellar, with gasoline up to their armpits, arguing about which one of them has the most matches.

What can I do?

I can grapple with the interpretation and application of New Testament principles of citizenship in relation to the political system of which I am a part. I can try to understand the significance of these principles in other systems. However, I will not presume to pass judgment on the manner in which my brothers and sisters in Christ seek to live by these principles in the respective political systems.

I cannot accept a posture of engagement. I will study. With every resource at my command I will learn the big picture.

I can share with fellow believers as God gives me grace and opportunity, testing my views against theirs. Teaching, at times, and learning. Trying hard, and it is not easy to do one's homework on complex issues, to relate my faith to what is happening in the world, Bible in one hand, newspaper in the other.

I can reach out to those in other churches, other faiths, other lands. One biblical mandate is that we care for all the world. If God so loved the world, so do we. A world view, a global vision, a Great Commission perspective will purge us all of narrow nationalisms, parochial prayers, and self-satisfied citizenships. As G. K. Chesterton said, "We are all in a small boat on a stormy sea and we owe each other a terrible loyalty."

I can act in ways, however small, to advance my vision of God's Kingdom. While we think globally we must surely act locally. No cup of cold water in His name, no prayer for peace, no witness to the saving power of Jesus Christ is wasted.

In fact, we may have overstated ambitions for the church in the world, religion affecting politics, Christians shaping government. The opportunities we have known in the United States, United Kingdom and some other democracies may have given us a false sense of power. We may well have grown too big for our britches.

Dr. Gerald Mann, in an earlier meeting of this Commission, appealed to us not to think more highly of ourselves than we ought. He reminded us of a biblical model that we may have forgotten.

We were called to be yeast (Matt. 13:3) in the loaf of the world, but we keep trying to be the loaf itself. The loaf is the world with all of its institutional structures—political, social, economic, and religious. It is the world required as a result of the Fall. God does not force people to believe in Him or to worship Him. Humanity's choice not to believe and worship, necessitated political, social, economic and religious structures. They are tributes not to our sin, but to God's integrity.

Political order was therefore given by God, as a gift to a humanity who was not forced to believe in Him (Rom. 13).

We are called to be "in the loaf" but not "of the loaf." We are yeast, not loaf. But we have repeatedly succumbed to the temptation of forgetting that our "Kingdom is not of this world."

Christianity was never meant to be a success-philosophy in the political sense. Our role is to permeate, to spiritualize, in whatever world we find ourselves, from the inside out. Ours is the yeasting role. The greater our success in yeasting, the greater our temptation to forget that we are yeast and to believe that we are loaf.

I have discerned a pattern in the history of relations between Christians and government: The Church's spiritual power to influence its society's values is inversely proportionate to its political power to enforce these values. The more political power it has to enforce values, the less spiritual power it has to influence them.

The Early Church was powerful in its role as yeast in Graeco-Roman culture. Then Constantine and Theodosius made it the loaf and it ceased to influence values. Once the idea was accepted that Church and State could be united in one commonwealth, the church lost is power to spiritualize society from the inside out.

Perhaps you see the church-state relationship with other biblical models. The church, the people of God:

as *plumb line*, measuring justice, insisting on truthtelling;

as *light*, exposing evil, providing the one essential commodity for vision;

as *salt*, preserving those traditions worth keeping, protecting the memory of what God has done in ages past, with hope springing from that memory;

as *mustard seed*, reminding all how God uses the minuscule to confound the mighty;

as *towel*, symbolizing the selfless service to the least of these that is always appropriate and never popular enough;

as *dove*, extending the work of the Spirit for peace.

Whatever strategy we choose, whatever model appeals to us, it must be one in which we begin with ourselves—the Christian community. We must be transformed before we can transform. This transformation begins with a reaffirmation of the Christian hope. What is the Christian hope? First of all, it is the recognition that Christianity has flourished under every political system conceived by man: tyranny, oligarchy, monarchy, anarchy, fascism, naziism, socialism, communism, democracy.

No political form has ever stifled the Church except the ones of its own making! Thus, our hope is not in a social or political reform. It is that God is the Lord of history, and as such, empowers his people to transform whatever society in which they find themselves.

"Citizens worthy of the Gospel,". . . may each of us aspire, persevere, realize that sublime appellation.

James M. Dunn is executive director of the Baptist Joint Committee on Public Affairs in Washington, D.C., U.S.A.

Women's Issues

Beth H. MacClaren

Early last November questionnaires were sent to all 141 executives of the BWA member bodies. A slightly different questionnaire was sent to 142 women holding positions of leadership in these member bodies. The charts show the countries and/or conventions and unions form which responses were received, and who responded. Thirty-three executive secretaries of member bodies responded, as did 94 women.

The number of responses speaks volumes about WOMEN'S ISSUES: 1) Women want to be heard. 2) Women took seriously a request from the BWA Women's Department.

Questionnaire Goals

My goals in the questionnaire were basically threefold: 1) To get a profile of what women are dong in the churches and denominations, 2) To test policies and attitudes regarding equal opportunities for women in ministry, and 3) To find out from the women themselves the issues of most concern to them and women in their areas.

Regarding Goal #2, questions were directed to both groups for comments on women's ordination and pastoral roles in the conventions and unions.

Introduction

Women are a majority in Baptist congregations around the world. They love the Lord. They are devoted to the Church. They are finding fulfillment in service to God and others. Although these are not startling discoveries, this is exciting news. Nevertheless, women are struggling. They are struggling on every continent. The struggle is everywhere and takes many forms. For some, the struggle is tangible. It is related to survival—survival from poverty, illiteracy, disease, wars, and on and on. For others, the struggles are intangible, related to other forms of survival, such as emotional well-being and self-esteem. These are nonetheless real.

There is a lot of pain expressed. The pain comes from those who are marginalized in society and in the Church. Yet, there is power in the struggles. There is courage, determination and purpose. A number of the women profess a lack of self-confidence, but they possessed the courage to answer a questionnaire1

A large part of the struggle relates to women's roles in the Church. There is not a consensus among these women that ordination is appropriate or necessary in order to minister, preach, or, even in some places, to pastor a congregation. Many women expressed mixed feelings. A number are opposed. Many more support ordination as a recognition of equality.

Ordination aside, a large part of the struggle has to do with affirmation of women's gifts, their value and usefulness in the Church. This is a unifying issue for women. I think that women want to move from what they perceive to be "servitude" to "partnership" and, with men, find a true "servanthood" within the Church.

I. Africa

Issues

In Africa, the chief issues are: Illiteracy, polygamy, divorce, absentee husbands, inter-religious marriages, inheritance laws, cultural barriers and lack of education and leadership training. Additionally, a lack of respect for women and their opinions, moral issues, disease, AIDS, health care, equal job opportunities, unemployment with all its related family problems, widowhood and poverty.

Roles in the Churches

Women are filling traditional roles in the churches: Teaching, children's and women's work, tending to orphans and the poor, and, generally, working in a caring capacity. A few are deaconesses, especially in Nigeria, but women in Togo describe their roles as "somewhat limited."

In the Central African Republic, women play a very important role "because they are an overwhelming majority." In Tanzania, "they can teach the mixture of men and women in Bible study." In Zimbabwe, they are mainly involved with "ladies work, Sunday School, flowers, music and catering and sometimes tough work." In the Baptist Union of South Africa they work in "caring capacities." In burkina Gaso, it is "participation by observance only," according to one missionary.

In Sierra Leone, our woman correspondent said the unique thing about her church is the equality of the sexes, preaching and witnessing. "The pulpit is open," she reported.

Ordination

Nigeria does not have a policy on ordination, because they have not been faced with this matter, according to the executive there. A woman leader said that women who are called and trained, should be ordained. A missionary in Nigeria said women are asking why they cannot be ordained.

Ghana has only ordained deaconesses. In Togo, "there would be considerable resistance." The response from Malawi was simply, "We don't ordain them." In the Baptist Union of South Africa, presently women are not able to be ordained, but this matter is to be reviewed in the 1989 assembly. In Zimbabwe, the general feeling is that "it wouldn't go through very easy." In Burkina Paso, "no ordination." There is "no problem" with ordination of women in Liberia. In Tanzania, there is a "cultural custom of no ordination." In Cameroon, "not quite supportive."

In the Central African Republic, a woman leader from Banqui said she would like to see someone "do something about this problem as women also have qualities and abilities they have received from the Lord." Her hope is that "the All-Powerful will give women the necessary possibilities in order that the women's ministry may be emancipated."

In several African countries, the possibility of ordaining women has not been considered. Several said they are not opposed to a woman being ordained, but would prefer having a man as pastor. The response from Benin was, "Just as the saints mentioned in the Scriptures, the women do not have a very large place in the church."

Obstacles

Among the answers given about obstacles to ministry are these: It is not easy as a woman to voice opinions, women have little authority in this country (Burkina Faso); male colleagues who give us difficulties (Central African Republic); religious intolerance and imposed restrictions by traditional religions (Nigeria). A number of women noted their lack of education as an obstacle in ministry.

II. Asia

Issues

The issues listed by Asian women are: Equality of women, marginalization of women, women's struggle for recognition of their value and contribution to the Church, the need for more education and theological training, the abuse and exploitation of women socially and economically, illiteracy, poverty, unemployment, family problems, family planning, cultural mores such as ancestral worship, cultural taboos, marriage customs, inter-religious marriages, personal independence and being a whole person, self-understanding and self-affirmation, and Christian identity in non-Christian surroundings.

Roles in the Churches

A general secretary in India wrote that women are double in number in church attendance. In village churches, 90 percent of the members attending church are women. In India, women are doing all the traditional roles of church work, plus fund raising, hospital and medical work, relief work with homeless and powerless, and numerous other social ministries. One of the men executives in India said that in spite of advancement in education and in other fields, a women in India "is expected to be a wife only. . . husbands claim superiority over their wives."

Ordination

In one of the Indian unions, there is "no bar with regard to ordination of women;" however, there are no women ministers, the executive of CBCNC said. He expressed support for women in the church, saying there is no difference between man and woman in the sight of God. "Where is the place to consider woman in any way less than man or inferior to man?" he asked. There are two women pastors (unordained) among 200 churches in CBCNC.

The same view was reflected by the executive from the Bengal Orissa Bihar Convention, but he said, "The time is not yet ripe" to consider women's ordination.

In Burma, there are five ordained women and an undetermined number of women serving as unordained pastors. In the Philippines, there is ordination of women, but few women apply. Ordination is "an esoteric issue" said a young spokesperson, and "should not receive top priority in a society where so many problems revolve around poverty and survival."

While ordaining women as deaconesses is a common practice in Korea, there are no ordained women ministers. Indonesia has no policy regarding ordination of women, but there seems to be no objection.

Several of the women raised questions about the meaning of ordination for men and women, the special privileges it accords, the status it implies, and its necessity for effective ministry. One woman educator in India, noted her mixed feelings, saying, "Ordination does help, but women not ordained are also being used greatly by the Lord."

Obstacles

The attitudes of men toward women is an obstacle in Korea, declared a women's leader. "Men underestimate the knowledge and abilities of women. . . women's roles and men's roles shouldn't be so divided. . . women who are qualified would be given responsible positions and allowed to do the work and to be compensated comparable to men," she wrote.

"Just being a woman is sometimes an obstacle," declared a well-known "proclaimer" in India. In Burma, "contemporary women struggle daily for self-understanding and self-affirmation." In Indonesia, one woman claimed that "restrictions come from the part of male ministers" who do not allow women to establish independent women's groups."

The chief obstacle to a woman leader in the Philippines comes from the State, where a strong Roman Catholic influence prevails. A respondent reported receiving a lot of criticism from the State because of her social activities on the side of the poor and powerless. "This criticism has been carried over into the Church," she said.

It is "abominable" that we have no women pastors in India, wrote one woman. Women can preach in women's conventions and meetings, but not on Sundays in worship services. A woman from Japan, writing for "every Japanese woman" said that many pastors still do not accept women as co-laborers.

III. South West Pacific

Issues

The issues are: Unemployment, drugs, drinking, abuse of women, lack of spiritual life, being faithful to the Gospel, creative ministries in the Church, finding quality time for family, avoiding the workaholics of male pastors (this from a woman pastor), learning how to work alongside men in ways which transform church structures, outreach to unchurched persons, bridging the gap between the older and younger generations, reaching working women and un-churched women, good family relationships and having women more involved in decision-making in the churches and denominations.

The men who responded to the question about women's issues listed these additional ones: violence toward women and child abuse, conscious and un-conscious discrimination against women (for example, "sexist language" in the church), decline of morals and social concerns, particularly "those related to women, children and family."

The issues faced by women in New Zealand, said one woman, "are those of an affluent society, rather than those faced by the Third World."

In Papua New Guinea, the issues have a different ring: Husbands who do not trust their wives to go away for Bible conferences, retreats and conventions, the inability of women to make their grievances known in public without being mocked, single parenting and being the breadwinner for the family. "Tradi-tionally, women carry heavy burdens and husbands walk away with lighter loads," our Baptist women's leaders from Papua New Guinea said. "Woman bring up children alone, husbands don't take part."

Woman in the Churches

All roles are equally open to women, although they are not yet equally taken, said a woman pastor. There are women pastors in New Zealand and Australia. The Baptist Union of New Zealand has been ordaining women since 1974, and it "is not an issue," one executive said. However, he added that there are few churches that would call a woman to be senior pastor.

This executive said also, "Churches should take their own women much more seriously. Women are one of our greatest untapped or unrealized resources, who have a great deal more to offer in leadership and ministry." Other executives echoed the same affirmation for women's gifts for ministry. The executive of the Seventh Day Baptists there, a woman, noted that they have no women pastors and no policy regarding ordination of women.

Papua New Guinea—Women in the Churches

Women in Papua New Guinea "do not speak in church until they are asked by the elders of the church," responded our women's leader. Also, women are "not allowed" to be ordained. At this time, Baptist women are not aware of the possibility of ordination for women, as it has not come to their notice. "If it does," she said, "our men folks will put it away."

South West Pacific—Other Attitudes Toward Ordination

Not all the women are fully supportive of ordaining women, even among two women pastors who wrote. One expressed her disagreement with "women being in authority over men," and urged against bringing a "way out" feminism into the church."

One of the laywomen, in explaining her views on ordaining woman, said that it must be evident that "she has the gifts of Christ and be capable in her exposition of the Scriptures. She must not concentrate on women's issues..." Another expressed her uncertainty about it, saying sue's inclined to wish she were "more liberal and tolerant," but that she "would not want a woman ministeri"

IV. South America

Issues

The list goes like this: Lack of education and equal job opportunities for women, limited career opportunities, economic and family problems, social and political problems, counseling and ministering to families with children in war zones and persons affected by the war (Nicaragua), women participating in the Church and society, illness and health care, subjugation and marginalization of women, marriages between Christians and unbelievers, resistance to new ideas, and personal fulfillment.

The executive secretary from El Salvador expressed this concern: "We have to struggle still to recognize the equal value of women. Mainly here, where Latin American women are the marginalized people from every aspect of life." He noted further that 75 percent of the Baptist women in that country are poor.

Roles in the Churches

Women are listed as doing all the traditional work in the churches, plus preaching, teaching in seminaries and serving on executive committees. Among the Haitians, women fill "any role except officers in men's classes or the pastorate." In El Salvador, "in the last four years, every field and role has been opened to women." In Nicaragua, conditions are "improving" and women are moving from the roles of cooking and cleaning in the churches to positions of leadership, theological training and teaching.

Ordination

Answers from member body executives about women's ordination go from acceptance and encouragement to "Nuts." From Nicaragua, "We accept and encourage. . ." From El Salvador, "We accept. . . even as pastor." From Cuba, "We have not had any cases of women aspiring to the ministry." From Haiti, "Nuts."

"Personally, I never felt the need to be ordained." She told of participating in a seminary discussion on this, and she came to the conclusion that the problem with women's ordination is "who administers the sacraments?" Noting the Roman Catholic background for this attitude, she concluded, "It seems that administering them is who remains with the power."

In Chile, they have not ordained women, and "there is a certain prejudice about it." In Cuba, the women's leader of the Eastern Convention noted that though they do not ordain women, women do have an important role in the church, but not necessarily as pastors or senior ministers.

The woman leader from the Western Convention in Cuba, formerly a national women's department president, and a pastor's wife, said that many young members in their congregation wish that she were ordained. "However, adults would never get used to such an idea. . . it would not be acceptable on higher convention levels," she said. The Cuban leader noted further that in that society a thorough fulfillment of women is intended at all times. She added, "It is very peculiar that non-Christian people do not accept a woman as a minister."

In Honduras, it is not accepted. In Mexico, a missionary respondent said, "It is not acceptable." She went on to say that she doesn't think it is necessary. "We can work up a storm without that." In Panama, it hasn't been discussed, but no woman has been ordained. Our respondent further said that women should fulfill other kinds of work in the church and allow the men to have a full-time call to serve. Also, "women are not prepared" for full-time work in the churches.

One respondent said that "single women should not alienate as feminists" in seeking the right of ordination. "We have been being pastors, so let them be pastors."

Obstacles

Among the obstacles encountered by women in South America, concerning fulfillment of their calls, these seem significant: Having five children for

30 yearsı "A bit of resistance and years of work" to get women on the convention executive committee and seminary council; some family resistance; hindrances when others do not recognize individual gifts and capacities; policies of restriction and marginalization within the convention.

Three of the eight women who responded said they had not encountered any obstacles to doing what they felt the Lord wanted them to do.

V. Europe

Issues

The long list of issues includes these: Breakdown of the family, coping with teenagers, living a simple life-style, unemployment, poverty, concern for the poor, refugees, homelessness, education, health services, care of the elderly, personal safety, child abuse, alcohol and other drug abuses.

Of special concern among European women is their role in the churches, and the challenge to accept responsibility for ministering to other women. One leader said that women's issues could be solved, "if only we could educate the menı"

Roles in the Churches

Women in these 16 countries are in all the usual roles in the churches. Also, many are pastors and denominational leaders. In Denmark, about 50 percent of the deacons are women. In Italy, it is hoped that "soon a woman will become president of the Baptist Union." In Swedish-speaking Finland, "Traditionally, women have occupied the "servant places" in our churches, but things are changing." In Switzerland, women "have equal rights."

In England, 21 women are ministers "in sole charge of a church." In Sweden there are a number of ordained women serving as pastors. The general secretary of the Swedish Baptist Union is an ordained woman. In Hungary, "women are in partnership with men."

Others said: "Women sit in the benches and listen, but things are changing (Finland—Swedish-speaking Union)." "Very seldom they preach." (Yugoslavia) "We almost have no organized work among women in our Union. Our women are being organized in prayer circles, they visit homes, hospitals, etc." (USSR).

Ordination

In England, the Baptist Union has had no objection to women's ordination since 1925. In Scotland, a church can ordain a woman to the ministry, but support for such a ministry cannot come from Central Baptist funds, according to present regulations.

The general secretary of the Baptist Union of Scotland said he wants that Union to recognize women as equally gifted, and for women to have opportunities to fulfill their ministries. "Women have particular aptitudes for pastoral concern. . .which men sometimes lack, and there is much to say for women exercising such ministries within the life of the church."

Finland (Swedish-speaking) Union has ordained women for ministry since 1973. Denmark "welcomes women as pastors." Switzerland has had two ordained women serving as pastors. In Italy, women's ordination is the same as for men. Sweden first ordained women for the ministry in 1958.

In Israel, the Baptist convention is "against" ordination of women. In Yugoslavia, it is "not accepted, till now." In Czechoslovakia, there are no ordained women in the churches, "Nor do we reckon on having them in the future." Poland does not ordain women. It is also not accepted in the Netherlands; however, the general secretary from there listed "ordination" as one of the issues of most concern to women. He wants their convention to "pay more attention to the gifts given by the Spirit to women."

The same sentiment came from the general secretary of the Swedish-speaking Union of Finland: "Women do have gifts and qualities which men do not have." It is not a question of choosing between a man and a woman, "but a question of choosing the best qualified person for a special task."

Women's Attitudes on Ordination

There were mixed opinions from the women on ordination. One women in England said, "I'm all for it." One in Scotland said, "I'm very much against this." Another in England said, "I believe it to be the will of God."

Other comments were: "I would be willing to accept...providing the criteria were similar to those accepted for men" (Scotland). "It is quite right" (Sweden). "I feel uncomfortable, but not unwilling to consider it" (Cyprus), adding that in Arab cultures, "it would never be considered." In the Finnish-speaking Union of Finland, it is "considered unbiblical."

There is no ordaining of women in the USSR, but it is a question "of the future," our respondent from Moscow said, noting that in the USSR there are women preachers.

One woman from England, an international officer in the Women's Department, said her hope is that "women's ministry. . . will cease to be "an issue" and become a normally accepted part of life."

Another, an executive for women's ministries in the United Kingdom, declared: "If anyone is called of God, to any ministry, male or female, young or old, black or white, rich or poor, who are we to put obstacles in his or her way? If we hinder anyone, because of our prejudice, we have a lot to answer for."

Another woman from England wrote that she had been reading reports and books for the subject for the last 40 years, and sometimes despairs "at the slow progress in the recognition of women's gifts in the service of Christ."

VI. North America

Issues

Social issues, family-related concerns and equality of opportunity within the denominations denominated the long list of issues.

There were no surprises in the list. There were two issues added that had not been mentioned by women in other countries: Abortion, both the pro and the con side, and Peace.

The Canadian women listed: Abortion, child care, Christian life-style and being recognized and affirmed as having gifts for ministry. A few cited the need to grow in acceptance of themselves and having their personhood affirmed in the church. Canadian women mentioned also the need for equal pay for equal work, the need to be included in the "language" of denominational references, and the lack of women executives in the denomination.

The five English-speaking countries of the Caribbean listed these issues: Drug addiction, especially among young women, hunger, homelessness, teenage pregnancies, single parenting, demands on women to be both breadwinner and housewife. One need is for women "to feel good about themselves." Another said women need "stimulating and meaningful activity to enable them to enjoy the fullness of life." One said the need in her area is for more male leadership in the churches.

In the United States, the issues were much the same, with the addition of "Peace" on the list. Abuse of women and children, drugs, economic justice for women and equality of men and women in the Church were mentioned by several women.

Women in the Churches—Caribbean

"If the women were not involved in church work, there will be no church: the doors would be closed," declared the women's leader on one of the islands. The involvement of women in most every role was reflected in the questionnaire from the Caribbean.

Regarding ordination of women, some of the churches welcome it "with open arms," according to one leader. Another noted that there are no ordained women in her convention, but the matter is to be discussed at a national assembly. One said women in her convention do not mind women preachers, but they still feel ordination is for men.

Women in the Churches—Canada

Canadian women are filling all roles in the churches, except senior minister positions. There are a number of women deacons and leaders in other executive committees. Recently, Mrs. Chirley Bentall served as president of the Canadian Baptist Federation. (Her name must be mentioned in this paper, along with the recommendation that you read the paper she presented last year to the BWA Commission on Human Rights on "Baptists and Freedom of Expression Without Discussion as to. . .Sex.")

Regarding ordination for women, each one who responded supports this. "It is appropriate and should be encouraged; our churches need the gifts that women bring," one woman executive said. Two others said women are called by God as well as men. One of these added that she personally dislikes women who feel that "women's gifts are inferior to their own. Ministry is partnership," she wrote.

Women in the Churches—United States

Women in congregations and denominations in the United States are filling nearly all roles available, except deacons and pastors in some denominations. Even where ordination of women is acceptable, women have difficulty finding pastoral positions. Regarding equal pay for equal work, one woman executive described it as "a policy in place" in her denomination, but feels it is not being carried out since few women are in executive staff positions and the denominational structure is "male oriented." She added that women rarely rise to the positions where pay is high and women are kept in secretarial or subsidiary roles "even when their abilities are superior to their supervisors" except in women's organizations. "The opinion is that the male is worth more," she concluded.

Another women executive wrote that in her convention there is not intentional inequality, "except it doesn't employ women to "equal work" positions."

The policy and practice of ordaining women covers the spectrum of "no" to "mixed feelings" to "no problem" to the practice of ordaining women for 40 years in one convention and for over 100 years in another.

A couple of women voiced objections to ordination for men or women, but added: "If ordination is valid for anyone, it is valid for women," and that if any are to be ordained, "sex should not be a criterion." Another cited scripture as the reason for her church doesn't ordain women.

One denomination executive in women's work said that she wishes she had sought ordination, but was discouraged in doing so earlier in her life. "I feel we do a disservice to women, to the Word of God and the Church by limiting women in this rite of the Church," she wrote.

The general secretary of the Seventh Day Baptist Convention, one of the two member body executives to respond, wrote that he is "proud to be a part of a conference that...provides an equal opportunity for women and men considering their abilities as the only limiting factor." That conference has ordained women for over 100 years. American Baptist Churches have ordained women for more than 40 years.

Obstacles

Several women mentioned their own lack of confidence as an obstacle to ministry. This was reflected in a number of other responses citing low self-esteem as a great need to be addressed among women.

One state executive for women cited the "subtle obstacles" which she experienced from childhood that were a form of "denigration" of Christian rights and freedom. Another said she grew up accepting obstacles by society for women's choices. "Now" she noted, "younger women notice the obstacles and rightly object."

One young woman, a pastor's wife, said she was fortunate to have worked with men who encouraged her. Another expressed gratitude that she worked with two men who would "fight" for her rights and for equal pay for her. Several women said they had encountered no obstacles.

Conclusion

In spite of the pain in some of the voices we have heard, it has been encouraging to have the responsiveness of women from around the world. It is even more encouraging to see their willingness to stand together in service to the Church, whatever role they are permitted to fill in their churches and society, and to know their devotion to the Baptist World Alliance.

Another source of encouragement has come from a number of men who commented on the need to recognize women's gifts as an untapped resource for the Church. I would like to cite two more comments from men executives. A general secretary in Japan urges women not to give up on "improving the situation even if it takes a long history." The president of the Baptist Evangelical Union of Italy wrote that "Galatians 3:28 is as revolutionary for the Church today as Romans 1:17 was in Reformation time: let's take up the challenge!"

Among the women whose voices you have heard are, in my opinion, some 20th century versions of Biblical women. When the roll call of the faithful is sounded, I believe they will be on the list along with Sara, Miriam, Deborah, Esther, the Prophet Anna, Priscilla, Phoebe, several women "church planters" named by Paul, and scores of Marys and Marthas. There are some, I dare to suggest, who would be contemporaries of the Apostle Paul, Barnabas or Peter.

God's power is at work among women. Women may not have denominational "power" as such, and they are not in the "limelight" in most places. Yet, they do not give up. They are being faithful to their calling in Christ. Women are ready to accept the challenge of Christ, to risk being God's person in a particular place.

God has given gifts to women that cover the whole spectrum of Christian service and ministry. Many have gifts that we associate with pastoral, administrative and executive positions. Some are gifted as proclaimers, prophets and teachers. As Baptist Christians we handicap our mission and witness in the world when we relegate such persons to secondary roles in our churches and denominations.

Many more women are gifted in other ministries such as arranging flowers, keeping the children during workshop times, and making our places of studying and worshipping comfortable and appealing. They are also *nurturers* of our congregations.

Ordination is not the issue here. Affirming the gifts of women *is* the issue. To use ordination as a sole standard for including women in church ministry is to lose sight of the inclusive call of all to be persons used by God whatever their gifts.

In conclusion, here are more questions to ask:

Why is there so much pain in North America and in Western Europe about affirmation of women in churches?

Why don't women have more support for women as pastors and "spiritual" leaders? Is it a fear of change? Does low self/social image influence this?

Are our churches and denominations doing something to address the issue of low self-esteem among women? Are men admitting a similar need about themselves?

What can the Baptist World Alliance do to affirm women where cultures degrade, devalue, denigrate and often denounce the value and contribution of women?

How can the Baptist World Alliance support women in their struggles?

As we move into the next decade, which we hope will be a "Decade of Evangelism" for our world Baptist family, and then into the next century, there's a lot of work and ministry to be done. It can best be fulfilled as women are affirmed as full partners in this Mission. The words of Jesus say it best: "Whoever does the will of my Father is my mother, (my sister), and my brother."

Beth H. MacClaren is the executive director of the Women's Department of the Baptist World Alliance, Washington, D.C., U.S.A.

The Modern Diaspora
Displaced People, Human Migrations, Refugees, and Homelessness

John N. Jonsson

Issues of homelessness relating to the aged, the mentally deficient, the physically disabled, human delinquents, and women have been excluded deliberately in this presentation. These would feature in municipal treatments dealing with homelessness and poverty. In this paper specific attention has been given to homelessness within the international context of human migrations and refugees.

I. The Global Phenomenon

Victims of natural catastrophe, human holocaust, social revolution, and political upheaval have created a new mass of people known as human migrants, asylum seekers, the homeless, the people within the transition of loss of personal identity. Intolerable threat, loss of life and liberty, oppression, persecution, deprivation, civil strife, poverty, earthquake, drought, flood, and famine are among the devastating circumstances contributing towards this global phenomenon of displaced persons - the modern diaspora.[1]

1. Change in Focus Towards Humanitarian Interests

Televised appeals for financial help for victims of disaster invariably stress the depressed conditions caused by some natural catastrophe. Rarely are the problems treated symptomatically, however, with focus on the socio-ethical and politico-economic problems of dependency and injustice.[2] The primary problem of Third World dependency, of international economic imbalance, and of covert action by the super powers is rarely highlighted by the media, and is glaringly absent in evangelical presentations.[3]

The radicalities of human migrants, refugees, and the homeless, has been a specific feature of international law during the 20th century.[4] People fleeing across frontiers, however, have come to be accepted by commentators as an inevitable contingency of conflict, whether this be due to external aggression, radical internal policies, political injustice, or social change. Only recently has dissatisfaction been expressed concerning the manner in which statistical data has been processed, and how the existing mechanisms and procedures have been allowed to operate in so-called problem solving. The structures dealing with these issues at international and municipal levels together with commentaries treating the subject, have failed to keep abreast with current issues and have failed to treat the ethico-human concern as being kernel to the problem.

With the 1980s attention began to be focused on an essential ethical premise, vix., that refugeeism ought to be considered to be the exception and not the rule; that legal and political measures ought to be directed to the rights of people to live in peace, free from persecution and prejudice; that where these rights are highlighted, resolutions towards voluntary repatriation become a priority treatment; that political realities in affected countries are not facing up to the possibility that these are ethical, humanitarian issues which must head the discussion in negotiations. This changing perspective means that the foundation and framework of international law is having to concentrate on answering three basic questions, viz: 1) how are we to define a refugee, 2) what does "asylum" for refugees entail, 3) how are we to protect refugees?"[5]

This new approach, gives specific accent to the human being having inviolable rights, regardless of color, class or creed. This necessitates broader, more comprehensive, more explicit interpretations of what a human migrant as refugee and homeless person implies. Basic to this assumption is the principle conception, that such a person, or group of people, is worthy of being assisted and given refuge from injustice. This includes home-life and job-opportunity being made available.[6] The *Shorter Oxford English Dictionary* defines "refugee" as one who, owing to religious persecution or political troubles, seeks refuge in a foreign country. "Refuge" inter alia is shelter or protection from danger or trouble, help sought by or rendered to a person; a place of safety or security; a shelter, an asylum, a stronghold. This is precisely what refugees, migrants and the homeless are seeking to have.

2. Geographical and Demographic Research

The phenomenon of human migration, refugeeism and attendant homelessness, while persisting to occur across the globe, features in varying forms not making a general treatment possible. In Africa, urban migrations in Kenya, have been shown to be due to indigenous people rising up against old colonial policies.[7] The use of cheap black labor across frontiers, by industrial and mining operations in Africa, has regretfully been accepted by the "Big Five" powers as being an accepted norm.[8] In West Africa the demographic aspects of migration have been the feature of research.[9] Among the factors ingredient to migrations in Asia are the pressures of population explosion, want and war.[10] In the Americas, migrations of labor-seekers across the frontiers of Mexico and the U.S. have raised serious socio-ethical issues.[11] Cross-frontier migrations in search of employment have also been the concentration of research in Northwest Argentina and in Bolivia, together with other areas of industrial development.[12] The phenomenon of human migration in the European Community is also being researched in relationship to migrant workers.[13]

Human migration appears to take place wherever there is industrialization and modernization.[14] There is general consensus that migrants are being drawn into urbanized areas across frontiers of nationhood, race and ruralism. There is the general consensus among researchers that within such processes of transition, radical changes are inevitable in societal structures and in human relationships.[15] A constant factor in processes of urbanization and modernization, are the massive migrations which are taking place from rural areas. A dominant contributory factor which accounts for such trends, relates specifically to the absence of viable economies in rural communities in developing countries.

In more developed contexts, such as in the U.S. and Europe, there are new counterurbanization trends, new directions of movement from urban to rural migration.[16] This is a clear indication that, when rural economies are strengthened by smallholding, private ownership, the problems of homelessness in urban areas, caused by overcrowding, lack of job opportunity, and poverty, could be resolved by voluntary migrations back to rural communities. All efforts by authorities to strengthen rural economies are to be given our enthusiastic support.[17]

3. Apartheid Labor Laws and Homelessness

The phenomena of black migratory labor in South Africa relates specifically to a particular form of homelessness, in which the discriminatory labor laws destroy black family life. The influx control laws of the apartheid policy, in its application to black rural migratory workers in the white urban areas, is indicative of this. The laws of the white apartheid government which control the flow of black people into the cities, treat the black people as utilities of labor, to give support to the white economy of that country. Although these laws are said to be in the process of revision, the socio-ethical issue is not adequately being addressed by the white government in that country. This relates specifically to the deprivation of normal family life for the black migrant workers drawn from rural areas within the borders of South Africa to work in white urban areas.[18]

The labor laws in South Africa, affecting black migrant laborers in the white cities, stipulate that such male and female workers may not be allowed to bring their respective spouses and children with them to the city of their employment. During the course of their employment contract in the city, the black migrants are required by law to stay in black community centers in black townships adjacent to the white cities. Only after a black employee has worked for the same employer for more than ten unbroken years, may that black worker apply to the urban authorities for a house for his or her family. This deprivation of family life to the black workers is a basic violation of an inviolable human right, viz., the right to family life in the area of employment.

The shanty towns in Crossroads on the Cape Flats in South Africa represents black attempts to create family life. During our ministry and political involvement in South Africa, my wife Gladys and I were constantly addressing this heinous form of "homelessness" among black migrant workers. During a visit to South Africa in 1984, I approached Dr. Piet Koornhof, then chairperson of the Presidents Council. The relevant part of my letter read:

> "I have been shocked by the continuing inhumane manner in which blacks are being treated by regional authorities in the Cape Town area. . . The manner in which black homes were destroyed in a township near Crossroads in June 1984, on an evening when it was starting to rain, leaving women and children out in the dark, adds to the callous ruthlessness of a kind of mentality which refuses to consider that the blacks have a point of view. . . All the white authorities see in "shantytowns" are the hovels people live in. We do not give regard to the fact that because of the laws pertaining to the tenure of blacks in the cities, the "shantytowns: are often the only places in the cities where certain blacks are able to have family life. The forceful eviction of blacks from these areas is a complete disregard for the natural desire of family life among the blacks, something which is being denied them. Whereas the whites have laws which stress the dignity of family life, the present practice of black removal means that serious anomalies exist in the laws of the country. For when the law takes precedence over the needs of people in in section of the community, for the benefit of some at the expense of others, then justice is no longer seen to be done. . . These issues belong to the heart of the Gospel of the kingdom of God and his Christ, for they belong to the common dignities of human life and order against which there can be no law.[19]

4. International Law and Refugees

The international laws which protect human rights include the rights of displaced persons, - "refugees." In treaties concluded under the League of Nations (1922-46) a "refugee" was defined as someone outside their home of origin, without protection of government or state. This has proved to be an unsatisfactory definition, and the UN, through its offices of the High Commissioner for Refugees (UNHR), has helped give added content as to what constitutes a refugee.

Article 14 of the University Declaration of Human Rights (1948) of the United Nations, reads:

"1) Everyone has the right to seek and to enjoy in other countries asylum from persecution.

2) This right may not be invoked in the case of prosecutions genuinely arising from non-political crimes or from acts contrary to the purposes and principles of the UN"

In the light of global masses of migrants from trouble areas, this definition has become inadequate in application by UNHR.[20] Since 1975, UNHR has had to provide programs for displaced persons who were victims of war in Laos and Vietnam seeking asylum, and to people leaving the Indo-China peninsula in small boats. UNHR also has had to provide care and maintenance, and to promote programs for resettlements. In these the UNHR had to go beyond the parameters of the UN definition of a "refugee". When in 1976 refugees were spoken of as "asylum seekers," the definition of what constituted a refugee became a semantic issue, with differentiations being made between "refugees" and "displaced persons".[21] The Convention of 1951 and the 1967 Protocol had defined "refugees" to include:

1. those outside their country of origin;
2. those unable or unwilling to avail themselves of the protection of that country or to return there;
3. such inability or unwillingness being attributed to a well-founded fear of being persecuted;
4. the persecution feared being based on reasons of race, religion, nationality, membership of a particular social group, or political opinion.[22]

The UNHR recognized that "membership of a particular social group" could have very real political overtures.[23]

A number of member countries of the UN have both constitutional and enacted law provisions benefitting refugees.[24] Most states are all too conscious of the potential threat to their internal security from massive influxes of refugees, but none claim absolute right to return to a refugee to be persecuted. What has often happened, however, is that certain countries have evaded their moral responsibility to "refugees," by labelling those appealing for asylum as "illegal immigrants," "aliens," "deportees," "boat-people," or "stowaways."[25] Guy S. Goodwin-Gill, Legal Advisor in the Office of the UN High Commissioner for Refugees, for this reason contends that there is a need in international law to concentrate on: 1) the right for people to belong; 2) the right to move orderly in seeking of work; 3) the right to decent living conditions; 4) the right to freedom from strife.[26]

Measures to avert and to resolve refugee crises can only be achieved on the basis of international cooperation elaborated on the lines of two self-evident premises, viz., 1) that human rights, as fundamental freedom, is conditioned by opportunities of individuals and groups to participate in and benefit from the national politic; 2) that the right to seek asylum and the benefits due to refugees, include non-refoulement, with standards of treatment which are humane and humanitarian.

In 1980 the UN Commission on Human Rights expressed concern that large exoduses were frequently the victims of human rights violations.[27] This resulted in the General Council establishing a 17 member group of governmental experts to review all aspects of refugee problems, and to find a basis for international cooperation.[28] The Special Rapporteur to the General Assembly, the next year, proposed that there be an updating of refugees, of nationality, and of labor law, within the context of a "New International Humanitarian Order." The UN General Assembly responded to this by suggesting that there also be a reappraisal of the economic needs of developing countries in terms of the possible causes of such needs.[29]

5. Christian - Secular Dialogical Coexistence

Christian organizations concerned in bringing about radical change in refugeeism and homelessness, need to take serious cognizance of the trends of increasing sensitivity to the socio-human and ethnic dimensions in international law. Hopefully this will engender efforts to work in close cooperation with the offices of the U.N. High Commissioner for Refugees and the Commission of Human Rights. It is my considered conviction that only in this way will the multiplicity of our fragmented global efforts of relief be put to best effect. The need for coordination of our socio-evangelical effort in existing global relief ministries is a priority in itself. The need for a global mission conference of mission boards, service organizations in Eurica and Latfriasia is urgent. At the top of the agenda of such a meeting should be the issue of cooperation with secular powers within the framework of existing humanitarian efforts and international law. For this to happen it will be necessary for Christian leaders, worldwide, to reaffirm a much-neglected biblio-theological doctrine, viz., the presence and working of the living God of our Lord Jesus Christ within the human affairs of our contemporary world. We must respond positively, in dialogue, with all secular movements of a new "International Humanitarian Order."

II. A Socio-Ethical Christian Evaluation

Most U.S. and European analyses, of internal migratory trends, conclude that the causes of geographic mobility are due to the economic well-being which such movements will afford.[30]

1. A Methodological Problem

The assumption on which such postulates are made may well apply to the hegemonous context of "developed" countries, enjoying a common economy. However, reasons for human migrations across frontiers of "developing" countries is far more complex and cannot be reduced to one such cause or goal objective.[31] Tendencies to look for the causes of refugees, homelessness, and poverty, all too often evade the contextual issues within the actual human dilemma. This results in the refugee, the homeless, and the poor being treated as a normal problem, rather than their conditions being viewed as abnormal, necessitating attention and solution, regardless of the causes.[32]

The manner in which researchers tend to theorize on the causes of migrations, poverty, and homelessness, from the vantage point of western economic assumptions, is here being brought into question.[33] Statistics are not factual data, but highly interpreted and interpretative source material, used selectively by researchers for a variety of politicized reasons, not least that of the resistance of settled communities to influxes of migrants and refugees seeking shelter and employment.[34] Migrants constitute a destabilizing threat to settled communities in developed countries. We conveniently label the causes of migration, poverty, and homelessness as being economic, because movements of "displaced persons" in our direction, tend to disrupt our own economic stability and security.

Periodicals such as *Seeds* and *Sojourners*, consider western assumptions used to interpret homelessness and poverty as being unsatisfactory, because of western prestige, enculturation, and international politicization.[35] Patricia L. Bailey, professor of social work, contends that the role of research needs closer scrutiny, because of the manner in which statistics is utilized to give support to our own political theory, making this a serious philosophical and methodological problem.[36] Third World leaders, such as Vinay Samuel and Chris Sugden, consider this to be due to our multinational mentality, in which we as westerners express our parochial, self-accommodating interests in our missions approach to the world problems.[37]

2. The Priority of Housing

Overcrowded living conditions, the lack of proper sanitation, and the absence of clean drinking water, on a global scale, makes the provision of proper housing the top priority for public concern and interest, as a legitimate service to humanity. Though this be the case, Alan Murie, a social scientist in the British context, contents that the provision of housing has become, primarily, a market operation subject to economic policy, rather than a public service to meet basic human necessities for human well-being and security. Because the role of houses has become equated with the accumulation of wealth, Alan Murie concludes:

> It must be a matter of concern that the housing debate which was at one time focused on issues of health and child development is often carried out as if problems of meeting need were solved, and remaining inequalities no longer had importance for life changes.[38]

Vic George's basic theoretical premise gives the explanation to what accounts for the wealth or poverty of individuals within nations. After his analysis of major theories on this area, he adopts the structuralist explanation for analyzing statistical data of post-war economic and world inequality trends. Such trends, he concludes, proves how resistant to change we are in our economic security.

He shows that the extent or poverty within affluent countries still exits on a substantial scale. He also points out that the evidence of famine, starvation, and subsistence poverty in the Third World, highlights the fact that Third World poverty must be analyzed from within the context of the Third World and not from our First World vantage point. We can no longer project the analysis of our own internal perceptions onto the Third World, in attempts to give explanation of the global dilemma.[39]

3. The Root Cause of the World Problem

The issues of human migration, refugees, and homelessness necessitates a closer analysis of the root causes of poverty. Thomas D. Hanks points out how affluent peoples of the world treat "underdevelopment," poverty, and dependency, as being due to laziness, drunkeness, and to assumed racial or national inferiority of certain classes of people.[40] He points out that the Bible, however, has nothing to say about "underdevelopment" but has a great deal to say about oppression.[41] Oppression in the bible is shown to be the root-cause of poverty, with the word "poor" spelt out as "oppressed poor." Liberation movements and theologies, in the Third World countries, deal specifically with this imbalance as the basic problem to be addressed and remedied.[42] Thus Jon Sobrino highlights the experience of God in the poor in the church, as being a missing dimension in our understanding of God in the mission understanding of Christians in affluent society.[43] Affluent Christians tend to treat the plights of the homeless, displaced person in search of personal identity, with mindsets which no longer view justice from the viewpoint of the poor, deprived, and oppressed, but in terms of their prestige, their social standing, their economic security, and their political power.

4. Call for Socio-Human Action

Jan Lochman, in expounding the ancient Greek myth of "Prometheus," addresses this fundamental attitude. As in the myth, we have assumed the power role of Zeus in our mission leadership and in our theological orthodoxy. This legitimizes us putting Prometheus to death, where Prometheus represents the idea that people in their own right have legitimate claims to make for themselves. Theologically we reject this, because we have imbibed the haughty spirit of Zeus into our theological orthodoxy, and reject the legitimate socio-human claims of people within the existence of their orthopraxy.[44] The orthodoxy of our theological belief systems has desensitized us to the ethical priorities of the place of the human in scripture, and to the dilemma of people in their societal existence.[45] Albert Schweitzer complained about evangelical orthodoxy and religious liberalism in Germany in the 1930's, in the socio-ethical neutralism it had adopted, at a time when Hitler was entrenching himself in the Third Reich.[46]

As Christians we need to be liberated from the lethargy of our detached spirituality and piety, disrelated to socio-ethical issues, disengaged from the plights of our contemporaries in our societal world. If Jesus Christ is the watershed of history we can no longer persist in hammering away at constructing theological cliches behind church doors which are closed to the socio-ethical issues of our time. As the body of Christ, we should be up front at the cutting edge where socio-human issues belong, as the continuum of the Incarnation of Jesus Christ in our time. The Macedonian call in our day appeals to us to "come over and help" the homeless in society, the victims of holocaust, the human tragedies of displaced persons entrapped in mass movements of migration.[47]

David Hollenback interprets socio-human justice in the Bible as being a relational, conventual bond among people in community, a bond which protects and enhances the lives of individuals in mutual support in society.[48] Socio-ethics is creative in that it seeks to remake a socio-human context of fairness, with freedom towards new and more personal relationships between people. This is what "koinonia" (fellowship) is intended to be, namely, that of giving the homeless, the aging, the destitute, the deprived, and the poor a new sense of belonging. "Koinonia" is, for people in community, a new sense of human identity; a new appreciation of mutual self-respect; a new conception of one's own human worth and creative ability. It is freedom from inferiority, freedom from oppression, freedom from intimidation, freedom from dependency. It means being new creations in Christ Jesus (II Corinthians 5:17).

5. Inter-active Planning in the Kingdom of God

Patricia Bailey has expressed profound insight into the fundamental dilemma of Christian organizations in their humanitarian efforts today. She points out that there are hundreds of Christian organizations in most countries across the globe engaged in feverish efforts to deal with problems related to human tragedy and disaster. All too often there is excessive overlapping in their "in praxis" programs of relief. Her observations are poignant at this point. She contends:[49]

(a) There is little or no consultation among organizing bodies toward the coordination of their efforts, making their separate efforts ineffective, with little collective reflection or strategy of concerted effort.
(b) Many of the organizational efforts treat the socio-human problems as emergencies within particular crises, without addressing the issues of how to bring about stability and effective change towards normality.
(c) Emergency efforts are all too often transportations of western perceptions, of what we consider to be for the benefit of the victims, without implicating the local "helpers" and indigenous leaders within the decision-making and administrative processes of "in praxis" operations.
(d) Accordingly, we do not address the problems symptomatically, and do not deal with the basic socio-human problems which aggravate the well-being of people in society. (e) This in turn robs us of the most important ingredient for problem-solving, namely, that which uses the problems themselves, together with the participants implicated in what is germane to the problem and consequently is able to bring about healing within the hurting communities.[50]

Pat Bailey concludes, "I consider the kernel problem of homelessness, poverty and displaced persons basically to be a theological one, within the parameters of our western thinking." This devastating assessment is so crucial to our self-evaluation, because it highlights the ineptness of our abstract and theorized belief in God, in Christ, and in the Holy Spirit. It also brings to the surface of our awareness, the futility of our Christian leadership, which chooses to be neutral to socio-ethical issues affecting the dilemma of the Third World people in their economic dependency and deprivation.[51]

Albert Schweitzer's opening remark in his Hibbert Lectures at Manchester College, Oxford, England in 1934 under the title of "Religion in Modern Civilization," reads:

> I am going to discuss religion in the spiritual life and civilization of our time. The first question to be faced, therefore, is: Is religion a force in the spiritual life of our age? I answer in your name, and mine, "No!"[52]

Possibly in the words of J. Hoekendijk, we the church need to be "turned inside out." Probably we need in our theology a greater recognition of the veracity of God's transcendence at work within the human affairs of people in our world. Possibly we need to have a greater sensitivity in compassion at "gut level," where the cross of Christ is being enacted before our eyes today within the tragedies of human privation, human destitution, and human dereliction. Possibly we need a new infusion of spirituality, which incarnates our belief system into a mission that, in the words of Archbishop Desmond Tutu, "puts our bodies where our mouth is."[53]

Possibly we as Christian leaders, representative of our world family of Baptists, need in our mission understanding to give recognition not only to "mission Dei," the mission of God, not only to "missiones ecclesiarum," the mission of the church, crucial and cardinal though these may be. We need also to give full recognition to the authenticity of "missio hominum," the mission of secular people in society. This will necessitate our giving fuller recognition to the spiritual forces at work in our time, such as in the mission of the UN Commission on Human Rights and the High Commissioner for Refugees. We need to give recognition to the living God at work in global functioning bodies in our time. We need to seek counsel, and to act in consultation with such secular movements. In this kind of mutuality their endeavors will be enhanced, and our kingdom of God involvements in socio-human affairs will have a hope and a future under the providence and enabling of Jesus Christ and His eternal spirit. For in the ultimate issues of the kingdom of God and of His Christ, the poor, the deprived, the dispossessed, the displaced, the diaspora, and the homeless do not need us, but we need them.

John N. Jonsson is professor of Missions and World Religions at The Southern Baptist Theological Seminary in Louisville, KY, U.S.A.

Footnotes

1. J.A.Jackson, ed., *Migrations* (University Press, 1969). J. Mangalam, *Human Migration: A guide to Migration Literature* (Lexington: University of Kentucky Press, 1968) William H. McNeil and Ruth S. Adams, eds., *Human Migration: Patterns and Policies* (Bloomington: Indiana University Press, 1975.

2. Alexander Kirkland Cairncross, *Home and Foreign Investment: Studies of Capital Accumulation* (Clifton, N.J.: A. M. Kelley, 1975).

3. Michael N. Dobkowski, ed., *The Politics of Indifference: a Documentary History of Holocaust Victims in America* (Washington, D.C.: University Press of American, 1982). Beatriz Manz, *Refugees of a Hidden War: The Aftermath of Counterinsurgency in Guatemala* (Albany: State University of N.Y. Press, 1988.

4. Guy S. Goodwin-Gill, *The Refugee in International Law* (New York: Oxford University Press, 1983). Atle Grahl-Madsen, *The Status of Refugees in International Law* 2 volumes. (Leyden: A. W. Sijthoff, 1966). Robert Kee, *Refugee World* (New York: Oxford University Press, 1961).

5. Guy S. Goodwin-Gill, Ibid, pp. i-ii (ed) Gabriel Sheffer, *Modern Diasporas in International* °Politics N.M. St. Martins Press 1988.

6. Clifford J. Jansen, *Readings in the Sociology of Migration* (New York: Pergama Press, 1970).

7. Tabitha M. Kanogo, *Squaters and the Roots of Mau Mau* London, J. Currey, 1987.

8. Sharon Strichter, *Migrant Laborers* N.Y. Cambridge Press 1985. (ed.) W. R. Bohnong *Black Migration to South Africa: A Selection of Policy-Oriented Research.* Geneva, International Labor Office, 1981.

9. K.C. Zachariah, *Migration in West Africa*, N.Y. Oxford 1981 (ed.) Samir Amin, *Modern Migrations in Western Africa* International African Seminar, Dakar 1972. London, Oxford Press 1974.

10. Bruno Lasker, *Asia on the Move* N.Y. H. Hold and Co. 1945.

11. Stephen H. Sosnicic, *Hired Hands*, (Santa Barbara: McNally and Loftin, West 1978) Carol Norquest, *Rio Grande Wetbacks: Mexican Migrant Workers* (Alburquerque, University of New Mexico, 1972. Grace Halsell, *The Illegals* (New York: Stein and Day, 1978.

12. Scott Whiteford, *Workers from the North* (Austin, Texas: University of Texas Press, 1981) Julian Laite, *Industrial Development and Migrant Labor in Latin America* (Austin, Texas: University of Texas Press, 1981.

13. W. R. Bohning, *The Migration of Workers in the United Kingdom and the European Community* (New York: Oxford University Press, 1972). Arnold Marshall, *Migrants in Europe: Problems of Acceptance and Adjustments* (University of Minnesota Press, 1969).

14. William H.V. Clark, *Recent Research on Migration and Mobility* (Oxford, Pergamon Press, 1982). Barbara A. Johnson, *Internal Migration During Modernization in . . . Russia* (Princeton University Press, 1980). Guy Standing, *Labor Circulation in the Labor Process. . .within the Framework of the World Employment Program* (Dover, England: N. H., Groom Helm, 1985). Robert Repetto, *Economic Development, Population Policy and Demographic Transition in the Republic of Korea* (Harvard University Press, 1981). William J. Demarest, *Mayan Migrants in Guatemala City* (Guatemala: Seminario De Integacion Social Guatemalteca, 1984).

15. Robert N. Kearney, *Internal Migrations in Sri Lanta and Its Social Consequences* (Boulder, Colo.: Westview Press, 1987). R. Marshall Prothero and Murray Chapman, *Circulation in Third World Countries* (Boston: Routledge and K. Paul, 1985. J. Barry Riddell, *The Special Dynamics of Modernization in Sierra Leone Structure, Difussion and Response* (Evanston: Northwestern University Press, 1980).

16. A.J. Fielding, *Counterurbanization in Western Europe* (New York: Academia Press, 1980). David L. Brown and John M. Wardwell, eds., *New Directions in Urban-Rural Migration: The Population Turnabout in Rural America* (New York: Academia Press, 1980). Amos H. Hawley and Sara Mills Mazie, *Nonmetropolitan America in Transition: Research in Social Science* (Chapel Hill, NC: University of North Carolina, 1981).

17. John N. Jonsson, "Ferment in the Cities of Developing Countries," *Review and Expositor* Vol LXXXII, No. 2, Spring 1985, pp. 195-196.
Church bodies need to be proposing programs for strengthening the economics in rural areas, to stem the tide of movements into the cities. Support should be given to every effort being made to bring hope towards self-subsistence among the underprivileged of the world."
Mr. R. E. Hudson-Reed, a Baptist leader in civic affairs in Moor River, South Africa, has been responsible for hundreds of millions of dollars being dispersed among ordinary black people in Natal, in order to initiate and sustain a black rural economy controlled by black leadership, to provide black bargaining power in negotiations towards the dispensation of their equal rights and political involvement at the highest levels of the legislature and judiciary, in counter demand to the unjust apartheid system.

18. Cf. John N. Jonsson, *Retranspositionalization: Socio-Human Justice for South African Blacks* (Louisville: Nilses, 1987), pp. 34-37; x-xi.

20. In Africa the size of the refugee problem in the 1960's made individual assessment of refugee status impractical with machinery inappropriate for dealing with "group refugees." e.g., the crisis in Nambia in 1982, the Chinese refugees in Hong Kong since 1955, and the Algerians fleeing to Tunisia and Morocco to escape the effects of their struggles for liberation.

21. "Refugees were defined as those who crossed international frontiers, whereas displaced persons had not. Cf. Guy S. Goodwin-Gill, *The Refugee in International Law* (New York: Oxford University Press, 1983). This differentiation of what was international and what belonged to the internal matters of a state could not be justified, however. "Protection" implies both "internal" protection, the guaranteeing the life, liberty and security of a person, and "external" protection, providing diplomatic protection with documentation abroad, recognizing the rights of nationals to return to the place of their origin. "The right to return" became a real issue to be defended. The UNHR in dealing with specific cases of refugees challenged semantic differentiates which avoided the humanitarian rights of a person to be helped in time of distress by the international community of nations. E.g., the Afghanistans seeking assistance as fugitive insurgents in Pakistan, and Ethiopian refugees in Somalia considered by the Ethiopian regime to be "instruments of aggression and disruption." (UN Document A/AC.96/521 para. 105 nd A/C.3/34/AR.46 para. 58f).

22. Guy S. Goodwin-Gill, Ibid, p. 11-13.

23. CF. Atle Grahl-Madson, *The Status of Refugees in International Law* 2 Vols. (Leyden: A.W. Sitthoff, 1966), vol. I, p. 217.

24. Eg., The Federal Republic of Germany 1949 Article 16 (2) prescribed the right of asylum to those politically persecuted.

25. Guy S. Goodwin-Gill, Ibid., p. 19.

26. Ibid., p. 215. Cf. Sadruddin Asa Khan, *Study on Human Rights and Mass Exoduses* (UN Document E/CN.4/1503 para. 9).

27. *Commission on Human Rights Res 30* (XXXVI) of 11 March 1980. (UN Document E/1980/ 13, 191).

28. Expanded to 24 members in 1982. (*UN General Assembly Res 38/121*, 16 Dec. 1982).

29. *UN General Assembly Resolution 36/136*, 14 Dec. 1981.

30. Richard J. Cebula, *The Determinants of Human Migration* (Lexington, Mass.: Lexington Books, 1979), pp. 5-52. Dudley Baines, *Migration in a Mature Economy* (New York: Cambridge University Press) 1985). Frank Musgrave, *The Military Elite* (London: Heinemann, 1963.

31. Guy Standing, *Labor Circulation and Labor Process* (Dover: Groom Helm, 1985). R. Mansell Prothero and Murray Chapman, *Circulation in Third World Countries* (n.p.: Bosron, Routledge and K. Paul, 1985).

32. Robert Coles, *Uprooted Children* (Pittsburg: University Press of Pittsburg Press, 1970. Henry Hill Collins, *America's Own Refugees: Our 4,000,000 Homeless Migrants* (Princeton: Princeton University Press, 1941).

33. R. Paul Shaw, *Migration Theory and Fact: Review and Bibliography of Current Literature* (Philadelphia: Regional Science Research Institute, 1975). Kenneth George Willis, *Problems in Migration Analysis* (Lexington, Mass.: Lexington Books, 1974).

34. Samir N. Maamary, *Attitudes Toward Migration among Rural Residents* (San Francisco: R. & E. Research Associates, 1976. Daniel Kubat and Anthony H. Richmond, eds., *Internal Migration: The New World and the Third World* (Beverly Hills: Sage Publications, 1976).

35. Cf. Vic George, *Wealth, Poverty and Starvation* New York: St. Martin's Press, 1988). Alan Murie, *Housing Inequality and Deprivation* (London: Heinmann, 1983). 36. Patricia L. Bailey, *Poverty Course 3840*, The Southern Baptist Theological Seminary, to be introduced January 1990. Discussion with Professor Bailey.

36. Patricia L. Bailey, *Poverty Course 3840,* The Southern Baptist Theological Seminary, to be introduced January 1990. Discussion with Professor Bailey.

37. Samuel Vinay & Chris Sugden, "Mission Agencies as Multinationals,: *International Bulletin,* vol, 7, no. 4, October 1983, pp. 152-157. Cf. Orville L. Freeman and William Persen, "Multinational Corporations: Some Facts and Figures," *The Futurist* Dec. 1980.

38. Alan Murie, Housing Inequality and Deprivation Ibid., pp. 173-236.

39. Vic George, *Wealth, Poverty and Starvation*, Ibid., pp. 126-167.

40. Thomas D. Hanes, "Why People are Poor," in *Border Regions of Faith* (New York: Orbis: 1987), pp. 411-417.

41. There are 15 Hebrew and 2 Greek roots, used more than 300 times in all, in no fewer than 122 biblical texts.

42. Cf. Dean William Ferm, *Third World Liberation Theologies* (New York: Orbis, 1986), pp. 15-198.

43. Jan Lochman, *The True Church and the Poor* (New York: Orbis, 1984, p. 125-159; 253-301).

44. Jan Lochman, *Christ and Prometheus? A Quest for Theological Identity* (Geneva: W. C. C., 1988.

45. John N. Jonsson, *Putting an Ethical Horse in Front of a Theological Cart* (Natal, S.A.: University of Natal, 1966).

46. Cf. John N. Jonsson, *God's Eager Fool: Theologia Viatorium with Albert Schweitzer* (Louisville, Nilses, 1986), pp. 15-19.

47. John N. Jonsson, "The Church Turned Inside Out," *Retranspositionalization* (Louisville, Nilses, 1988), pp. 12-13.

48. David Hollenbach, "The Biblical Justice of Politics" in *Border Regions of Faith* (New York: Orbis, 1984), pp. 418-421.

49. A productive discussion with Patricia Bailey, Professor of Social Work, The Southern Baptist Theological Seminary, on 7 July 1989. Pat Bailey has been actively implicated in social field work in Skidrow, Chicago, Illinois, and in the West End of Louisville, Kentucky.

50. Cf. Vinay Samuel and Charles Corwin, "Assistance Programs Require Partnerships," *Evangelical Mission Quarterly*, 15, no. 2 (April 1979) pp. 97-101.

51. Cf. Steven G. Mackie, "Seven Clues for Rethinking Mission," *International Review of Mission*, vol, LX no. 239 (July 1971), pp. 324-327.

52. Albert Schweitzer, "Religion in Modern Civilization," *The Christian Century*, November 21, 1934.

53. A public statement made by Desmond Tutu on 21 March 1985 when 239 Christian leaders in South Africa were arrested in Cape Town in protest against the slaying of Black Christians in Uitenhage.

54. Mother Teresa made a similar statement when she received her Nobel Peace Prize Award: "The poor do not need us, we need the poor."

Commission
On Human Rights

Thorwald Lorenzen

The concern for Human Rights is intimately interwoven with the history and theology of Baptists.

The origins of the Baptist vision on the European continent, on the British isles and in North America is closely linked with the claim for religious liberty, for freedom of conscience, for freedom of opinion, and with freedom of assembly. The Anabaptists in 16th century Europe and the Baptists in 17th century England followed the voice of their conscience even when this led to conflicts with the political and religious authorities and institutions of their day. Their struggle became an important ingredient for the Human Rights that are codified and universally recognized today.

But the implementation of Human Rights lags far behind their theoretical codification, and their moral and juridical authority. People are being tortured by the very governmental authorities whose function it is to uphold the law. Children are being denied the right to life, education and medical care. Nations are being robbed of their right to self determination. Sexual, racial, and religious discrimination is rampant. Even within our own Baptist family, sisters and brothers have to pay dearly for their commitment to Christ. They are persecuted and imprisoned. They suffer educational and professional disadvantages. Both political, and religious institutions are known to deny human rights to Baptists.

This experience makes us Baptists sensitive to the tragic fate of others. What we claim for ourselves, we cannot deny to others. At every BWA Congress or BWA Council important resolutions give expression to our commitment to our struggle for the implementation of human rights. Thus in recent years resolutions have been passed on racism, apartheid, religious liberty, terrorism, peace, disarmament, shelter for the homeless, justice, prisoners of conscience, world hunger, hostages, minorities, the rights of children, and the equality of women.

As Baptists were are committed to the authority of the biblical message, and there we discover that God from the beginning was concerned not only with creating humanity and the world, but also with saving and protecting it. When His people are oppressed, He longs for their liberation, and He invites people like Moses to participate in that liberating activity. With the law codes in ancient Israel special structures were created under the providence of God to ease the fate of the poor, the slave, the widow, and the stranger. The prophets of Israel expose those leaders and institutions that destroy the dignity of human persons. Jesus announces liberation to the oppressed and promises grace to the poor, the hungry and the sorrowful (Luke 4:18f., 6:20f.) The Psalmist gathers up the intention of the biblical message when he says: "Give justice to the weak and the fatherless; maintain the right of the afflicted and the destitute." (82:3) and in Proverbs this concern for justice is related directly to the being and action of God: "the Lord will plead their cause." (22:22) "He who oppresses a poor man insults his Maker, but he who is kind to the needy honors him." (14:31) The early church tunes into this biblical message when it interweaves our relationship to Christ with our concern for human rights: as much as you have done it or not done to these the needy brethren, you have done it or not done to me, the Christ (Matt 25:31-46).

The Baptist World Alliance has given structural expression to this biblical imperative by creating the Human Rights Commission. To this Commission over 40 Baptist leaders from many countries have been appointed. The Commission meets once a year in conjunction with the BWA Council. Gazing over the activities of the commission during the last 5 years, we may highlight four main areas of concern.

There is, firstly, the area of theology and history from a Baptist perspective. Our commitment to the Bible as the Word of God has given us an immediate concern for and perspective to the world wide struggle for human rights. The papers by Dr. Athol Gill emphasizing a theological perspective from below, Dr. James Wood's reference to Baptist history and theology, and Dr. Saverio Guarna's contribution relating our commitment to evangelism to the struggle for human rights, are illustrations of this dimension of our work.

We have secondly dealt with concrete issues that are of interest to our churches and to human society. Papers were presented and discussed on issues such as torture, shelter for the homeless, equality between men and women, refugees, asylum seekers, and the fate of children in our world. From this branch of our activities we have included the paper by Shirley F. Bentall on the equality between men and women with special reference to us as Baptists, and the essay by Dr. Wolfgang Lorenz dealing with our responsibility to refugees and asylum seekers.

A third concern has been to be sensitive and respond to situations in which denials of human rights are daily experienced, and where our Baptist brothers and sisters have been involved. This has been a particularly sensitive and sometimes controversial area of our work. Denials of human rights are so widespread, reliable information is often difficult to get, people and churches need to be protected, so that we could only deal with a few selective situations, like South Africa, Nicaragua, El Salvador, the German Democratic Republic, Ruanda, Liberia, the Philippines, Cuba, Jordan and the Caribbean.

We have, fourthly, asked ourselves again and again the question how we can actually communicate our concerns, our information, our insights to our unions and churches. What good is it, we have asked ourselves, if once a year a few experts talk about human rights, if we do not find ways to share this aspect of the gospel with our constituency? We have tried to encourage our churches to observe a Human Rights Sunday once a year and we have made information available; we have written press releases and have hoped that Baptist papers would publish them. This concern with the reception process is illustrated in the paper by Per Midteide.

As a fifth area of concern we have on several occasions dealt with the relationship of the Baptist World Alliance to the United Nations. The possibilities and responsibilities which the BWA has as a recognized "Non Government Organization" at the UN is discussed in the paper by Dr. Carl Tiller.

I hope that the following selection of papers conveys hope to the reader to become engaged in the struggle for the implementation of human rights. As Baptists we are committed to the biblical message as God's word to us. A word that forgives our sin and liberates us from our self interest so that we can creatively tine into God's healing passion for the world. At the same time, we are a world wide fellowship of believers in which we feel the agony and the joys of our brothers and sisters around the world: "If one member suffers, all suffer together; if one member is honored, all rejoice together." (1 Cor. 12:26) The closer we come to Christ, the more we shall hear the silent and spoken cries of men, women and children for whom Christ died. In our faith, our prayer and our life we can no longer bypass those whose human dignity is denied. Our commitment to the struggle for the implementation of human rights becomes an essential part of our faith in the trinitarian God.

Dr. Thorwald Lorenzen is Professor of Systematic Theology and Ethics at the Baptist Theological Seminary in Ruschlikon, Switzerland.

Human Rights: A Down-Under Perspective

Athol Gill

The theme of Human Rights has long been a favorite among Baptists. So much has been written that one might wonder if, apart from reports on human rights abuses in various parts of the world, there is anything more that can be said. Certainly the biblical material has been raked over many times. Liberation theology and the insights of scholars from the Two-third worlds, sociological exegesis and a rediscovery of many previously neglected themes of Scripture (prophetic concepts of justice, Jesus' proclamation of the Kingdom and good news to the poor, the corporate nature of Pauline theology and ethics among others), have, however, led to the development of a fresh perspective which has far-reaching, consequences for our understanding of human rights.

I have called this a "down-under perspective" for I think that is important that you understand the direction from which I am coming when I seek to interpret the Bible and when I speak of human rights as predominantly an "East-West" issue and that it was concerned primarily with questions relating to the freedom of religion. More recently, however, I have been forced to recognize that it is a "north-south" issue and that it concerns the totality of human existence.

Through our involvement with the House of Freedom and the House of the Gentle Bunyip Christian communities we have been introduced to some of the marginalized and oppressed people of Australian society and have been helped to see life from their perspective. International contacts have encouraged this process. Brothers and sisters from Central America have greatly helped me to read the Bible and to understand human rights from this perspective.

1. Biblical Perspectives for Human Rights

1.1 The new perspective on human rights of which we have been speaking does not rest upon an occasional proof-text from an obscure book of the Bible. It has its roots in one of the most fundamental aspects of theology, namely the nature of God and of God's relationship to humanity. For many of us, Christian concern for human rights has been awakened by the frightening injustice and sometimes overwhelming oppression of the world in which we live, but it is important for us to realize that this concern for human rights is ultimately grounded in the nature of God the creator and redeemer. As a result it can never be reduced to the level of an optional extra or even be considered simply as a necessary implication of the gospel. Social justice and the quest for human rights are at the heart of the gospel; they reflect the heart of God.

1.1.1 We must remember, of course, that within both the Hebrew and Christian Scriptures the doctrine of God is related as the story of the One who is actively involved in human history, seeking to establish justice and peace. In the Hebrew Scriptures God is described as the One who intervened on behalf of Israel when she was in slavery, liberated her from the oppressive might of the Egyptians and finally established her in a fine broad land, a land flowing with milk and honey. The Exodus is depicted as the foundational event of Israel's history and in that event God is revealed as the God of justice and liberation, intervening on behalf of the oppressed, responding to the cry of the weak who were groaning under the weight of their oppressors (Ex 3:1-20). To hear the cry of the poor, to intervene on behalf of the weak, to bring down the might of the oppressor is to join with God in the divine mission of liberation and salvation. The patriarchal stories, with their emphasis upon Israel as a chosen race through Abraham, were added to the Biblical tradition at a later stage in its development and ought not to be used obscure this vital insight concerning Yahweh as the God of the oppressed. The very name "Hebrew" may well be an indication of this perspective, referring not so much to a "race" as to a "social class" - "those who had sold themselves into slavery". Yahweh is identified as "the God of Abraham, Isaac and Jacob" who reveals his essential nature as the liberator of the oppressed. The liberation which the God of Israel brings is social and economic, cultural and political. It's ultimate goal is that the liberated people might worship "Yahweh" (3:12; 5:1, 7:16, 27; 8:27). When those who had been liberated from Egypt finally reached Palestine they joined forces with the marginalized elements of Canaanite society and together overthrew the Canaanite overlords and set about the task of establishing a new social order.

The distinctive feature of this new social order was its rejection of the stratification of the urbanized Canaanite culture and the attempt to establish an equality based upon social units of the extended family. Even though the stories have been refashioned under the influence of the later social and economic status of Israel, we cannot ignore the fact that were originally understood from the perspective of those who had been oppressed and marginalized. The vehicle of God's liberation is Israel the oppressed, not Egypt the oppressor.

1.1.2 Israel was created by the justice of God and was called by God to continue God's mission of justice in the world. Israel's failure to become involved in this divine mission resulted in the repeated denunciation of the nation by the prophets of Yahweh. Rather than being a center for justice, the nation became a haven of oppression. Religion remained popular, justice and respect for human rights became rare commodities.

The introduction of the monarchy into Israel had far-reaching social, economic and religious consequences for Israel as elements of Canaanite culture and social organization were re-established, destroying whatever semblance of equality existed between the clans and extended families of Israel. Under Solomon state expenditure outran income with his mammoth building projects, extensive army and lavish support of the Jerusalem cult. Heavy taxation was imposed and forced labour gangs were introduced. During the ninth century the disintegration of Israelite society placed the poor at the mercy of the rich. The story of Naboth's vineyard (1Kgs 21) indicates both the tyranny of the wealthy and the role of the prophet as the bearer of God's judgment upon those who failed to recognize basic human rights. The eighth century was a time of political stability and economic prosperity and as archaeological evidence clearly shows the rich were becoming richer and the poor poorer. The "down-under" perspective was in danger of being lost as the lifestyle and economic policies of the rulers of Israel were increasingly influenced by those of the nations round about.

In stark contrast to the perspective of the developing dominant culture Amos (eighth century B.C.E.) attacked the exploitation of this early capitalism as an affront to the God who had liberated Israel from oppression in Egypt. Because the large property owners and leading merchants had perverted justice and oppressed the poor and deprived them of their rights, even to the extent of selling them into slavery, the reluctant prophet declared that the nation would be reduced to rubble (Am 2:6-8; 3:1-2, 9-11; 4:1-3; 5:1-17; 8:4-7).

After denouncing the neighboring nations for their crimes against humanity (Damascus, Gaza, Tyre, Edom, Ammon, Moab), the prophet launches into an even more stringent denunciation of Israel:

"*Thus says the Lord,*
For three transgressions of Israel and for four,
will not revoke the judgment;
because they sell the righteous for silver,
and the needy for a pair of shoes -
they trample the head of the poor into the dust of the earth,
and turn aside the way of the afflicted." *(2:6-7)*

In contemporary theology, oracles against other nations were traditional-

ly followed by a promise of salvation based on belief in God's covenant relationship with Israel. Amos' conviction, however, was that the Exodus experience
had become the basis of judgment: *"Listen, Israelites, to this prophecy which Yahweh
pronounces against you, against the whole family who I brought up from Egypt:*

"You alone have I known of all the families of the earth,
that is why I shall punish you for all your wrong doings." (3:1-2)

The inaugural visions (7:1-9; 8:1-3) are the key to the prophetic perspective for, when Yahweh declares his judgment upon Israel and the prophet in-
tercedes on behalf of his people, he bases his appeal not on the covenant or
size status of Israel, but on the simple fact that the nation was so small: How
can Jacob survive, being so small?" (7:2,5). Yahweh is recognized as the God
of the small and the lowly and Yahweh responds to his recognition: "It will
not happen," said Yahweh (vv3,6). Eventually, however, the nation's oppression of the needy is greater than the prophetic plea and Yahweh announces final
judgment:

"Listen to this, you who crush the needy
and reduce the oppressed to nothing,
you who say, "When will New Moon be over
so that we can sell our corn,
and Sabbath, so that we can market our wheat?
Then, we can make the bushel-measure smaller
and the bushel-weight bigger
by fraudulently tampering with the scales.
We can buy the weak for silver
and the poor for a pair of sandals,
and even get a price for the sweepings of the wheat."
Yahweh has sworn by the pride of Jacob,
"Never will I forget anything they have done." (8:4-7)

Basic to the prophetic understanding is what we have called the "down-
under" perspective, the understanding that God sees reality from the perspective of the poor and the lowly and is determined to protect their rights against
the onslaught of the wealthy and the powerful. When the people were an oppressed minority in Egypt, Yahweh had intervened on their behalf, liberated
them from the might of Pharaoh, gave them a land and brought them together
as a nation. But when social and economic stratification became a reality in their
nation and the wealthy minority enjoyed the fruits of economic prosperity at
the expense of the poor, Yahweh again revealed himself through the prophets
as the God of the lowly.

A little later, in the southern kingdom, Isaiah of Jerusalem (seventh century B.C.E.) continued the prophetic attack on the exploitation of the poor
by the landowners, the corruption of the judges and the manipulation of the
system by state officials. In the face of a national theology which had domesticated
Yahweh into the guardian of the State, the prophet's message was that national
idolatry and social injustice would result in God's devastating judgment on the
city and the nation (Isa 1:21-28; 3:12-15; 5:8-10; 10:1-4). Again, God reveals
his "down-under" perspective by denouncing the mighty for the depriving the

lowly of their rights to a just and human existence:

"The Lord has taken his place to contend,
he stands to judge his people.
The Lord enters his judgment
against the elders and princes of his people:
It is you who have devoured the vineyard,
the spoil of the poor is in your houses.
What do you mean by crushing my people,
by grinding the face of the poor?"
says the Lord of hosts." (3:13-15)

The prophet reveals the divine perspective when he pronounces judgment on lawmakers who use their power to enact oppressive legislation:

"Woe to those who enact unjust decrees,
who compose oppressive legislation
to deny justice to the weak
and to cheat the humblest of my people of fair judgment,
to make widows their prey
and to rob the orphan." (10:1-2)

As the national situation deteriorated and the Babylonians threatened Jerusalem, Jeremiah (sixth century B.C.E) found himself standing almost alone as he denounced kings, judges, prophets, priests, rich merchants and state officials for their idolatry and injustice (Jer 5:26-29; 6:11-13; 7:1-20; 22:1-19).

When commanded to deliver the word of the Lord to the king, he declares: "Thus says the Lord, "Do justice and righteousness, and deliver from the hand of the oppressor him who has been robbed. And do no wrong or violence to the alien, the fatherless and the widow." (22:3-4).

Later in the same chapter he denounces King Jehoiakim:

"Woe to him who builds his house by unrighteousness,
and his upper rooms by injustice,
who makes his neighbor serve him for nothing.
and does not give him wages. . .
Did not your father eat and drink and do justice and righteousness?
Then it was well with him.
He judged the cause of the poor and the needy;
then it was well.
Is this not to know me? says the Lord." (vv13, 15-16)

The great-pre-exilic prophets od Israel understood God as active on the side of the poor and the lowly, seeking justice for the oppressed and downtrodden. They understood that justice and human liberation belonged to the very character of the God whose message they so fearlessly proclaimed. Liberation to justice was an essential part of the heritage and mission of Israel and, as far as the prophets were concerned, this process of liberation and justice was always seen from the perspective of the poor and the oppressed.

1.1.3 The various Law Codes enshrined in the Hebrew Scriptures were formulated at different periods of Israel's history, but they all recognized the fundamental concept of the justice of the liberating God established in the event of Exodus. The Book of the Covenant (Ex 20-23) was probably formulated during the period of the Judges and proclaims that justice must be afforded to the marginalized, even to those who were regarded as having lost all human rights through selling themselves into slavery. These early laws sought to alleviate the suffering of the poor by regulating the relationship between the poor and the rich through a prohibition against usury, an injunction against oppressing the widow, the orphan and the stranger, the establishment of a fair system for the administration of justice, and the introduction of a fallow year during which the poor may feed from the produce of God's bounty.

During a later period of changing economic and political conditions the Deuteronomist reinterpreted Israel's legal heritage so as to produce a series of inter-related laws which would protect the poor from new devices designed by the powerful to exploit and oppress the poorer sections of the community. The new laws were designed to break the perpetual cycle of poverty in which the poor were unable to regain economic and social independence. The basis of these humanitarian regulations was, once again, given as: "You shall remember that you were a slave in Egypt and that the Lord your God redeemed you from there; therefore I command you to do this" (Deut 24:18). Even though it was recognized that poverty was probably inevitable in Israelite society the new law codes sought to alleviate suffering and to protect the poor from the worst excesses of the rich. A characteristic of Israelite law was the special concern for the widow, the orphan and the stranger who is within your house shall come and be filled; that the Lord your God may bless you and all the work that you do" (14:29).

During the Exile, when the people of Israel were suffering under the yoke of foreign domination, the author of the Holiness Code (Lev 17-26) again reinterpreted his legal heritage in the hope that one day, when his people finally returned to their own land, a just and equitable system of justice might be established for all. To this end he designed a Year of Jubilee (Lev. 25) as a time of liberation when all the land would be returned to its original owners, all debts would be cancelled and Israelite society would return to a position of substantial equality.

1.4 In the Psalms, the great songs of faith composed throughout Israel's history, special emphasis is placed upon the justice of God who stands on the side of the poor and oppressed. yahweh is described as "father of the orphans, defender of widows (Ps. 68:5) who is "a stronghold for the oppressed" (9:9) and "listens to the laments of the poor" (10:17-18; cf 69:33; 86:1). God is acknowledged as creator, preserver and governor of the world and is increasingly seen as the one who is particularly interested in the well-being of his humbler subjects. Yahweh is worshipped as the One who will "judge the world with justice and the people with God's truth" (96:13; cf. 98:9) and it is seen that "the heavens proclaim his justice and the people behold his glory" (97:6) for "righteousness and justice are the foundations of his power" (97:2) as "he stands at the side of the poor to save their lives from those who sit in judgment on them" (109:31). As "the Avenger of blood. . .God has not forgotten the cry of the poor" (9:12). A brilliant post-exilic hymn expresses this fundamental understanding of the majestic grace of the God of the lowly (113:58). Of special interest is the way that the hymns of Israel praise the God who has exalted the lowly speak of the God of justice and righteousness (89:14; 97:2,10,11; 98:7-9; 99:3-4; 145:13-21).

A later psalm pronounces blessing on the person whose hope is in the Lord who has not only created heaven and earth but also "executes justice for the oppressed, who gives food to the hungry" (146:5-7). Therefore all creation praises God (96:11-12; 98:4-8) and the people look forward to the day when "steadfast love and faithfulness will meet; righteousness [justice] and peace will kiss each other" (85:10).

> "Yahweh raises the poor from the dust,
> he lifts the needy from the dunghill,
> to give them a place among the princes of his people." (113:7-8)
> "Yahweh sustains the poor,
> and humbles the wicked to the ground." (147:6)
> "He keeps faith for ever,
> gives justice to the oppressed,
> gives food to the hungry;
> Yahweh sets prisoners free.
> Yahweh gives sight to the blind,
> lifts up those who are bowed down
> Yahweh protects the stranger,
> he sustains the orphan and the widow." (146:7-9)

In a magnificent prayer for the king, the Psalmist asks that the distinctive character of Yahweh might be reflected in the activities of the king, as Yahweh's representative:

> "God, endow the king with your own fair judgment,
> the son of the king with your own saving justice,
> that he may rule your people with justice,
> and your poor with fair judgment. (72:102)
> "With justice he will judge the poor of the people,
> he will save the children of the needy
> and crush their oppressors. (v4)
> "For he rescues anyone needy who calls to him,
> and the poor who has no one to help.
> He has pity on the weak and the needy,
> and saves the needy from death,
> "From oppression and violence he redeems their lives,
> their blood is precious in his sight." (vv-12-14)

The temple in Jerusalem was the dominating center of power within Israel and the presence of "the down-under theme" in the Psalms may well reflect the position of the Levites. They exerted an important influence in the composition of the great hymns of Israel but increasingly became a lower order of clergy, removed from the power of the priests. From their positions of powerlessness the Psalmists praised God from the perspective of the poor and oppressed and invite us to enter into this experience with them.

1.1.5 The later prophets, of the Exile and post-Exilic period, tended to despair of the possibility of finding righteousness in the midst of the continuing oppression that characterized much of Israelite existence. They looked forward in hope to the day when God's justice will be established on the earth:

"Violence shall no more be heard in your land,
devastation or destruction within your borders;
you shall call your walls Salvation, and your gates Praise." (Isa 60:18)

To the exploited labourers of Israel the beautiful promise is given:

"They shall build houses and inhabit them;
they shall plant vineyards and eat their fruit.
They shall not build and another inhabit;
they shall not plant and another eat;
for like the days of a tree shall the days of my people be,
and my chosen shall long enjoy the work of their hands. They shall not labour
in vain, or bear children for calamity;
for they shall be the offspring of the blessed of the Lord,
and their children with them.
Before they call I will answer,
while they are speaking I will hear.
The wolf and the lamb shall feed together,
the lion shall eat straw like the ox;
and dust shall be the serpent's food.
They shall not hurt or destroy in all my holy mountain,
says the Lord." (65:21-25)

When the people of Israel were fasting Isaiah, following the tradition of Micah, declared that God demands true fasting:

"Is not this the fast I choose:
to loose the bonds of wickedness,
and undo the thongs of the yoke,
to let the oppressed go free
and to break every yoke?
Is it not to share your bread with the hungry
and bring the homeless poor into your house?
Then your light shall spring up speedily;
and your righteousness shall go before you
and the glory of the Lord shall be your rearguard." (58:6-8)

All of this can be expected because in the days to come, says the prophet, the character of God will be revealed in the community of the people of God. It will be a liberating community of justice and peace. The ground of these promises is again found in the nature of God who is the source of justice and peace (Isa 45:19, 25). The prophet provides the final rationale for "the down-under perspective" when he describes God, "the High and Exalted One," as saying: "I live in the holy heights, but I am with the contrite and humble." (Isa 54:15).

1.1.6 Of course, it would be foolish to suggest that all of the books of the Hebrew Bible, especially in their final form, reflect the "down-under" perspective in any significant way. Quite the contrary is the case in the wisdom tradition and in the major historical presentations.

The Wisdom Traditions were handed down in "wisdom circles" related to the courts and to other wealthy groups within the community. The book of Proverbs incorporates material gathered over a long period of time. The earliest layer of sayings is concerned with the education of the individual for a successful and harmonious life, the next layer is concerned for the community rather than the individual, while the latest layer seeks to relate ethical behaviour to God. The earliest stage has a dominating perspective (Prov. 12:11, 13:18 and many places), but in the latest it is recognized that God is on the side of the poor so that "he who oppresses the poor insults his Maker" (14:31; 17:5). The Book of Ecclesiastes stands a long way from the center of Israel's faith. It is the product of a wealth cynic who pours scorn on everyone and everything and yet still tells his people to be happy! Nothing moves him to involvement in life, for life is only to be observed and commented upon. He knows nothing of the "down-under" perspective.

The Historical Traditions of later Israel were handed on by court historians who were particularly concerned about the role of the kings and the ruling classes. The portrayal of Solomon's wealth and his wives, his cornering of the market in chariots and horses, and his forced-labour programmes (1 Kgs 9-10), for instance, all reveal the dominant perspective of the narrator. When these stories are taken up and reinterpreted by the Chronicler (2 Chr 1-9) his adoration is almost without restraint and reveals a perspective far removed from that of the major traditions of the Old Testament.

1.2 The fundamental nature of God as a God of justice, working for the liberation of the oppressed and the afflicted is not only a central feature of the Hebrew Bible; it is the background against which the teaching of the New Testament is to be interpreted, and it is seen most clearly in the mission and message of Jesus of Nazareth.

1.2.1 Western Protestants have generally been very slow in attributing theological significance to the life and mission of Jesus of Nazareth. Aspects of the mission of Jesus which have become central in the process of theological reflection in the Two-Thirds World are generally passed over in silence in the West, apparently regarded as "accidents of history" rather than as a deliberate choice of God. When we ignore such central factors of the Gospel tradition we again provide ample evidence of the cultural containment which we experience when we read the Scriptures. We are frequently unable to take the life of Jesus seriously because we are hemmed in by the constraints of our middle-class western culture which insists on interpreting everything through the paradigms of power.

The fact that Jesus spent most of his life in Nazareth is attested throughout all levels of the Gospel tradition, so much so that he is still called "Jesus of Nazareth". He may have been born in Bethlehem, but Nazareth was his town! Even the divine messenger, surrounded by the resurrection glory at the empty tomb, tells the women, "Do not be afraid; you seek Jesus of Nazareth who was crucified. He has risen, he is not here." (Mk 16:6) This identification of Jesus with Nazareth is culturally and theologically significant. That town is mentioned nowhere in the Old Testament or in any other writing prior to the time of Jesus. It was a tiny place without a past and with no anticipated future. Nathaniel's amazement is absolutely to the point: "Nazareth! Can any good thing come out of Nazareth?" (Jn. 1:46) Jesus was from an unknown town on the underside of history. He was from the margins of Galilean society, a long way from the center of economic and religious power in Jerusalem. From the beginning he interpreted human reality from the "down-under" perspective.

Growing up on the margins of society, Jesus became a partisan of the poor and afflicted. What a strange collection of people he regarded as his friends: lepers, whose physical appearance and supposed danger of contamination had led to their ostracism from society (Mk 1:40-45; Lk 17:11-19); the demon-possessed, whose strange behaviour could not be explained and so was attributed to one of the devil's underlings (Mk 1:22-26; 5:1-20); the sick and crippled, whose inability to work robbed them of their humanity as they were forced to beg for money to survive (10:46-52 and many places); Gentiles, whose ethnic background had resulted in their relegation to second-class citizenship (Mt 8:5-13; Jn 4:46-54); women and children, whose physical powerlessness was exploited by a male-dominated legal system that robbed them of their rights (Mt 8:14-17; 9:20-26); despised tax collectors, whose grubby employment and disreputable business practices had earned them their reputation (Mt 11:19; Mk 2:14-17; Lk 19:1-10); drunkards and prostitutes, whose habits and morality meant that they could never be admitted to the culture that created them (Mt 11:19; 21:32; Lk 7:37-50).

One of the really striking things about the ministry of Jesus was the way he enjoyed table fellowship with "sinners". He invited them into his house (Mk 2:15), reclined at table with them at festival meals (Lk 5:29, 7:37) and promised them places of honour at the messianic banquet of the people of God (Mk 2:17; Mt 5:5-13). In the East, even today, family and festival meals are occasions of great social and religious significance. To invite a person to a meal was an offer of trust and peace. To share a meal with a person wa to share oneself, to accept a meal from someone was to accept them, to reject a meal was a sign that you were rejecting them. Jesus' meals with tax-collectors and notorious sinners revealed the heart of his mission and message to the world. As he himself expressed it to the religious authorities who were indignant at his behaviour: "I did not come to invite the righteous, I came to invite sinners to participate in God's salvation!" (Mk 2.17). Such behaviour turned upside down all contemporary social and religious norms and customs. No wonder the representatives of the religious establishment were outraged at his behaviour!

When John the Baptist was imprisoned and expressed his doubts by sending two of his disciples to ask Jesus about his real identity, he replied:

"Go and tell John what you hear and see:
the blind receive their sight and the lame walk,
lepers are cleansed and the deaf hear,
the dead are raised up,
and the poor have the good news preached to them."
(Mt. 11:5-6; Lk 7:22-23)

The reply of Jesus to the messengers of John involves a free quotation of a number of Old Testament passages: Isaiah 28:18-19 and 35:5-7 (pictures of the Messianic Age) combined with Isaiah 61:1 (the prophet's call to preach the good news to the poor). As the concluding statement "and blessed are those who take no offence at me" clearly indicates, the emphasis in the reply of Jesus is upon the preaching of the good news to the poor. Many of the parables were, in fact, told in defence of his decidedly "down-under perspective" (Mt 20:1-15 the labourers in the vineyard, 21:28-31 the two sons, Lk 7:41-43 the two debtors, 15:4-7 the lost sheep, 15:8-10 the lost coin, 15:11-32 the prodigal son, 19:9-14 the Pharisee and the tax-collector). This perspective offended many people in the time of Jesus and the same is true in many circles today.

Jesus came proclaiming the good news of the kingdom and this proclamation envisaged a reversal of traditional cultural and religious values. It envisages a community in which "many who are first will be last, and the last first" (Mk 10:31). The poor (Mt 5:3), the persecuted (5:10) and the powerless (Mk 10:14) are the promised heirs of the kingdom, but the powerful rich oppressors will experience difficulty akin to that of camels trying to pass through the eye of a needle (10;25). The victims of injustice are promised liberation, but the perpetrators of injustice are warned of the coming judgment. The only saving hope for them is to repent and change their way of living. A total reorientation of life towards justice offers the only possibility of averting the fearful judgment of the rich in the coming kingdom (Lk 6:24:26). The rich and powerful religious and political leaders were indignant at such teaching and nailed Jesus to the tree, the poor and oppressed recognized in him their Messiah. God raised Jesus from the dead, attesting the validity of his life and his death, affirming the truth of the perspective from which he viewed reality.

1.2.2 If the new perspective on human rights has its roots in the justice of God and the mission of Jesus it also seeks to take seriously the preaching and teaching of the Apostle Paul. Paul has undoubtedly played a dominant role in Western thinking, but it has often been a domesticated Paul one who has been shaped by the dictates of our own culture. This is to be seen primarily in the way that the corporate nature of the Pauline gospel has been individualized and the all-embracing dynamic of faith has been reduced to the level of intellectual acceptance of a doctrine or creed and is preaching has been seen as the repetition of orthodox theological slogans. At the outset, let it at least be remembered that Paul saw himself as a minister of reconciliation (2 Cor 5:18) and as a servant of justice (Rom 6:18).

Paul's concern for the whole world arose out of his understanding of the gospel. It was impossible for him to think that the good news could be restricted to Israel, since through it God was seeking to reconcile the whole world to himself, establishing "a new world" in Christ (2 Cor 5:11-21), a new world in which all former distinctions between Jew and Gentile, slave and freeman, men and women have now been abolished (Gal 3:28). Here already in what was perhaps his earliest letter, Paul is striking at the heart of accepted religious, social and sexual norms of the first century, particularly of first century Hellenistic Judaism. Each morning the pious Jew gave thanks to God that he had not been born a Gentile, that he had not been born a slave, that he had not been born a woman. Josephus, the first-century Jewish historian remarked: "I consider that a woman is in every respect of less worth than a man" and such cultural understanding permeated much of the religious, cultural and political world of Paul's day. The Apostle, however, refused to accept such an understanding as normative. Rather he proclaimed the freedom of all people through Christ and he expected that this freedom would become the norm for all. Because of the circumstances prevailing in his day Paul was primarily concerned to see that the reality of the unity of all humanity be realized in the life of his churches. He bitterly attacked anyone who sought to block the realization of this unity of humanity (even if it was the Apostle Peter, the first disciple of Jesus and dominant leader of the early church).

Paul's concern for the unity of all humanity is seen also in the collection which he organized among the Gentile churches in order to relieve the suffering of the poor saints in Jerusalem (2 Cor 8 and 9). Paul says, "There is no question of relieving others at the cost of hardship to yourselves. It is a question of equality. At the moment your surplus meets their need but one day your need may be met from their surplus. The aim is equality (8:12-15). For Paul the collection was an expression of "fellowship". an act of "service", a response to the grace of God in Christ. Its ultimate inspiration is the grace of Jesus Christ who was rich yet for our sakes he became poor so that we, through his poverty, might become rich (v9). For further motivation Paul cites Psalm 112:9: "He scatters abroad, he gives to the poor, his justice endures for ever" and tells them that if the community is generous God "will increase the harvest of your justice" (9:9-10). The goal of the collection is equality, the unity of the church (and ultimately of all humanity) across national boundaries based on brotherly and sisterly love (Gal 2:10; Rom 15:27).

In the Pauline understanding, the sacraments likewise have a religious, social and political significance. Against the background of cultural divisions baptism is presented as the rite of entrance into a community where the old distinctions based on race, sex, and social class no longer play a role (Gal 3:27-28). Against the background of serious divisions of class and economic status ("the strong" and "the weak") Paul calls for unity and equality in the Eucharist (1 Cor 11:17-34) a unity and an equality made possible in Christ and realizable in the life of the Church and the world.

1.2.3 Space precludes the development of the "down-under" perspective throughout the rest of the New Testament. We have not the time to speak of the Magnificat with the promise that God will pull down the mighty from their thrones and lift up the lowly (Lk 1:46-55), of the cross as the only way to glory (Mk 8:27-9:1), or of the frontal attack on the Roman Empire as the embodiment of Satan (Revelation).

We must, however, draw your attention to the way that the author of Hebrews develops the powerful image of Christ crucified "outside the gate": "So Jesus also suffered outside the gate in order to sanctify the people through his blood. Therefore let us go forth to him outside the camp, bearing abuse for him. For we have no permanent city here on earth, we are looking for the city which is to come." (13:12-13). According to the author of Hebrews Jesus suffered outside the gate and he calls on us to go to him outside the camp, to find our place with the outcasts and lepers of society, among the marginaliz-ed and oppressed. He calls on us to bear society's abuse for the One who lives among the outcasts as we work together for the city that is to come. Only four verses earlier the author had spoken of "Jesus Christ the same yesterday, today, forever" (v8). He wa born in a stable, he worked with the outcasts, he was crucified outside the camp. Jesus Christ is the same yesterday, today and forever! To use our language, he has always viewed reality from the perspective of those who live "down-under" and will always continue to do so.

2. Some Theological and Practical Consequences

2.1 From what has been said already it will have to be acknowledged that the quest for human rights and social justice belongs to the heart of the gospel. it belongs to the heart of the gospel because it belongs to the heart of God. The God of the Hebrew and Christian Scriptures is a God of justice and the practice of justice and the quest for human rights is therefore as much part of the church's mission and ministry as is evangelism or worship.

The work for human rights, likewise, must not be restricted to a plea for freedom of worship. The liberation which God offers, and for which we work, is the liberation of the entire world. Every human dimension is included. The social and the economic, the political and the religious dimensions of human existence are all involved. We cannot work for human rights without being in-volved in one way or another in the quest for economic self-determination and political freedom.

2.2 From what has already been said, I hope that it will be apparent that the quest for justice and the struggle for human rights is a corporate respon-sibility and belongs to the mission of the whole church. In contemporary society we are obsessed with specialists and specialization. Soon we will only be going to our local general practitioner in order to get a referral certificate to the ear, nose, and throat specialist or to his counterpart responsible for some other part of the body. Specialists are necessary and within the New Testament it is recog-nized that there is a diversity of gifts. In the New Testament, however, it is stressed that all of the gifts are to work together in harmony for the building up of the body of Christ. Too often within the modern church the gifts have been separated and the mission of the church has been compartmentalized and entrusted to specialists who have sometimes even been known to work in competition with one another. The results have been quite disastrous for the Church.

We are all aware of the unfortunate consequences of the modern television evangelists who preach a popular gospel of nationalism, success and a middle-class way of life. But even nearer to home we are probably aware of the distor-tion of christianity which arises when pastors and evangelists preach a gospel which only calls for an individualistic type of repentance and faith. Christian community is an optional extra and questions of freedom, justice and human rights are left to others.

The traditional way of welfare work in the church has been to set up a division of social services and to employ social workers and welfare officers. The traditional way of working for human rights and social justice and to employ research and education officers. That is one way to go, but it is fraught with dangers. It leads to a compartmentalization of the church's mission and forces us into competition with the departments of evangelism and church growth. It tends to separate social work and political action from the life of the local parish and congregation and this has meant that there has often been a lack of the necessary context of christian community and the insights from the human rights and justice divisions have often not flowed back into the life of the worshipping congregation.

Too often we have been guilty of fighting for human rights in the world when similar situations of social injustice have been allowed to exist within our own churches. I need only to mention here the position of women and of young people, to illustrate the point. Our ministry and liturgies frequently suffer from the outrages of male domination and our young people are rarely given the power and responsibility accorded them in secular society. The process of action-reflection involved in the quest for human rights requires a congregational context and the action-reflection of our quest for human rights.

2.3 From what we have already said, it will probably be clear that our work for human rights and social justice will need to be done from the perspective of the poor and the oppressed. The God who is revealed through the Exodus and the return of the people of Israel from the Exile in Babylon, the God who is revealed in the life and ministry of Jesus of Nazareth, the God who is revealed in the preaching of the Apostle Paul and others in the early church is a God who has taken his stand with the poor and afflicted, a God who is engaged in bringing liberation to the captives and recovery of sight to the blind. It is this God who calls us through Jesus Christ and empowers us by the Holy Spirit to service of the world. This perspective "from down-under" will have far-reaching consequences for our work in pursuit of human rights.

From this "down-under" perspective, we will undoubtedly seek to incarnate the liberating power of the good news of Jesus Christ into the economic processes which are shaping our contemporary society. In this sphere we will want to stand against the unjust distribution of goods, the exploitation of people and of the earth, the social oppression encouraged by inequitable tariff agreements and trade boycotts, and the ruthless pursuit of growth economies. We will want to work for social justice, solidarity and fellowship among peoples of all races and classes within society. This may well begin with the incarnation of the gospel in the lives of Christians and Christian communities in the depressed regions of our cities and our countrysides, but it will also carry through into education, employment and political representation.

From this "down-under" perspective we will undoubtedly seek to incarnate the liberating power of the good news of Jesus Christ into the political processes which are shaping contemporary society. We will undoubtedly wish to stand against the pressures exerted by trans-national corporations and the vested interests of the powerful, against the illegitimate use of force in order to establish or maintain unjust political situations, against the distortion of "news" by media controlled by powerful interest groups and others, against any moves which will seek to oppress one sector of society in favour of another. We will again want to work for political justice, for the acceptance of basic human rights as belonging to all members of every society, for the humanizing of all structures and processes, and for the alignment of our nation towards humanity.

From this "down-under" perspective we will undoubtedly seek to incarnate the liberating power of the good news of Jesus Christ into the social processes which are shaping contemporary society. We will undoubtedly wish to oppose any attempt to degrade migrants and ethnic communities as second class citizens, to regard aborigines as inferior to white people, to treat women a subordinate to men. As in all other areas we will be seeking social justice and humanization for all peoples and will undoubtedly involve solidarity with the oppressed and the poor whoever they might be for it is in this incarnation and identification that Christ is to be encountered again and again. We are called to seek out those areas of the world where Christ is at work liberating women and men from the shackles of bondage and oppression and there join with Christ and the poor in God's work of liberation. In so doing we will experience out own liberation, through Christ, the One who gave his life for others.

Athol Gill is Professor of New Testament at the Baptist Seminary in Melbourne, Victoria, Australia.

Baptists and Human Rights

James E. Wood, Jr.

Although the concept of human rights cannot be claimed as a contribution of Baptists to the modern world, there is profound significance to be found in the pioneer role Baptists played in their insistence upon liberty of conscience and the worth of the individual. Religious liberty is, in fact, the key to understanding Baptist thought on human rights. Baptist advocacy of religious liberty paved the way for Baptist involvement on behalf of human rights. In England, as in America, Baptist espousal of liberty of conscience, the worth of the individual, and the limited role of all civil authority, along with the generally humble social status of Baptists, inevitably resulted in active Baptist participation in social reforms. In England, for example, Baptists actively supported social change on behalf of universal suffrage, the abolition of the slave trade, and prison reform. Robert G. Torbet has written, "Running all through the interest of English Baptists in reform was the typically Baptist issue of liberty ... religious and civil liberty ... They gave sympathetic backing to social reforms because of an appreciation of the individual as a free person before God."[2]

Similar conditions attended the role of Baptists in America, in which they found their radically democratic view in more fertile soil and more compatible with the beginning of a new nation. The significant contribution of Baptists toward the adoption of the First Amendment and the entire Bill of Rights in the United States Constitution is widely acknowledged. William Warren Sweet wrote that "justice compels the admission that (Thomas) Jefferson's part in this accomplishment was not so great as was that of James Madison, nor were the contributions of either or both as important as was that of the humble people called Baptists."[3] Baptist views of religious liberty, the worth of the individual, and the secular state were harmonious with the American experience. At the same time, this American legacy has had a profound effect upon Baptist perception of human rights.

Baptists have a long history of involvement in human rights. British Baptists played an important role in the abolition of the slave trade in the British Empire in 1838. The contribution of the Baptists became vital to the birth of Jamaica - in emancipation, in education, and in the struggle for social justice and a free society.[4] Very early in the history of the United States, Baptists showed particular concern for the rights of American Indians and American Blacks. In 1789, the Philadelphia Baptist Association went on record as favoring the abolition of slavery and the following year the General Committee of Virginia Baptists adopted a resolution which declared "that slavery is a violent deprivation of the rights of nature and inconsistent with a republican (form of) government; and therefore (we) recommend to our brethren to make use of every legal measure, to extirpate the horrid evil from the land ..."[5]

This is not to ignore the involvement of many Baptists in the institution and defense of slavery, which resulted in a denominational schism in 1844 between Baptists of the North and Baptists of the South. Nevertheless, whatever the failures of Baptists have been relative to human rights, whether in principle or in practice - and, admittedly Baptist failures have been on both counts - "the rank and file of Baptists," Torbet noted, "have produced a significant impact upon society."[6] To the degree that Baptists have been sensitive to the rights of conscience and the worth of every individual person they have reflected, at least in some manner, a concern for human rights. Baptist champions of human rights have been many: John Leland, William Carey, William Knibb, Walter Rauschenbusch, Nannie Helen Burroughs, Joseph M. Dawson, and Martin Luther King, Jr., to name a few.

Baptist Pronouncements on Human Rights

Baptist concerns for human rights have found expression in various denominational structures as well as in official pronouncements of Baptist national and international bodies. For more than eighty years, one forum for channeling Baptist concerns on human rights has been through the Baptist World Alliance. In addressing the First Baptist World Congress, held in London in 1905, J. D. Freeman of Canada appropriately echoed for the Congress a view widely shared by Baptists. "In our postulate of soul-liberty." Freeman declared, "we affirm the right of every human being to exemption in matters of faith and conscience from all coercion or intimidation by an earthly power whatsoever.

Our demand has not been simply for religious toleration, but religious liberty; not sufferance merely, but freedom; and that not for ourselves alone, but for all men. We did not stumble upon the doctrine. It inheres in the very essence of our belief. Christ is Lord of all."[7]

The Second Baptist World Congress, held in Philadelphia in 1911, adopted a "Resolution on Social Progress," in which the Congress voted to name a committee on social concerns that would confer with similar committees of other religious of the world to combat the social evils of the day. Time was given to Russian delegates to share with the Congress a report of the sufferings of Russian Baptists at the hands of the Czarist regime.[8]

At the Third Baptist World Congress in Stockholm in 1923, E. Y. Mullins stressed that "religious liberty implies the greatest of human rights."[9] Economic rights were made the subject of a major presentation at the Fourth Baptist World Congress in Toronto in 1928, in which particular attention was given to the poor and the delegates were reminded that "there is no natural right to waste" or to extravagance.[10]

Meeting in Berlin the year after Adolf Hitler's rise to power, the Fifth Baptist World Congress forthrightly declared that "this Congress deplores and condemns as a violation of the law of God the Heavenly Father, all racial animosity, and every form of oppression or unfair discrimination toward the Jews, toward coloured people, or toward subject races in any part of the world."[11] This resolution was reaffirmed five years later at the Sixth Baptist World Congress in Atlanta, at which, for the first time, the Baptist World Alliance adopted "A Declaration on Religious Liberty." The Declaration made note that Baptists insist upon the full maintenance of religious liberty for every person "of every faith and of no faith."[12]

At the Seventh Baptist World Congress in Copenhagen in 1947, four resolutions were adopted that addressed human rights concerns, in addition t a "Manifesto on Religious Freedom." These included: "Resolution on International Relations," "Resolution on Race Relations," "Resolution Concerning the Jews," and "Resolution on Displaced Persons." The Congress declared that "un-Christian practices and abuses of people, such as lynchings, race extermination, economic and racial discrimination, unfair unemployment practices, and denial of political rights are contrary to the principles of Christianity."[13]

In 1950, two years following the adoption of the United Nations Declaration of Human Rights, the Eighth Baptist World Congress in Cleveland, Ohio urged all nations to support the Universal Declaration of Human Rights. In a manifesto entitled "Mid-Century Call to Religious Freedom," the Congress viewed with alarm the worldwide violations of conscience, even within the churches themselves. Once again, the Alliance expressly condemned, as it had done in the Congresses of 1934, 1939, and 1947, all forms of racial discrimination and urged Baptists of the world to "use their influence to have discriminatory laws repealed wherever they appear in their respective countries." The Congress also endorsed the United Nations Convention on Genocide and expressed the hope that it would be speedily ratified by the necessary number of governments and "thus become part" "of international law."[14]

The Golden Jubilee Congress of the Baptist World Alliance, held in London in 1955, adopted a "Golden Jubilee Declaration on Religious Liberty" in which the Congress urged "the extension of freedom in secular as well as in religious life." "We deplore," the Congress declared, "regimentation and enforced uniformity which hinder the full development ... in the liberty with which Christ has made us free." "We will not rest content until we witness the achievement and individual liberty throughout the world. We believe this is an essential part of our contribution to the thought of the church, as well as to the establishment of Christ's reign in the earth." Once again, resolutions on peace and race relations were passed, the latter reaffirming the previous resolutions of 1934, 1939, 1947, and 1950.[15]

At the Tenth Baptist World Congress, held in Rio de Janeiro in 1960, another "Manifesto on Religious Liberty" was adopted. Unfortunately, the document issued no call to action but rather was prepared to provide an exposition as to the meaning of religious liberty to which Baptists would give witness. Once again, resolutions on "Race Relations," "Underprivileged Persons," and "World Peace" were adopted. In a resolution on "Nuclear Testing," the Congress urged "the nations to dispense with all testing of nuclear weapons and the production of the same."[16]

The Eleventh Baptist World Congress, held in Miami in 1965, adopted a "Manifesto on Religious Liberty and Human Rights," in which the Congress declared, "We suffer with our generation ... in policies which deny basic human rights ... We appeal to the governments of all lands, not only to preserve law and order, but also to recognize and guarantee religious and civil liberty ..." This manifesto was the first and official declaration that specifically addressed "human rights" along with religious liberty, a recurring theme addressed throughout all Baptist World Congresses.[17]

In a "Manifesto" adopted by the Twelfth Baptist World Congress, held in Tokyo in 1970, specific attention was again directed to a broad range of human rights: "We seek equal civil rights" the Congress declared, "for all men and women and support the responsible use of these rights by all ... we will strive to conquer racism, achieve brotherhood, alleviate poverty, abolish hunger, and support morally sound population objectives."[18]

In a resolution adopted by the Thirteenth Baptist World Congress, held in Stockholm in 1975, the principles set forth in the United Nations Universal Declaration of Human Rights were reaffirmed. "We believe that God has made humankind in his own image and that he endows us with certain human rights which Christians are obligated to affirm, defend, and extend: The right to necessities of life includes the right of all persons to have access to life, liberty, food, clothing, shelter, health, education, the right to work, and the pursuit of happiness including a quality of life that allows for adequate development of human potentialities ... The right to maintain cultural identity includes the rights of racial, ethnic, and national groups to maintain their self-determined identities." The Congress also underlined the right of all segments of society to participate in political decision-making.[19]

The Fourteenth Baptist World Congress, meeting in Toronto in 1980, issued a "Declaration of Human Rights," which was prepared for presentation to the Congress by the Commission on Freedom, Justice and Peace. "Concern for human rights is at the heart of the Christian faith," the Declaration declared. "Every major doctrine is related to human rights, beginning with the biblical revelation of God." The document marked the first time a Baptist World Congress adopted a separate declaration on human rights. The Declaration affirmed that the theological foundation of the Christian faith obligates Christian concern for specific human rights, such as: "the right to choose a religion freely" and "to share religious faith publicly with others"; "the right to a health environment" "the right to be employed" "the right to participate in the political processes"; "the right to privacy"; "the right of dissent"; "the right to cultural identity"; "the right to be free from violence against one's person"; "the right to be free from arbitrary arrest and imprisonment"; "the right to a just and open trial"; "the right to equal protection under the law"; "the right to nationality ... and the right to travel"; "the right to freedom of peaceful assembly"; "the right to freedom of association"; "the right to leisure, rest, and recreation"; and "the right to an education." The Congress affirmed that "to declare human rights is not enough," rather "to strive to promote and to defend human rights within churches and society at large is also our responsibility."[20]

Meeting in Los Angeles in 1985, the Fifteenth Baptist World Congress passed a series of resolutions directly bearing on human rights and urging Baptists to take action, including calling upon their respective governments on behalf of various human rights concerns. In a resolution on "The Fortieth Anniversary of the United Nations," the Congress commended the United Nations in its efforts directed toward the improvement of health services, food production, disaster relief, and the standard of living in developing countries; the elimination of racial discrimination; and compliance of all nations with the Universal Declaration of Human Rights. In separate resolutions the Congress condemned racism in general and apartheid in particular, expressed concern for the sufferings and East-West tensions in Nicaragua and called upon Baptists to press for an end to the conflict and the economic blockade there, reaffirmed its adherence to the basic human right of religious liberty, and deplored terrorism by any group "as a violation of international law as well as an assault on the conscience of humanity." In a resolution on "Peace and Disarmament," the Congress called "upon the nuclear powers to enact immediately a verifiable moratorium on the manufacture of all nuclear weapons and to seek mutually the abolition by negotiation of all nuclear arms."[21]

In North America, Baptist concerns for human rights have been repeatedly given corporate expression in the actions and pronouncements of the Baptist Joint Committee on Public Affairs. The issue of human rights was the primary reason which brought about the formation in 1939 of the Baptist Joint Committee. In 1936, the southern Baptist Convention established a Committee on Public Relations that was assigned the task "to confer, to negotiate, to demand jut rights that are being threatened or to have other ... dealings with our American or other governments."[22] The initiative for this step was first precipitated by religious persecutions in Rumania. With the close of World War

II, the Baptist Joint Committee sought to foster a universal declaration on religious liberty which would bring an end to religious persecutions throughout the world.

In april 1945, with strong support for the formation of the United Nations, the Baptist Joint Committee named four well-known Baptist representatives to the United Nations Organization in San Francisco. Their assignment, supported by 100,000 petitions from Baptists - North and South, black and white - was to secure a provision for religious liberty in the United Nations Charter. Joseph M. Dawson, the first Executive Director of the Baptist Joint Committee, presented the petitions from Baptists. While Baptist efforts in this case were not entirely successful, the preamble of the United Nations Charter does imply the idea in principle.

Faithful to its original charter, the Baptist Joint committee on Public Affairs through the years has addressed a wide variety of human rights concerns at home and abroad. Concern for human rights has dominated the agenda of this agency in both national and international affairs. It has constituted the ultimate concern of this joint North American Baptist witness in public affairs. In addition to religious liberty, these concerns have included, among others, the right of conscientious objection, nondiscrimination with respect to race or religion or sex, the right to privacy, the right to food, the right to employment, the right to an education, the right to vote, and the rights of displaced persons. Through the years it has meant opposition to Universal Military Training and repeated reaffirmations of support for the United Nations and the Universal Declaration of Human Rights. Particular attention has been given to the elevation of human rights in United States foreign policy and in the United Nations. Thus, in March 1977, the Baptist Joint Committee voted unanimously to commend President Jimmy Carter for his commitment, "in word and deed," to the implementation of human rights in U.S. foreign policy and to the elimination of "all nuclear weapons from this earth."[23]

In October 1977, the Committee reiterated its strong support for "human rights throughout the world."[24] In anticipation of the Belgrade Conference for the Implementation of the Helsinki Final Act, the Baptist Joint Committee voted that "we affirm our strong belief that all actions which are signatories to the Helsinki accord should seek to show in every way possible respect for human rights and fundamental freedoms, including freedom of thought, conscience, religions, or belief."[25] The Committee has also urged the U.S. Senate ratification of the United National human rights covenants and treaties.[26]

The American Baptist Churches in the U.S.A., in both 1958 and 1965, urged that its churches initiate studies of the United Nations Declaration of Human Rights, and called on the U.S. Senate "to place itself on record as being opposed to forced labor, arbitrary arrest, and genocide"[27] and for the U.S. Senate "to ratify the U.N. Conventions (treaties) on the Political Rights of Women, Slavery, Forced Labor, and on Genocide."[28] In 1963, the Southern Baptist Convention adopted a resolution on human rights, which declared, "We reaffirm our historic stand for human freedom, self-government, and religious liberty for all people. We pledge to fellow Baptist and to all others who do not enjoy true freedom that we will ... work continually with them for the ultimate realization of their right to full freedom of religious and the other inalienable liberties with which all mankind is endowed by the Creator.''[29] Several other resolutions on human rights have been subsequently adopted. In its Eighteenth Annual Session, the Progressive National Baptist Convention, Inc. passed a resolution which declared, "The President's human rights offensive must universally proclaim and promote the right to work, the right to vote, the right to own property, the right of self-defense, the right of equality before the law, and the right of self-determination for all persons and groups in the world - beginning in America.''[30]

Toward the Implementation of Human Rights

However important is the espousal of human rights even when based upon solid theological foundations, the more fundamental issue is the translation of that commitment into action. The ultimate concern cannot be for human rights as abstract ideals, but their realization. In the accomplishment of the task, Baptists are called upon as members of the community of faith to defend human rights and to suffer with the oppressed, namely to be a force for liberation and justice for all. By working for the implementation of human rights, Baptists give witness to the work of the authenticity of their human rights pronouncements and their theological foundations. This genuine concern for human rights imposes upon Baptists a solemn obligation to defend human rights in the context of today's world and to do so in the light of certain basic realities and principles.

1. Although human rights are almost universally espoused in principle by most of the nations of the world, in actual practice human rights are expressly denied throughout the world by nations large and small. The truth is that the almost worldwide ratification of the Universal Declaration of Human Rights has by no means been accompanied by a steady advance of human rights among the nations of the world.[31] Political persecutions have become widespread resulting from charges of "political crimes" against the state. Baptists must be concerned about an evidence of flagrant violations of human rights, both at home and abroad. Baptists must ever work for and witness to an even wider and more complete recognition of basic human rights for all persons.

2. There is evidence of a growing concern for human rights all over the world. Much of the impetus for this concern has resulted from the far-reaching implications to be found in the Universal Declaration of Human Rights, to which Baptists and the churches at large made a major contribution for the inclusion of religious liberty and other concerns.

3. Human rights must be made an authentic and expressed concern of governments in international affairs. Up to now this has not been realized either within the framework of the United Nations or the foreign policy of any single nation-state. As O. Frederick Nolde rightly declared, "The myth that human rights, especially race relations and religious liberty, are a matter solely of national concern must give way to the recognition that international involvement in what happens in any country has very considerably diminished the area of

domestic jurisdiction."[32] Commitment to human rights and human values must be made prior to chauvinistic appeals of "national interest."

4. Human rights must be rooted in the concern for the inviolable rights of all persons. These rights are appropriately symbolized in minimal terms in the freedoms verbalized in the Universal Declaration of Human Rights. Freedom *and* justice must become a matter of primary concern in the struggle for human rights. The times require that governments show regard for human values, encourage in every way possible the elevation of human values in both national and international affairs, and seek to ensure through both national and international law the protection of human rights for all persons. In supporting the cause of human rights at home and abroad, a nation is thereby contributing to the stability and strength of itself and the world community to the benefit of all mankind. For a nation to do less is not to serve mankind, but to serve as an end unto itself and to diminish the cause of human rights.

5. Human rights must be perceived as embodying both personal and social rights: freedom of religion, freedom of thought, freedom of assembly, freedom of speech, freedom of the press, freedom of movement from within and outside of one's own country, and freedom to take part in government as well as the right to employment, food, shelter, education, and health care. Human rights must also include freedom from governmental violations of the integrity of the person, such as freedom from torture, freedom from degrading treatment or punishment, and freedom from arbitrary arrest or imprisonment. Any denial of a fair and public trial is a denial of one's basic human rights.

To ignore the social context of a person is to deny the wholeness of that person. Therefore, the advance of human rights for the vast majority of the peoples of the world requires that systemic changes be made that will provide greater equality and justice for all who are oppressed by the evils of poverty, disease, and ignorance. As Dwain Epps has perceptively observed, "Any approach to human rights that takes the individual out of his social context is like an attempt to empty the sea with a bucket."[33] Without recognition of cultural and social rights, personal or individual rights may be virtually empty of meaning and without any real fulfillment.

6. Finally, it is necessary to comprehend human rights as indivisible and to recognize the interdependency of all types of human rights violations. Both freedom and justice must become joined in the struggle for human rights. Religious liberty must be seen as a part of a larger whole. As people of God, Baptists dare not focus their concern on religious rights while ignoring other civil and political rights or economic and social rights. "Human rights need to be deepened and enriched by the more holistic biblical view that goes beyond intrinsic self-interest or self-authenticating value to interacting, covenanting communities."[34] Nor can Baptists justify deploring human rights violations only against Baptists or other Christians, while ignoring violations of human rights to others. To be genuine, concern for human rights must be for all persons everywhere. This principle was well articulated in the mandate given the Baptist Joint Committee of North America at the time of its inauguration in 1939. "Believing religious liberty to be not only an inalienable human right, but in-

dispensable to human welfare, a Baptist must exercise himself to the utmost in the maintenance of absolute religious liberty for his Jewish neighbor, his Catholic neighbor, his Protestant neighbor, and for everybody else."[35] In human rights, concern must be expressed for all who are oppressed, based on God's concern for all humanity.

There has never been greater need than today for Baptists to demonstrate their genuine and unequivocal commitment to human rights and their profound concern for human values within the social and political structures of today's world. In this, Baptists can claim to possess no special competence, no superior wisdom, and no ready-made formula for the implementation of a program of human rights, at home or abroad. Nevertheless, impelled by a biblical faith, Baptists must not fail now, or in the future, to identify themselves with the cause of human rights for all persons everywhere. In doing so, Baptists will reflect a noble part of their heritage on the sanctity and infinite worth of the human person.

James E. Wood, Jr. is Professor of Church-State Studies and Director of the J.M. Dawson Institute of Church-State Studies at Baylor University, Waco, Texas, USA.

Notes

1. This fact is acknowledged by a wide range of Baptist and non-Baptist scholars alike. In the seventeenth century when Lord Chancellor King sought to recognize John Locke as the author of religious liberty, Locke forthrightly declared that "the Baptists were the first and only propounders of absolute liberty - just and true liberty, equal and impartial liberty"; Stanford H. Cobb, *The Rise of Religious Liberty in America* (New York: Macmillan Co., 1902), pp. 64ff. Writing almost a century ago, the distinguished historian, George Bancroft, affirmed that "the paths of Baptists were the paths of freedom"; George Bancroft, *History of the United States*, 6 vols. (New York: D. Appleton and Co., 1892), 1:608. An important source of our heritage of religious liberty, Cecil Northcott wrote, "Lies in the witness of the Baptist churches whose devotion to this idea, through years of persecution in ... Europe, makes their place a foremost one in the history of liberty"; Cecil Northcott, *Religious Liberty* (New York: Macmillan Co., 1949), p. 28. Similarly, E. Y. Mullins, former president of the Baptist World Alliance, declared, "The greatest fact of modern history was the discovery of the idea of liberty, and that discovery was made by Baptists"; E. Y. Mullins, *The Axioms of Religion* (Philadelphia: Griffith and Rowland Press, 1908), p. 269.

2. Torbet, *A History of the Baptists*, 494.

3. William Warren Sweet, *The Story of Religion in America* (New York: Harper and Brothers, 1950), 193. Former Chief Justice of the United States Supreme Court, Charles Evans Hughes, himself a Baptist, declared that "this contribution /of Baptists to religious liberty/ is the glory of the Baptist heritage, more distinctive than any other characteristic of belief or practice. To this militant leadership all sects and faiths are debtors ..."; Address of Charles E. Hughes at the Laying of the Corner-Stone of the National Baptist Memorial to Religious Liberty," *Religious Herald* 90 (27 April 1922):4. See also, Anson Phelps Stokes, *Church and State in the United States*, 3 vols. (New York: Harper and Brothers, 1950), 3:485-86; Joseph M. Dawson, *Baptists and the American Republic*

(Nashville: Broadman Press, 1956), and James E. Wood, Jr., ed., Baptists and the American Experience (Valley Forge, Pa.: Judson Press, 1976).

4. See Inez Knibb Sibley, *The Baptist* (Kingston, Jamaica: The Jamaica Baptist Union, 1965).

5. Garnett Ryland, *The Baptists of Virginia, 1699-1926* (Richmond: Board of Missions and Education, 1955), 151.

6. Torbet, *A History of Baptists*, 494.

7. *The Baptist World Congress, London, July 11-19, 1905* (London: Baptist Union Publication Department, 1905), 23.

8. Baptist World Alliance, *Second Congress, Philadelphia, June 19-25, 1911* (Philadelphia: Harper and Brother Co., 1911), 333-334.

9. Mullins, "The Baptist Conception of Religious Liberty," in *The Third Baptist World Congress, Stockholm, July 21-27, 1923*, 66.

10. *Fourth Baptist World Congress, Toronto, Canada, 23-29 June 1928* (London: Kingsgate Press, 1928), 261-266.

11. *Fifth Baptist World Congress, Berlin, August 4-10, 1934* (London: Baptist World Alliance, 1934), 17.

12. *Sixth Baptist World Congress, Atlanta, Georgia, U.S.A., July 22-28, 1939* (Atlanta: Baptist World Alliance, 1939), 13-14.

13. *Seventh Baptist World Congress, Copehagen, Denmark, July 29-August 3, 1947* (London: Baptist World Alliance, 1948), 98-100.

14. *Eighth Baptist World Congress, Cleveland, Ohio, U.S.A., July 22-27, 1950* (Philadelphia: Judson Press, 1950), 336-338.

15. Baptist World Alliance, *Golden Jubilee Congress*, (Ninth World Congress), *London, England, 16-22 July 155* (London: The Carey-Kingsgate Press, Ltd., 1955), 369-370.

16. Baptist World Alliance, *Tenth Baptist World Congress, Rio de Janeiro, Brazil, June 26-July 3, 1960* (Nashville: Broadman Press, 1960), 296-303.

17. *The Truth that Makes Men Free: Official Report of the Eleventh Congress, Baptist World Alliance, Miami Beach, Florida, June 25-30, 1965* (Nashville: Broadman Press, 1956), 482.

18. *Reconciliation Through Christ: Official Report of the Twelfth Congress, Baptist World Alliance, Tokyo, Japan, June 12-18, 1970* (Valley Forge, Pa.: Judson Press, 1971), 248-250.

19. *New People for a New World - Through Christ: Official Report of the Thirteenth Congress, Stockholm, Sweden, July 8-13, 1975* (Nashville: Broadman Press, 1976), 255-259.

20. *Celebrating Christ's Presence Through the Spirit: Official Report of the Fourteenth Congress, Baptist World Alliance, Toronto, Canada, July 8-13, 1980* (Nashville: Broadman Press, 1981), 246-250.

21. *1985 Yearbook of the Baptist World Alliance, Minutes of the General Council Meeting, Los Angeles, California, July 1-6, 1985*, pp. 65-69.

22. *Southern Baptist Convention Annual, 1936*, 96.

23. See *Report from the Capital* 32 (April 1977):6.

24. Ibid.

25. *Report from the Capital* 32 (October-November 1977):7.

26. *Report from the Capital 34 (November-December 1979):12.

27. *Yearbook of the American Baptist Convention, 1958*, p. 60.

28. *Yearbook of the American Baptist Convention, 1965-1966*, 73-74.

29. *Southern Baptist Convention Annual, 1958*, 60.

30. Adopted by the Progressive National Baptist Convention, Inc., at its Eighteenth Annual Session, New Orleans, Louisiana, 6-12 August 1979.

31. For some major comprehensive studies, including primary documents, see Louis S. Sahn, and Thomas Buergenthal, *International Protection of Human Rights* (Indianapolis: Bobbs-Merrill Co., Inc., 1973); Richard P. Claude, *Comparative Human Rights* (Baltimore: The Johns Hopkins Press, 1976); Thomas Buergenthal, ed., *Human Rights, International Law, and the Helsinki Accord* W. Thompson, ed., *The Moral Imperatives of Human Rights: A World Survey* (New York: University Press of America, 1980); and Robert A. Evans and Alice Frazer Evans, eds., *Human Rights: A Dialogue Between the First and Third Worlds* (Maryknoll, N.Y.: Orbis Books, 1983).

32. See O. Frederick Nolde, *The Churches and the Nations* (Philadelphia: Fortress Press, 1970).

33. Dwain C. Epps, "Three Mistaken ideas about Human Rights," *Church and Society,* July-August 1974, 61-62.

34. Miller, "A Biblical Approach to Human Rights," 174.

35. *Southern Baptist Convention Annual,* 1976, 113.

According to the Scriptures: Evangelism and Human Rights

Saverio Guarna

This presentation aims at exploring the search for faithfulness to the Lord in accomplishing the mission which He entrusts to His church today. It stems from the experiences of the ministry of the Italian Baptist Union's Department of Evangelism in which I serve and which supplied countless opportunities for reflecting upon and redefining a viable understanding and practice of evangelism in our present historical context.

The prolonged dialogue with our congregations resulted in a policy of the Department of Evangelism which sees an intimate and unseparable interconnection between the theology of evangelism and the ethical responsibility of the churches to respond to the challenges of the present time.

I consider it a privilege to serve in the Italian Department of Evangelism, where the salvation of the individual person and the salvation of the world are equal concerns, where evangelism in the traditional sense and responsible social ethics go hand in hand, where proclamation of the Christ-event for the conversion of men and women and interest for Human Rights and Rights of the Peoples are complementary and undivided.

Introduction

If evangelism means proclaiming the Gospel to the world, the church ought to enquire first what the Gospel is about. The question is of fundamental importance and seeks the clearest possible answer, for the church's attitude towards the world, as well as its approach to the issue of Evangelism, are dependent on what the church believes to be the nature and content of the Gospel.

Further questions follow from this first one, and they are equally important: why, how and when is the Gospel proclaimed. Appropriate answers to such questions can only be investigated when the first and fundamental question has been dealt with.

At the same time, human rights are a priority on the world agenda today, and yet their violations continue to be perpetrated on a world-wide scale. Churches are called to take a stand in this area: Christ's life and teaching challenge us to leave neutral grounds and engage ourselves in the struggles for human dignity. Commitment to the implementation of human rights appears to be a very significant service that churches can and should render to the world.

This presentation views both evangelism and human rights in the context of the Mission of the Church, which expresses the totality of the believers' obedient commitments to the Lord and is a comprehensive concept including both evangelism and human rights, together with many and various other aspects which need not be dealt with here but should not be considered less important.

It seems appropriate first to assess the understanding of evangelism and then relate to it the human rights issue.

The unavoidable necessity of any theological discussion to anchor the reflection on biblical grounds immediately suggests two specific texts as starting points; they appear at the same time, emblematic for synthesizing the presentation. They are: Mark 1:1 and 1 Corinthians 15:1-5.

Evangelism in a Broad Sense

Mark 1:1

As explicit designation of a book, the word *euaggelion* appears only towards 150 AD in Justin Martyr. It is evident, however, that in Mark 1:1 it denotes if not a book, certainly the report of a series of events that begins in Mark 1:1 and ends in Mark 16:20. The narrative develops during a definite period of time and in a definite place and includes healings, conflicts, parables, sayings and so forth. Thus, *euaggelion* is the unfolding of the life of Jesus as the story of the Son in whom God accomplishes His way. The word *euaggelion* has, then, a wide inclusive meaning which reflects the sense of the *missio dei* being accomplished in the mission of Jesus. God's mission and the mission of Jesus interlock in the unfolding of the events: the narrative which reports all of this is the *euaggelion*, the Gospel.

A Comprehensive Concept

Speaking of evangelism on this basis means including in its definition all that the Gospel witnesses about Jesus, characterizing it as a global task comprehensive of all that the Church is sent to do in the world by its Lord: in practice the concept of evangelism in a broad sense coincides with the concept of the mission of the Church.

According to the Scriptures, God sends messengers and prophets through the centuries, but at a given point in time He sends His Son to proclaim to humankind that God's rule is present in history. With His presence, proclamation and action, Jesus brings the "Kingdom" among men and women, He brings *shalom*, which means at the same time justice, reconciliation, wholeness, freedom, brotherhood, harmony and peace. Hence all God's activity in creation and redemption has a missionary character and is geared to the salvation of the world. The Son is the highest expression of God's missionary activity towards humankind. The many aspects of his ministry: healing, cleansing, teaching and so on, constitute Jesus' mission in their totality, which embodies God's mission. The Son sends the Church to act similarly in the world and the totality of the things which the Church does in obedience to Jesus' mandate constitutes the Mission of the Church, or we could say, Evangelism in a broad sense.

Christian Ethics

The abundance of ethical teachings which constitutes a large part of the Gospel passes naturally also into the understanding of evangelism in a broad sense. It asks for the saving ministry of Jesus to be presented and interpreted in the midst of suffering and the struggles of humankind. Evangelism in a broad sense appeals to believers to actualize the personal and communitarian ethical implications of the message of salvation as members of the community of God's economy, of the new age. To this pertain concepts such as credibility, presence, service, witness, solidarity, and so on.

The Challenges

As to the challenges which interest evangelism in a broad sense, five areas have been indicated and seem to summarize the complexity of the possible and responsible involvement of the Church: a) the integrity of the human person; b) the alienation between persons; c) oppression; d) justice and peace and the dominion of peoples against peoples; and e) the integrity of creation. All these areas can be summed up in the expression: Human Rights and the Rights of Peoples. These have been specified as: a) civil rights, which serve to protect all those aspects of the personality considered important for the complete realization of the individual person (equality before the law, personal freedom, protection of private life, political asylum, citizenship, freedom of thought, religion, etc.); b) political rights, which permit the citizens to participate in the government of their own country (the right to vote, the right to public office, to participate in elections, etc.); c) economic, social and cultural rights (social security the right to work, to a just salary, health, education, etc.); and d) the right of peoples (self-determination, national independence, full sovereignty, etc.).

The Picture is Complex

Having established that evangelism in a broad sense is all inclusive of the mission of the Church, and that the ethical implications of the Gospel constitute a large part of it, it still needs to be said that the total mission of the Church appears to be centered on the proclamation of the Word, around which all other activities are organized and from which they are deduced.

In fact, if we wish to consider the mission carried out by the Church, not just a mission, but the mission, then we cannot bypass the characteristics which pertain to its origin, its motivation, its modality, its contents and its purpose. As for the origin, it is the initiative of God who sends; as for the motivation, it consists in the awareness that those who are sent by God; as for the modality, it embraces the lifestyle of the believers and Christian ethics; as for its contents, it derives from the teaching of the Gospel; as for its purpose, it consists in the commitment to the divine project of redemption for the world.

Eventually it is again the *euaggelion*, this time in a narrow sense, which characterizes the Mission of the Church as over against all other missions. And now we search for the essential element which, if lacking, leaves no Christian Mission at all, and which is the center from where every other aspect of the mission of the Church, or evangelism in a broad sense, descends. When we speak of evangelism in a strict sense we no longer draw the understanding of the term *euaggelion* on the basis of Mark 1:1, but we draw it from 1 Corinthians 15:1-5.

Evangelism in a Narrow Sense

I Corinthians 15:1-5

The starting point for the definition of evangelism in a narrow sense is Paul's use of the term *euaggelion* in I Corinthians 15:1-5. The term denotes here exclusively an item of news, which, as such, calls for the proclamation of a definite content: briefly, Gospel is what the proclamation of the news communicates. An item of news is something which can only be said, communicated, transmitted by language, and as such does not belong to the ethical commitment of the Church, rather to its message: it refers to the person of Jesus and calls attention to the experiential dimension behind the propositional form. And this Gospel is so vital for Paul that he doe not hesitate to stress for the Corinthians the importance of receiving it, remembering it, standing firm on it. From it they draw their salvation if they believe it in the way that Paul passed it on to them.

After these strong warnings on the vital importance of what he is going to say, Paul outlines the contents of the *euaggelion* stressing that it is not his own invention, but that he received it from others who were called by God before him.

The Christological Formula

The Christological formula in I Corinthians 15:3b-5 is pre-Pauline by Paul's admission and proposes in synthesis the earliest formulation of the Christian message: the Gospel to be transmitted is the confession of faith, the *depositum fidei* received by Paul from the Early Church tradition.

It is relevant to clarify that the doctrinal formulation epitomizes the faith of the early Church and not the "reality" itself, which originates that faith. The essence of that faith cannot be based on any propositional formula, but rather is an experiential encounter with the "person" of Jesus as "Way, Truth and Life". And the fact that the Christological formula has a stereotyped flavour, rather than diminishing, confirms and heightens the importance of the affirmation, for it shows that the truth which it affirms was so fundamental that it led progressively to the formalization of the language.

The Gospel as a Punctual Event

Before discussing the sense of this formula we underline that Paul's understanding of the Gospel is quite different from the understanding which the term has in Mark 1:1.

While in Mark 1:1 *euaggelion* is a series of events, a history, the history of Jesus, in Paul's writings it is a precise moment in this history, that is, the moment of the death and the resurrection of Jesus, which chronologically happens at the end of his ministry and theologically at the beginning of it, since Jesus is understood as the Christ, Son of God, from the perspective of the post-Easter faith. That this is true also in Mark is shown by the process of formation of the Gospel tradition, within which the first collection of stories about Jesus constituted the Passion narrative, which begins in Mark, Chapter 14, and has led to the definition of Mark's Gospel as the Passion narrative preceded by a long introduction.

On the basis of I Corinthians 15:1-5, we understand that evangelism may have a narrower sense, when it indicates the communication of the Gospel as a particular truth about Jesus' life, that is a particular event, punctual in time, his death-resurrection. And this leads to an understanding of evangelism in a narrow sense, definitely different from that of evangelism in a broader sense which is based on the meaning of Gospel in Mark 1:1, as a linear series of events which developed during a certain time between Galilee and Judeah.

The relationship between evangelism in a broad sense and evangelism in a narrow sense is such that the first one is comprehensive also of the second, constituting in effect its nucleus as well sa the heart of all Christian existence. Conversely, evangelism in a strict sense does not limit indeed the range of action of evangelism in a wide sense, otherwise the whole ethical dimension of discipleship would be excluded.

Both Understandings of Evangelism Are Necessary

But there is more to it. To bring the Gospel of salvation to the world implies also interpreting the saving ministry of Christ in the context of the struggles of humankind. Christians cannot avoid going back from the event death-resurrection of Christ to the history of Jesus if they want to actualize in their mission the characteristics of the salvation offered in the proclamation of the Gospel. Therefore both evangelism in a broad sense and evangelism in a narrow sense are unavoidably interwoven, reciprocally necessary and complementary to each other.

The New Testament has been written in the context of the faith professed by the Church about Jesus crucified and resurrected, but the Church was also aware of the historical tension between the Christian experience of the Christ of faith in the community of believers and the memory of the life of Jesus of Nazareth, and they knew that the Christ resurrected was the same Jesus of Nazareth who lived, fighting for the redemption of the underprivileged. If faith in Christ loses its tie with its reference point, that is, with the life of Jesus of Nazareth, the resurrected and exalted Christ becomes a mythical figure and the world of faith is no more than the realm of fantasy produced by a spirit of individualism.

It is not by chance that we have in the New Testament besides the Epistles also the Gospels, where alongside the saving event of Jesus' death and resurrection his works and teachings are related.

The Contents of the Gospel

The answer to the question about the content of the Gospel is very important, because the whole attitude of the church toward the world, and her approach to evangelism, is dependent on what the content of *euaggelion* in a narrow sense is believed to be as well as on its right relationship with the concept of evangelism in a broad sense.

While the presentation of the Gospel may vary, its content certainly cannot, for it is given, otherwise there would be as many Gospels as there would be preachers. Preaching and teaching take care of proclaiming and interpreting the meaning of the *kerygma* in the historical context: the *kerygma*, which is the *depositum fidei* must be proclaimed faithfully, but it also must be followed by the interpretation of its relevance in history. It must be contextualized without being amputated or modified or augmented. Through the contextualization it becomes comprehensible to the listeners, it becomes a message of judgment and salvation, of denunciation and hope in the encounter of God's word with the human predicament.

The Structure of the Formula

The research on the primitive central message of the New Testament (*kerygma*) may be summarized in the pre-Pauline formula of I Corinthians 15:3b-5, which consists of two verses in parallelism: Christ died for our sins according to the Scriptures. He was buried. (Christ) resurrected on the third day according to the Scriptures. He appeared. In this formula there are different elements, equally important, but which play a different and distinct role: the mentioning of the event death-resurrection, its interpretation, the witness to it and its historical proof. The elements of the formula fall easily into four parts:

a) event
b) interpretation
c) witness
d) proof

the death and resurrection of Christ
for our sins, on the third day
according to the Scriptures
was buried, appeared

The Event and the Proof

The death and resurrection of Christ are facts chronologically distinct but theologically united and inseparable to the extent that they constitute a sole event. It would be impossible to reflect theologically on the Cross without at the same time thinking of the Resurrection, and vice versa. For the faith of the Church, the death-resurrection of Christ is the place of the revelation of God in history, it constitutes and saves the believers. The Christ-event is the basis and origin of the formula, and absolutely cannot be missed. Evangelism in a narrow sense proclaims this *datum*. The burial and the appearances of Jesus stress the truth and historicity of the event.

The Interpretation

The event death-resurrection of Christ is related to the forgiveness of sins and "the third day". These elements are only affirmed, not explained. Without God's forgiveness man remains in his original state of separation from God, in his existential condition of solitude. "On the third day" introduces the concept of fullfilment of God's promises.

The Witness

What concerns us strongly in our discussion is the historical witness of the event by the Scriptures, which relate God's activity in history. The Christ-event is for Paul, as for the Early Church, the full revelation of God's promises. That the death-resurrection of Christ happened "according to the Scriptures" means essentially that it belongs to God's plan for the salvation of the world. It is therefore no extemporary, contingent, casual event, but one which, in its historical specificity, temporal and spatial, is inscribed at the center of the divine design, pre-ordained of old. "According to the Scriptures" introduces in the Christological formula the reality of the God of Abraham, Isaac and Jacob, of the Exodus deliverance, of the *shalom*, of the Kingdom. It introduces into the *kerygma* the understanding that the same God who intervened in the Christ-event intervenes in history for the deliverance of his people and other peoples (Amos 9:7) and for the dignity of the human person (widow, orphans, foreigners, etc.).

At the center of the *depositum fidei* of the Early Church, we thus find from the beginning that the proclamation of the Christ-event for the Salvation of men and women and of the entire world, is strictly connected with the understanding that in the person of Jesus Christ, God reveals himself as God for the respect of human dignity and the dignity of peoples.

Conclusion

This presentation hopefully expresses the complexity and the riches of the task of evangelism to the Church. It has distinguished between two distinct, and yet strictly related concepts of evangelism: evangelism in a wider sense, which is the global Mission of the Church, and evangelism in a narrow sense, which constitutes its heart and has to do with the proclamation of salvation in Christ to non-believers. We deduce that the issue of Human Rights and the Rights of the Peoples are strictly connected to both concepts of evangelism; it is in large measure the content of the ethical Christian endeavor in the understanding of evangelism in a broad sense; in evangelism in a narrow sense it is strictly connected with the *kerygma* and offers the interpretation of the *kerygma* in its earliest formulation. If we wish to let the Bible speak for itself, we ought to recognize that it keeps the two concepts of evangelism distinct and yet inseparable, as distinct and inseparable are the proclamation of the message of salvation and the call to faithful discipleship to the demands of Jesus, the Christ.

The Challenge

The Gospel confronts the person with a radical decision for life. It situates the listeners before a judgement and invites them to salvation in Christ. This is the sense of Paul's insistence before the Corinthians. The invitation to repentance and faith is structurally included in the proclamation of the Gospel and must always accompany it.

Repentance is not simply a bad conscience, it is also a radical change which happens in a person by God's initiative and produces a life motivated, lived and spent with sentiment and thoughts inspired by God. Repentance and faith appear to be the two sides of one same coin, conversion: repentance and faith, past and present, man is called to conversion, which marks the border between repentance and faith, past and present, old and new, judgement and salvation.

The understanding of evangelism in a narrow sense helps us to invite persons to become children of God in faith, evangelism in a broad sense helps us to invite them to become disciples of the same God whose love goes beyond the believers and the Church to the world, which he loves and cares for and wishes to save in Christ, "according to the Scriptures". Human Rights and Rights of Peoples must be a true concern for individual believers and the church. This expression summarizes all the concerns for the injustices today perpetrated on a world-wide scale against the human person as well as against entire nations. The Church, willing to serve, will faithfully respond to the challenge.

Saverio Guarna is Secretary of Evangelism for the Italian Baptist Union, Rome, Italy.

Baptists and "Freedom of Expression Without Distinction as to . . . Sex"

Shirley F. Bentall

Introduction

The *Universal Declaration of Human Rights* proclaims that all human beings are born free and equal in dignity and rights (Article 1). It states further that "everyone is entitled to all the rights and freedoms set forth in the Declaration, without distinction of any kind, such as race, color, sex, language, religion, political or other opinion, national or social origin, property, birth or other status..."

In 1967 a further *Declaration on the Elimination of Discrimination Against Women* was adopted by the General Assembly of the U.N., providing that women shall hold equal rights with men regarding voting, election to public bodies, the holding of public office and the exercise of public functions.

In 1980 the 14th Baptist World Congress issued its own *Declaration of Human Rights* which declared that "concern for human rights is at the heart of the Christian faith." It went on to list 20 rights "which ought to be of concern to persons everywhere and especially to those who follow Jesus Christ." The list included the right "to share religious faith publicly with others" and freedom of expression or "the right of dissent." The Congress affirmed that "to declare human rights is not enough ... (but) to promote and defend human rights within churches and society at large is also our responsibility."[1]

At Singapore, in 1986, it was ironic that the Human Rights Commission, after hearing papers regarding Baptist concern for human rights, went from the Commission to a session of the General Council, where Edna Lee de Guiterrez, president of the Women's Department, began her report with a statement about the importance of her department "because so many women in so many of our churches and conventions are not allowed to speak."

As the Rev. Per Midteide pointed out in a presentation to the Commission in Amman, "there is a considerable gap between the content of our resolutions ... and the ability to follow up the intentions of the resolutions within the BWA."[2] Others have expressed the same concern, including James E. Wood, Jr., who stated that even more fundamental than the espousal of human rights based on solid theological foundations "is the translation of that commitment into action."[3]

Wood went on to acknowledge that "although human rights are almost universally espoused in principle by most of the nations of the world, in actual practice they are expressly denied through the world by nations large and small." We could paraphrase his statement, "Although the rights of women as human persons have been endorsed in principle by every Congress of the BWA, in actual practice women are expressly treated as inferior in my Baptist churches and conventions or unions throughout the world."

The Credibility Gap

Discrimination on the basis of sex takes place in two different arenas of a Christian woman's life - in the church and in the home. (It also happens in the marketplace, but that is not the concern of this paper.) In both cases it is eloquently rationalized on the basis of scriptural texts. We have a dichotomy at the heart of our denomination. We believe that "the concept of human rights has a solid theological foundation, rooted in the nature of God."[4] But we give evidence on every hand of believing that half of humanity is not intended to have rights in relation to the other half and that this permanent subservience, inequality of dignity and curtailment of freedom is based upon God's Word.

As one Christian writer states, "The Church has dug itself a great credibility gap. You cannot claim to be light to the Gentiles, lag behind the Gentiles in sexual justice, and have your claim found credible."[5]

Are Women Fully Human?

Not in every part of our Baptist world, but in many parts, woman are undergoing an immense struggle. Some are leaving the church, finding that for them the "good news" of the gospel is eroded by interpretations that disparage their sense of personhood and human dignity. Some men as well as women are finding that the ongoing debate is undermining their confidence in the authority of scripture or the reality of the love of God.

One writer talks about the pain of women who have been nurtured in a faith that urged them to personal commitment, as they have felt led of the Spirit, only to be told that they are not worthy or acceptable to God for service in his kingdom. Patricia Gundry refers to the anguish of such women and states that the question, "Are women fully human?" is "the central and watershed question in this conflicted issue." She says:

> If the answer is yes, then say a clear yes, not yes, but ... Yes, but ... is not yes. It is closer to maybe, or not yet, or even no, because yes, but ... always carries restrictions and prohibitions that intrinsically deny that full humanity expression, opportunity or essence. Usually it denies all three.[6]

The "yes, but ..." experience of many women who are in graduate schools today, having received a call to ministry, is described by one woman who has experienced it herself: "Yes, you can aim for a graduate degree in philosophy but not one in theology." Yes you're an excellent and promising graduate student but there's no point in continuing..." "Yes, you are as competent to teach and lead as any man in our church, but those areas of service are inappropriate for you because you are a woman."[7]

Are Women Fully Redeemed?

It is not only for the sake of women who are feeling dehumanized, but for the sake of God's kingdom and his righteousness that Christians, including Baptists, need to formulate a credible theology of redemption. For example, in Rom. 1:7, when Paul addressed "all in Rome who are loved by God and called to be saints," was he writing for men and women, or for men only? He said:

> Now a righteousness from God, apart from law, has been made known, to which the Law and the Prophets testify. This righteousness from God comes through faith in Jesus Christ to all who believe. There is no difference, for all have sinned and fallen short of the glory of God, and are justified freely by his grace through the redemption that came by Christ Jesus (Rom. 3:21-24 NIV).

If women are fully redeemed by the atonement of Christ, the judgment passage of Gen. 3 should not be quoted to bind women, either in the church or the home (as it is not quoted to confine the role of men).

It should be common information that the verbs in Gen. 3:15 are not in the future imperative but the simple future tense, describing what would happen as a result of the fall. Statements like those of Tertullian to women ("Do you not know that you are an Eve? God's verdict on the sex still holds good, and the sex's guilt must hold also") should have been rejected long ago, but, in fact, they are still being used today.[8]

If women are fully redeemed, with the Gen. 3 judgment set aside by the atonement, those who have confidence in the authority of scripture should be prepared to find that the "problem" Pauline passages regarding the role of women in the church have long been misinterpreted and that Gal. 3:28, stating the broad principle that "there is neither Jew nor Greek, slave nor free, male nor female, for you are all one in Christ Jesus" is a key passage - after having been so "spiritualized" for centuries as to have no earthly significance. F. F. Bruce writes of this verse, "Paul states the basic principle here; if restrictions are found elsewhere in the Pauline corpus, as in I Cor. 14:31f or I Tim. 2:11f, they are to be understood in relation to Gal. 3:28 and not vice versa."[9] A growing body of interpretive material from responsible evangelical scholars makes it evident that this is not only possible but essential and urgent.

If women are fully human, fully redeemed, and male and female are "one in Christ." we need to gain some understanding, also, of the passages in which the husband is described as "head" of the wife, or man as "head" of woman, for example, in Eph. 5:23 and I Cor. 11:3.

Theologians seem to have moved recently from bluntly stating women's inequality to claiming that women can be one or equal with men (in keeping with Rom. 3:22-24, Gal. 3:28 etc.) and inferior at the same time. I am not sure that they would be convinced by their own arguments, if they were in the secondary role themselves - if, for instance, all blue-eyed men were destined to be equal but subservient to brown-eyed men (or vice versa) all their lives. I suspect that they would have some problems with the concept of equal inferiority or inferior equality.[10]

One wonders why scholars of personal and spiritual integrity, especially those who call themselves "inerrantists," would fail to acknowledge that when we read the word "head" (kephale) in the New Testament, used as a metaphor, it is highly improbable that it conveyed any sense of authority, superior position, leader, director or decision-maker, to Greek readers in Paul's day. Convincing evidence of this was presented by Berkeley and Alvera Mickelsen (of the Baptist General Conference) to the Evangelical Colloquium on *Women and the Bible*[11] held in Illinois in 1984. In response to their paper, Philip Barton Payne said that they had actually understated their case from Greek usage and that three prominent specialists in ancient Greek literature, whom he had consulted, all agreed that the idea of "authority" was not a recognized meaning of *kephale* in Greek.[12]

As Payne points out, "The ancient Greek world through the time of Paul commonly believed that the heart, not the head, was the center of emotions and spirit, the "central governing place of the body." Aristotle held that the heart was not only the seat of control but also the seat of intelligence."[13]

The New Testament "head" passages come alive in an entirely different way when we read them with the understanding of *kephale* as "source" or "nourisher."[14] In the I Cor. 11 passage, we realize that Paul was building a case to stop Jewish male Christians from wearing the traditional head covering (called a "tallith") to worship, as a symbol of guilt. Paul used the order of creation here to help prohibit men but to allow women to wear the head coverings that were important to them for social propriety. He then carefully balanced his statement about woman having been created from man (i.e. man as the source) by the statement that man is now born of woman (she has become his source). But, he concluded, "everything comes from God (7-12).

In Eph. 5:21, 22) which, as we know, shares one verb) the word frequently translated here for wives to "submit" comes from the Greek *hupo* ("next after") and *tasso* ("I arrange"). It does not infer compulsion but the voluntary surrender of self-interest for the sake of others, in keeping with the teaching and example of the Lord Jesus Christ. In order words, Paul addressed Christian wives (and, later, Christian slaves also) as free moral agents although they were not free in their society. He called them to take the voluntary initiatives of love, out of their reverence for Christ and their responsibility to present a credible witness to him in their milieu. Paul then challenged husbands to (if anything) an even deeper kind of caring, a sense of responsibility and loving, voluntary surrender of their self-interest also. The instruction is basically reciprocal, with verse 29 reaffirming the directive to "nourish." Paul knew that the relationships of Christians within their marriages, as within their community of faith, were windows through which others could see what differences the Lordship of Christ had made in their lives.[15]

Much more could be said about these passages but the point is this: if women are, indeed, fully redeemed members of humanity, and if the few passages of scripture that have been used for so many years to repress women's freedom in both the church and the marriage relationship have not been adequately understood or correlated with the whole message of the gospel, it is surely time to ask whether Christians, in general, and Baptists, in particular, are faithfully representing God's Word and His righteousness in our world today.

A Brief Review of Our Baptist Story

We know that there were Baptist women preachers in Western Europe in the 17th century because Thomas Edwards, an English Churchman, described them disdainfully as "she-preachers" in 1646. Even earlier, John Smyth, who founded the first identifiable Baptist Church in modern history in 1609, had written in that same year, "the Church hath powre to Elect, approve and or-deyne her own Elders, also: to elect, approve and ordeine her owne Deacons both men and women."[16]

A woman named Dorothy Hazzard was the founder of the first Baptist church in Bristol, England, according to an account by Leon McBeth.[17] Mrs. Hazzard, a young widow and devoted Christian, had gathered a group of dissenters, both women and men, who met in her home for Bible studies and prayer. When John Canne, a Baptist preacher, came to Bristol in 1640, she per-suaded her group of friends to be baptized as believers and to form themselves into a Baptist church. She, herself, was an effective teacher, leader, soul-winner and preacher.

In colonial America it seems that the earliest women took a less active role, although there were exceptions, including Catherine Scott, whose witness to Roger Williams led to the founding of the first Baptist church in North America. (Catherine's sister, Anne Hutchinson of Boston, was probably the first woman preacher in America, but she was not a Baptist.) We should realize that there is a tendency for the contribution of women to be lost in the writing of history.

By 1765 (the year of the British Stamp Act which caused a storm of col-onial protest about "taxation without representation," until Britain repealed the law), the Philadelphia Association of Baptist churches ironically debated for half a day "whether women may or ought to have their votes in the church." The men delegates finally gave consent and then wrestled with how a woman could give testimony to her conversion if she was not allowed to speak. They concluded that "a woman may, at least, make a brother a mouth to ask leave to speak, if not ask it herself; and a time of hearing is to be allowed ... yet ought not they to pen the floodgates of speech."[18]

Other associations and churches did not hold such cautious or restrictive views. A book by Morgan Edwards in 1774, entitled *Customs of Primitive Churches*, indicates that many of the Baptist churches in America had both deaconesses and eldresses, and that the eldresses sometimes preached (being veiled if men were present). By 1800, however, there was a growing tendency toward restraint of laymen as well as women.

"Regular" Baptists, whose main strength was in the settled coastal cities, had united with "Separate" Baptists, who had come out of the revival known as the First Great Awakening, which had swept with evangelistic fervor across some of the southern states (especially in the backcountry) involving women in leadership roles as ordained deacons, sometimes eldresses, and as popular preachers. In the union, the Separates set the tone in theology, evangelism and organization, that was later followed by the Southern Baptist Convention, but the active role of women was rejected.

A national organization for foreign missions was established in 1814 and for home missions in 1832. Then, in 1845 the North-South division took place, largely because of tensions related to mission work and to the slavery issue.

Women had become keenly interested in missions but the missionary role was not opened readily to them. When Adoniram Judson, America's first Baptist missionary in Burma, was asked if he could use single women in his work, he replied quickly, "Yes, a shipload." But the shipload was not sent, as Sarah Frances Anders points out. "Single women who asked to be appointed were firmly refused. In effect, they were told that if God wanted them on the mission field, he would send them husbands.[19]

However, single women persisted in seeking the freedom to express their response to God's call and were finally accepted for missionary service. Lottie Moon, who was not the first single woman to go overseas but has been called "the patron saint of Southern Baptist missions," went to China in 1873. Her work was not without frustration. She wrote, "What women want who come to China is free opportunity to do the largest possible work." And, "Simple justice demands that women should have equal rights with men in missionary meetings and in the conduct of their work."[20]

In 1879, H. A. Tupper, secretary of the Southern Baptist Foreign Mission Board, stated, "I estimate a single woman in China is worth two married men."[21]

During this past decade, China has opened her doors to other countries again, and it has been thrilling to discover that the Christian faith, planted there many years ago, is still alive and flourishing. It seems that house churches have been the significant factor, as they were in the first century (with leaders like Mary, Lydia and Chloe, in Acts 12:12, 16:14, I Cor. 1:11). When Arthur Glasser, editor of *Missiology*, visited mainland China in 1981, he reported that "fully 85% of the leaders of house churches thriving in the People's Republic of China are women."[22] (Today, I understand that some 80% are women, and 50% of the students in Nanjing Seminary are women.)

Glasser went on to state his opinion that the modelling of Christian commitment by missionary women and their indigenous counterparts, the Bible women, have been "responsible for a major share of the evangelism and Bible teaching that brought to birth the churches of the Non-Western world."[23]

Meanwhile, Baptist women had been busy forming mission societies all over North America. Women's missionary societies became organized into missionary unions, raising significant amounts of money through exemplary patterns of stewardship. Northern Baptist Women appointed their own missionaries, while the Southern Baptist WMU was auxiliary to the Southern Baptist Convention. It was gradually recognized that women were "becoming one of the most fruitful sources of missionary influence and income."[24]

"Despite their contributions," Leon McBeth states, "Southern Baptist women faced adamant resistance to any church leadership roles. Most of the men held the most restrictive view of Bible passages relegating women to silence and subjection. Moreover, they feared women would be tainted by (those who) were demanding the right to vote, attend college and hold property.[25]

At the Southern Baptist Convention of 1885, when it was realized that Arkansas Baptists had sent women as 2 of their 7 messengers, a long debate resulted in the SBC changing its constitution to exclude women as messengers. One pastor from Virginia stated, "For 40 years the Convention has been in existence and never yet has a female taken part in its deliberation."[26] It was true that even the report of the WMU was regularly read by a male.

Almost another 40 years passed before the constitution was changed back (in 1918), to admit women, and that, in spite of some dire warnings that it would lead to women serving on committees, making motions, speaking in public, and even serving as officers of the Convention. In 1929, when a woman addressed the Convention, several men tried to prevent her from speaking. On the other hand, McBeth points out that in 1978 "it was a woman who drew the largest crowd and the most publicity as she addressed the Pastors' Conference before the Convention."[27]

Writing in 1979, McBeth had an optimistic view of the expanding role for women among Southern Baptists, pointing to the practice of ordaining women as deacons, that had mushroomed in the 1970's and to the number of women who had been admitted to seminaries, with 50 or 60 having been ordained to ministry, beginning with Miss Addie David in 1964. He mentioned that "since 1973 every meeting of the SBC has had to deal with the role of women, making this one of the most controversial issues facing Southern Baptists today."[28]

The picture in 1983 is not so favorable for women. Many more have been ordained in the interval but, in 1984, at the Convention held in Kansas City, the messengers adopted a resolution that cited Eve's role in the fall from Eden as reason to exclude women from pastoral functions or any leadership roles entailing ordination. The Home Mission Board has further ruled that it will not give "pastoral aid" funds to newly established churches that hire women pastors, and a number of local associations have disfellowshipped churches that ordain women as deacons or pastors.

Currently, according to *Folio*, the quarterly journal published by the Women in Ministry Network, there are more than 450 Southern Baptist women ordained for pastoral ministry, of whom only 11 are serving as pastors or co-pastors, and only 4 of those as senior pastors. One of the 4, Nancy Hastings Sehested, was called to the 235-member Prescott Memorial Church in Memphis, Tennessee, after the Search Committee had reviewed more than 100 resumes and interviewed a number of well-qualified candidates, both men and women. The church, which is dully aligned with the SBC and the ABC (the American Baptist Churches in the USA, formerly the Northern Baptist Convention), has been disfellowshipped by the 120-church Shelby Association of the SBC.

Looking to the Future

The serious question that we need to address is whether this age-long dispute has been honoring Jesus Christ, or actually dishonoring His name, denying his purposes. If the latter, upon whom will God's judgment fall?

One realizes that some church leaders, pastors and theologians, have built up such a case for the "divine order" and the subordination of women (in spite of Jesus' example and teaching, as in Mk. 9:35; 10:15, 42-44), that it must be difficult and undesirable for them, personally, to make any kind of change.

In fact, it is difficult for anyone to give up privilege and power to which one has become accustomed. More than a century ago, British philosopher and humanitarian, John Stuart Mill, pointed out that any form of domination that has become customary always seems to be natural to those who exercise it (as slavery seemed to those who called on the authority of scripture to defend it). So, "they come to worship their own will as such a grand thing that it is actually the law for another rational being." And, "there is nothing which men so easily learn as this self-worship; all privileged persons, and all privileged classes, have had it ... Philosophy and religion, instead of keeping it in check, are generally suborned to defend it."[29]

In a sense, this became the battleground between Jesus of Nazareth and the Jewish leaders of his day, steeped as they were in the legalistic defence of their own entrenched interests. Jesus had grown up, himself, "on the margins of society," as Athol Gill pointed out in his paper, presented to the Human Rights Commission in 1987, and he became "a partisan of the poor and afflicted," including women, in keeping with his stated mission (Luke 4:18) and his claim to reveal the very nature of God (Jn. 14:9,11).

However as Gill stated:

> Western Protestants have generally been very slow in attributing theological significance to the life and mission of Jesus of Nazareth. Aspects of the mission of Jesus which have become central in the process of theological reflection in the Two Thirds World are generally passed over in silence in the West, apparently regarded as "accidents of history," rather than as a deliberate choice of God. When we ignore such central factors of the Gospel tradition we again provide ample evidence of the cultural containment which we experience when we read the scriptures. We are unable to take the life of Jesus seriously because we are hemmed in by the constraints of middle-class western culture which insists on interpreting everything through the paradigms of power.[30]

We should be humble enough to admit that we all bring our personal backgrounds, knowledge and opinions to the interpretation of Scripture, and we bring our own responses or reactions to all that has happened to us, as well as all that is happening around us. We develop "our canon within the canon" of Scripture. There are passages or verses to which we attach ourselves, because they express, or we want them to express, what we already believe. The danger is that we will idolize our own interpretations (our own "isms") and defend them as the sole "authority of Scripture," whether or not they are in tune with the life and lordship of Christ, or the real message of the gospel.

It is because this has happened all too often in the past that Christianity's record - in spite of its basic distinctiveness - is not too different from that of other world religions regarding womanhood. Buddhist women have been barred from leadership in their religious communities. Islam has made a woman's witness only half the witness of a man. Jewish males thanked God for not creating them as females. While Christians have not cast widows on their husband's funeral pyres, as Hindus used to do, and have never bound women's feet, they have engaged in a binding of the spirit, not unrelated to the Confucian attitude of traditional "honour" for women, stemming form their acceptance of bondage.[31] The principle of female inferiority and of women living their lives through their husbands and children, has been essentially the same, not allowing for full personhood or "responseability" akin to that of men, in either the home or church.

And this, in spite of Jesus' parable of the talents, his commissioning of disciplines, both men and women, in the Upper Room, and Pentecost, when the Holy Spirit filled and empowered people of both sexes (Acts 1,2). It is also in spite of the equity expressed repeated in 1 Cor. 7 and Rom. 16.

Today we are living in a world where women in many cultures are insisting upon taking their own abilities and opportunities seriously. We see women involved effectively in business, management, medicine, the media, sports, entertainment, education, law, government, and as elected heads of state.

A long process has been going on, especially in Western societies, toward the erasing of what psychologists call ascriptivism - the determination of one's role in life by the status and occupation of one's father, together with one's race, religion, ethnic and sexual identity. As more and more people become accustomed to the privilege of personal choice based upon their own interests and abilities (or sense of call) they become less tolerant of control, even in the name of the church. And this applies to women as well as men. As one writer points out, "Most of those who complain most loudly about the movement of Christian feminism would themselves be confined to spending their lives as indentured farmers and servants if this vast social process had not taken place."[32]

In our modern world, an increasing number of committed Christian women, feeling called of God, want to serve within the church. They offer themselves freely in the Lord. Or they want to enter marriage as a partnership where husband and wife are both subject to each other in mutual love and reverence for the Lord. When they encounter masculine determination to stifle or subordinate their womanhood, even when it is wrapped in scriptural references, it looks more like a manifestation of fallen human nature or fallen human relationships than redemption and the fellowship of the redeemed in Jesus Christ.

In Conclusion

I believe that Christians have been entrusted with a message that the world desperately needs to hear: a message about the nature of God, His love and forgiving grace in Jesus Christ, offered freely to every person, to bring that person into a new relationship with Him and with others, in Christ. Every Christian is intended to become an ambassador for Christ, an agent of His reconciliation. Paul expressed it unforgettably in II Cor. 5:16-21:

> So from now on we regard no one from a worldly point of view ... Therefore if anyone is in Christ, he is a new creation: the old has gone, the new has come! All is from God, who reconciled us to himself through Christ and gave us the ministry of reconciliation ... We are therefore Christ's ambassadors, as though God were making his appeal through us ... God made him who had no sin to be sin for us, so that in him we might become the righteousness of God (NIV).

My final questions, in closing, are these: How can half of God's ambassadors want to curtail and confine the other half? There is so much need in the world! If it is possible to interpret "problem" passages of scripture in ways that do not conflict with the full meaning of other key passages, how can any disciples of Jesus Christ not be eager to do so? How long must women wait to have their personhood and their redemption affirmed by the churches to which they belong?

In the meantime, there is such a waste of time and energy in debate, and an incalculable loss of human resources as well as the failure to model relationships of oneness and mutuality in Christ. The credibility of the gospel and confidence in the authority of the scriptures are undermined. The social conscience of Christian churches lags behind the social conscience of the United Nations.

The question of how to effect change among Baptists must be left with each person, each church, association and convention. In my view, it is vitally important for male theologians, pastors and denominational leaders to become aware of what this situation is actually saying and doing to women (inside and outside the church) and to discover ways in which they can make a difference within their own spheres of influence and action. It seems more appropriate for men to insist upon the rights of women than for women to be put in the position of having to defend their own rights, even their own calling in Christ.

For years our denomination has affirmed the Human Rights Declarations of the United Nations and has passed resolutions paying lip service to "freedom of individual conscience and to the worth and inherent rights of each individual being." The time has surely come, and is long past, when we should measure up to our own yardsticks for human justice based on our understanding of the love of God and our commitment as ambassadors for Christ.

Shirley Bentall, of Calgary, Alberta, Canada, is a former president of the Baptist Union of Western Canada and of the Canadian Baptist Federation.

Endnotes

1. From the BWA Congress in Toronto, quoted by James E. Wood, Jr., "Baptist

Thought on Human Rights" (1986 Baptist Human Rights Commission Paper), p. 10.

2. Per Midteide, "Human Rights Within the BWA and the Reception Process (1987 BWA Human Rights Commission Paper) p. 1.

3. Wood, op cit., p. 12.

4. Ibid. p.4.

5. Denise Carmody, *Feminism and Christianity*, Nashville: Abingdon, 1982, p. 89.

6. Patricia Gundry, *Why We're Here. in Women, Authority and the Bible*, ed. Alvera Michelsen, Downers Grove, Illinois: InterVarsity Press, 1984, p. 20.

7. Gretchen Gaebelein Hull, *Response+to. to Why We're Here*, in Ibid, p. 22.

8. Quoted by Charles Ryrie, *The Role of Women in the Church*, Chicago: Moody Press, 1958) (3rd printing 1981) p. 113. Ryrie states of Tertulian, "there is not one false ring in his writing."

9. F. F. Bruce, *Commentary on Galatians*, Grand Rapids, Mich: William B. Eerdmans Publishing Co., 1982, p. 190. 10. In this connection, it is interesting to note that at a final meeting of the International Council on Biblical Inerrancy in 1986, 300 inerrantist scholars produced a final "Chicago statement on Application of Scripture," which included the following sentence:

"We affirm that in the marriage pattern ordained by God, the husband as head is the living servant-leader of his wife, and the wife as helper in submissive companionship as a full partner with her husband."

What does "submissive companionship as a full partner" mean?

11. Berkeley and Alvera Michelsen, "What Does Kephale mean in the New Testament?" in: *Women, Authority and the Bible*, op. cit. pp. 97-110. The Michelsens refer to the 2000 page *Greek-English Lexicon*, covering Homeric, Classical and Koine Greek (by Liddell, Scott, Jones and McKenzie) which lists 25 possible figurative meanings of *kephale*, in addition to its literal meaning, but does not include the concepts of authority, supremacy or superior rank. Heinrich Schlier's article in the *Theological Dictionary of the New Testament* provides 27 possible metaphorical meanings outside the New Testament, none of them conveying the meaning of authority.

12. Philip Barton Payne, "Response to What Does *Kephale* mean in the New Testament?" Ibid., p. 118. The linguists consulted by payne were David Armstrong of the University of Texas and Michael Wigodsky and Mark Edwards of Stanford University. Payne pointed out that "including its 1968 supplement, the Liddell and Scott lexicon lists forty-eight separate English equivalents of figurative meanings of *kephale*. None of them implies leader, authority, first or supreme."

13. Ibid, pp. 119, 120.

14. Interpreting *kephale* as "source" or "nourisher" and not "authority" is not to say that Christ does not have authority over his church. Indeed he does, but it is stated in other passages, in other ways, eg. *exousia* in Matt. 28:18f, Jn. 17:2, II Cor. 13:10, II Thess. 3:6.

15. For an interesting study of the way Paul balances masculine and feminine concerns and relationships, see I Cor. 7 and note v. 5 re: decision-making in marriage.

16. William T. Whitey, ed. *The Works of John Smyth*, (Cambridge: University Press, 1959) Vol. II, p. 509.

17. Harry Leon McBeth, "The Changing Role of Women in Baptist History",

in *Southwestern Journal of Theology*, Vol. 22, Fall 1979, pp. 86, 87.

18. A. D. Gillette, ed. *Minutes of the Philadelphia Baptist Association from A.D. 1707 to A.D. 1807* (Philadelphia: American Baptist Publications Society, 1851) p. 53. Quoted by McBeth, Ibid, pp. 87, 88.

19. Sarah Frances Anders, *Woman's Role in the Southern Baptist Convention and its churches, as compared with Selected Other Denominations*, in *Review and Expositor*, 1972 (1) p. 39.

20. Quoted by Ruth Tucker, *Female Mission Strategists: A History and Contemporary Perspective, Missiology*, 1987, 15 (1) Jan. p. 74.

21. Ibid, p. 74.

22. Quoted by Frances Hiebert, "Missionary Women as Models in Cross-Cultural Context", in: *Missiology*, Vol X(4) Oct. 1982, p. 460.

23. Ibid, p. 460.

24. *Annual*, SBC, 1881, pp. 61, 62. Quoted by McBeth, "The Role of Women in Southern Baptist History," op. c,t. p. 6.

25. McBeth, "The Changing Role of Women in Baptist History," op. cit. p. 92.

26. Ibid, p. 93.

27. Ibid, p. 85.

28. Ibid, p. 84.

29. John Stuart Mill, *The Subjection of Women*, New York: D. Appleton & Co., 1869, pp. 22, 77.

30. Athol Gill, "Human Rights: A Preliminary Sketch of "A Down-Under Perspective"," (BWA Human Rights Commission Paper 1987) p. 9.

31. See Carmody, op. cit., pp. 14, 15.

32. Nicholas Wolsterstorff, "Hearing the Cry," in *Women, Authority and the Bible*, op. cit., p. 288.

For We Are Strangers Before Thee and Sojourners . . .

Wolfgang Lorenz

I. The Problem of Refugees and Asylum Seekers With Particular Reference to the Situation In the Federal Republic of Germany And in West Berlin

I have been asked to present a paper dealing with the problem of refugees and asylum seekers from the viewpoint of my home city, West Berlin. I cannot do this without first referring to the distressing recent history of my country, for the experiences with National Socialism have shown in a most extreme manner how human rights can be abused, and how minorities can be discriminated and persecuted.

Until the Spring of 1940, i.e. before the war touched the German civil population, the number of refugees from Germany that found acceptance in

Western Europe, North America, Latin America and the other parts of the world has been estimated at about 800,000. The number of those, however, who at that time found no asylum and for that reason suffered death is unknown.

These experiences led the founders of the Federal Republic of Germany to include an article into the constitution which says: "Politically persecuted persons enjoy the right of asylum". Nevertheless there are still tremendous problems in our country in order to meet the refugee problem of our world with the necessary legal and charitable measures.

According to the figures of the United Nations High Commissioner-for Refugees (UNHCR) (Nov. 1986) there are at present 12 million refugees who had to leave their home because of political, racist or religious persecution, to say nothing of war, civil war and economic catastrophes. The majority of these seek and find refuge and shelter in their respective neighboring countries in the Third World. Only 5% of them reach Western Europe and clearly less than 1% the Federal Republic of Germany. The predominant number of refugees would desire to remain in their own region. Many of those refugees who desire to come to Europe are being handicapped in their desire
- because the ways of escape are blocked,
- because the refugees cannot afford the travel costs,
- because the air-lines will not transport refugees who do not possess a valid visa.

A comparison of the number of refugees in the relationship to 1000 citizens shows the difference between the "first" and the "third" world:

Sudan	41, 7
Pakistan	36, 0
Somalia	14,15
Sweden	5,15
Switzerland	4,98
Belgium	3,56
France	2,95
Austria	2,78
Great Britain	2,49
Norway	2,42
FRG	1,91
The Netherlands	1,01
Denmark	0,70

By evaluating these numbers, however, one has to consider that there is no common criterion to define the status of a refugee. With reference to the Federal Republic of Germany we also have to remember the fact that until the year 1961 a great number of refugees from the German Democratic Republic and from the countries east of the Oder-NeiBe-line - the contemporary border between the People's Republic of Poland and the German Democratic Republic - were integrated into the Federal Republic of Germany.

The numbers of asylum seekers in the Federal Republic of Germany for the years 1980 - 1986 are as follows: (Source: The Ministry of the Interior, press service of 5.11.86.)

1980	approximately 108,000
1981	49,391
1982	37,423
1983	19,737
1984	35,278
1985	73,832
1986	91,100 (until Oct. 31)

In West Berlin during 185 22,908 applications for asylum were made and during 1986 32,567. This shows an increase of 42%. The increasing number of asylum seekers - particularly the quota in Berlin - is a source of serious problems and poses a great challenge for all who are in authority. The Federal Republic of Germany as well as other West European Countries have been reacting with an increasingly restrictive policy to cut down a continuous stream of asylum seekers.

We are experiencing loud voices who claim that our ability to assume and integrate asylum seekers has reached its limits. These voices are echoed by a great percentage of the population and encourage a climate that is not conducive to helping to solve the problem of the refugees.

In all of these problems the ones who have to suffer most are the refugees themselves. Their flight from their country into an uncertain future was not undertaken lightly. Persecution or a life threatening need led them to this step. To eliminate the reasons for fleeing from one's country is a long term problem. Our governments and all those who have political responsibility must be challenged

- to bring about an end to critical conflicts between countries and to support everything that can be done to prevent the outbreak and consequence of such conflicts;

- to encourage and support processes for a permanent, effective and quick overcoming of poverty and material need in the developing countries.

A responsible policy for the matter of asylum has to be based on the principles that

- every political refugee must have a chance to reach the border of the Federal Republic of Germany in order to apply for asylum;

- an expulsion or deportation to their country of origin may only take place, if that implicates no life threatening danger for the refuges.

The Ecumenical Council of West Berlin in which 19 Churches, Free Churches and Fellowships work together, has recently adopted the goal to encourage a dignified and humane association with inter-change with refugees. It is also in close contact with responsible political agencies to promote a quick and efficient legal process for the benefit of the refuges.

The Council is further concerned with the situation of those, who find themselves in deportation quarters. It continues a dialogue with the Senate of our city and has brought about a demand for the cancellation of the order to expel ca. 4000 citizens of Lebanon living in Berlin. All Member Churches of the Ecumenical Council have been encouraged to continue to support their charitable efforts in this area. In addition to the Ecumenical Council of Berlin and the individual Churches other interested agencies support a refugee counselling centre. More activities of this sort we also find in the structures of the two larger Churches of our country, the Evangelical (Lutheran) Church in Germany and the Roman Catholic Church.

In all of this one fact is underlined The question of refugees is a humane and a political question. However, where Churches and individual Christians become involved the question of faith and confession to Jesus Christ is raised. And therefore it is my opinion that after this short description of the situation it is our task first of all to seek the biblical point of view concerning our problem, and subsequently to explore the consequences for the work of the Baptist World Alliance and of all the Unions united with it, as well as to describe the concrete task for the local churches.

II. The Biblical Witness

Introduction

The Bible - this is our claim - is the guideline for our life and for our service both in our churches and in the world. This has universal validity. Particularly where we have to ask for our spiritual and practical stand concerning social and political challenges and where we discover new ways and insights that are not always conformable to the society in which we find ourselves. The wellknown English preacher Charles Haddon Spurgeon is the author of this admonition: "Brothers, read those bible passages most, that hurt the most." This is the situation in which we find ourselves when we approach the word of God with the theme that has been given to us, the theme of the refugee and the situation of the asylum seeker.

"To be a Stranger" — the Old Testament Meaning

In the centre of the biblical recollection of Israel stands the experience of God freeing his people from alien domination and oppression. In ancient Israel three types of strangers must be distinguished: Firstly, there was the *stranger who was travelling through*. He was a guest for a few days and for his benefit the command of hospitality was given. Secondly, there was the *stranger* who was often called a sojourner or a refugee. He was placed under special protection of the law. Thirdly, there were *whole nations*, "strangers" for whom Israel was predestined to become a blessing. Our concern here is with the second type, the stranger who has to flee and live in another land. The lexicon of Kohler/Baumgarten (VETERIS TESTAMENTIS LIBROS, Leiden, 2. edition 1958, column 192) says: "The stranger is a man who either alone or with his family leaves his home because of war, unrests, hunger, plague or some other catastrophe where he, as far as his rights and possession, marriage, justice, worship and war are concerned, has somewhat been cut short, and looks for refuge and sanctuary."

Biblical examples for this definition are: Abraham, the "foreigner by command", as Johannes Busch has called him, who comes to the Hetites and asks for a burial place for his dead wife (Gen. 23;4) or Ruth, the Moabitess, who finds reception as a foreigner with Boas. Finally, Israel itself was a stranger in Egypt, later also a stranger in Babylon, and even today is scattered among all lands. These figures become a type for Israel's existence as a stranger, and they assume a paradigmatic dimension.

A stranger, according to the Old Testament, is one who has been driven away by a catastrophe or is on flight, with the exception of Abraham who was a "foreigner by command". On the other hand the foreigner is one who is also trying to find a way of economic life and to develop new relationships. In spite of this, compared with the locals, the natives of the country, he is a man who enjoys fewer rights and privileges. He doesn't own land and for this reason he has no civil rights. He is economically and legally weak and therefore in need of protection.

Relations With Strangers According to the Old Testament

Israel was in the habit of practicing hospitality for all who were travelling through or for those who, as strangers, became settlers in the country. Examples for this kind of hospitality are the three men who came to Abraham in Genesis 18, the two angels who visited Lot in Genesis 19, the angel who appeared to Gideon, Judges 6, or the angel who visited the parents of Samson, Judges 13. There are also negative examples for hospitality that is denied. In the conclusion of the book of Judges 19,22f this evil murder was avenged so that almost the whole tribe of Benjamin was eradicated. Therefore hospitality is one of God's highest mandates and commands. Israel has this responsibility as a foregone conclusion without any reward. When strangers settled in Israel they had the right of protection.

In the Ten Commandments - albeit in a little hidden place - we find this again in the command of the sabbath (Exodus 20;10). The sabbath shall also be observed by the stranger, the slave and the cattle. That means, by all who are weak. In the Book of the Covenant, the old collection of laws, we find: "You shall not wrong a stranger or oppress him, for you were strangers in the land of Egypt" (Exodus 22;21). Or in Exodus 23;9 we read also: "You shall not oppress a stranger; you know the heart of a stranger, for you were strangers in the land of Egypt".

Strangers, we see, belong to the class of people who are economically and legally weak. Therefore they have been and remain the object of particular care by the people of God. This is also stressed in the later Israelite laws, for example in Deuteronomy or in the so-called Levitical Laws in Leviticus 9;3-4. There are certain rules as to how one is to help the strangers:
- they have the right of the second cutting of the harvest (Deut. 24;17f)
- they shall not work on the sabbath (Exodus 20;10)
- as slaves they shall not be deported (Deut. 23;16-17)
- they shall not be economically exploited (Deut. 24,14)

- the foreigner is to be granted refuge and asylum just as the sons of Israel (Num. 35;15).

We may summarize: The divine law commands that the underprivileged stranger is commended to the particular care and concern of the people of Israel.

Israel's Experience of and With God as Its Motivation

The biblical legislation in this area shows a remarkable difference to that of other countries in ancient orient. The Codex Hammurabi, for example, also demands concern for the stranger from the Babylonians and other nations; nevertheless the difference consists in the fact that the law of hospitality for Israel does not spring from a mechanical sense of obedience but rather from an obedience based on conviction. For this reason we read in Exodus 23;9: "You shall not oppress a stranger; *you know* the heart of a stranger, for you were in the land of Egypt".

The mandate to protect, to respect and to love the stranger does not spring from a particular social principle nor from an idealistic picture of humanity but from Israel's own historical experience. The experience of and with God.

In Deuteronomy 5;12-15, where the command to keep the sabbath is further expanded, we read: "You shall remember that you were a servant in the land of Egypt, and the Lord your God brought you out thence with a mighty hand and an outstretched arm; therefore the Lord they God commanded you to keep the sabbath day." This belongs to the basic confession and experience of the people of Israel (see also Deut. 6;20-21).

The command to love the stranger, to give him protection and help, commands nothing more than that what God himself does, as we read in Deut. 10;17-19: "For the Lord your God is God of gods and Lord of lords ... He executes justice for the fatherless and the widow, and loves the sojourner, giving him food and clothing. Love the sojourner therefore; for you were sojourners in the land of Egypt."

Israel's Continuing Existence as a Stranger Before God

In the last part of Leviticus we find agrarian and property rights. Here we read in Lev. 25;23-24: "The land shall not be sold in perpetuity, for the land is mine; for you are strangers and sojourners with me. And in all the country you possess, you shall grant a redemption of the land". This means that Israel owned its property land under the condition of the previous and continued possession of God. They own the land conditionally because it was Jahwe's land unconditionally. Israel lived as a stranger and guest with Jahwe. Jahwe is the true land-owner. it is essential that this be remembered, because according to Israel's legal understanding, all the other civil rights were connected and had their origin in this right of ownership. Ownership of land was the source of the right to participate in worship, in war and in the practice of justice and legal litigation "in the gate". Possession, ownership and settledness must never be taken for granted.

In the Psalms we read: "Hear my prayer, O Lord, and give ear to my cry. Hold not thy peace at my tears! For I am thy passing guest, a sojourner, like all my fathers." (Ps. 39;12). In view of the ultimate threat of death and in fear of being shut out from the land of the living, the prayer of the Psalmist cries out to the Lord of the lands, namely to God, for a prolonged permission to remain in the land of the living: "O lord, who shall sojourn in thy tent? Who shall dwell on thy holy hill? He who walks blamelessly ..." (Ps. 15;1f). In the 119th Psalm we read: "I am a sojourner on earth; hide not thy commandments from me." (V.19) And finally we have in this context a classical text from the Chronicles 29;15: "For we are strangers before thee, and sojourners, as all our fathers were; our days on the earth are like a shadow, and there is no abiding." This is a sentence from the prayer in the last public service of David. After this Salomon assumes the throne and David dies, old and, as it is recorded, in "a good old age, full of days, riches and honor." And in this, his last service, David as the typological king of Israel bears witness to the fact that Israel fundamentally has to live its life as a stranger in its total existence not only in Abraham's days or later during the exile. Even the times of the kings; all time is lived as a stranger. The transitory nature of life and all existence breaks through again as a witness to Israel. They are the undomesticated. Israel, the people of God, has no enduring city.

The Sojourner Existence in New Testament Context and Background

This theme is treated in the New Testament in various contexts. The early Christians read in their Bible that Abraham in the Old Testament is recognized as the father of faith. In Hebr. 11 we read: "We have here no abiding city but we seek one to come". We find this motif again and again in the New Testament. Most clearly it is in 1 Peter: "To the exiles of the Dispersion in Pontus, Galatia ..." (1;1) Here the admonition is: Conduct yourselves with fear throughout the time of your exile". (1;17)

The Roman Catholic exegete Norbert Brox describes the sojourner existence in the context of 1 Peter as follows: 1. To be a Christian means to be a member of a minority, to live in isolation (4;12). 2. There exists a sort of polarity and antithesis between the congregation and the world (2;1-10). 3. Within the congregation there exists a solidarity with the persecuted (2;10). 4, Encouragement takes place through the example of Jesus Christ. He, too, was rejected (2;21-25, 4;1-13). Finally we mention the parable of the Last Judgement where the Son of Man is coming again and says: "I was a stranger and you welcomed me ... I was a stranger and you did not welcome me ... Truly, I say to you, as you did it not to one of the least of these, you did it not to me" (Matth. 25;31-46).

III. Theological Consequences

With these mandates, experiences and stories of the Old and the New Testament we meet central biblical themes. These themes are not isolated, but they are to be seen in a further context that leads to a basic biblical conviction of faith that belongs to the orientation of the Christian congregation, which is both binding and abiding for all times. In view of the world-wide crisis of refugees and their difficulties, we as Christians and parishes have tasks that are placed before us. It is important that we continue to receive the encouragement and aid from the biblical background, and witness in our practice to meet these tasks and problems.

God, the Creator of all Mankind

All people are by definition creatures of God. And the earth has been entrusted to all. From this we derive the basic responsibility to administer and care for the earth which, though entrusted to us, is the possession of God, and to share its goods and fruits, its resources and possibilities with all people. In the reception of the stranger, therefore, we have an element of this sharing in the gifts of God. Responding to the need of the stranger with what we possess we respond to God, because God is the creator of the world and the father of all humanity. It includes one's relationship to other human beings, those who are near and those who are more distant. In people who, as refugees, look for protection and a chance to live we meet the unsolved problems of our common humanity, problems of development, of peace and human rights. Salvation and well-being, righteousness, justice and peace are divisible. The one humanity lives in a multiplicity of race, languages, cultures and peoples. The differences do not exist to create opponents; they are changeable, reversible and can be negated when they are not in harmony with the mandates of God. So the more distant co-human being can become a neighbor for whom I am directly responsible. We asked the question: Could it be that god is knocking on our doors through the refugees, the asylum seeking foreigner, in order to challenge our egocentric viewpoints, our prejudices and our boundaries, that we might ultimately change the situation in view of our world-wide responsibility? Could it be that in this sense the stranger and pleader at our door is a teacher of God, knocking on the doors of our churches to show us anew the wideness of the creation of God and the universality of His kingdom?

To Work for Reconciliation

From the very beginning the Scriptures reckon with the reality of evil. It consists in humanity's disregard for the command of God; it rejects Him and, by doing so, also rejects his creatures. Understanding among human kind is frustrated because man rebels against God, and for this reason rejection, oppression and exploitation plays such a role in life. The reality of evil, however, does not have the last word according to the proclamation of the scriptures. Through the crucifixion of Jesus Christ God has brought about reconciliation between Himself and the world. His resurrection is the victory over evil. The reconciliation that God has effected is unconditional. Nevertheless this reconciliation with God through Jesus Christ leads to acceptance, and even more, to the love of the neighbor. Reconciliation is to be lived. In life it develops its freeing and uniting strength. Therefore Jesus gave us the mandate to love as the basic orientation of our Christian existence. And this mandate to love is also valid for the relationship between nations, between citizens and foreign refugees. Many things of course can obstruct our living reconciliation: e.g. prejudice and fear that stems from ignorance about the stranger and his strange customs. Or reaching back into a colonial past to find justification and guilt for the stranger's position. Stubborn ideological viewpoints which also in turn lead to a despising and a rejection of man in his worth. Fear of loosing one's security and possession can make us bitter. It continues to remain a challenge for the Christian congregation, how to meet the needs of the foreigners in their midst. By means of our behavior, our talk and our acts, we continue to witness to our faith.

The New Fellowship

In the church, boundaries and animosities are not simply erased, but they stand under a new perspective. "There is neither Jew nor Greek, there is neither slave nor free, there is neither male nor female; for you are all one in Christ Jesus." This is the message of Galatians 3;28. In the overcoming of the boundaries of race, sex, class and nation, people who were previously divided up into nations, cultures and social groups have been led together to a new fellowship, the body of Christ. Many refugees and asylum seekers are Christians. Christian congregations should open themselves to these people and their needs. Work among refugees, however, can not be restricted only to Christians, because the mandate to love has validity for all those who are in need and is specifically not distinguishable by color of skin or nationality, culture or religion. Love gives the refugees who come into our country - those who are chilled inwardly and externally - the necessary warmth and security. And so the congregation takes a stand for the right of the weak to life, and resists the tendency to reject and segregate the refugees. This action of the Christian congregation is a living sign and announcement of the future world of God.

IV. Conclusions and Consequences
For the Baptist World Alliance (BWA)
And the Churches

Positions and Resolutions from Meetings and Conferences of the BWA

The Baptist World Alliance in line with the basic biblical convictions of all related agencies has from the very beginning taken a position for the respecting of freedom of religion and freedom of conscience, as well as against every form of discrimination of peoples, races and nations.

This has taken place in the context of the work of this commission in the past years and has been attested to. As a result I would like to point to a few of the documents. The Fifth Baptist World Congress which took place in the year 1934 in Berlin passed a courageous statement to the governments of all countries in view of developing National Socialism. In connection with the race question we find the following words:

> This congress that represents the world-wide fellowship of Baptists in all peoples and races knows that in spite of all racial differences the unity in Christ exists. This congress further condemns all racial enmity and every form of suppression or injust treatment of Jews, coloreds or *people living under another nation as minority* as a transgression of the law of God, our heavenly father.

In the Resolution of the Fourteenth Baptist World Congress 1980 in Toronto we find under VI: Refugees:

> Feeling the deepest disquiet over the plight of the homeless peoples of the world, we plead with all governments to give care and human rights to the dispossessed peoples within their jurisdiction so they may live with hope and security within their own country.
> We urge the governments of all countries to act with humanitarian concern towards persons seeking shelter as a result of personal dispossession or exclusion from their own nations, and we commend those governments which have already done so.

The BWA Council stated in Singapore 1986 in Resolution 8 in reference to the situation in Afghanistan the following:

> The 1986 BWA Council in Singapore
> 1. is aware of the present situation in the country of Afghanistan and notes with concern the plight of some three million refugees;
> 2. also notes that the refugee situation has created serious problems for neighboring countries, particularly Pakistan;
> 3. urges the countries involved with the help of the United Nations Organization to reach agreement for the creation of conditions for restoring peace and the withdrawal of all foreign forces, so that the refugees from Afghanistan may return to their homes with honor and dignity.

Dr. Gerhard Claas, the General Secretary of the Baptist World Alliance, in an interview in February 1986 in Germany had the following to say to the question of refugees and asylum seekers:

> The UNO-year of the homeless has caused us in the BWA to appeal to all member unions to renew their concern for the poorest of the poor. We appeal particularly to those countries who do not have a broad middleclass, and therefore a very thin upper-class, that their churches should accept and open themselves to peoples who are the victims of sickness, unemployment, abuse of alcohol and drugs. These people, who are not in a position to find their way back into society, have to receive a sign of hope from us as Christians. We are to be to them a light, which means that the Churches are to be opened and that food - and clothing - programs must be established. In all of this we have to keep in mind their reintegration in society by having con-

fidence in them, saying: You are not written off, but you have the possibility of a new beginning. All this is involved when we pass this resolution."

The Tasks and Possibilities of the Churches of Today

Just as in the public and political realm we have different opinions with respect to these problems in our congregations. The discussion is at times very controversial and heated. Generally speaking, we observe that biographical and contemporary viewpoints and experiences play a greater role in this argumentation than spiritual and theological motives.

It is important that this discussion continues to be open, objective and patient in the context of our congregations. Principally our churches are to orient themselves on the guidelines of scripture. For this reason it is a major task of the sermon to draw attention to this area, to counteract prejudices and anxieties, to sharpen conscience and to encourage our congregations to accept the strangers and the refugees. The best preachers in this area are the refugees themselves. In addition to the sermon the practice of the church should be directed to giving assistance and help in overcoming the human and the social problems of the refugees. I would like to list a few practical examples of such work among and with refugees:
- Reception and care of newly arrived asylum seekers at the airport or in the transit rooms;
- General care and counselling in the mass-quarters, camps and hostels;
- Counselling and care related to the transition to private and decentralized housing;
- Sponsorship of housing, particularly for qualified and integrated groups;
- Legal counsel;
- Qualified psychological and social counsel;
- Counselling and support in cases of repatriation or continued seeking for asylum;
- Language instruction, orientation-courses, job-offers;
- Specific care for families and children;
- Support in keeping and/or getting families together;
- Help in finding living-quarters; help in integrating the refugee in professional and social respects;
- Support of all self-help initiatives in cultural and other areas of the life of the refugee;
- Political representation towards government and society;
- Defense of humanitarian principles by public engagement of citizens and by practical initiative like "Sanctuary".

All this can take place when the church understands itself as advocate of the weak, and therefore particularly as advocate of the refugee.

Refugees have to be treated as human beings in every phase of their temporary or permanent residence in our midst. The church leadership of the Baptist Union in Germany issued a word to the situation of the refugee and the asylum seeker in our country in September of 1986. In this "Word To The

Churches" practical suggestions for the work on the local church level are given.

> According to our Free-Church understanding of congregation- of Jesus has always taken a stand for freedom of conscience and religion as well as observance of human rights. For this reason we find it necessary and salutary to define the right of asylum so that it will be granted to those who are persecuted for political, religious or racist reasons. Therefore we ask our congregations: 1. Let the love of Jesus condition your contacts with the stranger. Accept the one who is looking for protection. Open your churches. Offer them rooms, meeting places, youth-groups and language-courses. Invite them to your worship-services and to participate in the church life, so that they can experience security, hospitality and human warmth. 2. Have no part of inconsiderate generalizations and remain sensitive and vigilant where anxieties are stirred up and moods are misused. Assist the stranger in his accommodating to a strange or different culture and particularly stand by him when a repatriation is threatening that could result in torture or death in his home country. 3. Do not be lax in your intercession for all those persecuted and deprived of their rights, as well as for those who are concerned for these people. The love of Christ equips you with courage and creativity to witness to the stranger the Gospel in word and deed.

V. Conclusion

In this paper we have reviewed the situation of the refugee and the foreigner with particular reference to my home-country. Then we have heard the biblical witness along with the resulting theological conclusions and pointed to a few consequences for our churches. Now, in conclusion, I would like to summarize, on the basis of my personal experience, and say that the central question is the question of our mobility. How versatile and flexible are we in our work and service and witness if we are truly strangers and pilgrims of God according to the Bible. I think that this question is also linked to the question of the ability and the readiness of the BWA to declare itself in solidarity and help the congregations who suffer with this problem in other countries. In times past a favorite book of Christians was John Bunyan's *Pilgrim's Progress*. Are we still people who are pilgrims, travellers with a degree of homesickness and a desire to come home, or are we sitting on our upholstered chairs here in this world, proud of what we have already accomplished? Another problem related to this question is the experience of the difficulty of creating a relationship with foreigners in our midst. Connected with this is the question: have our riches hindered us in our obedience to the biblical word? Have we become so adapted to the status quo that we no longer are mobile, we no longer can change? What price have we paid for this stance? Could it be that we have so many difficulties in understanding the refugees, the minorities, the despised because we ourselves are no longer in the situation of the despised and no longer live under these conditions? As Baptists we are getting on in years, and this is not only a matter of our social status but also has to do with our thinking and feeling. john F. Kennedy, as he once visited my home city of Berlin, spoke this well-known sentence: "Ich bin ein Berliner - I am a Berliner". This was nothing other than the ability in a particularly challenging, politically tense situation to declare himself in solidarity with the people of the city. Nothing else is asked from us when we meet the strangers and the refugees in our city and in the congregation - give of yourself to them in the name of Jesus Christ.

In the conclusion of the gospel of Luke we find the story of the two men who go for a walk and meet a stranger. They continue their walk with him and invite him in for a meal. And behold, later they notice and are convinced: it was the Lord. "I was a stranger and you welcomed me" (Matth. 25;35)

Sisters and brothers, the truth of the Scriptures will not save us, unless it is a truth that conditions and controls our hearts and our lives. I have tried to speak particularly from the biblical background - and I hope that it has been a salutary provocation for us all as we are strangers and sojourners "in the Lord".

Wolfgang Lorenz is a Baptist pastor in West Berlin, Federal Republic of Germany.

Notes

1. Norbert Bros, Situationen und Sprache der Minderheit im Petrus-Brief, CYROS, 1977.

2. W. Eisenblatter, Biblische Perspektiven zum Thema "Leben mit Auslandern", *Impulse*, Nr. 5, 1985.

3. Fluchtlinge und Asylsuchende in unserem Land, hrg. vom Kirchenamt EKD, EKD-Text Nr. 16, Hannover 1986.

4. Aktuelle Texte zur Asylrechts-Diskussion, epd-Documentation 38/86, Frankfurt/Main.

5. Interview mit dem Gerneralsekretar des BWA, Dr. Gerhard Claas, Gemeinde-jugendwerk - Aktuell, Nr. 2, 1986, S. 24ff, Hamburg.

6. Bischof Kamphaus, Hirtenbrief zur Asylfrage, Limburg, 1986

7. Resolution of the BWA Congress in Singapore, 1986.

8. Resolution of the 14. Baptist World Congress, Toronto: *Celebrating Christ's Presence Through the Spirit*, Nashville, Tennessee, USA. S. 241ff.

9. Wort der Bundesleitung an die Gemeinden zur Zituation der Asylanten, BEFG 1986.

10. Asyl in unserem Land, hgg. EkiBB (West), Berlin 1985

11. Refugees, No 35, hrsg. vom UNHCR. Genf 1986.

Human Rights Efforts Within the BWA
And the Reception Process

Per Midteide

I. The Problem

Baptists have an historical tradition concerning human rights issues that we like to be proud of. We have been in the forefront when principles of freedom and fundamental human rights were discussed and we can number among our leaders outstanding men and women who fought for human freedom from the time of the Anabaptists up to this century.

"What do Baptists stand for today in these matters?"

To answer this question it is very convenient to refer to the many resolutions accepted by the Baptist World Alliance through the years concerning burning issues within the area of human rights. In several papers presented to our Commission it has been demonstrated that there are a number of printed resolutions and other material from the Alliance proving that we really as a world body have been concerned about the violations of human rights, warfare and human suffering all over the world.

Important work is done on the national and local level by some Baptist groups or leaders. We know that the leadership of the BWA has played a vital role in a number of cases where violations of human rights have been taken up and problems solved. And yet - there is a considerable gap between the content of our resolutions, the good will and wish behind these strong words, and our ability to follow up the intentions of the resolutions within the BWA. The gap is no smaller when it comes to the relationship between the resolutions, the official BWA stand on the one hand and that which reaches the national Baptist conventions and local churches in a way that will cause any change in priorities, attitude and program making on the other.

We have to admit that questions concerning human rights, peace, social justice are *not* given the attention among Baptists in general as could be expected from our Baptist tradition. These issues are *not* given the attention among Baptists in general as it is given in the objectives of the Constitution of the BWA.

When this is our situation - no wonder we have a problem in regard to the reception process. The problem is rooted in our priorities - but is it not also rooted in our structure?

We do have a Commission on Human Rights within the Alliance. What can such a commission do about the problem of the reception process. What are we supposed to do or what do we have the right to do from the role we are asked to play within the Alliance?

II. The Position of the Human Rights Commission Within the Structure of the BWA

It is fair to say that the Human Rights Commission (alongside the other study commissions) has a rather weak position in the structure of the Alliance. The Commissions are not mentioned in the Constitution of the BWA - apart from the list of members of the General Council where study commissions may be represented: In the article VI, 2 of the Constitution it reads:"...Not more than twelve additional members, any of whom may be coopted by the General Council at any time, to serve until the conclusion of the next General meeting. In making such cooptions, the General Council shall give consideration to, but not limited to, representation of the committees, Division committees and study commissions which assist the Alliance in the work."

Accordingly the commissions are not a fundamental part of the BWA structure. This becomes even more evident when we look at the Bylaws of the Alliance. The Commissions are not mentioned by name even here. Article VII however deals with "Programs" which "shall be organized to promote and implement the objectives of the Alliance as set forth in Article II of the Constitution."

In VII, 2. we find "Program of assistance to the member bodies.." These programs are defined within four areas:

(1) Evangelism and Christian Education.
(2) Mission Strategy.
(3) Study and Research.
(4) Lay Development.

The aim of the Study and Research Division is "to bring about the exchange of ideas on topics relating to the Christian experience and mission; to encourage creative new solutions to the Christian mission in today's world."

To reach this aim the Division of Study and Research may establish study commissions (not more than five at any time). The members of these commissions will (in principle) be appointed by the General Secretary of the Alliance. However, it seems to be clear from the text in the Bylaws that it is up to the Division of Study and Research to decide which and how many commissions the Alliance needs. In fact without changing any part of the Constitution or the Bylaws of the Alliance, the work of the Commission on Human Rights can be terminated.

This seems to be the case even through the BWA clearly has stated as one of its basic objectives to "Act as an agency of reconciliation seeking peace for all persons, and uphold the claims of fundamental human rights, including full religious liberty." (Article II,5).

Furthermore, in the Bylaws are mentioned four fields or possibilities of cooperative action (separated from the point where the commissions are mentioned):

(1) Regional Fellowships (Federations).
(2) Relief and Development.
(3) Representation - to make the voice of Baptists heard in matters of human rights and religious liberty for all people.
(4) Cooperation - to make common cause with other religious or Christian bodies in areas of mutual concern.

Human Rights issues and the BWA concern for matters within this field seem to have a central position in the work of the Alliance. But the Commission on Human Rights seems to play almost no role in this work when we look at the structure. Programs and actions are the responsibility of the administration or the General Secretary and there seems to be no direct channel or link between the executives of the Alliance and the Commission on Human Rights.

It is often underlined in our commission that we are working within a *study commission* and that we are not in the position to take any action or to have any direct line of information or influence on any regional, national or local Baptist body. What we want to say, we have to present to the Council which will accept or not accept our motions or resolutions. What we want to do we have to appeal to the General Secretary to do (through the Study and Research Division or through the Council).

In our meeting in Singapore we experienced a clear tension coming to the surface: the tension between lectures, studies, and discussions on the one hand, and the expression of need for action and practical support to those groups who are suffering daily from the lack of very fundamental human rights. People from countries where the governments were suppressive, persecuting Christians and political opposition, were standing up in our Commission meeting challenging us. Some said: "we do not know what will happen to us when we return home... We don't need papers and study documents, we need active support from the Baptists of the world!"

It could of course be said that this tension would exist even if the BWA structure would allow the Commission to take concrete and practical action. It is evident that we never will be able to do what we should do in his field. However, I fear that if we do not face this tension constructively, the interest in the work of the Commission on Human Rights can easily diminish and our potential influence will be reduced - also because people who are sincerely interested in human rights and have a deeply felt concern for other people, feel they can use their efforts and their initiative better in another context.

III. How Is the Material On Human Rights Coming From the BWA Used In the Member Bodies?

In preparing this paper I wanted to know more about the fate of the resolutions and the lectures given in our commission meetings. I sent a questionnaire to each member of the commission asking some questions that I hoped would give a more precise picture of the situation.

22% of the Commission members responded. This was less than I expected but still I think the returned questionnaires give a representative picture of the level of reception in different parts of the world. Let me present a short summary of what was said in these responses (coming from Bangladesh, Canada, England, India, Nigeria, Norway, Switzerland and the USA (4).

The questions were:

1. To which extent do the people in the local churches of your Convention know about the work of the Commission on Human Rights?

2. In which ways are the resolutions from the BWA Council meeting in general and the resolutions on Human Rights issues in particular made known to the Baptist Union(s) and local Churches in your country?

3. Is the material from the Human Rights Commission or the discussions there in any way reflected in the life of the Church?

The material in the responses showed:

1. Two or three members indicated that they themselves had shared some information when visiting churches or written some articles about the work of the commission. But the overall impression is very clear and simple: Baptists

in general know very little if anything about the work of our commission.

2. There seems to be no regular procedures. In the US the resolutions are occasionally printed in Baptist state papers. In some countries the resolutions are reported at the national Baptist convention or council. In some European countries the resolutions are printed in Baptist papers - in other countries this is not so. The same seems to be true in other parts of the world.

3. One replied that the young people were happy to see the BWA being concerned with these issues. Some said that similar questions were discussed in some churches and taken up in some magazines, but this was done independently of what is done in the BWA context. In fact it seems that the material presented in our commission does not reach any Baptist body outside the commission itself.

IV. Obstacles

If we want to intensify the work of the Commission on Human Rights and the influence this commission can have in Baptist life and work, and facilitate the reception process, there are a number of obstacles that have to be overcome. I want to list the most important of them as I see them: Non-involvement, Structure, Communication, Theology and Politics.

1. Non-involvement.

Especially in western countries the society is growing colder, people become estranged from one another and an individualistic culture is causing people to be less sensitive to what happens to other people. The interest is focused on oneself and one's family and close friends. "Others have to look after themselves . . . I will have to take care of my own problems first . . ."

We get to know so much of human suffering that we can not take it in. so many are exposed to a kind of immunization that prevents them from even thinking of getting involved in questions of human rights. They don't care, they don't think it makes any difference, they don't think it is their business. This also has to do with overemphasizing the personalistic understanding of the Christian faith. The Christian responsibility for people in the community and the corporate responsibility for evil structures in different parts of the world is completely neglected.

What this amounts to is non-involvement. People are indifferent to sufferings of others and this could be the greatest danger - also for us as Baptists.

2. Structure.

We have already pointed out how the structure of the Baptist World Alliance easily may represent a hindrance for a Commission on Human Rights. The commission is defined as a "study commission" with a very weak base for its existence and with no formal channels to reach any recipient outside itself.

Whenever a critical situation concerning human rights occurs anywhere in the world the commission has to mandate to take any action in order to help or to protest. Certainly we do know that some quiet diplomacy is done by the BWA administration in order to help individuals (and we are aware that this in some cases has been very helpful), but the BWA does not have resources to make specific human right cases a high priority matter of concern. With the limited staff in Washington it is hard to see how this could be possible.

The structures can also be an obstacle on the national level. If the leadership is not sufficiently motivated to give the necessary attention to issues concerning human rights in Convention or Council meetings as well as on the local level, what we say or do in the BWA context will have little or no influence.

As the link between the BWA Council and the smaller Baptist unions often is a one or two-person contact we see how vulnerable this process can be.

3. Communication.

Obviously the commission members themselves will have to ask critical questions concerning their own role in the communication process. The same is true for the BWA office and the national offices.

a) The commission members are not all of them present at the meetings. Usually less than 50% of them can be there. We know that the problem of funds to cover the travel expenses is the main reason for this but still it represents a serious problem for communicating what happens in the commission.

b) We also have to admit that commission members often are far too passive in communicating appeals and messages from the commission or BWA in general on serious human rights issues.

c) The report from the commission meetings including papers and other relevant additional material is often sent to the commission members a long time after the meetings took place.

d) The material sent from the BWA to the national Baptist headquarters stays in the office of the executives and nobody knows that important material really is available.

e) There is no direct line from the BWA or the commissions to Baptist weekly magazines or papers. The editors don't know which issues have been discussed.

So far the best we could hope for was to have resolutions printed in Baptist papers. But resolutions definitely are not the best way of communicating a message to our churches. Often they just turn people off. Resolutions aim at encouraging churches to take practical steps, but they need to be motivated. They need a deep understanding of *why this is important*. We have to communicate the urgency of these issues and the Christian responsibility for standing up for the suffering people. This is a serious problem clearly felt on all levels in the life of the church. We sense it in the local church as well as in the council meetings of the BWA.

4. Theology.

We are talking about the Church and its Mission. This mission is often defined as *proclaiming the gospel of Jesus Christ to the world*. This is not the place for a discussion of the right understanding of mission but we all know that a number of devoted Christians stress the given definition heavily and say that nothing should divert our attention from this one and only obligation. Nobody will say that we do not also have an obligation to help people in need - but this is often felt to be a secondary responsibility which is not a part of the real nature of the Mission of the Church - it is understood to be an optional addition to the real task of a Christian.

The process that brings an understanding of the Christian responsibility as including the totality of man - not only his/her spiritual life - is moving too slowly. At least in the West the suspicion of not being sufficiently Biblical or Evangelical has too often emerged when this message has been focused. We can even identify an opposite trend attacking those who encourage the churches to engage in the work for human rights as an integrated part of our Christian responsibility, saying that they mislead the believers - especially if this work is done in cooperation with non-Christians!

Therefore, it is important that people like Dr. John R. W. Stott who, I believe, has confidence in different groups within the Christian Church, makes it very clear when speaking about the Mission of the Church:

> "Therefore, if we love our neighbour as God made him, we must inevitably be concerned for his total welfare, the good of his soul, his body and his community. Moreover, it is this vision of man as a social being, which obliges us to add a *political* dimension to our social concern." (*Christian Mission in the Modern World*, 1975, p. 30).

and he continues:

> "And there is no reason why, in pursuing this quest, we should not join hands with all men of good will, even if they are not Christians."

In a number of cases reservations which have been labeled "theological reservations" boil down to one word: FEAR. Engagement in and discussions to the church of human rights issues are in many cases bound to be controversial. And many churches cannot handle controversies: "We have enough controversial issues as it is and we don't want to run the risk of unrest, or may be even splits over human rights issues . . ." This fear, which I clearly see as lack of faith, very often arises from a deep concern for avoiding the church getting involved in politics.

5. Politics.

The conviction of separation of Church and State should give Baptists a better chance of being free to speak up against persecution, suppression and an unjust rule wherever it appears. But to many Baptists the "doctrine" of separation of Church and State has created an almost paralytic attitude to vital issues in the society. It is all right to talk about Christian responsibility for human suffering in general, but as soon as this general talk becomes specific, gets faces, names and addresses, then it is a job for politicians . . .

This was clearly demonstrated when the Lutheran Church in my own country published a lengthy statement on the question of the involvement of the Christian Church in peace efforts. It became controversial, not because the Church wa talking about peace in general, but because the statement recommended concrete and specific steps taken to reduce the nuclear threat.

Not a single case of violation of human rights is non-political and it is essential for our churches to realize this and at the same time to understand that this doesn't mean that the church will end up as a political battlefield because of involvement in questions of human rights.

We readily admit that the political aspect of human rights issues may represent a problem. This is felt also in the Commission on Human Rights and in the BWA where for example the tension between East and West sometimes can cause problems for the wording of resolutions. Often it is easier to criticize what happens in smaller countries than what is done by super-powers with many representatives on the Council.

Every piece of bread given to the hungry, every appeal for release of a Christian *or a non-Christian* political prisoner has political implications. The principle of separation of Church and State gives the churches a chance to speak a prophetic word in our time and age - to be the voice of the voiceless.

It is difficult to be objective, to keep the right balance in important and complicated questions. This is a matter of great concern also to our commission. One of the questionnaires returned pointed out that the resolutions of the BWA would be more readily received if they were more objective and not biased in any direction - it was felt that the resolutions were anti-American. It *is* important to aim at the greatest objectivity possible. On the other hand, a government which is criticized and rightly so, will always accuse any resolution or criticism for lack of objectivity!

We should also take another fact into consideration: In a number of countries the authorities will look upon any attempt to focus on human rights with suspicion - if it is not directed towards groups or nations this authority regards as enemies. This fact in itself represents a serious violation of the freedom of speech and is an indication that the government has something to hide in this respect.

V. What Can Be Done?

A number of ideas have come from commission members and I am going to include some of them in this section (without giving anybody credit by name...)

1. Other churches are also working to find a better structure through which they can be more effective in this field. The Methodist Church does not have any specific department for human rights, but they have included this concern within the Department for Social Responsibility. It also seems that they have a larger staff at the UN Church Centre. In the US they play an important role in the Human Rights Office of the National Council of Churches and the United Methodist Church also supports Amnesty International directly - using their material in local churches. They do organize groups working with specific countries, like the group in the US working on South Africa.

The Lutherans have one assistant general secretary of the Lutheran World Federation working full time with human rights questions. They seem to be concerned about this work, not as an isolated field of attention in the church, but integrated in the regular life of the church. They have set aside one Sunday during the time of Advent and one of the Christmas days for prayer services for persecuted people all over the world.

The Roman Catholic Church instituted in 1967 a new forum for social, ethical and human rights questions named "Justitia et Pax". The headquarters are in Rome but this department is supposed to have local committees in every diocese. In my country they have instituted a *"World Peace"* Sunday where the concern for peace and other human rights are reflected in the liturgy. They also had seminars for church leaders on the national and local level to present a more wholistic understanding of the Christian responsibility in this world.

2. I think we need to discuss with the leadership of the BWA the role of the Commission on Human Rights aiming at a more effective way of working for human rights within the frame of the Alliance. If this cannot be done within the context of a commission, we need to discuss what status could be given to the work for human rights within the BWA.

3. The role of the commission members will have to be upgraded or intensified. It is important that the members are people who have a sincere interest in and concern for human rights as well as time and energy to do something about it - including visiting churches to speak about our Christian responsibility in this field and to present material from the BWA as well as other sources.

It would also be worthwhile to look into the procedure of appointment commission members.

4. Better information concerning BWA material and more efficient distribution.

a) Papers presented in the Commission on Human Rights could be printed (perhaps in a concentrated form) in national Baptist magazines.

b) BWA communication people should be present in the Commission meetings and press releases written immediately after the General Council and Study Commission meetings.

c) Annual Human Rights Newsletters distributed to Baptist Unions or even to individuals upon request.

5. The commission members could establish a network where important news concerning human rights, prayer concerns and experiences could be shared. When a critical situation occurs somewhere, the members of the commission could alarm the chairman of the commission or the BWA administration.

6. The Commission could try to make available human rights material: films, books, papers, resolutions or program ideas for practical steps to be taken by local groups. These resources could be offered through the BWA office to national conventions or churches.

7. Sermon-suggestions on human rights questions could be made available for pastors. The Commission could produce programs for special services. Topics for discussions at conferences for ministers and Convention meetings could be offered. This could be printed in a leaflet and offered to Unions and pastors.

8. Each Baptist Union should be encouraged to appoint a national committee working with human rights. Contact should be established between these national committees and the Commission on Human Rights.

9. The work for human rights should be more closely connected with

Christian Education aiming at presenting the Gospel not only in personal terms but also in corporate and global terms.

In cooperation with other Baptist organizations (Youth Department, Commission on Christian Ethics, Evangelism and Education Committees...) Bible Study material where human rights issues are incorporated should be produced.

10. A closer contact with agencies working for human rights outside the Baptist family would be helpful. (Amnesty International, World council of Churches, United Nations, etc.)

11. One Sunday each year is suggested as Human Rights Sunday. More should be done to encourage churches all over the world to take this opportunity to pray for all those who suffer from violations of elementary human rights which most of us so easily take for granted.

Per Midteide is Professor of Practical Theology at the Norwegian Baptist Seminary, Trondheim, Norway.

The B.W.A. Opportunity at the United Nations: Let's Make Baptist Influence More Effective

Carl W. Tiller

Nature and Scope of the Opportunity

Objectives of the Baptist World Alliance

The Baptist World Alliance is a religious organization, composed of more than 140 church bodies with a constituency in over 100 countries. Its constitution identifies eight objectives. Some of the objectives are readily seen as "spiritual" or "churchly".[1]

Other objectives are directed towards the application of faith in the direction of dealing with world problems: "act as an agency of reconciliation seeking peace . . . ," "uphold the claims of fundamental human rights," "serve as a channel for expressing Christian social concern . . . ," and serve also as a channel for "alleviating human need." Peace, human rights, social justice, humanitarian activities — these are as much as the objectives of the B.W.A. as are the more "spiritual" or "churchly" aims on which attention is often focused.

The B.W.A. has established a Division of Evangelism and Education to lead activities which might be called "churchly," and a Division of Communications to help maintain fellowship within its own ranks. It has a Division of Baptist World Aid for humanitarian assistance. But the issues of peace, human rights, and social justice are not committed to any structural entity with responsibility for *action*; they are at most perceived as objects of *study* within a Division of Study and Research.

Purposes of the United Nations

The United Nations if a secular organization, composed of 159 states and responsible to their respective governments. The preamble to its Charter lifts up four "ends": international peace, fundamental human rights, justice, and social progress (the latter being defined as "better standards of life in larger freedom"). The U.N. has established a General Assembly, three Councils, and various commissions and committees for the tasks, and a Secretariat of U.N. employees (international civil servants) to "staff" the structure. The activities are based at three sites where staff is permanently stationed: New York (headquarters), Geneva, and Vienna.

The phrase "the United Stations system" embraces the U.N. itself and a number of specialized agencies (other international governmentally-comprised bodies) such as the Food and Agriculture Organization, the International Labour Organization, the U.N. Educational, Scientific, and Cultural Organization, the World Health Organization, and the International Atomic Energy Agency.[2]

The U.N. includes, in addition to much relating to security and peace, and the work of the specialized agencies, such activities as those of a Disaster Relief Coordinator, a High Commissioner for Refugees, an Environment Program, a Children's Fund, and a Centre for Human Rights.

From the first Baptist World Congress after the U.N. was formed (Copenhagen, 1947), the B.W.A. has spoken its approval of the U.N. concept, and has given encouragement to U.N. aims and activities.

Consultative Status at the U.N.

Article 71 of the United Nations Charter provides in part that:

> "The Economic and Social Council may make suitable arrangements for consultation with non-governmental organizations which are concerned with matters within its competence."

The granting and continuation of "consultative status"[3] for a non-governmental organization (NG) is discretionary with the U.N. The status is coveted by many private, non-profit bodies. It is not easy to obtain; some applications are rejected and others deferred each biennium. Organizations in consultative status (classified in three levels by the U.N.) have the privilege of addressing various U.N. commissions and committees, and of having their communications to the U.N. circulated to all delegations — sometimes only in the original language, sometimes translated into the various official languages of the U.N.

The General Council of the B.W.A. (at that time called the Executive Committee), after a long period of examining and deliberating over the matter, voted in 1973 to seek consultative status at the U.N. The B.W.A. request was granted by the U.N. on April 22, 1974. At the U.N.'s recurring review of B.W.A. status, at four-year intervals, the situation has been continued without interruption.

Comparatively few NGO's in consultative status are religious in nature. The Vatican, enjoying the unusual position of being a "city-state" as well as a religious entity, has a special role. Several Roman Catholic organizations, such as Pax Christi, have consultative status. There is an Eastern Orthodox NGO. Among Protestants, the Baptist World Alliance, the Salvation Army, the Lutheran World Federation, and an organization of Methodist women have been granted consultative status. In addition several multi-denominational bodies are so accredited; these include the World Conference on Religion and Peace, the Christian Peace Conference, and the Churches' Commission on International Affairs (WCC).

The B.W.A.-U.N. Relationship in Practice

A good relationship with the U.N. can be carried on properly only in person; it cannot be done from a distance, hence a consultative status calls, as a minimum, for someone to be at hand frequently at U.N. headquarters.

The task of liaison with the U.N. has been carried on mainly by an unpaid volunteer in New York under the general direction of a staff member at the Washington (McLean) headquarters. When the volunteer, a homemaker named Eleanore Schnurr, was hospitalized with cancer in 1980-81, Carl Tiller, then employed full-time elsewhere in New York City, became a spare-time substitute for her. She resumed her role when her disease went into remission, and Tiller continued in "partnership" with her. Her death in December 1988 left Tiller (by that time, retired) as the lone spokesperson for the B.W.A. at U.N.-New York.

B.W.A. representatives at New York meet with other NGO representatives in committees, task forces, and working groups where they can benefit from an exchange of information and viewpoints. Schnurr served in the leadership of several such NGO groups; Tiller was at one time the Treasurer of the Religious NGO Committee, and currently is on the executive subcommittee of the NGO Committee on Disarmament.

Eleanor Schnurr was good at one-on-one relationships with ambassadors and U.N. staff. The B.W.A. has made a few formal interventions, in writing or orally; none in Council, some in committees. The B.W.A. did submit its resolutions of a pertinent nature to the Second Special Session of the General Assembly on Disarmament, and to the U.N.-sponsored international conference on Disarmament and Development. The B.W.A. witness in NGO committees has been significant, though not easily measured.

B.W.A. representatives have sought to keep the B.W.A.- constituency informed — Schnurr in the early years through an occasional "International Corner" newsletter which examined a few subjects in depth; Tiller in the decade of the 1980's through brief news notes on a wide variety of subject matter. Those notes, 800 to 1000 words at a time, and up to 70 times a year, are sent to McLean, intended for dissemination to the Baptist press and to B.W.A. leadership.

Given the mutuality of interests, the U.N. expects non-governmental organizations in consultative status to work at advancing common goals. A NGO representative is likely to gain a good hearing at the U.N. if he/she reports that the organization's constituents are active in dealing with the problem on which an NGO viewpoint is being presented.[4]

The B.W.A. has not done well in this respect. At the General Council meeting in 1988, a plea was made from the rostrum for Member Bodies to give the New York representatives information on what Baptists are doing about matters on the U.N. agenda, such as drug abuse, illiteracy, the need for clean water in developing countries, the need for the enhancement of women, etc. At the time of reporting statistics on churches and membership, B.W.A. Member Bodies were invited this past year to supply information on resolutions adopted relating to U.N. interests. But information on what we *do* (not just what we *say*) is not available.

Eleanor Schnurr was often at the U.N. five days a week, and sometimes all day and into the evening (the U.N. keeps late hours!). The present writer is limited by various factors to one or two short visits a week. At least two volunteers or one person employed half-time is needed in order to recover for the B.W.A. the prestige which it had been building.

For the Geneva and Vienna posts, the B.W.A. named as representatives persons who were otherwise fully employed, and in the case of Geneva someone at a distance - Thorwald Lorenzen of Rueschlikon for Geneva, Alphonse and Irene Lamprecht for Vienna. (Baptist churches in western Switzerland are not affiliated with the Baptist Union of Switzerland or the B.W.A.)

When an U.N.-sponsored international conference has been held elsewhere (for example, Nairobi, Bangkok, Rome) a local Baptist leader has sometimes been asked to observe on behalf of the B.W.A. This writer is not informed of cases where they were authorized to speak. Only rarely have such representatives reported to the B.W.A. on the event.

Activities of Other Religious NGO's

Many of the other NGO's in consultative status, and some which do not have that status, have full-time paid employees at the U.N. in New York; some do so at Geneva and Vienna. The Lutherans, Quakers, and Roman Catholics are outstanding in that respect; some non-Christian bodies — Jewish, Muslim, Buddhists, Baha'i — also provide good coverage at the U.N. Several American NGO's, with only observer status, have full-time "lobbyists" at the U.N.-New York, among them the Presbyterians, the United Church of Christ, the Unitarian-Universalists, and the Evangelical Covenant Church of America.

The Lutheran World Federation and more than one Roman Catholic group have made oral presentations to U.N. bodies — most noteworthy to meetings in Geneva on human rights, but also to meetings in New York on disarmament.

The substance of the presentation and the previous build-up of confidence in the person speaking are, of course, important. Also relevant to effectiveness are: the interest of the NGO body in the U.N. (as evidenced by the extent of its representation), the recognition by Member States' delegations that part of their own citizenry is represented by the speaker, and the evidence that the speaker presents that the NGO and its affiliates are actively pursuing the mutual objectives.

With regard to specific programs within the U.N. system, particular NGO representatives have established special rapport with a U.N. agency. In disaster relief some NGO's ("private volunteer agencies" in disaster relief parlance) have good working relationships with the U.N., especially on the transportation of relief goods. On development, the U.N. agency regularly publishes articles about NGO activities in the developing world. This is also the case on women's and children's interests, and on public health matters.

Some NGO's have responded well to the entreaties of the U.N. Environment Programme that their people be encouraged to attend to their responsibilities for stewardship of the earth on at least one Sabbath each year.

Recommendations for B.W.A. Action at U.N. Sites

The Baptists can impact the world more effectively if at the three major U.N. sites the B.W.A. would:

—Strengthen its witness by having at least two volunteers or at least a half-time employee at New York, and a minimum of weekly volunteer visits to Geneva and Vienna.

—Keep before the U.N. Secretariat and the diplomatic delegations the relevant information on the breadth and depth of the B.W.A. constituency.[5]

—Intervene more frequently in U.N. meetings where the B.W.A. is welcome, utilizing a B.W.A. officer for that purpose on occasion.

—"Lobby" more promptly and effectively for the viewpoints expressed in resolutions of a Baptist World Congress, the General Council, and the Executive Committee.

—Demonstrate to the U.N. and the diplomatic delegations that Baptists are doing something constructive (more than just adopting resolutions) about the concerns which the B.W.A. and the U.N. share.

—Represent the views of a B.W.A. Member Body, as expressed in its own resolutions, more often.[6]

B.W.A. representations, except when limited to speaking on behalf of a particular affiliate, must always be constrained by the B.W.A."'s postures on an issue, and by the limitation that the B.W.A. must not bring embarrassment or increased oppression on a Member Body by an inadvertence at the U.N.

Suggestions to Implement the Foregoing Recommendations

In order to have a more effective Baptist witness at the U.N., implementing actions in B.W.A. structures and practices would be helpful:

1. (a) The B.W.A. might change its provision relating to human rights and other U.N. matters from a "*study* commission" to an *action* body.[7] (b) An alternative: The B.W.A. might create a commission to provide guidance and

"moral support" for the U.N. representation.[8] It should be authorized to hold telephone conferences as well as meetings closely aligned with the Executive Committee meetings.

2. Leadership on B.W.A.-U.N. matters might be recognized more fully in the job titles and descriptions of the assigned headquarters staff member.

3. Each Member Body should be requested to appoint a leader to act as its liaison on U.N. matters.

4. Representatives of the B.W.A. at the three major U.N. cities, and the U.N. liaison person in the B.W.A. Secretariat at McLean should all be in regular communication with one another. Training for such persons would be in order; also a consultation at the time of General Council meetings.

5. Modest financial provision for additional travel expense would be welcome, particularly in the case of representation at Geneva where inter-city travel is necessary to the handling of B.W.A. interests at the U.N.

6. The B.W.A. could arrange for more complete coverage of U.N.-sponsored conferences held away from the three U.N. sites, and for very prompt reports by the B.W.A. representatives at such conferences.

7. Consideration of contemporary world problems, from the viewpoint of Christian/Baptist insights and the objectives in the B.W.A. constitution, could have a place on the agenda of each B.W.A. General Council meeting.

Carl Tiller, of Teaneck, New Jersey, USA, a volunteer representative of the B.W.A. at the United Nations in New York City.

Notes

1. The use of the words "spiritual" and "churchly" for some of the B.W.A. objectives should not be construed to imply that the other objectives are any less spiritual. In fact, the other types of objectives occupied much of the B.W.A."s attention historically. Almost from the beginning, negotiations for religious liberty were a major activity, after 1920 relief became major, and after 1939 religious liberty interests were caught up in a concern for the larger field of human rights.

2. In this paper the words "United Nations" and the initials "U.N." are occasionally used to include the specialized agencies as well as the U.N. itself.

3. Consultative status granted by the Economic and Social Council should not be confused with the observer status which has been given by the U.N. Department of Public Information to various national bodies, mostly American (including three Baptist conventions in the United States). Their accreditation to the U.N. resembles in many ways the accreditation of press representatives in that they may observe what happens and they have access to U.N. documentation, but are not invited to present their viewpoints either in writing or orally.

4. For example, acceptable activity could include: teaching in Church School against the use of narcotic drugs and against sexual promiscuity, making literacy efforts a part of a mission in places where educational opportunities are limited, helping opium farmers to shift to a substitute cash crop, constructing residences for the homeless, taking part in specific efforts against apartheid, etc.

5. The Baptist World Alliance is the most widespread Protestant family of faith (the Lutheran World Federation exceeds the B.W.A. in its membership count, but is

in fewer places; no other Protestant group comes close to the B.W.A. or L.W.f.). The B.W.A. has a larger constituency than most secular NGO's. The B.W.A. is the one NGO, religious or secular, with the greatest spread of constituency among nations of East and West, North and South; B.W.A.'s greatest strength numerically is in the U.S.A., the U.S.S.R., India, Brazil, and Nigeria. What a variety of political, economic, and cultural situations!

6. B.W.A. representatives in New York have presented British Baptist and Italian Baptist views to a U.N. body (once for each), clearly noting that they were the views of an affiliate and did not necessarily represent a B.W.A. viewpoint.

7. The beginnings of the present B.W.A. Division of Evangelism and Education were in the "study commission" mode.

8. A more advanced proposal would be to create a B.W.A. Division, with a Division Committee and assigned staff responsibility, for each of the "neglected" objectives named in the Constitution: (a) reconciliation and peace, (b) human rights and freedoms, and (c) social concerns generally. If this were done, it might be appropriate to create a commission on the U.N. which would include representatives from those three division committees, plus one from B.W.A., and one each from the departments of women, youth, and men.

Commission on
The Ministry of the Laity

The Commission on the Ministry of the Laity has its focus on all God's people fully sharing the ministry of the church.

During the past quinquennium the Commission has divided its sessions between theological principles related to the laity and practical or methodological aspects, including illustrations of how ministry of laity is implemented. It has throughout this time been the sincere wish of the Commission to take advantage of regional and local contributions available from the different areas of the world where the meetings have taken place.

The Commission has also had its attention particularly directed to ways of ministry that can be fulfilled in times of crisis or strife. More than once, the location of the meetings has made the regional contributions illustrative of ministry during critical circumstances. Such was the case when in Singapore a report was given from the Philippines after civil strife, and also in Naussau as participants from Nicaragua and El Salvador gave their testimonies of ministering in their areas, suffering under ongoing political pressure.

In the meetings in Yugoslavia, a report was given from Lebanon. That presentation by Mrs. Mona Khauli is included here.

Regional contributions have exposed the Commission to a variety of ways in which churches are carrying out their ministry through their members—the laity. In Singapore the Rainbow Community Baptist Church shared its success in growth through outreach activities by a well-trained group of laypersons. In Amman, Jordan we were exposed to the necessity of laypeople's ministry in churches which are extremely small and which serve within certain restrictions. From the Baptists in Yugoslavia we learned not only that lay-led congregations are a necessity due to the limited number of members, but also that some Yugoslavian Baptist groups prefer lay leadership on principle.

Training programs and tools for equipping the laity for ministry are another area of interest for the Commission. A presentation was given describing how a Mexico City congregation offers a complete program for training members for personal evangelism, spiritual growth and caring ministry. In Yugoslavia, a nationwide program for theological education by extension and lay training was described. A list of programs offered at a number of institutions is being prepared to facilitate the sharing of ideas, curriculum, books and other resources. This list should be available in 1990.

The Commission on the Ministry of the Laity is happy to present these papers hwich deal with theological and practical dimensions of laity in ministry. George Peck of Andover Newton Theological Seminary, who has contributed considerably to the work of this Commission, has paid particular attention to the right of laity to be included in theological training. He is the author of the paper "Toward a Theology of Christian Ministry". Ruth Sampson of Melbourne, Australia, who has experienced a variety of ministries — congregation-centered as well as community based — addresses an extremely vital issue in her paper "United or Separated in the Ministry of the Church". Birgit Karlsson of Sweden in her paper "Clergy and Laity Trained for Their Ministry", makes a plea for a deeper understanding of the unity of the church in its ministry, for its spiritual growth and for its mission to the world.

Two papers included illustrate the work of the Commission on specific areas of the ministry of the laity. "Christians in the Workplace" is a theme addressed by both George Peck and by John Sundquist, Valley Forge, USA.

Finally, we share on of the presentations offered on the milnistry of laity during times and in areas of strife. Mona Khauli of Beirut, Lebanon, for more than fifteen years working in Christian social ministry, presents her experiences referring to the Scriptpure passage "I shall not die, but live, and achieve the work of the Lord".

The work of the Commission on the Ministry of the Laity encompasses a wide area in which to face these issues, searching out both methods and programs and sharing both successes and failures. To focus on laity in the life and mission of the church is of great importance to many—yes, we believe of importance to all—since we are all made the people of God.

Birgit Karlsson

Birgit Karlsson is General Secretary of the Baptist Union of Sweden.

Toward a Theology of Christian Ministry

George Peck

Introduction

The word "toward" in the title must be taken very seriously. To claim to have developed a full theology of Christian ministry in one short paper would be presumptuous. I can hope only to set down an outline of what I believe has to be taken into account and to suggest directions which ought to be pursued in filling that outline. I propose also to limit myself to a consideration of the *biblical* bases for a theology of ministry, and I shall therefore not touch at all upon the large body of historical and constructive material which would have to be brought into a complete study. Even in dealing with Scripture I shall have to be brief, given the time available for presentation and discussion.

I shall first review the Bible's understanding of ministry in summary fashion. From that quick biblical survey I shall next choose the fundamental image, namely "the body of Christ", and offer a series of reflections upon it as it concerns the church's ministry. It is from this latter exercise that I believe we shall derive the most instruction and profit in our exploration of the ministry of the whole people of God in the world and in the household of faith.

I. Ministry in the Bible

If anything is clear it is that the Bible provides us with no absolute "blueprints" for the structuring of ministry in the church today. By that I mean that we cannot find in Scripture patterns of ministry which can be carried unchanged into our time in such a way as to provide us with unquestionable prescriptions to be followed in detail. There are many significant theological and spiritual injunctions about the nature of ministry, its meaning and purpose, but any attempt to take a supposedly uniform biblical "order of ministry" as that on which our contemporary manner of doing things can be based is sure to fail, for the simple reason that the historical situation of the people of God in ancient times is so different from ours that the transfer of what was appropriate then to conditions in our different places must result in distortion. It must also be stressed that one important factor in the biblical state of affairs is that patterns of ministry had simply not yet been firmly set. They were fluid and in the process of developing; they were also not the same in every church or in every region in which the church was established. That a certain list of ministries is found in a letter to the church in Corinth, for example, cannot be taken to mean that the same ministries could be expected necessarily to occur in other churches.

Indeed, it is evident as one reads the New Testament that there was considerable variety in the way in which different ministries were understood and expressed from area to area. Even within the seventy years or so represented in the New Testament documents there was plainly a shift in patterns of ministry as the church matured and began to adapt itself to changing conditions. The impression given by the later documents is that ministry is still emerging in form and style as the church moves toward the future. The notion that the Bible as a whole, or the New Testament in particular, can be used as a point by point guide to specific types and structures of ministry today does not take sufficiently into account the realities of biblical interpretation and the dynamic character of the history of the early Christian community.

With this as background, let us now look in summary fashion at what the Bible has to say about ministry, in preparation for our examination of the implications for ministry of Paul's characterization of the church as "the Body of Christ".

A. Old Testament

We can use the Old Testament for our purposes only indirectly, but there are nonetheless important affirmations to be found in Israel's literature which both undergird much in the New Testament and present us with interesting pointers and challenges today. In the Old Testament, if anyone is called to ministry it is the *whole people*, Israel. Again and again it is stressed that Israel has been elected, chosen by God in order that the whole community might acknowledge, worship, and serve God in the midst of the nations. It is Israel as a unity, as a collective body, which is called to be a light to others, to bear witness to the name and purposes of Yahweh throughout the earth. (Is. 43:1-13; Ps. 67, 126) It is only in that context and under that qualification that particular individuals are summoned to specific roles: religious leaders (Moses), military leaders (Joshua), judges (Gideon, Deborah), priests (Aaron), kings (David), prophets (Elijah, Jeremiah). All Israelites are called as part of the people, all are called to serve the Lord in their position among the people (the life of the nation depends on that), and some are specially called to positions of leadership within the nation, in order that as a whole Israel might fulfill the intention of God.

B. New Testament

The overall pattern discernible in the Old Testament is not unlike that which is to be found also in the New Testament. Here as well we find the stress upon the calling first of the *church* to the ministry of Christ, with the individual ministries of the members expressed and realized as part of the embodiment of the service and witness of the whole. It is this above all that the image of the Body of Christ makes clear. But before we draw out the implications of this image, let us look briefly at what may be found regarding individual ministries in the New Testament, the provisos outlined above being kept in mind.

If anyone were to imagine that by simply listing the ministries mentioned in the New Testament we would have provided ourselves with all we need to know about structuring ministry today, he or she would have failed to observe how complex the picture in fact is. For instance there are several positions of leadership referred to, together with a variety of titles. There are the twelve apostles, but the word "apostle" is also found in other places under circumstances which suggest that it was not at all limited to those who had been physically with the Lord. (Acts 14:14; Rom. 16:7) Was it intended that the church should continue to be led by "apostles" or was this an office appropriate to the founding period but not beyond it? There is no plain injunction one way or the other on this issue, and there is evidence that the use of the term was already fading as the New Testament time comes to an end. Certainly the title is not used later, and eventually comes to be restricted to those who had been specially called for particular ministries having to do with the establishment and spread of the church in the original, formative years.

Or consider the interesting situation with "elders" and "bishops". For the most part in the New Testament they are barely distinguished, and several times they are explicitly intertwined. For example, in Acts 20:17 and 28, Paul addresses the elders of the Ephesian church, and refers to their role as one involving "oversight" of the church (i.e. the elders are *episkopoi* or bishops). Similarly, Titus is instructed to appoint elders in Crete (1:5), but in the same context they are immediately referred to as "bishops" (1:7). For the most part it seems that the word "bishop" is actually being used to denote a leadership role in a logical congregation (i.e. not having to do with the outreach of the kind associated with the use of the term "bishop" in some denominations today). When reference is made to a "bishop" in I Tim. 3:2 or Titus 1:7, the office involved is actually that of the elder in a local church. To add to the complexcity, it is worth noting that in I Peter, the apostle, who might have been expected to have thought of himself as a bishop, actually calls himself a "fellow elder" (5:1). (In other words, apostle, bishop, and elder can all be pointing to the same person!) It would be very hard indeed to find in all this a blueprint for modelling ministry in the contemporary church.

And what are we to make of lists which include expressions such as prophet, evangelist, healer, administrator, pastor, teacher, miracle worker, discerner of spirits, deacon, speaker, leader (cf. I Cor. 12: 12ff. Eph. 4:4-16, I Pet. 4:10-11, Rom. 12:6-8)? The question is made the more pertinent when we recall (as was pointed out earlier) that by no means every church contained the same group of offices. It is possible, for example, that some churches did not use the title "elder", while others did; there is no evidence that the gifts of the Spirit were uniform throughout the New Testament churches, scattered as they were from one end of the Mediterranean to the other.

In order to give some unity to this rather confusing collection of data, I think it is worthwhile to attempt some generalizations, which I offer in rather staccato fashion.

1. The New Testament churches seem to have been more concerned with function in ministry than with position and status. That is, there were certain tasks to be performed on behalf of the community, and the Spirit called people to carry them out. As the tasks varied, the callings and the ministries changed with conditions and needs. Little, if anything, of the detail was meant to be "fixed in concrete".

2. It is very hard to find in the New Testament the pattern according to which each congregation had one "pastor" as its primary leader. Certainly it is not appropriate in New Testament terms to apeak of "the minister" of the church and to mean the "pastor" in our sense today. Of that usage the New Testament knows nothing at all. Probably churches had multiple "pastors" (in the sense of primary leaders). At times "elder" is the preferred term here, while "bishop" is also used. The chief ministry of such people was probably to preside at the Lord's Supper. They do not appear to have been "the preachers" in a congregation as we would think of them now. The form with which we are so familiar (each congregation with its "pastor", assisted in some cases by various "associate pastors") is clearly a later development, having no exact parallel in the New Testament. That is not to rule it invalid, but it is certainly to suggest that it is not sacrosanct.

3. Since in the New Testament, ministry is not associated in any significant way with status or position, the emphasis is not upon rights or powers or even authority, but upon service to God, to the Gospel, and to one's fellow-members in the community of faith. If a special standing or authority of even

power is to be linked with particular ministries, this is under no circumstances an end in itself or a privilege to be used for the benefit of the individual. It is justifiable solely as the necessary means to carry out the vocation which one has been given in the Spirit.

If we are to get at the true heart of a theology of ministry in a New Testament form, we cannot do it simply by gathering the New Testament data about the particular shapes which ministry assumed in the earliest churches. We shall make more progress, I believe, if we turn instead to the fundamental theological principles which are to be found at certain key points in the New Testament's witness, one example being the concept of "the priesthood of all believers" which occurs in two important texts (I Pet. 2:9; Rev. 1:5-6). The clear implication that all Christians are "ministers" before God on behalf of others, or that all believers are called to be the means (the "media)) by which others are blessed and brought into touch with Christ (the traditional role of priests), could be drawn out in ways full of challenge and instructive import for the church today. But for the moment I am content to leave the exploration of this possibility to someone else. I have found my inspiration in recent years more in the study of the meaning of the image of "the Body of Christ", and it is to that image that I now wish to turn.

II. The Body of Christ and the Meaning of Ministry

The church is depicted as the Body of Christ in I Cor. 12:4-27 and Eph. 4:1-16. A careful study of these passages, together with concentrated reflections on the implications of the Body, bring to light, I believe, a powerful, and potentially revolutionary theology of ministry. There is within the image a certain logic which gives rise to a movement of thought concerning ministry which may be outlined as follows:

1. When we think of ministry, the primary ministry to which we must refer is Christ's own ministry. This is where we have to begin when we try to comprehend what ministry is, to whom it applies, and how it should be implemented. The Body is the Body *of Christ*, and Christ is its Head. The Body therefore exists and lives to express and implement Christ's ministry. It is the instrument of Christ's mission, the means of Christ's presence in and outreach to the world. To speak of Christian ministry in the first instance is to speak of the ministry of Christ himself.

2. But there is then a *second* step in this movement of thought which must be taken. If the Body fulfills Christ's ministry on earth, then that ministry is actualized or brought into effect fundamentally in the ministry of the church as a *whole*. Since the Church is the Body of Christ, it is in the activity of the total community that the mission of Christ in the world is fulfilled. In Paul's biblical realism, the Body, the church, is in a sense Christ himself in ministry. In the texts, look closely at the frequent emphasis on the unity of the whole and the interdependence of the parts. The parts cannot be thought of in isolation from one another. If we are to define ministry, we cannot turn to one of the parts of the body, or a selection of parts, and define ministry as such purely in those terms. If ministry is to be defined properly, it must be in such

a way that every individual ministry of every individual member of the body, can be seen as implementing the ministry of the total Body, which is Christ's Body, Christ himself in ministry. After Christ, under Christ, it is primarily the church as a whole which ministers.

3. The *third* step is then obvious. Christ's ministry through the church depends on the call and equipping of *all* the people for their ministries. "Everyone has been given a gift, a *charis*, a due portion of Christ's bounty" (Eph. 4:7). In Greek *charis* refers to a gift of the Spirit with a view to ministry, and every believer, through baptism and the outpouring of Spirit, has such a gift. (cf. I Pet. 4:10: "As each has received a *charisma*, use it in service...like good stewards of the varied grace of God."). To be a member of Christ's Body, and to be called to ministry, go inextricably hand in hand. The call and equipping of all the members for ministry is part and parcel of the image of the Body of Christ. There can be no members, no parts or organs of the Body, which are not in principle called to ministry. Christ's ministry, the ministry of the whole church, is expressed in the individual ministries of all the people who are members of the Body. The Body functions in ministry through its interrelated, interdependent organs and limbs. It is fully itself, fully alive and well only when it is functioning as it should through each of the limbs and organs which make it up.

4. We come finally to the *fourth* step in the movement of thought required by the Body image. In the Body there are varieties of ministry, but there is none which is a mere appendage. There are varieties of gifts, as there are varieties of service, varieties of forms of work, and it is the same Spirit who is at work in each case in a particular way, for some useful purpose (I Cor. 12:4-7). The Body cannot be reduced to one organ, and no organ can say to another that it is not part of the Body or part of its ministry. All the gifts have a function in the ministry of the Body, no matter how lowly or hidden they may seem to be. No one is excluded, and no one can in ministry be treated as insignificant. Nothing is clearer than this if the Body image is allowed fully to make its impact on our theology of ministry.

In summary, then, reflection on the image of the church as the Body of Christ brings us irresistibly to a theology of ministry whose focus is the ministry of the whole people of God. It is there that we must begin, and out development of the theory and practice of ministry must be consistent with that focus. The ministry of the whole people of God is rooted in theological reality. It is of the Gospel and mandated by the Gospel. It is absolutely demanded by the central biblical image of the Body of Christ. The ministry of the laity, the *laos*, cannot be an option for us, to be picked up or discarded as we choose. It is a theological necessity. Our theology of ministry must be oriented in this direction, or it is an inadequate, distorted theology of ministry. When the image of the Body is faced squarely, it is plain that the ministry of the whole people of God is not a peripheral issue. The ministry of all the members if crucial to what Paul is saying about the Body. The Body and its many parts, the gifts of the spirit, the variety in unity, the multiplicity, the interdependence, the mutuality of the different ministries, all of that is *essential* to Paul's argument, not incidental. The ministry of the laity simply cannot be avoided as the foundation of everything else we say about ministry.

One important thing which this means is that we have to do here with much more than just a principle of human organization ("it's a good thing for everyone to have something to do in the church; that's how you keep people involved and interested, and so on"). The principle before us is grounded in the will and purpose of God. It is an expression of one of the highest doctrines of our faith, namely the Incarnation. The Incarnate Christ has chosen to continue his ministry in a world through the church, which is his body, and that ministry can be fully expressed only by means of the individual gifts of the Spirit granted to the members of the body, that is, through the ministry to which all of them are called and for which they are to be equipped. The ministry of the whole people of God is rooted in the profoundest theological reality there is, the Incarnation of the Son of God for the redemption of the world.

III. The Ministry of the Body in Practice

Having laid the groundwork for a theology of ministry, I want in this last section to underline the significance of what has been said by pointing to some practical implications for the way in which we approach ministry in the life of our congregations. I do not mean to offer detailed practical advice but rather to stress certain things which must be kept clearly in mind as we seek to fulfill our calling in ministry as the whole people of God. There are four assertions on which I would insist.

1. The Whole People of God Should Minister in the World.

This is bound up with one of the most obvious impressions conveyed by the word "Body". A body is tangible and visible. It can be touched and seen in the day to day world, and it can reach out and have an effect upon that world. If Christ is to be tangible and visible in the world of the workplace, in the world of our institutions, from the home, through the places of our daily employment to the centers of our government, it must be through the witness and activity of the whole church which lives and serves in that world. The Body, through its members, its laity, is plainly called to ministry there, and for that ministry it must be prepared and strengthened.

2. The Whole People of God Should Minister Within the Fellowship of the Church.

This is the ministry of the people of God viewed inwardly, as the other is that ministry viewed outwardly. The implication is expressed more than once in the New Testament texts: each member of the body has a role to play in the upbuilding, the growth, the maturing of the whole. "Bonded and knit together by every constituent joint, the whole frame grows through the due activity of each part, and builds itself up in love." (Eph. 4:16) That it is the responsibility of only a select few to minister in the church cannot be reconciled with the image of the Body of Christ. On the contrary, that image requires that each member deal with this question: To what ministry am I called for the benefit of the fellowship of which I am a constituent part? Just as the image requires also that every member answer the question: What ministry am I called to fulfill in the world?

3. The Ministry of Every Member Should Be Affirmed and Supported in and by the Church.

The Body image leaves no room for rivalry, or for any system of "caste" in the church's structures of ministry. It implies collegiality in the most serious way. There are differences of calling and role and function, and there will of necessity be leaders with authority as well as responsibility. But each ministry will intersect with the others in mutual interdependence which will make anything like a "lone ranger" model completely inappropriate, if not sinful. If everyone's ministry is an expression of Christ through the church, if the primary ministry is Christ's implemented by the church as a whole, then no one form of ministry can be "the" ministry in terms of which all other ministries must be understood and on which they must be modelled.

To put it bluntly, the ministry of the laity, of the whole people of God, cannot be defined and limited as though it were just another form (a kind of pale reflection) of the ministry of the ordained. In the Body of Christ, the ministry of the ordained will be a very important form of ministry, but it cannot be the whole of ministry. The Body image makes it crystal clear that the ministry of every member should be affirmed and respected, even as it has made it crystal clear that every member does indeed have a ministry, the gift and calling of the Holy Spirit. And that has to mean also that the church must attend seriously to the matter of providing for all the members the preparation and support they need if they are to be effective in their calling.

4. The Pastoral Office in the Congregation Should Be Understood and Practiced in the Light of the Ministry of the Whole People of God.

The question will inevitably come up, and it must therefore be addressed directly. What does all of this imply about the ministry of the pastor, the ministry of the ordained? In our answer we must make it abundantly clear that the pastoral office is in no way being downgraded. It is not a matter of denigrating the ministry of the ordained, but of making sure that the ministry of the whole people, including the pastor, is celebrated as it ought to be. In the interests of the ministry of the laity there is no need to undermine the ministry of the ordained, and *vice versa*. In fact, the undermining of any ministry in the church would be a violation of the plain sense of the Body image.

However, in affirming the ministry of the pastor, we must at the same time stress that this ministry must be interpreted and put into effect in the context of the vision of the ministry of the Body as a whole. We must have done with the notion that the pastor is paid by the congregation in order to perform the congregation's ministry as a kind of proxy ("we don't have time to do it so we will set the pastor aside for it in our place"). When we do set people aside for ministries (i.e. commission them), it must always be as one further expression of the ministry of the whole people, not as the assertion of the idea that some people are in ministry while others are not. (We really must repudiate the concept of a call to "full-time Christian service" for just a few in the church, as if we are not *all* called to be full-time ministers of Christ!) There will be missionaries, and evangelists, and chaplains, and so on, but their ministries, like those of the leaders in our congregations (our pastors, Christian educations, and such), will be specific realizations of the ministry of the Body in which each of us should be engaged as the Body's members.

The pastor will therefore have as one of his or her main responsibilities to see to it that all the people of God are empowered and prepared for their ministry. The pastor's ministry is intended to be with, of, and for the *laos* in the ministry to which it is called. It should be the pastor's constant concern to ensure that in worship, spirituality, Christian education, pastoral care, and all the other ministries of the congregation, the ministry of the whole people of God is given its proper place, through these ministries the whole Body being inspired, grounded, equipped, cultivated, and motivated for its total calling. It would contradict the Body image for the pastor to try to do all of this alone, but the pastor should take the lead and make the resources of her or his training available in all possible ways to this end.

Conclusion

If a theology of ministry is to be worked out in its fullness and applied in detail to our structures and patterns, a great deal more must be done than I have been able to accomplish in so short a space. Many topics would have to be dealt with which I have touched upon only in passing or, in some cases, not even raised at all (e.g. the whole question of the ministry of church leaders who serve in structures and organizations beyond the local congregation). But I am confident that however we were to press such issues in the exploration of ministry, we would have to treat them always in relation to guidelines developed from theological study such as we have carried out with regard to Paul's image of the Body of Christ. Lacking a detailed biblical plan which we could simply take over, no other course is available to us. Nor would it be appropriate to expect that any view of ministry could be justified which did violence to what is so emphatically laid out in what the Bible says about the Body. The challenge to our churches today is just this: When are we going to take with absolute seriousness, under the Lordship of Christ and the guidance of the Spirit, the ministry of the *whole* people of God?

George W. Peck is president of Andover Newton Theological School, Newton Centre, MA, USA.

"United or Separated In the Ministry of the Church?"

A Look at Issues Involved in Ordination, Authentication, Recognition and Commissioning of Ministry

Ruth Sampson

Introduction

Several weeks ago, I joined the Barn Team in their weekly meeting. This group of a dozen or so ("lay") members of our congregation pursues its call to ministry through a full-time support and training program to unemployed young people. They do this in association with a government-funded scheme, in which three out of four paid project officers are members of The Barn team and half the annually-elected local management committee are members of our congregation. (Half of the remainder are members of other local churches of different denominations.)

The weekly team meeting involves Bible study, prayer, personal and ministry support. As we gathered, one of the project officers, with great amusement and obvious satisfaction, related this event from that day:

Sue, a young single mother who had been attending The Barn for more than a year, had picked up a stray copy of our weekly church bulletin, left behind after morning tea the previous Sunday. In utter astonishment she yelled out, "Hey look at this! It says here that Dave is a Reverend! Is that right?" Dave is an (ordained) member of our pastoral team, who periodically calls in at The Barn to chat with participants and to keep in touch with how things are going. Sue had sometimes talked with him, but had no idea he was "a Reverend".

Her astonishment grew upon reading that not only is Dave a "Reverend", but so too is Bruce (listed in the bulletin as an honorary member of the pastoral team). Sue was incredulous upon being told that Bruce is also a Professor of Pastoral Theology! Not only had Sue met Bruce, as she had Dave, at The Barn, but a fortnight before, she had become his next-door neighbor. For Sue and her baby had moved into a church-owned unit, located in a group of five. The other four units are owned and lived in by congregational members (including three members of The Barn team), to enable long-term ministry to people like Sue. In all her dealings with Dave and Bruce, she had never once suspected that either was a "minister." Perhaps it would be better to say that she had never perceived any difference between them and the other church members who had ministered to her through The Barn.

This simple episode implicitly raises many aspects of our topic: the diversity of ministries (both individual and corporate) given to the church, the primacy of mission to the world in its need, the enabling call of God to every believer, the relation between "lay" and "ordained" ministers, the stereotyped perceptions of "ministers" by people outside (and inside?) the church, and so on.

If I state that this event (though sadly, not the whole of our congregational life!) represents significant movement towards my vision of what the church
in her ministry is called to be, I begin to reveal my theological assumptions.
It is to a brief outline of these that we now turn.

I. Theological Foundations

It is impossible to outline a theology of "lay" or "ordained" ministry
in isolation from a general theology of ministry. This, in turn, is impossible outside the context of a theology of the church. As John Stott reminds us, unbalanced notions of "clergy" and "laity" and their interrelationships are due
to unbalanced notions of the church. Our starting point must always be the
biblical view of the church, for it is the whole church which participates in the
fundamental ministry of Christ, as both a blessing to be received and a commission to be obeyed.

The call of God comes to each of us as individuals and that same call
simultaneously summons us to respond to the gospel of Christ, joins us to him
and his body and therefore ordains us as his servants, his "ministers", to participate in his own continuing ministry in the world (e.g. Mi. 1:16-20, Rom.
1:1-7, Eph. 4:1-7, I Pet. 2:9-10). All this - and more - is expressed in baptism.
The New Testament nowhere refers to any "call" other than this primary call
which has been experienced by every believer. Additional directions for the
development and extension of ministry are given, but all mentions of "call"
refer back to our primary, common call as Christians.

This call is comprehensive. It comes to us all for the totality of our lives:
for all of our days and years (we can never "retire" from the ministry of Christ)
and for all of our activities in life.

> It is our "Sunday ministries, i.e. for our "churchly" or "ecclesiastical" activities.
> It is for our "seven day" ministries, i.e., for our every day activities with fam-
> ily, friends and neighbors.
> It is for our "Monday morning" ministries, i.e., our work activities during
> the week, whether our "work" is centered in the world or the church, the
> home or the neighborhood, and so on.
> It is no less for our "Saturday night" ministries, i.e., our lives in leisure, enter-
> tainment, sports and holidays.

Each of us shares this commission to live the whole of our lives as Christ's
servants with the entire church: together we are called to respond to God's call.
So we can expect mutual support, sharing of resources, practical training and
so on.

All such expressions of fellowship, however, are derived from the fellowship
God offers us in Christ through his spirit. We can embrace our call to ministry
with joy and confidence, knowing that each is empowered by God's Spirit and
endowed with specific gifts which enable us to minister in particular ways. Our
own gifts will complement the variety of ministries given to our brothers and
sisters. Since these gifts are freely distributed by the sovereign Spirit, to be exer-

cised for the common good under the Lordship of Christ, there is no room in the church for distinctions of status or prestige; no room for hierarchial structures which are used to coerce, to elevate the gifts of a few or to devalue the gifts of many; no room for passivity, for "spectators", "armchair critics" and the like. Such principles of ministry life in the church are consistent with our Lord's teaching about life in the kingdom community, as it is recorded in passages such as Matthew 23:8-12 and Mark 10:35-45.

The overall picture presented in the New Testament as I understand it, then, is one of an harmonious, non-hierarchial fellowship in which each individual participates in a unique and valued way in the shared ministry of the community under Christ. Unity is experienced as diverse ministries are recognized, affirmed and exercised together, all directed towards a common goal: to share in the servanthood of Jesus through his church for the sake of the world.

II. Authentication of Ministry

Such a vision of the church's essential nature as a missionary and a ministerial community has spread throughout the Christian church during the past forty years or so. We have been stirred to hear the Word of God afresh in this area through many currents: the church renewal movement, the ecumenical movement, the charismatic movement, the experiences of the church through war, persecution and rapid growth are but a few examples. Embodiment of this vision has been slow and limited in many places, though, as firmlyentrenched structures, assumptions and practices are threatened and difficult problems have surfaced. Many of these center around issues of authentication/recognition/commissioning of ministry, all of which are sharply focussed in the relationship between "ordained" and "lay" ministries. Confusion abounds. Clearly, we need to examine our understanding and practice of "ordination" afresh in this contest. (It would be more accurate to say "understanding and practices, in acknowledgement of our characteristic Baptist diversity!)

Assuming the view of the church and her ministry so briefly outlined above, one could naively assume that authentication of ministry should be a non-issue. After all, one might ask, if every believer has been called by God himself and commissioned to a life of discipleship and ministry, what further authentication could be needed?

Of course, things are not as simple as that.

To begin with, many Christians are simply unaware of their high calling or have forgotten it in the press of life. Such people need appropriate teaching and regular reminders and reassurances, following apostolic example (e.g. Rom. 1:1-6, I Cor. 1:1-9, Eph. 4:1-7). The level of ignorance in this area presents a profound challenge to our evangelists, preachers, teachers and others.

Secondly, since this dimension of Christian life is only newly-discovered (or is still to be discovered) in many of our churches, we are generally unpracticed in discerning the specific shape of the ministry given to each of us as individuals. We find it difficult to specify our gift. In such circumstances, our call can seem an uncertain and fragile thing. Again, reassuring teaching and practical helps such as those in Drummond's book need to be offered regularly in our church communities.

Thirdly, people's emerging ministries need to be authenticated within the church community through an appropriate process of testing, recognition and commissioning (Acts 6:1-6 and 13:1-3 are instructive here). The benefits of such a process are many. For example:

It enables an individual or group to check their perceptions of God's call in the context of the unity of the ministry of the wider church community.

It is most affirming for the people concerned in such a process when it is seriously and sensitively carried out.

It invites support from the whole church community for the ministry so recognized.

It acknowledges the God-given authority bestowed in that area of gift.

It reminds people that ministry is never solely an individual matter, though it is intensely personal.

It enables a process of accountability to be established.

It acts as a teaching event (through example, if nothing else).

Without a process of congregational discernment and recognition of some kind, the fostering of gifts and ministries will almost certainly degenerate into the chaos of rampant individualism - a problem with which many Baptist congregations are already too familiar! On the other hand, denying the opportunity for individuals and groups to explore the specifics of their call to ministry with their church community usually leads to increasing stagnation and rigidity in congregational life - another familiar problem. The movement of the wind of the Spirit is all too easily missed when we do not actively encourage the emergence of new forms and directions in ministry, in response to the commission of the ever-sending God.

Fourthly, authentication needs to be seen as an on-going process, with continuing acknowledgement and affirmation of recognized ministries, in worship and other areas of congregational life. Training, support and regular, honest review are all important (e.g. 2 Tim. 1:6, 1 Tim. 4:6-8, Titus 2). What message is given to the laity by the grossly disproportionate level of resources committed to the training of the few (the clergy) for ministry? This issue needs to be addressed urgently.

The prospect of incorporating such a process into our congregational life to authenticate God-given ministries ought to come as no surprise to us. After all, in principle it is no different from the testing and recognition process which normally precedes the commissioning for ministry which we call "ordination." Let me illustrate this with an extended quote from the *Report of the Study Commission on Ordination*, produced at the direction of the Baptist Union of Victoria, Australia (1978). In response to the question, "What is meant by a "call" to ministry?", the Report answers:

"The call to ministry includes at least four elements:

(i) **The call to discipleship.** The Spirit works in the community of the church. It is inconceivable that anyone could minister to the people of God without first belonging fully to that people. All those appointed to ministry will know the call of Christ to repentance, faith and discipleship and will have sealed their Christian identity in baptism.

(ii) **The inward call.** No one can enter the ministry without an inner sense of summons, namely that personal conviction or experience whereby an individual feels himself directly invited or commanded by God to take up the work of the ministry.

(iii) **The providential call.** The exercise of ministry pre-supposes the presence of those spiritual gifts which belong to that form of ministry. These gifts are not acquired except through the agency of the Holy Spirit (Acts 8:18-24). Those who would minister on behalf of others must demonstrate the gifts and talents necessary for the exercise of the office and show the continuing control of the Spirit in all circumstances of their lives (cf. II Tim. 3:1-9; I John 2:18-19).

(iv) **The churchly call.** The ministry is not a private enterprise. It is exercised in and at the behest of the body as a whole. The other aspects of the call, therefore, must be confirmed by the fellowship, which acknowledges the validity of the call by inviting the one who has it to undertake the work of ministry within the life of the community.

The testing of a call to ministry is an important task both for the church and for the individuals who feels the sense of call. The validity of a call must be evaluated in the light of the four elements outlined above." (pp. 11-12).

There seems neither logical nor theological reason for limiting such a process of authentication to one manifestation of ministry alone. Yet this commonly occurs. We often accept the appropriateness of a testing and affirmation process, prior to the recognition of "ordination", yet express surprise at the prospect of extending a similar process to other ministries.

Does this surprise betray a lingering suspicion that one form of ministry really is "more important" than other forms, and is therefore to be taken seriously, while all other "less important" ministries may be dealt with more casually? Or perhaps our surprise is merely a response to the unfamiliarity of viewing the issue of authentication from the "underside" of the long-standing clergy/laity divide.

III. The Trouble With Ordination

Coming at the issue from the perspective of the whole ministry given to the whole church obviously raises questions about the place of ordination. Many now ask: "If every believer's divine call and commission is expressed in baptism, why do we hold a separate additional, ordination service for a select few within the church? Is there any good reason why a tiny minority should be so singled out for special treatment? Isn't it time we completed the Reformation and at last began truly to embody our cherished belief in the priesthood of all believers? If we began to take really seriously the testing, recognition and commissioning process of every member, could not those with gifts of pastoral leadership be tested and recognized on the same basis as their brothers and sisters?" And so the questions keep coming. It is little wonder that the ordained ministry has been called "The Perplexed Profession" and that signs of profound uncertainty about their role are common among both ordinandi and established pastors. The numerous reports on ordination and church leadership commissioned by our member bodies in the last decade or so are a further sign of widespread questioning.

We have time only to look briefly at ordination specifically as it relates to our theme. We shall do so under three headings:

A. Baptist Perspectives

Our founding fathers and mothers, the English Baptists of the seventeenth century were, of course, heavily influenced by the Reformation in their understanding. In theory, they rejected a sacramental view of ministry and for a time, there were disputes as to whether or not ordination was necessary or appropriate. Very quickly, however, in response to strong criticism and persecution, the need for a "separated ministry" was affirmed in the interests of "good order" in the church. Ordination wa usually performed within local congregations who "set apart" suitably gifted men or women (deacons, who were ordained, could be male or female). They generally performed this by the laying on of hands with fasting and prayer. With the growing urge for evangelism and the move to establish associational ties, ordination sometimes came to involve extra-local representatives as well. Such ordination was not believed to confer special rights or status of any kind - it was merely a congregation's recognition that a certain person had "the gift of ministry", exercised through preaching, so education and training were highly valued. As early as the mid-seventeenth century, structures began to rigidify, in reaction to the growing threat of Quakerism, with its denial of an institutional church, a separated ministry and visible sacraments. Among the Baptists, preaching and the administration of the ordinances became generally restricted to the ordained ministry.

The use of Scriptures to justify this understanding and practice of ordination was inconsistent. During this same period, some Baptists introduced the laying on of hands at baptism (and only at baptism), some use the practice at both baptism and ordination, while others restricted it to ordination. The same texts were often used in support of each of these practices! It is hard to escape the conclusion that historical factors, rather than biblical principles, shaped the patterns which emerged. The same could be said of some significant later developments, such as Charles H. Spurgeon's total rejection of ordination and the laying on of hands, largely in reaction to the High Church Oxford Movement.

Present-day Baptist understanding and practice of ordination varies considerably worldwide and it would be impossible to cover all the variations here, even if I were aware of them! Suffice it to say, that some Baptists restrict "the ministry of word and sacrament" to ordained ministers except in "abnormal" situations, while others are more flexible; most (?) Baptists practice the laying on of hands with prayer at ordination. (In Australia, for example, ordination is almost totally in the hands of the Unions of churches).

Even such a cursory look at Baptist traditions can help us place our own local practices in a broader perspective. Always, though, these practices must be tested against Scripture, so it is to Biblical foundations that we now briefly turn.

B. Biblical Precedent

New Testament references to ordination are scanty and their meaning is vigorously debated. The key texts generally referred to are I Tim. 4:14 and 2 Tim. 1:6, with additional evidence being adduced from passages such as Acts 6:1-6, 13:1-3, 14:25 and I Tim. 5:22 where the laying on of hands and prayer are associated with setting apart for ministry. There are other occasional references to the laying on of hands (e.g. Acts 9:17, Heb. 6:1-2), but there is disagreement as to whether the reference is to the occasion of baptism or to a "commissioning" for ministry (the first incorporates the second in a general way, in any case).

Most scholars agree that none of these texts refers to an elaborated ceremony such as we associate with "ordination" today. Ministry forms and structures are clearly still fluid and seem to vary according to the need of the situation. So, too, does the process of authentication vary; a variety of actions is mentioned (laying on of hands, prayer, fasting) and a number of different terms are used to refer to the process (appoint, set apart, choose, enrol). No one gift or form of ministry is alone recognized in this way and there is no sense in which such an appointment is to be a "professional position."

Debate has centered on the meaning of the laying on of hands, which rapidly came to be seen as the crux of ordination. Is it a sign of apostolic succession (the sacramentalist notion that it effects succession has generally been rejected by Baptists)? Is it a sign of fellowship and blessing? Is it a sign of the presence and gift of the Spirit? Resolution of this issue is clearly impossible in this paper but it is worth noting the recent contribution to the debate offered by a Baptist in Canada, Marjorie Warkentin. In an extended treatment of ordination in its historical and total biblical (N.T. and O.T.) context, she argues that we misunderstand the references to the laying on of hands when we try to link them with ordination per se. The spasmodic mentions of the practice in the N.T. are related to specific "moments" in the economy of God, she contends, and cannot be taken as evidence of a general practice. To quote:

". . . the laying on of hands heralds key moments in the history of redemption, moments when the "hand" of God is manifestly shaping the destinies of his people. Its essence is of the "times and seasons" that are under the authority of God alone (Acts 1:7 cf. I Thess. 5:1)."

(Warkentin, p. 187)

Whatever the variety and development in practice evident in the N.T. and whatever the specific elements included in any one instance of "setting apart" for a specific ministry, it seems clear that the church was responding to three legitimate needs:

> -First, the need to regulate some abuses and excesses in ministry, affirming that the ministry is given to the whole church, not to individuals in isolation.
> -Second, the need to ensure faithfulness to the apostolic tradition.
> -Third, the need to provide for stability and permanence, in view of the passing of the original apostolic witnesses.

At base, ordination is a public recognition that God calls individuals and appoints them to the ministry of Christ, for which task he equips them with appropriate gifts. The church affirms God's prior actions in a particular individual and acknowledges his or her authority to exercise ministry in and through the whole Body. In other words, ordination facilitates the legitimate use of authority in the church. The fact that the reverse has often sadly been the case highlights the problems associated with the practice of ordination.

C. Issues Arising

I believe that the problems are not so much due to the practice of ordination itself, as to the fact of its restriction to so few within the church, while little or no recognition is offered to the majority of Christ's ministers. The issues are compounded when only one person in each congregation is so recognized, in contrast to the pattern of shared leadership attested to in the N.T. The destructive consequences of this state of affairs are legion and only too well-known to most of us. I will simply list what seem to me some of the more obvious and important:

1. *Ministry is concentrated in one person*, so that:

> authority and power in the church are centralized. This is the most dangerous and far-reaching consequence of our common practice - a problem which quickly became evident in the post-apostolic period and has plagued the church ever since. Hierarchial structures of ministry have almost universally developed, as legitimate and God-given authority has been abused and used to dominate and devalue others. Instead of liberating and empowering them to share fully and appropriately in ministry.
> -expectations of giftedness become focussed in one person.
> -a "professional" view of the ministry is fostered. Unhealthy tendencies in this development can be seen, for example, in the relationship between money and "ministry." We have lost something more precious than we realize when we think primarily of the ministry of Christ in terms of a "paid profession." In a world increasingly dominated by the mentality of the advertising industry, where "experts", "celebrities" and others are paid handsomely to promote a produce, the credibility and integrity of the proclamation of the gospel is eroded when we rely almost exclusively on paid professionals to do the job.
> -a "spectator mentality" readily develops among congregational members. At best, the laity are seen merely as potential "helpers" of an overstretched professional.

-unrealistic expectations of "the minister" abound, contributing to frustration, stress, burn-out and so on.
-clergy often feel lonely and isolated.

2. *Ministry is stressed in only one area of life, our "Sunday" activities,* (see I. above), so that:

-the church easily becomes introverted, focussing on its own internal affairs, rather than giving her life away for the sake of the world. This reinforces the perception so common today that the church (and hence the gospel we proclaim) is essentially irrelevant to everyday life and needs.
-the laity, who live out most of their lives through their "seven day", "Monday morning" or "Saturday night" activities (see I. above) feel devalued as a "second-class citizens" within the church. Little serious affirmation is offered to them in these areas of life, let alone specific help given to equip them for effective ministry there.

Such a catalogue of woes amply demonstrates that although, theologically, we affirm the fundamental unity of all believers in the ministry of the church, in practice, we usually experience separation. Rarely do we glimpse the unity in diverse ministries witnessed to in the storm from The Barn with which we began. What is to be done? Can we see a way forward?

IV. Prospects and Possibilities

It should be evident that, despite the magnitude of the problems referred to, I see no reason to discontinue the practice of ordination per se (although I admit to being tempted to advocate that solution at times!) After all, it embodies some important N.T. principles of ministry such as those summarized in III.B. above. Also, it has the capacity to meet contemporary needs very similar to those experienced in the late and post-apostolic period. Reform of our approach to ordination could enable us to witness more faithfully to these perspectives.

Urban Holmes, for example, urges us to take as seriously as the N.T. evidently does, the diversity between church communities, with their differing leadership needs and gifts. He suggests that, rather than starting with the individual, we start with the Christian community, which discerns the leaders who have been gifted in ways which meet the specific needs of that situation. These people may then be given training and ordained in recognition of their God-given "presbyterial" role in that particular community. This would reinforce an understanding of ordination as commissioning for a particular ministry, rather than as admission to a special status group within the church at large. Obviously, there would be significant implications for theological training.

The issue, then, as I see it, is not so much to withdraw authentication/recognition/commissioning from one form of ministry as it is to extend it appropriately to all forms of ministry given to the church. I have suggested important features to include in this process in II above. Other specific and practical ideas are offered for your inspiration (and use!) in the Appendix. A fruitful beginning point would be to develop the theological understanding of baptism as every Christian's ordination to ministry. Both our instruction and our practice may need to be modified to bring together baptism, church membership and commissioning for ministry.

I am excited by the possibilities which are opened up by the challenge before us to traverse the gulf which too often still separates ordained from unordained ministers in the church and to experience in new ways the unity offered to us, as together we participate in the ministry of Christ in the world. The task will require of us energetic and sustained commitment and all the creative and rigorous thinking and acting we have to offer. Well may we ask with the apostle: "and who is equal to such a task?" His reply offers us reassurance and hope as we tackle the job: "Our sufficiency is from God, who has been pleased to make us effective ministers of his new covenant with men. (2 Cor. 2:16, 3:5-6).

Ruth Sampson is a Baptist pastor in Melbourne, Australia.

Clergy and Laity Trained For Their Ministries

Brigit Karlsson

Introduction

Some presuppositions need to be indicated as introductory steps. The Church is best described through concept as the Body of Christ, the People of God, the True Vine. The Christian individual is best understood as a part of the Body, a personal member of the People, a branch of the Vine. Unity with God and community with each other, dependance on God and mutual interdependence on one another describe the basic conditions for life. The Church as body, people, vine has its genuine purpose—its ministry. That ministry is in the world and it can only be fulfilled through a fully functioning community. In short, we need one another in a true community in order to fulfill our common ministry to the world.

The Picture and the Real Life

The fact is that none of us (or at least very few and very seldom) have seen the fully functioning Christian church. It is a wide gap between the picture we have of what the Church community should be like, and the experiences most of us have. One may question the picture, or one may question life. There is a tension between the map and the landscape whenever we are travelling. We are making our journey facing our contemporary world with a biblical material and with a load of traditional collections of models and patterns in our luggage. More often than not our experience of a genuine community is only a brief glimpse from a worship hour, not a coherent pattern of the total life. There is a gap between Sunday worship and Monday ministry, between our Sunday faith and our weekday world.

Effects on Split Between Clergy and Laity

Our painful predicament could be described with many more examples. It is enough to state that the suffering of this gap between the picture and the reality is to be taken seriously because it limits the efficiency of the Church's total ministry to the world and deprives the world of a model for reconciled unity and community and it limits the individual's growth towards spiritual maturity. In this paper we are paying attention to only one aspect of the problem—the effects of the split between clergy and laity.

Many have made profound studies attempting to explain how this split came about. Not going into any depth analysis of the cause of this illness, I restrict myself to stress that it is worth paying attention to some of the historical facts that point out where some original principles were forsaken and the development was turned into another direction. Only made aware of what is lost, can we look for its restoration.

I am anxious to stress the fact that principles are more appropriate to look for than patterns when we search the biblical material for advice how to understand concepts at Church and Ministry. There is in fact no single detailed pattern in the New Testament, rather do we meet a developing adjustment in ways of ministry and mission according to changing society circumstances.

A Common Responsibility

My intention is to underline the common responsibility of clergy and laity for the restoration of the church for her ministry. A common responsibility, although responded to in different ways. I used to think that the clergy carried a greater responsibility and this were those from whom to expect the initiative for change. Honestly, I have been forced to rethink my view points in that respect. Today my hope for a renewed Church is with the laity. Let me try to explain why.

Once I thought that the clergy had greater access to the theological sources which are needed for correction and renewal of Church life, ministry and mission. I meant that one main task of the clergy was to maintain a solid and true identify of the Body, a task fulfilled through teaching, preaching, worship and counseling the members how to lead a spiritual life. I still believe trained Clergy have access to theoretical biblical knowledge, historic facts and the tools by which to dig in the vast material.

Need For a New Theology

However, I have come to the point where I recognize a desperate need for a new theology, a theology that is relevant to all the People of God. It seems to me that such a theology is not formulated in seminaries, libraries, or even in the pastors' studies alone. In this statement, no criticism at all is directed to the Clergy. They are just not placed where this necessary theology can be formulated.

There is also a matter of role expectation that affects the Clergy. The pastor is traditionally expected to be the one who watches over the flock and who cares for its preserving. Such a role almost with necessity leads to a life style where change is not the first goal to work for—especially if one takes into account that change always has its cost.

The World as Field For Theological Reflection

I think it is not unfair to state that the flow of ideas, values, modes and issues at stake is so much faster in the daily world where laypersons live, than within the institutional Church where pastors mainly have their main time spent. Therefore Laity are constantly exposed to new needs and problems of the society where their Christian faith is challenged. There is the place where theology is made. My definition of theology is plainly, reflection over God's revelation to the human being and the interpretation of that revelation.

In summary, the Church needs for its restoration a theological work done by laity, as well as by clergy. Only thus can the theology serve all the people of God in the ministry of the world. Only then does the theology reflect the needs of the world.

Two Worlds Made One

We started out with pointing to the gap between Sunday's faith and Monday's ministry. Let us return there and ask how that gulf can be bridged, for bridged it must be. As it is today, too many laypersons feel that they are living in two worlds totally separated from each other, with two totally different sets of languages and concerns. Nothing of relevance is to bring from the worship life to the everyday life, and the questions of Friday afternoons are not understood and recognized in the Sunday morning sermon. Thus the two worlds must be made one. That requires that it is met, faced and embraced in the same manner as Jesus did. Only the Body of Christ in its totality can do this, i.e. Clergy and Laity together.

Reconsider the Nature of the Church

We must reconsider the nature of the Church, its conditions and its purpose in order to recapture a whole world in which to live and serve. This includes the fact that to live in the Christian community is to accept two dimensions to life, two modes of appearances—one when the believers are gathered for worship and one when the believers are spread for service. But the parts of the Body are as much parts of the Body when they are at work in the outside world as when they are resting and being restored in their worship hour. Should these forms be more separated from each other and be more strange than are the different modes of rest and work in the individual's physical life? In both cases we recognize a law of nature given by God, from creation and through reconciliation. Equal importance must be given to both dimensions. Worship and renewed strength is a necessity for the ministry and the function of the gifts for the world is a necessity for a healthy life. This is a normal rhythm of life for the total body with all its parts.

The different parts are made interdependent and together only ultimately dependent on Christ. This has obvious consequences for the understanding of the often felt tension between clergy and laity. Different ways of serving, but the same value must be ascribed to both categories. There is no hierarchic order, but a system of coordination that rests in Christ's lordship over the total body.

In order to restore a whole world for the Church and its members in which to live and serve we need to be more careful with the language we use and the manners we develop. As long as we say that Laity *go* to church and at least at times think that clergy *are* the church, we have not understood the church as our place of residence all days and all hours whatever we are occupied with. As long as we talk about Clergy as "full-time ministers" and assume that Laity is ministering only now and then, we have not understood what ministry means as a way of life for every member of the People of God. As long as we separate even the Laity in different categories, and tend to see and give recognition only to those who carry certain offices in the institutional setting of the congregation, we have not fully understood the ordinary life as an environment where Christian presence is the most efficient form of ministry. I am only suggesting the area where rethinking of ordination, installation, recognition etc. is of utmost importance.

Listening to the Messengers

A couple of years ago in my country the Council of Free Churches founded an Institute for Research. One of the first initiatives taken within the frame of this institute was to summon a conference for all interested to suggest areas where study and research work needs to be done on behalf of the Christian churches.

The consultation was an extremely exciting experience. Seldom have I met such a crowd of Christians, qualified and skilled to represent all the areas of the society, and seldom have I heard so many new and fresh aspects formulated regarding the Christian faith's necessity and possibilities in all these areas. I joyfully discovered that the Church moved out there, in new and challenging areas of the modern society, through all these brothers and sisters of whom I had heard and seen so little before. How rich is not the Church as we recognize its totality in ministry.

For the few clergy present, I believe this experience was a very helpful lesson in the necessity to share responsibility, we were reminded that there are persons to be trusted as Christian ambassadors almost everywhere. And those are the messengers from the world to the worship part of the Church, and from the Sunday worship to the every day world for ministry.

That consultation was also a common Christian reflection over the daily life's Christians—if it is not too pretentious—we did some theological work together. This experience served as an example of what can be done, as one practical result of the consultation initiative has been taken by seminaries to arrange conferences for Laity and Clergy interested in theologically to address certain issues—particularly ethical questions born out for a new scientific eras with effects for the individual as well as on humanity. Those conferences have been well attended and appreciated, and we believe that there is a road to travel.

Varied Ministries

This example has brought us into the specific area where the Church's ministry through Laity mostly takes place. That is the work place—be it market place, educational settings, hospitals and homes, institutions and industries, factories and farms, research centers, etc. In all these environments all kinds of human experiences are present. This is the fabric of the world and there is the Church present through its members.

William E. Diehl, a sales manager in a large steel industry and most known for his book *Thank God, It's Monday*, givers in another of his books *Christianity and Real Life* a number of examples of how the Christian presence is made relevant in the society. He uses the term *The Ministry of the Aid Man* and he describes pictures and network of Christian laypersons who are skilled to detect needs, are prepared to be close to those who need support and able to listen and respond.

Further Diehl points to *The Ministry of Words* and gives it three ways to be implemented in the working place—by the way the Christian person expresses his own values, outlook on life and style of life, by the way he expresses his viewpoint on issues of the day, and finally, by expressing the teaching of his personal faith. In a brief chapter in this book, Diehl applies to the term *The Ministry of Ethics* and gives practical examples on how ethical dilemmas occur and need to be faced from the Christian viewpoint.

The World's Agenda for the Church's Training

These three main aspects on the Laity's ministry all actualize specific needs of the layperson—not only to be trusted and recognized by his Church, but to be trained, equipped and constantly supported for the demanding ministry. All too often laypersons do not feel that those needs are met through the Church. Again, I quote Diehl who says that he misses the down-to-earth level of discussing for instance the ethical issues when such fields are dealt with in the Church's teaching and preaching. Theologians often stay with the top level of the issues—important as they are as they make parts of corporate policy—but overlook or are unable to enter into the types of ethical decisions which are common to most people in their daily life.

If the Church lets the needs of the world, as those are reflected through the ministries of the Laity, write the agenda for training programs offered, themes of lectures and courses, some improvement is sure to occur. The total Church, Laity and Clergy alike, will benefit from such a development.

Community for Support

One very important factor for the Laity's ability to serve successfully is what sort of support groups are available. It is taken for granted that the congregation always provides fellowship that is nourishing, loving, restoring, developing and strengthening when it comes to coping with the demands of everyday life. Few articles in the Christian faith store are more over advertized than is fellowship. On few areas are we as human beings more vulnerable than when we are left out, left alone in times of severe needs, and left with a feeling of not belonging. If the community part of the church life does not meet these urgent needs of the Laity, the signs are declining attendance in the worship and fellowship life and an increasing development of non-church related training opportunities and support systems. I believe we are discovering such a tenency in some places.

Role of Seminaries

One final point about the concern for training efforts that are beneficial for all the People of God in ministry is the role of theological seminaries. Having some seminary experience I have seen hopeful signs and I have also seen discouraging things take place, in spite of the best intentions.

The encouraging things I have seen are the great interest from the part of the Laity when courses are offered on times that are adjusted to their life schedule, on topics that are burning in their world, and in a methodological way that fits the content, mostly dialogue and discussions and guided research for individuals and groups.

Too little awareness, however, has been made to the value in mixing Clergy and Laity for those programs. At times there has also been a tendency to build programs of theology for the Laity in an easy or popularized version of academic theology, rather than facilitate a forum where theological work is done not only for, but by the Laity. A final observation I have made with regard to what takes place when laypersons are exposed to the seminaries' courses is that some dedicated and devoted laypersons during the period when they attend some of a seminary's offer, do change their view on ministry. From having taken their service as teacher, clerk or doctor as a God-given avenue for ministry, they lean toward a church-centered type of ministry for themselves. I do not deny that for some this can be the road God intends to guide them, but I do fear that some do find a profile to a ministry in that setting, and miss an equally clear defined picture of the Laity's ministry. Then something is missing in the program, something that needs to be worked on.

Closing Remarks

The responsibility for bridging the gap between church-centered ministry and society-centered ministry and the responsibility for giving all God's people one whole world where the Christian faith is relevant, that responsibility is a shared one for Clergy and Laity.

My greatest hopes and my most exciting dreams for a new and living, and serving Church are bound to the Laity who are prepared to deliver itself from their silent captivity in the pews. I urge them to act strongly and to act soon—for the benefit of all, including the Clergy who are captured in the institutional system. I urge them to look hard and see all the rich experiences they daily do as Christian laypersons in our fast changing society, so that young Christians will discover the contemporary "saints" they need as models for leading a spiritual life today.

If those of us who are appointed for this commission although we are Clergy, have the right to speak—let us appear to our laity-friends to start a liberation movement or to join in with groups here and there within the Christian church families. In my view, it is high time for us as Baptists to reclaim our identity as a lay movement, when more established Churches make major changes in their liturgy, structure and life as they have listened to the majority who have been silent for so long. Now it is time for us as Baptists to reclaim our true identity and to develop and cultivate our specific contribution for the ministry of all God's people in all God's world.

Birgit Karlsson is General Secretary of the Baptist Union of Sweden in Stockholm, Sweden.

Christians in the Workplace:
Toward an Understanding of Ministry
From an Institutional Perspective

George W. Peck

Around the world millions of Christians, Baptists among them, spend a great deal of their lives in places of work. From homemakers to coal miners to business executives to politicians, the people of God use their gifts and talents to fulfill the roles they have assumed as part of the public order within which they find themselves. The economic and political systems vary greatly, the opportunities and possibilities are often quite dissimilar, but whatever the circumstances church members take their place and contribute to the common health and good.

In virtually every case, this activity is carried out in *institutions*. They may be small and simple (the home), or they may be vast and complex (a government department or multinational corporation), but they are all structures in which human beings relate to and cooperate with one another for some overarching purpose. This purpose may be poorly defined and comprehended, but it nonetheless exists. Each institution is gong somewhere and achieving something and in the process is having an effect on the lives of those within it and making a difference (positive, negative, or partly both) to the people on whom it impinges.

Are these institutions which collectively make up any human- society spheres of ministry? Are the people of God as a whole called in the Gospel to practice ministry in such places? Or is the church the only institution to which the word "ministry" can be legitimately attached? The purpose of this paper is to argue for an affirmative answer to the first two of these questions. I hope to show (albeit in brief outline) that there is a "ministry to and in institutions" which is an aspect of the redemptive purpose of God, and that all Christians are indeed summoned to exercise it in its multifarious shapes and forms.

I

Consider first the way in which the Bible depicts God's intentions with respect to human institutions in general. Here the crucial questions run like this: Is God really involved with human institutions understood as I have suggested above? Does God have plans and purposes for them? Are they part of the overall divine "scheme of things"? Is God up to something with regard to them? If the Bible were to depict God as simply concerned about individuals, as dealing only with private citizens, as leaving the world's institutional structures to function by their own devices alone, then we could perhaps conclude that our interest in them is misplaced except insofar as within them we look out for the welfare of their people one by one. But the story really comes out quite differently if we read the Bible carefully.

For example, in the Old Testament, is not God continually involved with and concerned about the calling, character, purpose, and future of the *nation* Israel? To say that for the Old Testament God is interested only in individuals and not in Israel as a totality, and therefore as, in a sense, an institution, would be to misrepresent the texts very seriously. Are there not pages and pages of legal instructions given to Israel implying that God is greatly concerned about how a nation is run? Do not the books of Kings and Chronicles depict in detail how Israel was ordered politically, under God's direct guidance? Nor is Israel the only nation within the divine purview. Throughout the Old Testament the God of Israel is held forth as the God of the nations in general. What Assyria does, or Babylon, or Egypt is all gathered up in God's overarching providential rule. Amos speaks of God as monitoring the morality of the deeds of many nations besides Judah and Israel (cps. 1 and 2), and makes it clear that God was active in the destinies of the Cushites, the Philistines, and the Aramaeans as well as in what happened to the children of Jacob (9:7-8). Isaiah 44:27ff makes a not dissimilar point when it is announced in remarkably explicit language that Cyrus, king of Persia, someone who does not even acknowledge the God of Israel, is the Lord's "shepherd", carrying out God's purpose, one who has been

anointed (the Hebrew word is "messiah") and for whom the Lord has sub-
dued nations, undone opposing kings, and effected many surprising things to
make it possible for him to advance as he has, with his people.

And this is by no means all the Old Testament evidence that could be
adduced. In fact, nothing is clearer than that in the Bible God is as much a
participant in the life and well-being of nations as collective units (or institutions) as in the experience of individual human beings. It is this same God of
whom Paul speaks in Romans 13 when he asserts that even the Roman empire
is an agent of God's will, and about whom Jesus tells the parable of the Great
Judgment in which it is the nations of the world who are held accountable for
the way they have treated the least of his "brethren" (Matt. 25:31ff). Then
if we add to all these references to nations the amount of stress placed upon
the role of the home in God's purpose (the home is surely an institution), or
upon how God wants people to conduct themselves in their business dealings,
it becomes obvious that God is profoundly concerned about how institutions
should be ordered and about how they should affect the lives of men, women,
and children. God is a God of institutions as much as of you and me taken
one by one. When then should we believe that God would be less involved
in the institutions of *our* contemporary societies than in the institutions of an
ancient time? If we are speaking of the same God, ought we not now to affirm
the divine purpose for farms, schools, universities, corporations, charitable
organizations, and the like in today's world, as much as for analogous communities long ago?

II

On this basis, then, it is impossible to insist that the people of God should
not take lightly their calling to approach the institution in which they live and
work as arenas of *ministry*. If our institutions, from homes to multinationals,
are instruments of the divine intention, ought we not to consider ourselves to
be responsible to do more in them than just to exist and make our living? If
in their own varied ways they are serving God, should not that have an effect
on our service in them? Nor ought we to be put off here by the objection,
"But what about purely secular institutions, or even atheistic institutions which
are explicitly inimical to the announced purpose of God?" Cyrus's God was
not the Lord, and the Roman Empire could hardly be called a friend of the
Risen Christ. A lack of explicit acknowledgement does not mean that institutions are beyond the pale of God's great order of things. Even when that
acknowledgement is totally lacking and could never in the normal course be
expected, it is possible for the people of God still to go to work each day in
the conviction that God has chosen them in this institution to minister in Christ's
name.

In this respect, I am very fond of some things expressed several years ago
by the Czech theologian Jan Milic Lochman, in his book *Church in a Marxist
Society*. Writing from within a nation which could hardly be said to be consciously
seeking to do God's will, Lochman speaks of what he calls the "civilian pro-

clamation" of the Gospel, witness given by believers who are "out of uniform", who are not wearing the robes appropriate to church services, but are dressed for their daily chores. It is time, says Lochman, for Christians to reestablish "the theological honor of the working day", not detracting from the significance of what is done in the midst of the church on Sunday, but making it clear also that there is ministry to be performed as well from Monday to Saturday. "The Church .. can .. never be content to be the Church of a single day. It will always claim the whole week." And that implies, he goes on to argue, that in any society we should anticipate finding Christians "in unexpected places". That is, ministering beyond the organizations and institutions of Christian life. "A living Church always appears also in unexpected places (as her own Master, Jesus of Nazareth, did from the manger in Bethlehem to the cross on Calvary)." Which forces us further to conclude that in such a context we are speaking especially of the role and witness of the *laity*, because it is they who are "the real bearers of the apostolic witness" in society's institutions, people who, engaged in the fullness of their professional and human tasks, are at the same time acting as professing members of their Christian communities.

Is not something very like this suggested by all those in the Old Testament who seek to do God's will in carrying out their tasks on behalf of the nation? Is it not implied by the exhortations in the New Testament to do everything with our whole heart, as if we were doing it not for human beings, but for the Lord (Col. 3:23)? Nor is it without significance that the latter urging is delivered in the first instance to household slaves and the reference is to the carrying out of their ordinary duties! One is reminded, indeed, of the remarkable twist that was given to the concept of "vocation" in the thought of the great Reformers, Luther and Calvin. For the European church of the Middle Ages, the word "vocation" was restricted to those who were called to church-related ministries (priest, monks, nuns, the members of religious orders). But Luther insisted that all believers are called in Christ to express their Christian status in the particular spheres of life in which they have been placed. The clericalizing of the idea of vocation was radically contradicted. Even purely worldly, supposedly secular occupations could and should be treated as Christian vocations. Christians were to "work out their salvation" not by fleeing to monasteries or into churchly roles, but by doing properly and well, for the sake of Christ, the job they were given in society to do. For Luther, oddly enough, the only ones who did *not* have a true vocation were the monks and nuns who were cut off from the world!

John Calvin in turn took this view of Luther's a few important steps further. Luther understood society as ordered by God into a fixed hierarchy of callings, and the responsibility of the Christian was essentially to stay where one was put, where one began, and there to do one's best. But in Calvin's judgment God deals with people in such a way that they can expect, if they have the ability, to move from one calling to another. The Christian certainly fulfills her or his life and profession in a specific task (even if it is a secular one), but believers need not accept submissively what has been ordered beforehand. They should strive through the exercise of their gifts to improve themselves and to advance the society of what they are a part. The task of the Christian in the world is to seek to build the Holy Commonwealth, to redirect society according to the vision of the Kingdom of God. Working in and through their institutions, the people of God should endeavor to implement (as much as it lies in them) the will and purpose of God for their communities. This is their "vocation", their daily calling. And with the use of this kind of language we are not far from speaking of the Christian's daily "ministry" in the workplace.

III

It remains, finally, for us to look into one other set of issues with regard to our theme. If God has a purpose for institutions, and we are to regard this as the basis of our calling to minister in them, what should such ministry involve? What would be examples of its content? What would qualify as "ministry" in distinction from just "work"? Here we must begin by acknowledging that God" intention in and for institutions is twofold. On the one hand, God wishes the institutions themselves to be wholesome, humane communities, tending toward the enrichment and not the injuring of those who make them up. Then on the other hand, God would clearly want the same institutions in society at large to work for the welfare of the people, for their enhancement as human beings made in the image of God. Institutions should be just, caring, rewarding places contributing to the development of just, caring, rewarding societary systems. And our ministry in them, therefore, should be directed to such ends. To this we are called.

One valuable way to envisage what this might mean would be to look at ministry in the workplace in accordance with the model of what has traditionally been called the "threefold office" of Christ himself. In Scripture and in Christian thinking Christ has often been depicted as fulfilling the roles of prophet, priest, and king (ruler, sovereign). Since in the world the Church is the Body of Christ, Christ's representative, the tangible, visible Christ in the midst of humanity, what if we saw ourselves as called to be also prophets, priests, and rulers in his name in, for, and on behalf of our institutions? The prophet proclaims and projects the vision, the Good News of what God has revealed and done in Christ, the promise expressed in God's purpose of human beings and systems. The priest acts on behalf of those whom he or she represents, praying for them, serving them as an agent of reconciliation, solidarity, and unity, if necessary bearing a share of suffering in order that the vision might be realized. The ruler acts to effect what the vision portends, assuming the responsibility to see to it, as far as can be done, that the vision is enacted. Only Christ, of course, can do all this to the full, and most Christians will be able to carry out such ministries only very partially, especially since many will have relatively low-level positions in the institutions they serve. But given our varying conditions it is possible to conceive of any Christian in any situation being each of these figures among those with whom he or she lives and works. Cannot a mother in a home hold forth the vision of what a home should be (prophet), pray constantly for those whose home she shares (priest), and take daily the steps needed to bring the home closer to the promise the vision embodies (ruler)? Even an assembly line worker in a factory or a laborer on a farm who appears to be devoid of real power to make a difference could be some things day by day that would qualify as acting out this threefold calling. Can we not without difficulty imagine how that might be? And would not a Christian who is in an executive position in government or business have a special responsibility, since here we would have someone who could "rule" as well as speak and intercede? It is not really farfetched to take this image of the threefold ministry of Christ, apply it to ourselves, and regard it as a pattern by which to guide our daily witness and action. Here are some examples of what might result from such a model: evangelism, personal caring ministry, the mediation of disputes, ensuring the proper functioning of the institution, taking stands for justice and equity, and insisting on environmental stewardship. And these are but a few of all that are possible. In one sense, we would all become trustees, no matter what our status in our institutions, trustees of our own communities, trustees of society itself. There are not many states of human affairs that would not be enriched were the church to take such a view of ministry seriously.

And where, you might ask, does the local congregation fit into this picture? Are we leaving out of the picture altogether that sphere of ministry? Not really. Are not our churches also institutions, and should we not minister there too? And why should not our congregations be seen as those communities in which, week by week, the people of God are nurtured, instructed and inspired in order that they might be precisely what this paper has proposed they should be? Let us worship, study and care for one another to the greater glory of God and in such a way that everyone who takes the name of Christ may be empowered to be His minister in those "unexpected places" into which life carries most of us for much of our time.

George W. Peck is President of Andover Newton Theological School in Newton Centre, Massachusetts, USA.

Ministry of the Laity in the Workplace

John A. Sundquist

For more than two decades now, there has been a rather universal emphasis within the wider Christian Community on the ministry of the whole people of God. While there is plenty of mystery about the divinity of Christ, there is no mystery about Christ's servanthood, nor of His calling to *diakona*, or serving. Diakona applies to every believer who serves Jesus in any way. All of God's people have a calling to salvation, and all of God's people have a calling to serve.

Tragically, however, in spite of the clear teaching of the New Testament and recent widespread preoccupation with the ministry of the whole people of God (the laos), traditional divisions of labor and specialization between so-called "clergy" and "laity" remain. Clergy preach; laity listen. Clergy baptize; laity are baptized. Clergy serve the Lord's Supper; laity receive the Lord's Supper. Clergy teach; laity are taught. Clergy spend God's money; laity give God's money. Clergy care for their laity; the laity are the cared-for. Clergy go to their study; laity go to work.

As always, Jesus is our model. The great text of Philippians 2:5-11 describes how this one, who was very God of very God, chose to live as a servant. He humbled and emptied himself, and took on the form of a servant. We who follow Him are also to choose servanthood as the shape and style of our living.

Therefore, in spite of centuries of conditioning, the whole people of God must continue to struggle not only for the mind of Christ, but also to model Christ in servant ministry to the world.

All of God's people are called to this ministry. The impulse toward service to the world is not something either contrived or learned, but given. It is a gift from God and the indwelling Spirit. (Ephesians 4:11ff)

For Baptists, one of the blocks that prevents us from eliminating this unbiblical, and even heretical, division of labor between clergy and laity is our highly personalistic and legalistic understanding of salvation. If conversion is seen exclusively, or even primarily, as a divine transaction for the forgiveness of sin, then the initial turning, or decision, becomes the whole experience and an end in itself.

If God is transforming the kingdoms of this world into the Kingdom of our God, then God has a job to be done in this world and a people gifted to do it. (2 Corinthians 5:17-21) The goal of salvation is the establishment of the Kingdom of God, so that all things—persons, institutions, nations—and the whole created order may enjoy God and praise God forever. All of us, as God's people, are called and gifted to give of ourselves and our resources to that grand end. (Romans 12:4-21) All of us are ministers of Jesus Christ. Through the ministry of the Holy Spirit, we know that we are created by God, redeemed by Jesus Christ, and gifted and called to follow our Lord in service to our world. That knowledge in our very bones gives us an energy and boldness to claim our world for Christ, wherever that world may be.

Only a very few of God's people are engaged in "church careers." In many ways, these are the fortunate servants, for their roles are fairly clear and their expectations often rather low. Servant ministry for everyone else is filled with hard realities: getting and keeping a job, running a family, maintaining a house, and relating redemptively to neighbors and to the world community. They must confront and respond to the difficult questions of life every day: Why is there no answer to my prayers? What would Jesus do in this situation? What is happening to our world? How can I reach my son or daughter? How can I tell my co-worker that I care?

Vocation, security, financial resources, integrity, recreation,- justice, family, all take on reality in the world. It is in the world, not in the Church, that real ministry takes place. In the world, where moral decisions are not always clear, where insecurity and chaos seem the norm, where justice hits the road in the workplace, where work is often difficult or tedious, where families fracture and faith falters, the people of God minister. In the world, where there is an enormous pull toward safety, a longing for simple solutions and authoritative answers, the temptation is always present to fall back into the old divisions of labor where the clergy minister and the laity are ministered to. It is not easy in the world; yet in the world we find our calling, and it is in the world that we will receive power. (Matthew 26:32; 2 Timothy 2:7)

The people of God are found in every vocation and profession. There, they serve God and people with an energy, wisdom, insight, and courage beyond themselves. In, through, and around them, the breeze of the Spirit blows to transform people and situations to the glory of God. At times, the servant may be aware that God is working through him or her; at other times, totally unaware; but always, the servant is the vehicle for the release of power not his or her own.

In the workplace, the Christian lives not only for self and family, but also for neighbor, community, and world. There, Christians become Christ to others, releasing the acceptance, affirmation, forgiveness, and love which they have experienced in Christ. In the workplace, God's people often live a sacrificial love, respond to a spirit above self-interest, and do justice because they can do nothing else.

Examples of ministry in the world and in the workplace are many and varied. As one in a "church career," I have been deeply moved and at times shaken and judged by the selfless ministry of the people of God. When my friend, Emmett Johnson, was stricken with Hodgkins Disease and his body ravaged by the effects of massive chemo and cobalt therapy, his physician was Dr. Clarence Arlander, a faithful member of the church where Emmett was pastor. Each morning at 6:00 a.m., Dr. Arlander would make his rounds and sit by the bed of his pastor. He would encourage him, urge him not to lose hope, and share his own faith in the Great Physician. One morning, after being in the hospital for several weeks, Emmett noticed that Dr. Arlander was wearing knickers, and complimented him on his "new look." The doctor smiled and said, "Yes, I've been on vacation for the last two weeks, and am on my way to the golf course." Emmett says that as his brother in Christ, his physician, left that morning, he [Emmett] recalled the anger and frustration of his congregation's nominating committee when, year after year, Dr. Arlander refused to serve as a deacon or trustee. Emmett said, "Now, I understood. His ministry was here, by his patients' bedsides."

In my own life, I thank God constantly for several incredible lay persons, who were "ministers of Christ and stewards of the mysteries of God." (2 Corinthians 4:1) First and most importantly, I think of my father, who was a marvelous example of Christian love and care, a respected deacon of our church, and, vocationally, a telephone-man from age 17 to retirement. When he went home to glory, I still remember my shock when I discovered that, on a weekday morning, his home church was filled beyond capacity for the memorial service I was to conduct. It was only then that I began to understand the incredible influence of this quiet man on the lives of so many.

I had the powerful privilege of having Kenny Wahlgren as my Sunday

School teacher from the sixth grade through high school. This masonry contractor took seven boys from the city of Chicago under his care, and not only gave them an hour every Sunday morning, but allowed them to interrupt his life at all hours of any day. Not only was he always available, he carved out big chunks of his time to take them to ball games, concerts, and even on long fishing trips. It is no accident that all "his boys" are committed to Christ and the church, and three of the seven are in "church careers."

In college, I was profoundly influenced and pointed toward ministry by a warm and humorous psychology professor, Swan Engwall; who, in my eyes, radiated the power and passion of the Gospel.

Recently, I was the guest preacher at the First Baptist Church of Waterloo, Iowa. My host for the day was a man I guessed to be my age, by the name of Merlyn Christensen. When I discovered that he was already retired, I was overwhelmed. I could not imagine that one so young could be retired. Just before I left him later that day at the airport, I risked asking him about his retirement. He gave me a wonderful testimony to the power of the Gospel in his life. Merlyn was a graduate Civil Engineer who had had a long and distinguished career with the Army Corps of Engineers. In the United States, the Army Corps of Engineers employs primarily civilians to build dams, bridges, roads, and other public service construction projects. Mr. Christensen had been engaged in a most responsible position in relation to flood control within the Great Plains. He found his work consistent with his commitment to Christ, making a significant contribution to the good of the community, nation, and world. However, during the second term of the current American President, it became clear that the Army Corps of Engineers was going to do less civil work and more military work. Convinced that his faith commitment would not empower him to use his skills militarily, he retired early, with significant financial loss to him and his family.

This story of Merlyn Christensen is particularly important in our day and time, for integrity always carries a cost. The tensions of conflicting demands and interests in our interdependent, modern world often tear at people's values as well as their emotions. It is refreshing and delightful when someone is able to declare, as did Merlyn, "As for me and my house, we will serve the Lord."

Some time ago, it was my privilege to meet an incredible woman by the name of Retha Tillman in White Oak, Tennessee. This middle-aged woman began to have a deep concern for the way women were marginalized and pushed toward poverty within her Appalachian hill community. Through her efforts, a cooperative was established for the purpose of developing cottage industries; and soon, a day care center was established for the children of these women. In a very brief period of time, her program, created out of nothing, became the county's largest employer of women.

It was while I was pastoring at Minneapolis that I came under the influence of Robert McGarvey. Bob was an active layman within the life of our church and the owner of the area's largest supplier of restaurant coffee. Bob was a recovering alcoholic and an active member of Alcoholics Anonymous. His commitment to the Church of Christ spanned all denominational barriers.

He was a person of great kindness and generosity. Perhaps his most important contribution was that his large and successful firm employed person after person who would never have been accepted by any other employer.

Two years ago, I was preaching in Connecticut and met a delightful elderly woman named Laura Cummings during the covered dish dinner which followed the service. She shared with me that her husband died at the age of 67, nearly 20 years ago, of a heart attack. This absolutely outgoing and bright woman had fully captivated my attention. There was something electric about her, and it was obvious that she had an unlimited ability to love the world. She wore a vest made by the Nagas of northeast India that she had purchased at a mission craft bazaar that her church had sponsored. Laura told me that before her husband died, she had never driven a car. When I asked if she had then gone out to learn how to drive, her response was, "I wasn't gonna be tied down like a horse!" Later I learned that Laura recently learned how to play the harmonica so that she could entertain the elderly and shut-ins she regularly visited. Before I left the church that day, the pastor told me a most moving story about this incredible woman. The pastor has a 35-year-old, severely retarded son, who is institutionalized. The boy had a starvation of oxygen to the brain during birth and has been institutionalized since he was eight years old. He does, however, spend each weekend with his family and is usually in the church every Sunday. Recently, the boy had been working on painting a picture of the Last supper. Though the pastor didn't say so, I had the feeling that it was, perhaps, a paint-by-number picture. When he asked his father if he could bring it to church to display it in the narthex, his dad said, "Certainly." When he brought it to the church, Laura Cummings was the first to see it and admire it. Laura asked the young man if it was for sale, and he assured her that it was. She asked, "How much do you want for it?" and quickly he responded, "Fifth dollars." According to the pastor, his son has hardly any sense of the difference between fifty dollars and fifty cents, or for that matter, five hundred dollars. But Laura quickly pulled out her billfold and wrote the young man a check for fifty dollars and took the painting home.

The pastor told me how he had spoken to Laura, thanking her for her generosity, but expressing to her that her gesture was really too much. He said her response was priceless: "She told me, "If you worked as many hours in preparing your sermon as he did in painting that picture, we couldn't pay you enough." She then added, "I will buy only one painting, but I want you to know, it was worth every penny of the fifty dollars."

These people are the ministers of the church. These are they who radiate the light of the Gospel and reflect to a needy world the reality of our Christ.

John A. Sundquist is Executive Director of the American Baptist Board of International Ministries in Valley Forge, Pennsylvania, USA.

Ministry in Middle Eastern Context

Mona Khauli

"I shall not die, but live, and declare the works of the Lord"
Psalm 118:17

This is a very significant verse for the survivors in Lebanon who have come through fourteen years of armed conflict that has raged endlessly on Lebanese soil, endangering our lives, threatening our national sovereignty, intimidating and terrorizing us beyond any human description or imagination. As we embark on our fifteenth year of desolation, we cannot but thank the Lord for his miraculous intervention at times of great danger and risk, whence He delivered us from death, deprivation and mental distress.

It is not an overstatement to declare that God has brought us through disastrous times for a divine purpose. Nevertheless, bearing in mind Jesus' comment to His disciples in Luke 15:1-5, on the plight of galileans who suffered an ugly death at the hands of Pilate; and the eighteen dwellers of Jerusalem who perished under the falling tower of Siloam, reminding them that all these people were neither more sinful nor deserving death above others, but all needed repentance in order to be spared. As such, we are persuaded that as Christians, saved by the precious blood of Christ, we have been kept for the purpose of uplifting fellow sufferers by sharing with them the bliss of present day partnership with the Lord and the treasures of eternal life upon transiting from this world. The reality of death, haunting our existence, day and night, under the intensity of warfare, kidnapping and killing of innocent civilians, is often turned into a wishful prayer that we utter in despair as a means of escape from the escalating madness.

Therefore, each new day is a gift of life and a challenge to Christian service in a country that has been repeatedly condemned to die by its friends and foes alike, a death which it has resisted by sheer faith and trust in the power and goodwill of the Prince of Peace, in the absence of the power and goodwill of the nations that have claimed our rescue.

Historical Background

At this point it is needful to share with you a brief overview of the Lebanese plight which has claimed over 150,000 civilian lives, and that has precipitated very serious social and economic problems as represented by:

30,000 widowed women,
50,000 orphanned children,
60,000 handicapped, the majority being children,
100,000 youths suffering from drug abuse or addiction,
870,000 displaced civilians, practically one third of our 3/2 million total population.

News coverage of our once peaceful country far exceeds the space it covers on this earth. It is a strip of only (4000 sq. miles) 10,000 square kilometers, mostly rugged mountains, on the eastern shores of the Mediterranean Sea. Since Old Testament times, the Phoenicians inhabited its coastal towns of Tyre, Sidon and *Byblos* where the alphabet, our contribution to world civilization was invented and the name of the word of god "The Bible" was derived from. Its present population, a quarter of whom are non-Lebanese refugees, represents two major religions, Christianity and Islam. It is the only state in the Middle East with a Christian identity which dates back to the times of Christ and it has been the mainstay as well as the refuge for Christians in the surrounding Arab States whose totalitarian regimes have imposed varying degrees of repression on them. With its strategic position on the eastern shores of the Mediterranean, it was the passageway of all great armies thru history and repeatedly a focus of political struggle and armed confrontations.

Our independence in 1943 was shortlived as the year 1948 saw the creation of the state of Israel on the land of Palestine with a massive influx of refugees into our country. Their mounting anger and frustration at their plight, especially after the expulsion from Jordan into Lebanon of 400,000 armed Palestinian revolutionaries, disrupted the delicate sectarian balance and created for us a state within a state. The turmoil in the Middle East at this time as well as the escalation of the arms race reflected negatively on the stability and life of the country. 1975 witnessed the beginning of the present state of war and belligerence when many Christian communities got armed to defend their areas as fighting broke out with Palestinian revolutionaries who allied themselves with Moslem groups. In 1976 the Arab League deployed a deterrent force which subsequently withdrew leaving the Syrians in actual occupation of most of Lebanon. This period witnessed widespread clashes among several Arab and foreign states on Lebanese soil using local agents and mercenaries who had crossed illegally into Lebanon. The Israeli invasion of 1982 added a new chapter to the grim history of our young nation which ended with the intervention of the American and European multinational force who withdrew prematurely creating for us a new crisis. Throughout these long years of war, the independent spirit of the nation was not quelled as the Lebanese have been determined to retain their identity and dignity by extreme perseverance coupled with hard work, personal initiative and resilience that enabled us to endure and survive to this day.

Against this very grim background, our evangelical churches continued to bear witness for Christ to a suffering, disillusioned population of Christians and Moslems alike, with utter dedication and commitment.

The Ministry Among Non-Christians

Lebanon is as ancient as the Bible, and Christianity in Lebanon goes back to Christ. We find Lebanon mentioned on more than one occasion and in more than one context. As early as Deuteronomy and throughout the Psalms and the Prophets, Lebanon is given geographic recognition, historical value and most importantly its name and meaning are synonymous to beauty, elevation, purity and sanctity. The righteous are likened to the Cedars of Lebanon which the Lord has planted (Ps. 92:12 and Ps. 104:16).

Moreover, the bride shall be called out from Lebanon (Songs of Solomon 4:8). The smell of her garments is like the smell of Lebanon. She is a garden enclosed, a fountain sealed, a well of living waters and streams from Lebanon (v. 11-15). Could this mean anything less than a faithful Church that teaches and disseminates the word of God in a thirsty land. The Christian ministry has prevailed amongst a population of about 3-1/2 million, half Christian and half Moslem. Their composition is roughly: 1 million Shiite Moslems; 1/2 million Sunni Moslems; 1/4 million Druze Moslems; another 1 million Maronite and Catholic Christians; 1/2 million Greek and Armenian Orthodox Christians; 1/4 million other Christian sects, among them some 40 thousand Protestants. Naturally, the weight of evangelistic out-reach falls on this last group, comprising Protestant churches of which the Baptists number approximately 2000.

To say the least, our contemporary Christian ministry is a very delicate one, given the recent upsurge in militant Islamic fundamentalism that has a strong base in Lebanon, with a few committed Christians trying to reach out to a multitude of other than, or nominal Christians. This difficulty is compounded by the fact that they all believe in the one and same god, however, with individual deep-rooted divergencies. For example, the traditional Christian constituencies have their respective patron saints to whom reverence is due on a par with Christ. Moslems on the other hand, have a high regard for Christ as the greatest of prophets but refuse his divine nature as reflected in the Trinity. These two groups are equal in their resistance to Christ's lordship as savior from sin and as the only mediator between God and man.

In what manner then have we been able to preach Christ as Son of God, fellowman, crucified and resurrected as savior of humanity??

Dialogue invariably fails, leading from friendly discussion to heated argument and often ending with negative overtones, misunderstanding and a complete block-out on further conversation.

Door to Door visitation is often refused and visitors harshly rejected, accused of being related to various political parties, Jehovah's Witnesses or even burglars in the guise of good men.

Drawing People to church or to evangelistic meetings has given minimal results as conservative groups hesitate to be seen entering a church building for fear of harassment by their own families and religious leaders (our local communities are very small and privacy in those matters is nonexistent).

What ministries then have succeeded where others have failed??

Campus Ministries have had far reaching results as college students exchange ideas, carry on with Bible study or just live honestly letting Christ speak through their lives and Christian ideals. More non-Christian youths are drawn through this mutual friendship approach and eventually join our churches, than through direct confrontation and overt evangelistic campaigns. Similarly, Christian education offered by the Baptist High School in West Beirut is still well received by non-Christians, despite strong religious fundamentalism.

Clubs for Children and youth held in homes, or even in our church buildings on weekends, have also attracted large numbers. These activities offer variety; and the informal discipleship of young people working together and sharing their Christian experience is very appropriate. Whereas parents object to their children's attendance of formal church meetings on Sundays, they do not resist non-formal activities in the church building or basement facility.

Camps for Christian leadership are extremely popular at all age levels. This wholesome approach to personality development where participants are taught certain skills, leadership mechanics, outdoor activity and team work, has also opened the way to mature discipleship that leaves its lasting mark on leaders and campers alike.

These and similar forms of ministry have won many individuals to Christ who have not matured in grace and have assumed leadership roles with younger groups. The sad thing, however, is the lack of cooperation between churches and youth fellowships for lack of trust and often just sheer stubbornness that all ministries must be church-centered, church-guided or church-oriented. The reason behind this dogmatic approach is invariably the indiscriminate, undiscerning adoption of church patterns that have succeeded in other cultures and communities, and in good faith were carried to us by competent evangelistic leaders, rarely taking into account local social patterns and religious customs. My observation at this point is for both Christian teachers and local communities, who must together plan appropriate evangelistic methods bearing in mind the models that Christ exercised which always took note of individual needs and respected social traditions.

Our Ministry During Wartime

This is an era of our lives better erased and forgotten on account of its length, its pain and its hardship. From 1945-1975 our country enjoyed peace and a development boom that earned it a high rating equal to the most developed countries of the West. This high standing was slowly and systematically eroded by a protracted regional conflict that worked its way into Lebanon in 1975, abusing its hospitality and using its religious and cultural differences to fuel and perpetrate wild militarism that has taken its toll of our lives, our possessions and our land. The war technology introduced to keep this war ablaze is the worst and most lethal, comprising the most up-to-date bombs and explosives that were tested on civilian populations to measure their power of destruction, i.e. phosphorous, cluster and vacuum bombs have been used in Israeli aggression against unarmed city communities.

We live in constant fear of imminent violence and sudden danger as car bombs and rocket launchers take us unawares. Hooked to our radios, we listen where the shelling has hit next. Is it our home, our child that is the latest casualty? There is no safe place, no sense of certainty about anything. Except the certainty of God's love, his care and protection that we have come to know in a very real way and pass it on.

Emergency Relief became a necessity for everyone, owing to mass displacement of whole communities that reduced the bulk of our population to the poverty line. This was aggravated by high inflation and a deteriorating economy that touched the working sector with incompatible salaries and unemployment.

Sadly, it took some time for the Baptist communities abroad to address the physical needs of their brethren in Lebanon. While all social and political movements stepped up their relief efforts towards feeding, clothing and housing the homeless, our Baptist churches stood helpless except for local generous sharing among the brethren out of their meager means that had to stretch over repeated crises and hardships.

Even now, it took a lot of negotiation to convince our mission relief committees that assistance should be administered cordially and according to physical or medical need so as to preserve the dignity of the recipient who is already humiliated and traumatized by his loss.

Education and Vocational Training are two areas of ministry now badly needed. Economic deprivation and forced eviction have stripped families of all their resources, their homes and farming lands. They resort to education or vocation to insure a living. In this realm, the YWCA was instrumental in creating skills training for fast earning jobs for which it raised enormous funds in scholarship to enable the displace and destitute. Subsidies have been generous for youth enablement and widows' income generating workshops, but very little of it was matched by Baptist support. Whereas the YWCA is based on Christian principles, it does not have a mandate to preach the gospel like the church, except where Christian commitment exists and this is where I have been blessed by both. My social ministry as Lebanon YWCA director is enriched by my Christian calling which has helped me on occasion to couple church involvement with social outreach. But the fact remains that compassionate action by church support groups in emergency situations is lacking, contrary to the initiative of the apostles in Acts 4, 6, and 11.

Here I stress the need to undergird the ministry of the Baptist School with repairs, after its recent extensive damage, with equipment and scholarship assistance that it may continue to nurture new generations.

Before concluding, a tribute is due to our Lebanese youth and women who played a significant role in upholding the ministry by investing their lives and their talents alongside the menfolk to keep the churches alive and active when many pastors emigrated.

Our women have excelled in all respects, whether in the business sector in senior administrative posts or in the realm of social service where the challenge is gigantic. More importantly, they have operated as peace makers through their influence on members of their households, by instilling in them such noble values that contribute to harmonious and peaceful co-existence with others. Like their ancestor the Canaanite woman who pleased with Christ to heal her child, they do not take no for an answer and are never deterred by the lack of resources. On countless occasions they have launched their initiatives by faith and the Lord has greatly blessed and increased their potential.

In closing, let me stress the value of your support to the Christian ministry in Lebanon. Bearing in mind Lebanon's traditional role as a haven for minorities, both Christian and Islamic, its present trauma has implications for the future of christianity in the Middle East. Also remembering that "Neither is he that plants nor he that waters anything but God that gives the increase. For he that plants and he that waters are one, and everyone shall receive his own reward according to his own work. For we are fellow workers with God."

Let us be partners together in the planting and the watering so that we may change the wilderness into a fruitful garden and so fulfill the prophecy of Isaiah which reads: "Is it not yet a very little while and Lebanon shall be turned into a fruitful field?"

(Isa 29:17)

We are the labourers in the field, we know the language, we are familiar with the culture, we are conscious of the needs and are committed to withstand all the dangers and hazards in order to steer our country through this turbulent era. You are the labourers in God's free world where you have the advantage of using your time and energy to bring about change to our crisis area of the world. This you can do through

Pressure on your governments to convene the proposed international peach conference on the Middle East as called for by the United Nations and halt the sale of arms to the area.

Bring an end to the war in Lebanon and press for the withdrawal of all intervening armed forces from the country.

Build up public awareness regarding the root causes of the conflict in the Middle East and press for their elimination through peaceful measures.

Form support groups in the church and in the community for- prayer and program exchange with our crisis areas.

Provide financial support for education, vocational training, nutrition, health and other human development programs for the poor, the refugees and the displaced in Lebanon.

For by so doing you shall be restoring life and dignity to a country that has been condemned to die and that has been sadly broken under the crushing weight of self-interest power politicking. So let our theme for this day be

"Come let us Build"

Mona Khauli is President of the Young Women's Christian Association of Lebanon in Beirut, Lebanon.

Commission on Pastoral Leadership

Just as the pastorate is a multi-dimensional form of ministry, the pastor is a multi-relational person. Any responsive and responsible pastor is shaped by a variety of relationships as well as challenged to effect for good a large number of relationships.

At the beginning of this quinquennium, members of the Commission on Pastoral Leadership of the Baptist World Alliance decided to spend at least three years intensely studying pastors from a relational perspective. Though both ministers and ministry are influenced by their unique national and cultural context, views of the basic relationships out of which pastors work and to which pastors contribute remain amazingly the same throughout the international community of Baptists.

The first and by far the most fundamental relationship in the pastor's life is the pastor's relationship to God. A variety of significant concerns fall under this focus: the pastor's call to ministry, the pastor's authority as a minister, the pastor's spirituality, the pastor's primary identity. Papers and discussions within the commission devoted attention to these general topics. However, since this primary relationship was the object of our attention in Singapore, we looked specifically at the Asian context of ministry. Out of the pastor's own relationship to God come an understanding and a commitment to evangelism and church growth. Asian Baptist pastors provide good models for assuring both personally and institutionally, the Good News is discovered in their relationship with God.

A second relationship which directly affects and is greatly affected by the pastor is the pastor's relationship to the church, the local church in which the pastor serves. Predictably a large number of topics for discussion cluster around this particular perspective on the pastor's life and work: the pastor as a worship leader, the pastor as a team minister, the pastor and the ordinances, the pastor as administrator, the pastor as preacher, the pastor as problem solver, and the pastor as a spiritual leader. Very beneficial were three statements on structuring the church to discover God's will presented by persons from Western Europe, Eastern Europe, and the Caribbean. Acknowledgement that the pastor's spouse and other family members are significant factors in the pastor-church relationship resulted in a consideration of the special pressures which impact these people.

The third major dimension of pastoral relations involves the community. Obviously in this realm, the nature of the national/political context of ministry can be decisive. Civil involvements which invite responsible pastoral participation in some governments are impossible in other governments. Nevertheless, a study of the pastor's relationship to the community resulted in directing attention to: the pastor as prophet, the pastor as community leader, the pastor as an enabler, the pastor as social activist, and the pastor as care-giver. In a dialogue which brought together numerous different national points of view, a significant amount of consensus developed regarding the pastor's role in the community.

Edited papers representative of the work of our Commission on pastoral relations follow. We claim no final word on any of the topics treated; only one more word intended to encourage more reflection and discussion.

C. Welton Gaddy, Chair

C. Welton Gaddy is Pastor of Highland Hills Baptist Church, Macon, Georgia, USA.

The Pastor as Leader of Public Worship

C. Welton Gaddy

Worship is a necessity for the people of God. Holy Scripture is filled with statements which record the divine invitation to worship and reveal God's expectation of a worshiping congregation. First among the memorable mandates of the Decalogue was the requirement to worship only the one true God. Prohibition and admonition were intertwined. People were not to worship false gods in order that Yahweh could be worshiped. Chronicler, prophet, and psalmist agreed on the priority of a human response to the divine requirement for worship and praise.

> Ascribe to the Lord the glory due his name;
>   bring an offering, and come before him!
> Worship the Lord in holy array; (I Chron. 16:29)
> O Come, let us worship and bow down,
>   let us kneel before the Lord, our Maker! (Ps. 95:6)
> . . . all flesh shall come to worship before me,
> says the Lord (Isaiah 66:23)

Jesus recognized the divine expectation in this regard and encouraged his followers in an involvement that would move toward that time "when the true worshipers will worship the Father in spirit and truth, for such the Father seeks to worship him" (John 4:23). Out of his own personal pilgrimage, John came to acclaim on Patmos what Moses had understood on Sinai: "Worship God" (Rev. 22:9).

So integral is worship to the life of faith that one without the other is unthinkable. Gerhard Delling has made this point powerfully asserting that, "there is no possibility of being a Christian in the New Testament without worship."[1] In reality, the New Testament itself, like its Old Testament counterpart, developed in and was preserved by a worshiping community of faith. Worship preceded both theology and scripture.

Essentially worship is a verb. Etymologically the Anglo Saxon "weorthscipe" became "worthship" and finally "worship." At stake are ascriptions of worth—words, thoughts, and actions which are obedient to the instruction of the Psalmist.

> Ascribe to the Lord the glory of his name;
> worship the Lord in holy array (29:2)

To worship God is to give glory and honor to God, to adore God, to exalt God. A. S. Herbert described worship as "the recognition and acknowledgement at every level of human nature of the absolute worth of God."[2] Similarly, William Temple saw worship as "the submission of all of our nature to God...in adoration."[3]

Human expressions of divine worship vary considerably—formal, informal, orderly, chaotic, emotional, rational. In reality, no one individual can tell another precisely how to worship honestly. Congregations differ in their understanding of meaningful worship. However, certain general guidelines can be helpful. All worship should reflect conformity to biblical teachings on worship (such as the importance of order, the necessity of understanding and the centrality of praise), a dignity in expression which is complementary to the holiness of God (the means of worship should not communicate a denigration or compromise of the nature of God), and a variety in forms sufficient to provide for the diversity of human needs (means of worship which match personal tastes, abilities, and levels of spiritual maturity). Though such worship may occur privately, by definition it is fundamentally congregational.

Worship leadership is the responsibility of every pastor. Indeed, William Willimon judges it to be the "primary...revelatory pastoral activity."[4] Numerous studies have discovered that lay persons place worship leadership at the very top of their list of expectations regarding ministerial functions. In reality, for pastors, leadership in public worship is both the extension of a crucial act of ministry professionally and an expression of their own spirituality personally.

Consider the role of the pastor as leader of public worship. Fundamental responsibilities related to basic congregational activities highlight the various dimensions of the pastor's spiritual identify.

Prompter of the Congregation

The pastor's identity as congregational prompter stems from Soren Kierkegaard's famous analogy comparing corporate worship with the Danish theatre. According to the renowned philosopher, in the drama of worship members of the congregation are the actors. Ministers are the prompters. God is the audience. Congregations of believers gather before God in order to offer worship to God. Ministers prompt—encourage, enhance, facilitate—the experience.

Immediately obvious are serious discrepancies between the philosopher's descriptive model and dominant popular concepts of corporate worship. In numerous worship settings today, God is considered the prompter, ministers are seen as the actors, and the congregation is established as the audience. Such a model is the source of the burdensome expectation that the pastor perform satisfactorily in front of his people. The efficacy of a particular sermon has more to do with its value as a gift to God than with the nature of its reception by the congregation.

Kierkegaard's opinion is not without biblical foundations. Repeatedly God has invited worship from his people and established an official person to help them. Old Testament worship integrally involved assistance from prophets and priests. Likewise in the New Testament apostles, bishops, and deacons served as worship leaders. Contemporary ministers of the gospel stand in this sacred tradition when they prompt the worship of a congregation.

Essential in an experience of corporate worship are agreement and understanding regarding the meaning of certain words and actions. Thus, liturgy is important. This term "liturgy," which was used to translate the Old Testament *sharath*, meaning to minister on behalf of the community, came to designate the act of worshiping God (it was applied to the efforts of the Christians at Antioch in Acts 13:2). Though many people fear this word in relation to worship, liturgy—literally, "the work of the people"—is simply a reference to the service which a congregation offers to God.

Having noted the necessity of shared meaning in congregational worship, Stephen Winward has explained that "a pattern of words is a rate, a pattern of actions a ceremony, and a combination of both a ritual."[5] Thus, ritual makes congregational worship possible. Liturgy—the service of the worshipers—incorporates our rituals—formal or informal, prescribed or assumed, novel or traditional. Liturgy is that action of the congregation which enables each member to understand the meaning and purpose of all that is said and done.

Evidences of common liturgies are prevalent in New Testament scriptures. In fact, various forms of worship were the derivatives of different confessions of faith. Expressions of praise were primary. Frequently, members of a congregation voiced togehter "Maranatha," "Abba," and "Amen." sometimes a congregation declared, either spontaneously or according to a prescribed order, "Jesus Christ is Lord." Psalms were sung by the congregation as were other kinds of songs and humns. Numerous types of prayers were offered by congregational participants. Some New Testament students view Acts 4:24-30 as a model congregational prayer regularly incorporated in public worship.

Pastors serve as liturgists—facilitators and directors of the "work of the people"—encouraging individuals' involvement in worship and assuring a shared understanding among the people. In fact, the pastor is a key factor in whether or not a liturgy works. William Willimon has observed, "The presider of the liturgy sets the tone of the assembly, educates by his very presence and attitude, provides coherence and unit to the community's celebration, helps move the congregation toward its desired goal, and reminds the congregation under whose grace and judgment we all stand."[6] Guarantees of openness and hospitality within a service as well as a spirit of confidence are dependent upon the pastor. Of great consequence for a congregation's worship is the pastor's acceptance of the prompter role. The pastor represents the whole people of God. Hear Willimon again, "While the priest is neither the primary actor nor responder in the liturgy, the priest is the primary instrument of action and response...The presiding pastor gives visible expression to the faith and devotion of the congregation and to the graceful community forming work of Christ among his people and thereby becomes an agent of faith and formation."[7]

Prior to the Reformation, worship had become the almost exclusive possession of the clergy and monks. Active participation on the part of ordinary believers "apart from adoration, not unmixed with superstition" at the elevation of the consecrated elements in the Mass, was confined to communicating, in the bread only, once a year at Easter."[8] No such apathy and abstinence on the part of the congregation must be allowed to develop again—whether by thoughtless default on the part of lay believers, by jealous assertions of privilege on the part of the clergy, or by the ratings-minded commendation of television preachers who attempt to "put-on" worship for people to see. Participation by all people is essential if worship is to be truly congregational and thus biblical. Every conscientious pastor labors toward that end.

Intercessor in Prayer

In corporate worship, prayer is corporate. The pastor prays with and for the members of the congregation. Personal concerns like private prayer should be reserved for sessions of solitary worship. Though only one person—usually the pastor—speaks aloud, the goal is a unison prayer such as the one found in Acts 4:24.

Incumbent on the pastor is an articulation of the situation of the congregation before God. In a sense, it is in the pastor's prayer of intercession that all of the community's needs are to meet and coalesce. Biblical precedent for this pastoral act can be found in the ministries of Abraham (Gen. 18:22-23), Daniel (Dan. 9:3-19), and Ezra (Ezra 9:6-15). Of course, both Jesus and Paul repeatedly prayed for the church.

Leander Keck of Yale Divinity School has characterized the pastoral prayer as "a bowl of wet, soggy noodles dumped on a helpless congregation."[9] Perhaps the reason for such a stinging critique resides in the fact that most ministers spend a great deal if time preparing what they will say to people and very little, if any, time preparing what they will say to God. George Buttrick always advised his students to devote the same kind of meticulous attention to the pastoral prayer that is devoted to the sermon.

Common ingredients in the pastor's prayers with and for the congregation are the adoration of God, praise and thanksgiving to God, confession before God, and petitions to God related to the needs of others. Often the pastor can formulate in words thoughts and concerns which the people only know how to feel. Genuine communication with God can be established with the result that the community is strengthened.

Obviously the ability of any minister to function as an effective intercessor is directly related to that person's actions as a pastor. The concerns and needs of the community of faith can be represented only if the worship leader has heard the cries of troubled families, shared the grief when a loved one has died, participated in the joy of new life, and otherwise been involved in the lives of the people.

Interpreter of the Word of God

Donald Coggan has observed "that between the forgiveness of God and the sin of man stands—the preacher! That between the provision of God and the needs of man stands—the preacher! It is his task to link human sin to forgiveness, human need to divine omnipotence, human search to divine revelation."[10] To exercise responsibility in this crucial position the preacher needs insights, thoughts, and words beyond his or her own wisdom. In fact here is further incentive to be faithful to the role of an interpreter of the Word of God.

If pastors fail to speak about God they lose their *raison d'etre*. Indeed, every sermon should treat a theme that is in some manner addressed in scripture. William Willimon is correct in his conviction that "Congregations are more likely to hear our prophetic preaching if they are convinced that it arises out of the church's weekly confrontation with Scripture rather than out of the preacher's private need to be relevant, abrasive, and controversial."[11]

When is preaching biblical? Numerous authors have addressed that question. Simply quoting the Bible is not an adequate solution. George Sweazey has offered a good summation of the criteria essential for a positive response to such an inquiry. Preaching is biblical when it presents a major biblical theme and biblical attitudes; when it is related to the Bible's central message of salvation through Jesus Christ; when it refers to what the Bible says; and when it is formed around the two foci of the Bible and a present need.[12]

In reality the key to biblical preaching is the pastor's own personal relation to the Bible. The sermon is his or her primary act of worship—the pastor's offering to God. Thus, that which is said for God and overheard by the people must be grounded in the Word of God. Crucial to the ministry of every pastor are hearing, interpreting, and applying the Bible.

Listening to the Bible

More basic than the responsibility of interpreting the Word of God is the pastor's identity as a sinful person needing to hear the Word of God. Paul stated unequivocally that salvation comes only by hearing. That truth is for all persons. A pastor cannot interpret that which has not been heard. A professionally-based preoccupation with "What should I say?" must be replaced by the more fundamental interrogation "What is God saying?" Full attention to the Word of God is the very least that any pastor can given to God.

Pastors must listen carefully to God's Word in scripture. Every resource available should be utilized in an endeavor to hear and to understand a given text. Each passage of scripture studied should be allowed to speak its own deepest intent which may involve calling the pastor into question, interpreting the listener, or throwing light on the meaning of contemporary life.

With the challenge, encouragement, and instruction of writers like Robert McAfee Brown and Gustavo Gutierrez, pastors need to learn to listen to the scripture with third world ears.[13] The meaning of various texts is almost completely transformed when a pastor has accurately identified the wealthy and the poor of the world. Very helpful in this regard is Ernesto Cardenal's four volume work *The Gospel in Solentiname*. Cardenal provides a transcript of the discussions of various gospel texts among the poor citizens of the village of Solentiname in Nicaragua.[14]

Interpreting the Bible

Before raising the question of what a given text means, attention should be devoted to what the text says. An accurate answer to this inquiry requires careful interpretation. James Cox offers a helpful declaration of homiletical questions which various preachers have used to address biblical texts on their journey from the original setting of a text to its situation in contemporary life. Note that each question establishes an agenda for interpretation.

1. What is the text about?
2. What does the text mean to you?
3. What critical exegetical issues in the text might bear on a correct interpretation?
4. What is the significance of the text in relation to Jesus Christ and the history of redemption?
5. What has the text meant to other interpreters?
6. What is the point of immediacy? Where does the text strike closest home in your life?
7. What is there in the text that would make it difficult to communicate?
8. Can the truth in the text stand alone, or does it need to be seen in relation to a counterbalancing truth?
9. What are some of the causes of the condition or situation discussed or suggested in the text?
10. What are the logical implications or practical duties that grow out of the truth of the text?
11. What objections may be raised to your conclusions about the implications and applications of the truth of the text?
12. What would be the results of knowing or failing to know, believing or failing to believe, or doing or failing to do what the text suggests?
13. What must you do to make the message of the text real and true in your own life?
14. What is there in general literature, in biblical resources, in personal counseling, an in personal observation and experience that will exemplify or illustrate the truth of the text?[15]

Applying the Bible

The aim of biblical preaching—the objective of the interpreter of the Word of God—is to cause persons to enter into biblical events as the story of their lives so that the text becomes God's Word to them. The text is brought into contact with human experiences in such a manner that it illuminates the meaning of who we are and what we have been doing.[16] Gerhard Ebeling states the situation this way: "The word that once happened and in happening became the text must become a word with the help of the text and thus happen as interpreting word."[17]

James Cleland declares that "A Word of God is always the Good News (or an aspect of it) immersed in a Contemporary Situation."[18] Where God's Word is found, a "thus saith the Lord" is joined to a local situation. In Cleland's words, "The Word of God is bifocal. It has its head in the heavens, but its feet are on the ground."[19]

Whether one begins in the Bible and moves to the contemporary situation or begins where people are and moves to the Bible, preaching within the context of Christian worship causes these two worlds to intersect. Truth comes forth as the message of the scriptures and the content of the daily newspaper are engaged in dialogue.

A truly authentic interpreter of the Bible never will ignore the really significant issues of our time. A study of Jesus' feeding of the five thousand may call upon the church to reconsider its "five loaves and two fishes" in the context of a starving world. Expositions related to the "Jerusalem offering" may provoke some serious questions about the role of the church and the government in present-day welfare programs. Attention to Amos" denouncement of those who "sell the righteous for silver, and the needy for a pair of shoes...that trample the head of the poor into the dust of the earth and turn aside the way of the afflicted" creates concern about the general relationship between the have's and the have not's of our world.[20] As Gerhard Ebeling has said, "We cannot speak responsibly about God without speaking about the world in whose affairs he confronts us, and we cannot speak with ultimate meaning about the world and its issues without speaking about God."[21] Having listened to a text, interpreted it and been interpreted by it, and applied it to contemporary life a pastor delivers the Word of God. Such a sermonic offering is both pleasing to God and beneficial to members of the congregation.

Announcer of the Invitation to Redemption

Essentially worship is an offering. Members of the congregation gather not so much to receive a blessing as to make an offering. When the drama of redemption has been celebrated by a congregation, an invitation to respond with an offering has been implied. The pastor simply makes explicitly in language what is implicit in the liturgy and sermon. In reality, no person has truly worshiped God apart from the gift of the self to God.[22]

Historically God has called unto himself a people. Truly to worship God is to respond positively to the God veiled in mystery and revealed in redemptive activity. God has entrusted to the church the divine summons to redemption. As a worship leader of the church, the pastor is privileged to announce this invitation. The human call is based on the divine call. Likewise human responsiveness is made possible by divine grace.

The place and importance of the invitation in congregational worship are patterned after the relationship of the indicative and the imperative in biblical presentations of the gospel. The indicative always comes first. Announcement of the good news takes precedence over all else. However, demand inevitably follows gift just as responsibility invariably accompanies blessing. After the indicative of the gospel—"The time is fulfilled, and the Kingdom of God is at hand"—comes the imperative of the gospel—"repent, and believe in the gospel." The pastor articulates the imperative in the form of an invitation.

Worship is fake if it involves anything less than a person's total being. Humanity is the result of God's creative activity. Thus, the invitation extended in worship in no way encourages a forfeiture of one's humanity. Rather, persons are encouraged to become all that God has intended them to be. In redemption one discovers true humanity. Like Isaiah of old, worshipers hear the invitation from God to live as servants. Acceptance of that invitation comes with an affirmation of a new identity—"Here am I! Send me."

Surely other dimensions of the pastor's role in the leadership of public worship can be discussed. However, here are four priority functions. Each has to do with a responsibility in relation to the congregation and with the nature of the pastor's own identity as a person. A pastor faces no greater challenge and no higher calling than that of leading a congregation in an authentic experience of the worship of Almighty God. Toward that end, John Oman has the best final word—"I have often been puzzled about what makes a service worship. It does not depend either upon having a liturgy or wanting it. It does not depend on the sincerity or even the piety of the minister. More and more I come to think that it depends on worshiping with the congregation, and not merely conducting their worship."[23]

C. Welton Gaddy is Pastor of Highland Hills Baptist Church, Macon, Georgia, USA.

Note

1. Gerhard Delling, *Worship in the New Testament*, trans., Percy Scott (Philadelphia: The Westminster Press, 1962), p. xii.

2. A. S. Herbert, *Worship in Ancient Israel* (Richmond, Virginia: John Knox Press, 1963), p. 47.

3. William Temple, *Readings in St. John's Gospel* (London: Macmillan and Company, 1940), p. 68.

4. William H. Willimon, *Worship as Pastoral Care* (Nashville: Abingdon Press, 1982), p. 210.

5. Stephen F. Winward, *The Reformation of Our Worship* (Richmond, Virginia: John Knox Press), p. 54.

6. Willimon, *Worship as Pastoral Care*, p. 214.

7. Ibid. p. 215.

8. Raymond Abba, *Principles of Christian Worship* (New York: Oxford University Press, 1966), p. 23.

9. Willimon, *Worship as Pastoral Care*, p. 216.

10. Michael Marshall, *Renewal In Worship* (Wilton: Morehouse-Barlow, 1985), p. 100 citing Donald Coggan, *Stewards of Grace* (Hodder & Stoughton, 1958), p. 18.

11. William H. Willimon, *The Service of God: How Worship and Ethics Are Related* (Nashville: Abingdon Press, 1983), p. 156.

12. George E. Sweazey, *Preaching the Good News* (Englewood Cliffs, New Jersey: Prentice-Hall, Inc., 1976), p. 161.

13. Robert McAfee Brown, *Unexpected News: Reading the Bible With Third World Eyes* (Philadelphia, The Westminster Press, 1984) and Gustavo Gutierrez, *A Theology of Liberation* (Orbis Books, 1973).

14. Ernesto Cardenal, *The Gospel in Solentiname*, 4 volumes, trans., Donald D. Walsh (Maryknoll, New York: Orbis Books, 1984).

15. James W. Cox, *A Guide To Biblical Preaching* (Nashville: Abingdon Press, 1976), pp. 49-57.

16. Merrill R. Abbey, *The Word Interprets Us: Biblical Preaching in the Present Tense* (Nashville: Abingdon Press, 1967), p. 51.

17. Ibid. p. 42 citing Gerhard Ebeling in James M. Robinson and John B. Webb, Jr. editors, *The New Hermeneutic*, (New York: Harper ¿ Row, 1964), p. 68.

18. James T. Cleland, *Preaching to the Understood* (Nashville: Abingdon Press, 1965), p. 44.

19. Ibid. p. 45.

20. C. Welton Gaddy, *Proclaim Liberty* (Nashville: Broadman Press, 1975), pp. 71-73.

21. Abbey, *The Word Interprets Us*, p. 54 citing Gerhard Ebeling, *Word and Faith*, (Philadelphia: Fortress Press, 1963), pp. 354-362.

22. Winward, *The Reformation of our Worship*, p. 50.

23. Abba, *Principles of Christian Worship*, p. 116 citing John Oman, *Office of the Ministry*, p. 11.

Spirituality of a Pastor

Y. K. Dukhonchenko

Among all the services in the Church the service of a pastor holds a special place.

We, Christians-Baptists, profess the principle of universal priesthood, but it does not mean that all members of the Church are called upon to be pastors. It rather means that we have a direct access to God through Jesus Christ, that all members of the Church, in accordance with the spiritual gifts, are called upon to conduct the service like that in a beehive where every working bee knows its place and its job. The same in Jesus Christ: "Now there are varieties of gifts...and there are varieties of services...but to each is given the manifestation of the Spirit for the common good" 1 Cor. 12: 4-5, 7.

Undoubtedly, every member of the Church is a man reborn from above. Nobody can be a spiritual man without being reborn of the Holy Spirit, who gives a new life to man in Christ. Because "that which is born of the flesh is flesh, and that which is born of the Spirit is spirit". Jn. 3, 6. And "if any one is in Christ, he is a new creation". 2 Cor. 5:7.

It is impossible to be a spiritual man without getting a new life, which is given to all who embrace Jesus Christ as their own Saviour, who believe that Jesus Christ is the Son of God (I Jn. 5:13). The birth from above is an indispensable condition for every believer and the more so for a pastor who in accordance with the Scripture "must hold firm to the sure word as taught, so that he may be able to give instruction in sound doctrine and also to confute those who contradict it" (Tit. 1:9); he is called upon to dress the wounded and to appease the madmen and to guard the flock "against the wolves", to preach the word, be urgent in season and out of season (2 Tim. 4:2), to "see that no "root of bitterness" spring up and cause trouble" (Heb. 12:15), to carry the sound doctrine of Christ to the Church and keep it intact. Moreover, he should do it even when not all understand him and do not always support him. Therefore, this service can be performed only by the spiritual man, the man filled with wisdom and the Holy Spirit, having God as the source of his force and knowledge, life and strength; the man who in his life and service leans upon God, confiding everything in Him.

There may be cases in a local church when a pastor is a man not born from above. Through such a servant God cannot bless the church and with such a pastor it cannot grow up spiritually as he plays the role of a blind man who must lead others.

But even if he is born from above a Christian called upon to be a pastor should possess certain qualities characterizing him as a spiritual man. The Scriptures depict the life of a Christian and the more so the life of a pastor as "a city set on a hill" (Mt. 5:14), therefore his personal, family and social life must be irreproachable.

What Is the Spirituality of a Pastor?

Nothing makes a pastor, filled with the Holy Spirit and wisdom, so Christ-like as the precious, powerful life of Christ manifested in his character and his blessed service through the fruit of the Spirit. In his message to the Galatians the Apostle appeals: "Walk by the spirit and do not gratify the desires of the flesh. For the desires of the flesh are against the Spirit, and the desires of the Spirit are against the flesh; for these are opposed to each other". Having enumerated the works of the flesh the Apostle characterizes the fruit of the Spirit as "love, joy, peace, patience, kindness, goodness, faithfulness, gentleness, self-control." Gal. 5:16-17; 22, 23.

Love

Love ranks first. It is not by chance because "God is love, and he who abides in love abides in God, and God abides in him" (I Jn. 4:16). From the Scripture we know that "God so loved the world that he gave his only Son, that whoever believes in him should not perish but have eternal life" (Jn. 3:16).

In accordance with the presence of love the Lord gives a commission "Free my lambs, tend my sheep" (Jn. 21, 15-17). To those who do not have love God does not give such commissions. This is also the reason why love ranks first. And prompted by love the pastor, imitating Christ who "came to seek and to save the lost" (Lk. 19, 10), always "go in search of the sheep that went astray (Mt. 18:12), so that, according to Apostle's word "be able by all means save some" (I Cor. 9, 22).

Joy

This is the inner state of all the Christians and, in the first place, that of a pastor. The joy of salvation, the joy of the fulfilled will of God, the joy of the conversion of a sinner: all this is well known to the heart of a true pastor. It is to this hard, self-sacrificing and firm service of the pastor that the following words of the Scripture can be referred in the first place: "May those who sow in tears reap with shouts of joy! He that goes forth weeping, bearing the seed for sowing, shall come home with shouts of joy, bringing his sheave with him". Psalm 126, 5:6.

Christ sent all his disciples and commanded all his Church to be the witnesses in peace. The testimony of Christ is aimed at showing people "The Most Beautiful of Human Sons". This testimony often ends with what the Samaritans said to the woman: "It is no longer because of your words that we believe, for we have heard for ourselves, and we know that this is indeed the Saviour of the world". Jn. 4, 42. The fruit of the testimony of Christ is the conversion of sinners to God.

Not only heaven and angels rejoice in one repentant sinner but the Church and the pastor rejoice in each soul converted to God. And equally the pastor grieves over each stolen soul, over each soul turned away from God.

Peace

As is known, sin destroyed the peace of Man with God, Man with Man and split the creation. But with the Nativity of Christ the Saviour the humanity found "on earth peace among men" (Lk. 2:14). Apostle Paul states "Therefore, since we are justified by faith, we have peace with God through our Lord Jesus Christ" (Rom. 5:1). The consequence of the peace with God is heavenly peace as a state of the spiritual man. This is the state of which the Scripture says: "Great peace have those who love thy law; nothing can make them stumble". Ps. 119:165. Such a man is sure of his future for he knows who possesses the key for the future. The awareness that we are in God's hands gives us inner peace. Peace for a Christian does not mean any absence of a conflict, it means a profound and constant peace among all circumstances. David experienced it when he exclaimed: "the Lord makes me lie down...he restores my soul". Ps. 23:2, 3.

The pastor is a peacemaker also when the peace is broken in the Church, when factions appear in the Church. The pastor should always be above any splitting. And when peace is broken in families he brings peace there as well. The following words can be referred to such: "How beautiful upon the mountains are the feet of him who brings good tidings, who publishes peace" Is. 52:7.

The pastor who serves reconciliation from God must have "the word of reconciliation" for people. As it is written: "So we are ambassadors for Christ, God making his appeal through us. We beseech you on behalf of Christ, be reconciled to God" - 2 Cor. 5:20.

Patience

Patience is an indispensable quality in the service of a pastor. The Apostle writes: "The signs of a true apostle were performed among you in all patience . . ." - 2 Cor. 12:12. Patience including compassion, understanding, and indulgence to the mistakes of others is so necessary for a minister!

Patience makes us capable of enduring weariness, tension, bearing feeblenesses of others (Eph. 4:1-2). Patience makes us Christ-like and therefore the Scripture calls on us to be "strengthened with all power, according to his glorious might", for all endurance and patience with joy" (Col. 1:11).

Here is a story of one large patriarchal family with several sons, daughters-in-law and grand-children. An old father or grandfather was at the head of the family.

Peace, order, respect and obedience reign in the house...

"How have you managed to rule your family in so wise a manner?" the old man was asked.

"In patience", he answered.

"Is not it all the same that we must have seen in God's Church but only in the holier, lighter, more joyous and more loving form? The Scripture teaches that those "who are strong enough to bear with the failings of the weak", ought to help the spiritually weak, be mutually forgiving, encourage the faint-hearted, be mild, reserved, reasonable, patient (Rom. 15:1-2; Thess. 5,14).

That is why the Apostle ends one of his messages with the following wishes: "May the Lord direct your hearts to the love of God and to the steadfastness of Christ" - 2 Thess. 3, 5.

Therefore, the pastor, too, must be understanding, patient and forgiving in his relations with people.

Kindness

The word "kind" in the language of the Scripture means to be as God because no one is good but God alone (Mk. 10, 18). Kindness is something more than mere goodness. This is love in action, gratuitous doing of goodness from the bottom of the loving heart. And in the first place this is manifested in the life and in the service of a pastor.

The pastor in his service meets different people: the prosperous in their spiritual life, the wounded and tormented by sin; those who are aware of their state and those who are scoffing at everything, who are maliciously slandering, who are speaking in a haughty manner. The pastor manifests kindness and severity of God, kindness to those who continue in his kindness and severity towards those who have fallen (Rom. 11, 22).

Kindness is not to indulge sin but rather a means to provide salvation to sinners.

The Apostle Paul drawing a boundary between light and darkness says: "For the fruit of light is found in all that is good and right and true", Eph. 5, 9. The light of Christ makes his followers including pastors, useful citizens of this world; makes them as people always performing their duty before the people, Fatherland and God.

Goodness

What an indispensable quality for a pastor - goodness! "Holding sin in contempt one can be rough and unkind towards a sinner...Some people are so righteously fervent that they have no room for compassion towards those who sin" (Charles Allen).

No matter how eloquent is the pastor, how good is his schooling and how gifted is he but if he lacks cordiality and goodness he will not be able to bring many to Christ. Goodness makes the pastor capable to mourn for one who has fallen so that he return to the Source of Blessing.

Only goodness makes the pastor capable to behave in such a way as Apostle Paul writes: "Who is weak and I am not weak? Who is made to fall, and I am not indignant?" 2 Cor. 11:29. Like the Apostle the pastor again and again experiences the birth pains of those who stopped in their growth in Christ: "My little children, with whom I am again in travail until Christ be formed in you!" - Gal. 4, 19.

Faithfulness

Faithfulness in question does not mean faithfulness through which a man receives remission of sins and salvation, but rather a faithfulness as devotion or faithfulness produced by the Holy Spirit in the heart of Man who entrusted his life to God.

Faithfulness not only in great things but in small things too. "You have been faithful over a little, I will set you over much" - Mt. 25:21. The Apostle writes: "It is required of stewards that they be found trustworthy" - 1 Cor. 4, 2.

The pastor's faithfulness to God is expressed both in the personal and family life and in service entrusted to him. The violation of faithfulness before God deprives the minister of the blessing in life and successes in service. The pastor ought to guard those who are entrusted to his care from various heresies, dogmas, splittings, because he is responsible before God for the souls entrusted to him.

It is very important for the pastor to allocate his time in a proper way and to be careful in his promises. "What I have promised I shall fulfill" should be the motto for the pastor too. Faithfulness is rewarded by the Lord. Therefore it is said: "Be faithful unto death, and I will give you the crown of life" Rev. 2:10.

Gentleness

Gentleness is an indivisible feature of a pastor's disposition; it is displayed in a responsive, delicate manner, in respectful relations with others, in mildness of his heart. An example for every minister is the Lord who said: "Learn from me; for I am gentle and lowly in heart" - Mt. 11:29.

Gentleness is especially needed in treating spiritually ill and opponents of the truth. That is why the Scripture calls: "correct his opponents with gentleness" (2 Tim. 2:29) and restore the sinners in a spirit of gentleness (Gal. 6, 1).

Self-control

Self-control (moderation) is of great significance in the life of a pastor. Self-control is control over oneself, this is the "spiritual brakes" in life. We know how many accidents occur in transport due to failure of brakes of this or other means of transportation. And how many accidents occur in the spiritual life of people, in the church because the pastor's "spiritual brakes" fail!

Abstinence in food, words, in manifestations of irritability and wrath, modesty in clothing, moderation in various pleasures and tact in dealings with associates - all this should be indicative of the pastor's life.

The need for self-control or abstinence in every aspect of life was always relevant but it was never so urgent as at present.

The Apostle Paul is a good example for us in this respect. Being aware of the importance of self-control he wrote: "Every athlete exercises self-control in all things. They do it to receive a perishable wreath, but we are imperishable. Well, I do not run aimlessly, I do not box as one beating the air; but I pommel my body and subdue it, lest after preaching to others I myself should be disqualified" - 1 Cor. 9, 25-27.

We live among the people who do not always accept our testimony of Christ. But to show Christ to them through his life is always possible for a Christian. That is why Christ said: "Let your light so shine before men, that they may see your good works and give glory to your Father who is in heaven" - Mt. 5:16.

One of the episodes of the spiritual awakening in our country can be recollected. Second half of the 19th century. Dr. Bedecker came to Petrograd to announce about Christ to the common and to the noble.

Once, upon completion of the divine service Dr. Bedecker had a talk with a man who after his sermon turned to God. And that man told him: "You perhaps saw that during the sermon I went out; I came to the coachman and asked: "You had brought this preacher?" Having received a positive answer, I asked the second question: "Does he live as he preaches?". And I was surprised to hear what he said. He said: "No, Dr. Bedecker cannot preach so well as he lives. He lives better than he preachers".

Let us remember that words teach and deeds persuade. The pastor's service is not simply a profession. The Apostle Peter implores: "Tend the flock of God that is your charge, not by constraint but willingly, not for shameful gain but eagerly, not as domineering over those in your charge but being examples to the flock". - 1 Pet. 5:2-3.

Spirituality will never manifest itself in the service of such a pastor who is self-interested. The Apostle Paul characterizing a pastor says: "A bishop must not be...greedy for gain", (Tit. 1, 7).

Any affection, save life to God, will not contribute to the spiritual growth of the pastor.

Naturalness, good-will, piety and ability to sacrifice characterize a true pastor.

The spirituality of a pastor is displayed in that he becomes "an example for believers in speech and conduct, in love, in faith, in purity" (1 Tim. 4, 12). One can say of him that he is "strong in word and in deed". And it means that all his life: personal, family, social, he agrees with the Word of God. His words are "leaves of the tree of life", which bring curing for the sick, encouragement for the tired, strength for the weak and accusation for the resisting. When he admonishes, the objective of his admonishment is "love that issues from a pure heart and a good conscience and sincere faith! (1 Tim. 1:5).

The pastor has a correct attitude towards human praise. When someone is ready to make a sacrifice, he, like the apostles, is ready to exclaim: "Men, why are you doing this? We also are men, of like nature with you..." (Acts 14:15). He understands that "every good endowment and every perfect gift is from above, coming down from the Father of lights" - Jas. 1, 17).

The pastor does not respond with evil-speaking to evil-speaking. He ought to act as it is written: "We who are strong ought to bear with the failings of the weak, and not to please ourselves; let each of us please his neighbor for his good, to edify him. For Christ did not please himself: Rom 15: 1-3. Spirituality does not detach the pastor from the problems of the people. On the contrary, the higher is spirituality, the closer are the problems and sorrows of the people. The Acts of the Apostles tell about a priest, Joseph, a good man, full of the Holy Spirit and of faith (Acts 4:36; 11, 24). It is known that the apostles surnamed him Barnabas, which means "Son of encouragement". This name was given to him because wherever he went he brought encouragement with him. It was in him that the word given at one time to Abram came true: "you will be a blessing" (Gen. 12, 2). It is said in the Scripture: "Contribute to the needs of the saints" (Rom. 12, 13). The pastor shows himself in all respects a model of good deeds (Tit. 2, 7).

Thus summing up the reflections on the spirituality of a pastor one should turn attention once again to what intention God has in relation to his followers.

"For those whom he foreknew he also predestined *to be conformed to the image of his Son*" (Rom. 8:29), i.e., the aim of God in the life of the pastor, as in the life of every Christian, is that "we may be filled with all the fullness of God" (Eph. 3:19).

The mind of Christ (Phil. 2, 5), the wisdom of Christ - all this is manifested in the varied life and activity of the pastor

But the pastor as any believer does not stand still he ought to grow "to the measure of the stature of the fullness of Christ" (Eph. 4, 13).

What contributes to the spiritual stature of a pastor?

1. Further surrender of oneself to God.
2. Continuing in the Word of God.
3. Continuing in the prayer.
4. Fellowship of the pastor with believers.

1. Further surrender of oneself to God

For the spiritual life it is important who dominates in it. The surrender of life to God is the first step towards constant walking in the Spirit. This step transfers a man from the realm of wilfulness to the realm of God's will. He provides us with the basis for a further spiritual growth. Surrendering ourselves to Christ we choose God's will as a guiding principle for all our life in the future. And it means that we speak so as Christ spoke in the desert, in Gethsemane, in Golgotha, generally in all his earthly life: "Your will be done!" If we give ourselves to the power of Our Lord Jesus Christ, then from this time on we take a commitment to act under all circumstances, at any time not by our, but his will.

The surrender of oneself to God is the beginning, entering the domain of the spiritual life. By knowing God and His will further in everyday life, the pastor gives Him that that has not yet been given, because any Christian belongs to "another", to him who has been raised from the dead, in order that we may bear fruit for God" (Rom. 7, 4).

2. Continuing in the Word of God

The spiritual stature of a pastor depends on constant continuation in the Word of Christ. "If you continue in my word, you are truly my disciples" (Jn. 8, 31). A Christian continues in Christ only to that measure to which his word continues in him. The constancy and success of our spiritual life depend on our attitude to the Word of God. It was not just one worker on the field of God that lost his force in service only because he was negligent in the Bible. The inevitable result of this negligence was a substitution of a human word, beautiful, but empty phrases, like "the sound of cymbals", seemingly wise reasoning for the word of God. Like for any Christian so for the pastor it is necessary: long for the pure spiritual milk, that by it you may grow up to salvation (1 Pet. 2:2) and have success in service (Josh. 1, 8).

3. Continuing in the Prayer

Continuing in the prayer along with continuing in the word of God is indispensable condition for the spiritual growth of the pastor. The need for a prayer follows from the natural need of a human soul longing for communion with God. The pastor encounters many difficulties in his service and can weaken spiritually. This is also why he needs and looks for a communion in prayer with the One in Whom he has force and life. Someone became convinced when he said: "A lot of praying - a lot of force; little praying - little force".

Like Christ who, when He was in Gethsemane, was heard by God and in response to this prayer an angel appeared to him from heaven, strengthening him (Lk. 22, 43), so the pastor too prays, begs, receives and thanks. That is why it is said, "that they ought always to pray and not lose heart" (Lk. 18, 1).

4. Fellowship of the Pastor With Believers

The pastor has a need to communicate with faithful men. The history of the church of the first apostles kept an interesting case. Apollos, an eloquent man, well versed in the scriptures came to Ephesus. There he met a good Christian family, Aquila and Priscilla, who explained to him the way of God more precisely and it inspired him for a further successful preaching among the Jews that Jesus was Christ. Acts. 18, 24-28. Similarly, the pastor has to communicate with faithful people because communicating with the people the pastor not only gives but also receives. Especially it is important when he, as an ordinary man, is tired and depressed. For Paul the meeting with the brethren brought happiness and encouragement. It is said: "And the brethren there, when they heard of us, came as far as the Forum of Appius and Three Taverns to meet us. On seeing them Paul thanked God and took courage" (Acts 28:15). It was no accident that the apostle John appeals: "So that you may have fellowship with us; and our fellowship is with the Father and with his Son Jesus Christ" - Jn. 1, 3.

The service of the pastor requires constant growth. There should not be a stop in gaining the experience, not laziness of action, delay in development. The following words of the apostle may characterize the pastor's mission: "Brethren, I do not consider that I have made it my own; but one thing I do, forgetting what lies behind and straining forward to what lies ahead, I press on towards the goal for the prize of the upward call of God in Christ Jesus" (Phil. 3, 13-14).

The normal state of every spiritual man, and the more so the pastor, is to go ahead. He is not satisfied with what "the fruit" can bring, his heart encourages him to bring "much fruit". For it is written: "By this my Father is glorified, that you bear *much fruit*" - John 15, 8.

Ya.K.Dukhonchenko is Superintendent of the Baptist Churches in the Ukraine, USSR.

Pastors Under Pressure

(Part I)

Paul Beasley-Murray

I. Surveying the Scene

High Calling

There is no higher calling than that of pastoral ministry. James Stewart, addressing future pastors, rightly said: "To bring men face to face with Christ has seemed to you a matter of such immense or overwhelming urgency that you propose to devote your whole life to nothing else and...it is a thrilling and noble enterprise. It demands and deserves every atom of a man's being in utter self-commitment . . . To spend your days . . . actually offering and giving men Christ. Could any life work be more thrilling or momentous? Yours is the greatest of all vocations." The pastoral ministry is indeed a "gift of grace" (Ephesians 3.7).

High Stress

Yet there is another side to pastoral ministry. For many the high calling leads to high stress, or so it appears today. For today, at more than any other time, pastors feel under pressure. Increasingly such terms as "stress," "burn-out," and "marital breakdown" are being used of the ministry. Pastors it would appear are themselves in need of pastoral care!

No doubt to the average man in the street, for whom the parson is "six days invisible, and one day incomprehensible," such talk of pressure comes as a surprise. "You only work one day in the week," is the constant quip. "Sunday is your busy day," Although that may be true of some, for the majority that is not the case; most of our pastors are hard-working and many are exceedingly hard-pressed.

Something of the nature of the problem is indicated by the Australian Baptist, Rowley Croucher, who in an unpublished dissertation reported that one major American denomination "found that three out of every four ministers reported feeling stress severe enough to cause depression, anguish, anger, fear and alienation," Roy Oswald of the American Alban Institute paints an equally depressing picture, when in a treatise on burn-out (burn-out = the result of chronic stress) he writes: "17% - one out of five - clergy are burned out. This does not imply that they are inactive in parish ministry. They are still able to perform their pastoral functions with skill and concern. The difficulty is that they have lost their zest and enthusiasm for ministry. They appear to be hollow, dull and uninteresting, with little life or creativity left in them. The tragedy is that these are probably our most dedicated and committed clergy. They are not really dull and uncreative; they simply have given too much of themselves for too long."

II. Analyzing the Pressure

What are these pressures that are causing terms as stress, burn-out and marital breakdown to be increasingly common in discussions about the ministry?

Long-Standing Pressures

Some pressures have been with us for a long time. One such pressure is the matter of image. Consciously or unconsciously people put their ministers on a pedestal - they expect him to be perfect. Indeed, not only is he to be a saint, he has to be seen to be a saint!

But does the problem simply lie within the expectations of the church members? It could be argued that the problem lies within the pastor: i.e., the pressure is primarily self-imposed, rather than imposed by the church. Ministers put themselves on a pedestal.

The Australian John Mallison writes of ministers who act as though they are (or should be) beyond the frailties of human existence: without doubts, illness, limited abilities, family problems or discouragements. Such ministers are often dominated by "the tyranny of the should." In this respect he quotes Leroy Ardern: "Our captivity is expressed in various ways, for example, when we act out one of the following thoughts: I should be well-liked and respected by my people. I should be able to speak relevantly to my congregation and deliver a good sermon every Sunday. I should be able to meet all the needs of my flock. I should be available to my congregation every minute of the day, even if my family is neglected. I should have no other interests of concerns beside the church. I should be able to take almost anything people say to me.

Linked with the problem of image is the pressure of visibility, the phenomenon of living in a goldfish bowl. The pastor's life - and indeed the life of his family - is observed more closely than anybody else in the community. As D. P. Smith put it: "He is continually on display - many of his role performances are in public and the manse may be next door to the church where even his personal life is likely to be observed."

Needless to say, this particular pressure is closely linked with the preceding pressure of "image." Unlike almost any other job, there is a close connection between a pastor's work and his personal life. Indeed, his continuance in his job is dependent upon his having an ideal marriage and family life. Woe betide if things go wrong!

Pastors are also *scapegoats*. As the head of the organization - at least in human terms - the pastor is inevitably blamed when things go wrong in the church. There can be no passing of the buck. He alone is responsible.

If young people are not coming forward for baptism, it's his fault. If dissatisfied members leave to go to another church, the pastor bears the responsibility. If the offerings don't keep up with inflation, the pastor is at fault also. I sometimes say that the best way for a church to raise money is for it to sell off images of its pastor, together with the necessary pins to stick in!

Another pressure on the pastor is that of *time*. Unlike most mortals, the

the pastor has no set hours of work; instead of a 9 to 5 job, he is at work 24 hours a day. His it eh pressure of total availability. Living "above the shop," there is never a moment when he is truly off, not even if his "day off" is publicly stated in the church news bulletin.

There are so many expectations of his time. Selwyn Hughes tells of how members of a Christian congregation in the USA were given a questionnaire in which they were asked to state how many hours they felt their minister should devote, per week, to the following tasks: administration, pulpit preparation, committee meetings, promotion, visitation, youth work, counselling and personal prayer. The total on the answers averaged 82 hours per week. One member proposed 200 hours (a week has only 168 hours!)

There are so many demands on his time; there is always more to be done. The pastor, if he is not careful, can go around with a perpetually guilty conscience. Alternatively he may seek to appease his guilty conscience and end up by becoming a classic workaholic.

Financial matters can present a troubling situation. In spite of the Scriptural inunction, "the labourer is worthy of his hire," in some contexts at least pastors have long suffered from the "keep them humble, keep them poor" syndrome. pastors are not always paid a fair living wage. In part this may be linked with the very first pressure we mentioned, viz image. "Pastor, you're meant to set us an example of holy poverty!"

Linked with finance is the problem of long-term housing. Many ministers live in church homes, which although providing short-term benefits in fact deprive the minister involved from investing in the housing-market and thus providing for his retirement needs. The resultant pressure can be intense on both the pastor and his wife, and can affect the marriage relationship.

Loneliness is another pressure that is often present; the pastor tends to have no meaningful relationships with his people. Margareta Bowers has described the clergy as "lonely set-apart people. The sick clergy were even more lonely." Similarly the Roman Catholic Henry Nouwen says "the priest in being friendly to everybody, very often has no friends himself. Always consulting and giving advice, he often has nobody to go to with his own pains and problems...(So) looking for acceptance, he tends to cling to his own counselees...He spends long hours with them, more to fulfill his own desires than theirs. The paradox is that he who is taught to love everybody, in reality finds himself without any friends."

Pastors sometimes find themselves in the position of being *powerless*. The church is a voluntary society, with the result that pastors have to work with volunteers. This creates difficulties: on the one hand they can't "order" any one to do things - instead they have to coax and persuade people, and then be happy with the results, whatever they may be. On the other hand, they can't choose their volunteers; instead they have to work with the material they are given, however awkward and difficult it may be. The pastor, alas, is not able to hire and fire his people!

Another aspect of the church being a voluntary society is that nobody has to stay. If people don't like the way the pastor operates, they can always move on to another church. Fear of offending members, thus causing them to leave the church, adds to the feelings of powerlessness.

Baptisms and church attendance apart, it is almost impossible for any pastor to measure what God has achieved through him. For most of the time he has little if any knowledge of what has been wrought in other people's lives. The grace of God apart, there is little to fall back upon in his darker moods. He asks himself, "Has all my sermonizing been in vain? Have they truly understood what I have been trying to say? If they did, then why is their commitment so seemingly superficial? What have I achieved through my visiting? Have I simply been passing the time of day, or have I spoke to someone's heart? Questions like these arise, and this side of Jordan there are no easy answers. All this seems to contrast with the world of business, where the profit/loss balance is seen all too clearly!

The job of the pastor is never finished - there is always more that can be done. This creates another pressure related to that of time. The Anglican psychologist John Sandford describes the pressure in these terms: "The carpenter, for instance, finishes the table he is making; the engineer can stand back and admire the bridge he has built; the surgeon may have the satisfaction of seeing his patient recover; the lawyer will eventually wind up the case with which he has been wrestling. Not so the ministering person. The ministering person is like Sisyphus in Greek mythology, whose fate it was to have to push a great stone up a mountain only to have it roll down again before reaching the top. This feeling that the job is endless, that you can never reach the top of the mountain no matter how hard you try, can lead to exhaustion."

This leads to the problem of differing if not contradictory expectations. Within any given church there are normally a wide variety of views as to how the pastor should devote his time and energy. There are those who would have him spend time with the young people, whereas others would have him major on caring for the old. Some would like him to spearhead the church's work of evangelism, whereas others believe he should be move involved in the community and its affairs. In terms of worship, there are those who would have him be dignified, whereas another section of the church long for him to become more free and easy. In such a situation it is possible for the pastor to feel himself torn into all sorts of different directions.

So far we have been describing pressures that have long been with us. But in addition to these long-standing pressures many pastors find themselves having to cope with a number of new pressures too.

One such pressure is the current theological whirlpool. Theology has always had its fashions, but never have the fashions seemed to change so quickly as today. Churches are changing rapidly. Many churches today are unrecognizable compared with even just ten years ago. Worship patterns are in a state of constant flux and leadership patterns are experiencing radical change. In Britain, at least, must of this upheaval is consequent upon the emergence and development of the charismatic movement. In such a situation as this, where members seem to be increasingly fickle in their allegiance, the pastor is called to lead. Unfortunately not all pastors know how to manage change, with the result that sometimes they and their churches are sucked into a whirlpool that leads to destruction.

Somewhat related is the fact that the mainline churches in Britain, as indeed in much of the West, have experienced substantial numerical decline. In an article entitled *Christian Survival in a Cold Climate*, the Dean of St. Paul's, Alan Webster, wrote, "There are lean times for the churches in England. It is tragic to see so many of them struggling for survival." The pressure increases on the pastor as there are less people around to do the work. It sags away at his confidence and he feels pushed to the edges of society.

Fortunately in England Baptist churches overall have begun to grow again. But such growth creates problems. On the one hand, it creates problems for the pastor experiencing growth - expanding congregations simply increase the pressure of work, unless the pastor knows how to effectively delegate and share the work. Indeed, sometimes the church simply grows beyond the pastor's capability.

On the other hand, church growth presents a very real threat to the pastor in a situation showing no growth. To quote Rowley Croucher: "I believe very many pastors today are disillusioned by the church growth approach, not because it's not valid for some, but because it becomes a yardstick for measuring worth - both of the pastor and the church. One experienced pastor I spoke to recently said he believes this single factor alone has been most responsible for most of the clergy breakdowns he has witnessed in the last ten years."

Another more recent pressure is the democratization of education. In times past the pastor was the "parson," i.e. the "person": he, along with the squire of the village, was the only educated person in the community. Today, however, many of his members are better educated than he. This in itself can pose a treat to an insecure pastor: his members are able to think for themselves and are no longer prepared to accept things on his say-so. This, coupled with the current anti-authoritarian climate in the West makes it more difficult to lead as a pastor used to.

Another pressure is the influence of a competitive society. We live in the day of the "rat race" - and this spirit has affected the church. Just as many people expect to go places, so too do some pastors! But this is not so easy for them, simply because the Baptist ministry at least provides no progression. There are not a series of recognized steps to be trod before one becomes an archbishop. In theory, at least, we have no hierarchy. True, there is a progression between smaller and larger churches, but the smaller churches can become larger and vice versa. For some pastors at least, this lack of a career structure can pose problems of motivation in a society which is so success-oriented.

It is perhaps debatable as to what extent the complexity of moral issues is a problem for most pastors. Indeed, in some senses it might be argued that this is a commendable pressure to experience—at least it denotes an openness and understanding of what is going on in the wider world.

Many of today's moral issues have become increasingly complex - the questions that are raised cannot be viewed in terms of black and white. If the pastor is to guide his people, what should be his stance over against the current nuclear debate? Can nuclear arms be justified? Or in the field of medical ethics, is abortion always wrong? Is genetic engineering always indefensible?

Then there is the matter of the development of the welfare state. From a social viewpoint the development of the welfare state in many countries is to be welcomed. The needs of the young, the sick, the old, the unemployed are cared for. Thanks to welfare, life, in some respects at least, is not as hard as it used to be.

From a pastoral point of view, however, it is possible that the welfare state has produced a softer breed of minister. Many of today's ministers are used to everything being provided for them. It comes as a shock to the system to discover that life in the ministry can be hard. To quote Bernard Green: "I find many ministers nowadays without the expectations which are given to me when I started. These include awareness of financial restriction, hard work, frustration and disappointment - the bit of Isaiah 6.8 which we seldom reach."

Next there is the slowing down of mobility. In a British context at least, there is a tendency towards longer pastorates. In part this may be due to the influence of church growth teaching, but in part too it is due to our present economic climate, which has created a difficult job-market for wives wanting to pursue their own careers. This latter fact means that many wives are reluctant to move, with the result that it is now less easy for pastors to move away from their problems.

Dennis Duncan has written of "difficult phases" coming in ministries around the four or five year mark: "For the first two years or thereabouts, expectations are high, the willingness to back up new ideas and endeavours is real and congregations are, on the whole, ready and willing to "go along" with whatever the minister suggests. By year three or thereabouts, latent opposition so far held in check, may begin to be present. If things do not go well, then the difficulties of the fourth/fifth year era may be very real." In the past this has been the moment when many pastors have sought a move. But that is not so easy today!

There is uncertainty in the role of the pastor. Perhaps of all pressures this is the greatest. The Anglican John Tiller in *A Strategy for the Church's Ministry* speaks of an almost paralysing uncertainty about the proper role of the clergyman. He quotes the anonymous contributor of the Preface to Crockford's Clerical Directory 1980-1982 who refers to "a crisis of confidence in the hearts of many ordained ministers, who work hard but are not sure that it is work which they ought to be doing."

For some these doubts have their source in the defects of radical theology. But evangelicals too are affected by the same sense of uncertainty. With the present rediscovery of the ministry of all believers, there is now uncertainty as to what is the role of "the minister." Questions are increasingly being raised as to the meaning of ordination: "What am I?" "Who am I?"

III. Clarifying the Pressure

This is an age of stress. It is important for pastors to realize that they are not unique in feeling the strains and stresses of life. Indeed, life in the 80's has been described with three words: hurry, worry, and bury. Or to sum it up in one: stress!

Jan Markell writes: "Of the 10 leading causes of death in America today, 8 are attributed to stress. Experts agree that the average business executive has a 1 in 3 chance of dying of a heart attack by 60." Stress leads more than 20 million Americans to develop ulcers at some time in their lives. Twenty years ago only one woman suffered from ulcers for every 20 men. Today the ratio is 1 to 2."

From all this is can be seen that stress is now reaching epidemic proportions. Needless to say this is causing concern not just to the medical community, but also to the business community because of its economic implications. Thus in 1978 it was variously estimated that American industry was losing between $17 - $60 billion dollars annually through lost work days, hospitalization and early death caused by stress. In 1983 in Australia the costs of coronary heart disease through lost production, etc. were put at £2.8 million per day for a population of 15 million!

However, it is important to realize that although stress may be a killer, it is not of itself necessarily harmful. Indeed, stress can be good for us. We need a certain amount of stress if we are to live full and meaningful lives.

Stress in fact is often needed to motivate and energize us. Thus Dr. Howard of the University of Western Ontario has produced a graph which shows the relationship between stress and productivity in his stress productivity curve: In any task a certain amount of stress is needed to get us moving and to keep us on our creative edge. From the graph it will be seen that productivity increases with stress until a certain critical point. But beyond that critical point, productivity drops rapidly.

Stress in itself is not necessarily negative. This is helpfully illustrated by Ted Engstrom and Edward Dayton: "Stress is the spice of life. In all types of activities we are involved in stress. When we exercise our muscles we are stressing them. When we exercise our minds we are stressing them. Life without stress would be dull indeed. But the problem most of us face far too often is excess stress and strain. It seems so hard to cope."

Therefore, excess stress is what is to be feared. The term currently being used to describe the negative effect of stress is strain. Expressed in different terms, "hyperstress (too much stress) is bad for us but so too is "hypostress" (too little stress). What is important is to gain the right balance, vix, "eustress"!

What are the major determinants of stress? Broadly speaking three groups of "stressors" have been identified.

First is job environment. Such "organizational factors" include job qualities (e.g. work pace or control; work overload or underload; physical conditions such as pollution, noise), roles in the organization (e.g. role conflict, role ambiguity, responsibility for people), relationships at work (e.g. poor relationships with supervisor or peers; difficulties in delegation and communication), and career development (e.g. under/over-promotion; job insecurity; frequent company moves).

"Extra-organizational stress factors" include births, death and marriages; serious illness; financial difficulties; anxiety about the children. Clearly an individual's ability to cope with such stress is greatly influenced by his support from his family and friends. A man can cope with difficulties at work - but not so easily with difficulties at work and at home.

Some individuals tolerate stressful conditions better than others and/or have more skills in copies with these conditions. Indeed, some people actually generate stressful circumstances for themselves.

To a large extent stress factors in the ministry simply parallel stress factors in the world. As we have already indicated, pastors can suffer from work overload ("lack of time"). role conflict ("differing if not contradictory expectations"), role ambiguity ("the uncertainty of the role"). They can also suffer from poor relationships (with deacons, with church members!).

However, in contrast to most jobs, not only is the pastor often under stress, his wife is also. She has to cope with difficulties relating to role expectation (an unpaid curate?), lack of pastoral care (can one be husband and pastor to the same person), lack of support (is a pastor's wife able to share her true feelings?), living in a church house . . .

In Christ we may be a "new creation," yet basic psychological characteristics still exist. Some pastors will be more prone to stress than others.

IV. Coping With Pressure

Having looked at the pressures as perceived by pastors, and then having clarified our thinking by taking a brief look at the general nature of stress at work, we are not in a position to address the problem itself: how can we help pastors to cope with the pressures of ministry?

Secular stress management has basically three approaches for dealing with stress in organizations:

Treat the Symptoms of Stress

This strategy seeks to treat individuals who are already suffering from the effects of stress. It is designed to alleviate the pain of those individuals who are already hurting. An example would be employee health and counselling services in which professionals diagnose individuals' problems and offer appropriate relief. This strategy essentially neutralizes the impact of stress. It clearly does not change the stress-producing factors nor does it necessarily prepare the individual to handle stress better the next time. It simply seeks to mitigate the adverse effects of stress.

Change the Person

This strategy seeks to reduce vulnerability and to develop better and/or coping responses to stress. Here individuals are taught to cope more effectively with stress and to be more aware of their own stress. Popular techniques include meditation, relaxation, exercises, and diet. Another coping mechanism is the encouragement and provision of support groups, where individuals are able to share their feelings.

Change and/or Remove the Stressor

This strategy seeks to get at the root of the problem by eliminating, ameliorating or changing the stress producing factors in the job. Examples include introduction of flex-time, job-restructuring, changes in policies and procedures.

Clearly these three different approaches are available in the church:

Treat the Symptoms

This first approach is the least positive approach. It offers only partial relief. A church, sensing that its pastor is under strain, will tell him to take a fortnight's extra holiday - indeed, it might even pay for him to have a trip to the Holy Land in the hope that his might enable him to recharge his batteries. But nothing changes the situation - nothing changes the man. Within a few weeks back at work, he's back to square one - struggling with life. Another way to treat the symptoms is to send an experienced pastor round to talk things through: this in itself is often a great help. Loneliness is often part or the problem; it does help to get things off one's chest. But at the end of the day, the problems are still there unless the counseling has actually helped to change the person and his attitudes towards the situation.

Change the Person

This second approach is infinitely better than the first. There is no doubt that pastors need to develop coping mechanisms to help them get to grips with the many pressures that are upon them. They too can benefit from meditation, relaxation, exercises and diet. Even more importantly, they can benefit from support networks in which they can share themselves and their feelings. Likewise there is much to be said for pastors going on time-management courses, where they can learn how to be more effective in their work. It is interesting that much of the present pastoral stress literature involves basically a Christianizing of secular stress management programmes, which seek to change the person.

Change and/or Remove the Stressor

In coping with pressure in the ministry, this surely is the key. There are no doubt many helpful coping mechanisms, but if pastors truly wish to exercise a rich and rewarding ministry, this is the area which needs attention. Just as secular management helps to eliminate or at least ameliorate stress by job-restructuring, so in church terms pastors will find the pressures begin to disappear once they accept a fresh job-definition.

V. A Fresh Definition of Pastoral Ministry

Pastoral ministry is God's ministry. In the first place pastors are called to be ministers of Christ, and not minister of his church. It is God who called them into the ministry - not the church. The church in setting them aside for ministry was simply recognizing what had already happened in their lives.

True, God calls pastors to serve his church. True, it is the church which pays their salaries. True, they have a certain accountability towards those who called them and pay their salaries, but ultimately they are accountable to God.

This can be a fearful thought; for unlike the church, God is ale to see into a man's very inmost being. He sees us as we actually are, and not as we would like to be seen. But it is also a liberating thought. Ultimately pastors are not dependent upon what others may think of them - it is not their judgment which counts.

In spite of recent Church Growth teaching, God does not call pastors in the first place to be successful - he calls them to be faithful. Faithfulness will often result in fruitfulness, but ultimately the latter is not their concern.

Pastoral ministry is shared ministry. The "monarchial episcopate" enjoyed by many Baptist churches receives no justification in Scripture. The New Testament knows nothing of a one-man ministry. In the New Testament church there was always a plurality of leadership. As Andrew Le Peau rightly says: "Organizations that are built on the preaching, teaching, thinking, entertaining, fun-raising charisma of one person - of which there are many in Christendom - are built contrary to Scripture. These are not bodies. These are grotesque mutations." Pastors need to develop team leadership. Where team leadership is exercised, there pressures are shared. However, shared ministry involves more than shared leadership. Every member has a ministry to exercise. Rightly understood, a church's membership roll is in fact its ministry roll. This is a lesson which many of our lay-people need to learn. But it is also a lesson which many pastors need to learn too! In this respect pastors are often their worst enemies.

Pastoral ministry is specialist ministry. Within this general context of share ministry, the pastor has a particular ministry to perform. He is not called to be a Jack of all trades called to fix anything and everything. As pastor he is called to fill a particular role:

- in the first instance, he is called to be *a man of God*. To lead, he needs to be led.

- in the second instance, he is called to be *a leader*. Under God he is called to lead the flock.

- in the third instance, he is called to be *a teacher*. As pastor he must needs feed the flock.

- in the fourth instance, he is called to be *an "equipper."* As pastor he must seek to "equip the saints for the work of the ministry."

Of course the pastor is called to care for those within the fellowship ("pastoral care"). Of course he is called to care for those outside the church ("evangelism" and "social action"). But in these areas of pastoral care, evangelism and social action the work can so often be shared. Difficulties, however, arise when these areas become the prime focus of a pastor's unshared ministry!

VI. Reassessing the Pressures

In the light of the foregoing we are now in a position to begin to reassess the various pressures that are upon pastors. We shall see that although the pressures are still there, they need not be so intense. They may merely cause stress, but, if properly handled, need not cause undue strain.

Firstly, we should note that pastors can render their people no better service than to be truly genuine. It is an interesting fact that the sin which Jesus attacked most was the sin of hypocrisy - time and time again he accused the religious leaders of his day of "play-acting." It does their people no good - not indeed themselves if pastor try to wear a mask and pretend to be what they are not. For a start, they won't be successful - the mask is bound to fall. And what is more, by adopting a mask they will only be encouraging their people to do the same.

Secondly, and perhaps even more importantly, is the point that churches don't need pastors who pretend to be perfect. Rather they need pastors who are seen to be striving to be men of God, men who constantly seek to live out their lives in his presence. The example needed is not one of a static perfection, but a dynamic one of following. As they see their pastor seeking to follow Jesus, so they too in their turn will be encouraged to follow him. Needless to say, this is still an awesome responsibility for the pastor, and emphasizes all the more his need to a major on his relationship with his God.

Thirdly, there is no need for pastors to feel that they must be seen to be omnipotent. No one person has all the gifts. Rather, pastors must be seen to be exercising the girts that God has given them. In this respect Dayton and Engstrom cite Romans 12.3: "Do not think of yourself more highly than you should. Instead, be modest in your thinking and judge yourself according to the amount of faith that God has given you. "This," they comment, "is not to put us down. Rather it means that we are to be accepting of who we are. Christians of all people should be able to accept themselves, to see that their gifts and experiences are given to them as stewards of God's grace...Strive for excellence in a few things. Understand the limits of your abilities, and with those abilities do the best you can. Do not strive for perfection. This is almost always unobtainable. It is the perfectionists who are the most frustrated of all people."

Visibility, the problem of living in a goldfish bowl, is surely related to the problem of image. Or to put it another way, the higher the pedestal, the more exposed the pastor! Once the pastor is seen to have rejoined the human race and no longer belongs to some spiritual elite, that moment the pressure begins to ease. True, the pastor may still be a leader, but hopefully his leadership is now shared. There are others upon whom his people may focus their attention. Furthermore, if the pastor is willing to acknowledge his humanity, then the goings-on in his household no longer hold the same interest. Thus if he is truly one of "us," then what's so special that he has problems with his teenage children - don't we all?

The pressure of the pastor as *scapegoat* has its roots in the old on-ministry model. Where the pastor made all the decisions, then clearly he had to take the responsibility for the consequence of those decisions. However, where decision-making is a shared responsibility, then deacons and church members alike share the responsibility when things go wrong. Indeed, one would hope that in a situation where things went wrong, far from blaming one another the church would then enter a period of mutual heart-searching; how is it that we so badly failed to discern the mind of Christ?

We cannot stress too strongly that if the church is truly functioning as the body of Christ, if all members of the bvody are playing their part, there can be no scapegoat. There is only one head - Jesus Christ himself!

The pressure of *time* is above all a question of priorities. Herodotus claim-ed that the bitterest sorrow is to aspire to do much and to achieve nothing. Not so, maintains James Simpson, the bitterest sorrow is to aspire to do much and to do it and then discover it was not worth doing!

Charles E. Hummel wrote a small pamphlet entitled, *The Tyranny of the Urgent*, in which he distinguished between the important and the urgent. "The important task rarely must be done today, or even this week...But the urgent tasks call for instant action...The momentary appeal of these tasks seems irresist-ible and important and they devour our energy. But in the light of time's perspec-tive their deceptive prominence fades; with a sense of loss we recall the import-ant tasks pushed aside again. We realize we've become slaves to the tyranny of the urgent." What is the solution? Quite clearly a daily seeking of God's will, as Jesus sought God's will. "By this means he warded off the urgent and accomplished the important. It gave him a sense of direction, set a steady peace, and enabled him to do every task God had assigned."

In other words, the pastor's first priority - which all too often becomes his very last - is spending time with his Lord in prayer, in study, and in reflec-tion. It is in such "quiet times" that priorities can be discovered.

Again, linked to this question of time is the issue of shared ministry. If a pastor truly believes in the ministry of all believers, then he will not seek to be a "job collector." Rather, he will happily share tasks with others and con-centrate on what he believes God would have to be the main thrust of his ministry.

Finance can be a real pressure and mustn't be underplayed. However, as with so many of these pressures, it has a theological root. Where the pastor operates a one-man model of ministry, he limits the church's role to that of being his employer, which can indeed have disastrous results. But, where the pastor encourages the ministry of all believers, where the members are taught to love one another, pray for one another, encourage one another, care for one another, bear one another's burdens - indeed to fulfil all the various aspects of New Testament fellowship - there will be inevitable spin-offs for the pastor! For where membership is understood in covenant terms as commitment to one another, then the church will be committed to its pastor - emotionally, spiritu-ally, and also financially. The members will want to see to his needs. Yes, shared ministry results in shared resources.

Needless to say, in such a situation the pastor must be prepared to be open with his people. If he conceals his needs and allows his people to think that like Elijah he too is fed by ravens, then he should not be surprised if finance becomes a problem. if on the other hand he is willing to acknowledge his humanity - he too has to feed his wife and children! - financial problems can be shared.

Next we turn to the pressure of *oneliness*. "It is not good that the man should be alone," said the Lord God of Adam (Gen. 2.18). Likewise, it is not good for the pastor to be alone. He needs friends, just as our Lord needed friends who would stand by him (see e.g. Luke 22/28). Friendships are important for a pastor's (and his wife's) social well-being. However, they are also important for their spiritual well-being. Whether from within or without the church, the pastor and his wife need to belong to some small "growth" group, where their spiritual needs can be met. Howard Clinebell writes: "Growth stimulating relationships are warm, caring and trustful, at the same time they are honest, confronting and open. Caring and confrontation = growth. This is the growth formula." Clinebell is speaking generally, but his words can surely be applied to the pastor and his wife. They too need to be in the kind of relationship where on the one hand they can be cared for, but on the other hand they can be confronted.

In part loneliness is also a question of "image." If the pastor insists on setting himself on a pedestal, then naturally enough he will be a lonely figure. However, in the normal course of events, shared ministry leads to shared friendships.

In part, loneliness is also a question of time - time has to be made if friendships are to be developed. But if such friendships are seen as important, and surely they are - then other calls on his time will have to be set aside.

In some senses *powerlessness* is more a problem of leadership than of power. Lord Montgomery of Alemein defined leadership as "the capacity to rally men and women to a common purpose, and the character which inspires confidence." A leader, he wrote, "must exercise an effective influence, and the degree to which he can do this will depend on the personality of the man - the incandescence of which he is capable, the flame which burns within him, the magnetism which will draw the hearts of men towards him." An example of such magnetism wa expressed by one Southern Baptist pastor, who said: "My church would charge hell with a thimble-full of water, if I said this wa where God wants us."

Yet if the truth be told such enthusiastic leadership can be a very human quality. What is needed is that spiritual enthusiasm which proves to be contagious. Such enthusiasm ultimately comes from God himself: for, etymologically at least, an enthusiast is the one in whom God is. It is the man of God, who by his very integrity, can inspire those in his charge to follow his lead. In other words, here again we have a question of priorities!

We live today in a success-orientated age. Alas, the spirit of the age has affected the ministry. Pastors look for results. The first step, therefore, in dealing with this pressure is to recognize that it is indeed a "worldly" pressure, and withstand it.

Secondly, pastors need to recognize that the Lord did not call them in the first place to be successful, but to be faithful. As Paul said to the Corinthians: "This is how one should regard us, as servants of Christ and stewards of the mysteries of God. Moreover, it is required of stewards that they be found trustworthy" (1 Corinthians 4:1,2).

Thirdly, pastors need to recognize that even if they were able to measure "success," it would not necessarily be seen as successful by the Lord. The words of Samuel in this respect are salutary: "God does not see as man sees; man looks at appearances, but Yahweh looks at the heart" (I Samuel 16:7).

In one sense the task is endless, and yet it need not be unbearable. The task is made bearable when the ministry of all believers is taken seriously and work is delegated and shared.

A familiar example of delegation in Scripture is found in the story of Jethro and Moses. "What is this you are doing to the people?" said Jethro to his son-in-law. "Why do you alone sit and judge, while all these people stand around you from morning to evening? What you are doing is not good. You and these people who come to you will only wear yourselves out. The work is too heavy for you; you cannot handle it alone" (Exodus 18: 14, 17f). Jethro then proposed that Moses should continue to act as God's representative, responsible for the teaching of spiritual principles and exercising his legislative functions, but that he should delegate other areas of judicial responsibility to competent men. Linking Exodus 18 with Exodus 38.26 Ron Trudinger has calculated that in this way Moses involved 78,600 leaders!

The pressure *of differing if not contradictory expectations* eases once a pastor gets his priorities right; in the first place he is accountable to Christ, and only secondly to the church. He is a servant of the church only insofar as he is a servant of Christ. Paul brings this fact our fairly starkly when he writes to the Galatians (1.10): "Am I now seeking the favour of men or of God? Or am I trying to please men? If I were still pleasing men, I should not be a servant of Christ!"

Ultimately it is to Christ that pastors owe their allegiance: He it is who gave pastor-teachers to His church (Ephesians 4.11). In one sense this is a fearsome responsibility. But over against the differing if not contradictory expectations of a church, it can be a liberating responsibility - the pastor doesn't have to give an account of his ministry to the many, but to the one (Hebrews 13.17).

These are demanding days. "Constant change is here to stay" seems to be the motto of our times. If pastors are to survive, then they need to develop more self-confidence - or rather, they need to develop confidence in their standing with their God. For he alone is the great unchangeable. He is the rock amidst all the theological storms. So here again we are back at the pastor's priority to be a man of God. Important as it is to be able to handle the process of change - and undoubtedly there are management techniques to be learnt - this is the key.

For some - not least those pastoring in the inner city - the numerical decline of the mainline churches can be a very real pressure. It can indeed be debilitating to pastor a church whose glories are all past. Humphrey Vellacott, an experienced reviver of apparently dead inner city causes in London, put his finger on the real need. . . ." Our problems lie not in techniques, physical resources, manpower. We have these in abundance. The need is to deal with God and to be the man of God." Although Humphrey was not right in all he denied, he was most certainly right in what he affirmed. Ministry in the inner city is tough: it has its disappointments, its failures. But the acids of disillusionment and frustration can be neutralized by a continuous relationship with our God.

On the other hand, church growth, however welcome, can prove threatening unless a pastor learns to let go and share the leadership. But this will involve changing structures, changing patterns of ministry. This can prove a challenge to the pastor, who perhaps up to that point felt he had to have a finger in every "pie". It can, however also prove a challenge to the church, who because of their determination not to lose the "personal touch," expect the one pastor to personally minister to their need. Sharing the leadership and encouraging the ministry of every member is the answer to this pressure.

As for those who feel threatened by the growth of other churches, they need to focus their sights on their Lord rather than upon other churches. For Christ has an individual plan, not only for our lives, but also for the life of our churches. What he may want to do in one place, he may not want to do in another. The incident in John 21. 21,22 comes to mind: "Lord, what about this man?" asked Peter. Jesus answered: "What is that to you? Follow me!" Again we are back at a pastor's relationship with his Lord!

Where the pastor is concerned for his pedestal, *the pressure of more educated or more gifted people* can be a threat. However, where the pastor is concerned to mobilize the laity, the presence of such people can be a godsend. Andrew Carnegie, the great industrialist of the late 19th and early 20th century, was once asked the secret of his success: "Always having people around me who are smarter than I am," was his answer!

It is a false concept of ministry to believe that the pastor must be "topdog," must be some great "know-all." In the first place the pastor is not called to be an educated man. He is called to be God's man. His authority lies not in his academia achievements, but rather in his relationship with his God.

Next we turn to the *influence of a competitive society*. The writer to the Hebrews encourages his readers to "look to Jesus, "the leader" . . . who for the joy that wa set before him endured the cross, despising the shame" (Hebrews 12.2). Or in the words of Count Zinzendorf: "I have one passion, it is He, He alone." Again the key is the pastor's relationship with his God.

Yet perhaps the question of ambition is not as simple as that. Jaroslav Pelikan writes: "There is perhaps no greater need in Christian thought today than the development of a theology of ambition . . . Christian theology has had comparatively little to say about the sin of refusing to become everything that one can be." There is a sense in which a better stewardship of our God-given gifts may move us from one position to another.

The complexity of moral issues is, in part, a question of image: once he acknowledges that he is not called to "know it all," a pastor can freely admit that he is as puzzled and uncertain as anybody else.

To some extent this is also a question of shared ministry: the pastor, for instance, may not know all the issues involved in the current abortion debate, but the gynecologist in membership with his church most certainly will! This is not to argue that the pastor has not theological insights to offer in questions of a technical nature, but rather to say that sometimes an approach needs to be jointly worked out.

Lack of mobility may be a pressure when difficulties arise, but very often those very difficulties are a means of maturing and developing a pastor. As the Arab proverb puts it: "All sunshine makes a desert." Or in J. B. Phillips version of James 1.2-4: "When all kinds of trials and temptations crowd into your lives, my brothers, don't resent them as intruders, but welcome them as friends! Realize that they come to test your faith and to produce in you the quality of endurance. But let the process go on until that endurance is fully developed, and you will find you have become men of mature character with the right sort of independence."

James Glasse in *Profession: Minister* makes a wry observation about one kind of preacher talk. He observes that preachers often say to one another, "I have been at this church five years. I think I have done all the good I can do here." Other preachers nod their heads in sagacious agreement. Glasse asks: "Does a doctor say, "I have been here five years. I have won all the cases I can win?" Glasse concludes, "If a minister says he has had 15 years experience, what he means is that he has had five years" experience three times over." And "If a minister keeps moving, the only thing he really has to change is his address."

Finally we come to the uncertainty of the role of the pastor. At this stage another paper is required! The theological issues raised need far more space than a mere paragraph. Hopefully, however, the definition we have given of pastoral ministry is a beginning!

Paul Beasley-Murray is Principal of Spurgeons College, London, England, UK.

The Pastor and Stress

(Part II)

Paul Beasley-Murray

I. The Pastor Under Pressure

In my paper, "Pastors Under Pressure", presented to the Study Commission at Singapore in 1986, I devoted much space to analyzing pressures - both longstanding and more recent - experienced by pastors in today's ministry. As last year's Commission meetings revealed, clearly this was not exhaustive list: pressures abound! When I sought to tackle a similar theme at the 1987 Spring

Conference of London Baptist ministers and their wives, the following additional pressures were identified: denominational pressures (time and more), ministers' fraternals (not always the model of Christian community!), the presence of ethnic minorities (whether Jewish, Hindu or Muslim), the shortage of skills in small churches, the mobility of congregational leaders. In particular, attention was drawn to three pressures:

1. Team Ministry

In England at least, professional team ministry tends to be something of mixed blessing. A large proportion of them - a figure as high as 50% has sometimes been mentioned - end up in disaster. In part this may be a matter of personality. In part it may stem from insecurity (it doesn't help when the Assistant proves to be more gifted). In part it may reflect a lack of training (the rapid growth of team ministries in England is a relatively recent phenomenon). However, team ministry is not limited to the professionals - many English Baptist churches are experimenting the "elderships" or lay leadership teams. But what was intended to share the load can in fact increase the load, particularly when such leadership teams are in the adolescent process of development.

2. A Crisis in Personal Faith

Needless to say, this is not a pressure limited to pastors, but it is perhaps helpful to be reminded that pastors do suffer from doubt. One leading London pastor cited two particular causes of such doubt: first, the multi-faith society which is increasingly characterizing the life of many English cities - religious pluralism does pose all kinds of fundamental questions regarding the faith. Secondly, the moral failures of fellow pastors - an adulterous affair is a very denial of the gospel which claims to transform lives.

3. Pastors' Wives

(Pardon the sexist language, but by and large it is the wife of a pastor, not the husband of a pastor, who feels under particular pressure.) Indeed, according to Roy Oswald of the Alban Institute, stress among pastor's wives is as high as for pastors Pastors" wives have been termed by Mary La Grand Bouma as "the walking wounded". Certainly in my experience probably a greater proportion of spiritual casualties are to be found amongst pastors" wives than amongst any other group. This is compounded by the fact that by and large the one person a pastor cannot pastor is his wife. In some cases the wife's distress results in the pastor leaving the ministry; in many more cases the pastor may remain, but clearly his ministry is affected.

Yes, pressures abound, but the question arises: how do we deal with such pressures?

II. The Pastor Under God

In my first paper I suggested that the key to coping with pressure is for the pastor to redefine his or her ministry, and in the first place recognize that pastoral ministry is God's ministry. He or she is God's servant, not the church's servant. Therefore it behooves the pastor to be, in the first place, God's man or God's woman. William Temple, the future Archbishop of Canterbury, when enthroned as Bishop of Manchester, spoke these words: "I come as a learner with no policy to advocate, no plan already formed to follow. But I come with one burning desire: it is that in all our activities, sacred and secular and ecclesiastical and social, we should help each other fix our eyes on Jesus, making him our only guide...Pray for me, I ask you, not chiefly that I may be wise and strong, or any such thing, though for these things I need your prayers. But pray for me chiefly, that I may never let go of the unseen hand of the Lord Jesus and may live in daily fellowship with him. It is so that you will most of all help me to help you". We too would surely wish to echo these words. In the first place pastors are not people *with* authority but *under* authority. Pastors are but under-shepherds. If they are to tend the flock of God, then they must be followers. Or, to put it another way, we need to be reminded that "being a shepherd isn't the same as being a sheep-dog!. Caring for people doesn't mean fussing around them in the morning hours, when a man should be in his study - on his knees".

Jesus had enormous pressures on him during the three years of his public ministry. Yet, as we read the Gospels, we see that he maintained a relationship with his Father that daily sustained and renewed him. Whether early in the morning or late in the evening, he made the time to withdraw. If daily withdrawal was a top priority for Jesus, it dare not be any less for his followers, and especially for those of us who lead in his name. The Quaker, John Edward Southall, underlines this fact when he writes: "We cannot go through life strong and fresh on constant express-trains; but we must have quiet hours, secret places of the Most High, times of waiting upon the Lord when we renew our strength and learn to mount up on wings as eagles, and then come back to run and not be weary, and to walk and not faint." Yes, if we are to cope with pressure, we must make time to wait upon God, to feed upon his Word, to gain the strength that is mediated through prayer. This leads me on to say that as we pray, we will be able to get our priorities straight for the coming day. Heroditus claimed that the bitterest sorrow is to aspire to do much and achieve nothing. Not so, maintained James Simpson: the bitterest sorrow is to aspire to do much and to do it, and then to discover that it was not worth doing. The pressurized pastor, if he or she is not careful, can all to easily become what William Cowper once described as "the busy trifler". Let me quote Charles E. Hummel, who wrote a small but seminal pamphlet entitled *The Tyranny of the Urgent* in which he distinguished between the urgent and the important: "The important task rarely must be done today, even this week...but the urgent tasks call for instant action...endless demands, pressure every hours and day...the momentary appeal of these tasks seems irresistible and important and they devour our energy.

But in the light of time's perspective their deceptive prominence fades; with the sense of loss we recall the important tasks pushed aside again. we realize we have become slaves to the tyranny of the urgent." What is the solution? A daily seeking of God's will as Jesus sought God's will - "by this means he warded off the urgent and accomplished the important. It gave him a sense of direction, set a steady pace, and enabled him to do every task God had assigned".

III. The Pastor Undergirded By Friends

Some years ago, Mrs. Norah Coggan, the wife of the then Archbishop of Canterbury, gave an address to clergy wives entitled, *Who helps the helpers?* The title was in fact taken from Juvenal in one of his satires. Literally, Juvenal said: "Who is to guard the guards themselves; who is to watch over those who are doing the watching?" In its original context this had something to do with a woman who comes to entice the guard, but the quotation is capable of a more general application. Thus Norah Coggan wrote, "The time comes when we (the helpers) have lifted too many burdens and we really are worn down, exhausted and depressed. Maybe our faith is cold and also our lives with witness for the Lord. Perhaps we feel we are in a dark tunnel. Depression comes over us. What then?" Yes, what then? The fact of the matter is that there are times when we cannot go on alone - we need help, we need friends. But to whom can we turn?

For those of us who are married, in the first instance we can and should turn to our spouses. That is where mutual help and comfort are to be found. And yet, if we are honest, there are times when it is insufficient to turn to our spouses for support for they too need to be helped. They too need to be supported. Together, both husband and wife need to find support.

For some, it may be possible to discover a couple in the church with whom they can share the dark days as well as the good days of life. Others may have to turn to a couple (another pastor and his spouse?) who are outside of the church. Howard Clinebell speaks of the need of growth groups: "Growth-stimulation relationships are warm, caring and trustful, at the same time they are honest, confronting and open. Caring and confrontation equals growth. This is the growth formula." Although Clinebell is speaking generally, this surely can be applied to the pastor and his spouse. They need to be in the kind of relationship where, on the one hand, they can be cared for, but on the other hand they can be confronted. Or maybe a better term than a growth group is a covenant group. As David and Jonathan committed themselves to one another totally (see 1 Samuel 18:1-4) and in so doing found new strength in their togetherness, so there is much to be said for pastors and their spouses covenanting with another couple. In this way their hands can be "strengthened in God" (1 Samuel 23:15-16). It is perhaps of significance that I have not spoken of fraternal relationships. Unfortunately, my own experience of organized Fraternals has not always been the best. Interestingly, Roy Oswald confirms my own view when he writes: "Fellow clergy, better than anyone else, understand the hazards and pressures of parish ministry. Unfortunately, clergy peer support groups usually don't work. Rarely does such a group have enough trust and confidence to explore their pain, fear and vulnerability. We all need a place where we can share our hurt, loneliness and threats."

If Fraternals are not always of help, a "spiritual director" may prove supportive. In England at least an increasing number of pastors are looking for people to act for them as "fathers in God". Initially, Baptists, with their doctrine of the priesthood of all believers, have tended to be very wary of such a role - but does the superficiality of the unexamined life have anything to commend it? Surely, whatever leads to the deepening of the spiritual life is to be welcomed - not least when it enables a pastor to cope all the more effectively with the many and varied pressures that are upon him.

Yes, supportive relationships are vital. Unfortunately, such relationships demand time with the result that the pressurized pastor is tempted to dispense with them. But such support systems are not luxuries in the pastoral life - they are essential both for our survival as also for our ongoing growth and development. Such relationships may prove to be costly in time and energy, but in the long run they will prove to be exceedingly rewarding.

Paul Beasley-Murray is Princpal of Spurgeons College, London, England, UK.

By Whose Authority?

Brian Jenkins

Introduction

What is the nature of authority in the Kingdom of God and in the Church? Who holds such authority and how is it to be applied? As the Christian Church approaches the end of the 20th Century these are some of the emerging issues. Amongst Baptists, such current concerns as inerrancy, the role of the pastor, the role of women in the church and the nature of the Kingdom of God have, at their very heart, questions about authority.

Such questions are not new; the nature of Kingdom authority has quite literally bedeviled the church from the first. For Baptists, however, the issue is of vital concern because of our commitment to Biblical concepts, our strong emphasis on the liberty of the individual conscience and our insistence upon the autonomy of the local church. These have been regarded as essential aspects of Baptist life from the outset. The issue also has a great practical urgency as churches and even entire groups of churches are torn apart in argument over issues which are claimed to be doctrinal, but which often eventuate as a struggle for power and control.

The following paper is intended only as an introduction to the topic.

Authority in the Scriptures

Authority is the term used in English language translations of the New Testament for the Greek word exousia. In its strict sense, exousia implies a derived authority which, for the Christian, comes from God (John 19:11, Romans 13:1f). However, if the authority is to be effective it must also have the strength to make it work. Hence in Matthew's Gospel in the KJ version exousia is translated *power*.

Frequently, the word *authorities* is used of those to whom authority is given, whether they be secular governments or angelic beings. The source of their power again is God. Satan also has his agents, the evil spirits, who together form the exousia (dominion) of darkness from which Christ has freed us but against which we now are now involved in a fight. For the present, Satan claims authority over the kingdoms of the earth. Indeed, Satan offered this authority to Jesus if he would acknowledge Satan's superiority, thus giving him the greater power. Ultimately though, the Devil will be defeated and Jesus will become the controlling ruler of the world.

The resurrected Christ is said to be far above every authority (Eph. 1:21, Matt 28:18) and his greater authority is passed on to his followers. In sending out the Seventy, Jesus said "I have given you authority to trample on snakes and scorpions, and to overcome all the power of the enemy." (Lk. 10:19). Paul spoke of the authority the Lord gave me and significantly adds it is for "building you up, not tearing you down". (2 Cor. 13:10, 10:8). In Revelation 2:26 there is an indication that this extends beyond the apostles: "he who overcomes and does my will to the end . . . will have authority over the nations . . . just as I received authority from my Father".

The nature of his authority must be clearly understood, however. Jesus says "The kings of the Gentiles lord it over them; and those who exercise authority over them call themselves benefactors. But you are not to be like that" (Lk. 2:25, 26). Again, in Lk. 22:26, Jesus tells his disciples "The greatest among you shall be the youngest, and the one who rules like the one who serves . . . I am among you as one who serves". In Mt. 23:8 he says "But you are not to be called "Rabbi" for you have only one master and you are all brothers . . . the greatest among you will be your servant".

In summary, when a Christian has authority it is not something he has earned (though it may need to be demonstrated over a period before it will be recognized by others), but rather something given by God. While it may be seen particularly in appointed leaders, it is not theirs exclusively. It could be described as more a quality than a position. Indeed, a Christian's authority will be best seen when his servant-attitude is most obvious. All Christians are in a struggle with those whose authority comes from Satan and who tend to control the sources of power in this world.

Channels of Authority

Traditionally, the three main channels of God's authority have been the

Church, the Bible and personal experience. The New Testament writers naturally drew heavily on the third, but it was the first that dominated Christianity thereafter and right up until the 16th Century. (Indeed it could scarcely be otherwise since people were largely illiterate and the Bible had to be laboriously copied by hand.) Following the Reformation and the invention of printing, however, the Bible because the main channel of God's authority especially amongst Evangelical Protestants. From their beginnings, Baptists have always given a preeminence to the authority of the Bible, even to the point of stating it to be "the final authority in all matters of faith and conduct".

Yet it must be remembered that God remains the final source of authority and that he made his more authoritative statement in the Word-who-became-flesh. The significance of this was not lost on the early church; one of the earliest debates was about how authority is transmitted from Father to Son to Holy Spirit. Paul clearly describes Jesus as "the head of the body" (Eph. 1:22, 5:23) - thus establishing Christ's right to control and direct those who are in the community of Believers. Additionally, in 1 Cor. 2:22f, he says that no one can interpret the mind of God except for the Spirit of God, which implies that understanding for the Church must come through the mediation of the Spirit, while the Lord himself, in Acts 1:8 describe the Holy Spirit as the source of true power for the believer.

The fact that the Bible is inspired by God and furthermore, that it is our only account of the Word-who-became-flesh, makes it a very important channel for us. It is the control by which a person's own experience and the teaching the church has given him can be tested. At the same time, the current emphasis on contextualization brings a healthy reminder that the Scriptures are read with limited and biased human eyes and must be interpreted with care and understanding. The increased awareness of the work of the Holy Spirit is also a necessary corrective to interpretation that depends on human intellect rather than the Divine spark set alight in the heart of the reader.

But What About?

Two specific problem passages need to be considered.

The first, in Matt. 16:19 and 18:18 refers to "the keys of the kingdom", by which whatever is bound on earth will be bound in heaven. There is some uncertainty as to whether this is said in reference to Peter alone or to the whole church but the matter is clarified by the second passage. The subsequent verse relates this to any two or three who come together in God's name. Thus God's authority is available to all believers, not just to Peter or even the pastor. There are three conditions to be noted, however, - more than one person should be involved, there should be agreement over what they are asking, and God should be present. The pastor alone, or even on his own, does not have God's binding authority.

The second passage is the story of Peter's dream and the subsequent conversion of Cornelius. When he senses that God is telling him to "kill and eat" Peter refuses outright and appeals to the current theological interpretation of the Scriptures as his authority. In his reply, God emphasizes that He has the greater authority.

As a result, Peter breaks away from the accepted teaching and practice of his religious leaders. In no longer isolating himself from an "unclean" household he discovers a whole new experience in preaching the Gospel to a Gentile. Here is an example of a Christian leader claiming direct authorization from God to do something which was at odds with the teaching of the best theologians of his day and with the practice of God's people. (In doing this, of course, he was following in the steps of his master whose views on the use of the Sabbath, for instance, were radically different from the religious leaders of the time).

Yet it was not Peter's personal vision which finally gave- authority to the action, but, significantly, the same three factors mentioned earlier. Peter took other Christians with him, so he was not alone. He sought their agreement before he baptized Cornelius and above all, God's approval was demonstrated by the action of the Holy Spirit in the situation in an observable way. Later, their interpretation of events was confirmed before an assembly of the whole church in Jerusalem.

This should serve as a reminder that the authority given to the pastor does not extend to a Divine imprimatur on his interpretation of Scripture, or for that matter, of his experience, unless it is confirmed by other Christians and above all by the obvious activity of the Holy Spirit.

The Authority of Jesus

The most characteristic reaction of people to Jesus, whether they were friend or foe, seems to have been surprise at the authority with which he spoke and acted. His authority in healing was hard to refute; his authority in preaching was envied; but it was his claim to have authority to forgive sins which brought the greatest opposition. It was stated that God alone had the authority to forgive sins which brought the greatest opposition. It was stated that God alone had the authority to do this.

In his teaching, Jesus commends obedience to civil authorities, but severely criticizes some of the recognized religious authorities, notably the Pharisees. (Mt. 23). His comments were directed mainly at their emphasis on status, position and outward appearances as the evidence of their authority, instead of an inner reality. Similarly, he attacked their rigid observance of laws rather than a dynamic application of principles.

If "authority" lay at the heart of much of his conflict with his enemies it is also true that it was one of the chief problems among his friends. At the most significant times of crisis, it is noticeable that his disciples were preoccupied with arguments over position. (Lk. 9:46, 22:24; Mt. 20:20-28). They still thought in terms of a hierarchy in which the higher the place the greater the authority. Those who recognized that Jesus spoke not as other men but with an authority that was not of this world showed greater insight.

The job of those watching the crucifixion was that he could not save himself, but this involved a deliberate decision not to use his power, which is different from losing his authority. Yet it could be suggested that Jesus did temporarily lose his authority on the cross. It is reflected in his anguished cry . . ."My God, why have you forsaken me?"

After the resurrection, though, Jesus confidently states again that all authority on heaven and in earth had been given to him. (Mt. 28:18) and he continues by authorizing his followers to make disciples baptize them and teach all that he had commanded. His authority had been restored in even greater measure.

Any discussion of the authority of Jesus must also note the attitude with which that authority was exercised. Paul sums it up so magnificently, in Philippians 2, when he encourages us to have the same mind as was in Christ Jesus. He then describes this as a "servant" attitude which is not concerned about what people think nor is it fired with ambition to the point of seeking to be equal in place and power with God. Paul echoes Jesus' own statement to be equal in place and power with God. Paul echoes Jesus' own ambition that he had come "not to be served, but to serve" (Mt. 20:28). In today's ambition driven, profit-centered world these words carry even deeper significance for the Christian leader.

Christ's own action in washing his disciples' feet was a dramatic demonstration of his attitude. The interplay between Jesus and Peter is also significant in considering the Christian's authority. Jesus showed Peter that he needed to be wiling to receive the service on the one hand, but not to demand more than was essential on the other. (Jn. 13:6-10) This may suggest an appropriate attitude for people towards their pastor, while the action of Jesus in being willing to wash fee, sums up the right attitude for the pastor towards his people.

The Nature of the Pastor's Authority

In his excellent book, "The Radical Kingdom", Nigel Wright of Spurgeon's College, London, has a very helpful chapter on authority in the church.[1] Though the book is written in response to the Restoration Movement in England, it is a wide-ranging defence of historic Baptist (and Biblical) principles. He makes some significant comments about authority and the church.

He reminds us that *the church and the kingdom are not identical*. "The church is the gathering of those who have received the kingdom of God . . . but it is not itself the kingdom of God. God's kingdoms seen in his immediate and direct rule over us.[2]" Furthermore, *the church is not a hierarchy*. There are two ways of seeing the decision-making in the church - as a hierarchy from the top down or alternatively it can be seen from the bottom up. In the former, great store is placed on the "apostolic foundation" as the source of authority, but in the latter, decision-making is seen as arising from the presence of Christ among his people. Therefore all the people must be given and must take the opportunity to be involved. To fail to do so is to shirk our God-given responsibility and to deny the very nature of the church.

Thirdly, *delegated authority is a misleading concept*. Wright quotes Mt. 10:40,

41; "He who receives you receives me, and he who receive me receives the one who sent me. Anyone who receives a prophet because he is a prophet receives a prophet's reward . . . ." The prophet, for his part, must demonstrate that he has received true authority from God for the role he is undertaking. The congregation for their part, must recognize this and submit to what God is saying through the prophet. The prophet must be careful not to step beyond the role God has given to him. As Wright says of the minister of God, "In all these things he exercises a ministry towards God's people, an enabling and serving ministry focused on Christ.[3] For Baptists, the pastor's authority is seen to have certain distinctives:

1. It Is Derived - Not Inherited

The authority of God is passed on, but to whom and under what circumstances? This remains a major question for the church. Is it inherited through a form of episcopal succession or is it derived from the direct activity of God? This is not unrelated to the issue of the authority of the Scriptures. Ironically, it was the invention of printing which, in many ways, made possible a shift from the collegiate interpretation of the Scriptures by the Church to direct interpretation by the individual. At the same time the concept of episcopal succession was also changed. Amongst the Anabaptists, the need for an external check was still recognized, but not it could be exercised by the land congregation using their own copies of the Scriptures to check out what the pastor said. The pastor's authority is derived from God, but it is affirmed by his fellow members.

Amongst Baptists the issue is still an important one. In some cases it has become traditional for a convention or union to authorize the pastor after he has completed approved theological training and demonstrated his ability to minister in the field. In other countries there is a pattern of individual churches taking upon themselves the authority to appoint pastors - frequently from their own ranks - with a different set of criteria emphasizing spiritual adequacy rather than education. Significantly, where the former has been the practice, there is an increasing tendency for churches to act in the latter manner today. Perhaps the reverse is true also.

This raises questions. Is it sufficient that God's authority in a man be recognized by the nuclear Christian family in the local church, or does it need the confirmation of a wider family? Is it a "once for all" status or a dynamic authority that must be repeatedly confirmed by the Spirit's activity? How does the denomination as well as the church recognize when God's authority for a particular role is withdrawn from a man?

2. It Is Demonstrated - Not Demanded

Even though Baptists may not accept the doctrine of episcopal succession there is still a tendency for graduates of theological seminaries to feel they have an automatic right to a church position. They sometimes act as though their preparation has given them a higher level of authority and that the role of their congregation is to hear and obey. Yet few Baptist congregations see their new pastor as the vicar of Christ! On the other hand, when a man has been successful and has proven himself over a number of years, few denominations give more authority to their pastor than Baptists. This can be a very happy yet sometimes, a very false relationship. The danger lies in the congregation *confusing* organizational or communicational ability with true spiritual authority. When God gives us a piece of his mind it is not always what we want to hear!

3. It Is Devotional - Not Legalistic

In practice, most church members sense the pastor's authority more in the closeness of his relationship to Christ, his understanding of Christ's mind and his appropriate counseling, than the purity of his interpretation of the teaching of the church. There is a tendency in the structured church, however, to emphasize doctrinal purity or traditional orthodoxy rather than loving relationships - as seen first in the Jewish Scribes and then in the Councils of the Church. In our own day there are still many who will judge a pastor's authority on the basis of his doctrinal purity - by their interpretation. The need for an objective assessment of any person's understanding of Scripture is important, but the demonstration of a Kingdom lifestyle by the pastor is even more telling. What impressed the disciples about Jesus was not so much the adequacy of his exposition of the Scripture, but the fascinating closeness of the relationship he had with God. He even dared to call him "father". This they saw as the source of his authority and that encouraged them to submit to him.

Authority Structures in Baptist Churches

A clearer understanding of the nature of authority could prevent many of the problems that arise in churches. Unfortunately, the followers of Jesus have not changed or learnt much it sometimes seems. The major preoccupation of many churches continues to be with whom will hold the real power.

For theological reasons already discussed, Baptists believe that decision-making authority should lie in the gathered community of Believers. There is a natural tendency - and in larger churches, an almost inevitable need - to hand over the decision-making to a few, and in some cases to one. The few are usually the deacons, the elders, a pastoral team or a prominent family. The one may be the pastor, but he may equally be the chairman of deacons or the church secretary.

It is an irony that it is usually the smallest and largest congregations that suffer most from these transfers of authority. The demagogic pastor who builds the church around his own personality or the powerful board of deacons who "run" everything can easily dominate the larger church. In the smaller church it is more likely to be a deacon and his family. Whatever the particular nature of the concentration of power it always lessens the possibility of God conveying his mind to the congregation because they confine Him to working through them. Even if the final decisions are made by a few it is always wise to have an open forum where any member can express his or her perception of what God is saying to the church.

People with significant authority in the church have often earned it by dedicated service. The respect in which they are held becomes a trap if it leads the congregation to avoid its responsibilities or too easily accept the person's authority in relation to all matters. The end results can be quite tragic. Those who were once so helpful end up being a millstone slowly destroying the dynamic of the church. They have created structures they are comfortable with and which sometimes run so well they no longer need interference from anyone, least of all God! The parable of the vineyard and its absentee owner is enacted afresh.

A Typical Story

There is a syndrome in churches that is all too common. It can be described as follows: The young pastor of a smallish church has had a good beginning. The people and in particular, the authority figure (who shall be called "Mr. Brown") have welcomed him warmly and told him of the great expectations they have for his ministry. After two years of good response, criticisms begin to surface and slowly intensify. Sometimes they come from unexpected people, to the surprise and hurt of the pastor. Eventually open dissatisfaction is expressed in the deacons' meeting and the issue is taken to the members. At the meeting debate rages back and forth, until finally Mr. Brown, with apparent reluctance, confirms his belief that in the circumstances it would be best for the pastor to go. Voting usually follows fairly quickly after this because the pastor's fate is now sealed, whatever the justice of the situation. When they vote, the members will not be thinking about what God is saying in the matter, but what Mr. Brown feels.

It is easy to blame the pastor. He has failed to establish his authority as the one the church can trust to interpret the mind of God to them. A look at the history of the church reveals a sequence of pastorates lasting three and a half years at the most. The facts of the situation are more likely to be that as the pastor began to grow in authority the existing authority figure felt threatened. He wanted a pastor because it gave his church status, but consciously or unconsciously, he wanted a tame pastor who would not challenge his authority in the church. Because he cannot admit to such feelings he rationalises the situation by pointing to the pastor's weaknesses. He raises these publicly by working through loyal mouthpieces. Until the very last he never works with direct accusations but always by insinuation and "innocent questions. The pastor is always at a disadvantage. He is dispensable, but the congregation must continue living with Mr. Brown.

It is frequently only when Mr. Brown is removed from the scene that the church begins to go ahead. Such removal normally depends on his death or transfer . . . a very slow way of getting relief! Sometimes Mr. Brown loses his authority because the church finally wakes up to what is happening and, after a lot of heart-searching, summons the courage to take action. The results are usually bitter, with Mr. Brown departing in great hurt and with the church feeling must guilt in the midst of their relief. Sometimes, of course, it can be the pastor himself who becomes the "Mr. Brown" in the church. His long pastorate is finally ended by his retirement, or by a palace coup d'etat through the diaconate, an associate pastor, or by outright revolution as the "young Turks" in the church lead the opposition.

If this sounds altogether too like the power struggles of the world, it is so, and reflects again the difficulty Christians have in truly being people who live under the authority of God. Perhaps part of the problem lies with a confused view of the nature of the process within, a Baptist church meeting. It is common, in the West, at least, to think of this as democratic process, but no less a person than Britain's Prime Minister, Margaret Thatcher, has made a very appropriate comment on which she said: "Nowhere in the Bible is the word *democracy* mentioned. Ideally, when Christians meet, as Christians, to take counsel together their purpose is not (or should not be) to ascertain what is the mind of the majority but what is the mind of the Holy Spirit - something which may be quite different."[4]

A Name Above All Other Names?

The Church, universally, has rejected the idea of a continuing of "Apostle". Baptists go further, usually and avoid the office of "Bishop" while having a love/hate affair with "Elders". Deacons they will respect. The reason for this seems to be that the terms have become so identified with hierarchial structures adopted by the Church. This creates a tension for some who certainly accept that authority is derived from God, but who wonder if Baptists have not been over-zealous in rejecting that which the Early church recognized.

A few churches are now even recognizing the office of "Apostle". They see him as a man who is itinerant, a proven church-planter and who provides a sort of spiritual "covering" for the local work. The point to Paul, who though not one of the original disciples, considered himself to have been appointed to the office by God. It is quite true that some people seem to exercise the function of an apostle. In an informal, unrecognized way, many churches look to a person or a small group of persons in whom they have particular confidence, to give teaching and advice to the church from time to time. Unfortunately, where a church formally submits itself to such a person as their apostle it usually ends in withdrawal from the normal co-operative Baptist "coverings" such as an Association, Union or convention. This, again denies the potential of God to speak through another congregation or even the collective understanding of the wider family and can lead to the very problems of authority that Paul had to deal with in 1 Corinthians 1.

Keeping a Proper Balance

Here some basic principles regarding the use of authority and power by the Pastor.

1. The pastor does have an authority. It is bestowed upon him by God and recognized by the people. it is a particular authority within the congregation and is more a matter of degree than difference. he is worthy of special request.

2. The leader, be he pastor otherwise, needs to have a deep sense of the privilege of being a channel through which God has chosen to work. he must always keep in mind, however, that the authority he has is extended to him by God. He is a servant or ambassador from God to God's people.

3. Both pastor and people must guard against making "success" or "popularity" the evidence of authorization from God. They need to look for the recognizable confirmation of the Holy spirit's activity.

4. The theology of the Kingdom needs to be more widely taught and understood amongst Baptists. Structures or relationships that hinder or remove the possibility of being a people sensitive to God need to be better known and guarded against.

5. Unlike God, from whom the authority comes, the pastor is neither omniscient nor consistent. He is not equally authoritative in all areas and he will have both strengths and weaknesses. In a good situation these things will be recognized by both pastor and people and suitable compensations made using others in the congregation.

6. Similarly, the pastor will not always be consistent in his spiritual and devotional life. He will go through "dry" periods. Ideally both pastor and people would openly recognize this and take steps to help him through these times without destroying his authority in their eyes.

7. We must be careful to avoid solutions we would not regard as "Christian" in other circumstances. Too often churches react by annulling the marriage . . . ("We shouldn't have called him in the first place; he wasn't God's man for us".) . . . or by separation ("He was fine when he first came, but he's changed. We'll just have to go elsewhere") . . . or by divorce ("His time here is finished"). We are to demonstrate our message of reconciliation.

8. Pastors and churches change - sometimes quite radically. The influence of major movements such as Black liberation, Feminism, Charismatic renewal, or whatever, can create crisis points in the churches. The pastor's authority will be strongly challenged - either because he has changed too much, or because he hasn't changed enough. It has never been more necessary for church and pastor alike to openly seek God's mind together.

9. In the calling of a pastor, great stress is rightly laid upon seeking the mind of God and on all parties coming to the same conviction about it. This is usually the time when the church works best as a "brotherly Christocracy" as Barth called it. In the termination of a pastorate there is a much greater tendency to see the matter in a one-sided way . . ." We dismissed him." "I resigned." There ought to be equal concern for discovering together the mind of Christ in the termination of a pastorate as there is in the initiation of one.

10. The pastor has a responsibility to ensure that he maintains his relationship with God, while the congregation must guard against the pastor becoming distracted or weighted down with peripheral matters. He needs adequate

time for rest, reflection and stimulation from other people who are similarly seeking God's mind. He is then more likely to be a good channel for the authoritative message of God to the church.

11. In the training of pastors it is probably even more important to ensure that they have appropriate perceptions of themselves, their roles and their tasks than it is to impart formal knowledge. There is a crucial balance to be achieved in a pastor's attitude, between the servant who is the slave to everyone else's authority and the elder who believes he rules by Divine Right. The first gives no sense of authoritative direction, the second insists on the congregation going his way whether they are convinced it is God's will or not. Both are travesties of the true exercise of authority in the family of God.

Brian Jenkins is a Baptist Pastor in Auckland, New Zealand.

Endnotes

1. Nigel Wright, *The Radical Kingdom*, (Eastbourne, England: Kingsway Publications, 1986), p. 86.

2. Ibid., p. 91.

3. Ibid.

4. From a speech to the General Assembly of the Church of Scotland. Quoted in *Discipleship Journal*, March/April 1989, p. 9.

The Creative Resolution of Conflict

Gerald T. Marks

The issue of conflict resolution has been of growing interest in recent years. A number of books have been written on this and related subjects; and I get the impression that every second magazine I read has an article on conflict and the role of the Pastor or Church leader. I do not pretend that mine is an exhaustive study of the subject! All that I will be attempting to do in these six or seven pages will be to summarize my own observations and discoveries after four to five years of "not inconsiderable" involvement in Church conflict.

1. The Inevitability of Conflict:

This is where we must start. To be human, means that we will have conflict. We probably do not need to spend much time establishing this, except to say that it is part of our humanness and ought not to be regarded as failure. Conflict is inevitable because e are both social and intentional beings. Social in the sense that we do not live in isolation but in communities; and intentional in the sense that we all have ambition, expectations and needs that will clash with the intention of others.

The conclusion to all of this is firstly, that it is okay to have conflict, whether in our homes or in our Churches. We therefore must resist the impulse to suppress it as unhealthy and necessarily destructive. "In most of us there seems to be an innate desire for a conflict-free existence. Most of the great religions of the world promise a future pictured as a blissful, peaceful, conflict-free state. The Church also embodies this human desire to avoid conflict. The Christian faith is usually interpreted as being opposed to conflict. The Christian faith is usually interpreted as being opposed to conflict. As a result, most Churches develop norms rejecting behaviour that encourages conflict and rewarding behaviour that tends to suppress it." ("Resolving Church Conflicts" by G. Douglass Lewis).

And secondly, the inevitability of conflict means that as leaders we will often be thrown into the role of conflict managers. To avoid that role or even the expectation of it, is inevitably going to threaten the health and vitality of the Church and its members. This clearly has implications for the preparation of men and women for pastoral leadership. How well are any of us prepared for and trained in conflict management?

2. Conflict, the Catalyst for Growth

It is well understood that there is a dynamic and potential for discovery when a group of men and women work together, that would be denied those same individuals working in isolation. This is the thesis of those who teach synergetics, and it is, of course, Biblical. The Apostle Paul labours the point that we have gifts and experiences that differ and which are complementary. No individual has the genius or completeness that no longer needs the input or interaction with others.

Such a process almost inevitably involves conflict in one form or another, as individuals openly and honestly present their views and conclusions. To withdraw from such honest confrontation, will abort the process that can bring new discovery.

It could be argued that all progress in almost any field of knowledge and in almost any walk of life is the product of conflict. "The conquests of Alexander the Great in the 4th Century BC created social and international chaos but they also released powers of mind and spirit which have influenced the Western world ever since. The history of the trade union movement in this country is the history of conflict, which may be regarded as out of place now, but which, at the time, procured not only a living wage for the worker but a say in the democratic ordering of society. Churchmen still look back to a golden age, as they suppose it to be, when the Church was one and men lived by a faith universally recognized, if not always honoured. Yet that so-called golden age was an age of deepening corruption and inner apostasy from which we were extricated by the Reformation. Every great institution occasionally needs a "wild boar in its vineyard" if it is to remain vital and relevant. In the world of the intellect, in the world of the arts, in the world of science, the same holds true - the comfortable dogmas of a previous age come under threat and are drastically revised under the impact of conflict."

Ronald Kraybill (Director of the Mennonite Conciliation Service in Akron, Pennsylvania) writing in it. Leadership magazine, makes the point that "throughout Church history, conflict proves to be the arenas of revelation. More than any other moment, God speaks to humans when they stand face to face in disagreement. Look at Acts 15 - tremendous conflict, yet the setting in which God reveals stunning new intentions about the scope of salvation. Consider our Church creeds: virtually all we call orthodoxy emerged in its present form only because of conflict. The potential for hurt, pain and chaos is substantial. But let us begin by looking first for the goodness in conflict, not the darkness. If we rightly understand Scripture, Church history and human experience, we might realistically have the courage to say: "Well, what is God going to say to us this time?"

This being the case, I like to see the role of the conciliator like that of a mid-wife, who, in the midst of the pain and trauma, is helping to bring to birth the new discovery and life.

3. Principles for Conflict Management

Conflict of course has both the potential for destructiveness and hurt as well as for creativity and new discovery. If we continue with the analogy of childbirth, it would be helpful to recall that some decades ago, it was a much more risky business. Both mothers and their babies were very much at risk. Trained mid-wives and doctors, benefitting from years of research, have reduced both mother and child mortality rates to the place where the first question is no longer an enquiry about the health of mother or child, but whether it is a boy or girl. The other is simply taken for granted.

That rather long-winded analogy was intended to make the point that untrained "conflict managers" may well increase the incidence of "relationship mortality!"

The following are a number of principles that I have found helpful.

3.1 Creating the Right Climate
Douglass Lewis in the earlier quoted book makes the excellent point that to establish the right climate before there is any conflict, prepares a Church or leadership group to deal with difference much more constructively. He suggests that the best way of doing this is to help others feel good about themselves. When we feel good about ourselves, conversation flows, good ideas emerge readily and listening to others comes more easily. We are open, accepting, and not threatened by the ideas and actions of others. We can more easily affirm others' needs and goals and we have more energy to work on alternatives.

However, if we feel bad about ourselves, we are more defensive and hostile to others. Our inclination is to fight and to put others down. We become narrow in our vision, have less confidence in what we do or say and see fewer alternatives.

Therefore the first rule in conflict management is to help others feel better about themselves. Even better, is to create such a climate before conflict begins.

How do we help others feel good about themselves? Quite simply by listening to others and taking seriously their goals. The good conflict manager will look for and appreciate the strength and gifts of others. He or she will do all they can to affirm others' ideas.

"He who gives himself finds himself. He who is vulnerable to others, open to their needs, and not out to control them; he who can give power away, mysteriously receives personal power."

I am also discovering how important it is to help even the "perpetrator" to feel good about himself. It is too easy to isolate the perceived aggressor. All isolation does is reinforce the feelings of failure, guilt or grievance, thereby increasing their defensiveness.

3.2 Bring Conflict Out Into the Open

We are all aware of the temptation to suppress or avoid unpleasantness. We can do this by spiritualizing the issue (let's pray about it), avoiding the issue (either not talking about the contentious problem with the result that our relationships become rather superficial, or avoiding the person concerned!), or for someone to come into the situation with a heavy hand, suppress discussion, decide who or what is right and imagine that the conflict has been resolved.

Ronald Kraybill writes "My experience has taught me that whenever Churches have faced conflict openly, the congregations have grown stronger in the process. But whenever they have hidden from conflict, it has emerged when the congregations were weakest and least prepared. The longer the congregation hide, the more political and power-oriented the struggle becomes, and the more destructive is its impact.

The first and most important principle, therefore, is to allow conflict and even courage it. It's a paradox, but "if you want to experience less conflict in your congregation, try to have more. Invite differing views to be expressed."

3.3 Engender Hope

One of the most important things that we can do if ever we find ourselves in the role of a conciliator, is to encourage hopefulness. This is not wishful thinking, but a mixture of realism and commitment. Realism, because most new and creative ideas are born out of conflict; and commitment, because creativity through conflict demands a commitment to a process.

So whenever and wherever possible, there ought to be encouraged the expectation that we are on a journey of discovery that will require all parties to be willing to set aside grievances and privately held conclusions in the pursuit of the better alternative.

3.4 Decide On the Process

One thing that I have discovered, is to determine the process and objectives before you get embroiled in the issue. The process should include identifying the issue, deciding on how the points of conflict will be raised and what third parties, if any, will be involved. This understanding should be detailed and specific, and probably ought to be in writing, so that it cannot be challenged at a later date.

This is, of course, the rationale of Church constitutions. They are the "rules" of the Church or organization, in which the behaviour and process are decided, before the high emotion of a conflict situation.

As an aside, a number of our congregations in New Zealand have recently written new constitutions which have proved to be inadequate in contention. Most of these Churches have dispensed with the model constitutions written by the Baptist Union, in favour of a rule book that is "simpler and more easily understood". While the objective of having a constitution more easily understood by people is a good one, you can sometimes end us with a document that does not adequately prepare a Church for those tense situations that occur infrequently. A Church constitution needs to be written by or at least thoroughly checked, by people who have been involved in Church life for some years - if not decades!

What exactly should be the process? While everybody's lists would be different, they would probably include something like the following:

> -Try and work through, and then write down the specific grievance. In most cases this will take quite some time at a number of meetings! But it is very difficult to make any progress without defining the problem first.
>
> -Agree on the problem-solving process. I have written this elsewhere in the paper, but it is imperative, that the process is determined at the beginning and that it is quite specific. It is too late arguing about the specifics when you are trying to come to a conclusion. Again, it is probably better that this be in writing.
>
> -Try and find new solutions agreeable to both parties. Part of the whole rationale of hope in conflict, is that there are new solutions that have yet to be discovered. Instead of the conflicting parties defending their positions, they should be encouraged to brainstorm, to think more laterally and to find the better alternative.

3.5 Insist On In-Depth Listening

There are two keys to communication. The first is clear speech, and the second is listening. Of the two, the most important by far is listening.

I am sure I would not have written that five years ago. I am now convinced of it. For not only is listening imperative for communication, it also encourages greater honesty and openness from the speaker (if it is in-depth listening) and it creates a climate in which others are encouraged to listen more carefully.

One of the conciliator's most important functions, is to encourage those involved in conflict, to listen carefully (and this involves an attempt to understanding feeling, as well as reflecting, by occasionally checking what we are hearing).

This raises the question, how good are our communication skills? Ought we to provide training in listening and communication skills for the leadership groups with which we work?

3.6 We Offend More With Style Than With Substance

One of the other discoveries that I have just made recently, is that conflict involving a leader, is seldom over incidents. It generally has as its base, loss of confidence in the leadership and its style.

Let me illustrate. You are called in to help a Church where there is serious tension between the Minister and his leaders. More often than not a Minister will want to know the specific complaints of his accusers. He may persist in his request for a list of the specifics, in the mistaken assumption that this focus will resolve the conflict. When you turn to his accusers, you will often find that the list of misdemeanours seem trivial.

The reality is that it is not the list of what "he did or didn't do" that is at issue, but rather a break-down in the relationship. If a Minister's or leader's style is the problem; that is, he is autocratic, he does not listen, he cannot accept criticism, etc., then confidence in his ability to lead and to manage conflict will go. It is this lack of confidence in a leader that is most often at the root of Church conflict that involves a Minister and his people.

The tragedy is that Ministers will often not see this, and will emerge from such a confrontation believing that they have been dealt with unjustly. I sincerely believe that if there is confidence in the leadership, then almost any "incident" is survivable. If the relationship is becoming sour, then almost every incident will become an "issue" because the mechanism is no longer there to creatively resolve it.

The moral of this is not to be side-tracked by issues. Look for a possible loss of confidence which may be at the root of the contention.

3.7 The Power of Absorbing Anger

The New Testament in particular accepts the inevitability of conflict, and teaches us how we ought to act and react. One of the distinctively Christian reactions, is, in the spirit of Christ, to absorb and not deflect anger. In Paul's passage on litigation in 1 Corinthians Chapter 6, his complaint is not that they should be involved in conflict, but that they should use the services of a non-Christian conciliator. He goes on to those who believe themselves to have been wronged: "The very fact that you have legal disputes among yourselves shows that you have failed completely. Would it not be better for you to be wronged? Would it not be better for you to be robbed?"

Peter is even more explicit. "God will bless you . . . if you endure the pain of undeserved suffering because you are conscious of His will. If you endure suffering even when you have done right, God will bless you for it. It was to this that God called you, for Christ himself suffered for you and left you an example, so that you would follow in His steps. He committed no sin and no one ever heard a lie come back from his lips. When he was insulted, he did not answer back with an insult; when he suffered he did not threaten, but placed his hopes in God the righteous Judge." (1 Peter 2:19-23).

Christ demonstrated the power of faith in God (not simple- passivity) in the face of injustice. It was in such absorption of anger and injustice, that the world was redeemed. It is to this that we also have been called. To absorb anger ("If someone has done you wrong do not repay him with a wrong. Never take revenge, my friends, but instead let God's anger do it." Romans 12:17-19). We are encouraged to follow the example of Jesus, who trusted his Father, (the righteous Judge) to vindicate and to right the wrongs.

This is firstly a word to those who are personally involved in conflict. There is invariable a need for someone to act out the redemptive role. Its power is seen as others are encouraged to follow that example. But it is also a word to the conciliator, who will at times have to provide an ear to the angry and hurt. Allowing people to express their frustration and pent up anger will often be an important part of the resolution of conflict. It does, of course, have its price, as anyone will know who has had to listen to anger for any length of time.

"Few things amaze me as much as the power of good to overcome evil. Yet few things are as hard to do. Fallen human beings just don't act that way. We tend to respond in kind. If we are treated well, we generally respond well. But if we are treated badly, we tend to respond badly. Yet, New Testament passages constantly call us to handle conflict "differently": Turn the other cheek,,,If your enemy is hungry, feed him . . . Rejoice when you are persecuted and people falsely speak evil against you . . . Don't resist an evil person . . . Forgive . . . Love your enemies . . . If you are unjustly forced to give, give more than is demanded . . . Be submissive . . . Don't judge . . . Humble yourself . . . Be patient when you suffer for doing good . . . Give with no expectation of return . . . Don't complain or argue . . . Bless those who oppose you and do not curse them . . . Be defrauded rather than publicly press your case against your brothers . . . Deny your very self . . . Consider it a joy to face trials . . . Take up your cross daily.

It is an act of love to deal directly with conflict when you can. But the greater emphasis in the New Testament is on yielding in conflicts - even if the other person is at fault. The overwhelming affirmation is that fighting back is not the way to overcome evil. Indeed, fighting back is a feeble strategy compared to the power of returning good for evil. Returning evil for evil is an especially feeble strategy.

"Part of being a leader is that you must spend a considerable amount of energy absorbing other people's complaints. It is not the happiest way to spend one's time; but, if a group is going to run smoothly, people must have an opportunity to get the bile out of their systems. Providing this ventilation should not be an unbearable burden when you remind yourself that it is one of the ways you keep a group tightly motivated.

Anger is inevitable; and it is much smarter to let it ventilate upward, rather than allow it to smoulder down in the ranks, for it is such smoldering that often erupts into a major conflagration." ("Bringing Out the Best in people" Alan Loy McGinnis).

3.8 The Third Party
It is obvious that triangling must be avoided. The only justification for the third party, is when that person is needed to bring the parties to conflict

together. To encourage aggrieved parties to speak to third parties does absolutely nothing to remedy the problem, while spreading suspicion and discontent.

I have found helpful the involvement of a Select Committee when conflict has sometimes reached an impasse. Such a Committee can be asked for by either party, but its membership ought to be agreed upon by all concerned. The purpose of such a Committee ought to be to hear all the parties concerned, and to make some suggestion on the way ahead. This could, in extreme circumstances, suggest the resignation of a Minister, but more likely would recommend changed courses of action, or the use of a Moderator to work alongside the Church for a period of time. I have found it most helpful if the Church agrees that its findings, if unanimous, become binding on all parties. But whatever, it is imperative at the very beginning, that all concerned in the conflict understand exactly the Committee's brief and the process that all are going to embark upon.

4. Conclusion

I do not believe that anybody graduates in the school of conflict management! I always come out of such situations feeling tired, rather dirty and wishing that I had done it all a different way. I have the feeing that most of us come to the same sort of confusion. However, it is not something that we can avoid. And I have come to the other conclusion that I would still rather be in the conciliator's chair, than to give it to those of the old school who come in, castigate everybody for their behaviour, decide on the basis of very little information who is right and who is wrong, and then walk out thinking that the problem has been solved! Conflict can be highly creative and productive, and I believe that developing skills in its management, is one of the better uses of my time.

Gerard T. Marks is General Superintendent of the Baptist Union of New Zealand.

Structuring the Church For Discovering God's Will

Elimar Brandt

According to God's created order, God created man in His image (Gen. 1, 27). It is for this reason, that man seeks the will of God.

God wants communication with His creatures.

He revealed Himself as Jahweh (Exodus 3, 15) and as the living and active God to the fathers Abraham, isaac, Jacob and to the people of Israel . . . and He reveals Himself to all men in Christ.

The revelation of God's being is the one and only possibility given to man to know His will.

Throughout the history of the people of Israel, God has shown His love

. . . a love that is patient, unmistakable and indiscriminate. Despite the lack of faith and obedience from His people, He revealed, again and again, His will through His prophets.

The church, which has its origins in Jesus Christ, is the new people of God. he is the Lord and the head of His church.

Jesus Christ calls men to follow Him and enables His disciples to live a life according to the will of God.

It is through the crucifixion and resurrection of Jesus Christ that the number of believers grow in fellowship, living under the lordship of Jesus Christ.

Every church ordinance and all decisions in the congregation are based upon the redemptive work of Christ for His people.

The wandering congregation of God lives from the presence of the Lord through his Word and spirit. The visible signs of His presence are bread, wine, gifts and fruit of the Holy Spirit and the experience of brethren fellowship.

The life of the congregation in this time demands asking, seeking and finding the will of God as a concrete response to today's challenges under the scope of the eschatological redemptive work of God.

The fundamental and forever valid will of God has been laid out for everyone to see in the bible.

The pinnacle of this revelation is found in the incarnation of the Word in Jesus Christ.

All questions concerning the will of God remain tied to the gospel of Jesus Christ and to the practical fulfillment of faith in the living Christ.

As people who have been given our own will, who only find the fulfillment of, quote, "our will" by knowing God's will.

In the congregation, each individual will finds, through the unity of the spirit of God, correction and direction.

The congregation which understands itself as "familia dei" and which lives in an observable size in spacial proximity and in spiritual fellowship, will base its decision-making processes upon the will of God.

The structure of the congregation is not hierarchial, but rather a charismatic structure - a structure with the viewpoint solely of service; for the goal that should be reached is the building up of the body of Christ.

In order for the congregation to jointly find and know the will of God in concrete questions and situations demanding decisions, the congregation must regard the following essentials:

a) The common study of the Bible
   (There can never be enough Bible study within the congregation.)
b) The common experience of church services
   (In the church service, the congregation experiences the one Word and the might workings of the one spirit of Jesus Christ.)
c) The individual groups of the congregation must understand themselves to be ministry groups for the entire congregation.
d) To recognize the common priesthood of all believers and to be prepared to give equal attention to the voice of each member in the congregation.
e) Conscientious awareness of the ministries that are set forth by the Holy Spirit

(In questions concerning the will of God, it is good for a congregation to regard the counsel of experienced brethren in the life of faith.)

f) Capability to open oneself to the prophetic Word

(A congregation lives from the openness in which God, again and again, concretely speaks His Word to the situations of the congregation through prophetically gifted people.)

g) To maintain the balance between tradition and order with development and spontaneous forms

(Direct, spontaneous inspiration from the Spirit, must be measured according to the Word and to the historically proven structure of the church.)

Elimar Brandt is a Baptist Pastor in Berlin, West Germany, FRG.

Direction In Pastoral Practice

Ralph E. Elliott

Introduction

This paper is not intended to be in any way a sophisticated or academic effort. It came about in the following fashion.

In early October, 1985, Dr. Julian A. Cave, Jr., at that time the chairman of the Commission on Pastoral Leadership, wrote to a number of people asking for suggestions about the Commission's work during the current five-year period. In turn, I wrote a reply in which I listed some of my concerns. At the same time I indicated my feeling that we should do some substantive work as a Commission. Otherwise the large expenditures of time and money can hardly be justified. There is great strength in fellowship but my personal feeling is that our responsibility to each other and to our constituencies is larger than that.

I would like to see us produce some material which is helpful to us personally and which might likewise be of some catalytic value for the institutions and communions which receive our papers.

Ultimately word came that Dr. Cave had resigned and C. Welton Gaddy was asked to take the leadership. This paper is an attempt, at the request of Dr. Gaddy, to put some flesh on the skeletal suggestions which I had sent to Dr. Cave. What I share is simply one person's idea as to what might constitute a partial agenda for us. Perhaps what I share here may be useful in stimulating a discussion which will produce some kindred or totally other items from which our ultimate agenda might be made.

My assumption is that we are primarily concerned with the pastor and his/her pastoral practice. Therefore my discussion will center upon the pastor as theologian - a primary aspect of his/her work as I understand it, the roots of the theological context for the pastor's labors, and the pastor's relationship to contemporary issues in the kind of cosmos in which we find ourselves.

I. The Pastor As Theologian

What is the special and peculiar task of the pastor within Baptist ranks?

We have long been known for an emphasis upon the mutuality and interdependence of all of the people of God in ministry. Every Baptist as a minister or missionary is the genius of Baptist witness. Such an understanding is inherent in the "priesthood of the believer" emphasis as Baptists have transmitted the tradition. We believe in the appropriateness of an ordained ministry but yet wish to affirm that every believer has a ministry. Every person is ordained to his/her ministry at baptism. We have general agreement that *laos* includes the whole people of God.

As such there are very few, if any, facets of service which are by mandate restricted only to the pastor. Although the sacraments (ordinances) in their administration and the leadership of worship are generally reserved to the pastoral leader, it is not necessary that such be the case and in many parts of our Baptist community, non-ordained persons regularly minister and lead such.

Although many functions of the pastor are aided or assumed by all of the people of God and although no pastoral functions are absolutely the exclusive territory of the pastor, it is clear that she/he does have a distinct and primary function to serve as resident theologian.

Occasionally some pastor opts out of a discussion with the comment, "I am no theologian," Of course the pastor is a theologian. This is in keeping with the Baptist practice and tradition of interpreting the Scriptures and preaching the Word as the chief sacrament in the life of the Baptist community of faith.

The preaching task itself requires one to be a theologian. Dietrich Bonhoeffer in *Act and Being* spoke of preaching and theology as the reflective act. Theology is a reflection upon the remembered happenings of the community of faith, according to Bonhoeffer. Theology has the task of reflecting upon the mystery which has come into human history and such reflection gives birth to preaching. It was Bonhoeffer's view that right preaching involves both confession and theology.

The reflective act as theologian is also necessary if one is going to be involved in the other part of the pastor's task, the directive action. The pastor serves as theologian in discerning and interpreting the ways of God in relation to the world. The nature of society is no longer determined by individuals. It is shaped by institutions and theological activity is necessary in order to know how to evaluate and influence the corporate and institutional issues of life and society. The pastoral function in "equipping the saints for the work of ministry" demands hard theological work in order to gain appropriate insight on individual, corporate and institutional responsibility. Whether one's ministry is pastoral within a local church or in a larger judicatory, ecclesiastical or ecumenical setting, one has a strong responsibility as theologian.

This primary function of pastor as theologian directly ties him/her to the community of faith and strengthens the nature of the preaching ministry. When the task of pastor as theologian is grasped, she/he no longer is the agent *with* whom and *through* whom a congregation preaches. It is necessary for the pastor to be theologian if it is to be understood that the sermon is not just one more form of elocution. Theological attention is needed in the preparation and growth of a covenant community from which preaching comes. Amos may have done it without community but he was an exception. The great prophets were basically related to the cultic community. Great communities make great preaching but seldom do so-called "great preachers" make great communities.

In the light of the above, a major thrust of the Commission's attention over this five-year segment might be devoted to a study of the pastor as theologian. It would be necessary to wrestle with what this means. It would also be necessary to envision how "pastor as theologian" relates to the many and varied functional roles and duties which fall within the net of the pastor's responsibility.

II. The Roots of Theological Context

The pastor as theologian would necessitate a serious reassessment of the theological context in which she/he labors. Primary attention would be called to the Kingdom of God of which the church is but a part. Our primary attention is often focused upon the church. This myopia causes us to miss the relevant witness which our kind of world demands. It likewise contributes to a fragmented gospel and ministry whereby the individual and social concerns are separated and even viewed as competing witnesses. The pastor's ministry to, with and for the church is evaluated by and subsumed under the Kingdom of Christ. God's reign and realm is a context for all else. The pastor as theologian seeks to keep all things in a proper perspective for the Kingdom.

A. The Kingdom

God is the sovereign Lord of the universe where the whole structure, including the church, is joined together through Christ (Ephesians 2:21) who is supreme above all things and in whom all things hold together. The sovereignty of God over the entire realm is assumed. God's reign is expressed through Jesus Christ who calls the entire creation, personal and impersonal, into a redemptive relationship with himself. Neither the individual nor the world can "hold together" (Colossians 1:17) unless purpose is found in the Christ who holds the universe together.

It has long been recognized that Christ is Lord of the church. It needs to be recognized that Christ has the same relation to the so-called natural world as he does to the church and the "spiritual" world. The purpose of his reign is to reconcile all things (Colossians 1:20), and the "all things" has reference to both cosmic redemption and the redemption of individuals so that nothing and no one is alien to him. He is Lord of all.

The pastoral theologian has a responsibility to be alert to the present world in all of its technological and moral struggles and to recognize the kind of Christology which underscores that "God was in Christ reconciling the world to himself" (2 Corinthians 5:19). Mission and identity involve the entire world.

The pastoral theologian struggles to enable those with whom she/he labors to recognize that the Biblical vision of salvation therefore has an individual and a corporate, social and collective character. Every world issue is thus our issue. Theological direction is needed for serious attention to this world for it is on this earth and in this world that Christ develops his purpose and it is here that we find the central meaning of the human enterprise. Faith in God as the sovereign of all and in Jesus Christ as the Lord of history involves us in a faith in the future of this world.

This world cannot be given over to any other sovereignty. Under God's sovereignty, all creation is one, with every creature destined to be in community with the other under the will of God (Isaiah 2:2-4). The Biblical vision gives birth to the supposition that all are children of a single family and heirs of a common hope.

If the concerns of God's general sovereignty over the universe at large and God's particular sovereignty over the people of God have any validity at all, there are serious implications for the community of faith in terms of both mission and discipleship. The pastor as theologian will help his/her people work out what it means to follow Jesus in his prayer, "Thy Kingdom come, thy will be done on earth . . ." Although the ultimate fullness of the Kingdom may be in the future at another time and in another place, if God's reign on this earth is not a realistic expectation, then the prayer of Jesus was misdirected and a large segment of the prophetic hope is only fantasy. Of course no human group can produce the Kingdom but it can bear testimony to its realization. Therefore, to allow any eschatology or futurology to remove us from the recognition of God's sovereignty in this world is to contribute to a hopelessness which is counter to Biblical hope.

This articulation of the vision of the present as well as the future reign of God is an important work of the pastoral theologian. The pastor as theologian will seek to encourage the Christian practice within the context of a specific history. If the particular situation is of a hungry and politically exploding world, then it is there that the Kingdom call and character must be worked out. It will be done so under the unifying vision of the reign of God.

As was demonstrated on the part of God, the mission is always incarnational in that the word has to become flesh in every time and place. God's people have a gospel to share which is more than simply a matter of idea or inner spiritual experience. How is that to be done?

B. The Church

The context above places upon the pastor the task of theologian in helping the people of God (the church) to recognize its place in sharing the rule of God. The rule of God is shared with and through the people of God, the church.

From the first to the last, the Bible is concerned with God's purpose in creating a people for himself, or, as Peter summarized what he had borrowed from the book of Exodus: " . . . you are a chosen race, a royal priesthood, a holy nation, God's own people, that you may declare the wonderful deeds of him who called you out of darkness into a marvelous light." The Petrine epistle (1 Peter 2:8-10) describes the church (the body of believers) in terms of Israel as the holy people of God. The church is the church when it recognizes that it is the people of God in covenant with God who is the suzerain or sovereign willmaker. From his own grace and goodness, God wills to give a particular inheritance or assignment to a people who have certain claims connected with the will. The will or covenant (*diatheke*) is made between God and the people. The result is that those who enter into the covenant with God have a kinship with each other. They are brothers and sisters in the will as part of the family of God.

Those who are called into covenant with God and with each other constitute a special creation of the people of God elected to a special ministry for God in behalf of all humanity and addressing itself to all humanity. The people of God has a collective and an individual priesthood. The elect are a "peculiar" people or treasure in the midst of all peoples. All people are God's but these are chosen for a unique and particular use or function. The particular people of God are to live in the midst of all the people of God as a "kingdom of priests and a holy nation." The people of God are holy (i.e., distinct, different, set apart, unique) in order that they may serve as a "priest." The word "priest" means bridge-builder, go-between, intermediary or negotiator. The church is committed to a specific moral relationship as the people of God in order that it may aid in building a bridge between God and humankind, between humankind and God, and between the various segments of humankind itself. This is the essence of the church's purpose at any stage in its history. The church, in other words, points to Jesus Christ, the Lord of history, and is an agent of that Lordship.

Biblically, as the process develops through the two testaments, the form of the people of God is both changing and negotiable but its mission for the divine ruler is not. As the event in history is remembered as experience, and experienced again, how is it shared? Furthermore, how does ont continue to call the covenant community into being and how is it nurtured? These are questions for the pastor as theologian.

III. The Pastor and Contemporary Issues

If the pastor has a primary task as theologian and if the Kingdom provides the backdrop and the church serves as the context of the pastor's ministry, there are a number of current issues which deserve pastoral attention. These issues provide a challenge for ministry and they deserve some theological evaluation as to whether they do nor do not contribute to the authenticity of one's task. The issues relate to the context of both Kingdom and Church.

A. The Kingdom and Liberation Theology

With a Biblical understanding of Kingdom, how are we to relate to the issues of poverty, hunger, justice and peace as they have more graphically come to our attention through the media of the world and through the focus provided by the so-called "liberation theology"?

We represent various segments of the world and different ideologies and political systems. Yet we cannot be unaware of the pains and wounds of the world, near at hand and far away. I look at the people in my own city where there is massive poverty, and indeed in the very church of which I am a part. Many of our people are dispossessed in one way or another. A number have been political prisoners or have suffered political harassment. Through them I have come to see pains which I had not seen before; through them I have come to sense grace I had not known before, and through them I have had to search the Scriptures in ways I have not searched before and to make revelatory discoveries which blinded eyes did not see before. By looking into their needy faces, I at times have seen the face of Jesus.

What is my responsibility when often I know that in order to address these questions and these needs, I must address the very political system of which I am a part? What does the pastoral theologian discern about a religious issue which becomes a political issue?

The easy way is to turn away but a voice looms large when I am "not grieved over the ruin of Joseph" (Amos 6:6) and the voice of Jesus speaks strongly to me that what is required of the community of faith is an active concern for the dispossessed - the widow, the orphan, the poor, the prisoners; this indeed is central to what is expected in the lifestyle of a people who calls itself the people of God. The poor and the oppressed in both the underdeveloped and the developed world are the focus of liberation concerns.

If God's Kingdom is to be a kingdom of this world and the next, who can doubt that the Church has the responsibility to be, to speak and to do? Is Jose Miguez Bonino wrong when he speaks of faith, not as an intellectual assent but as "an attitude of engagement, in the light of God's design, with everything human, whether individual, social, economic, political, educational . . ."? If God takes His stand against the lofty and with the lowly, can the church do any less?

We live in the shades of another day when liberation was presented as a "by and by" dream, "up yonder some place" in the Jerusalem of the sky. It is not to be denied that liberation's fullness may come in some point beyond historical time. Is it true, however, suggested by Juan Segundo, that "total liberation is conditioned upon a liberation process in history"? What does the pastor as theologian say to the Black contention that "no magic in the hereafter will be able to make up for what human beings have failed to do here below?"

It is been suggested that a Biblical note is that God's Kingdom will come on this earth, yet everywhere the world is hostile to God and enslaved by the powers of darkness. On the other hand, the last book of the Bible announces that the kingdoms of this world "shall become the kingdoms of our God and his Christ." Mortimer Arias suggests that Jesus came announcing "the good news of the Kingdom of God" as being his mission and evangelization; he further suggests that we have confused "the plan of salvation" with Jesus" evangelism. Is there a conflict between the two? Are orthopraxis and orthodoxy in conflict? How much of our theology is to be formed through engagement?

There are many questions but one thing is clear - God has called us to incarnational Christianity. Both Bonhoeffer and the liberation theologians seem to have something to offer in requiring doctrinal statements to be worked out in the practical relevance of the earthly struggle. The struggle alongside the dispossessed calls for a church where theology becomes anthropology, the theology of a Christ incarnated and humiliated.

Questions or not, surely the more the church draws near to Emmanuel, God with us, the more the church draws near to the dispossessed. We cannot remain inside debating resolutions while outside the world is burning - or starving. Beyond that we cannot be satisfied with sending food to people in chains; we must find ways to cut the chains - or at least to accept the chains as our own. how do pastoral theologians in various parts of the world help their people to grapple with these issues of the Kingdom?

B. The Church as Essence and the Church as Institution

How then are the church as institution, known to all of us, and the church as essence, known in the mind of Christ, to be understood? One can hardly quibble with the necessity of church as an institution. Every organism needs organization as an expression of its life. Can there be a harmony of process in growing the church as Christ calls it to be and growing a successful and thriving institution? Does one call for the other or does either deny the other? To speak to the question is to be forced to deal with the issue popularly known as church growth.

It is crystal clear in the Scripture that the church is to share its witness and it is anticipated that the church shall grow in numbers as well as in the depth of discipleship and faith maturation and in the height of a changed lifestyle with ethical implications. The book of Acts details a growth process and who can doubt the mandated impact of the so-called "Great Commission" in Matthew 28:18-20? The recognition of the legitimate necessity of sharing the faith and a compassionate concern for those outside the church has led to a rather widescale adoption of methodological techniques for growth which have been accompanied by success.

The techniques, commonly called church growth techniques, have been found to be successful in achieving increased numbers. There are certain "givens" in the methodology. A prophetic stance of ministry is basically disallowed and the invitations for personal response are made to cater to the personal desires of the individual. A favorite slogan is to "find a need and fill it" so that the growth ministry of the church is directed primarily to "servicing" rather than "challenging" those who are recruited. A rather autocratic style of pastoral leadership is proposed with the pastor functioning as the chief strategist, assuming the "company commander" rather than the "enabler" stance.

But more basic than all of the others is the sociological foundation of the methodology, namely, that growing churches can only be built with homogeneous people. People "like to become Christians" without crossing racial, linguistic, or class barriers and they must be so accommodated if the church is expected to grow. It is believed by the adherents of the movement that sociological factors are far more a deterrent to Christian commitment than are theological factors. Therefore, it is better to go with the tide and make Christian decision as easy as possible. Since people do not easily become Christians individually, a "tribal consciousness" pattern with an emphasis upon multi-individual decision-making is encouraged. Utilization is made of sociological "people movements" and people are encouraged to become Christians this way.

But the obvious success of the movement leads to the question. Are essence and methodology one and the same? Who, if not the pastoral theologian, sorts out the strength and weakness, the truth and error, of any system? The growth of the church is more than technique and there are occasions when the success of methodology can actually violate essence. In the worldly, measurable sense, the church has not always been and is not always "successful." Numerical success and spiritual success can be one and the same. But there are times when there is a "cheap" grace and a "costly" grace, a time when technique and essence do not coincide. "Whatever succeeds" is not thereby mandated.

How can "God has made one blood all . . ." (Acts 17:26) be used as a directive for building separation? Does not the gospel call for a new humanity which refuses to recognize old barriers (Galatians 3:28)? Is not Acts 15 a challenge to relinquish exclusiveness and isolationism? Does not grace overcome barriers and unique people in the same fellowship without any necessity of meeting the peculiar conditions and customs of either group? Had homogeneity been a mandate, Paul's life-mission as an apostle to the Gentiles would have been denied. The spread of the gospel has to do with crossing barriers and building bridges. The body of Christ cannot be a reflection of earth's divisions, shaped by class and culture. Furthermore, although an emphasis upon homogeneity may give temporary success, it does nothing towards preparing the church for an increasingly heterogeneous world.

The pastor as theologian has the responsibility to scrutinize and test the motivation and validity of any "system" to see whether the system is consistent with the mission.

C. The Ecumenical World

Another issue demanding attention on the part of the pastor as theologian is the question of the ecumenical pattern of the church.

The oneness of the church is a given and there are many signs that we are in a position to respond to the gift of unity for which Christ prayed in John 17 and to which the Church is called (Ephesians 2:11-21). Unity appears not to be an option but rather, a scared gift and trust. If the price of a fragmented Church is a fragmented world, then the unity of the Church is absolutely essential for the unity of the world. Conversations in this direction abound and under the auspices of the Baptist World Alliance, we engage in conversations with Roman Catholic brothers and sisters.

Two very practical questions arise with reference to the theological base of ecumenicity. The first relates to the previous issue on church as essence and as institution. What is the result of ecumenicity with reference to the local institution? There are those who would argue that ecumenicity encourages a moral relativism "where anything goes." Furthermore, it is suggested that "to scatter the shot" weakens the local institution and denies the growth of a local congregation. But does the charge that mature ecumenism weakens theological stance and evangelistic endeavor prove to be the case? Some of the most serious theological and ethical struggles to be encountered anywhere will be found in ecumenical circles. Does not ecumenicity require one to become more solidly acquainted with one's own roots and thereby make stronger Christians, not weaker ones? It can be said that those who work ecumenically are generally more aware of the kind of world in which we live and this in turn strengthens the evangelistic imperative. Is not the fear of ecumenicity at least partly a result of a pragmatic style which gives "church" preeminence over the Kingdom of God? The call to the Kingdom is a costly call to newness with radical new allegiances. The evangelistic message to be sounded is a call to relationships which transcend both institutional church and denomination. On the other hand, how does such a call harmonize with the necessity of building a local nurturing community of faith?

The other question relates to the very nature of Baptists. Perhaps of all the things which we have had to contribute, the most characteristic one is our understanding of the regenerate nature of the Church as a body of visible saints. Traditionally this has led to a certain view of believer's baptism. It can be said that Baptist participation in the ecumenical movement has offered many opportunities for the acceptance of Baptist positions by larger bodies, as is evident in some sections in the World Council of Churches statement, *Baptism, Eucharist and Ministry*. Yet tremendous pressures are felt in the ecumenical world which suggests that unity in the Body of Christ makes baptism "an unrepeatable act." If baptism is a requisite to full obedience and entrance into the community of faith, and if baptism is to be administered only to believers, how do Baptists respond to other brothers and sisters in Christ?

If the pastor as theologian does not help his/her people with such issues, who does? What kind of agreements must we have in order to work together?

D. Personal Spiritual Development

One additional issue with which our commission might spend some time relates to personal spiritual formation.

Corporate worship in Baptist life has had a vitality too it when it has been an extension of the private devotion and practices of spiritual discipline and formation which were customarily part of daily living. In their early worship, Baptists tried to emulate initial Christianity as much as possible. Biblical material was much in evidence as Baptist preachers tried to "tell the story," lifted from the pages of both the Old and New Testaments. Great Christological passages like the litanies incorporated into Philippians 2:1-11 and Colossians 1:15-23 were lifted up as media for experiencing the centrality of Christ.

Solitude and community are joined together so that the corporate contributes to the personal and the personal contributes to the corporate. The Biblical message is not a strange happenstance in a weekly service but rather a deepening of a happy and familiar part of life. Christian spirituality is an interweaving of the personal and the corporate.

But pastoral theologians themselves need help with those personal disciplines of an inward nature so that our own activity in life and leadership is experiential rather than merely academic. How do we nourish that inner strength which keeps the vision sharp and the zeal undiminished? Is not a devotional thrust at the heart and center of it all?

How does the pastor as theologian find something for her/himself which is vital and authentic?

Conclusion

No attempt has been made here to be exhaustive or to cover the vast areas of pastoral responsibility. The one area for direction in pastoral practice, that of pastor as theologian, has been suggested as a theme which might be pursued with profit for ourselves who gather here and possibly as a contribution to those who view our work. A context for the pastor as theologian has been suggested, that of Kingdom and Church. Four areas of personal ambiguity and interest have been sketched as perhaps worthy of the personal attention of us all.

Perhaps the above will serve to generate other areas. These collectively might be categorized and organized with particular assignments to be made with responsibility for resource material to be provided for forthcoming meetings of the Commission.

Ralph H. Elliott is Pastor of the North Shore Baptist Church in Chicago, Illinois, U.S.A.

Theological Reflection On
The Practice of the Ordinances

Bruce Rumbold

Introduction

This paper is presented here in draft form, with only minor changes from the version tabled for discussion in Nassau. I should also state at the outset that I am particularly interested in the actual *practice* of the ordinances of Baptism and Lord's Supper in our different Baptist Conventions, Associations and Unions. These practices I believe reveal our operational theology; and this as we all know can be at variance with the formal theology propounded in our doctrinal statements! I would therefore appreciate it if a significant proportion of discussion time can focus on the issues of practice raised in Section D below, for I am very much aware that my own ministry experience is limited to Melbourne and a brief period in northern England.

Some comments on terminology might be appropriate here. I will use the term ordinance throughout to refer to Baptism and Lord's Supper, although the term sacrament is also common in contemporary Baptist writing. Communion and the Lord's Supper I will use interchangeable, noting that they are more familiar to Baptists than the term Eucharist which is common in ecumenical circles. I will however employ Eucharist frequently in the discussion of ecumenical perspectives.

Finally, it does not seem possible to conduct a discussion on the ordinances today without extensive reference to the World Council of Churches (WCC) document *Baptism, Eucharist, Ministry* (henceforth referred to as BEM). This document, sometimes also referred to as the Lima document, is the product of 50 years of ecumenical discussion in the Faith and Order Commission of the WCC, and for this reason alone deserves attention. A further compelling reason is that most recent Baptist discussions of the ordinances have been conducted in response to this 1982 document or its 1975 predecessor *One Baptism, One Eucharist and a Mutually Recognized Ministry*.

A. Baptist Tradition

1. Baptism

There appears to be general agreement among Baptists that the normative mode of baptism is to be by immersion in water upon confession of repentance toward God and faith toward our Lord Jesus Christ (Acts 20:21). Differences emerge as to the exceptions which will be allowed to this normative practice, particularly in respect of transfers into membership from other denominations. Some Baptist congregations will accept into membership only those baptized as believers by immersion; others are prepared to accept as valid the baptism by affusion of a believer; others again require only a confession of faith, making no firm baptismal requirement of those joining by transfer while continuing to practice only the baptism of believers within the congregation. When we link these baptismal practices with practices relating to the Lord's Supper, three broad groups among Baptists may be distinguished:

i. Those who believe in open membership and open communion.
ii. Those who restrict membership and communion to those who have been baptized as believers.
iii. Those who maintain a closed membership but open communion to all believers.

These groupings were in fact identified from questionnaire responses by a Study Commission of the Sixth Baptist World Congress in Atlanta, Georgia in 1939. (It is interesting to note that the Commission emphasized "the need for more thorough and systematic instruction in Baptist principles" on the basis of the responses received!) It seems that these distinctions have been there from the earliest days of the Baptist movement, and that they continue today.

2. Lord's Supper

Baptist views of the Lord's Supper need to be seen in the context of sixteenth-century Reformation debate. The initial challenge to the then-prevailing medieval Catholic doctrine of transubstantiation came from Luther, who rejected this doctrine's explanation of the real presence of Christ in the Mass, although he retained a clear understanding that indeed Christ's flesh and blood were truly present. Zwingli moved further from this position, rejecting not only transubstantiation but also any literal understanding of "This is My Body". For Zwingli, baptism and the Lord's Supper are "signs and symbols of holy things, but not . . . the things of which they are signs." The Supper becomes a simple feast of thanksgiving and remembrance. Calvin argued for an intermediate position. He criticized the Catholic (and to a lesser extent the Lutheran) views because in them the signs of bread and wine obscure the mystery; attention is drawn to the elements more than to that which is signified. He also criticized Zwingli, because in this view the sign is separated from the mystery. Rather, Calvin insists, the key to proper understanding is found in the ministry of the Spirit. It is by the spirit's power that communion is bestowed upon believers, who receive spiritual food as well as the outward symbols of bread and wine. Unbelievers in contrast receive only the outward symbols, and remain under condemnation not because they have partaken unworthily of the elements, but because without faith they cannot be nourished by the Spirit. This is, communion is effective through faith, the symbols are not effective in themselves.   Baptists emerged among the many movements of seventeenth century Non conformity, and from the beginning, both Zwinglian and Calvinistic strands were distinguishable among them. Strangely enough it was the Particular Baptists, strongly Calvinistic in their theology of election, who were the most Zwinglian in their approach to the Supper, and the General Baptists, Arminian in their doctrine of salvation, who held to a Calvinistic view of communion. With both strands of the Baptist movement however the themes of remembrance and fellowship were central, and while there were debates over "ordinance" v. "sacrament", openness of the Table tended to be more an issue of dispute than the mode of Christ's presence at the Table. The General Baptists tended to open the Table to all baptized believers "who appear to love the Lord in sincerity", while the Particular Baptists were concerned to limit communion fellowship to those who shared a common baptism, viz. by immersion as a believer.

In recent years (over much of this century) there has been remarkably little discussion of the Lord's Supper within Baptist circles. At the same time the Supper has slipped from a central place in the worship life of many congregations, often becoming in effect an additional service which merely supplements the main worship service. The discussions which have taken place, such as those catalyzed by the WCC Faith and Order Commission, tend to owe more to Calvin in their approach in that they acknowledge the real presence of Christ in the fellowship of the Table.

One further change has been the matter of presidency at the Supper. Until the middle of the nineteenth century, apart from some local exceptions among Particular Baptists, Baptist congregations insisted that the president be an ordained minister, preferring not to celebrate the Supper if a minister could not be found. This appears largely to have broken down today, although in most places it seems that a congregation will ask an ordained minister to preside if such a person is available.

B. Contemporary Baptist Statements

The majority of contemporary Baptist statements on baptism and the Lord's Supper have been made in response to the World Council of Churches Faith and Order Commission document *Baptism, Eucharist, Ministry*. Responses to this statement continue to be published (the sixth volume has just been released), including formal replies from the following Baptist bodies:

I. Baptist Union of Great Britain and Ireland (pp 70-77)
III. All-Union Council of Evangelical Christians - Baptists in the USSR (pp 227-229)
    Baptist Union of Scotland (pp 230-245)
    Baptist Union of Denmark (pp 246-253)
    Covenanted Baptist Churches in Wales (pp 254-256)
    American Baptist Churches in the USA (pp 257-263)
IV. Burma Baptist Convention (pp 184-190)
    Union of Evangelical Free Churches in the GDR (Baptists) (pp- 191-199)
    Baptist Union of Sweden (pp 200-213)

The Roman numeral prefix is the volume number of the series *Churches respond to BEM*, published by World Council of Churches in Geneva. Vol. I came out in 1986; Vols. III & IV in 1987. I also have access to a statement from the Baptist Union of Australia (published by the Australian Council of Churches, but not as yet by WCC), and a draft statement discussed by the BWA Doctrine Commission in Singapore in 1986.

The material that follows is based largely upon these statements. it is perhaps worth emphasizing that they are committee statements which have been in many cases considered and affirmed by the Union or Convention concerned as an official response to BEM. They are thus more likely to be representative of contemporary Baptist thought than the writings of individual pastors or theologians.

1. Baptism

In its presentation of baptism, BEM identifies five major dimensions of meaning:

    i. Participation in Christ's death and resurrection
    ii. Conversion, pardoning, cleansing
    iii. The Gift of the Spirit
    iv. Incorporation into the Body of Christ
    v. The Sign of the Kingdom

These dimensions are further developed in discussion of the relationship between baptism and faith; the relationship between baptism of infants and believers (including here the recognition that "baptism upon personal profession of faith is the most clearly attested pattern in the New Testament documents"); and the possibilities of mutual recognition of baptism among the diverse Christian traditions. In this second section lies one of the more contentious phrases for Baptists, where those who practice believers'' baptism are asked to avoid "any practice which might be interpreted as "re-baptism". (It is perhaps only fair to point out that churches practicing infant baptism are also asked to guard against "apparently indiscriminate baptism and take more seriously their responsibility for the nurture of baptized children to mature commitment for Christ".)

It may be helpful to recognize here something of what BEM has adopted from prior discussions with Baptist churches, in particular the Faith and Order Consultation at Louisville in 1979, where members of the WCC Commission met in dialogue with a number of Baptist leaders and theological teachers. (These proceedings were published in full as Vol. LXXVII of *Review and Expositor*, (Winter 1980; a report and some associated articles are contained in *Baptist Quarterly*, Vol. XXVIII, 1980). Five significant pints of agreement were recorded:

1. The acceptance that believers'' baptism is the most clearly attested practice of baptism in the New Testament, together with the recognition that infant baptism has developed within the Christian tradition and witnesses to valid Christian insights.
2. The statement that the personal faith of the recipient and continuous participation in the life of the church are essential for the full fruit of baptism. In believers' baptism the believing community has played its part in the nurture of that personal faith, whilst, in infant baptism, the supportive believing community surrounding the infant will nurture the child's personal faith as it moves toward discipleship.
3. The recognition in all the group reports that both forms of baptism require a similar and responsible attitude towards Christian nurture and a serious development in the concept of Christian catechumenate.
4. The reminder that the pressures of contextuality have always borne in on the understanding and practice of baptism and that in these present days contextuality requires radical rethinking by both groups as to what form of baptism they practice and why.
5. The conviction that indiscriminate baptism is seen as an abuse to be eliminated.

These insights have been incorporated in BEM, and with this at least two important developments in ecumenical baptismal discussions are made. The first is that the debate concerning Scriptural precedents for infant baptism is effectively over; the case for infant baptism must now be made on grounds other than apostolic authority. The second is that the richness and diversity of New Testament understanding and practice is better realized, with a consequent lessening of the pressure for one particular church to claim that its stance represents "pure" doctrine.

Baptist responses to the Baptism section of BEM have been for the most part quite affirming. The richness of the BEM interpretation of baptism has been welcomed, and is seen by many as assisting Baptists to deepen their own understanding of this ordinance. In particular the focus on incorporation into the body and baptism as a sign of the Kingdom have been welcomed. The former emphasis is seen to link baptism unambiguously with church membership, the latter underlines the "political" dimension of baptism insofar as a person pledges in baptism primary loyalty to Kingdom motives and values, making all other values and allegiances secondary to these.

Baptist responses are however virtually unanimous in questioning three aspects of the BEM perspective. These are a perceived tendency to present baptism as effecting the things it represents; the implied necessity of baptism for Christian faith; and the relationship between infant baptism and believers' baptism implied by mutual recognition of baptism.

Several responses thus question the content of statements like "baptism is . . ."; does hit mean that baptism *signifies* these things (new life, participation in Christ's death and resurrection), or that it *effects* these things? The former interpretation is of course acceptable to Baptists, the latter is not. Some responses would want to strengthen the statement in BEM that "baptism . . . implies confession of sin and conversion of heart". Here "implies" should be "demands", for these respondents suggest. That is, Baptist responses wish to focus more clearly the element of faithful individual response without necessarily rejecting the other dimensions outlined by BEM. (This is expressed most clearly in the responses from the USSR and the GDR, both of which suggest that the whole BEM document is in danger of putting church ahead of Christ rather, as the response from USSR says, "first of all the personal encounter between man and Christ should take place, and then it must be followed by baptism, eucharist and ministry".)

Several responses also suggest that BEM assumes implicitly that a Christian is one who has been baptized. If so, this is seen to be inappropriate or inadequate both in the light of Scripture and in recognizing confessional groups such as the Society of Friends and the Salvation Army which do not practice baptism. it is faith, not baptism, which is necessary for salvation.

The fundamental issue for all Baptist responses is however that of believers" baptism as compared with infant baptism. None of the Baptist responses can see that infant baptism is an adequate expression of the baptismal theology outlined in the BEM text. They maintain that only believers" baptism can represent this theology appropriately. This of course leads on to the difficulty of "re-baptism". Most Baptist responses see the BEM request (to avoid *any* practice which might be interpreted as re-baptism) as impossibly restrictive. They argue that if a person's infant baptism has not been accompanied by adequate nurture in the faith or followed by any evidence of personal commitment to Christ, then if he or she is converted and becomes convinced out of an instructed conscience that Christian obedience requires believers" baptism, this baptism should be administered.

The Baptist Union of Australia response in this respect is helpful, drawing as it does upon some of the extensive work of George Beasley-Murray on baptism.

> "I have now reached the point in believing that the churches will never solve their baptismal problems till they acknowledge (this conclusion). And it is this: *infant baptism is not the baptism of which the New Testament documents speak.* That it performs certain useful functions and embodies valuable truths is not to be denied, but its function is different from that which the New Testament writers attribute to baptism".
> (George Beasley-Murray *Baptism Today and Tomorrow*, 1966, p. 156)

> To identify similarities, real or imagined, between the two is to miss this basic point. It is not that we have different understandings of one baptism but that there are two different baptisms. Infant baptism certainly "witnesses to valid Christian insights" but not to valid Christian *baptismal* insights as expounded in the New Testament and summarized in BEM itself.

> This is not to reject ecumenical sharing but to advance a different base from which mutual recognition and sharing might proceed.

The submission from the Baptist Union of Great Britain and Ireland develops this further, also drawing upon the perspectives of George Beasley-Murray, in suggesting that while a plausible case cannot be made for equating infant baptism with believers' baptism, a case might be made for equating the full initiation process of the different church traditions. That is, the infant baptism followed by nurture, personal commitment, confirmation and acceptance into church membership might be recognized as equivalent to the Baptist process of the blessing of a child, followed by nurture, personal commitment, baptism and church membership. This would permit the transfer of membership to Baptist congregations from congregations of other denominations, even though that Baptist congregation would practice only believers" baptism.

2. Lord's Supper

BEM distinguishes five dimensions of meaning for the Eucharist or Lord's Supper:

> i. Thanksgiving to the Father
> ii. Anamnesis or Memorial of Christ
> iii. Invocation of the Spirit
> iv. Communion of the Faithful

v. Meal of the Kingdom

The accompanying discussion includes a recommendation that the Lord's Supper be celebrated frequently (at least once each week), and identifies diverse attitudes to and treatment of the elements and to those who may participate and preside. The particular issue of participation of children is noted, although it is not discussed.

In general, Baptist responses to the BEM section on Eucharist again tend to be affirmative, largely because it builds upon and broadens traditional understandings and adds fresh insights (such as those on anamnesis and meal of the Kingdom). In particular Baptists welcome the balance of the word with sacrament or ordinance, and for the most part also welcome and affirm the Trinitarian framework of Eucharist as thanksgiving to the Father, memorial of Christ, invocation of the Spirit.

Questions arise principally around the matter of "real presence". It is worth noting that this is the case not only for Baptists, but for all denominations. Catholic bishops regret the absence of a focus upon sacrifice; Baptists and Churches of Christ (Disciples) express caution about the very idea of "real presence"; Reformed theologians want to know more about what is meant by the term "presence" in BEM. In other words, a number of traditional issues are re-awakened here. BEM's treatment of *anamnesis* (the Greek word used for memorial in the words of institution) in the light of recent Biblical scholarship provides some bridge over these difficulties. it is pointed out that in Biblical understanding the act of remembering makes an event — or at least its benefits and responsibilities — present today. Remembering identifies us as participants in the story which is remembered, and calls forth a response from us; to remember is not only to recall, but to obey. Thus there is the possibility of holding together both "sacrificial" and "memorial" aspects of Eucharist.

Many Baptist responses express an interest in and willingness to explore the anamnesis (memorial) and real presence issues. They express however some concern with the statement that Christ's presence in the Eucharist is "unique". Most Baptist responses affirm the real presence of Christ within the fellowship (where two or three are gathered) and are wary of any tendencies to link presence specifically with Eucharistic fellowship let alone with the eucharistic elements. The tensions felt here are most plainly expressed by the Baptist Union of Scotland paper, which suggests that BEM places sacramental and evangelical theologies alongside each other without attempting any meaningful integration, and that the problems in applying the BEM position arise from two incompatible understandings of grace; grace through faith on the one hand, and grace effected through participation in the sacrament on the other (Whether such a clear distinction can actually be made is yet another matter for discussion.)

British Baptists make an interesting suggestion at this point. They feel that a theology of "elements" continues to dominate the BEM presentation rather than a theology of "action"; that is, there is still too much attention being paid to "bread and wine" rather than to "eating and drinking". They would focus Eucharistic understanding on fellowship; what actually happens in the sharing of the elements, and what is represented by that sharing. This seems to be a helpful insight, grounded in Calvin's perspective yet developing beyond it, and showing us a way of moving past the often-sterile debates of the past. It allows for a non-magical view of real presence in the Eucharist, opens the communion or eucharist to all faithful believers, permits the presidency of any member authorized by the congregation, and emphasizes the centrality of fellowship in discerning and experiencing the presence of God. These aspects — particularly open communion, lay presidency, and the centrality of fellowship — are stressed in all Baptist responses.

The recommendation that communion be celebrated at least weekly is queried in a number of Baptist responses, not so much because of the frequency suggested as for the apparent reasoning that, as the presence of Christ is centered uniquely in the Eucharistic celebration, frequent observation is important. (Danish Baptists even wonder whether BEM is implying that any service of worship is incomplete without eucharist.) Baptists however maintain that the presence of Christ is in the gathered community of believers, and so the communion service which celebrates this presence, while important, has less priority than the frequent gathering of believers together for worship and ministry. As the Swedish Baptist response puts it "if as in Baptist tradition other resources are considered as being of equal value (*to the Eucharist*), the question of how often the Eucharist should be celebrated is still important but not in the crucial way that the Lima document (BEM) indicates".

C. Some Pastoral Theological Strategies

A considerable amount of theological reflection has already been presented in the preceding section, and I will not enlarge further on this. Rather, I wish to offer here a series of practical theological comments and suggestions based on the preceding material, which should in turn stimulate further discussion. I will not attempt to argue a case for each, although in some instances I will indicate the basis on which I make it. It should also be understood that I make these not as statements of a final or unnegotiable position, but as a personal perspective developed through reflection upon the issues raised by BEM and in my own pastoral practice. I am open to the wisdom of the Commission on these and other points!

Ordinance or Sacrament?

It seems to me that the juxtaposition of these terms in common Baptist usage (as reflected in many of the responses to BEM) is unfortunate. The implication seems to be that there is little or no ground between "ordinance as mere memorial" on the one hand and "sacrament as creating faith" on the other. While wanting to resist any suggestion that immersion in water or the sharing of bread and wine can be effective in themselves for creating faith, it nevertheless is clear from pastoral experience than baptism and Lord's Supper can be very powerful events in people's lives, and are in this sense sacramental, mediating God's grace. Is it not possible for Baptists to use the term sacrament while avoiding the implication that God's grace is limited to these rites or that the rites themselves guarantee the delivery of grace?

Relationship Between Baptism and Lord's Supper

I suggest that the connection between baptism and Lord's Supper should be made explicit in our practice: that we should not administer baptism unless we also follow this with a celebration of the Lord's Supper at which the baptized persons are welcomed into the membership of the congregation and commissioned for ministry, preferably by the laying on of hands with prayer. I further suggest that at each Lord's Supper the link should be reinforced by offering the opportunity for communicants to reaffirm their baptismal vows, either privately or in some public (liturgical) form.

Baptism as Commissioning (Ordination) to Christian Ministry

The point has been made in the previous paragraph, but is worth emphasizing. The commitment of believer's baptism is worked out as the baptized person finds his or her place within the overall ministry of the congregation. Is it not appropriate that this be made explicit in an act of commissioning or ordination to Christian ministry through the laying on of hands with prayer?

Mutual Recognition of Initiation and Communion

Mutual recognition of communion is not a Baptist issue as such. The vast majority of Baptists appear to offer communion to anyone who believes in Jesus as Lord, and mutuality here depends rather on other traditions opening the Lord's Table to us. On the other hand, Baptists are restrictive about baptism as compared with other traditions; that is, most other traditions recognize believers'' baptism, but this recognition is not reciprocated by many Baptists.

While agreeing that it is not possible to equate infant baptism with believers' baptism, I suggest that we explore further the possibility of the mutual recognition of initiation processes as outlined above. This would allow persons baptized as infants either to enter into membership of a Baptist congregation through believers' baptism, or, if they believe that they have through nurture and confirmation appropriated their baptism as an infant, to come into membership by confession of faith. The membership of the congregation would thus be composed of persons baptized in either mode; but the congregation would proclaim and practice believers' baptism alone as the normative mode of baptism.

(It is interesting at this point to note another approach to convergence within the Uniting Church of Australia, which is currently considering a proposal that a service of "immersion as baptismal re-affirmation" be introduced for those who wish publicly to testify to their faith in this way.)

The Lord's Supper and Fellowship

While the theological emphasis in Baptist discussions of the Lord's Supper is upon fellowship (pages 6 & 7 above), in practice Baptist celebration of the Supper appears to emphasize individual private devotion which includes little or no recognition of other communicants.

I suggest that we need to find ways of restoring an emphasis upon corporate life in our celebrations of the Supper. For example, the Sharing of the Peace among communicants, if not already practiced, should be introduced as one means of expressing fellowship. Communion should be made central to the worship services of which it is part, and the whole service should focus upon the corporate life of that congregation through testimony, shared intercessions, stories of ministry, calls to mission and reports from groups within the life of the congregation.

Pastoral Leadership

For many years in our tradition there has been a strong tendency for ordained pastoral leadership to be associated with sole rights to preach, to baptize and to preside at communion. I think that we need to ask ourselves whether these tendencies do not in fact reflect a view of ordained ministry which is more strongly sacramental than we actually profess, and whether we should not be more active in seeking lay participation in these aspects of ministry rather than merely permitting lay involvement on the occasions on which an ordained person is unavailable.

The Status of Children

Baptists' clarity about baptism being for regenerate believers only, and the associated doctrine of children as God's little ones, makes the status of children within the Baptist congregation rather ambiguous. Somewhere along the line they stop being God's little ones and start being people who need regeneration. Where this transition occurs is rather unclear; and the earlier in life that it is placed the more difficult it becomes to link baptism with conversion on the one hand (so that many young people are baptized many years after conversion) or adequate comprehension on the other (for some children's initial conversion experience occurs well before they are intellectually capable of participating in a baptismal preparation class).

This ambiguity in status is focussed further by the question of children's participation in communion. What is there to stop God's little ones participating? And if the table is open to adults who have not been baptized by immersion, should it not also be open to children who have made some form of commitment to Christ which nevertheless it is perhaps not yet appropriate to express in believers' baptism.

I suggest that communion should be open to children of all ages (particularly if we have an understanding of communion as a meal of the Kingdom), but that responsibility for discernment should not be placed entirely upon the shoulders of each child (or the stewart who serves the communion!). Rather, a child wishing to participate in communion should sit with a parent or another adult friend who can assist in deciding if it is appropriate for the child to do so and can indicate this to the steward who offers the elements.

The Baptized Unbeliever

The problem of the baptized unbeliever is frequently noted as a consequence of indiscriminate infant baptism; but it is also an issue for most Baptist congregations where some, having been baptized as believers, have subsequently fallen away from faith. (A significant number of those baptized as teenagers come into this category.) I believe that we need to face this matter squarely, consider what it says about nurture prior to and following baptism, and ask whether in fact the baptism we administer may not be at times a recognition not so much of genuine conversion as of peer pressure within the youth group. In many congregations baptism is not closely associated with either the actual experience of conversion or a call into some form of ministry in the congregation. Should believers' baptism be in fact delayed until a person has some idea of his or her vocation in life? Or should we leave things as they tend to be at present, with baptism a sign that a person is now starting to take faith somewhat more seriously?

D. Contemporary Baptist Practice

As an outline of one Union's practice I append a copy of part of the response of the Baptist Union of Scotland to BEM in which they set out their normal practice of baptism and Lord's Supper. This could be a helpful framework for discussion, enabling us to note the points of similarity and departure in the practice of other Baptist Unions and Conventions represented on the Commission. Other issues for discussion include:

-Do Commission members feel that their practice adequately reflects the breadth of understanding of both baptism and communion as presented in BEM? (Should it?
-Is the practice of a blessing rite or dedication of the parents of new children common to most Baptists?
-How usual is it for unbaptized children to participate in communion?
-In what ways do congregations in your Union or Convention provide nurture for children? What instruction and support is associated with preparation for and nurture following believers' baptism?
-In practice, what is the minimum age for baptism in your Union or Convention?
-The impression gained from recently-published material is that almost all Baptists now practice open communion. Is this so, or are there sill Unions or Conventions where communion is offered only to those baptized as believers?
-Is the Lord's Supper a service added onto the usual worship service, or is it integrated into the service whenever it is celebrated? How frequently is communion celebrated in the churches of your Union or Convention?
-Who presides at communion? Who serves the elements at communion? Who

baptizes? If lay people from the congregation preside or baptize, what sort
authorization (if any) is required?
-Is open membership available in at least some of the churches of your Union
or Convention?

Bruce Rumbold is a Professor at Whitley College, Melbourne, Australia.

Appendix: The Practice of Baptism, Eucharist and Ministry in Scottish Baptist Churches.

Baptism

Because of the independency of Baptist churchmanship there are no hard
and fast regulations relating to baptismal practice. There is a minister's manual
(published by the Baptist Union of Great Britain and Ireland in 1960) which
many follow, but not slavishly. All that can be decribed in general practice -
to which there will be exceptions.

It is unusual for candidates to be baptized before their early teens (though
some have been baptized at 10-11 years of age). Because church membership
is normally (though not inevitably) linked with baptism it is thought prudent
to delay baptism until the candidate is mature enough to take on a church
membership responsibilities.

The request for baptism is normally left to the candidate's own initiative
though such requests frequently arise from a pubic appeal at the close of a baptismal service.

It is exceptional for candidates not to undergo a course of instruction
(lasting 6-8 weeks) before baptism and church membership. The course of instruction will cover such topics as personal faith, the biblical basis for baptism,
the meaning of baptism, baptist history and principles and church membership.
Interested enquirers are usually invited to join in such a course without any
obligation to go forward to baptism.

Applications for baptism are approved in many instances by the minister
alone though if the baptism is to lead directly into church membership the ap-
plicant is then interviewed by two church members who present a recommendation for acceptance to a church meeting.

The baptisms take place on Sundays in the context of a public service and
normally follow the sermon. Lady candidates are dressed in robes and men candidates in washable trousers and shirts (robes are no longer so common for men).
The minister usually wears waders and a robe though younger ministers are now
tending to favour a similar form of dress to the male candidates.

In many churches, prior to their baptism, candidates are expected to give
some confession of faith in a testimony or a text of Scripture. Once in the water
the minister usually puts a final question to the candidate regarding his or her
personal faith.

The minister immerses the candidate in the name of the Father, Son, and
Holy Spirit, by lowering him or her backwards into the water. The candidate
then usually leaves the baptismal pool after a brief pause for private prayer. In
some instances, though rarely at present, a minister may lay his hands on the

candidate and offer a public prayer.

Soon after baptism, sometimes at the same service, the candidates are welcomed into church membership in the early part of a communion service.

Eucharist

The Eucharist, or the Lord's Supper, as it is more familiarly known in our churches, has held a central position in worship and in the shaping of the pattern of Christian obedience. The sharing of the bread and wine of communion has been considered one of the greatest privileges of believers, and in accordance with the word of institution it has been a frequent celebration. In many churches the service is held weekly, on the Sunday morning, and in others fortnightly or monthly. Until the turn of the century it was held in the afternoon, and wa pre-eminently the members'' service, where matters of discipline and fellowship business could be announced and discussed. More recently the communion has been held at the end of the other service, and this has unfortunately led to its being devalued and treated as an extra service by some. Yet for most of our people it remains a previous meeting place with the Lord, and an indispensable act of love and obedience.

Liturgically the key word has been simplicity, and the atmosphere of the upper room, and of the meeting of friends has been sought. The words of Jesus are our warrant, and his action in prayer of thanksgiving is initiated by the deacons of the church. The minister normally presides, but any designated believer, authorized by the church, may on occasion be called on to lead the service. Bread is generally, but not always, diced, and the unfermented wine is served in individual cups. There is often a fellowship offering, originally a love gift of the membership for the poor of the congregation.

In several churches the Eucharist has been taken into the whole service, and in others a quarterly or monthly celebration is "integrated". This would seem to be a move back to an authentic Baptist tradition.

Faithfulness in the Community - The Pastor's Part

Linda C. Spoolstra

There are almost 5800 American Baptist churches distributed across the United States. They are located in rural villages, in the open country, in towns, suburbs, cities and on the edge of the sprawling metropolis. Each of these congregations should be asking the question: What is our mission and how can we minister in our community? Unfortunately, many congregations do not ask these questions with any seriousness. Perhaps they see themselves as too small to minister in their communities. Perhaps they are committed to more "eternal" matters than to be concerned about everyday needs around them. For others, their sense of mission has a global perspective and the needs of their own communities go unnoticed.

Often pastors are caught in the struggle between their vision of the Church as the body of Christ and servant to the world and the congregation's expectations that they have been employed by the church as the "in house" chaplain, paid to serve the congregation's needs and to offer only what little is left over to the community. The strongest tradition of pastor and church being involved in the community is found within Black and Hispanic American Baptist churches. More about that later.

Lest this paper begin too pessimistically, it must quickly be said that there are many churches in which the pastor is very involved in the community and many churches that commit a great deal of their resources to addressing the needs of the people in their communities. These churches are compelled by their understanding of the Scriptures to undertake projects, large and small, that bring justice and hope to their communities. In this way they witness to their faith in Jesus Christ as our Deliverer and our Peace.

One pastor in a small church in a depressed, coal producing area of Pennsylvania describes his ministry as "convincing folks that poverty housing is as much a cocnern of Christ's as another year of VBS (so we have VBS with Habitat for Humanity as a mission project and have kids bringing in nails and weather stripping instead of dimes and quarters); getting two or three who will step out and get the hands-on experience of ministry . . ." He goes on to say, "I feel strongly that we don't need to be filling people's precious time with church "busy-ess". Instead we need to help them see that every hour of every day is an opportunity to participate in God's redeeming the creation. We don't need to work as hard at getting folks into the church as we do getting the Church into the world."

As to the needs in our communities, there are many. Yes, the United States ia an affluent nation with a high Gross National Product, but there are injustices and a need for changes in our society. In the past ten years we have had an increase in the number of people living in poverty. A growing immigrant population, widening economic disparity, rapid technological change and the destruction of the environment adversely affect the economic well-being and personal and social fulfillment of persons. Dying rural communities, decaying urban ones, rootlessness and individualism conspire against communities becoming places of belonging and caring. Historically it was the churches in the United States that founded hospitals, schools and other institutions for community life. In recent years, however, the federal government in particular has reduced funding for community services which has resulted in great suffering. In the midst of this situation, some churches have become deeply involved in ministering in their communities in faithfulness to the gospel. sometimes they work alone, sometimes with other churches, community organizations and with governments at different levels.

Biblical Imperatives For Ministry in the Community

Churches which are vital and alive are often in mission in their communities in response to their understanding of the Bible. This section will consider some of the stories, images, and expectations of how the church can bring life, hope, peace and justice to the community. In the Old Testament, for example, there are these words from the prophet Amos: "Let justice roll down like waters and righteousness like an everflowing stream." (Amos 5:24) From Zachariah comes a vision for the city: "My cities shall again overflow with prosperity and the Lord will again comfort Zion and again choose Jerusalem." (Zachariah 1:17) "Old men and ole women shall again sit in the streets of Jerusalem, each with staff in hand for every age. And the streets of the city shall be full of boys and girls playing in the streets. (Zachariah 8:4-5)

What is—is not what has to be. There is a new vision for the city in the New Testament as well: "I saw a new heaven and a new earth; for the first heaven and the first earth had passed away . . . I saw the holy city, new Jerusalem, coming down out of heavy from God . . . God will wipe away every tear from their eyes and death shall be no more, neither shall there be mourning nor crying nor pay any more, for the former things have passed away." (Revelation 21:1,4)

From visions of what the city can become, we move to the teachings of Jesus. In Luke we read that early in Jesus' public ministry he went to the synagogue and read from the prophet Isaiah:

The Spirit of the Lord is upon me, because he has anointed me
    to preach good news to the poor.
He has sent me to proclaim release to the captives
    and recovering of sight to the blind,
to set at liberty those who are oppressed,
    to proclaim the acceptable year of the Lord. (Luke 4:18:20)

These words became the prologue to Jesus' ministry. They also become the outline of a compelling mission for churches in their communities. Whenever we labor on behalf of the rule of God and Kingdom-values, we provide for God's Kingdom to come on earth as it is in Heaven. Pastors who urge and equip their churches to work for community development are acknowledging that salvation is more than an individual's concern; the Gospel has a social dimension as well. Saving my soul and saving my city are related.

The Bible consistently advocates for justice. There are images of cities being places of caring and safety. Jesus claimed for himself a ministry to the oppressed, the poor and the blind. He taught us to pray and work for God's will to be done on earth as it is in heaven. He taught us that our faith must be acted upon by feeding the hungry, welcoming the stranger, clothing the naked, visiting the prisoners and giving water to the thirsty. Jesus cared about people in their community, like Zacchaeus, and he loved the city of Jerusalem and wept over it. He confronted injustice and attacked greed.

What is the greatest commandment? You shall love your neighbor as yourself? But who is my neighbor asked the lawyer of Jesus. We must ask ourselves this same question. In the past a community was understood to be a geographic area in which one lived. In the community were people one knew and whose family one knew. They were the business people, the people on the porch next door, the people one greeted by their first names. Currently in the United States our understanding of "community" is much more complicated. Face to face contacts with people in one's neighborhood have diminished while community with colleagues at work, in the carpool, with those who share the same sport or hobby, have increased, In metropolitan areas, in particular, people have new ways of experiencing a sense of community.

At the same time we have become increasingly aware of our interdependence as people in community. While we have become anonymous to one another, we find ourselves in communities bound together by the need for water, schools, sewerage, police protection, economic development, mass transportation, etc. Face to face contacts between homogenous people have declined. Yet our sense of being interdependent has increased. How might we describe community today? Conrad Hoyer has written: "Community is any continuing, meaningful relationship between people for their mutual benefit."[1] It can include the need for physical protection, economic security, spiritual enrichment, moral support, cultural advance and so forth. The emphasis is on the relationships between people and not the geography in which one lives.

Our understanding of community is more complicated and more multi-dimensional than thirty, forty or more years ago. The result is that the mission of the church to the community has many possible dimensions at many levels. For example, I ask myself, "What is my community?" Is it Radnor, the town of 1000 people and my mailing address, or is it Wayne, a suburb of 30,000 people in which the unincorporated section of Radnor is located? Is my community metropolitan Philadelphia, the mid-Atlantic region, the northeast section of the United States? Or is my community the whole world? Perhaps the answer is all of the above!

Given our complex understanding of community, one must ask, what tasks should be done by the individual, what by the congregation, what should be addressed at the city level, the metropolitan level, the state level, etc.? This is a difficult question. Some people in the churches are only concerned about the neighborhood within two miles of the church building. Others ae concerned about worldwide problems, but in doing so they fail to see what is at their doorstep. There is a slogan being used which give some advice about our situation. It says, "Act locally, think globally," Most people should be engaged in ministry as locally as possible while learning about and being committed to the global interdependence of all people.

The Church as "servant to the world" is certainly one of the most powerful and most Christ-like images that can motivate the local church to serve its community. "The one who is greatest among you shall be your servant; whoever exalts himself will be humbled, and whoever humbles himself will be exalted." (Matthew 23:11)

"Love your neighbor as you love yourself," said Jesus. When churches express their love for their communities, they are expressing God's love for the world. Jesus taught that we are to render under Caesar that which belongs to Caesar; we must obey civil laws. Taking our responsibility one step farther we also bear responsibility for social or societal failures that exist: the unequal opportunities for education, employment, and access to health services, etc.

Some of our churches are involved in addressing these issues. An example is the Providence Park Baptist Church in Richmond, Virginia, the state capital. The pastor is Miles Jones. The county was not providing adequate water to the citizens. Under the pastor's leadership, citizens petitioned for some of the same services from the county that were being provided to the city residents. To draw attention to their needs, they picketed and marched around the county headquarters. In the eyes of Jones, the county authorities were violating God-given rights to necessary human services that were being provided without equity. Sanitary conditions provided by water and sewer systems were being provided to some citizens and denied to others of God's children. As a pastor Miles said his concern was not for how the finances would be arranged to provide the services (there were others with expertise for that), but to proclaim what was right under God.[2]

Churches that minister in their communities value risk-taking. They search for new options for the future. They overcome the tendency of Americans to compartmentalize life: this part for work, this part for family, this part for recreation, this part for religion, etc. They do not draw a line between the sacred and the secular. They believe that all of life is sacred. Whatever concerns people concerns the church. They believe the Scriptures that the role of the church is to bring hope to people and that the church, as the body of Christ, is God's visible presence in the community

The Pastor Leads the Church in Mission

The pastor has a variety of pastoral tasks that are used to challenge, equip, and encourage people in developing a ministry to the community. Preaching, leading in worship, teaching, organizing, and modeling involvement in the community are some of these tasks. Before discussing these specific functions, it will be helpful to consider the pastor's overall role as the leader of the congregation's mission in the community.

A book, on the small church, *Developing Your Small Church's Potential*, provides insights for all-size churches on the role of memory, vision and structure in empowering a church to be involved in ministry to the community.

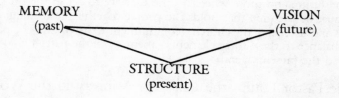

MEMORY
(past)

VISION
(future)

STRUCTURE
(present)

1. Memory

A pastor will build bridges to the past by evoking memories of what has transpired. The authors suggest that pastors "build on the church's memories, not of specific programs, but of stories about the energy, risks, and indignations that were embedded in the caring ministries of previous generations."[3]

Calling forth memories and making connections with the present provide a way to translate the universal gospel into the story of the community.

Soon after I joined Central Baptist Church in Wayne, Pennsylvania, I heard stories about the church's work with new immigrants to the community from Italy. That was in the 1920's and 1930's. The memory of the church reaching out to persons in need was celebrated and provides motivation to carry on this tradition in a variety of contemporary ministries to the community.

2. Vision

Linking the past to present concerns is not enough; there must be a vision of a new future. Imagination must be employed, the dreaming of dreams of what can be. The pastor is the chief spokesperson for the church's vision for the community is consistent with the congregational memory.) If, for example, the pastor articulates a vision of what the community could become to be a more livable place, then it is possible for some members of the congregation to see their part in making it so. Using imagination to think about possibilities yet unrealized can generate excitement and commitment.

3. Structure

Remembering the commitments of the past and having a vision of what can be are two components of the pastor's role in shaping the church's ministry. But there is a third part: the sense of mission must be organically connected to the present structure of the church. The pastor as leader and chief administrator will need to provide ways for members to have access to decision-making about the scope and shape of the church's ministries. This takes time. But if the people are to believe that they have the capacity to achieve goals they must set them for themselves and the church must be organized to be able to make and keep its commitments.

The pastor as leader unites those who remember the past, those who envision the future and those who have the capacity to act in the present. The pastor must be the glue that holds the people together, nourishing the relationships and stretching the church's commitment to its vision. The pastor can provide balance to these three elements - memory of the past, a vision for the future and the present agenda.

The Pastor Equips the Laity For Ministry in the World

In addition to leading the congregation to discover its corporate mission in the community, the pastor has a responsibility to equip the saints for the work of ministry in the world. The laity express their Christian vocation primarily in the secular world. Images of light and leaven remind us of the work of the church in society, often done individually. The pastor nurtures the laity's identity as Christians and as ministers of Jesus Christ. Unfortunately this is an area in which there are few helpful models. In far too many churches, the laity are reluctant to consider themselves ministers and the clergy are all too content to enjoy special privilege as the only "real ministers." One of the most challenging tasks for pastors is to help laity see themselves as ministers of Jesus Christ doing God's will.

The Pastor as Preacher and Worship Leader

The pastor uses the pulpit to instruct the congregation and increase awareness of the possibilities for community ministries. In addition to instructing the church, the pastor will speak prophetically, challenging the church to a servant role in the community. The pulpit can be a powerful platform to orient the congregation to a vision for ministry through a variety of means and by a variety of groups. Sermons will help the congregation to interpret how the gospel relates to the particular community in which they are located. The most important single voice to speak on behalf of ministry to the community is the Bible itself. The stories, words of God, and events cry out for a response from the people.

Prayers, hymns, and offerings can also unify the people's vision of ministry. Worship that sensitizes us for social responsibility is not some special kind of worship. It is any true worship that humbles and empowers us, deepening our faith to the point that we dare to act upon it, but preserving within us the humility that senses our limitations and our need for new light in every situation.

The Pastor as Communicator and Encourager

The members of the congregation will look to the pastor to communicate about the responsibility of the church to the community, not only from the pulpit but through other forums available, such as the church newsletter and in the work of committees. The pastor will be engaged in sensitizing the congregation to their mission and, with the laity, will be organizing, investigating, planning and acting on the vision for ministry in the community. The pastor's encouragement of the laity, which can occur through personal contacts, is always helpful.

The Pastor as Leader in the Community

Americans tend to relegate some things to the public sphere and other things to the private sphere. In the usual way that life is ordered, religion and the church belong to the private sphere. As a result it can be controversial for a pastor to become very involved in the community. Yet what better way to show how the Church should seek to be engaged in compassionate ministries and work for justice than for the pastor to become involved in the community? Many pastors have to take time to help their congregations see that some of their time must be spent beyond the internal life of the church.

It has been my experience that black churches are more supportive of this than anglo churches. An insight into why this is so was provided by Dr. J. Alfred

Smith, Jr., Pastor of the Allen Temple Baptist Church in Oakland, California. Dr. Smith explained that in black churches, there is an absence of the traditional cleavage between the sacred and the secular. The roots for this are in West Africa where there is no division between spiritual values and the values of political, economic and social liberation. The result is that even black churches with a conservative theology have a liberal social activism, based on Old Testament theology that called for Pharaoh to liberate the oppressed.[4]

A powerful illustration of a pastor's involvement in the community is Lucius Walker, Jr., pastor of First Salvation Baptist Church in Brooklyn, New York. In addition to being a pastor, Walker is the founder and executive director of the Interreligious Foundation for Community Organizations. This organization has helped develop over 80 community-based organizations within the United States and Central America by providing technical assistance, grants, training for organizers and using its global network of grassroots organizers to advance the struggles of oppressed people for justice and self-determination. Organizations that have been helped include the National Anti-Klan Network (now known as the Center for Democratic Renewal), the Ecumenical Minority Bail Bond Fund and the Black United Fund.

Perhaps less dramatic than community organizing, but very important, is the opportunity that pastors have to serve on community organizations such as boards of hospitals, Youth Commissions or Human Relations Commissions.

Churches and their pastors can and must work ecumenically as a witness to our unity with the people of God and to have a greater impact on the community. Unfortunately councils of churches are generally weak and even defunct in this period of our history. Hopefully the times will change and ecumenical organizations will once again be strong.

One way in which ecumenical cooperation continues to be effective is through the community's ministerium, the organization for the pastors, priests and rabbis of the community. This group can provide effective leadership for the religious organizations' work to address the needs of the community. An example of this is the ministerium of Skokie, Illinois, a Chicago suburb in which there have been large numbers of Jews living who survived the holocaust. In 1976 a neo-Nazi group threatened to march in Skokie. The Niles Township Forum brought all faiths together and stopped the march. The religious people continue to find unity in ecumenical services held at Thanksgiving.

Conclusion

Many churches have a significant impact on the physical health, economic stability and spiritual vitality of their communities. In the area of *hunger and nutrition*, churches operate soup kitchens, food pantries, and nutrition programs. Churches are involved in housing including building and renovating housing for the poor. Churches are involved in *health and healthcare* through health fairs and clinics offered to the community. Churches are involved in *education and literacy* programs. Writing letters to legislators, voicing opinions on decisions to be made, providing counseling to people seeking jobs, visiting in prisons,

nursing homes, and hospitals are additional examples of how churches are involved in ministering in their communities. Church buildings are often offered
as a meeting place for community organizations or to house a day care program, or recreation facility for the community. Sometimes churches are effective because of their wide connections, sometimes because they are not captive
to the mainstream, and sometimes because they can make decisions and take
action. Where churches are actively involved in their communities, it is almost
always because the pastor has a vision for this ministry.

These churches are distinctive from other churches. Being prophetic means
paying a price. Ministering on behalf of a community requires determination
and a willingness to respond to the Spirit of God. Martin Luther King, Jr. said
that the church has a divinely-ordained responsibility to be a vanguard in the
struggle for peace, justice and community. He warned that it will sign its own
death certificate and rob itself of a significant place in the annals of history if
it does not act on that responsibility. What he said twenty-five years ago is still
true today.

If the church takes this challenge and opportunity, the whole world will shout
for joy, but if we fail, some future Toynbee, writing the annals of a history
of our civilization, will say that in the hour of trial, the church and the Christian were weighed in the balance and found wanting, and this was the beginning
of the end of an age.[5]

*Linda Spoolstra is Executive Director of the American Baptist Churches Commission on
the Ministry in Valley Forge, Pennsylvania, USA.*

Notes

1. Conrad Hoyer, *Ecumenopolis U.S.A.: The Church in Mission in Community* (Minneapolis, Augsburg, 1971), pp. 41.42.

2. Miles Jones, *Kingdon Challenges and Community Development: A Biblical Perspective* (Valley Forge: National Ministries, 1989), pp. 7-8.

3. Carl Dudley and Douglas Alan Walwrath, *Developing Your Small Church's Potential* (Valley Forge: Judson Press, 1988), p. 78.

4. J. Alfred Smith, Jr. "The Responsibility of Black Churches to the Underclass"
in *The Disadvantaged Among the Disadvantaged: Responsibility of the Black Churches to the
Underclass, Report on a Conference* (Harvard Divinity School, October 23-25, 1987), p. 30.

5. Lewis V. Baldwin, "The Minister As Preacher, Pastor and Prophet: The Thinking
of Martin Luther King, Jr." *American Baptist Quarterly*, volume VII, June 1988, p. 93.

How a Local Church Makes Decisions In Romanian Baptist Churches

Ioachim Tzunea

On the general theme — Structuring the Church for Discovering God's Will — I was commissioned to prepare a paper on "How a Local Church Makes Decisions in Romanian Baptist Churches." I will deal with three aspects of this subject briefly.

Within the Baptist Church of Romania, the General Meeting is regarded as more than an ordinary business meeting. Rev I. R. Socaciu, a former professor of the Baptist Theological Seminary at Bucharest, told the students in his course on Practical Theology, "The General Meeting of the Church, when inspired by the Holy Spirit, will be an opportunity for great joy and will become a true experience of worship."

There is no doubt, however, that the General meeting by its very structure is a business meeting. At the same time it is more than that because the Church's main goal in any problems is to discern God's will regarding its tasks and activities as well as its worship and witness.

Due to this the participants of the General Meeting should not come with preconceived ideas or to impose their own without consulting one another in order to know God's will regarding every issue under discussion. This is to be done only through a close fellowship of all the Church members both with the Lord and with each other. In this way, the General Meeting is always a worship service as it should be. In connection with this, I want to mention that the General Meeting is always preceded by a 30-minute devotion led by the pastor of the church. He reads a Scripture appropriate to the purpose of the meeting and then he exhorts the members to be of one mind. These insights are followed by prayers for guidance by the Holy spirit regarding the problems to be discussed and the decisions to be made.

During a 34-year ministry I humbly share with you I have had such blessed experiences of true worship services at General Meetings. Unfortunately I cannot say this about all of the General Meetings I have attended!

The General Meetings in the Baptist Churches of Romania are led by democratic principles, but this does not exclude the theocratic type of leadership.

According to the rules, the General Meeting carries all the decisions unanimously, or at least with a quorum, assuming that substantial majority discern God's will. This requires, of course, a pre-existing harmony with one another and all with God in a prayerful desire to fulfill His will through their vote.

Ideally, all the decisions of the church should be made by a unanimous vote. This is made possible when all the church members are perfectly tuned to the Holy spirit. We have to admit, however, that we are not perfect and this gives rise to differing opinions.

In connection with this I would like to present an experience of a decision voted by the church I minister. The General Meeting decided to ordain five deacons. The church has 1,012 members and there are only two ordained deacons at the moment. With a view to understanding the biblical requirements for a future deacon, we decided to have a Bible study based on I Tim. 3:8-13. This Bible study was presented in a special service. Afterward, the General Meeting voted that the Church should bring the question of electing five deacons to the Lord in prayer for three months. Furthermore, it was decided that on the first Sunday of the month, at the Holy Communion, the whole church should fast and pray that the Lord would reveal His will on this matter.

Within three months, a substantial number of the church members nominated several persons out of which the committee made a list of eight people. This list of nominees was presented to the church in a General Meeting. After a time of prayer the General Meeting, by secret ballot, unanimously elected the five new deacons to ministry in the church. In this way both the principle of democratic leadership - expressed by the unanimous vote of the church - and the Holy Spirit's leading for fulfilling God's will were observed. The five deacons' ministry proved that the church was led by the Holy Spirit.

According to our regulations, at least 2/3 of the church's members must participate in a General Meeting. If the number of participants is below this limit the General Meeting should be postponed until the next when it may be held with any number of participants. Of course it is preferable to have a majority of the members at a General Meeting, but attendance varies according to the topics on the agenda. Full attendance of the church membership is required for major problems, such as the selection of a new pastor or deacon. Such decisions should be made with an overwhelming majority.

I must emphasize that in Romania, a pastor would accept a ministry in another church only if he received at least 80 percent of the votes of that church.

The general principles of our Creed are presented in the Confession of Faith based on the Holy Scripture and the general principles by which the Church must act are written in the Regulations of the Baptist Church of Romania. Consequently, Article 16 of our Regulation asserts that "the General Meeting, the Church Committee, and the members of the full Committee are enabled to lead and control the Church." It is also the pastor who leads the committee and the General Meeting because he was voted by the General Meeting and our Regulation entitles him to do so.

There are two kinds of General Meetings: the *ordinary* General Meeting, held annually, and the *extraordinary* General meeting that takes place whenever the Church must make important decisions. The General Meeting is summoned by the pastor according to the previous resolution of the Church Committee. The meeting and the agenda are to be announced in the church 15 days before the established date.

The Church Committee is voted by the ordinary General Meeting at the beginning of the year. The pastor would appoint a nomination committee and the General meeting votes through secret ballot the spiritual and able persons for various activities in the church. The General Meeting may add to the nomination list other names to be chosen in the committee.

I have to add here that, since in Romania a pastor ministers in more than one church, the committee members also take responsibility for spiritual activities such as leading a prayer meeting or a Bible study for young people, serving as sunday school teachers, etc.

In Romania the pastor should prepare the sermons, visit with the church members, give counselling once a week, make up the agenda of the committee meetings, and train lay preachers.

We do believe that the success of a General Meeting in voting a motion according to God's will is based on the pastor's communication with all the church members involved in the church activities. Good communication between a pastor and his fellow-workers enables him to know the situation in the church and the right time to make a clear decision that he is to present at the committee meeting and then at the General Meeting.

I would like to add that in my ministry, every year before the ordinary General meeting where there are important problems on the agenda such as election of a new committee, voting a new budget, making projects for various sections in the church (children, youth, women, etc.) we invite all the persons involved in the church activities for a special meeting. In this meeting we discuss the problems that are to make up the agenda of the General meeting. This proceeding almost always ended in good results and demonstrated the Holy Spirit's guidance in knowing God's will for the church ministry.

To sum up then, in Romanian Baptist churches, the pastors try to involve as many people as possible in the decision-making process. If there is good communication within the church, the pastor will better understand the will of God as it is revealed through the church's members. In this way, the pastor will be better equipped to use the structures of the church for the purpose of accomplishing God's will in the world.

Ioachim Tzunea is Pastor of Golgotha Baptist Church in Bucharest, Romania.

Index